WORDS AND DISTINCTIONS FOR
THE COMMON GOOD

Words and Distinctions for the Common Good

PRACTICAL REASON IN THE LOGIC OF SOCIAL SCIENCE

GABRIEL ABEND

PRINCETON UNIVERSITY PRESS

PRINCETON & OXFORD

Published by Princeton University Press
41 William Street, Princeton, New Jersey 08540
99 Banbury Road, Oxford OX2 6JX

press.princeton.edu

All Rights Reserved
ISBN: 978-0-691-24706-9
ISBN: (pbk.) 978-0-691-24705-2
ISBN (e-book): 978-0-691-24707-6

British Library Cataloging-in-Publication Data is available

Editorial: Meagan Levinson and Erik Beranek
Production Editorial: Jenny Wolkowicki
Cover design: Katie Osborne
Production: Lauren Reese
Publicity: William Pagdatoon
Copyeditor: Maia Vaswani

Cover image: alchena / iStock

This book has been composed in Arno Pro

10 9 8 7 6 5 4 3 2 1

a felicitas, alma y emilio; nadie encendía las lámparas

CONTENTS

Abbreviations

Activity DF	activity 'distinction goes first!'
Activity WF	activity 'word goes first!'
AI	artificial intelligence
d	placeholder for any distinction
F	placeholder for any object or thing
IAU	International Astronomical Union
NGO	non-governmental organization
NHDSC	National Hot Dog and Sausage Council of the United States
NSU	Nationalsozialistische Untergrund
OOI	object of inquiry
STS	science and technology studies
'w'	placeholder for any word

Typographic conventions

(1) Single quotation marks:[1]
   i. For words and expressions, when they're mentioned rather than used (e.g., the word 'word')
   ii. For speech
   iii. For scare quotes
   iv. Instead of double quotation marks within double quotation marks

---

1. These typographic conventions stem partly from Abend (2008a) and Lyons (1977).

(2) Double quotation marks:
   i. For meanings and definientia (e.g., 'barista' means "a person who makes and serves coffee to the public")
   ii. For quotations
   iii. For titles of articles
   iv. Instead of single quotation marks within single quotation marks
(3) Italics:
   i. For emphasis
   ii. For titles of books and journals
   iii. For words in languages other than English (e.g., the word *trapisonda*)
(4) Small caps: For concepts (e.g., the concept of TIME).
(5) Ellipses:
   i. Ellipses in square brackets indicate that at least a full sentence, sometimes whole paragraphs, are omitted.
   ii. Ellipses without the brackets indicate that it's only part of a sentence, a clause, or even a couple of words that are omitted.

PROLOGUE (OR, WILL SOCIAL SCIENTISTS' NEVER-ENDING DISPUTES OVER WORDS EVER END?)

THIS BOOK is an invitation. An invitation to you. To you guys. Here's my invitation.

———

This book is about the logic of social science research. How can social scientists' practices be improved? This is what I'm up to.

———

This book isn't about methodology. It's not a manual or how-to guide. However, its temperament is normative, like manuals and methodology. Should and shouldn't. Good and bad. Look, this is how social science research should be conducted. That'd be a wrong step. This is good stuff; the product of good work. If you want to obtain this and that, you should do thus and so.

———

Social scientists observe the social world. They measure and represent it. They advance and test truth claims about it. For these purposes, they classify things, they sort them into classes, they draw distinctions among them. 'In this article, we're going to look at four objects. Objects *A*, *B*, and *C* will be grouped together, but *D* won't. It's not like the others.' Electricians, physicians, and magicians share this property. They're similar to one another in this respect. Architects aren't. There are gay people, straight people, bi people, asexual people, and none of the above. Social scientists constantly need to draw distinctions. How to do this well? What are the criteria to determine if it's been done well?

Many social science projects, subfields, and literatures have at their core one key word, or a few key words. (Sometimes they get called 'concepts.') Journal articles report findings on 'neoliberal policies' and 'digitalization' in the twenty-first century. They contrast several types of 'colonialism,' and compare cases of 'populism' in Europe and South America. They make general claims about 'religions' and 'ethnic groups' around the world. What do these key words refer to? How to use them well? What are the criteria to determine if they're being used well?

———

Hold on. Why should empirical researchers care about these issues? It's not because of philosophical or speculative reasons, but because of their job description and responsibilities. Researchers' substantive claims about the social world are dependent on their key words and distinctions. According to the 'democratic peace theory' in political science, democratic states don't go to war with each other. Is this contention true? Evidently, it depends on what 'democratic state' and 'war' refer to. According to some sociologists, racial and ethnic discrimination is better accounted for by economic than by cultural factors. Is this contention true? Evidently, it depends on . . .

Social scientists ask if social movement participation is declining in the United States and Western Europe. Whether rates of major depression are growing among young adults. Whether social class and gender predict altruistic behavior, and if so, how. Their answers will be a function of how data are sorted into categories: social movement (or not), major depression (or not), altruistic behavior (or not). They'll depend on what participating in a social movement is, what altruism is, and what *a* behavior is. Whether depression and altruism are dichotomous variables, or they come in degrees, such that someone can be three times more depressed than someone else. Whether there are two genders, three, more, or many more. Two social classes, three, more, or many more. What 'social class' refers to in the first place.

———

Delmira's office hours. She's a sociology professor at a large Midwestern university. One of her smartest undergraduate students shows up. 'Please, have a seat.' They'd like to write an honors thesis on secularization in South America. 'I feel I need to define "secularization" in my thesis, but I don't know how. I've found tons of different definitions in the writings of sociologists and philosophers of religion. How should I choose among them?'

Delmira isn't sure either.

The student continues:

> My puzzlement doesn't end there. Secularization theories are about religious belief, religious values, and the authority of religious institutions.

Something like, these things are getting weaker, though the story has interesting wrinkles, and I think the South American story has intriguing specificities. Now, how should I define 'religion'? Christianity, Judaism, and Islam are easy cases, but I have no idea if Umbanda, Inti worship, the Aztecs' cosmology and rituals, and Candomblé should qualify as religions. It seems there are arguments to go either way. What's a scientifically sound approach to this?

Delmira isn't sure either.
Delmira is sure that the deadline for undergraduate theses is April 15.

––––––

Suppose you're a social scientist who sets out to investigate the causes of gender inequality, or the functions of corporate social responsibility in contemporary capitalist societies. As you carry out your project, you have to make decisions about distinctions, classifications, categorizations, and typologies. Decisions about how to use and define key words. But how? One consideration is your immediate research objectives and ulterior publication objectives. What you have in mind is your next step, your upcoming experiment or survey, how you'll give support to empirical claims. This is bread-and-butter social science work, on which observations, measurements, variables, and models rely (and eventually explanations, predictions, and policy implications). It's also relied on by evaluators, such as journal referees and university committees.

Yet, every once in a while, you wonder about the warrants for your words and distinctions. You get more reflexive about them. Lately, you've been wondering if your uses of 'altruism,' 'gender,' or 'religiosity' are good. Good enough. Better than others. And why that is.

As it turns out, you're not alone. Many social scientists have reflected on and clashed over these issues. Some have been accused of unethically redefining key words, reclassifying data, and gerrymandering concepts. Disputes over words and distinctions may get heated. Emotionally charged, since people are attached to their preferred word uses, definitions, and distinctions. Chess is definitely a sport! (No, it isn't!) Hot dogs aren't sandwiches at all! (Yes, they are!) Pluto is definitely a planet! (No, it isn't!) Dedicated conferences are organized; frequently dedicated to one key word. 'What is gender?' 'Defining "the family" in contemporary societies.' 'Toward a renewed conceptualization of ethnicity.' 'What is disability?' Harmonious conclusions are never reached.

Harmonious conclusions or not, the show must go on. Research must get done, journal articles must get written and published, and committees must give awards and make recruitment and tenure decisions. Whatever you may want to say about words and distinctions in social science, it'll have to take this pragmatic imperative into account.

———

Just like social scientists' methods shouldn't malfunction and let them down, their words and distinctions shouldn't either. Unfortunately, the quality of the literature on the latter (words and distinctions) pales in comparison to the literature on the former (methods). It's high time the latter got up to speed.

There'll be payoffs for social science communities' production of research and knowledge, but also for the relationships between social science and society. Words are needed to mediate between scientific findings and claims on the one hand, and their real-world relevance and policy implications on the other. Social scientists are expected to shed light on populism, religious participation, civil war, empathy, and diversity—in ways that matter to policy makers, think tanks, the law, university students, social movements, international organizations, the media, and the general public. This is why social science is valuable to societies and polities, and is deserving of attention and financial support.

It'd be no good for social scientists to arbitrarily stipulate the meaning of 'populism' or 'diversity' and take it from there. What's demanded from them is knowledge about populism and about diversity: how to explain the growth of populism and how to stop it, and how to boost the salutary effects of diversity in the workplace, education, and politics. Otherwise, social scientists could be living in a fictional world they'd made up for the convenience of their research, measurements, and models, whose objects and phenomena don't correspond to anything in the real world. Societies would be reluctant to fund these projects.

Key words like 'populism' and 'diversity' are vital building blocks for social scientists, whether they're talking to fellow researchers and research communities or to fellow citizens and societies.

Practical reason

In this book I'll distinguish two questions. At first glance, they might seem questions for an individual social scientist, or for a research team or lab. Questions to be answered by each project, by each paper, to suit *its* objectives, what *it* wishes to accomplish. I'll argue that, in fact, they're questions for a social science community (and possibly for its stakeholders as well). They should be collectively addressed and answered, with a view to the common good. I'll call communities to work together on them.

First, given word 'w,' how should it be used in our social science community? For instance, how should we use 'gender' or 'terrorism'? On which grounds? Alternative formulation: how should word 'w' be defined? Additionally: should word 'w' be used at all? Which words should and shouldn't be used in our community?

Second, should distinction d be accepted in our social science community? For instance, someone proposes a distinction between childhood, adolescence, adulthood, and old age. Or between 'White,' 'Black or African American,' 'American Indian or Alaska Native,' 'Asian,' and 'Native Hawaiian or Other Pacific Islander.'[1] Should it be accepted? On which grounds? Alternative formulation: should objects be classified according to distinction d? Additionally: which distinctions and classifications are good for our community?

———

I'll argue that neither question is truth-apt. Answers to them can't be true or false, in the sense that empirical research can deliver true claims, and in the sense that 'the capital of Uruguay is Montevideo' is true. There's no right answer to be discovered.[2] Not by a very, very smart person. Not by a committee made up of a discipline's elite. Instead, answers to them can be good, better and worse, in the sense that practical reason can deliver good outcomes and arrangements. Rather than discovered, they'll have to be arrived at by the community, by means of good procedures.

Which requires that the community figure out good in which ways, and good for what and for whom. 'The community,' you say? To be sure, what 'the community' picks out is open to question. It's a network or assemblage of people, organizations, practices, traditions, artifacts, and understandings. But which ones? What are its boundaries?

———

1. "About the Topic of Race," United States Census Bureau, n.d., https://www.census.gov/topics/population/race/about.html; "Race," United States Census Bureau, n.d., https://www.census.gov/quickfacts/fact/note/US/RHI625219.

2. I'm using 'truth' and 'true' in a non-technical way. For some philosophers, moral, aesthetic, and metaphysical statements can be as truth-apt as 'the capital of Uruguay is Montevideo.'

Both questions have philosophical aspects, and philosophical genealogies, but I won't tackle them from a philosophical perspective. I'll draw on philosophy to sharpen my tools and construct my arguments, but I won't contribute to it. Instead, I'll contribute to the practice of empirical social science. I want to help social scientists with the words and distinctions their projects make use of—no matter what their data are, and how they're collected and analyzed. So, my attitude will be pragmatic.

That's the plan.

———

ARGLE: Is homeopathy a form of medicine?

BARGLE: That depends on how 'medicine' is defined.

ARGLE: Sure, that's certainly the case, but then how *should* 'medicine' be defined? Are you suggesting that this definition is up to me? Am I good as long as I define my terms?

BARGLE: Well, your definitions should be useful. For example, it's useful to define 'medicine' as "the science that deals with preserving health and curing disease." Similarly, if you draw a distinction, if you propose a classification, they should be useful. For example, it's useful to distinguish between allopathic and alternative medicine, and between empathy and sympathy. It's useful to classify oranges with apples, and tomatoes with cucumbers.

ARGLE: Useful for what? Useful to whom? Speaking of 'usefulness' doesn't seem to be very informative. Plus, what's useful to you, your colleagues, and your organization isn't useful to me, my colleagues, and our organization. Whose usefulness should prevail? Or, if you insist: whose usefulness standard is most useful?

———

I don't think social science communities are clear about the preceding issues. Nor about the tools that might be apposite. Is providing a definition equivalent to providing a conceptualization? What sort of thing is the definiendum: a word, a concept, a thing, or something else? Does it matter? How do words, concepts, categories, notions, terms, and conceptions differ from one another? Does it matter?

Cans of worms are all around us. One is how to decide these things and who gets to decide them. Another is usefulness. Where it can be invoked and what its relativity entails. There are plenty more.

———

A critic of social science notices that something is awry: 'will social scientists' never-ending disputes over words ever end?' The charge is that their discussions about the definition of 'power,' 'empathy,' or 'capitalism' are futile. Always the same old song. There are lots of competing definitions, everyone is convinced that theirs is the best, the most insightful, the most useful. But nobody can convince the others. Why not? Because people are committed to two beliefs. Not only do you have a definition of 'w' (the best one, according to you), but also an understanding of how to compare the worth of definitions (the best one, according to you). Therefore, disputes never get anywhere. They never end.

The critic goes on: 'social scientists are tasked with describing, explaining, and predicting social phenomena. Making policy suggestions and advising policy makers, and thereby making a difference in the world. They should talk about the social world, not merely about words.' This is a version of the age-old 'logomachy' denunciation: you're just quarreling about words.[3] Not substantive, real things. Just words, words, words.[4]

There's something to the charges leveled by this critic, but I don't think they're clear about the preceding issues either. We've got a lot to think through here, so that social science communities can be confident in and at peace with their word uses, distinctions, and classifications. So that words, distinctions, and classifications do the jobs they ought to. We must begin at the beginning.[5]

———

The history of the social sciences is rife with fantasies. Certainty! Perfect certainty. Complete objectivity and value freedom. Total independence from philosophy and metaphysics. Linear progress. Absolute precision. A perfect scientific language: pure, unambiguous, stable, final. An algorithmic methodological machine: enter your data where the user guide tells you to, and it'll automatically produce results. Voilà! No human interference or human judgment; just follow the predetermined instructions. (The algorithm can also learn to write

3. G. Campbell (1776) 1823, 85: "logomachy, or in plain English, the art of fighting with words, and about words." Cf. Burke 2018; Kivistö 2014; Werenfels (1702) 1711.

4. Cf. Léo Ferré's 1980 "Words . . . Words . . . Words . . . ," Mina and Alberto Lupo's 1972 "Parole Parole," Silvana Di Lorenzo's 1972 "Palabras, Palabras," and Dalida and Alain Delon's 1973 "Paroles . . . Paroles. . . ."

5. Carroll 1911, 124.

up the results, submit the article to a suitable journal, and fill out the declaration of conflict of interests. It'll even learn to respond to reviewers' criticisms.)

These fantasies are alive and well in the twenty-first century, minus the self-assured and triumphalist tone of earlier times. They did and continue to do harm to social science. Expectations won't be lived up to and disappointment will ensue. But these expectations weren't sensible: nobody should have had them to begin with. Enemies of science say it's failed to deliver on its promises. On closer examination, the blame doesn't lie with science and scientists. They're doing OK. The blame lies with promises that nobody made or nobody should have made.

These fantasies are pernicious. However, it doesn't follow—it obviously doesn't follow—that social science is tantamount to subjective opinions, moral convictions, and political preferences. Nor does it follow that social science can make do without methodology and logic, without collectively reflecting on what constitutes better research and better knowledge claims. Nor that individuals' judgments, individual social scientists' discretionary judgments, can take care of the whole of it, thus making communal procedures and understandings superfluous.

Attending to the logic of social research doesn't commit you to scientism. It doesn't commit you to modeling social science after natural science, as idealized in undergraduate textbooks. You don't have to end up with a rigid, uptight, anal view of science, what it ought to do and attain.[6] Attending to the logic of social research doesn't strike me as philosophically or methodologically controversial. My aims are probably acceptable to everyone, or almost everyone, who makes a living in the social science business. It's good for researchers to understand how their words and distinctions work, and how their arguments and inferences work. Words may be used well, used badly, misused, perhaps overused: it'd be nice to have well-thought-out criteria to tell the difference between uses and misuses. Observations, measurements, and claims should be about what they're intended to be about. Social scientists' arguments may be sound or unsound. If you see the latter, don't hit the 'like' button.

An invitation

This book is about social science research. Regarding social scientists' words and distinctions, I think the status quo leaves much to be desired, so I ask what is to be done. My answer to this question is that I can't satisfactorily answer it.

---

6. It does commit you to some views—e.g., looking for witchcraft-substance in people's small intestines isn't scientific research (Evans-Pritchard [1937] 1976, 15–17). You get my drift.

It's not the sort of question an individual can answer by themselves. Which is where the community comes in. That means we. That means you. You guys.

We have to work together and make decisions together. We have to figure out how to use word 'w,' whether distinction d is acceptable, and on which grounds. We'd better get moving.

So, here's my invitation:

First Act

1

Sandwichness wars

1.1 A sandwich is a sandwich is a sandwich

Brooklyn, New York. November 10, 2015. The doors of The Bell House, a music and comedy venue, open at 7 p.m. for a momentous debate. The debaters are Judge John Hodgman and Dan Pashman. Hodgman is a comedian, author, and host of the *Judge John Hodgman* podcast. Pashman is a food critic and host of the podcast *The Sporkful*. The moderator: journalist Brooke Gladstone, of WNYC's *On the Media*. The issue: whether a hot dog is a sandwich, and, by extension, what makes a sandwich a sandwich.[1]

In 2014, Judge Hodgman had ruled that hot dogs weren't sandwiches—as he explained in his column in the *New York Times Magazine*, Judge John Hodgman Rules.[2] Ever since, Hodgman has argued for this view multiple times in multiple settings, from *Time Out* magazine to *The Late Show* with Stephen Colbert. He courageously stands by his ruling, despite threats to his and his family's safety: "It has been years since I offered a ruling on sandwich-ness. As you know, a hot dog isn't one, and none of your angry letters or FedExes of poisonous vipers will change that fact."[3]

The thrust of Hodgman's argument rests on the property of "cut-in-half-ibility," which he claims to be essential to sandwiches. That's the essence of sandwichness:

---

1. Dan Pashman, "John Hodgman v. Dan Pashman: Are Hot Dogs Sandwiches?," November 30, 2015, in *The Sporkful*, podcast, http://www.sporkful.com/john-hodgman-v-dan-pashman-are-hot-dogs-sandwiches/.

2. John Hodgman, Judge John Hodgman Rules, *The One-Page Magazine*, New York Times, accessed May 4, 2014, https://www.nytimes.com/interactive/2014/05/04/magazine/04-one-page-magazine.html.

3. Hodgman 2020.

Cut-in-half-ibility. Genial share-ibility! Eat some now and save some for later-ibility! Divide and serve with a cup of soup-ibility! Are all intrinsic to sandwiches. Even subs! Heroes. Hoagies. Grinders. Wedges. Sure, you can physically cut a hotdog in half. And maybe you would do so under the tyranny of a child. But one would never routinely cut a hotdog in half, in a public setting, without expecting and deserving some looks.[4]

Cut-in-half-ibility isn't a sufficient condition. That something can be cut in half doesn't imply it's a sandwich. But it's a necessary one. If you can't cut it in half, then it's not a sandwich. Once Hodgman's metaphysical claim is on the table, epistemology and methodology have to step up. How can it be shown that hot dogs lack this property? He asks you to imagine what "you will feel" if you cut one in half. This test yields strong evidence in favor of his argument: "All of right-thinking humanity is on my side. Sandwiches are meant to be cut in half. You would never, unless under extreme duress or madness cut a hot dog in half. Picture yourself at a ball park, or even at a restaurant, cutting a hot dog and you will feel an instinctive, entire repulsion at the very thought of it."[5]

In more vehement terms: "Let me apply the wisdom of Solomon: If your friend's hot dog is a sandwich, why doesn't he just cut it in half? HE CAN'T, CAN HE? Because it is not a sandwich, but a hot dog, indivisible and sui generis."[6]

Dan Pashman would have none of it. Hodgman's argument was plain wrong. While Pashman's field of expertise is gastronomy, he availed himself of jurisprudential doctrines to make his case: "I am the [Antonin] Scalia of Sandwiches, a strict constructionist: I believe that we must look to the Earl of Sandwich, to the framer's original intent, to understand the definition of a sandwich. The Earl wanted to be able to eat his dinner with his hands without

4. John Hodgman, "A Hot Dog Is Not a Sandwich," March 26, 2020, in *Judge John Hodgman*, podcast, MaximumFun, https://maximumfun.org/episodes/judge-john-hodgman/a-hot-dog-is-not-a-sandwich/; "Transcript, Judge John Hodgman: A Hot Dog Is Not a Sandwich," n.d., in *Judge John Hodgman*, podcast, MaximumFun, https://maximumfun.org/transcripts/judge-john-hodgman/transcript-judge-john-hodgman-a-hot-dog-is-not-a-sandwich/.

5. Tolly Wright, "The Case against Hot Dogs as Sandwiches," *Time Out*, November 4, 2015, https://www.timeout.com/newyork/comedy/the-case-against-hot-dogs-as-sandwiches. See also "Dan Pashman of WNYC's The Sporkful has been trying . . . ," John Hodgman's blog, July 18, 2014, https://www.johnhodgman.com/post/92161625121/dan-pashman-of-wnycs-the-sporkful-has-been-trying.

6. John Hodgman, Judge John Hodgman Rules, *The One-Page Magazine*, New York Times, May 4, 2014, https://www.nytimes.com/interactive/2014/05/04/magazine/04-one-page-magazine.html.

his hands getting all messy, so he put a piece of meat between two pieces of bread, and the sandwich was born."[7]

John Montagu, 4th Earl of Sandwich (1718–92), is widely credited with the culinary innovation. Rumor has it that he "wanted to eat his dinner with his hands" because of his gambling addiction. The rumor originates in French traveler and writer Pierre-Jean Grosley: "[An English] minister of state passed four and twenty hours at a public gaming-table, so absorpt in play, that, during the whole time, he had no subsistence but a bit of beef, between two slices of toasted bread, which he eat without ever quitting the game."[8] It's doubtful that this traveler can be trusted, and apparently there aren't any other sources to back him up. But his account does make for a good story (which is reason to have more doubts). The invention of the sandwich makes for a good story.[9]

Pashman underscores that "the original intent of the framer of sandwiches, the Earl of Sandwich" was twofold: "1. You must be able to pick up a sandwich and eat it with your hands *without* your hands touching the fillings," and "2. The fillings must be *sandwiched between* two discrete food items."[10] Importantly, Pashman argues that "there is one notable exception to having two separate halves to a sandwich: the hinged bun."[11] Therefore, a hot dog is a sandwich. A burrito is not.

Historians might worry about Pashman's evidence for the Earl of Sandwich's mental states. Legal scholars would deny that Scalia was a strict constructionist.[12] Philosophers might object to the very idea of intent. Metaphysicians might grill Pashman about the discreteness of the discrete food items between which fillings are sandwiched: what it amounts to and what its significance is.[13] I'll set these worries aside and ask who's right about sandwiches and hot dogs: Hodgman or Pashman? How to determine who's right about sandwiches and hot dogs: Hodgman or Pashman?

7. T. Wright, "Case against Hot Dogs."

8. Grosley 1772, 149.

9. W. Allen 1966. See also Edmund Blackadder, "Blackadder Series 3 Episode 2—Ink and Incapability Full Script," Blackadder Quotes, February 22, 2016, https://blackadderquotes.com /blackadder-series-3-episode-2-ink-and-incapability-full-script.

10. Pashman, "John Hodgman v. Dan Pashman."

11. Mo Mozuch, "Why a Hot Dog Is a Sandwich but a Burrito Is Not (According to Dan Pashman)," *Newsweek*, July 3, 2018, https://www.newsweek.com/hot-dog-sandwich-burrito-dan -pashman-835793. See also T. Wright, "Case against Hot Dogs."

12. Scalia (1995, 79, 98) referred to his "philosophy" as "statutory construction in general (known loosely as textualism) and . . . constitutional construction in particular (known loosely as originalism)." "Textualism should not be confused with so-called strict constructionism."

13. Varzi 2013.

According to dictionary publisher Merriam-Webster, it's Pashman. Indeed, Merriam-Webster made a point of it on its webpage Words at Play—A Fun Look at Language, Word Histories, and More. The beginning of the post, "Sandwich History: 10 Words You Can Chew On," was predictable: "Definition: 1) two or more slices of bread or a split roll having a filling in between[,] 2) one slice of bread covered with food." This definition is a premise. Then, hot dogs must be in, just like a meatball sandwich and a peanut butter sandwich: "We know: the idea that a hot dog is a sandwich is heresy to some of you. But given . . . the definition of sandwich . . . there is no sensible way around it. If you want a meatball sandwich on a split roll to be a kind of sandwich, then you have to accept that a hot dog is also a kind of sandwich."[14]

Merriam-Webster's definition of 'sandwich' forces you to conclude that a hot dog is a sandwich: you're just logically applying it to the case at hand. Supreme Court Justice Ruth Bader Ginsburg played a deductive logic card, too, in a 2018 exchange with comedian Stephen Colbert. Colbert asked RBG if a hot dog was a sandwich. RBG cunningly retorted: "you tell me what a sandwich is and then I'll tell you if a hot dog is a sandwich."[15]

Merriam-Webster was spot-on concerning the heretical character of its definiens. The heresy wouldn't go unremarked or unpunished. "Merriam-Webster Discredits Itself by Declaring a Hot Dog Is a Sandwich."[16] "Users took to Twitter with the hashtag #hotdogisnotasandwich to voice their disagreement. Numerous Twitter polls showed that anywhere from 75 to 90 percent of respondents agreed that the hot dog is not a sandwich."[17]

According to New York State's tax law, Pashman is right, too. The Department of Taxation and Finance's 2019 Tax Bulletin ST-835 is titled "Sandwiches." Under the heading "What is considered a sandwich," it reads:

> *Sandwiches* include cold and hot sandwiches of every kind that are prepared and ready to be eaten, whether made on bread, on bagels, on rolls, in pitas, in wraps, or otherwise, and regardless of the filling or number of layers. A

14. "Sandwich History: 10 Words You Can Chew On," Word History, Words at Play, Merriam-Webster, last updated April 17, 2022, https://www.merriam-webster.com/words-at-play/to-chew-on-10-kinds-of-sandwiches.

15. *The Late Show* with Stephen Colbert, "Stephen Works Out with Ruth Bader Ginsburg," YouTube, March 21, 2018, https://youtu.be/ooBodJHX1Vg.

16. Chris Fuhrmeister, "Merriam-Webster Discredits Itself by Declaring a Hot Dog Is a Sandwich," Eater, May 27, 2016, https://www.eater.com/2016/5/27/11800864/merriam-webster-hot-dog-sandwich-debate.

17. "Sorry, Merriam-Webster, but Hot Dogs Are Not Sandwiches," Arrant Pedantry, June 15, 2016, https://www.arrantpedantry.com/category/semantics/.

sandwich can be as simple as a buttered bagel or roll, or as elaborate as a six-foot, toasted submarine sandwich.[18]

This passage doesn't offer a definition, as a dictionary would. Nor a list of necessary and sufficient conditions. Plus, it uses the word 'sandwich' to explain what's considered a sandwich. It wouldn't help a Martian, or an Earthling who didn't speak any English and had never heard the word 'sandwich' before. To be fair to the Department of Taxation and Finance, though, seldom do foreigners and Martians consult its tax bulletins. For the New York public, especially for restaurant owners, this bulletin's long list of "examples of taxable sandwiches" is helpful. The list does include "hot dogs and sausages on buns, rolls, etc."

On Pashman's side, too: what are presently called 'hot dogs' used to be called 'hot-dog sandwiches' and 'frankfurter sandwiches.' They were a type of sandwich, subsumable under the broader category. Eventually, the word 'sandwich' got dropped, and we ended up with hot dogs. A noun rather than an adjective. For instance, in 1922 the *New York Times* reported that there was a "novel method of peddling narcotics by placing a small envelope containing drugs in the slit of a hot frankfurter sandwich." In 1934, President Roosevelt and his family enjoyed an "alfresco luncheon" at a "'hot-dog' stand." Two attendants "[prepared] a tray for the President and Mrs. Roosevelt, on which were two 'hot-dog' sandwiches and a glass of beer for Mr. Roosevelt." Five years later, King George VI was President Roosevelt's guest, and he was treated to "the favorite American snack." "Later it was ascertained that the King . . . came back for more hot-dog sandwiches."[19] Better known than the monarch's penchant for hot dogs is the 1927 song "Frankfurter Sandwiches" (Harry Pease/Al Dubin/Ed G. Nelson), which several artists have performed and recorded.[20]

By contrast, the magazine the *Atlantic* would declare Hodgman to be the winner. The *Atlantic* "developed a grand unified theory of the sandwich: a

18. New York State Department of Taxation and Finance, "Sandwiches," Tax Bulletin TB-ST-835 (April 8, 2019), https://www.tax.ny.gov/pdf/tg_bulletins/sales/b19-835s.pdf.

19. "'Hot Dogs' in Atlantic City Carry Drugs to Addicts," *New York Times*, July 10, 1922; "President Meets Daughter-in-Law," *New York Times*, June 24, 1934; "King Tries Hot Dog and Asks for More," *New York Times*, June 12, 1939. As the articles' titles show, the shorter form 'hot dog' was already acceptable. It's also noteworthy that in 1922 and 1934 'hot dog' is in quotation marks, but not anymore in 1939.

20. h/t Katha Pollitt. For example, Harry Rose and Al Lentz and His Orchestra recorded "Frankfurter Sandwiches" in the late 1920s, and Peggy Lennon and the Streamliners with Joanne (Rosemary Squires) in the 1960s.

FIGURE 1.1. Every night I bring her frankfurter sandwiches.

simple test to determine whether a given composite food product does indeed operate in the tradition of the peckish earl":

The Sandwich Index we created consisted of four points:

1. To qualify as "a sandwich," a given food product must, structurally, consist of two (2) exterior pieces that are either separate or mostly separate;
2. Those pieces must be primarily carbohydrate-based—so, made of bread or bread-like products;
3. The whole assemblage must have a primarily horizontal orientation (so, sitting flush with a plate rather than perpendicular to it); and
4. The whole assemblage must be fundamentally portable.[21]

Hence, a burger "qualifies" as "a sandwich." Oreo cookies and ice cream sandwiches do, too. But "the drastically misnamed open-faced 'sandwich'" doesn't. Burritos and hot dogs don't either.

Like the *Atlantic*, celebrity chef Anthony Bourdain would concur with Hodgman's judgment: "No. I don't think [a hot dog] is a sandwich. I don't think a hamburger is a sandwich either." Bourdain's rationale consists in anticipating the reaction of experts. One sort of expert anyway: hot dog vendors. "I mean, if you were to talk [to] any vendor of fine hot dogs, and ask for a hot dog sandwich, they would probably report you to the FBI. As they should."[22]

The National Hot Dog and Sausage Council of the United States (NHDSC) felt obligated to weigh in as well. This trade association views the hot dog as a sui generis category. A category of its own kind: "Just as politics and religion can both unite and polarize, the question of whether a hot dog is a sandwich has stirred its followers' fury, and unless settled soon, may go down has one of American history's most polarizing disagreements. [. . .] [A hot dog] is truly a category unto its own."[23] The sui generis account of hot dogs is likewise

21. Megan Garber, "It's Not a Sandwich," *Atlantic*, November 5, 2015, https://www.theatlantic.com/entertainment/archive/2015/11/its-not-a-sandwich/414352/. See also Megan Garber, Sam Price-Waldman, and Nadine Ajaka, "What Is a Sandwich? (No, Seriously, Though)," *Atlantic*, September 10, 2014, https://www.theatlantic.com/video/index/379944/what-is-a-sandwich-no-seriously-though/. The *Atlantic*'s "grand unified theory" preceded the debate between Hodgman and Pashman.

22. Anthony Bourdain (iamAnthonyBourdain), "I've noticed this question coming up again and again," Reddit, September 20, 2016, comment on CheesyMightyMo, "Is a hot dog a sandwich?," https://www.reddit.com/r/IAmA/comments/53p6kb/i_am_anthony_bourdain_and_im_really_good_at/d7v5fs7/.

23. "National Hot Dog and Sausage Council Announces Official Policy on 'Hot Dog as Sandwich' Controversy," NHDSC press release, November 6, 2015, https://www.hot-dog.org

championed by comedian Jimmy Kimmel: "By my definition, a hot dog is a hot dog. It's its own thing, with its own specialized bun."[24]

———

An objector may interject that NHDSC represents the interests of the hot dog and sausage industry. Its whole point is to "[celebrate] hot dogs and sausages as iconic American foods."[25] Obviously, its views aren't impartial; it has skin in the game; it has an axe to grind. It doesn't care about getting things right, be it the nature of hot dogs, the nature of sandwiches, or the distinction between sandwiches and hot dogs. Why listen to this organization? What can be learned from it?

No doubt, this objector is on the mark about NHDSC. If you work for it, partiality is your duty. You were hired to promote hot dogs. Combat their foes in society, culture, and government. Help increase their sales. You don't have to have a theoretical perspective on hotdogness. It'd be ridiculous to demand detachment from you.

Bringing NHDSC into the picture is thought-provoking precisely because of the overt partiality of trade associations, pressure groups, and lobbies. It makes you wonder. To what degree and in which ways are its staff members' job descriptions unique? Who can be impartial and detached? Who's unconcerned about the real-world consequences of these disputes? Perhaps nobody who participates in them is. Neither about 'sandwich' nor about 'genocide' and 'gender.' Neither about 'hot dog' nor about 'intelligence' and 'digitalization.' Neither about food words nor about social science words. Neither in courts of law nor in social science departments, conferences, and journals.

1.2 Criteria

Who's right: John Hodgman or Dan Pashman? Merriam-Webster or Jimmy Kimmel? They disagree about what a sandwich is, or about the definition of 'sandwich.' Their disagreement should be adjudicated somehow. But how?

For starters, whence the criteria to assess definitions and arguments? By 'criterion' I mean a standard according to which definitions of 'sandwich' are

———

/press/national-hot-dog-and-sausage-council-announces-official-policy-hot-dog-sandwich-controversy.

24. Tony Merevick, "Jimmy Kimmel's Perfect Response to the 'Is a Hot Dog a Sandwich?' Debate," Thrillist, June 2, 2016, https://www.thrillist.com/news/nation/jimmy-kimmel-joins-the-is-a-hot-dog-a-sandwich-debate.

25. "About," NHDSC, 2016, http://www.hot-dog.org/media/about.

evaluated, compared, and ranked (definitions or, as I'd prefer, proposals as to how 'sandwich' should be used). These criteria would determine who's right, which argument is better, which argument is the best. Ideally, we'd have clear and well-grounded criteria, which Hodgman, Pashman, and everyone else can agree to. Since it's criteria in the plural, we'd ideally have a clear and well-grounded way to combine and weigh them, which everyone can agree to.

My point isn't rocket science. Imagine a committee charged with coming up with a ranking of some sort. A ranking of restaurants, movies, museum exhibits, universities, contributions to scientific knowledge, soccer teams, or soccer players. No agreement will materialize about the best restaurant in town, or the best soccer player in history, or the most significant contribution to scientific knowledge in the twenty-first century, if committee members' criteria patently diverge. No agreement will materialize about what a sandwich is if criteria patently diverge.

Table 1.1 summarizes seven criteria that are apparent in the sandwichness wars.

Hodgman, Pashman, Merriam-Webster, Jimmy Kimmel, the *Atlantic*—along with most people who've passionately chimed in on the web—are missing something. They don't seem to properly appreciate that two levels (or more) are involved. At a first-order level, they express strong opinions about what a sandwich is and whether a hot dog is a sandwich. 'It definitely is!' 'It's definitely not!' 'It kinda is!' To support these claims, they provide various kinds of reasons. But they haven't given enough thought to their justification vis-à-vis possible rivals. What kinds of reasons should (and shouldn't) be accepted? Which ones should be given more weight? What kind of criteria should (and shouldn't) be used? This second-order level doesn't have to do with sandwichness itself, but with the evaluation of sandwichness reasons and the adjudication of sandwichness disagreements.

1.3 A burrito is a burrito is a burrito

'Judge' John Hodgman wasn't the first judge to rule on what a sandwich is. Judge Jeffrey Locke confronted the same question some eight years earlier. The case was *White City Shopping Center, L.P. v. PR Restaurants, L.L.C.*, heard by the Worcester County Superior Court in Massachusetts. PR Restaurants "d/b/a" (doing business as) Panera Bread, a "café style restaurant chain that sells sandwiches, coffee, and soup."

The story begins in 2001. On March 14, White City Shopping Center, located in Shrewsbury, Massachusetts, "entered into a ten-year lease . . . with PR for retail space to operate a Panera restaurant in the Shopping Center. Lease negotiations lasted several months partly because of PR's request to include

TABLE 1.1. Sandwichness criteria

	Criterion	Description	Critical response
1	Inventor	What the inventor of the sandwich said or believed. That'd be the Earl of Sandwich's intentions in the eighteenth century.	An eighteenth-century earl doesn't get to oversee twenty-first century societies. Social things change. It's good that social things change. They develop their potential, adapt to new contexts, and fulfil new needs. History isn't destiny.
2	Genealogy	Cultural and institutional genealogies of the practice of eating sandwiches.	Cultural and institutional genealogies aren't destiny either.
3	Etymology	Words' etymology and past uses. (If a word has a coiner, what they said or believed, too.)	Etymology and past uses aren't destiny either. Present-day uses of a word aren't accountable to its roots in Latin, Greek, or Quechua.
4	Dictionary	What the dictionary says: how it defines the word 'sandwich.'	There's no such thing as *the* dictionary. Which dictionary? Which dictionaries? What to do if two dictionaries' definitions don't fully overlap? (More on this below.)
5	Essence	Essential properties, which are "intrinsic to sandwiches."	How can you demonstrate that a property is essential? That "you will feel an instinctive, entire repulsion" isn't proof of anything. And who are you to begin with?
6	Expertise	What contemporary experts, like chefs, say or believe. Just like you'd ask an astronomer what a planet is or you'd ask a psychiatrist what schizophrenia is.	Who's an expert in this case? Is a chef an expert on sandwiches? Do they have to be employed at a sandwich restaurant? (More on this below.)
7	Consistency	If A is a B, then C must be a B as well. If D isn't a B, then E can't be a B either. Accepting this definition of 'sandwich' logically commits you to these consequences.	None that I'm aware of (but see Borges [1977] 1989). None to consistency itself, but what you're logically committed to can get controversial.

an exclusivity clause in the Lease. [...] The exclusivity clause that both parties initially agreed to restricted White City from entering into new leases with businesses that primarily sell sandwiches."[26] To be more precise: White City agreed "*not* to enter into a lease, occupancy agreement or license affecting space in the Shopping Center ... for a bakery or restaurant reasonably expected to have annual sales of *sandwiches* greater than ten percent (10%) of its total sales or primarily for the sale of high quality coffees or teas." Panera Bread pushed hard for this monopolistic clause. Five years later, however, its privileged position would come under threat. Qdoba, "a Mexican-style restaurant chain that sells burritos, quesadillas, and tacos," was gearing up to set up shop in the shopping center. "On or around August 22, 2006, White City executed a lease with Chair 5 ['a Delaware limited liability company and franchisee of Qdoba'] for 2,100 square feet of retail space in the Shopping Center."

PR/Panera Bread tried to legally prevent White City and Qdoba from moving forward with the lease. It "asserted that tacos, burritos, and quesadillas fell within [the] meaning of 'sandwiches.'" While you won't find 'sandwiches' on Qdoba's menus, it does have 'burritos.' Burritos are a kind of sandwich; they fall under the extension of 'sandwich.' Therefore, the exclusivity clause kicks in. Or so Panera's argument went.

Is a burrito a sandwich? This became a difficult legal question, because the lease "contained no definition of 'sandwiches,'" which could have settled the dispute.[27] PR Restaurants' attorneys, Demeo & Associates, noted that "under Massachusetts law, the meaning of a term used in a contract" was its "common meaning." Then, they quoted a dictionary definition of 'sandwich':

> Sandwich is defined in the dictionary as, "food consisting of a filling placed upon one slice or between two or more slices of a variety of bread or something that takes the place of bread (as a cracker, cookie, or cake)." Webster's Third New International Dictionary 2326 (2002). [...] In the last 350 years, sandwiches have evolved with the result that today, "sandwiches take so many forms in the modern world ... that a catalog would be a book." *Id.* The term sandwich now includes items such as wraps, gyros, and in this case, burritos, tacos, and quesadillas. Qdoba's offerings—tacos, burritos, and quesadillas—are all sandwiches because they are all food that consists of bread folded around fillings. ... For Qdoba's tacos, burritos, and

---

26. "Memorandum of Decision and Order on Defendant's Motion for Preliminary Injunction," White City Shopping Center, L.P. v. PR Restaurants, L.L.C., d/b/a [doing business as] Panera Bread, Commonwealth of Massachusetts, Worcester, ss. Superior Court Civil Action, October 30, 2006, at 2. Subsequent quotations are also from this source.

27. Florestal 2008; Madison 2006; Park 2019; Posner 2012; Scalia and Garner 2012.

FIGURE 1.2. *Ceci n'est pas un burrito*. Photo: Creative Headline on Unsplash. Free to use under the Unsplash License.

quesadillas, the bread is the tortilla. [...] All authorities recognize tortillas as a form of bread.[28]

In support of their claim about the breadness of tortillas, PR's attorneys cited a 1998 case, *Sabritas v. United States* (on which more below); "*Webster's New Word* [*sic*] *Dictionary of Culinary Arts*"; and, again, *Webster's Third New International Dictionary*. Whether "all authorities" are in accord, and who are "all authorities," they didn't discuss.

PR's attorneys wrote "defined in the dictionary," not "defined in a dictionary."[29] Nor did they write "defined in a controversial dictionary," let alone "defined in the most controversial dictionary ever published."[30] No surprise there. In courts of law dictionaries are used selectively and strategically

28. "Memorandum in Support of PR Restaurants, LLC's Application for a *Preliminary Injunction*," White City Shopping Center, LP, Plaintiff, v. PR Restaurants LLC, Defendants, Commonwealth of Massachusetts, Worcester, ss. Superior Court Department of the Trial Court, October 6, 2006, at 6.

29. Moon (1989, 60): "collections of lexical information come to be referred to as 'the dictionary': in the singular, with a definite article used as if there was only one extant dictionary, in a single edition and single version."

30. Morton 1994; D. Skinner 2012.

to bolster your claims and undermine your opponents'. Which has led legal scholars to reflect on the source and scope of dictionaries' authority, and how divergences across dictionaries can be legally decisive, insofar as the outcome might hang on the meaning of a word. They've also decried the Supreme Court's overreliance on dictionaries and "dictionary shopping"—that is, choosing "which dictionary and which definition to use."[31]

What transpired in the *White City* case was 'within-dictionary definition shopping'. *Webster's Third* was also quoted by Judge Locke in his ruling. But he didn't quote the same definition of 'sandwich' PR Restaurants' attorneys had:

> This court applies the ordinary meaning of the word. The New Webster Third International Dictionary describes a "sandwich" as "two thin pieces of bread, usually buttered, with a thin layer (as of meat, cheese, or savory mixture) spread between them." Merriam-Webster, 2002. Under this definition and as dictated by common sense, this court finds that the term "sandwich" is not commonly understood to include burritos, tacos, and quesadillas, which are typically made with a single tortilla.[32]

One and the same dictionary can give support to conflicting claims, since some entries have several senses and subsenses, distinguished by Arabic numerals and lowercase letters. In *Webster's Third*, 'sandwich' has this subsense, "1 a": "two slices of bread usually buttered, with a thin layer (as of meat, cheese, or savory mixture) spread between them." And then it has this subsense, "1 b": "food consisting of a filling placed upon one slice or between two or more slices of a variety of bread or something that takes the place of bread (as a cracker, cookie, or cake)." Panera Bread quoted the latter subsense, which is consistent with its claim that a burrito is a sandwich. Judge Locke quoted the former subsense, which is consistent with his ruling that a burrito is not a sandwich.

Neither Panera Bread nor Judge Locke took the trouble to mention that in the very dictionary whose authority they summoned, *Webster's Third*, there's another subsense of 'sandwich'—much less that this other subsense contradicts

---

31. Aprill 1998, 301; Lemley 2020; Solan and Gales 2016; Werbach 1994. On 'ordinary meaning,' dictionaries, linguistic intuitions, and corpus linguistics, as they bear on the interpretation of statutes and the cogency of textualism and originalism, see Harris and Hutton 2007; Kirchmeier and Thumma 2010; Manning 2001; Merrill 1994; Scalia and Garner 2012; Slocum 2015, 2017; Thumma and Kirchmeier 1999; Tobia 2020. A widespread metaphor is Judge Learned Hand's "fortress," which he used in *Cabell v. Markham* (1945): "it is one of the surest indexes of a mature and developed jurisprudence not to make a fortress out of the dictionary."

32. Quotation is at p. 5. In a footnote, Judge Locke observes: "The parties have submitted numerous dictionary definitions for the term 'sandwich,' as well as expert affidavits."

their argument. Both cherry-picked the subsense that was favorable to their argument and concealed its partial character.[33]

———

Addressing the legal question 'what is a sandwich?' is a special case of addressing the general, metaphysical question 'what is a sandwich?' The former must be answered and it must be answered as soon as possible. Either Qdoba will open a restaurant in the shopping center or it won't. It involves legal considerations, aims, and tools, as well as particular contractual and regulatory elements. Special legal procedures must be followed. The issue isn't metaphysical or linguistic per se, but practical. There's a conflict between parties' interests, often pecuniary interests. Everyone wants to get their way.

Given the legal context and the contract at the heart of *White City v. PR Restaurants*, the ordinary meaning of 'sandwich' and dictionary definitions of 'sandwich' were sure to turn up. Yet, other criteria were also brought into play. Expertise, for instance. Three "expert affidavits" emphasize their authors' experience and understanding. Christopher Schlesinger wrote:

> I have been in the food service industry since the age of 18. Following my graduation from the Culinary Institute of America in 1977, I have worked in 35 different restaurants, working with New England's most innovative chefs. [...] I am presently the chef and owner of All Star Sandwich Bar in Cambridge, Massachusetts. I am co-author of five cookbooks.... I have taught culinary students at the Culinary Institute of America and was the winner of the James Beard Award in 1996 for "Best Chef of the Northeast."[34]

33. *Webster's Third New International Dictionary, Unabridged* was published in 1961, under the editorship of Philip Gove. What's the exact wording of subsense "1 a"? Judge Locke, quoting "Merriam-Webster, 2002," writes "two thin pieces of bread." I've consulted three earlier reprints, 1966, 1981, and 1993, and they all read "two slices of bread." So, in 2002 the pieces of bread needn't be slices anymore and had to be thin. Or did Judge Locke misquote this phrase? Regrettably, I couldn't get ahold of the 2002 reprint. Thanks to Annika Henrizi (Zentral- und Hochschulbibliothek Luzern) and Michael Sauder (University of Iowa and Olio Township) for their help with this source.

34. Judith A. Quick: "I have worked in the food safety, labeling, science and technology industry for over thirty years.... I have served as the President of Judith Quick & Associates, a consulting firm specializing in food labeling and regulatory issues for the food industry. Prior thereto ... I held various positions at the Food Safety and Inspection Service ('FSIS') at the U.S. Department of Agriculture ('USDA')." Kerry J. Byrne: "I have been a food and drinks writer for the Boston Herald since 1998.... I consider myself to be an expert on culinary issues."

Schlesinger isn't merely a chef, but the chef at a sandwich restaurant. Why does this make a difference? Does it matter how long someone has been in the food industry? If you claim that experts have unique access to and knowledge of the nature of a thing, two additional issues come up. First, what makes an expert an expert in the relevant domain—for example, whether having worked for twenty years as a Thai restaurant's chef would suffice; whether having made sandwiches is necessary to know what a sandwich is, and if so, why having made sandwiches for your children is epistemically deficient.

Second, what sort of thing this is, such that only experts grasp its nature. What is a planet? What is schizophrenia? What is an offside in soccer? What is a stalemate in chess? What is zirconium? Not anyone can tell you. By contrast, you arguably know what a newspaper is just as well as a journalist or a newsstand vendor, and you know what an airport is just as well as a pilot or a flight attendant. Is sandwich more like newspaper and airport or more like zirconium and stalemate?

Admitting both experts' expertise and ordinary meaning necessitates that they be integrated. An expert's definition of 'sandwich' may be at odds with a dictionary's definition (assuming there's one dictionary only and it provides one definition only). An expert's definition may be at odds with another expert's definition. Would you then need a meta-expert's view on which of the two experts' views should be taken into account? What if meta-experts are at odds with one another?

In the Panera Bread case, experts also acted as meta-experts. They reported on other experts' views—that is, people they consider experts. "Credible" chefs or culinary historians. "I know of no chef or culinary historian who would call a burrito a sandwich. Indeed, the notion would be absurd to any credible chef or culinary historian"—wrote Schlesinger. "I know of no one in the culinary industry who would consider a burrito to be a sandwich"—wrote Byrne. To establish what a sandwich is, one method would be a survey of experts, even if informally conducted.

Schlesinger's affidavit mobilized cultural genealogy, too. A shared genealogy makes sandwiches sandwiches, so this is a good criterion to appraise burritos' sandwichness. "A sandwich is of European roots," while a "burrito . . . is specific to Mexico." (Schlesinger was empirically wrong. Burritos are a typical 'Mexican' food in the United States, but not a typical food in Mexico.) For its part, Byrne's affidavit put forward the sui generis argument. Like the theory of hot dogs of Jimmy Kimmel and NHDSC: "A burrito . . . is, simply put, a burrito. It is a separate and distinct product."

———

Judge Locke ruled that "burritos, quesadillas, and tacos are not commonly understood to mean 'sandwiches.' Because PR failed to use more specific language or definitions for 'sandwiches' in the Lease, it is bound to the language and the common meaning attributable to 'sandwiches.'" Which doesn't include burritos. "For the foregoing reasons stated, it is hereby *ORDERED* that the Defendant's [PR Restaurants] motion for preliminary injunction be *DENIED*." Panera Bread lost. Qdoba won.

"'We were surprised at the suit because we think it's common sense that a burrito is not a sandwich,' said Jeff Ackerman, owner of Qdoba franchise group. 'We're just delighted that the experts and judge saw it the same way we did.'"[35] Ackerman was happy qua businessperson, not qua metaphysician or lexicographer. His delight at the judge's decision wasn't metaphysical. He wasn't happy because the judge got the nature of reality right. Lo and behold, his claim about "common sense" about sandwichness is consistent with Qdoba's interests.

Metaphysics, shmetaphysics . . .

1.4 Bread

There are several competing definitions of 'sandwich.' Their differences notwithstanding, one common denominator is bread. The word 'bread' is in all of them. However, this common denominator may not be common after all, because there are several competing definitions of 'bread,' too.

In its legal dispute with White City Shopping Center, Panera Bread maintained that tortillas were "a form of bread." Indeed, it maintained that "all authorities recognize tortillas as a form of bread." If these assertions were true, one of burritos' ingredients would be bread, which is required for something to be granted sandwich status. Besides their sheer authority, what warrants authorities' views about the breadness of tortillas? Panera Bread's attorneys referred to *Sabritas*, a United States Court of International Trade case. "Plaintiffs, Sabritas, S.A. de C.V. and Frito-Lay, Inc. (collectively 'Frito-Lay'), challenge the United States Customs Service's ('Customs') classification of its import taco shells . . . as 'other bakers' wares: other: other.'" Instead, they argued, taco shells are a kind of bread: "Frito-Lay contends its import taco shells are properly classified as 'bread, pastry, cakes, biscuits and similar baked products' under HTSUS 1905.90.10, which carries duty-free status." As ever, taxes make the world go round.

Judge Nicholas Tsoucalas's decision went in Frito-Lay's favor:

---

35. *Boston Globe*, "In Court, Burrito's Defining Moment," *Denver Post*, November 11, 2006, last updated June 22, 2016, https://www.denverpost.com/2006/11/11/in-court-burritos-defining-moment/.

The Court begins its analysis by noting that tortillas are unquestionably commonly and commercially accepted as bread in the United States. [...] Evidence was introduced at trial demonstrating that the tortilla undergoes certain changes when fried. Namely, as Dr. Pintauro [Customs' expert, 'food scientist' Dr. Nicholas Pintauro] testified, and Frito-Lay's witness admitted, the introduction of oil and high temperature necessary to create a hard taco shell from a tortilla alters the flavor, color and texture of the original tortilla. [...] Nevertheless, relying on the testimony presented at trial and, more importantly, on several definitions and descriptions in food dictionaries and treatises, the Court concludes that the common and commercial meaning of bread encompasses flat, fried bread and, therefore, the taco shells at issue.[36]

What did Judge Tsoucalas base his conclusions on? "Several definitions and descriptions in food dictionaries and treatises," such as "John F. Mariani, The Dictionary of American Food [and] Drink" and "Jonathan Bartlett, The Cook's Dictionary and Culinary Reference." While both "The Oxford English Dictionary" and "Webster's Third New International Dictionary" were mentioned once in his opinion, these specialized dictionaries were more important in his ruling. Also: the judge spoke of a word's "common and commercial meaning." Common *and commercial.*

For my purposes, court cases are most valuable if they explicitly analyze the appropriateness and inappropriateness of criteria to adjudicate disputes. Why isn't this criterion, consideration, or method apropos? For example, Judge Tsoucalas's dismissal of this US Customs' argument: "The Court is unpersuaded by defendant's testimonial and photographic evidence purporting to demonstrate that the taco shells at issue are not bread because they were not found in the 'bread aisle' at a supermarket Dr. Pintauro visited." Not being placed in the same place, not being in physical proximity in the grocery store, doesn't entail that taco shells and bread aren't of the same kind. In terms of evidence, as the judge observed, *a* supermarket isn't enough. Moreover, just like you could cherry-pick the dictionary that strengthens your case and that'd be 'dictionary shopping,' you could cherry-pick the grocery store that strengthens your case and that'd be 'grocery store shopping.' Shopping among grocery stores, not to be confused with shopping at the grocery store.

The judgment that taco shells are bread might have raised some eyebrows back in 1998. The 2020 judgment that "Subway bread is not bread" certainly did.[37]

36. Sabritas v. United States, 998 F. Supp. 1123 (Ct. Int'l Trade 1998).

37. Sam Jones and Helen Sullivan, "Subway Bread Is Not Bread, Irish Court Rules," *Guardian,* October 1, 2020, https://www.theguardian.com/world/2020/oct/01/irish-court-rules-subway-bread-is-not-bread.

The news was widely reported: "Ireland's Supreme Court Rules Subway Bread Is Not Technically Bread."[38] The Subway chain claims to be in the sandwich business, especially submarine sandwiches, or subs. Yet, at least in Ireland as of 2020, this claim is false. Sandwiches must contain bread. If Subway 'bread' isn't bread, then Subway 'sandwiches' aren't sandwiches.

Again, it's all about taxes. The Subway franchisee in Ireland argued that it's not liable for value-added tax (VAT) on certain products. Although the case had several dimensions and complications, a central question was: "Did the bread used in the appellant's [Subway's] sandwiches fall outside the statutory definition of bread?"[39] The VAT Act 1972 exempts bread from VAT. For something to be bread, "the weight of ingredients such as sugar, fat and bread improver shall not exceed 2 per cent of the weight of flour in the dough." As Supreme Court Justice Donal O'Donnell pointed out: "the Act contains a complicated definition of an everyday product. The intention of the Act in making such a detailed definition is reasonably clear: it seeks to distinguish between bread as a staple food, which should be 0% rated, and other baked goods made from dough, which are, or approach, confectionery or fancy baked goods."[40]

This baked good may look like bread and may get called 'bread,' but it fails to meet that bread standard. It looks like a duck, swims like a duck, and quacks like a duck, but it's not a duck. As reported in the *Irish Times*, "the five-judge court ruled the bread [Subway's] falls outside that statutory definition because it has a sugar content of 10 per cent of the weight of the flour included in the dough."[41] As you'd expect, Subway didn't agree with Justices Clarke, O'Donnell, MacMenamin, Charleton, and O'Malley. A spokesperson said, tautologically: "Subway's bread is, of course, bread. We have been baking fresh bread in our restaurants for more than three decades and our guests return each day for sandwiches made on bread that smells as good as it tastes."[42] "Of course" was of course unwarranted rhetoric.

38. Alina Selyukh, "Ireland's Supreme Court Rules Subway Bread Is Not Technically Bread," NPR, October 3, 2020, https://www.npr.org/2020/10/03/919831116/irish-court-rules-subway -bread-is-not-real-bread.

39. Bookfinders Ltd. Appellant and The Revenue Commissioners Respondent, Judgment of Mr. Justice O'Donnell, September 29, 2020, An Chúirt Uachtarach, Supreme Court, at 5.

40. Bookfinders Ltd., at 45.

41. Mary Carolan, "Subway Bread Too Sweet for the Irish Tax Authorities," *Irish Times*, September 30, 2020, https://www.irishtimes.com/business/agribusiness-and-food/subway -bread-too-sweet-for-the-irish-tax-authorities-1.4367663.

42. Reese Oxner, "For Subway, a Ruling Not So Sweet. Irish Court Says Its Bread Isn't Bread," NPR, October 1, 2020, https://www.npr.org/2020/10/01/919189045/for-subway-a -ruling-not-so-sweet-irish-court-says-its-bread-isnt-bread.

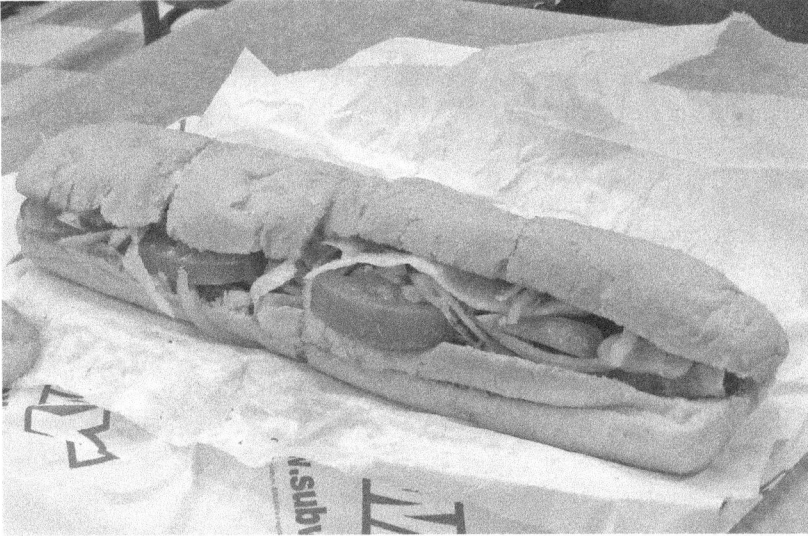

FIGURE 1.3. Not bread (*níl sé sin arán*). Thanks to Sarah Moriarty for the Irish translation. This file is licensed under the Creative Commons Attribution-Share Alike 3.0 Unported license.

The Irish Supreme Court's decision might have been legally impeccable, given the facts of the case, statutory definition, and pertinent laws. Its assignment wasn't to reveal the essence of bread. Still: why "fat, sugar and bread improver... shall not exceed 2 per cent" of the weight of flour? Why is this the correct definition of 'bread'? I grant that I might be raising trick questions. Perhaps there can't be a non-arbitrary percentage of flour. The law's cut-off point must be to some extent, or wholly, arbitrary. While justifications pretend to be well-grounded, they're actually just that: justifications. Legal institutions' face-work.[43]

In any case, Subway wasn't in a position to say. Like any firm, it was driven by its business interests. Like any capitalist firm, it must always act in its business interests, lest it be outcompeted and go bankrupt. And these Irish bread wars were legal wars, whose mechanics and rules are specific to the legal domain. Discussions about the properties of bread, what counts as bread, and how to define 'bread' reflected economic and legal forces.

———

43. Goffman (1955) 1967.

While we're on the subject of baked goods, what is a cake? Are ice-cream cakes and chocolate teacakes cakes[44]? Surely Jaffa Cakes, "Britain's greatest invention after the steam engine and the light bulb," are cakes.[45] Or are they? As a matter of fact, Jaffa Cakes used to be biscuits. But they did become cakes in 1991. Under UK law, VAT is levied on biscuits, whereas cakes are a staple food, and therefore they're zero-rated:

> The manufacturer, McVities, had always categorised [Jaffa Cakes] as cakes and to boost their revenue the tax authorities wanted them recategorised as biscuits. A legal case was fought in front of a brilliant adjudicator, Mr D C Potter. For McVities, this produced a sweet result. The Jaffa Cake has both cake-like qualities and biscuit-like qualities, but Mr Potter's verdict was that, on balance, a Jaffa Cake is a cake.[46]

Potter took into account several "facts and considerations," such as name ('cakes'—"a very minor consideration indeed"), ingredients, texture, size, packaging, marketing, and the fact that a "Jaffa Cake is moist to start with and in that resembles a cake and not a biscuit; with time it becomes stale, and last becomes hard and crisp; again like a cake and not like a biscuit." At the end of the day, he concluded that Jaffa Cakes "have sufficient characteristics of cakes to qualify as cakes."[47] Cakes have definite properties, even essential properties. That's how you can tell whether something is a cake. Subway's subs aren't. Jaffa Cakes are.

You may or may not agree with Potter's approach and with his verdict. Some commentators have qualms about the underlying dichotomous taxonomy, which everyone's claims presupposed. Why only two values? Paleontologist Adam S. Smith has advanced the argument, "based on a scientifically sound cladistic methodology," that "the implementation of a three-way classification

44. "Sales of Ice Cream Cakes and Similar Items," State of Wisconsin Department of Revenue, November 8, 2010, https://www.revenue.wi.gov/Pages/TaxPro/2010/news-2010-101108c .aspx; "I Scream, You Scream, We All Scream for Ice Cream," scene from *Down by Law* by Jim Jarmusch (Criterion Collection, 1986), YouTube, May 28, 2007, https://youtu.be/7rK3s _BP9kE.

British department store Marks & Spencer's chocolate teacakes were treated as biscuits and hence subject to VAT between 1973 and 1994. These "dome-shaped marshmallow thingys" might be depicted as "half cake, half biscuit, and this is where things have gone wrong" (Farrer 2007).

45. Edmonds 2017. Thanks to Nigel Pleasants for bringing Jaffa Cakes' cakeness to my attention.

46. Edmonds 2017.

47. "Jaffa Cakes," Tim Crane's website, n.d., http://www.timcrane.com/jaffa-cakes.html.

is necessary." There needs to be "a new group of biscuit-cake intermediaries, the pseudobiscuits."[48] Jaffa Cakes are pseudobiscuits.

Even if you're sympathetic to Potter's approach and adhere to the underlying dichotomy, you might not be at one with him concerning a cake's properties. Which ones are common and essential, and which ones are common but accidental? What warrants these classificatory judgments?

1.5 Meat and dairy

The issue is, what is chicken?

—*FRIGALIMENT IMPORTING CO. V. B.N.S. INTERNATIONAL SALES CORP.* (1960)

Sandwiches, burritos, and bread bring to the fore some issues I'll bring to bear, mutatis mutandis, on the practice of social science. Sandwiches, burritos, and bread are illustrative, maybe exceptionally illustrative, but not illustrative due to exceptional reasons. Many other things are contentious in these cultural and legal ways. Many meat and dairy products, for example. It'd take you only so far to know that a sandwich consists in "two slices of bread usually buttered, with a thin layer (as of meat, cheese, or savory mixture) spread between them" (one of the subsenses of *Webster's Third*). It's got bread, butter, meat, and cheese. You might not be sure about the extension of 'bread.' Nor about the extension of 'cheese,' 'butter,' and 'meat.'

In August 2013, the "world's first lab-grown burger [was] eaten in London."[49] On live television. The alimentary revolution was indeed televised. 'In-vitro meat' (or 'cultured,' or 'clean') was hailed as a scientific breakthrough. The research project was led by Mark Post, a University of Maastricht professor, and funded by Sergey Brin, one of Google's founders. To produce it, scientists take an animal's "'myosatellite' cells, which are the stem cells of muscles":

> When we want the cells to differentiate into muscle cells, we simply stop feeding them growth factors, and they differentiate on their own. The muscle cells naturally merge to form "myotubes." [...] The myotubes are then placed in a gel that is 99% water, which helps the cells form the shape of muscle fibres. The muscle cells' innate tendency to contract causes them to start putting on bulk, growing into a small strand of muscle tissue. [...]

48. A. Smith 2005, 2.

49. "World's First Lab-Grown Burger Is Eaten in London," *BBC News*, August 5, 2013, https://www.bbc.com/news/science-environment-23576143.

When all these strands are layered together, we get what we started with—meat.[50]

At the 2013 televised event, cultured burgers, also referred to as 'stem cell burgers,' were cooked by a chef and tasted by food critics. They were judged to approximate "the real thing," though they weren't exactly like it.[51] Seven years later, in 2020, lab-grown chicken started to be commercialized. The Israeli startup SuperMeat opened the world's first cultured chicken restaurant in Ness Ziona, a suburb of Tel Aviv. Per one report, its chicken burger "tastes . . . like a chicken burger."[52] In another significant first, the Singapore Food Agency approved the sale of lab-grown chicken "as an ingredient for chicken nuggets, making it the first lab-grown meat to earn regulatory approval."[53]

In addition, there've been impressive technological advances to get plant-based products to better reproduce the look, texture, feel, and flavor of animal meat. Not only burgers and sausages, but also chicken, turkey, and fish. They're becoming more and more commercially successful—and hence more socially, economically, and politically significant than older generations of veggie burgers, and tofu and seitan 'meat substitutes.' While lab-grown meats promise to transform the market in the not-too-distant future, plant-based meats are already a substantial market reality.

Both plant-based and in-vitro meats have been afforded much public attention, so it's hardly surprising that the standard metaphysical questions would be broached. Are they *really* a kind of meat? Or, rather, are they another kind of thing altogether, which is masquerading as true meat, trying to pass off as true meat? Nor is it surprising that metaphysics would blend into legal-cum-semantic conflicts, in which powerful organizations and corporations have a stake (no pun intended).[54] Are the words 'meat' and 'burger' being misused? Can they legally appear in products' packaging and marketing? Thorny questions multiply: whether 'Impossible Burger,' 'Beyond Sausage,' 'THIS Isn't Chicken,' and 'Tofurky Roast' are covered by legislation and regulation of 'meat' production, sale, and consumption; whether 'Impossible Pork' is kosher and halal; whether 'kosher bacon' is truly kosher.[55]

50. "Growing Beef," Mosa Meat, n.d., https://www.mosameat.com/technology.

51. Hogenboom 2013.

52. Holmes 2020.

53. Aridi 2020. The producer is Eat Just, a San Francisco–based startup. Its brand is called 'GOOD Meat.'

54. Salisbury 2020; Tai 2020.

55. Aymann Ismail, "Impossible Pork Is Testing My Faith," Slate, September 28, 2021, https://slate.com/human-interest/2021/09/impossible-pork-muslims-halal-yum.html; Jacob Gurvis,

This much is certain: this is all bad news for cattle ranchers and meat lobbies and trade associations. They don't like what they're seeing. So, they call dibs on "nomenclature associated with protein sourced from livestock production."[56] They claim historical and etymological ownership of the word 'meat'—even though it used to refer to food of any sort, not just the flesh of animals. They lobby legislatures to pass draconian laws that "impose fines of up to $1,000 for every plant-based and cell-based meat product, such as 'veggie burgers' and 'tofu dogs,' marketed or packaged with a 'meat' label." They run ads depicting 'fake meat' as unhealthy and unnatural.[57] Not real meat.

Things can get surreal. To put its point across, the European Union's umbrella agricultural interest group turned to surrealism. Its campaign paraphrased René Magritte: *ceci n'est pas un burger; ceci n'est pas un steak.*

'This isn't a cheeseburger' might express skepticism about any of its essential ingredients. The burger patty doesn't seem to you to be a real burger patty. The bread doesn't seem to you to be real bread. The slice of cheese doesn't seem to you to be real cheese. Disputes over dairy products have a long history, as exemplified by the US Oleomargarine Act of 1886, and the butter industry's all-out war on margarine. Fast-forward to the present and "non-dairy milk alternatives are experiencing a 'holy cow!' moment."[58] The popularity of non-dairy milk, cheese, yogurt, cream, and butter (or, non-dairy 'milk,' 'cheese,' 'yogurt,' 'cream,' 'butter') is growing. Up to a point, the dairy industry didn't feel threatened by a bit of soy milk here and a bit of almond milk there. But now things are going too far. 'Cow-nterfeits' ought to be crushed. "Big Dairy is after your almond milk."[59] *Ceci n'est pas du lait.*

"World's Largest Kosher Certifier Won't Endorse Impossible Pork," *Times of Israel*, October 3, 2021, https://www.timesofisrael.com/worlds-largest-kosher-certifier-wont-endorse-impossible -pork/; David Zvi Kalman/JTA, "Impossible Pork Shouldn't Be Kosher—Opinion," *Jerusalem Post*, October 7, 2021, https://www.jpost.com/opinion/judaism-often-thrives-on-new -technologies-that-doesnt-mean-impossible-pork-should-be-kosher-681284; JTA and Jacob Gurvis, "Kosher 'Pork' Is Hitting the Shelves. Well, Not if You Ask the Rabbinate," *Haaretz*, October 1, 2021, https://www.haaretz.com/food/kosher-pork-is-hitting-the-shelves-well-not-if -you-ask-the-rabbinate-1.10258253; Nathaniel Popper, "Meat Labs Pursue a Once-Impossible Goal: Kosher Bacon," *New York Times*, September 30, 2018, https://www.nytimes.com/2018/09 /30/technology/meat-labs-kosher-bacon.html.

56. The quotation is from the *2019 Policy Book* of the US National Cattlemen's Beef Association.

57. O'Connor 2019.

58. Kateman 2019.

59. M. Roberts 2018.

FIGURE 1.4. *Ceci n'est pas un burger.* COPA-COGECA (Committee of Professional Agricultural Organisations–General Confederation of Agricultural Cooperatives in the European Union). https://copa-cogeca.eu

As usual, the dairy wars have a semantic front.[60] Dairy lobbies will push for bans on "dairy-style names" for plant-based products, as the European Court of Justice did in June 2017 and the European Parliament reaffirmed and extended in October 2020. They banned any reference or parallel to dairy—for example, yogurt-style, cheese-style, cheese substitute, dairy substitute, milky taste (excepting the well-established 'peanut butter' and 'coconut milk'). These lobbies can thereby attempt to control and police the extension of the words '*Milch*,' '*leite*,' '*formaggio*,' '*queso*,' '*beurre*,' and so on. Attempt to *legally* control and police it, that is, because ordinary language isn't so docile. As a consequence, vegan products are forced to get creative and come up with alternative names: 'cheeze,' 'drink' (instead of 'milk'), or 'block' (instead of 'butter').

The dairy industry and trade associations intend to harm plant-based companies' bottom line and market share. The excuse, or at least doubtful empirical claim, is that innocent consumers are confused. They're being misled. Grocery store customers are incapable of understanding that 'vegan cheese' isn't ordinary cheese and 'almond milk' isn't ordinary milk.

Again, this is all predictable. Companies are always looking to increase their profits. They form associations and hire advertising agencies and lobbyists to

60. Sandis 2019.

represent their interests.[61] Simple capitalist dynamics. While my examples have been foodstuffs, similar stories could be told about any class of products or businesses, and their efforts to be defined and classified in an advantageous fashion.[62] Legally, but also socially defined and classified. Businesses, but also other organizations, groups, and ideas. In order to avoid taxes or regulation, to get public funding and support, or to get another sort of practical benefit, prestige, recognition, attention, or good publicity.

Bread, burritos, and cheese are just like motorcycles, casinos, and the distinction between bolts and screws. Beauty salons, luxury goods, and medical devices. Sport, religion, and educational institutions. Art, music, and concerts.[63]

1.6 Law and social science

> To the legal profession . . . words and their meanings are a matter of supreme concern. [. . .] [O]ne of the chief functions of our Courts is to act as an animated and authoritative dictionary.
>
> —LORD MACMILLAN (1937)[64]

What is an *F*? What is *F*-ness? What does the word 'w' refer to? How should 'w' be defined and used?

These are the questions I've been looking at, in their general form. The capital letter *F* stands for any thing, entity, object, phenomenon. The letter 'w,' in single quotation marks, stands for any word or expression.

The debate between John Hodgman and Dan Pashman was at a Gowanus venue. There were no legal implications, no legal context, no judge or jury. Even if Hodgman is a 'judge'—and has been sympathetically called "America's preeminent fake jurist."[65] For the most part, though, I've been considering

---

61. Another illustration is products' names furthering national and regional economic interests; e.g., geographical indications and designations of origin: 'champagne,' 'port,' 'jerez,' 'zinfandel,' 'tequila,' 'Roquefort,' 'Gruyère.' Cf. Bowen 2015; Jurca 2013.

62. See also the US Supreme Court's decisions in 1889 than beans are vegetables (*Robertson v. Salomon*) and in 1893 that tomatoes are vegetables (*Nix v. Hedden*) (the Tariff Act of 1883 imposed a tax on vegetables, but not on fruit); and the British Supreme Court of Judicature's decision in 2009 that Pringles are potato chips (i.e., 'crisps') (A. Cohen 2009).

63. "Is techno really music? Is it a concert when a DJ plays music?" (Radomsky 2020; my translation). In 2020, the German Federal Finance Court (*Bundesfinanzhof*) answered 'yes' to both questions. Concert halls get a tax break; so do clubs.

64. Macmillan 1937, 147, 163.

65. "These Judge John Hodgman Food Rulings Are Established Culinary Law," AllRecipes, n.d., https://www.allrecipes.com/article/these-judge-john-hodgman-food-rulings-are-established-culinary-law/.

actual legal wrangles, which have legal—and dollars-and-cents—consequences. Asking what *F* is, or how to define 'w,' isn't an end but a means. It's an argumentative tool, which lawyers don't value in itself. Instead of metaphysical or semantic truths, they seem to be thinking about worldly, material interests. Their clients' and their own. Money, power, and status. Getting a tax break, being awarded damages, or being acquitted. This is so across the board, be it about food labeling, private contracts, taxation, patents, or the Constitution.[66] Be it about the definition of 'sandwich,' 'chicken,' or 'terrorism.'

What is an *F*? What is *F*-ness? What does 'w' refer to? How should 'w' be defined and used?

These questions ineludibly arise in the formulation, interpretation, and application of the law. Whatever a law says about a kind of thing, there'll be disputes over what it does and doesn't comprise; where borderline cases fall. Think of the legal history and vicissitudes of marriage, life and death, person, rape, sex, and consent.[67] Think of art, pornography, manslaughter, insanity, religion, nightclub, and book.[68] Their construal in courtrooms and legislatures might be ontological—that is, what those things are. Or it might be semantic—that is, what those words refer to. In either case, higher-order, methodological, philosophy-of-law problems await.[69]

Who's to say what a sandwich is (and whether burritos and hot dogs are included)? Who's to say how to determine what a sandwich is (and whether burritos and hot dogs are included)? Do professionals and experts outweigh dictionaries and ordinary or plain meaning, or vice versa?[70] Do metaphysicians' reflections on sandwichness matter?[71] To decide what a problematic word picks out, should you focus on the text itself (e.g., a statute or a contract) or on authors' intentions and purposes?[72] Is 'I know it when I see it' a defensible method?[73] Do departments of taxation have ontological powers to rule that hot dogs are sandwiches?

---

66. See Lemley (2020) on patent law in the United States, how *Texas Digital Systems v. Telegenix, Inc.* (2002) brought about "chaos and uncertainty," and how *Phillips v. AWH Corp.* (2005) overruled it.

67. Bergelson 2014; Dembroff, Kohler-Hausmann, and Sugarman 2020; Sommers 2020.

68. Bokulich 2014; R. Dworkin 2011,158; Ludlow 2014.

69. H.L.A. Hart (1953) 1983.

70. Slocum 2015; Tobia 2020. Ordinary or plain meaning has many synonyms in the law, as documented by Slocum (2015, 287–88). On 'original public meaning' and 'original intent' as camps of originalism, see Kay (2009) and McGinnis and Rappaport (2019).

71. K. Fine 1999; Koslicki 2007.

72. L. Alexander and Prakash 2004; Manning 2006; Nelson 2005; Sinnott-Armstrong 2005; Solan 1993.

73. *Jacobellis v. Ohio*, 378 U.S. 184 (1964). Cf. Gewirtz 1996.

Legal arguments depend on claims about what F is or what 'w' means. This is so across the board, be it about food labeling, private contracts, taxation, patents, or the Constitution. Be it about the definition of 'sandwich,' 'chicken,' or 'terrorism.' In this sense, legal cases pave the way for what I have in store. Yet, in other ways, the law is peculiar. It's peculiar what's at stake and how these cases can be tackled. Natural language, dictionaries, and common sense may be consulted and may have the last word. Parties' interests are so obvious, so conspicuous, they're so much at the forefront, and they'll be directly advanced, or not, by a legal judgment. Not to mention that lawyers are playing their own litigation game, which has its own rules. They unequivocally set out to win the case, no matter what.

In light of these prima facie peculiarities, you might wonder if my legal examples generalize to other domains. Aren't these processes specific to the workings of the law and legal institutions in contemporary capitalist societies?

In the respects I'm interested in, I think they aren't peculiar. What they suggest isn't tied to any particular domain, field, or locus. Outside the law, legal/dollars-and-cents consequences may be replaced by status/social/cultural consequences. There are causal relations between the former and the latter, but they aren't the same thing. Take the countless clashes on the internet and social media about sandwichness, hotdogness, and burritoness. People argue, passionately, about what these things really are, what their nature or essence is. It matters to them. They want to be right. But their ardent posts make no difference whatsoever to the law, regulatory agencies, or public policy (thank goodness).

Sometimes you and your friends butt heads over what is and isn't a sport. You care about the status of chess, darts, fishing, breaking, Barbie Jeep Racing, or esports. Their social recognition and attention, among your coworkers, family, acquaintances, and elsewhere. You'd psychologically enjoy their achieving higher status. In your opinion, they absolutely are sports, real sports, and you're ready to argue for this. But you aren't thinking about the pecuniary effects of recognition and attention, which will accrue to leading practitioners, associations, brokers, and media companies. You aren't thinking about tax breaks, public support, and other legal and political benefits. Being a sport has positive social and cultural consequences. What matters to you and motivates you are these consequences, in and of themselves. You may go even further. To you and many of your friends, the fact that breaking will become an Olympic sport, starting in Paris 2024, isn't a valuable means but a valuable end. It's true and it's right.

———

The topic of this book isn't food. It's science. Especially, but not exclusively, social science. I'm going to look at F and 'w' in scientific research and arguments. As ever, concerns about scientific exceptionalism may surface. Aren't scientists' words and concepts governed by objective scientific methods, an airtight scientific logic, or something along these lines? Isn't science unique? I'll argue that in some respects it is, but in other respects it isn't.

'Terrorism' can illustrate the road down which I'd like to go. Politicians and lawyers make arguments about what terrorism is, or the correct definition of 'terrorism.' They do so in legislative chambers, courts, international meetings, and rallies. Press conferences and interviews. These aren't contributions to metaphysics, semantics, or lexicography. They aren't intended to be perceptive accounts and novel additions to the social science literature on terrorism. Rather, it's political and legal practice. Politicians and lawyers have practical aims: scoring political points, increasing their popularity and power, weakening rivals, persuading judges, juries, and public opinion. They want to see the Palestine Liberation Organization (PLO), the Ku Klux Klan (KKK), Antifa, or Robespierre delegitimized (or not). Ineffective (or not). Outlawed (or not). Obliterated by the police and counterterrorist units (or not). To punish organizations and individuals you hate, get them to be considered terrorists. By public opinion and by the law. Like Israel's president accused Ben & Jerry's of "a new kind of terrorism."[74] Plan B: get them to be considered communists or Nazis. Or, even better, both. (In the United States, communism would be overkill. Socialism is enough of a bogeyperson.)

Meanwhile, in the remote confines of the ivory tower, social scientists keep busy writing learned papers about the nature, causes, and history of terrorism. They organize academic conferences on the multiple definitions of 'terrorism.' They argue that science helps resist the spread of terrorist ideologies, so research funding organizations aren't misspending their money. For their part, lexicographers are working on clear and concise definitions of 'terrorism' for their dictionaries. They're hard at work finding out how English speakers use this word, how many senses it has, its etymology, and how its meaning or meanings might have changed over time.

Scientists and lexicographers are engaged in scholarly research. Some of their work has good applications, which are profitable to society, from education

74. TOI staff, "After Ben & Jerry's Snub, Herzog Calls Israel Boycotts a 'New Kind of Terrorism,'" *Times of Israel*, July 21, 2021, https://www.timesofisrael.com/citing-ben-jerrys-snub -herzog-says-israel-boycotts-a-new-kind-of-terrorism/; Johanthan Lis, "Israel's President: Ben & Jerry's Boycott Is Part of 'A New Form of Terrorism,'" *Haaretz*, July 21, 2021, https://www .haaretz.com/israel-news/2021-07-21/ty-article/.premium/israels-president-ben-jerrys-boycott -is-part-of-a-new-form-of-terrorism/.

reform to bilingual dictionaries. Aren't they unlike lawyers who'll do anything to win a case, anything so their client gets off scot-free, and who'd laugh society's welfare out of court? Aren't they unlike politicians who must worry about reelection, fundraising, partisan politics, public opinion, and the childish tweets of their country's president?

Scientists and lexicographers try to get it right. Their job is to make true knowledge claims. Proven true by looking at reality. Not shaped by people's preferences, wishes, or taste. By contrast, socialist, social-democratic, conservative, and libertarian views are dissimilar political orientations. They correspond to people's dissimilar preferences, priorities, values, and worldviews. Therefore, they aren't capable of truth or falsity, are they? You may like the red party better than the white party, you may endorse conservative social policies, you may be convinced that Chicago should elect a socialist mayor, but that's just your subjective preference, isn't it?

In sum, aren't scientists the polar opposite of politicians and lawyers? Isn't politics antipodal to science?

Not so fast, buckaroo.

2

The problem

2.1 What's the problem?

The problem is as practical as they come. Scientists are in the business of making true claims about the world. Their claims are neither about words and concepts nor about statistical results and mathematical relationships. Rather, they're about subatomic particles, stem cells, holobionts, herbivores, platypuses, planets, welfare states, and populist regimes. But here's the thing. The things about which science makes claims don't have badges announcing what kind of thing they are. 'Hi, I'm a planet!' 'Hi, I'm a gene!' 'Hi, I'm an institution!' 'Hi, I'm empathy (not sympathy)!' 'Hi, I'm a cult (not a religion)!' That would have been nice of them, had they taken the trouble. Even worse for social science: unlike astronomers', chemists', and biologists' things, social things may have badges, conspicuously displayed badges, but they can't be trusted. 'Hi, I'm (totally, totally) a democratic organization!' 'Hi, I'm a religion (not a mere cult or sect)!' 'Hi, I'm a profession (not a mere occupation)!'

Nor do things have badges announcing that they are one thing, one distinct thing, as opposed to two things, several things, or one part of a thing. 'I'm one social class!' 'I'm one process or one event (I begin right here and end right there)!' 'I'm one practice, not three interrelated practices!' 'I'm an action or a behavior!'[1] 'I'm one organism, neither several organisms nor one part of a larger organism!' Even worse: there's no exhaustive catalog of kinds of things, which could inform scientists of their options when they're sorting stuff out. It'd be convenient for scientists, and for librarians, to have exhaustive and unchanging lists of subject headings. But there aren't any.

Typically, a scientist's object of inquiry isn't an individual—that is, one singular thing. There are exceptions, though. You may observe and make claims about the moon: that'd be a selenography project. You may observe and

---

1. Anscombe 2000, 45; Austin 1957, 27; Davidson 1963, 686; Longino 2013.

make claims about Pepe Mujica, from Tupamaros member in the 1960s to president in the 2010s: that'd be a political biography project. You may observe and make claims about Donald Trump's election and presidency: that'd be a disaster studies project. If you're asked what your claims are about, you may respond ostensively, pointing to it. 'That white, round thing up there. Made of green cheese.' 'That guy on your TV screen. Petting a three-legged dog.'

But that's uncommon. In general, scientific claims are general: they are about planets, pandas, chlamydiae, and religious rituals. Social movements, criminal behavior, and discrimination on the basis of race and gender. They're about relationships between sets, classes, types, categories, or kinds of things. While in general they have scope conditions, they are general claims. Their truth or falsity depends on what's in the set, class, type, category, kind, or taxon. Suppose you're going to investigate the properties of planets, OCD (obsessive-compulsive disorder) patients, and terrorist organizations. That's going to be a function of what you take a planet, OCD patient, and terrorist organization to be. Looking at it from the other side, whether Pluto and Eris are planets, Antifa and the KKK are terrorist organizations, koala bears are bears, whale sharks and beaked whales are fish, and Trump's and Chávez's regimes were populist. This isn't brain surgery: how many books there are in your library is a function of whether you count pamphlets, encyclopedia volumes, journals, and audio books.

Are you writing a paper about F-things? Do you describe the set of F-things? Do you explain it, make predictions about it, give an account of it, tell its history, shed light on it? It seems you have to know what's an instance of it. What makes this object here, and that object there, and that other object belong to the class: *these* are the significant similar properties among them (while their differences aren't significant). You have to draw a boundary between F-things and other things. Between the phenomenon you're explaining and neighboring phenomena. Between the kind of thing you're describing and neighboring kinds. These are demarcation or delimitation tasks. Looking at it from the other side, you have to know what F is not; what it does not encompass.[2] At least, you need to roughly know this about your F—roughly as

2. These points have been expressed in many ways: what F is and isn't; what F-ness is and isn't; what constitutes F; what counts as F; what qualifies as F; how to individuate or pick out F; what passes or masquerades as F (in critical remarks). Also: how to apply F; what is and isn't an F-token; what's the definition of the word 'w' (which stands for F); what falls under F; and what falls into the extension of word 'w' or concept c. Distinctions produce classifications, taxonomies, categorizations, and typologies, in which you have F-things and other things. There's a boundary between F and non-F. This is a rough-and-ready laundry list, which lumps

opposed to accurately, certainly, definitively. That's a lower, less ambitious bar. But some such bar must be there.

My friend Diego is a demographer. To make claims about population growth in South America in the twentieth century, he needs to distinguish between countries that are and aren't in South America (hint: Uruguay is, Nicaragua isn't). My friend Wyman is a historical sociologist. To make claims about the causes of revolutions, she needs to say what is and isn't a revolution. A genuine, bona fide revolution, not just something similar to it. Arguably, this shouldn't be up to her, up to her discretionary 'definition,' lest she gerrymander F, so her causal claims come out true. Whether her explanandum comprises France 1789, Spain 1868, Uruguay 1904, and Nicaragua 1979 shouldn't depend on these data points' welcome or unwelcome effects on her statistical results. My friend Elena is an anthropologist. To make claims about the most frequent characteristics of religions across the world, she needs to say what is and isn't a religion. A genuine, bona fide religion, not just something similar to it, like a cult or a sect. Arguably, this shouldn't be up to her, up to her discretionary 'definition,' lest she gerrymander F, so her frequency claims come out true.

My friend Diego is one lucky social scientist. His demographic research can rely on a widespread convention, an institutionalized classification and naming convention. Venezuela, Uruguay, and Paraguay are in South America. Nicaragua, Guatemala, and Mexico aren't. Diego is aware of this convention, audiences and journal referees are aware of this convention, and that's all there is to it. Elementary school geography. He doesn't have to bother with kinds, natural kinds, and other dangerous things (with regard to South America—he shouldn't start celebrating just yet). But what in the world are Wyman and Elena supposed to do? They're aiming for claims about causes and frequencies, respectively, which require knowing what F is and isn't. Is this a revolution? Is that a religion?

The answer isn't to be found in 'the literature'—that is, the historical sociology of revolutions or the anthropology of religion. Much to the contrary: what you find in the literature is recurrent disputes over what's a revolution, what's a religion, what's an institution, what's populism, what's power, and what's pretty much anything social scientists have ever devoted their attention to.

These disputes are common in social science disciplines and subdisciplines. They're historically familiar, too. They repeat themselves. Time and time again you see analogous conflicts, parties, standoffs, and cul-de-sacs about the very

---

together things, phenomena, concepts, categories, and words. I'll say more about this mess in chapter 4.

same words. Logically, these disputes have direct implications for social scientists' empirical claims, models, hypotheses, and theories. Truth, predictive power, and policy relevance are affected by what does and doesn't fall under their key word or concept.

The history of all hitherto-existing social science is the history of such struggles. One part of its history, anyway.

––––––––

The problem is as practical as they come. You may not be into social theory and epistemology stuff, never mind philosophy of language and metaphysics, but we're talking business here. We're talking about what to do tomorrow morning at your lab, field site, archives, or computer. Not highfalutin social theory and philosophy, but how to select your data, code them, and design experiments. What to observe and what to sample. We're talking tomorrow morning. The problem is as practical and urgent as they come.

Practical, urgent, and decisive in five interconnected ways. First, your research will yield claims about F. Whether they're true is partly dependent on what F is and comprises. Second, whether the evidence you collected is evidence about F. Third, whether you're studying the same thing as other scientists and labs are, and hence your findings can corroborate or refute theirs. Or, rather, they're interested in the same area or topic, but what they're observing, measuring, and explaining is slightly different. Fourth, whether you can find F in ancient China, Capetian France, Uruguay in the 1950s, and contemporary Germany. What historical and comparative claims can be made about it? Fifth, in presentations and interviews about your work, whether you should do air quotes each time you mention F. That'd be tiring. Perhaps unintentionally funny as well.[3]

In this sense, words (or concepts) are essential workers. Unlike the claims of mathematics and logic, which are formal all the way down, the claims of science must somehow hook up to things in the world. They must be about real-world phenomena and processes—and normally about classes of real-world phenomena and processes. It's controversial whether the goal of scientists' claims is to correspond to the way the world is, or to mirror the world.[4] It's uncontroversial that scientists' claims need to be about the world.[5]

3. "Friends: Joey Doesn't Understand Air Quotes," YouTube, May 27, 2020, https://youtu.be/6C4ZV4TW86g.

4. Kitcher 2002; Leeds 2007; Rorty 1979.

5. The pivotal word 'about' isn't straightforward. On mental states' aboutness, directedness, or intentionality, see Brentano (1874), Goodman (1961), Ryle (1933), and Searle (1983). The pivotal word 'correspond' isn't straightforward either ('correspond to the way the world is').

This isn't to deny that science avails itself of formalization, simulation, and fictional assumptions. Thought experiments, lab experiments, and models. But these are means. The end is actual reality, the actual world. And a key mediator is language. Mediator, intermediary, connector, bridge, or middleperson. Whether this is a curse or a blessing, human beings' grasp and accounts of reality are mediated by language.[6] Scientists do many things. One of them is to make statements about what the world is like. Science produces many things. Statements, representations, explanations, interpretations, and accounts of reality. Technologies, machines, instruments, policies, and interventions. There's knowing that and knowing how. Succeeding by being true, by being illuminating, and by working. There's a lot more. I don't imply any hierarchy or priority. Making true statements about the world is one way for scientists to do well.

The problem concerns so-called 'qualitative' research as much as so-called 'quantitative' research. Findings about qualities and attributes as much as findings about quantities and relations. Small-N and large-N studies. Ethnographic, historical, and statistical data and methods. Data science, computational social science, and digital social science: access to large datasets and powerful methodological techniques doesn't mean 'what is F?' can be relegated to an afterthought, a post hoc 'framing' issue.[7]

Comparative and historical sociologists, who generally like generalizations, confront a special form of the problem: 'what is your case a case of?' How to establish if this is a case of F? Is it a case of F despite its dissimilarities to these undoubted cases of F? What can your claims be generalized to? In virtue of what is a phenomenon comparable and analogous to another?[8] Historians and anthropologists confront another special form. They study culturally distant objects. Some of their words (e.g., contemporary American English words) are cumbersome tools to pick out and depict such phenomena, institutions, and practices. They sound unnatural. Charges of anachronism, presentism, and ethnocentrism ensue. There was no F at that time—indeed, there couldn't be! There is no F in that place—indeed, there can't be! You can't speak of 'religion,' 'secularization,' 'racism,' 'nature,' or 'democracy' there and then.[9]

6. One mediator is language. There are other mediators: material, embodied, and social. Mediators, intermediaries, connectors, bridges, or middlepersons. Thanks to Sabina Leonelli for her comments on these issues.

7. Case in point: neuroscientists who study morality, empathy, love, art, and religion. Novel brain-imaging techniques won't tell you what the resulting neural correlates are neural correlates of (Abend 2017, 2018b; Pardo and Patterson 2013).

8. On comparative history's comparisons, see Bloch (1928), Hill and Hill (1980), and Sewell (1967). On how to go "beyond comparison," see Werner and Zimmermann (2006).

9. Barton and Boyardin 2016; Guhin 2014; Nongbri 2013; J. Smith 1998.

Policy scholars get phone calls and emails asking if F is good, what its effects are, and how to further it. Calling, or emailing, are governments, firms, educational institutions, NGOs (non-governmental organizations), and other organizations. They want to hear social science's predictions: how their organization will profit from more diversity, empathy, and trust; what the consequences of beefing up their gender equality or corporate social responsibility strategies will be. But F's identity is left up in the air.

Quantitative social scientists confront yet other special forms of the problem. They have to defend the categories and subcategories, types and subtypes, used in analyses, models, measurements, and questionnaires. Why they went for a categorical variable here and why they chose this reference category there.[10] They have to forestall objections of arbitrariness, or even deviousness, as to how they split and lump the data, what they group together with what, what they exclude, and their chosen scales and cut-off points. These methodological choices aren't cosmetic, but significantly associated with statistical significance and goodness of fit. They're prone to being exploited by unethical researchers and data analysts.

What's your object of inquiry? What are your claims about? What do they not apply to? Why to this, but not to that? Regardless of how data are collected and analyzed, scientists have to have answers to these questions. More or less rough around the edges. Sooner or later. But they can't be sidestepped. Whatever it is you're investigating, you'll be asked what it includes and why. You'll be expected to understand the classificatory or taxonomic rules that determine what's in and what's out, along with their rationales. Else, your object of inquiry may be faulted for being a pastiche, ad hoc, random, capricious. Immorally gerrymandered, uncritically adopted, or generated by an opaque algorithm.

In its general form, the question is: 'what is F?' You may recognize it as a metaphysical question, prominent in the history of philosophy.[11] However, I'm not putting this question to philosophers but to social scientists, who do empirical research for a living. A version of it, in fact. I'll argue for and work with a question about words: how word 'w' should be used. Not about ontology: what thing F is. Nor about concepts and conceptualizations. Bear with me.

———

Is the preceding discussion applicable to both social scientists and natural scientists? Isn't natural science off the hook to some extent? It's hard to say

10. Johfre and Freese 2021.
11. R. Robinson 1941, 1950; Wolfsdorf 2003a, b.

without inspecting the purported dichotomy between the two kinds of scientific inquiries. Both 'social science' and 'natural science' are big tents. Maybe research on polonium and protactinium is off the hook, research on protons and photons is to some extent or under certain conditions off the hook, whereas research on planets and pandas isn't at all.

Social scientists study institutions, norms, interactions, and language. They study people's feelings, thoughts, ideas, and intentions. Pluto is an inanimate, unfeeling, unthinking object, if ever there was one. But planetary scientists won't stop fighting over its status (see the appendix). Is it a planet, a dwarf planet, or something else? The planethood wars show that the problem ultimately lies with us, not with our objects. It's not you, planets and other celestial bodies, it's us.

Be that as it may, the problem has been more salient in the social sciences, broadly conceived: sociology, political science, international relations, social work, history, anthropology, management and organization studies, gender studies, science and technology studies (STS), education, economics, and so on.[12] To some observers, this fact underscores the epistemological distinctiveness of social science. Critics see here the canary in the coal mine. While all of these disciplines have encountered 'what-F-is' difficulties, sociology is salient in my account. My rationale isn't principled, but a more or less unfortunate biographical accident.

———

The problem is as old as they come. Philosophers have worried about it from two points of view: that of metaphysics, and that of language and mind. From the former, they've analyzed what it is to ask what F is; what a kind is; whether there's such thing as natural kinds; what an essential property is; whether there are abstract objects or, rather, just particulars or concrete objects. From the latter, they've asked how words relate to the world; how cognition and representation are conceptual; what words and concepts are; how to deal with their vagueness. Meanwhile, social scientists have mostly worried about the problem as a methodological one: how to identify and measure social things; how to identify and measure social things cross-culturally, comparatively, or

12. Economics isn't a main character in this book, despite the important policy implications of its definitions and measurements, and their patent moral aspects. Hopefully I'll encourage others to look in depth at economists' words and distinctions. Philosophy and jurisprudence are special cases, because their research isn't empirical like normal social science (except for experimental philosophy and experimental jurisprudence). Thanks to Steven Lukes for his comments on economics.

historically; what makes a type a type; how to determine what empirical findings are about; whether social scientific knowledge can cumulate and make progress.

And yet, old though the problem is, it remains a thorn in social science's side. Social scientists aren't sure what to do about it and why. Key words (or concepts) remain the Achilles' heel of their otherwise rigorous methodologies. While methodological techniques get increasingly more powerful and sophisticated, this Achilles' heel is as vulnerable as ever to Paris's arrow. Just look at present-day scientific practice, as well as discussions about good scientific practice. Look at scientific publications, especially journal articles' introductions, conclusions, and 'data and methods' sections. The warrant for social scientists' word and distinction choices isn't clear. Multiple criteria coexist within communities, fields, literatures, conversations, and exchanges—reasons to use this word rather than that one, and reasons to criticize someone else's word use. Social scientists feel free to pick and choose from these criteria, without having definite criteria to choose criteria. There are multiple options. Why invoke this one, rather than that one, at this point?

No offense, but social scientists' thinking on these issues hasn't been top-notch. For example, as Becker observes, some researchers "deal with all difficult conceptual questions by saying, *authoritatively*, 'Well, it all depends on how you define your terms.'"[13] Sure thing. It always does.

- "Is the threat of cyber war underplayed or overhyped? This depends on how you define cyber war."[14]
- "When will we know the pandemic is over? [...] That depends on how you define the pandemic."[15]
- "Does money make you happy? [...] [I]t all depends on how you define happiness."[16]
- "Do you trust politicians? Depends on how you define trust."[17]

13. Becker 1998, 1 (emphasis added).

14. "Risk of Cyber War" 2017.

15. Zoë Read, "Is the Pandemic Really Winding Down? And if Not, How Will We Know When It Is?," WHYY, July 5, 2021, https://whyy.org/articles/is-the-pandemic-really-winding -down-and-if-not-how-will-we-know-when-it-is/.

16. Diana Yates, "Can Money Buy Happiness? Gallup Poll Asks, and the World Answers," Illinois News Bureau, Research News, July 1, 2010, https://news.illinois.edu/view/6367/205589.

17. "Do You Trust Politicians? Depends on How You Define Trust," MSU Today, May 15, 2019, https://msutoday.msu.edu/news/2019/do-you-trust-politicians-depends-on-how-you -define-trust.

No eye-opener there. What it'd be fantastic to learn is how these words should be defined, what's a good or the best definition. Do you believe that any definition of 'cyber war,' 'pandemic,' 'happiness,' and 'trust' is as good as any other, so everyone's free to make up their own? If so, it's not good enough to loudly declare it, let alone to quietly assume it. At the very least, you owe an argument to the rest of us, why that's so, and what its implications are.

Social science communities' uncertainty is most evident when disagreements arise. In a disagreement situation, word choices need to be spelled out, examined, and defended. Implicit criteria become explicit. Reasons are pitted against one another. Social scientists are compelled to argue for their uses of key words. Which arguments, I think, leave much to be desired.

2.2 Objects

Social scientists do research on many and varied topics. Table 2.1 provides a bunch of examples.

These lengthy lists aren't exhaustive, they're probably tedious, and the disciplinary pigeonholing is somewhat artificial. My point is simply to illustrate the diversity of social scientists' objects of inquiry (*OOIs*). By 'object of inquiry' I mean that on which social scientists advance knowledge claims. What they do research, collect data, and develop testable theories and predictions on.[18] For this early part of my argument, *OOI* is conveniently broad—or, to be less forgiving to myself, conveniently vague. It's agnostic as regards what sort of thing *OOI* is. Whether a phenomenon, word, concept, representational device, construct, something else, some or all of the above. Whether a mental item, a language item, or something in the world. I'll also speak of 'ooi,' in single quotation marks, to refer to the English word or expression that stands for *OOI*.

To do research and make claims about *OOI*, social scientists have to observe it. Measure it. Or observe and measure indicators of it: manifestations, expressions, proxies. Which in turn means they have to conceptualize and operationalize it. Eventually, on the basis of their research and analyses, social scientists put forward statements about the properties, structure, causes, and effects of *OOI*. They tell us why it occurred, why it came into being, why it increased or decreased, and, if they like evolutionary theory, why it evolved. Subsequently, *OOI* figures in social scientists' recommendations for public

---

18. 'Object of inquiry,' or 'object of study,' or 'object' *tout court* (Bourdieu, Chamboredon, and Passeron 1968). 'Object' doesn't mean an individual, material object in the world, like my bass or your bike. It's an abstract entity, or collection, or idea of some sort.

TABLE 2.1. Social scientists' objects of inquiry

Discipline	Researchers advance and test claims about
Sociology	class, race, racism, ethnicity, status, stratification, family, identity, diversity, art, music, multiculturalism, collective memory, immigration, integration, socialization, social cohesion, social movement, revolution, knowledge, work, profession, sport, religiosity, secularization, crime, discrimination, poverty, inequality, capital, social capital, cultural capital, cultural schemas, social structure, action or agency
Political science	democracy, democratization, socialism, totalitarianism, nationalism, xenophobia, populism, polarization, the state, the welfare state, rights, freedom, political culture, civil society, citizenship, war, civil war, genocide, corruption, terrorism
Anthropology	religion, magic, ritual, sect, cult, myth, folklore, witchcraft, gift giving, rationality, play, dance, personhood, kinship, indigeneity/Indigenous peoples, colonialism
Organization and management studies	corporate social responsibility, sustainability, stakeholder, organization, institution, management, bureaucracy, entrepreneurship, leadership, business, businesses
Psychology	cognition, emotion, creativity, imagination, intelligence, consciousness, happiness, well-being, altruism, reciprocity, empathy, extraversion and introversion, suggestibility, love, compassion, automaticity, the self
Clinical psychology and psychiatry	anxiety, stress, hyperactivity, attention, addiction, paraphilia, depression, mental health, all the mental disorders identified in manuals like the *Diagnostic and Statistical Manual of Mental Disorders*
Many social science disciplines	science, globalization, capitalism, markets, neoliberalism, empire and imperialism, development, slavery, gender, sex, sexuality, power, culture, practices, social imaginaries, frames, morality, values, ideology, law, bias, community, morale, friendship, health, disability, the environment, nature, trust, trustworthiness, legitimacy, decision-making, language, technology, information, communication, system, artificial intelligence, digitalization
Social and cultural neuroscience	some of the above, focusing on their neural correlates
History	much of the above, focusing on their past

policy, politics, or therapy. They prospectively estimate its good and bad causal effects. The word 'ooi' occurs in the titles of their journal articles and books. In the titles of their grant proposals, research statements, and conference presentations. Blog posts, Substack posts, and TED talks. They're invited to podcasts and television shows as experts on *OOI*.

But here's the thing. Social scientists can't agree on what *OOI* is. Even, or especially, experts on 'it'; the people who spend their professional lives studying 'it.' They can't agree either on how to pick it out or individuate it. What makes it the case that you have an instance of it before you, as opposed to an instance of something else. What makes it the case that you have a piece of evidence about it, not about something else. Since the very beginning of research in this area: take two papers where 'ooi' is in the title, and they won't necessarily be describing and explaining the same object, process, or phenomenon. This also changes over time, so *OOI* (or 'ooi') has an eventful genealogy. Intellectual and conceptual historians document its creation and emergence, its metamorphoses and splits, and its demise and disappearance.[19] These genealogies aren't universal, but vary across disciplines and traditions.

Take any of the examples in table 2.1. Disputes over them regularly come about, which play out in public and private forums. Journals devote special issues and conferences devote thematic sessions to what *OOI* is: its nature or character; its best conception, conceptualization, or definition. Because of *OOI* and 'ooi' issues, book manuscripts, article submissions, and grant applications are turned down. Tenure files are voted down. Published book reviews are critical owing to the author's conceptualization of *OOI* or definition of 'ooi,' which doesn't square with the reviewer's own. This happens since the very beginning of scholarship on *OOI*.

Things unfold in predictable ways, as if they were scripted. In any scholarly community or community of inquiry. In the history of any field, literature, discipline, subdiscipline. Community members have often expressed views about how to (best) conceptualize, operationalize, and measure *OOI*. What's a good (or the best) *OOI* concept. What *OOI* is 'best seen as' or 'best understood as.' Some people are vocal and assertive about it. They claim to know what *OOI* really or truly is; what's the real or true meaning of the word 'ooi.'

As a result, the community ends up with a variety of such views. A large variety, if *OOI* is central in the field and the community is large. This is costly, like inflation. It's time-consuming. Frustrating. Community members complain: there are too many competing 'conceptions,' 'conceptualizations,' 'construals,' 'constructs,' 'views,' or 'understandings' of *OOI*, which are inconsistent or

19. Danziger 1997.

incommensurable. We aren't sure what *OOI* is anymore. The word 'ooi' is defined and used in too many different ways; it means different things to different people; it has too many 'meanings' or 'senses.' There's no consensus in the literature on what counts as, qualifies as, or falls under *OOI*.

I bet you've heard and read things like this in your areas of expertise. The "notion of ['ooi'] has accumulated a bewildering variety of subtly different connotations. . . . This confusion is nowhere better documented than in the proceedings of the Conference on [*OOI*]."[20] "Research on [*OOI*] has always been characterized by an open and ongoing debate about how to define the phenomenon."[21] At present, there's a "dizzying proliferation of different definitions unaccompanied by an understanding as to how they might speak to each other."[22]

Books and papers on *OOI* tend to begin with the word 'unfortunately' or a synonym thereof. Particularly literature reviews, *Annual Review* pieces, and other accounts of the state of the art. 'Unfortunately, there's no agreed-upon definition of "ooi" in the literature.' 'Unfortunately, our field hasn't been able to agree on what *OOI* is.' 'There are as many definitions of "ooi" as *OOI* researchers.' Therefore, "for all the talk about [*OOI*] . . . it is far from obvious that we know what we are talking about."[23] Such a terrible state of affairs for a scientific field! On a more positive note, the community is at long last aware of the problem: "for some years there has been a growing realization among social scientists that the [*OOI*] concept needs a careful reexamination."[24]

Further, in their meta-analysis moments, review pieces point out that so many review pieces point out "the lack of clarity about the concept" (and "[cast] doubts about its usefulness"). Pointing this out "has become almost a cliché."[25] In brief:

---

20. Allcock 1971, 378. The "Conference on Populism . . . was held at the London School of Economics, in May 1967." "There is not space in this essay to examine in detail the progress of the two days of the conference discussions: suffice it to say that the congregation of such an assembly of experience and interest, having such a diversity of personal and academic viewpoints, tended if anything to compound rather than simplify the problem of defining 'populism.'"

21. Rovira Kaltwasser et al. 2017, 12.

22. Gagnon et al. 2018, v.

23. Müller 2016, 2.

24. Blumenthal 1954.

25. F. Panizza (2005, 1): "It has become almost a cliché to start writing on populism by lamenting the lack of clarity about the concept and casting doubts about its usefulness for political analysis."

Although frequently used by historians, social scientists, and political commentators, the term is exceptionally vague and refers in different contexts to a bewildering variety of phenomena. [. . .] If we dig deep enough, can we find some central core, some esoteric essence uniting them? Scholars have made valiant attempts to identify such an essence, but the results are not encouraging. [. . .] [T]he conference 'To Define [*OOI*]' . . . demonstrated that the term was being used to describe so many different things that some of the participants doubted whether it could be said to mean anything at all.[26]

A few people complain about these complaints: they are meta-complainers. Things are fine as they are. Community members don't have *OOI* and 'ooi' troubles, but standard empirical disagreements about its properties, causes, and effects. They know what it is. They understand one another. Language use can regulate itself! Even specialized, technical languages, like scientific disciplines' languages. In a word, no action is needed. Neither defining 'ooi' nor specifying the conditions under which something falls under its extension. Nor organizing yet another conference on what *OOI* is, in an effort to finally pin down its identity and nature.

Other meta-complainers go further. That a social science community lacks a consensus on *OOI* and 'ooi' isn't a liability. Key words' polysemy, multivocality, ambiguity, vagueness, and contested character are assets. They shouldn't be minimized, curtailed, or done away with, but capitalized on. They're sources of creativity. They're generative. They help social scientists apprehend reality. Yet other meta-complainers argue that it's impossible to do away with polysemy and ambiguity anyway, so the whole matter is moot. Ought implies can, and linguists and philosophers of language have shown that you can't.

A few people complain about both complainers and meta-complainers: 'Everyone's wasting their time and should instead go back to their labs, computers, field sites, and archives, and carry on with their empirical research. Stop talking and get your hands dirty right now!' For all their bossiness, these meta-meta-complainers stand on shaky logical ground. Complainers and meta-complainers don't enjoy being bossed around and hasten to retort: 'Your view is self-defeating. You're yourself participating in this dispute, instead of

26. Canovan 1981, 3, 3–4, 5. Like Allcock (1971), Canovan (1981, 5) is referring to the conference To Define Populism at the London School of Economics in May 1967 (I. Berlin et al. 1968; Macrae et al. 1967). "The fact that it brought together so many of the experts in 'populism' with the object of attempting 'to define' it is in itself significant" (Ionescu and Gellner 1969, 2–3). Conference papers were published in *Populism: Its Meanings and National Characteristics*, edited by Ghiţa Ionescu and Ernest Gellner (1969).

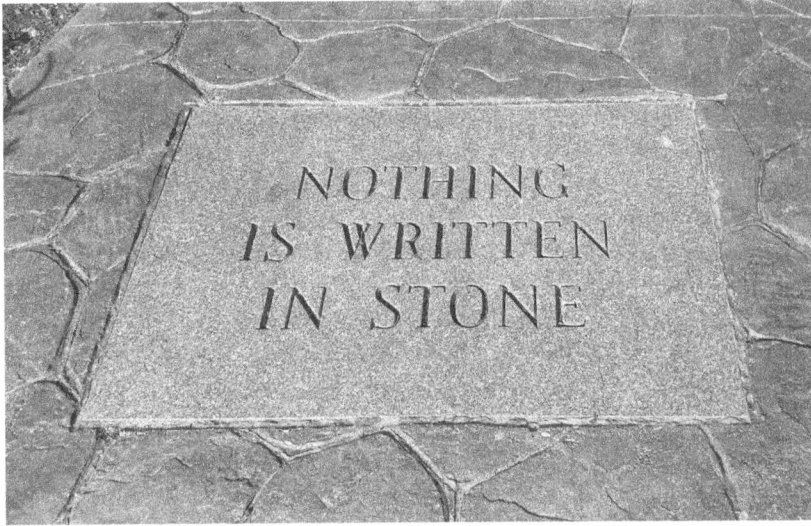

FIGURE 2.1. Nothing is written in stone. Photo: brewbooks. This file is licensed under the Creative Commons Attribution–Share Alike 2.0 Generic license. Seen at Northshire Bookstore, Manchester Center, Vermont.

carrying on with your empirical research. You aren't getting your hands dirty right now, but talking to us.'[27] You could have kept your mouth shut, but if you're meta-meta-complaining, you're performatively contradicting yourself.

———

I've been saying that *OOI* is that which social scientists empirically investigate. Ordinary features of the social world. Social phenomena, practices, institutions, processes. However, a special case is reflexive. It refers to social science itself: *OOI* is said to individuate a discipline as a whole. It's that which a discipline is about, or mostly about, or ultimately about. It unifies a discipline's parts and knowledge claims. For example, society (sociology), mental health and illness (psychiatry), cognition (cognitive science), communication and media (communication and media studies), information (information science), crime (criminology), education (education), the economy and the market (economics), the polity and the state (political science). Gender studies. Disability studies. Migration, urban, cultural,

27. Maslíah 1999.

performance, religious, or organization studies. Environmental (or conservation) studies (or science).[28]

OOI is involved in disciplines' boundary work and jurisdictional conflicts.[29] This is sociology, but that . . . that's not really sociology. What we do here is legitimate political science research, what you guys do isn't. He gets to sit at the table (he's an economist), she doesn't (she isn't a true economist). If you want to give funding to gender studies, you've got to fund us, not them. Gatekeepers thus include what's desired and exclude what isn't. Higher-ups make the case that something falls within or outside the boundaries of their discipline, on the grounds that it does or doesn't deal with the right sort of object.[30] Falling within or outside disciplinary boundaries can also be morally consequential, as disability studies, psychiatry, and genocide studies illustrate.[31]

'Thick concepts' and 'categories of practice' are morally laden.[32] 'Corporate social responsibility,' 'diversity,' 'refugee,' 'democratization,' 'development,' and 'socialist,' for instance. Predictably, they're perennial battlefields. What about social scientists' 'categories of analysis' that aren't simultaneously 'categories of practice' in social, organizational, and political life? What about words that don't look so immediately moral? They aren't free from trouble either. Social scientists still can't agree on what *OOI* is.

2.3 Characters

The story has recognizable characters and plot lines.

At some point, somebody will make 'the infancy move.' The absence of definitional and conceptual order is customary during scientific disciplines' early years. During their infancy or youth. In a mature science, "definitions, ergo, the conceptual scheme [should] be commonly accepted." But the social sciences still have childhood sicknesses:

> In this regard the social sciences, especially sociology, are separated by a
> wide gulf from the natural sciences, where the basic concepts are common

28. Development studies, genocide studies, indigenous studies, digital studies, sport studies, among others. In German, these are called '*Wissenschaften*.' On health economics, see Ashmore et al. (1989) and Mulkay, Pinch, and Ashmore (1987).

29. A. Abbott 1988; Gieryn 1983; Hamann 2018; Lamont and Molnár 2002.

30. Compare 'this isn't *X*, because it doesn't deal with *OOI*' to 'this isn't *X*, because it doesn't approach *OOI* the right way or it doesn't use the right methods (e.g., they aren't scientific).'

31. S. Lee 2010; Pleasants 2016; Schneiderhan 2013. On being *the* Holocaust, unique and sui generis, see J. Alexander (2002), Margalit and Motzkin (1996), and Pleasants (2016).

32. Abend 2019; Brubaker and Cooper 2000; B. Williams 1985.

to the majority of scientists. The lack of agreement results in numerous terminological controversies, the childhood sickness of young sciences. Their presence inhibits the communication and preservation of knowledge and diverts to pseudo-problems a good deal of mental energy.[33]

This character argues that the situation should get better over time. They're optimistic and underscore that it's a temporary malady: there's no agreement and order *yet*. They can already discern a few signs of maturity, and they see no "insurmountable obstacles against [terminological or definitional] unification."[34] But their judgments keep turning out to be too optimistic. The problem keeps resurfacing. It never seems to go away.

At some point, somebody will make 'the etymological move.' According to the script, it goes like this:

> The Greek and Latin etymologies of 'ooi' have been unduly neglected. We should study them and abide by their teachings. Only then will our field be in a position to understand what *OOI* is. Only then will we be able to conduct research on it. It's a pity that newly minted social scientists can't read Greek and Latin. Any time gone by was better. Also, who now reads the *Cratylus*?

The etymological move is a classic in the history of social science. It's a classic in the history of the humanities and philosophy, too.[35] A word's or expression's etymology is said to have semantic implications today, normatively impinging on present-day social scientists' uses. Besides, etymology is said to have metaphysical import. A word or expression stands for a thing. The etymology of the former sheds light on the nature of the latter. Consider how we got from Latin '*colere*' to 'culture,' or from Greek '*theōria*' to 'theory.' These historical semantic facts aren't curiosities, but should help social scientists determine what 'culture' and 'theory' refer to, and possibly what culture and theory are. At a minimum, they're deemed relevant. A word's etymology suggests something interesting about its meaning or referent. Few eyebrows will be raised.

---

33. Timasheff 1947, 202.

34. Timasheff 1952, 186.

35. On its point in Plato's *Cratylus* (390e–427d), and its alleged satirical point, see R. Barney (1998, 2001), Ewegen (2014), Hoenig (2019), Keller (2000), Sedley (1998, 2003), and Trivigno (2012). Barney (1998, 64) argues that *Cratylus* commentators have been obsessed with one question: "whether the etymologies are *Scherz oder Ernst*—whether Plato is expounding dogma or enjoying a (fairly private) joke." Sedley (1998, 140; 2003, 40) challenges the "assumption . . . that Plato must think the etymologies as ridiculous as we do."

Etymological moves are rhetorically seductive. Plus, they entice scholars to show off their chops (John 8:7). But they're based on fallacious inferences.[36] In fact, etymology has no normative force.[37]

At some point, rest assured, somebody will propose a moratorium. According to the script, it goes like this:

> Most of us are fed up with this endless mess. There's only one way forward: declaring that, in our social science field, 'ooi' is banned, and then enforcing the ban. Nobody should use it anymore. Nobody should be allowed to use it anymore. To talk about these issues, new words and concepts are needed. We have to leave this mess behind and start afresh. That's the solution to our problem.

Fresh starts, blank slates, tabulae rasae, can be tempting. If the situation we find ourselves in is complex, perplexing, historically messy, it's tempting to turn the page, start all over again, start from scratch. Invent a perfect brand-new language, a perfect brand-new constitution, a perfect brand-new philosophical system. Leave everything behind and start a new life in Cabo Polonio, on the Atlantic coast of Uruguay. Are these just tempting, deceitful mirages? Or, rather, do moratoria have something going for them?

In any event, moratorium proposals are ubiquitous. And yet, they fail to have significant effects on scientific practice. Scientists' language use flouts them.

Another cyclically reappearing character will say: 'I've got it! I've discovered the source of our problem and standoff. What's going on is that there are types of *OOI*. Just like there are types of table: dining tables and coffee tables. Types of computer: desktops and laptops. Types of reptile: crocodiles, turtles, tuataras, and lizards and snakes.'

To this standard character there's a standard response:

> You're right that dining tables, coffee tables, poker tables, and ping-pong tables are types of table. They are all pieces of furniture consisting of a smooth flat slab fixed on legs. But what makes your types types of *OOI*? Whence this larger, more comprehensive entity, of which they're said to be types? I don't see what warrants your claim that these five things over here are types of *OOI*, whereas those three things over there aren't. That's

---

36. Lyons 1977, 244.

37. Objection: you're caricaturizing the etymological move! Etymology isn't to look up words in etymological, Greek, or Latin dictionaries. It's to offer genealogies of language and culture. Which do have normative force. Communities have traditions, habits, shared histories and understandings. Current practices should be mindful of them.

precisely our problem, which claims about tables, computers, and reptiles aren't susceptible to. That's precisely what we can't agree on.

And back to square one. (Variations on this theme: *OOI*'s varieties, facets, faces, or dimensions; *OOI* "with adjectives.")[38]

Yet another cyclically reappearing character is an advocate of scientism.[39] For scientism, science is the measure of all things. Where 'science' refers to traditional, textbook, experimental science. Research in biology or chemistry, as represented in reputable textbooks, as understood by policy makers, teachers, and journalists (with any luck).

This character will make three points about social science:

(1) Science is about things, not about words. Sadly, social scientists don't seem to get this plain fact. 'Look, no real science cares about words. Newton and Max Planck didn't care about words. Why do you guys keep talking about words, words, words? Why do you keep having disputes that are merely verbal? Just call it what you want! Language is just a conventional instrument. Inasmuch as you take it to be more significant than that, you won't be doing science anymore.'[40]

(2) They'll rehash an old point, which social scientists are reminded of—and have ritualized conflicts over—on a regular basis: the projects of the social sciences and the natural sciences are alike.[41] The former ought to logically and methodologically emulate the latter as much as possible, which emulation comprises the use of words and the formation of concepts.[42]

(3) Following up on that, this character will deplore imprecision and vagueness in social scientists' work, as "precise deduction from vague terms is impossible." They'll go on to commend logic and the virtue of clarity: "Many, if not yet most, leading sociologists are accepting the necessity of learning the lessons that logic has to teach. In this direction may well lie the developing maturity which will, hopefully, in the future, lead us also to a convergence regarding at least the minimum terms of our discipline—terms of clarity and precision which hopefully may aid in developing an adequate sociology."[43]

38. Collier and Levitsky 1997; Lukes 2021a, b; Simko and Olick 2021.

39. Bannister 1987; Boudry and Pigliucci 2017; Hayek 1952; J. Isaac 2012; Platt 1996; Solovey 2020. Some people would say instead 'positivism'—on which, see Steinmetz (2005, 2020).

40. Cf. Outhwaite 1983.

41. Dodd 1951; Ellwood 1931; Lundberg 1945; MacIver 1931.

42. Hempel 1952.

43. C. Benson 1971, 122; cf. Ogburn 1930, 301.

———

From time to time, someone will propose that a committee be set up to streamline and standardize the use of 'ooi' or *OOI*. Or to standardize key concepts or words in the whole field. If this someone is a powerful someone, their proposal will be heeded and a committee will be set up.

In 1937, the American Sociological Society established the Committee on Conceptual Integration. As announced in the *American Sociological Review*: "The Committee for Conceptual Integration is a democratic group open to all who are interested in its two-fold purpose: (1) a critical study of the relative merits of technical terms in sociology and (2) promotion of agreement among sociologists in the usage of such terms."[44] In 1941, "the C.C.I." "set up three committees to guide its activities": Future Organization and Policy, chaired by Dwight Sanderson; Definitions, chaired by Earle Eubank; and Definition of Definition, chaired by Hornell Hart.[45] Besides its chair, Duke University's Hart, the members of the Sub-Committee on Definition of Definition were L. L. Bernard, Albert Blumenthal, F. S. Chapin, Lewis Dexter, and Maurice Parmelee.[46] Not to nitpick, but: these people's talents notwithstanding, it must have been challenging to work toward a definition of 'definition' if they didn't already know what a definition was.[47]

Comparable ambitions were behind political scientists' and sociologists' Committee on Conceptual and Terminological Analysis (COCTA) and Committee on Concepts and Methods, starting in the 1970s.[48] These committees continue to be active, rechristened RC01 Concepts and Methods and RC35 Conceptual and Terminological Analysis:

> COCTA developed out of an Open Meeting at the 1970 World Congress of the International Political Science Association (IPSA) and was initiated

44. "Current Items" 1939, 709; see also Blumenthal (1940) and Blumer (1940b).

45. "Current Items" 1941, 391.

46. Bernard 1941; Hornell Hart 1943; cf. Swedberg 2020b, 439.

47. "If I should attempt to state the most useful definition of definition, as the chairman has requested," said L. L. Bernard (1941, 510) at a 1940 meeting:

it would of necessity proceed from an attempt to condense and summarize the discussion which precedes. [. . .] Thus, to put it in a single sentence, definition ranges all the way from the low level of accuracy of indicating (pointing out) an object or process, through naming and describing it in a literary manner, to various stages of symbolic condensation and functional conditioning, and ending in the formulation of an ideal hypothetical norm which is a sort of compromise between the generalization of inadequate experiential reality and a projected reality which is yet to be attained in its entirety.

48. Sartori, Riggs, and Teune 1975.

by Fred Riggs and Giovanni Sartori with the aim of providing a forum for the clarification of basic social science concepts. COCTA was recognized in 1976 as IPSA RC01 (now active as 'Concepts and Methods'), in 1978 as RC35 of the International Sociological Association (ISA), and has at times also been institutionally represented within the International Social Science Council (ISSC) and the American Political Science Association (APSA).[49]

The standardization of social science terminology was also on the agenda of UNESCO, the United Nations Educational, Scientific and Cultural Organization.[50] It established the Interconcept program, "within the framework of UNESCO's Division for the International Development of Social Sciences," to foster the "analysis, clarification, and disambiguation of concepts used by social scientists."[51] One of its concrete goals was an "automated terminology bank," for which there was a "fundamental need." Therefore (surprise, surprise), "substantial financial investments" would be warranted.[52]

In the 1990s, Princeton sociologist Walter Wallace proposed "that the American Sociological Association appoint a *Committee on Basic Sociological Concepts* to investigate and recommend the official adoption of a basic conceptual language in American sociology"—which he elsewhere called "ASA Committee on Basic Substantive Nomenclature."[53] Wallace was an ardent advocate of scientism, so it makes sense that he'd ask: "what alternative do we have as long as we believe in sociology's potential as a science?"[54] In an article in *American Sociologist*, "Standardizing Basic Concepts in Sociology," he stressed that the committee should consider "all points of view" and join "similar efforts . . . by sociologists in other countries":

> The charge to this committee would be (1) to begin moving immediately— using any means (commissioned reviews of the literature, formal depositions, hearings, periodic pollings) that helps assure open and fair consideration

49. "RC35 Conceptual and Terminological Analysis," International Sociological Association, 2022, https://www.isa-sociology.org/en/research-networks/research-committees/rc35 -conceptual-and-terminological-analysis/. "The Committee on Concepts and Methods (C&M) is a Research Committee of the International Political Science Association (IPSA). Founded by Giovanni Sartori and friends, it was the first research committee recognized by IPSA in 1970" ("About," Committee on Concepts and Methods," n.d., http://www.concepts-methods.org).

50. Gould and Kolb 1964, ix–x; UNESCO 1956.

51. ISA 1979, 13; see also Felber 1977; Gould 1977; Riggs 1979, 1986, 1988.

52. Riggs 1981, 7.

53. W. Wallace 1990, 352; 1996, 633.

54. W. Wallace 1971; 1990, 357.

to all points of view—toward the official adoption of a basic conceptual language in American sociology, and (2) to join and otherwise support any similar efforts by other social scientists, and by sociologists in other countries.[55]

The following year, Wallace tried to get the "Section on Theoretical Sociology" (later renamed "Theory Section") to "[petition] the Council of the A.S.A. to establish a committee charged with recommending a glossary of basic socio-logical concepts for adaption by plenary session of the American Sociological Association annual meeting."[56]

Wallace's piece in the section's newsletter, *Perspectives*, prompted many re-actions, both approving and disapproving. Jeffrey Alexander argued that "such a proposal is utopian" and "displays a fundamental lack of seriousness in a sociological sense." Conceptual dissensus is "rooted in necessity"; "it may be less an affliction than a sign of health." Donald Levine wasn't on board either. He did applaud "efforts to clarify and deliberate the meaning of con-cepts": "for sure, sociologists should be as clear as possible about the meanings of their terms." But a glossary would be "a superficial and misleading docu-ment." Michael Faia endorsed Wallace's proposal, while David Maines accused the section of "collective amnesia": the Committee on Conceptual Integration and Blumer hadn't been mentioned at all.[57]

As Chris Prendergast, then editor of the newsletter, observed: "[Wally Wal-lace's] proposal—that the theory section present a cogent set of basic defini-tions to the ASA for approval—was a bombshell. We published eight replies to it over the next three issues. [...] The Wallace essay changed the way section members read and used the newsletter."[58] In the end, however, the "Council decided ... not to endorse his [Wallace's] call for a glossary of basic sociolog-ical terms."[59]

Arguments for conceptual streamlining, along with plans and initiatives to implement it, have been put forward across the social sciences throughout their history. They're comparable to—and occasionally inspired by—natural language standardization policies, and technological, administrative, legal,

---

55. W. Wallace 1990, 357; see also W. Wallace 1992, 1995.

56. W. Wallace 1991, 1.

57. J. Alexander 1991, 2; Levine 1991, 6; Faia 1991; Maines 1991.

58. Prendergast 1992, 2.

59. "Theory Section News in Brief" (1991), *Perspectives* 14 (4): 3. The Council made this deci-sion "despite its high regard for Walter Wallace." Wallace "resubmitted his resolution on stan-dardizing basic concepts in sociology" the following year. "Wallace Resolution Reinstated" (1992), *Perspectives* 15 (2): 12.

industrial, and commercial standardization efforts, within countries and internationally.[60] These domains and activities couldn't work, or couldn't work smoothly and efficiently ('rationally'), without standardization. Without common terminologies, procedures, criteria, weights, and measures.[61] Nor can scholarly work. Or so some social scientists have argued.[62]

2.4 Levels

The problem seems intractable. Like their predecessors, contemporary social scientists continue to struggle with it in their research projects, conference panels, and recruitment committees. Uncertainties about what *OOI* is, or what 'ooi' means, continue to give rise to obstacles to the practice of social science. To the production and evaluation of research and to communication and interaction with society. These aren't marginal obstacles, which only a few fields and literatures confront. They're apparent everywhere in social science research.

What makes the problem so hard? Can social science communities do anything about it, can they crack it, or must they throw their hands up in the air? First things first. The first to-do item is to dissect the problem well. Clarify what the issues are, how to tackle them, what it'd be to solve them, and what a solution should accomplish. I'll argue that one vital step is to distinguish the levels at which social scientists might disagree. Another vital step is to grasp what's at stake and who might benefit from different outcomes and arrangements. Who stands to gain from this use of 'institution,' of 'culture,' of 'nature,' of 'artificial intelligence'? Which research programs will be hamstrung?

I'll argue that the problem is a practical reason one. Interests are involved, so communities have to assess which interests are legitimate, more and less legitimate, and downright illegitimate. I'll argue that the chief beneficiary should be the common good. The community as a whole. Not one sector, group, or party. Not one approach or school. Not you, an individual, who's doing research in your field, writing up your results, and looking to get them published. Not you, an individual, who's writing a book about the problem.

60. See, e.g., "ISO/TC 37: Language and Terminology," International Organization for Standardization, n.d., https://www.iso.org/committee/48104.html.

61. Espeland and Stevens 1998; Timmermans and Epstein 2010.

62. Not that this is specific to social science. On the "stabilization of botanical nomenclature," see Daston (2004b). In biology, medicine, and computer science, unified 'ontologies' are intended to facilitate data sharing and international collaboration, such as gene ontology, hypertension ontology, or spider ontology (Leonelli 2016). For more examples, see the Open Biological and Biomedical Ontologies (OBO) Foundry: http://obofoundry.org/.

I believe social science communities aren't thinking clearly about the relationships between objects of inquiry, key words, and distinctions. They don't appreciate what prevents disagreements from being settled, and what it'd take to settle them. This isn't because of insufficient methodological proficiency. The social sciences are indefatigably at work to perfect their research methods and techniques. But what's causing trouble here is the logic of social inquiry. The logic of social inquiry inquires, logically, into the mechanics of scientific research, inferences, arguments, questions and answers. Given a question, what it is to get it right. Given an inconsistency or disagreement, what procedures to follow; what sorts of arguments, data, and methods are pertinent. Social scientists have good methods to address empirical questions and settle empirical disagreements. But they aren't well prepared to settle disagreements about a word's uses or whether a distinction should pass muster.

There are disagreements in the sense of discrepancies and disagreements in the sense of disputes. The verb 'to disagree' and the noun 'disagreement' can refer to "the state of being at variance" or to "the act of disagreeing."[63] An example of the former is a difference, inconsistency, or disparity between two social science practices. Alba's and Blanca's techniques, measurements, or claims are discrepant. An example of the latter is a quarrel between them. They talk. They aren't of the same mind about the best way to go. Both the former and the latter can be observed in social science communities. They shouldn't be confused, but they can be addressed concurrently. If two persons come to agree on the best way to go, they'll presumably go that way.

One significant distinction is between discrepancies and disputes. Another significant distinction is between disagreement levels or orders.[64] Social scientists disagree about the empirical properties of objects and phenomena ('level zero' or 'zero order'). Which are dependent on disagreements about words ('first level' or 'first order'). Which in turn are dependent on disagreements about first-order disagreements ('second level' or 'second order'). Which could lead us to further higher-order levels.

Level zero: empirical differences. Different social scientists provide different descriptions and explanations of *OOI*. Discrepant claims about its characteristics, causes, and consequences. Imagine three labs that are investigating what accounts for the increase of trust in a group or society, what increases the

63. *Merriam-Webster.com Dictionary*, s.v. "disagreement," accessed September 13, 2022, https://www.merriam-webster.com/dictionary/disagreement.

64. Abend 2014, 2017.

likelihood that you'll trust an unfamiliar person or organization, and whether trust is "rigid or malleable."[65] But their findings are consistently at odds with one another.

First level: object of inquiry/word. As it turns out, these three labs' findings diverge because they didn't start out with the same *OOI*. Their most powerful explanatory factors diverge because each lab's explanandum is a bit different, even though they all speak of 'trust.' This discrepancy is about what *OOI* is, what counts as *OOI*, or what the extension or definition of '*ooi*' is. If social scientists miss it, they'll talk past one another. They'll mistakenly believe to be disagreeing about the properties of one and the same object. They'll blame one another's methods and analyses.

By contrast, if they do correctly grasp what's going on at the zero level, they're likely to have explicit disputes about *OOI*. Papers, talks, and conferences on what trust is and on the nature of trust will proliferate.

Second level: criteria. Social scientists might also disagree about how to adjudicate their disagreements about what *OOI* is. Roughly, on which grounds you're entitled to say that one definition of 'trust' (or one TRUST concept) is better than another. At best, they'll have explicit disputes about this. They'll give reasons to favor particular criteria and procedures. This doesn't by itself solve the problem, but it's a positive development. It can ward off muddles, and it sends a signal to that effect. At worst, they'll be unaware of or unclear about what's going on. They might be unclear about the distinction between these levels. Or they might see the distinction between zero order and first order, but miss the second order.

If social scientists aren't aware of the first-order issue ('we aren't speaking of the same trust you guys are speaking of!'), the second-order issue doesn't arise at all. Yet, they might be aware of the first-order issue and still be unclear about the second level, what it's about, and how it works.

In addition to all of that, further higher-order levels mean that an infinite regress looms on the horizon.

———

You set out to do research on trust, how it varies, and what accounts for these variations. You ask yourself how to observe and measure it, whether it's in natural settings or in textual sources. If your study is experimental, how to elicit and measure it in the lab. As recommended by your methods teachers and textbooks, you consult the literature on trust. It's an extensive one, so, time

———

65. Paxton and Glanville 2015.

being scarce, you decide to begin with sociology. (Great decision, if I say so myself.) Sociologist S says that "trust . . . is a particular level of the subjective probability with which an agent assesses that another agent or group of agents will perform a particular action."[66] Sociologist T says that "TRUST IS A BET ABOUT THE FUTURE CONTINGENT ACTIONS OF OTHERS."[67] Sociologist U furnishes this "definition": "a belief about another person's trustworthiness with respect to a particular matter at hand that emerges under conditions of unknown outcomes."[68]

You see similarities and overlaps in these three experts' TRUST and 'trust,' but you see dissimilarities as well. Sociologist V argues that they're all mistaken: trust isn't necessarily about mental states, such as beliefs. Those are unduly mentalistic definitions. To which a more fundamental objector adds: trust isn't a kind of belief at all. If you study trust by collecting data on people's beliefs, probability assessments, what they think about others, what they expect others to do, you wouldn't be studying trust. Trust is only about actions.[69] Not to be undone, sociologist W affirms that 'trust' as such is undefinable. A person's trusting another person has nothing to do with 'generalized trust.'[70]

That's one view, that's another view, that's yet another view, and then what? One possible course of action would be inaction. There are possible worlds in which inaction would be fine. They might be lovely. In our actual world, however, inaction is precluded by social forces and constraints. Views need to be compared to one another. Reasons to prefer one of them need to be evaluated. Their merits assessed with the same metrics, benchmarks, criteria. At this point, the subject matter isn't trust per se anymore, but the logic of social research. What makes a word use good? Where should social scientists' words come from? It's the logic of social research, as it meets 'metasemantic' or 'metalinguistic' issues. Or as it meets 'conceptual engineering' of social scientists' 'representational devices' (more on this below).[71]

---

66. Gambetta 1988, 217.

67. Sztompka 1999, 25.

68. Robbins 2016, 976.

69. Dumouchel 2005, 424.

70. Adding philosophers of trust and trustworthiness to the mix would be wise, but a lot of work, since it'd massively enlarge the pool of options and foci. See Baier 1986, 1992; M. Hartmann 2011, 2020; Hawley 2019; K. Jones 1996; O'Neill 2002.

71. Ball 2020, 2021; Burgess and Sherman 2014; Burgess, Cappelen, and Plunkett 2020; Cappelen 2018; Plunkett 2015, 2016; Plunkett and Sundell 2013, 2021. A metalinguistic usage "is where a speaker uses a term (rather than mentions it) to express a view about the meaning of that term, or, relatedly, how to correctly use that term. A metalinguistic negotiation is a metalinguistic dispute that concerns a normative issue about what a word should mean, or, similarly,

As a matter of fact, sociologists of trust may not perceive this second-order level. Their discussions may proceed as though there were only one level, the first-order level, whose subject matter is trust. They may unintentionally get the two levels mixed up. In which case, these discussions won't get anywhere. One of the sources of their disagreements belongs to the second order. As different sociologists have their own second-order standards, their first-order trust will be the best trust they can have. The best *they* can have, each one of them. But not others, given their respective premises.

Wherever the second-order level *is* perceived and brought to the fore, that's surely great news. It's already a step forward. However, a satisfactory outcome may not transpire either. It may or it may not. Agreements about second-order standards and criteria aren't any easier than agreements about first-order definitions of 'trust.' Even if everyone does see the distinction.

In sociologist *A*'s opinion, you should look up the word 'trust' in *Webster's Third*, and take it from there. Your research project should measure trust, as 'trust' is defined in the most famous American dictionary. This definition will tell you if what you ethnographically observed yesterday evening was trust or something else. In sociologist *B*'s opinion, you should look up 'trust' in a dictionary or encyclopedia of social science, and take it from there. Of social science? Sociologist *C* substitutes a dictionary or encyclopedia *of sociology*.

For sociologist *D*, dictionaries have no bearing on sociological research. *Webster's Third* is beside the point, because it reports on the English language, which isn't the language of science. Specialized social science and sociology dictionaries aren't helpful either, because they simply represent their authors' views on what trust does and doesn't encompass, following their theoretical preferences and methodological leanings. Theirs is one more first-order position, as valid as any other sociologist of trust's position. But these dictionaries, despite their authoritative title and aura, aren't impartial judges of real meaning or true nature.

Sociologist *E* argues that dictionaries and encyclopedias aren't helpful, because each work offers more than one answer: either several senses of 'trust' (English dictionary) or several understandings or interpretations of TRUST (social science dictionary or encyclopedia). How are you going to choose among them? Finally, a less conventional sociologist, *F*, suggests that this conceptual or semantic disagreement can only be resolved by the Oracle of Delphi. The Pythia will put it to rest.

That's one view, that's another view, that's yet another view, and then what? There are possible worlds in which inaction would be fine. In our actual world,

---

about how it should be used, rather than the descriptive issue about what it does mean" (Plunkett 2015, 828).

however, these views need to be compared to one another. Views neither about trust, the thing, nor about TRUST, the concept. Nor about 'trust,' the word. Rather, these are views about the relationship between social science and natural language, the proper role of dictionaries in social science research, the proper role of dictionaries of social science in social science research, and the proper role of oracles in social science research. Reasons to go with *Webster's Third* or, rather, to ignore it altogether. More generally, reasons to prefer particular criteria over others. Reasons to go with particular procedures to adjudicate social scientists' disagreements about *OOI* and/or 'ooi.'

2.5 Human

The problem is as practical as they come. It concerns social scientists' research; it concerns their day-to-day travails. It's about their ongoing efforts to observe, measure, describe, and explain social phenomena, get reliable results, do good science. It can't be put to one side, because 'level zero,' 'first level,' and 'second level' are interdependent. Scientists' passion is empirical. They're after empirical findings and claims. But they're stuck with higher-order issues, words and criteria, semantic or conceptual stuff, whether they like it or not. Furthermore, tangible payoffs are up for grabs. Epistemic payoffs are tangible enough, but material payoffs will tag along, for an extra dose of tangibility.

The truth-value of social scientists' claims turns in part on what *OOI* turns out to be. Take descriptive or explanatory claim *p*. Whether *p* is true or false will be determined by evidence that tracks what the world is like, as well as by the contents and boundaries of the classes of things *p* refers to. Both the classes of things being explained and described, and the classes of things doing the explaining and describing. Therefore, when social scientists argue about what *OOI* is, they aren't arguing about *OOI* alone: they're also arguing about the worth of their own work. Per your definition of 'social movement,' you have developed a pathbreaking theory of social movements. Unfortunately, the journal's reviewers and editor object. Some of your cases aren't actually social movements. That's not how the literature on social movements defines 'social movement.' Your findings are an artifact of your arbitrary definition. Your paper is rejected. Forget about getting your dream job at Fancy University.

Speaking of jobs, consider the job of recruitment committees (on which more below). The Department of Sociology at the University of Montevideo, Minnesota, is seeking to hire a tenure-track assistant professor in the sociology of *OOI*, while the Department of Sociology at the University of Eureka, Illinois, invites applications for a tenure-track position at the level of assistant professor in the area of *OOI*. Naturally, for an applicant to get an interview, their research has to make major contributions to *OOI*: say, the sociology of culture, morality, art, or digitalization. Regrettably, the recruitment committee can't agree on what counts as research on culture, morality, art, or digitalization (beyond a few prototypical examples). It's contentious which applicants have contributed to *OOI*. Committee members aren't sure either what to do about this disagreement, where it's a matter of opinion and taste, and how to move forward now. But move forward they must. Invitations must be sent out to finalists. Hotel rooms must be booked. One of the candidates must be hired by the end of the fall semester.

Enter a critic of social science, who's wary of its epistemological and methodological credentials. They insist that committee members' claims about the extension of 'ooi' is shaped by extraneous factors, such as their training, research agendas, and predilections in social theory. At best, these are unconscious influences on their ideas and judgments. This would be bad, but statistically normal. Even if you're always on the lookout for unconscious epistemic vices and implicit biases, they're sneaky and tenacious, and you may not have control over them.[72] At worst, committee members are intentionally drawing gerrymandered boundaries, such that their favorite candidate qualifies and their most challenging competitor doesn't. Absent clear principles and methods to determine the extension of 'ooi,' powerful and high-status members will, on average, get their way.[73]

Harsh critics have this worst-case scenario in mind. Social science communities and practices aren't exceptional. They're akin to social, legal, administrative, and political processes in which definitions get instrumentalized. Meanings are means to achieve ulterior ends. Semantics is a slave to self-interest.[74] Much like meat and dairy lobbies. Much like homophobic groups, organizations, and politicians, who are out to prevent the LGBTQ+ community from obtaining recognition, rights, and equality. Their definition of the word 'marriage' is designed to further their repugnant political goals. What they want is to push their ideology and demands, which claims about words' meanings and uses are crafted to serve.

72. Brownstein 2018; Cassam 2019; Levy 2015.

73. To empirically study this, four important variables are: (1) how deans and university administrators participate in recruitment processes, (2) how recruitment committees are formed (whether there are fixed rules for their composition and whether these rules are democratic), (3) whether recruitment committees may or must have student members, and (4) how the specificity of job announcements varies across academic job markets (e.g., assistant professor in sociology v. assistant professor in the sociology of technology, with special emphasis on artificial intelligence).

74. Schiappa 1993, 2003; Stevenson 1938, 1944. 'Persuasive definitions' are also referred to as 'definist fallacies.'

Wait a second. Aren't these harsh critics of social science going too far? How dare they compare science to meat lobbies and homophobic organizations? I think they'd reply by going empirical themselves. Giving social scientists a dose of their own medicine:

> My analogies are defensible if you look at the actual practice of social science. Actual meetings and collaborative work, recruitment and award committees, grant applications and decisions, and journal review processes. As STS has taught us, textbooks are mythological. We shouldn't be misled by formalized and sanctified rules, and by oh-so pretty rational reconstructions. In reality, scientists' careers and reputations are at stake. Status, power, and money. Which is all breeding ground for immoral behavior. The evidence about scientific misconduct speaks for itself: fabrication, plagiarism, and cutting corners are widespread. Scientists are as morally unscrupulous as anybody else.

In other words, social scientists are thoroughly strategic about OOI. Their word uses are self-interestedly calculative and hence immoral. They have a stake. An axe to grind. What's more, they deliberately conceal their true motives, like lobbyists and homophobic politicians. They pretend to have scientific rationales for their lexical semantic or conceptual choices. Tricksters! They just want their papers to get accepted for publication, their publications and presentations to get more attention, their competitors to get fewer citations, and their friends and students to get coveted jobs.

What to make of these critics? They should be taken seriously, I think, as they might be onto something. They're right to look at actual science and to refuse to put scientists and scientific organizations on a pedestal. However, I fear they're moving too quickly and jumping to conclusions. The devil is in the details. For one, they haven't shown that social scientists are necessarily strategic about what OOI is or how they'll define 'ooi.' It's an empirical question how often this is the case (assuming people's motives can be discerned empirically). Plus, not all interests are alike. Nor are they all equally problematic. Nor do all interests work in the same way. You need to distinguish kinds of having an interest, kinds of being driven by interests, kinds of having an axe to grind. Then, you can reassess these critics' analogies and their defensibility.

What *is* necessary is that social scientists' words have practical effects. Effects on their communities, and effects on their own standing qua individual social scientists and qua social science communities. In this sense, definitions of 'ooi' can't be neutral. Answers to what OOI is, or what 'ooi' means, can't be neutral. Their epistemic and practical payoffs aren't egalitarian: there'll be winners and losers. My point now isn't about processes of definitional work, and how they're shaped by individuals' preferences and outlooks and (sometimes) morally dubious strategies. Instead, it's about their consequences. Whatever a community does about the extension of 'ooi,' whatever it decides, however 'ooi' ends up being used, whichever usages end up being acceptable: some people and organizations will benefit. Some goals, perspectives, values, and interests will be advanced as a byproduct of a community's word uses. They'll be advanced to the detriment of others. This is the nature of the beast. A familiar inequality beast. Any attempt to address the problem must accommodate it.

Any attempt to address the problem must be addressed to creatures like us. On pain of impracticality, it must be addressed to creatures with abilities, dispositions, and social and organizational contexts like ours (more on feasibility below). Social, cultural, and language animals.[75] Epistemically and morally limited. Who have desires, hopes, values, and interests. Live in stratified and unequal social worlds and are constrained by social structures. All of which apply to scientists (they're human beings, too). They wish to be happy and have fulfilling careers. They hope their claims will turn out to be true and their work will turn out to be influential. They don't live and work on a desert island. The practice of science is a social practice. It's organizationally embedded. Scientific organizations are social organizations. And so on.

What's waiting for us at the other end of the spectrum (at the good end, that is)? What's the opposite of trying to get the word 'meat' to mean whatever will maximize your company's sales and profits? What's the opposite of hiring lobbyists and bribing politicians if need be? Off the top of your head, you might respond that it's a value-free, objective, unbiased, disinterested, detached, neutral, or impartial definition of 'meat.' It's above the fray. Noncommittal morally and politically. Independent from anybody's goals. It doesn't take sides in any way at all. But I'm not sure you'd be thinking of value freedom, objectivity, unbiasedness, disinterestedness, detachment, neutrality, or impartiality for humans and human institutions.[76] You might retort that your definition only took scientific considerations into account. Intellectual, theoretical, or scholarly considerations alone. But I'm not sure you'd be thinking of a science for humans and human institutions.

75. C. Taylor 2016.

76. These words sound similar to one another: how do they differ? How about 'above the fray,' 'non-committal,' 'not taking sides,' 'not having a stake,' 'not having an axe to grind': are these synonymous? On neutrality, impartiality, and autonomy in science, see Lacey (1999, 2013). On objectivity, neutrality, and impartiality in history, philosophy, and literature, see Haskell (1990), Midgley (1974), and K. Murphy and Traninger (2014).

Thanks to scholarship in STS, cultural sociology, philosophy of science, and epistemology, we have a better idea of what can be hoped for. It's cemented a more insightful and credible picture, which transcends earlier Manichean controversies. Science and knowledge can't be pure, uncontaminated, perfect. Who'll be surprised to hear they aren't a divine creature, they aren't omniscient, and they don't live in paradise? Community members aren't angels either. When it comes to *OOI* or 'ooi,' like anywhere else: don't shoot for a perfect solution or you'll fail.

It doesn't follow that anything goes, and science is but politics, rhetoric, and power.[77] The bar must be set right. To address the problem, the bar must be set right.

2.6 What we talk about when we talk about 'bread,' 'planet,' and 'religion'

Consider the differences and similarities between these three cases:

(1) Much hangs on whether Subway's 'bread' is bread/falls under the extension of the word 'bread.' For example: Subway's reputation, tax obligations, and bottom line.

(2) Much hangs on whether Pluto is a planet/falls under the extension of the word 'planet' (see the appendix). For example: the theories of planetary scientists about the properties of planets, the status of NASA's New Horizons mission, shows and exhibits at planetariums, and the feelings of many children.

(3) Much hangs on whether Scientology is a religion/falls under the extension of the word 'religion.' For example: the claims of sociologists of religion about the properties of religions across the world, their claims about the causes of religious participation, and the reputation, tax obligations, and bottom line of Scientology organizations.[78]

The three cases have real-world, worldly, material consequences. Cases (2) and (3) have consequences for science. For the truth claims of scientists working in active, fertile, and competitive fields. At the same time, both Scientology and Pluto have social, cultural, and economic consequences. But there's more by way of similarities. Sociologists of religion are as much in a bind as astronomers and planetary scientists. Natural scientists aren't sheltered

---

77. Latour 1984, 257.
78. Urban 2011.

from conceptual doubts and definitional disputes. They're sparser than in sociology, political science, anthropology, and history, but they do occur. For instance, 'species,' 'microbiome,' 'holobiont,' and 'life' in biology; 'gene' in genetics; 'time' in physics; 'health' and 'disease' in medical science; 'disease' and 'disorder' in psychiatry; 'culture,' 'language,' and 'morality' in ethology; and 'intelligence,' 'neuron,' and 'consciousness' in plant science.[79]

It's true of cases (1), (2), and (3) that there are rival answers to 'what is F?' or 'what does "w" mean?' None of them is universally assented to. Their competition may be more or less explicit. Some people and organizations carry out definitional work, and scrutinize and criticize one another's.[80] Much of the discussion is bedeviled by unclear assertions. No doubt, there are exceptions. There are judges, astronomers, and sociologists who are analytically lucid and think clearly about F or 'w,' disputes over them, and why they never end. They see where individuals' and communities' errors lie. In general, though, confusion tends to be rampant.

Consider the differences and similarities between these four cases:

(4) Legal arguments and judgments about what a sandwich is

(5) Hodgman and Pashman's debate about what a sandwich is, blog posts and tweets about what a sandwich is, magazine articles and late-night drunk conversations at parties about what true love is, or what friendship is, or what art really is

(6) The arguments of sociologists of religion about what a religion is or how to define 'religion'

(7) The arguments of planetary scientists about what a planet is or how to define 'planet'

The problem is widespread. It isn't only a problem for the law: we've seen that it also manifests itself aplenty on the internet and at hipster events in Brooklyn. It isn't only a problem for the law and Brooklyn hipsters: it also manifests itself at social science conferences and in social science journals. It isn't only a problem for so-called 'soft' scientists like sociologists and anthropologists: it also manifests itself in so-called 'hard' sciences like astronomy. Go figure, not even astronomy is safe—which Comte called "celestial physics," the

---

79. Alpi et al. 2007; Baluška and Mancuso 2020; Berg et al. 2020; Beurton, Falk, and Rheinberger 2000; Boesch 2012; Brenner et al. 2007; Cleland 2012; Darwin (1859) 1909, 69, 525; Dupré 2012; Keil, Keuck, and Hauswald 2017; Langlitz 2020; Marchesi and Ravel 2015; D. Robinson, Draguhn, and Taiz 2020; Schnittker 2017; Stotz and Griffiths 2004; Stotz, Griffiths, and Knight 2004; Taiz et al. 2019; Wakefield 1992; Whooley 2019; Wilkins 2003, 2009a, b.

80. Ashmore et al. 1989; Mulkay, Pinch, and Ashmore 1987, 237–38; Swedberg 2020b.

science whose phenomena are "the most general, the simplest, the most abstract."[81]

Cases (4) and (5) can appeal to natural language and the intuitions of the person in the street. To their spontaneous reactions. 'Your suggestion is inconsistent with how people tend to see love.' 'It contradicts what's customarily understood as love.' 'It's at odds with the dictionary definition of "love."' Are (6) and (7) permitted to appeal to natural language and the intuitions of the person in the street, too? Few scientists would be willing to defer to them. Traditionally, they don't get a say in science. I'm not so sure.

———

The problem is general and pervasive. It doesn't beset the practice of social science only, it doesn't beset politics and the law only, but language and communication as a whole. 'What is F?' 'How should "w" be used?' These questions are widespread in social life, organizational life, and culture. For many important words, communities are unsure as to how to use them. Organizations use them erratically. People use them unclearly and imprecisely. In some areas of life, this isn't harmful. It's business as usual and there's nothing wrong with it. Indeed, it can be good. Good for them. Let them be.

Elsewhere, it does cause harm. It results in miscommunication and confusion. Waste and anxiety. Discussions about the right use of words feel necessary and urgent, but they end in deadlocks, because nobody knows how to tell who got it right. Dissimilar second-order criteria are invoked. The impact of second-order levels isn't appreciated. This happens to 'love' and 'happiness,' 'friendship' and 'race.' To 'art' and 'indie rock,' 'diversity' and 'Latinx.'

You're starving, but the fridge is empty. You text your awesome roommate if they'd be so kind as to buy you a veggie sandwich on their way home. They bring you a veggie hot dog, which you've never liked that much. You wonder: 'either I'm mistaken about a hot dog's not falling under the extension of "sandwich," or I'm mistaken about my roommate's falling under the extension of "friend."'

And yet, while social science communities aren't special in some respects, they are special in others. In which respects? In which ways are they relevantly different to communities of natural language speakers, to social and cultural communities, and to the groups, networks, and organizations of which society is made up? Along with four collaborators, we're starting a new research project on F, funded by a lavish grant. Tomorrow is Monday. Of course, we'd like

81. Comte (1830) 1934, 50 (my translation); see also ibid., 48.

to ensure that our research, evidence, and general propositions will be about what they're supposed to be about. It'd suck to eventually be bashed for failing to count as F something that actually is, or for counting as F something that actually isn't. Did I mention that tomorrow is Monday?

The problem is general and pervasive. While they aren't alone in this, it's imperative for social science communities to develop a well-thought-out way to address it.

3

Nine ways to decline

I had no choice but to appeal to first principles, that is, create my own language.

—DE ÍPOLA (2006)[1]

Does not this curious right ["to define one's terms"], which we have come to grant as soon as we deal with matters of importance—as though it were actually the same as the right to one's own opinion—already indicate that such terms as 'tyranny,' 'authority,' 'totalitarianism' have simply lost their common meaning, or that we have ceased to live in a common world where the words we have in common possess an unquestionable meaningfulness . . . ?"

—ARENDT (1961)[2]

3.1 What's your problem?

Many a social science textbook paints it as straightforward. So you wanna do social science? So you wanna make social scientific claims? You've got to observe a slice of social reality in a methodologically rigorous fashion. Observe it and measure it. This requires the operations of conceptualization and operationalization. Conceptualize, then measure. Or, conceptualize, then operationalize, then measure. These are frequent prescriptions in social science methodology. You find them in textbooks, primers, and undergraduate and graduate classes at universities. Prescriptions that go on to live applied lives. They materialize in journal articles, 'data and methods' sections, methodological appendices, interactions between advisors and advisees, group meetings, and elsewhere in the practice of social science. This is one way to tell you aren't an essayist or a journalist, but a social scientist. Whether you conduct experiments, ethnographies, statistical and

---

1. De Ípola 2006, 60 (my translation; author's italics omitted).
2. Arendt 1961, 95. Thanks to Monika Krause for pointing me to this passage.

computational analyses, content analyses, or comparative and historical research, the underlying logical structure and mechanics are taken to be basically the same.

Textbooks don't suggest that conceptualizing, operationalizing, and measuring social phenomena is a piece of cake. On the contrary, you have to exhibit much ingenuity and work hard at it. Be sure to purchase good textbooks to assist you. "Consistency in conceptualization and measurement" necessitates carefulness, attentiveness, and skill.[3] The "process by which concepts are translated into empirical indices" involves several steps: "an initial imagery of the concept," "concept specification," "selection of observable indicators," and "combination of indicators into indices."[4] There are hazards at each of them. Yet, the underlying logical structure and mechanics are taken to be basically unproblematic.

This general methodological picture is widely accepted in mainstream social science research, but it has variants. One is to put all your eggs in the measurement basket. Historically, this was the thrust of 'operationalism' (or 'operationism') and its 'operational definitions.'[5] Conceptualization and definition aren't autonomous, but byproducts of, or identical with, measurement. As physicist P. W. Bridgman put it: "we mean by any concept nothing more than a set of operations; *the concept is synonymous with the corresponding set of operations.*"[6] In the following years, the idea would be imported into psychology and sociology. It promised to mitigate their conceptual troubles, and hopefully dissolve them altogether.[7]

George Lundberg (1895–1966), a leading US sociologist and 1943 president of the American Sociological Society, was convinced: "Since Einstein, at least, [physicists] have blatantly declared that space *is* that which is measured with a ruler; time *is* that which is measured by a clock; force *is* that which makes pointers move across dials."[8] (The italics are tellingly his.) Lundberg maintained that, for physicists, definition and measurement were one and the same thing. Sociologists should learn from them:

3. Firebaugh 2008, 69.

4. Lazarsfeld 1958, 101.

5. On the history of operationalism, its strengths and weaknesses, and how to update it, see H. Chang (2004, 2021), Feest (2005), Green (1992), Hardcastle (1995), J. Isaac (2012), Vessonen (2019, 2021a, b).

6. Bridgman 1927, 5; see also 1938.

7. Adler 1947; Alpert 1938; Chapin 1939; Dodd and Shanas 1943; Hornell Hart 1940, 1953; Hearnshaw 1941; Stevens 1935a, b.

8. Lundberg 1936, 711; 1939, 60; see also 1942.

No platitude is more common in sociology than the remark that in order to measure, we must first define, describe, or 'know' what we are measuring. The statement usually passes as a self-evident fact which needs no examination. That measurement *is* a way of defining, describing and 'knowing' seems to have been overlooked. If one confuses words with the things they signify and regards the process of definition as a mysterious intuitive revelation, instead of an ordered and selective way of responding to a situation, the idea of measuring anything without first defining it (in words supposed to possess some final essence), seems the height of absurdity. In the meantime, however, it happens that physical scientists have proceeded in just this manner. [. . .] Today the *definition* of force and its *measurement* turn out to be the same *operation*.[9]

Electricity and intelligence are good illustrations of Lundberg's viewpoint. You should "define what electricity is in terms of what it does. It is *that which* under certain circumstances kills people, make trains go . . . , makes the hand of the voltmeter move to a certain score, etc., etc." Only "certain types of philosophers, children, and other more or less semantically deranged persons" wouldn't be down with this "definition." Similarly, Lundberg considered the "voluminous controversy over whether what the tests tested really was intelligence." He argued that indeed it was. It's an "entirely defensible definition" to "[define] intelligence as *that which* the test tested."[10]

Operational definitions extend an appealing offer.[11] It can be extremely appealing to social scientists, in light of their recurrent quarrels over words and concepts. The promise is that, as long as social science communities consensually consent to these definitions, they should have no ulterior conceptual troubles: measurement would seal the deal. This strategy has had its fans, but it's not itself without troubles and unpalatable implications. Since its early days, it's had many critics. Early critics in sociology included University of Chicago's Herbert Blumer, Columbia University's Robert MacIver, and Harvard University's Pitirim Sorokin.[12] Lundberg and Blumer had a public debate on "definitions in sociology" "at a session of the American Sociological Society devoted

9. Lundberg 1936, 710–11; 1939, 60.

10. Lundberg 1939, 59, 62. Cf. Boring 1923, 1945.

11. Kerlinger 1979, 41–44.

12. Blumer 1940a; MacIver 1942; Sorokin 1956. Three presidents of the national organization of US sociologists: MacIver in 1940, Blumer in 1956, and Sorokin in 1965. (Known today as the American Sociological Association, or ASA, but till 1959 as the American Sociological Society, or ASS.) Blumer left the University of Chicago and joined the University of California at Berkeley in 1952.

to sociological theory." "The argument, as fallible memory recalls, waxed warm at times."[13]

The operational approach was appealing in some quarters, but it didn't manage to become dominant across the social sciences. Its demands are too drastic, too uncompromising. Many social scientists have felt that it's missing something. Some form of conceptualization has to be prior, more fundamental, a foundation for operationalization and measurement. A foundation for empirical research. MacIver's objections to operational definitions in the 1940s have never lost their resonance: "Professor Lundberg applauds the definition of intelligence as that which the intelligence tests test. Is it unreasonable, then, to ask, 'Very well, but what is that?' Presumably the testers have some notion of what they are testing when they construct their tests."[14]

Such misgivings have been persistent in social science, despite dissimilarities in "what is meant by the term measurement."[15] How much you trust the powers of 'measurement,' and what you trust them for, depends on how you're using the word, including how broadly or narrowly.[16] While the meanings of the word vary, MacIver-type misgivings stick around. Besides, social scientists and philosophers have come to realize that 'measurement seals the deal' doesn't really seal the deal. Measurement isn't unidimensional, mechanical, mechanically objective. It can't fully dissociate itself from values, morality, and metaphysics. Not only in political science, anthropology, disability studies, gender studies, and sociology, but also in psychologists' and economists' measuring instruments, in psychometrics and econometrics—despite their alleging to be untouched by those profane things.[17] As if there were a magic wand to insulate scientific research from the unwanted influences of society and language.

13. Bierstedt 1959, 121–22.

14. MacIver 1942, 158. He didn't reject "operationalism . . . understood in a less absolute and more defensible sense."

15. Stevens 1946, 677.

16. For example, Cartwright and Runhardt (2014, 267) use it broadly: measurement "involves three different kinds of activities: *characterization*—laying out clearly and explicitly what the quantity or category is, including any features of it that we intend to make use of in assigning a number or category to a unit; *representation*—providing a way to represent the quantity or category in our scientific work; and *procedures*—describing just what must be done to carry out the measurement successfully."

17. Alexandrova and Haybron 2016; Cartwright and Runhardt 2014; H. Chang 2004; Chouhy 2021; Dupré 2007; Michell 1999, 2020; Putnam and Walsh 2012; Reiss 2017; Wijsen, Borsboom, and Alexandrova 2022.

I think most social scientists, from Lundberg's time to the present, do attempt to "define, describe, or 'know' what we are measuring." (The scare quotes are tellingly his.) Conceptualize, then operationalize, then measure. Hence, conceptualization is a methodologically pivotal step for social research. What does it consist in? Blalock's 1982 *Conceptualization and Measurement in the Social Sciences* summarizes a standard view, which many students have been taught as the ABCs of research:

> Conceptualization involves a series of processes by which theoretical constructs, ideas, and concepts are clarified, distinguished, and given definitions that make it possible to reach a reasonable degree of consensus and understanding of the theoretical ideas we are trying to express. [...] [C]onceptualization refers to the theoretical process by which we move from ideas or constructs to suggesting appropriate research operations, whereas measurement refers to the linkage process between these physical operations . . . and a mathematical language.[18]

Along similar lines, Babbie's popular textbook *The Practice of Social Research* explains that conceptualization is the "mental process whereby fuzzy and imprecise notions (concepts) are made more specific and precise. So you want to study prejudice. What do you mean by 'prejudice'? Are there different kinds of prejudice? What are they?"[19] Or take compassion:

> The process through which we specify what we mean when we use particular terms in research is called conceptualization. Suppose we want to find out, for example, whether women are more compassionate than men. [...] We can't meaningfully study the question, let alone agree on the answer, without some working agreements about the meaning of compassion. [...] We don't need to agree or even pretend to agree that a particular specification is ultimately the best one. Conceptualization, then, produces a specific, agreed-on meaning for a concept for the purposes of research.[20]

To cite another formulation of Babbie's (which goes from 'terms' to 'concepts'): "In social research, the process of coming to an agreement about what

18. Blalock 1982, 11–12; see also Blalock 1969, 1979a, 1986.
19. Babbie 2013, 166.
20. Babbie 2013, 169.

terms mean is conceptualization, and the result is called a *concept*."[21] Again, methodologists and methods textbooks acknowledge that, in practice, conceptualization might not be easy. But in principle they see no problem there.

Do we really have one? I'm calling social scientists to reexamine their words, distinctions, and logic of research. But objectors will find my whole undertaking to be unwarranted. Provoking unnecessary stress. A tempest in a teapot:

> Don't make such a big fuss over this stuff. Don't make it look as if you'd discovered a new problem. We're all well aware that our empirical research is based on key concepts or key words, and we know how to deal with them. Long ago our teachers, advisors, and textbooks told us how. In graduate school. Even in our undergraduate methods classes. Social science literatures are making fine progress by discovering more and more features of their objects and phenomena, better describing them, and better explaining them. Relax and stop worrying.

For a moderate objector's money, I'm overstating the significance and difficulty of the issues. They're actually small potatoes. For an all-out objector, this is but a pseudo-problem. There isn't one at all. What are their arguments? What were they taught, back when they were graduate or undergraduate students, such that they can now relax?

3.2 Nine arguments and nine responses

I'm extending an invitation to social scientists to consider and work on an important problem. An invitation to you. To you guys. Objectors say 'boo!' They either see no problem here or see only a minor one, which the community can take care of as a matter of course. So, they'll decline my invitation. On which grounds?

I believe there are nine arguments an objector may put forward: (i) the argument from stipulative freedom, (ii) the argument from theoretical vocabularies, (iii) 'they'll tell you!' (iv) the argument from usefulness, (v) the argument from dirty hands, (vi) 'that's too static!' (vii) 'that's unsophisticated!' (viii) 'leave things alone (nothing should be done),' and (ix) 'leave things alone (nothing can be done).' These objections shouldn't be taken lightly. In what follows, I consecutively present each of them, along with my response to it.

––––––

21. Babbie 2013, 166.

(i) Argument from stipulative freedom

Your research project is about democratization processes in the developing world, how social movements come into being, or the causes of terrorism. You're free to stipulate the meanings of 'democratization,' 'social movement,' and 'terrorism' however you wish. You're free to do that, provided you clearly communicate these meanings to your readers, provided you explicitly define your terms. Stipulation wouldn't be an option if you were speaking a natural language. But this isn't a natural language and these aren't any old words: they are social science's 'technical terms' or 'terms of art.'

Your words and definitions are up to you. And that's that. After all, it's your book, paper, or presentation. And this is reportedly a free country.

RESPONSE TO (I)

I have three lines of response:

(1) Suppose your colleague, a political scientist, defines 'democratization' à la Humpty Dumpty: "four-legged animal that barks."[22] Your sociology colleague says that, for them, 'religiosity' means "amount of rainfall that falls on a country's churches in deciliters/month." In their articles' and talks' introductions, they diligently inform readers and audiences of their definitional choices. Then, they go on to make empirical claims about democratization and religiosity. Their articles are titled "A New Theory of Democratization" and "Explaining Religiosity in Contemporary Societies." Dogs figure a lot in the former. Rain figures a lot in the latter.

You feel a strong urge to tell your colleague that their definition isn't OK. It can't be right. They've gone crazy. What's rainfall got to do with it? To which they'll reply: 'but you said I was free to define my terms however I wanted!'[23]

The argument from stipulation—also known as 'define your terms and nobody gets hurt'—has untenable consequences. You have no such freedom. (Legally, I suppose you do. Yes, this is reportedly still a free country.)

(2) If each scientist (or research group or lab) is free to define and use words in whichever ways they please, definitions and uses of 'w' are likely to mushroom. Since stipulation is cheap and it's not

22. Carroll 1911, 220–21.
23. Cf. Arendt 1961, 95.

disincentivized, overpopulation is the probable upshot. 'W' would be used to refer to more and more things, to do more and more tasks. But key words' overextension is detrimental to the community (more on this in chapter 6). Even if a community ended up with only a few definitions of 'w,' this could still undercut collaboration and cumulation.

Gervasio and Hildegard are political sociologists. They independently undertake to explain democratization processes in the developing world. The former produces a study that nicely explains 'democratization$_G$'—that is, democratization according to Gervasio's definition. The latter produces a study that nicely explains 'democratization$_H$'—democratization according to Hildegard's definition. Both definitions sound fine to you, they're both reasonable, they're both based on reputable sources in the literature. However, Gervasio's and Hildegard's empirical results aren't commensurable. They can't correct, amend, or qualify each other. They don't have the same dependent variable. How are they to collaborate, say, to identify general causal mechanisms, to specify the conditions under which democratization processes are robust, or to compare the pace of democratization in various countries and regions?

(3) Not only does the argument from stipulation undermine substantive cumulation objectives, whereby social scientists' studies and claims should add up to stronger conclusions, it also undermines social science's standing as advisor to society—as a reliable, consistent, credible advisor. A government agency has decided to invest more resources in diversity, democratization, or gender equality. A university is planning to expand its research and teaching on digitalization, and to create a new institute to study it. But 'diversity,' 'democratization,' 'gender equality,' and 'digitalization' as per whose definition? Who knows what they'll wind up investing in!

And it also undermines data collection, organization, and sharing.[24] It licenses each dataset, survey, or test to use words and classify things in its own way, in accordance with its preferred, freely chosen stipulations. No questions asked. They're accountable neither to social science communities' practices nor to natural language. Publicly available, institutionalized, collaborative datasets have to pick sides. You get the picture.

———

24. Leonelli 2016.

(ii) Argument from theoretical vocabularies

How to define and use your key words isn't a decision you make as an individual. Rather, it's supplied to you by a 'theory,' 'theoretical perspective,' 'theoretical framework,' 'theoretical tradition,' 'theoretical school,' 'theoretical paradigm,' or 'theoretical approach.' No social scientist is an island entire of itself.[25] Research questions are posed and empirical investigations are done within traditions, schools, approaches.

Your starting point is the 'theory' or 'theoretical approach' you subscribe to: feminist theory, Marxist theory, critical theory, postcolonial theory, poststructuralist theory, structural-functionalist theory, ethnomethodology, systems theory, rational choice theory, or whatever it may be. It suggests what's interesting and what's not worth your time. It provides you with premises or axioms. And it provides a vocabulary and grammar, so that you know how to speak this special and specialized language. Lexicon and syntax. Sentences' grammaticality and compositionality.

People who subscribe to a theoretical school share these premises and axioms, vocabulary and grammar. Other people subscribe to other theories, so they speak in their ways, which are governed by different syntactic and semantic rules. Each school defines and uses its key words differently, as it sees fit.

RESPONSE TO (II)

Argument (ii) is a version of argument (i). Instead of an individual social scientist who stipulates key words' meanings and uses, now it's a collective entity's stipulation: a theory, approach, school, or paradigm. Therefore, the preceding three lines of response apply to (ii), too.

I do appreciate the positives that the argument from theoretical vocabularies brings to the table. First, it underscores that your empirical research can't be perspective-free or 'theory'-free. Scientific claims aren't self-standing propositions. They're embedded in conceptual frameworks—in the absence of which they'd have no point, and arguably they'd make no sense. Not even evidence and observation are theory-free. Scientists would love to have aseptic 'observational terms' ('observation sentences,' 'observation language,' 'protocol sentences'), but this ambition is doomed. It keeps failing over and over again.[26]

Second, it underscores a usual way of doing things in social science research. As a matter of fact, people use key words however they're used by their

---

25. Donne 1624, 415. An "*Iland*, intire of itselfe."
26. Achinstein 1965; Duhem 1906; Feyerabend 1958; Hanson 1958; Poincaré (1902) 1917.

teachers, by the scholars they like and draw on, and in the literature they're speaking to. You use key words how you were socialized to use them. This is patent in 'multi-paradigmatic' disciplines and fields, like contemporary sociology. Many schools coexist, each of which has a vocabulary, conceptual framework, style of thought, thematic and methodological preferences, and favorite words. They have least favorite words, expressions that are looked down on, and, unsympathetically put, dog whistles. Two schools may investigate broadly the same topics, yes, but from different perspectives, focusing on different aspects, and calling them differently. (This is crude. A more fine-grained empirical account would have to specify where, when, under what conditions. Anecdotal evidence suggests that this configuration is more institutionalized in Germany and France than in the United States.)

Be that as it may, the problem I'm addressing in this book is ultimately normative. Not how words are used in a community, but how words should be used in a community. Not the distinctions it draws, but the distinctions it should draw. Not how things are at present, but how to improve them moving forward. Social research textbooks and methodology teachers are normative just in this sense. Yet, the argument from theoretical vocabularies is normatively unsatisfactory. It considers a social science discipline, like sociology, to consist in the conjunction of a bunch of schools or paradigms. These schools are internally consistent, they all believe to be doing sociology, to deserve jobs in sociology departments, to deserve grants from national science foundations, and to deserve the ear of policy makers and the media. But they can't talk to one another and produce knowledge together.

They can't. They're unable to. I'm not saying they don't like to talk to one another, because of self-aggrandizing patriarchs and their feuds, or because students are encouraged to be orthodox, even loyal, and are discouraged from reaching out to other schools, attending their conferences and classes, and (heaven forbid) reading and citing their patriarchs. This might be the case more often than it should, but it's not my concern here. Rather, I'm highlighting the fact that schools speak dissimilar languages. Their grammar and lexical semantics diverge. All of them make empirical, testable claims about 'law,' 'culture,' 'institutions,' 'art,' and 'social structure,' but they don't mean the same things by these words. Perhaps these claims are intelligible across languages, but they're untranslatable and incommensurable.[27]

Even more troubles await the argument from theoretical vocabularies. Within each school or paradigm, the question arises again: What if there's a

27. Abend 2006; Feyerabend 1981; Hoyningen-Huene 1990; Hoyningen-Huene and Sankey 2001; Kuhn (1962) 1970, 1977; Sankey 1993, 1994.

disagreement about how a word should be used? What if two card-carrying members find themselves disagreeing about the meanings and uses of 'w'? Such disagreements might be rare. Supporters of a theoretical school should have learned to use key words in the same way. In the right way. Like any socialization process, there are incentives to comply. Carrots and sticks. Discipline and punishment. But this is no normative consolation. What if, for whatever reason, a disagreement does arise?

This raises an additional worry about these ecologies, in which scientific disciplines are populated by schools that are more-or-less autarkic. Each controls resources, publishes journals and books, trains and socializes students, awards awards and fellowships, and has its own status systems. Within each school, there seems to be a consensus on words' meanings and uses. That sounds nice; it guarantees smooth operations and productive 'normal science.'[28] But I worry about the origin of this apparent consensus. Whether it was arrived at through acceptable processes, or, rather, it's the product of top-down decrees, decreed by schools' leaders. These are the abovementioned patriarchs, full professors, chair holders, who have job security, power, and status. Because of their structural position, they don't have to be fair and democratic. They don't have to take everyone's views and interests into account.

(iii) 'They'll tell you!'

Your research project is about religious practices and organizations in Uruguay, or about financial support for artistic work in Paraguay. It's wrong for you to provide definitions of 'religion' and 'art.' That's wrong not only methodologically but also morally: your project would be parochial and ethnocentric. Instead, this is an empirical question. You should find out what Uruguayans' own definition of 'religion' and Paraguayans' own definition of 'art' are. This is what you'll collect data on, and this is what you'll describe, analyze, and explain. After you complete your research, you'll offer descriptions, analyses, and explanations of that which Uruguayan people call 'religious practices' or that which Paraguayan people call 'artistic work.'

Differently put, you should be open-minded about the nature of religion and art. Be open to variations in the very definition of 'religion' and 'art,' through which societies tell religion from non-religion (e.g., cults and sects)

28. Kuhn (1962) 1970.

and artworks from non-artworks (e.g., crafts, design, porcelain urinals, Camp-bell's soup cans, primary school kids' art projects, and failed attempts at pro-ducing art). They (research participants) will tell you (researcher) about their social worlds: what things there are, what they're like, where one category ends and another category begins, and what things and categories are called.

Uruguayan 'religion' and Paraguayan 'art' throw this concern into sharp relief. However, the argument isn't restricted to faraway places with strange-sounding names. You're doing social science research in the United States, in your own 'culture,' be it about gender and class inequalities, diversity, eth-nicity, discrimination, or sustainability. But this doesn't mean you're in a position to say what 'gender,' 'class,' 'diversity,' 'ethnicity,' 'discrimination,' and 'sustainability' do and don't encompass. This would involve normative state-ments, which are anathema to scientists. It's again an empirical question what people take those things to be and how people use those words—where 'people' refers to the people you're observing ethnographically, historically, or experimentally.

Your rationale now wouldn't be to eschew ethnocentrism and parochialism. It wouldn't be the virtues of intercultural understanding, respect, and toler-ance. But the point remains the same. They'll tell you.

RESPONSE TO (III)

I'll respond with the help of another thought experiment. Rather than Uru-guay or Paraguay, the story takes us to Uqbar.

You're a sociologist of culture and organizations, who teaches at a North American or Western European university. Your current research is about libraries and librarians. Using comparative-historical, statistical, and ethno-graphic methods, you're investigating libraries' organizational structures, classification and storage practices, digitalization of collections, and librarians' accounts of their work: how they vary across societies and their causal effects.

Uqbar is one of your 'cases.' Having secured funding and institutional re-view board (IRB) permission to observe and interview 'human subjects,' you've moved to Uqbar's capital and are getting your fieldwork started. You're now in front of the building pictured in Figure 3.1.

The building's facade resembles the libraries you're familiar with from home. Next to the main entrance, two big words are carved on the wall, ele-gantly and imposingly: 'Uqbar Bibo' (not shown in the photo). You don't speak the Uqbar language fluently yet. But you do carry your Uqbar-English diction-ary at all times. It translates 'bibo' as "library." Great. This must be one of Uqbar's national libraries. Let the fieldwork begin.

FIGURE 3.1. Uqbar building's facade. Photo: Andrés Franchi Ugartemendía / CC BY-SA. https://creativecommons.org/licenses/by-sa/3.0.

You enter the building, and, to your astonishment, you see what's pictured in Figure 3.2 (turn over the page).

What on earth is going on? Two options suggest themselves:

(1) According to argument (iii), you have a Western understanding of what a library is. Uqbar culture's understanding is dissimilar to yours. Indeed, you set out to find out how libraries vary, didn't you? What you're finding so far, then, is this: libraries in Uqbar are radically different from libraries where you come from. People don't go there to borrow and read books, but to play and watch futsal. A most surprising finding!

(2) You got the translation wrong. The authors of your Uqbar-English dictionary did a terrible job of it. The Uqbar word '*bibo*' actually means "futsal court."[29]

---

29. There are other possibilities. For instance, this building used to be a library. It later became a futsal court, but the owner has never gotten around to putting up a new sign. But this possibility is immaterial here. It can be discarded by talking to Uqbar people, who confirm that this is a *bibo*. You show them figure 3.2 and yeah, this is what you do in a *bibo*. You ask them about '*Uqbar Bibo*,' and yeah, it's the right name, there's no need to change it.

FIGURE 3.2. Uqbar building's interior. Photo: Blancoyrojo / CC BY-SA.
https://creativecommons.org/licenses/by-sa/4.0.

My thought experiment shows that 'they'll tell you!' isn't a good argument. Libraries will vary to some degree and in some regards. Your Uqbar participants, or Japanese participants, or sixteenth-century primary sources do have a say on what libraries are and what the extension of their word for 'library' is. That's the grain of truth in it. (Caution, though: how can you know what their word for 'library' is in the first place?) But then, you, a Western European or North American researcher, an English-speaking academic, must establish the limits of permissible variation. You logically must. A general idea of what a library is, the basic definition of 'library,' its basic features: they'll have to be your own. As Foot puts it, you must establish "some content restriction on what can intelligibly be said to be" a library.[30] Beyond these limits, it'd be another sort of institution. This building doesn't count as a library anymore. The people working in it don't count as librarians.

The bite of my thought experiment doesn't depend on the Uqbar language and translation. Imagine that Uqbar's official language were English, and the words carved on the wall were 'Uqbar Library': argument (iii) wouldn't be off the hook. Are their libraries very dissimilar to ours? Or, rather, is their way of using the word 'library' very dissimilar to ours? In either case, your project

---

30. Foot 1995, 3.

isn't about futsal, but about "[places] in which literary, musical, artistic, or reference materials (such as books, manuscripts, recordings, or films) are kept for use but not for sale."[31] That's what *you* take libraries roughly to be and the word 'library' roughly to refer to.

Argument (iii) is well-meaning. You don't want your research project to be ethnocentric, Eurocentric, or Americentric. You want to understand difference, be tolerant, and be respectful. Respect cultural worldviews and ways of life that aren't yours, whose beliefs and values you don't share, such as Uqbar's. The promise of argument (iii) is attractive. Its spirit is laudable. Unfortunately, it can't deliver what its proponents hope for.[32]

———

(iv) Argument from usefulness

The argument from stipulative freedom is partly right: your definitions are up to you. But it doesn't mention a crucial factor: they need to be useful. In your paper, you might write something like, 'it's useful to define "democratization" in this way.' Or, 'it's useful to define "empathy" in that way.' Then, your paper will have to make good on these promises. And that's that.

RESPONSE TO (IV)

'Usefulness' is a tricky word. It's elliptical; it doesn't say enough. It underdetermines your next steps, and in particular it underdetermines your definitions and uses of key words.[33]

'Usefulness' is sometimes deployed in the methodological section of papers and books, as if it were a justification in and of itself. 'Doing X is useful; hence, I can go ahead and do X.' But this is no good. If you leave it at that, we, your readers, will suspect that something fishy is going on. We'll suspect that you want to do X, you feel like doing X, you'll get good outcomes and rewards if you do X, but you need a justification for doing X that doesn't solely appeal to your wants, desires, and interests. So, you say it's useful.

31. *Merriam-Webster.com Dictionary*, s.v. "library," accessed September 14, 2022, https://www .merriam-webster.com/dictionary/library.

32. Davidson 1984; Foot 1995; Hallen 1995; Hollis 1967; Hollis and Lukes 1982; Putnam 1981; Quine 1960. Thanks to Anthony Ossa-Richardson for his comments on these issues. In one sense, argument (iii) is a version of (i) as well. But I use (iii) to bring out a specific point: you can't delegate the definition of key words to the society, group, and language your project is about.

33. Duhem 1906; Quine 1951, 1975.

Suppose sociologist Delmira writes in her paper, 'my definition of "altruism" ["creativity," "intelligence," "digitalization"] is useful.' Or, 'it's useful to define "altruism" ["creativity," "intelligence," "digitalization"] thus and so.' Then, she'd be expected to explain useful for what and for whom: what goals will thereby be furthered, whose goals are these goals, and who and what might be adversely impacted by them. Delmira's usefulness considerations need to be subjected to public scrutiny. They may or may not turn out to be acceptable. This is the crux of the matter.

Say Delmira goes on in one of these ways:

(1) 'My definition is useful for my dependent variable or explanandum to be free from outliers and otherwise inconvenient data points—which are then excluded "by definition," as they say.'

(2) 'My definition is useful for my paper to get published in a top journal.'

(3) 'My definition is useful for my paper to get published in a top journal, and therefore for my CV and my odds of getting tenure.'

This won't fly. Journal referees and conference audiences would balk at (1), (2), or (3) (and would be befuddled by their candidness). From a scientific point of view, from scientific communities' point of view, these aren't valid reasons. If a definition is claimed to be useful, it must be useful to obtain scientific or epistemic goods, such as the advancement of science and knowledge. Admittedly, that doesn't say too much either, but it does sanction adequate beneficiaries: the scientific community, society, the common good, our common store of knowledge. Not just Delmira herself. In other words, knowledge might always be shaped and driven by interests, but not all interests are created equal. Only some of them are acceptable. Acceptable to whoever and whatever should have a right to judge.

Juana is a social psychologist and neuroscientist. Along with her postdocs and doctoral students, they're doing fMRI (functional magnetic resonance imaging) research to discover the neural correlates of romantic love.[34] Juana's latest paper starts with a succinct definition of 'love' she came up with. 'This definition is useful, useful to us and our project, because fMRI scans are expensive, experiments can't take too long, and we're only able to scan one person at a time.' Is this scientifically kosher? Surely to some extent it is. Experimental doability and tractability are reasonable considerations. So are deadlines and time pressures: 'I need to finish my PhD, I can't stay forever in graduate school.' On the other hand, these considerations will take you only so far. It's a big plus for a scientist's definition of 'love' to be tractable. To be

---

34. Abend 2018b; Bartels and Zeki 2000.

attuned to the technological and experimental conditions under which they're working. But this isn't the sole yardstick.

In sum, 'usefulness,' by itself, is at best uninformative. It can be a red flag. It can be irresponsibly used and abused. It can help scientists get away with methodological, conceptual, or semantic choices they didn't think out well. That said, the argument from usefulness does have important things to offer. To play a positive role, it must get more specific. It must specify useful for what, and useful for whom, and at what cost to whom. These specifications must pass communal acceptability and desirability tests (more on this below).

――――――

(v) Argument from dirty hands

Neuroscientist Michael Gazzaniga's remarks on consciousness are totally on the mark: "You don't waste your time defining the thing. You just go out there and study it."[35] That nails it. Don't waste your time mulling over philosophical quandaries about words, concepts, and things, which are unsolvable anyway. Get your hands dirty. Go back to your actual research.[36]

RESPONSE TO (V)

Gazzaniga chastises scientists who waste their time "defining the thing." Instead, they're urged to "just go out there and study it." But what do 'the thing' and 'it' refer to? If the relevant scientific community already knew what the thing was, it'd have no problem to begin with. Regrettably, the field is unclear and can't stop disagreeing about 'its' identity. Different scientists do research on different things, and they all claim to be getting at 'it.' They all claim to be offering descriptions, explanations, and theories of 'it.' Following Gazzaniga's suggestion would amount to burying one's head in the sand.

There are circumstances in which his advice may be advisable, though: if it's certain, or reasonably clear, what 'the thing' refers to, what's picked out by the word 'w.' (For the sake of argument, assume that being 'certain' and 'reasonably clear' aren't themselves problematic.) Sensibly, Gazzaniga would urge astronomers not to waste time defining 'Saturn.' Just go out there and study it. He'd urge political scientists not to waste time defining 'presidential elections

35. Quoted in Ledford 2008, 1028.
36. The abovementioned meta-meta-complainer is a proponent of argument (v).

in Uruguay between 1920 and 2020.' Just go out there and study them. This is sound scientific practice.

However, in these cases nobody is asking for advice or help. These scientists have had their hands dirty all along. If, instead, 'the thing' is consciousness, populism, the welfare state, social class, or happiness, the argument from dirty hands puts the cart before the horse.

———

(vi) 'That's too static!'

The purported problem will go away if you leave Socrates and Meno behind. Leave behind the idea that your definitions or concepts must be ready from the get-go. Ready, fixed, solid, and final. Either you have them or you don't. Leave behind the idea that your object of inquiry must be identified, delimited, and defined at the very beginning of your social science investigation.

This idea is naive, and it's out of touch with scientific practice, with how research actually works. It's too demanding and unnecessary. Instead, you should allow for diachronic interactions among your object of inquiry (roughly defined), your broader topic, existing knowledge about them, what you begin to find, and how your findings cohere with other people's findings and claims.

Your definition, conceptualization, or concept formation shouldn't be static, rigid, or temporally prior. They're processes. They're dynamic, flexible, iterative, interactive, fluid, dialectical, or something along these lines. You can dynamically revise your definitions and conceptualizations as you go along. Amend, adjust, fine-tune them. It's a flexible back and forth. You'll thus get closer and closer to establishing what your claims are about, exactly.

A visual metaphor can shed light on this process. You aren't progressively adjusting your focus to better see what you're already directing your eyes toward—you're looking the right way, at the right thing, but not seeing it well yet. Rather, you're progressively improving your selection of what to look at, what to direct your eyes toward—you're looking not quite the right way, not quite at the right thing yet.

You'll only be clear about your object of inquiry, what it is and what it's not, at the very end of your project. A "definition emerges properly only as one of the results and consequences of inquiry"; "it is unrealistic . . . to insist that they be clear and precise at the beginning of the process."[37]

37. Bierstedt 1959, 121–22. That was Blumer's response to Lundberg at an American Sociological Society session on "definitions in sociology." See also Mauss (1909) 1968, 385–88, 401–2, 414.

RESPONSE TO (VI)

Few people, if any, would welcome a depiction of their ideas as static and rigid. 'That's too static!' and 'be more dynamic!' are rhetorically effective, aside from their substantive force. Aside from rhetoric and pragmatics, though, I agree that social science projects don't need to know at the very start what exactly 'w' refers to or what exactly their object of inquiry is.

True, you can't start to find out if *'yerba mate'* is consumed with *'azúcar'* or with *'pimienta'* without knowing what these Spanish words mean. Get a bilingual dictionary first. Socrates couldn't start to find out if Meno was rich and noble without knowing who Meno was (*Meno* 71b). Picking out the word's referent can't be put off till later. But these analogies are questionable. Socrates might have been wrong to draw a parallel between 'Meno' and 'virtue,' and to transition from claims about the former to claims about the latter. This is a live topic for Plato scholars, in terms of the alleged 'priority of definition principle' and the alleged 'Socratic fallacy.' It "remains open and hotly disputed" what it is that Socrates endorses.[38] Yet, an indisputable conclusion is that definitions needn't always be prior. At least, not prior to everything else.[39]

In this regard, social scientists' objects of inquiry differ from proper names like 'Meno' and from Spanish words like *'azúcar'* and *'pimienta.'* I agree that, for a social scientist, it might be good enough to have a rough definition, a preliminary definition, that is in the ballpark. A rough idea of the word's extension can suffice to begin your study of 'it' (roughly). In these situations, you can indeed be 'less static' and 'more dynamic.' Your definition or conceptualization isn't prior. It'll develop. It'll be, in some ways, responsive to your epistemic gains. This is a process.

Nevertheless, this argument doesn't solve the fundamental problem at stake, much less dissolve it. This is because of two reasons. First: for your research to get going, you don't have to have a precise definition of your object of inquiry, but only a rough and preliminary one. Nice. But how are you going to get that? What if researchers disagree about this, too? In the preceding, so-called 'static' condition, we needed criteria to adjudicate disagreements about what 'w' picks out or what F is. In the present, so-called 'more dynamic' condition, we need criteria to adjudicate disagreements about what 'w' roughly picks out or what F roughly is. These criteria are needed because dynamism

---

38. H. Benson 2013, 155.

39. H. Benson 1990b, 2013; Beversluis 1987; J. Clark, forthcoming; Futter 2019; Geach 1966; Nehamas 1987; Prior 1998; Santas 1972; Wolfsdorf 2004. Benson's (1990b, 19) formulation of "the priority of definition principle" goes: "If A fails to know what F-ness is, then A fails to know anything about F-ness."

isn't anarchy. The risk is ending up again with pseudo-contradictions. Your paper makes descriptive, explanatory, and predictive claims that appear to contradict mine. In point of fact, they aren't about the same phenomenon.

Second: I wrote "in some ways, responsive to your epistemic gains" with malicious intent. In some ways. But which ways? Speaking of dialectical, fluid, and iterative processes doesn't give you any concrete guidelines or prescriptions. So, once again, what if researchers disagree about this? Advocates of 'that's too static!' in philosophy and social science are united by their rejection of the priority and fixedness of definitions. They aren't united by any positive proposals about the unfolding and assessment of the iterative, fluid, dynamic process. Without such proposals, supported by cogent arguments, the risk is ending up again with definitional arbitrariness, gerrymandering, or confusion. Each researcher would decide how their investigation and data impinge on the revised extension of 'w' (which is expected to become increasingly less rough). They'd be a second-order Humpty Dumpty.

My response to 'that's too static!' recognizes and is compatible with two standard scientific practices: exploratory research and retrospective casing. First: a scientist may explore an empirical area and, as they go along, search for their objects, phenomena, explananda. They examine this area without knowing yet what about it they're interested in, nor what object it'd be worthwhile to describe and explain. Figuring this out is what exploratory research is for. It also enables scientists to adjust their plans and preclude future fiascos. You'd planned on doing research on object F_1. However, as your investigation proceeds, you come to realize that 'it doesn't work.' So, you switch to F_2, a different object in the same area. This is ordinary scientific practice and it's not an objection to my response. At some point, whatever object you end up focusing on, its boundaries will come up. Questions about the extension of 'w' will come up. At this point, my response will kick in.

Second: retrospective casing, as opposed to case selection and categorization early on, at the research design stage. You've completed your sociological research, using historical or ethnographic methods. You've meticulously observed a certain phenomenon or process, and you've tested a set of claims about it. With these descriptive and explanatory achievements under your belt, you ask yourself, 'what is my case a case of?' Either you ask yourself or journal reviewers eventually will. What you're being asked is to fit your knowledge claims into a more general body of knowledge.[40] What more general category does your object belong to? What more general proposition do your claims give

40. Becker 2014; Krause 2021a; M. Morgan 2020; Pacewicz 2022; Ragin and Becker 1992; Small 2009; Wagenknecht and Pflüger 2018.

support to, prove or disprove, specify or moderate? So, you go ahead and answer these questions, to everyone's satisfaction, at this late point—after having done your research, even after having submitted your book or article manuscript, due to the referees' feedback. This is ordinary scientific practice and it's not an objection to my response. It doesn't matter if you deal with casing before, during, or after data collection and analysis. Whenever you do, you'll have to struggle with 'w,' what it refers to, and the distinction between F and non-F. Does your case belong to *it* or fall under *its* extension?

———

Another worry stems from the apparent circularity of dynamic processes of definition and redefinition, or conceptualization and reconceptualization. It's comparable to worries about validation in contemporary psychology:

> There is something of a chicken-and-egg problem in that, if we already knew exactly what correlations a measure should exhibit, we might not have much need for the measure. One piece of evidence that a well-being measure is valid, for instance, might be that it correlates to some significant degree with money. But then, on the other hand, the correlation between well-being and money may be precisely one of the things we hope to find out using the measure.[41]

The issue isn't exclusively epistemic. Proponents of 'the preregistration revolution' decry the morally unsavory consequences of dynamism.[42] Adjusting your 'w' or fine-tuning your F in light of a first round of empirical results would fly in the face of their plan:

> Preregistration, in its simplest form, is a one-page document answering basic questions such as: What question will be studied? What is the hypothesis? What data will be collected, and how will they be analyzed? In its most rigorous form, a 'registered report,' researchers write an entire paper, minus the results and discussion, and submit it for peer review at a journal, which decides whether to accept it in principle.[43]

By preregistering their studies, scientists limit their "degrees of freedom"—that is, their "flexibility in data collection, analysis, and reporting."[44] Fishing or

---

41. Alexandrova and Haybron 2016, 1103; see also H. Chang 2004; Tal 2019.
42. Nosek et al. 2018.
43. Kupferschmidt 2018.
44. J. Simmons, Nelson, and Simonsohn 2011.

p-hacking no more. Nor emulating political gerrymanderers, who manipulate boundaries to their advantage. Preregistration ensures that scientists can't modify their hypotheses, predictions, statistical tests, models, variables, categories, coding criteria, concepts, or definitions after seeing how the data turn out.[45] Methodological regulation will thus deter unethical behavior.

I can't appraise the arguments for and against preregistration at this time. It's complicated. Preregistration enthusiasts may have a flawed picture of science. Still, what matters here is that their worry isn't crazy. To them, dynamism is a vice. At least, an incitement to be vicious. For their money, 'that's too static!' authorizes methodological whitewashing; it confers respectability on sketchy scientific practices.

———

(vii) 'That's unsophisticated!'

The purported problem will go away if you give up your unsophisticated views on words and concepts. Give up your outdated framework of necessary and sufficient conditions, which either are or aren't met, and for which vagueness is a bug. It's a feature. Deal with it. Abandon the "classical picture" you're beholden to, for which "the job of classificatory concepts is to sort or segregate things into classes by providing a system of pigeon-holes, by placing a grid over reality, by demarcating areas of logical space."[46] Instead, if you read up on what linguists, philosophers, and cognitive psychologists have been up to, you can avail yourself of more sophisticated accounts of word meaning, extension, or "range."[47] Of the nature, structure, and point of concepts. Of falling under a category or being a member of a class or set.

Stop looking for the necessary and sufficient conditions for a politician to be populist, for a practice to be altruistic, for a chunk of matter or string of sounds to be an artwork, or for a song to be an indie rock song. You're better off relying on prototypes. On fuzzy sets and degrees of membership.[48] Or, if you're into Wittgenstein, on "family resemblances":

> Consider for example the proceedings that we call 'games.' I mean board-games, card-games, ball-games, Olympic games, and so on. What is

45. Chambers 2017; Chambers et al. 2013; Nosek et al. 2018.

46. Sainsbury (1990) 2002, 71.

47. Ludlow 2014.

48. Geeraerts 1989; Mahoney 2021; Mervis and Rosch 1981; Ragin 2000; Rosch 1973.

common to them all? [. . .] [W]e see a complicated network of similarities overlapping and criss-crossing: sometimes overall similarities, sometimes similarities of detail. I can think of no better expression to characterize these similarities than "family resemblances"; for the various resemblances between members of a family: build, features, colour of eyes, gait, temperament, etc. etc. overlap and criss-cross in the same way.—And I shall say: 'games' form a family.[49]

Much work has been done on prototypes in psychology and on fuzzy sets in comparative sociology and political science. Alluding to family resemblances is relatively common among social scientists. Besides these three, there are many other options on the market to replace your old, obsolete CONCEPT. Their origins are diverse and each has dedicated fans. Essentially contested concepts.[50] Open texture or porous concepts.[51] Concepts without boundaries.[52] Sensitizing concepts.[53] *Ballung* concepts.[54] Radial concepts or categories.[55] Concept matrices.[56] Polythetic classes.[57] Cluster concepts, including type clusters, family resemblance clusters, and law clusters.[58] Homeostatic property clusters.[59] Take your pick.

That social science needs to make some such move has been suggested by many commentators—though social science research hasn't adjusted in a consistent manner. There are recent versions of this suggestion, which build on recent advances in linguistics and philosophy. But the basic idea isn't new. In 1950s and 1960s sociology, for example, Blumer distinguished between "definitive" and "sensitizing" concepts:

---

49. Wittgenstein (1953) 2009, §§ 66–67.

50. Collier, Hidalgo, and Maciuceanu 2006; Connolly (1974) 1983; Gallie 1956; MacIntyre 1973; Ruben 2010; Viola 2019; Waldron 2002.

51. Waismann ([1956] 1968, 41): "I owe this term [open texture concepts] to Mr Kneale, who suggested it to me as a translation of *Porosität der Begriffe*, a term coined by me in German."

52. Sainsbury (1990) 2002.

53. Blumer 1954, 1969.

54. Cartwright and Runhardt (2014, 268, 269): "In order to describe this fuzziness we find in concepts like *civil war*, we call them *Ballung* concepts: concepts that are characterized by family resemblance between individuals rather than by a definite property." They "take the term from left-wing leader of the Vienna Circle between the Great Wars, Otto Neurath." See also Cartwright et al. 1996, 190; Uebel 2007, 115–16.

55. Collier and Mahon 1993; Lakoff 1987.

56. Calise and Lowi 2010.

57. Needham 1975.

58. D. Cooper 1972; Gasking 1960; Gaut 2000, 2005; Parsons 1973; Putnam 1975b, 52.

59. Boyd 1999.

A definitive concept refers precisely to what is common to a class of objects, by the aid of a clear definition in terms of attributes or fixed bench marks. [. . .] A sensitizing concept . . . gives the user a general sense of reference and guidance in approaching empirical instances. Whereas definitive concepts provide prescriptions of what to see, sensitizing concepts merely suggest directions along which to look. The hundreds of our concepts—like culture, institutions, social structure, mores, and personality—are not definitive concepts but are sensitizing in nature. They lack precise reference and have no bench marks which allow a clean-cut identification of a specific instance and of its content. Instead, they rest on a general sense of what is relevant.[60]

Whatever variety of this line of argument you favor, it'll benefit social science research, knowledge, and its applications, such as public policy. Special laws and regulations apply to bars. But being a bar shouldn't be black or white: there are degrees of barness. It's a continuum. Therefore, regulations apply to different degrees. Special tax breaks apply to bread and to religious organizations. Breadness shouldn't be black or white: it comes in degrees. Tortillas have a lower degree of breadness than baguettes. Tax rates would be prorated accordingly. Being a religion shouldn't be black or white . . . [61]

RESPONSE TO (VII)

Few people, if any, would welcome a depiction of their ideas as unsophisticated and outdated. 'That's unsophisticated!' can be rhetorically effective, aside from its substantive force. Aside from rhetoric and pragmatics, though, it's good advice to go beyond traditional accounts of concepts and words.

Proponents of this argument are encouraging social science communities to seek out better technical tools. For this, they deserve credit. Nevertheless, their argument doesn't solve the fundamental problem at stake, much less dissolve it. My response to argument (vii) is akin to my response to argument (vi). Terrorism, diversity, religion, institution, the welfare state, civil war, artificial intelligence, altruism: the interminable quest for lists of necessary and sufficient conditions is over! But don't get too excited just yet. You still have to establish which features or properties are relevant to your family resemblance, Ballung concepts, sensitizing concepts, or prototype claims. Why are eye color and nose shape more important than hallux length? Do irascibility and lactose intolerance count?

---

60. Blumer 1954, 7; 1969, 148.

61. If you prefer prototypes: laws and regulations could be based on a prototypical bar, from which instances or tokens deviate more or less.

Some features will count, others won't. Even without necessary and sufficient conditions, even without dichotomous variables or categories, even if boundaries own up to the inevitable fact of vagueness. That DEMOCRATIC ELECTION, TALL PERSON, TABLE, and RED are vague means that, unlike PRIME NUMBER and CONVICTED FELON, they have borderline cases. Their vagueness doesn't entail you can't distinguish democratic from non-democratic elections, or from military coups, or between tables and chaise lounges, between tables and avocados, or between tables and an infinite number of non-tables. You can. Indeed, you often can do it without a sweat (despite borderline cases remaining a potential pain in the ass). In a similar vein, you might argue that concepts don't "assign things to classes or sets," fuzzy sets included. Rather, they're "boundaryless"; they "classify without setting boundaries."[62] Very well. But RED, HEAP, CHILD, and BALD still have to get their classification job done somehow.[63]

Bottom line: necessary and sufficient conditions may be clumsy, traditional accounts of words and concepts may be outperformed by more sophisticated ones, but the latter still need some sort of boundaries, some sort of criteria. Given word 'w' or concept c, social scientists still need to know what these (upgraded) boundaries and criteria are, and how to determine what these (upgraded) boundaries and criteria are.

––––––––

(viii) 'Leave things alone (nothing should be done)'

Nothing should be done about what you call 'the problem.' Popularly known as: if it ain't broke, don't fix it. There are two alternative rationales for this:

(1) Everything is alright. Members of social science communities know how to use their key words and concepts. They understand one another. When difficulties arise, they're satisfactorily dealt with. Scientific research isn't hampered.

62. Sainsbury (1990) 2002, 72.

63. Which they can: "[contemplate] the colour spectrum. . . . Looking carefully, we can discern no boundaries between the different colours: they stand out as clearly different, yet there are no sharp divisions. There are bands, but no bounds. This does nothing to impede the classificatory process: the spectrum is a paradigm of classification. [. . .] We could, perhaps, think of such concepts as magnetic poles exerting various degrees of influence: some objects cluster firmly to one pole, some to another, and some, though sensitive to the forces, join no cluster" (Sainsbury [1990] 2002, 77).

(2) What you're presenting as an undesirable situation is actually a desirable one. That there are disagreements about key concepts is a good thing. That the extensions and intensions of key words are contested is a good thing. It's profitable for social scientific knowledge and understanding. It stimulates progress.

RESPONSE TO (VIII)

Rationale (1): you're making an empirical claim that strikes me as false. No doubt, sometimes you do observe unproblematic understanding and friction-less interaction, comparable to a conversation among speakers of a natural language. Competent, native speakers. No 'strange' accents, no three-year-olds. A conversation that isn't intellectually bewildering or emotionally disturbing, so it's easy for them to say what they mean. Interactions proceed effortlessly, spontaneously, naturally.

When things go well, that is. But I think setbacks abound in social science communities, and their consequences aren't negligible. Social scientists misunderstand and talk past one another. Even when they understand one another, even when words' extensions and intensions are transparent, their disputes aren't up to par. It's not apparent what arguments and methods are called for, and how to make headway. Complaints, meta-complaints, and meta-meta-complaints periodically reemerge.

What winds up transpiring is that powerful people and organizations tend to win out. Their semantic preferences or inclinations carry the day. Little wonder, since structural and cultural advantages aren't kept in check. Nor are their semantic preferences or inclinations seen for what they are. Social science communities, left to their own devices, will produce unequal outcomes. Like any community: doing research on inequality is no antidote to inequality. People's and organizations' starting points are unequal, so some get less of a say than others. Clear standards and procedures are lacking, which, like the rule of law, could have counteracted these patterns to some degree.[64]

The caveat is that I can't be sure about these empirical claims, because of the quality of my evidence. I've collected tons of data over the years, but they aren't statistically representative. My measures of 'misunderstanding' and

---

64. My claims aren't about intentions. But you could ask whether powerful people and organizations are deliberately imposing their preferred meanings on others, and then obscuring this very fact. This would explain why a community is receptive to 'leave things alone (nothing should be done).'

'talking past one another' are informal, 'abound' is imprecise, and so on. Wanted: systematic empirical tests.

Rationale (2): I see where you're coming from. Yes, semantic or conceptual disagreements can be generative. In some settings and moments, ambiguity and polysemy are a boon for a community, and "grace and charm" are preferable to "plain and direct speaking."[65] Mathematicians, computer programmers, and logicians would be hindered by ambiguous and polysemous signs, and by contested, unsettled, unstable, multiple, or in-flux meanings. These aren't at home in administrative and bureaucratic documents either. But they can be welcome elsewhere. In poetry and art. In therapeutic and self-knowledge projects. In parts of politics, international relations, and organizational life. In social interaction. They help people get along and get things done. They're thought-provoking. They're epistemically, morally, and aesthetically welcome.[66]

How about the projects of philosophy? That's a long story—a story at the heart of the divide between 'analytic' and 'continental' approaches. Per a standard story, 'analytic philosophers' fetishize clarity and despise ambiguity. In 'continental philosophy,' the former isn't a virtue and the latter can be. In reality, the story isn't so straightforward.[67]

How about the projects of social science? Levine answers in the affirmative: yes, for some social science projects as well. Or some parts of them. Challenging the "modern assault on" and "flight from ambiguity," he argues that

> the disposition to flee from the ambiguities of human life and utterance has produced three characteristic failings in modern social science. These failings reflect (1) a trained incapacity to observe and represent ambiguity as an empirical phenomenon; (2) insufficient awareness of the multiple meanings of commonly used terms in the social sciences; and (3) where such awareness exists, an inability to realize the *constructive* possibilities of ambiguity in theory and analysis.[68]

Levine's challenge isn't indiscriminate. Social scientists have to have a closer look, so as to recognize the difference between good and bad effects, and to "know what time it is."[69] Where to exploit the "constructive possibilities of ambiguity," as ambiguity is more "productive" than clarification of meanings

---

65. Levine 1985, 2. On sociological theory, see Crosbie and Guhin (2019) and Deener (2017).

66. Adorno 1970, 360; Deener 2017; Empson (1930) 1949, 234–36; Goffman (1955) 1967, 30; Levine 1985; Ossa-Richardson 2019.

67. Beaney 2013.

68. Levine 1985, 8; see also Levine 1965, 1997, 2015.

69. Levine 1985, 220; see also ibid., 39–40, 217, 219–20.

and agreement on uses.[70] Where keeping things ambiguous is the way to go. Where, even though being unambiguous is better than being ambiguous, ambiguity ought to be tolerated. Where to prioritize "the evocative representation of complex meanings and the bonding of a community through diffuse symbols." And then, where the priority should instead be to prevent "inconsistent applications of apparently clearcut [*sic*] categories in empirical studies; unwitting use of the same concept with different meanings in differing discursive contexts; and failure to appropriate adequately the different senses of polysemous terms even when their ambiguities have already been pointed out."[71]

Viewing natural language as a peril is familiar from the history of social science and philosophy. Supposedly, they can't get their job done without resorting to formal languages, or at least straightening out the bits of natural language they'll work with. Levine has a beef with this view, rooted in scientism, which holds that objectivity can only be attained by fleeing from ambiguity. He condemns social scientists' "disposition to *believe* that to be scientific means to be unambiguous, that what they do is 'scientific,' and therefore that what they do is properly unambiguous." However, he does acknowledge that "some of the consequences of this belief and its intermittent practical realization have been beneficial."[72]

———

Where does this leave rationale (2) as a way to decline my invitation? Two considerations are vital. First, I'm looking at a collective problem. What needs to be assessed is the good of the community, not the good of an individual. "Multiple meanings" and "ambiguity" are beneficial if they benefit the community as a whole, not the speaker, writer, or thinker themselves.

The balance sheet is mixed. On the one hand, they can be used to bullshit, obfuscate, and mislead. Politicians, attorneys, and sophists spring to mind. On the other hand, they can have positive effects on social solidarity, and be associated with attentiveness to style and beautiful writing. Overall happiness would go up if fewer papers were unimaginatively and formulaically composed, stylistically dry and bland. More solidarity and beauty would be communal goods.[73]

70. McKeon 1998, 2005.

71. Levine 1985, 14, 217.

72. Levine 1985, 7–8. "These consequences include the clarification of murky subjects; the detached analysis of topics charged with passions; the improved communication of findings among fellow scholars; the cumulative advancement of research traditions."

73. Objection: the circle isn't wide enough. It's no good if ambiguities benefit us, our community, while they harm other people, other communities, or the world.

Second, this is a case-by-case issue. It depends on what we're trying to accomplish, the character of our specific endeavor. That is, what we're up to, what might be of help, and what hurdles there might be. If we're trying to accomplish many things, their relative importance. Not all social science undertakings are alike. I'm looking at standard empirical ones, such as making descriptive and explanatory claims about social phenomena—against the backdrop of a literature, a joint effort, which expects individual studies to be commensurable. In these situations, Levine's assault on the modern assault on ambiguity isn't opportune.[74] My concern is precisely communities' confusions as to what exactly they're referring to. Social scientists who aren't sure if their findings can corroborate or refute one another's, because their observations may not be observations of the same phenomenon. Collective uncertainties about key words' extensions that can be taken advantage of. I've argued that these are precisely the respects in which the situation is problematic.

You might double down and retort that all of this is a good thing. Or, more moderately, it's not a good thing, but other good things make up for it. I don't see it, but I'm open to being shown how it benefits social science communities, how its pros overshadow its cons, where its fruitfulness and constructiveness lie. Digging deeper, you might retort that I'm wrong about all of this, because I'm wrong about the aims of social science. For example, social scientists' chief goal shouldn't be to provide true knowledge claims about terrorism, welfare states, artificial intelligence, empathy, and religion. Instead, social scientists should be doing X, Y, or Z. It's beyond my remit to engage these foundational philosophy-of-social-science debates, but I could reply in two ways. First, there's a robust consensus that the aims of social science have to do with true knowledge claims about social stuff. (Granted, this consensus might be mistaken.) Second, my arguments are conditional: if the aims of social science are such-and-such, then we should do so-and-so. (While I believe the antecedent is true, it might turn out to be false.)

Alternatively, you could claim that this is a matter of degree, a continuum of sorts. In the situations I'm looking at, less ambiguity is desirable, fewer semantic disagreements are desirable. What's not desirable is the eradication of such ambiguities and disagreements, because we would miss out on their good effects. My reply: I'm not sure. But you have to tell me more. Much work is needed to spell out your argument and how to evaluate it. Then, we'll have to look at one case at a time. We'd have to see your analysis of it—for example, your cost-benefit analysis—and your reasons for striking the particular

---

74. Levine may be opportune if you're trying to interpret and shed light on social phenomena, pique people's curiosity, or offer a 'diagnosis of the times' (Osrecki 2011); if you have therapeutic, political, or satirical goals; etc.

balance you believe should be struck. Either way, this view isn't inconsistent with my arguments, so I can leave the matter open.

Last, I'm going to argue that communities, not individuals, should decide what to do. It's a practical reason problem. Decisions about words and distinctions are up to the community. What if it ends up deciding that nothing ought to be done, either because the situation isn't too bad or because it's actually good? That's surely a legitimate outcome. Significantly, though, the community would have already done something. It would have already accepted my invitation to consider the problem and decide what to do. It would have collectively made a decision.

———

(ix) 'Leave things alone (nothing can be done)'

Nothing can be done about what you call 'the problem.' Unlike the formal languages of logicians, computer programmers, and mathematicians, the languages of social science communities can't be amended, fixed, regulated, directed, or controlled. Not in the way that addressing the problem would require. This is impossible.

Put differently, you can't actively shape social science languages. You can't do with them what you're envisioning. Proposals to direct language practices, in social science and elsewhere, are as frequent as they're hopeless. All there can be is spontaneous change, without intention, without direction, without coordination, without a telos.[75]

RESPONSE TO (IX)

Social science languages are neither natural languages nor formal languages. They share some properties with the former and some properties with the latter. They're somewhere in between. Neither unbounded, chaotic, and always on the move, like Spanish, nor tidy, well-organized, and rule-following, like propositional logic. Formalization and formal elements play a part in social science, without being its protagonists. Moreover, social science communities are much smaller than their natural language counterparts. They have traditions and genealogies, organizational structures and norms, and their members share institutional contexts and cultural understandings. There's face-to-face interaction and collective memory. This doesn't really constitute a 'way of life,' but some components of it are there.

---

75. The abovementioned meta-complainer is a proponent of argument (ix).

Because of these characteristics of social science languages, I think their development can be influenced by the community. To some extent. Not like logicians, computer programmers, and mathematicians, but to some extent alright. I can't offer a knockdown argument to this effect. However, I do resist argument (ix), whose analogies with natural language strike me as hasty and undiscerning. They aren't a winning move.

An objector could take another route. They'll set aside philosophical objections about what's in principle possible and impossible to do. Instead, they'll look at historical evidence. Communities' past experience gives rise to skepticism: 'Earlier proposals didn't have major effects on social science communities. They didn't manage to transform languages and language practices. Why would yours succeed? Are you a naive person or a wishful thinker? Do you have delusions of grandeur? You've never heard of the pessimistic induction (or meta-induction), have you?'[76]

My reply: we'll have to wait and see. I realize my proposal is demanding and aims at profound changes. I also realize people have a lot on their plates. Maybe few social scientists will listen to what I have to say. Fewer will be persuaded. Plus, you can be persuaded by my arguments but not prepared to act on them. I'm going to call for hard work; the hard work of collective organization and participation. Isn't this an unrealistic expectation? Chances are that no significant changes come about.

And yet, this may be a likely outcome, but it's not a sure one. Significant changes may be unlikely, but they aren't impossible (on which more below). Earlier proposals were relevantly different from mine. Social science communities have themselves changed in relevant respects. The world has changed. Hell, I may strike lucky! I don't know that this can be predicted. We'll have to wait and see.

Even if it were impossible for the language of social science communities to be shaped, I'd have one more card up my sleeve. Understanding. One of my messages to social scientists, to you guys, my colleagues and friends, is that the issues at stake must be rethought and reanalyzed. Understanding can independently improve the current state of affairs. Diminish the incidence of miscommunication and misconceived disputes. Fewer attempts to answer unanswerable questions. Less frustration and waste of time and paper (and coffee and cookies).[77] Important questions about language, words, and

76. Laudan 1981; Saatsi 2005; Wray 2015.

77. Several functions are served by coffee and cookies, and by the conferences and events at which they're served. Epistemically and socially good functions. Also, enjoying coffee and cookies is good for independent reasons, objectively good, in the grand scheme of things, from the point of view of the universe. It's not my intention to detract from these forms of goodness.

distinctions are forced on social scientists by the practice of research. Social science communities are well advised to pay attention to them.

You're not a philosopher, or a social theorist, or a political theorist. It's qua social science researcher that it behooves you to understand how words hook up to the world, how to establish what key words refer to and how to handle disagreements about them, and what definitions can and can't do for you. And why stipulation isn't the answer. And what 'what-is-F?' questions commit you to and why you should stay away from them.

This understanding has payoffs, real payoffs, despite their not being immediately tangible. The higher these payoffs turn out to be, the lower the probability that this book is a massive waste of time and paper. And coffee. Lots of coffee.

3.3 Envoi

As far as I can see, the foregoing nine arguments fail. I hope their failure isn't due to my failure to represent them well, charitably, as forcefully as possible. Provided the foregoing nine responses weren't responses to straw persons, I hope you—you guys—won't decline my invitation.

4

Technical FAQs

4.1 Introductory FAQs

What's this chapter about?

In chapters 2 and 3, I argued that there are issues with social scientists' key words and distinctions. They have been noticed, in one way or another, by many people over the years. People who've bemoaned their effects and made suggestions for improvement. One reason social scientists haven't addressed them successfully, I think, is a substandard toolkit. For the most part, they've poorly formulated the questions. They've sloppily used key words like 'word,' 'concept,' 'definition' and 'to define,' 'conceptualization' and 'to conceptualize,' 'term,' and 'notion.' Double quotation marks, single quotation marks, and italics have been sloppily used as well. This isn't a stylistic defect, but methodologically and logically detrimental to their arguments.

Help is available in linguistics, lexicography, philosophy of language and mind, and metaphysics. Unfortunately, seldom is this scholarship on the radar of social science researchers. They say 'concept,' without having a good grip on what makes a concept a concept, what it is to have a concept, and what sorts of things can be conceptualized. In much published research, it's unclear if definienda are words or concepts or both or something else, if there are several types of definitions, and where stipulation is OK, if anywhere. It's unclear whether and how 'word,' 'term,' 'notion,' and 'concept' differ from one another.

This chapter is about the toolkit with which I'll work. A technical toolkit or logic-of-inquiry toolkit.

I don't enjoy reading technical stuff. What's the point of this chapter?

This chapter is needed for the same reasons social science articles need 'data and methods' sections. They may bore you, you may skip them, but you're still glad they're there. If an article doesn't openly probe its data and methods, its results are less trustworthy, and its arguments are more likely to be misunderstood.

Up to now, my terminology has been lax. I've talked about objects of inquiry (*OOI*), words ('w'), concepts (c), and things (*F*). Key words and key concepts. Definitions. Semantic and conceptual disagreements. I also mentioned constructs and representational devices. Because it's "conveniently broad" (or "conveniently vague"), I've been using 'object of inquiry' as a catchall expression. It's now time to get more precise. In my arguments I'll go for words and word uses, and I'd like to explain why.

I'll try and keep things minimalist. I'll clear the ground and give reasons for my choices. Like the rest of the book, this chapter is guided by my practical aims: contributing to the practice of social science. Big philosophical quandaries about language, thought, and the social world will be all around us, but oftentimes they can be safely circumvented. Or so I hope. Like Goffman, I've got to hope "their treatment is not necessarily required before one can proceed. So here, too, I will let sleeping sentences lie."[1]

Social scientists disagree about power, capitalism, diversity, and empathy. You've sometimes presented these disagreements with the disjunction 'or': they're about what power is or what 'power' means; what capitalism is or what 'capitalism' means. Ontology or semantics. Which is it?

Let me break down this question into three. You might be asking (Q1) what social scientists believe their disagreements to be about, things or words. Or (Q2) what I believe their disagreements to be about, things or words. (If the latter, they can be about meanings, uses, or definitions.) For both Q1 or Q2, a further issue is whether you can tell what a disagreement is really about, and if so, how. Third, you might be asking (Q3) what I believe these disagreements should be about, things or words (or something else).

(Q1) A lot of social scientists run things and words together. A lot of discussions switch back and forth between the two, assuming them to be interchangeable. This is no good. Further, their unclarity is compounded by 'concept,' which presumably is neither a word nor a thing, but is connected to both. In any event, I can't answer Q1 in general. 'Social scientists' is a large and heterogeneous group. 'A lot' is an unverified conjecture. They'd have to be surveyed.

(Q2) I can say this. Even where they talk about words, concepts, and things, all of them, social scientists' claims about things are too

1. Goffman (1974) 1986, 10.

frequent to be dismissed as a tic. Social science communities frequently try to establish what *F* is. It makes sense to investigate what power is, what capitalism is, what empathy is, or what creativity is. Arguments and discussions proceed as if there were a way to find out what they are, even empirically. All the while, some social scientists would gainsay ontological pursuits and favor words' uses or definitions.

(Q3) I'll reject 'what-is-*F*?' questions (on which more below). To my knowledge, there are no good arguments to justify them in social science. Social scientists aren't in a position, epistemologically and methodologically, to answer them. By contrast, I can think of good reasons for someone to ask what an electron is, what Alzheimer's disease is, what a powwow is, or what a *charango* is.

So, what will you do? What are your arguments about?

In chapter 5 I'll argue that there are two distinct activities social science communities may engage in. Each has a distinct starting point, objectives, and challenges.

First, a community may start with existing words, and make collective decisions about their uses. Roughly, which uses of a word we're OK with. In brief: word goes first! For short I'll call it '*Activity WF.*' Second, a community may put language and words to one side, and instead make collective decisions about distinctions: which ones are worth drawing and why. Roughly, which classifications it'll accept and reject; which ways of classifying things and forming groups are acceptable. It's inconsequential how these groups are named. In brief: distinction goes first! For short I'll call it '*Activity DF.*'

These activities may be undertaken well or badly. In both of them, there'll be disagreements, conflicting proposals, conflicting reasons. These disagreements may be adjudicated well or badly. I want to figure out what's well and badly here.

4.2 FAQs about definitions and concepts

You distinguish two activities. In the first one, Activity WF, aren't those definitions?

Someone might describe *Activity WF* as: how to define key words. The aim is collective definitions. This is understandable, as 'definition' and 'to define' recurrently turn up in both ordinary language and social science. By the same token, someone might diagnose social scientists' problem as a definitional one: they have discordant definitions of 'gender,' 'diversity,' and 'capitalism.'

I wouldn't like to put it that way. The word 'definition' isn't doing irreplaceable work and it can be a troublemaker. 'To define' is polysemous, which can be misappreciated or pass unnoticed. 'Definition' may lead to blind alleys about acceptable definienda and definientia; what makes good definitions good and whether they have truth-values. People may associate it with dictionary definitions; with the definitions of geometry, mathematics, and logic; or with essences and 'real definitions.' These associations would muddy the waters.

I'm not intransigently against 'definition,' 'to define,' and 'definitional.' However, for the social science activity I'll be considering, *Activity WF*, I prefer word uses.

I have to push back on that. Isn't it obvious what a definition is and what it is to define something?

No, it isn't.[2] 'Definition' has diverse uses. There are many types of definition and many types of types of definitions—that is, ways of classifying them. Their genealogies are extensive.[3] These diverse types and typologies aren't always apparent to social scientists who present 'definitions' in their work.

One traditional distinction is between nominal and real definitions. It's been relied on by many: from Aristotle and Arnauld and Nicole's *Port-Royal Logic* to Spinoza and Locke.[4] In a real definition, the definiendum is a thing. It's not about language. Socrates is after real definitions of justice, piety, beauty, and temperance. He wants to know what these things are, what their essences are (more on real definitions below). In a nominal definition, the definiendum is a word or expression. Dictionaries don't define temperance, but 'temperance.' As a Spanish teacher, you ask your students for a nominal definition of '*belleza*' to check if they've understood and can explain what this word means.

Reading social science, I can't always tell if what's being defined is a word or a thing. At times, the definiendum is said to be a concept, as in 'We'll define

2. Gupta 2019; Hanks 2016; R. Robinson 1950.

3. Chapin 1939; Kennedy-Day 2003; Sager 2000; Timasheff 1947. I don't know how many there are at present, but in the early seventh century Isidore of Seville distinguished "fifteen kinds of definitions" (Sager 2000, 91).

4. Angioni 2014; Benardete 1993; Charles 2000, 2010b; Demoss and Devereux 1988. However, Whitaker (1996, 211) argues that the "distinction between real and nominal definition is not faithful to Aristotle's terminology." See also Bierstedt 1959.

the concept of diversity as . . .' But then I can't tell if defining DIVERSITY is considered to be equivalent to defining 'diversity.'

Another traditional distinction is between descriptive and stipulative definitions. The former are what *Webster's Third* and the *Oxford English Dictionary* offer: they tell you what ordinary English speakers mean by 'glory.' The latter is what mathematicians, James Cooke Brown (the inventor of the Loglan language), and Humpty Dumpty offer: they tell you what they chose 'glory' to mean.[5]

There are types of definition according to their purpose and object, but also according to their method—whose success should be judged on their own terms.[6] Given a sense of 'to define,' how do you do it well? What are you supposed to do? What's your definiens supposed to include (must have vs. can have/nice to have)?

These questions call for well-founded arguments, criteria and rules, or a 'theory' of definitions.[7] Of this, there's a long history, especially in logic.[8] As Robinson wrote in 1950, "there are certain traditional 'rules of definition,' four or five or six in number, originally collected from scattered remarks in Aristotle's *Topics*, and repeated with minor variations in textbook after textbook of logic." The sextet version is:

1. A definition must give the essence of that which is to be defined.
2. A definition must be *per genus et differentiam* (*sive differentias*).
3. A definition must be commensurate with that which is to be defined.
4. A definition must not, directly or indirectly, define the subject by itself.
5. A definition must not be in negative where it can be in positive terms.
6. A definition should not be expressed in obscure or figurative language.[9]

These are applied rules. But some of them require considerable philosophical and metaphysical support. For Aristotelians, things have essences. The definition of human being ('man') isn't featherless biped, nor mortal being, but rational animal. The proximate genus is animal, the specific difference

5. J. Brown 1960; Carroll 1911, 220–21.

6. R. Robinson 1950.

7. Belnap 1993.

8. M. Cohen and Nagel 1934; Joseph 1916; Suppes 1957.

9. R. Robinson 1950, 140–41.

is rational ('*definitio fit per genus proximum et differentiam specificam*'). For the rest of us, who aren't so metaphysically self-assured, these rules won't cut it.

If there are types of definition and types of types of definition, each one will need its own rules, criteria, 'theory' of what it does and how it succeeds at it.[10] All of them will face difficulties. Not only social scientists' definitions, which have to do with value-laden and culturally sensitive topics, but also lexicographers' definitions of everyday words. A lexical unit has phonological, graphematic, morphosyntactic, and semantic properties, so lexicographers have to decide which ones to provide in their dictionaries and how much of them. Maybe a word's definition should provide "its etymology, its frequency of usage, its semantic counterpart in other languages, or encyclopedic knowledge (thus, it is one thing to know the meaning of *bread* and a different thing to know various sorts of bread, how it is made, its price, its role in the history of mankind, etc.)."[11]

Lots of decisions. Where's the dividing line between the definition of 'w' and apparently optional elements, like "encyclopedic knowledge"? I wonder if my definition of 'bread' should contain a recipe. How to make this call, assuming length isn't an overriding factor (it's an online dictionary)?

You distinguish two activities. In the second one,
Activity DF, *aren't those concepts?*

Someone might suggest that the product of *Activity DF* is CAPITALISM, CIVIL WAR, TERRORISM, DIVERSITY. The activity could be called 'conceptualization,' and the resulting classes, categories, or groups could be called 'concepts.' If you make a distinction between food items that consist in two slices of bread with a filling in between and all other food items, this would be a conceptualization activity. You may refer to the former as 'sandwiches,' you may say you've conceptualized SANDWICH, you may piggyback on intuitions about the English word 'sandwich,' but you don't have to: what you call your categories is inessential and discretionary. What matters isn't the names, but the discrimination principles you came up with and followed, and the resulting group composition. Then, you may go on to make a distinction between types

---

10. You could argue, however, that the "applicability" of a "theory of definition remains invariant across . . . purposes." Belnap (1993, 117–18) is talking about "the standard theory of definition," which "seems to be due to Leśniewski." It "offers two *criteria* for good definitions," eliminability and conservativeness, as well as "some *rules* for good definitions."

11. Klein 2001, 8765.

of sandwich. This would also be a conceptualization activity, though of another sort.

You could put it that way, but it's not my favorite way of putting it. For my purposes, working with 'concept' or CONCEPT would be a liability. It causes more problems than it solves. It's got too many uses. Misunderstandings arise across disciplines, but also within them.

I have to push back on that. 'Concept' is ubiquitous in philosophers', psychologists', cognitive scientists', and linguists' work on thought and language, but also in the social sciences (and much of the humanities and natural sciences). What do people mean by 'concept'? Why are you so bent on avoiding it?

People's intended meanings vary. I've been saying that the extension and intension of 'culture', 'empathy', 'capitalism', and 'religion' are unceasingly controversial in the social sciences. 'Concept' can be added to the list. In most disciplines. Not to appeal to authority, but "the word 'concept' is too vague by far"; "concept' is a vague concept."[12]

At some point, someone laments that 'concept' "is used with an almost systematic ambiguity, and is rapidly reaching the point at which it will become almost useless for any meaningful discourse."[13] Consequently, "abandoning the very notion of concept is probably required to remedy the state of disarray of the current study of concepts."[14] For those unpersuaded by eliminativism, a less radical strategy is to divide and conquer: "most parties to the debate have, albeit tacitly, adopted the *uniformity assumption*: the claim that all concepts are a single, uniform kind of psychological entity. I will argue that, in fact, concepts are not constituted by a single psychological kind."[15] Once you have types, it'll be easier to agree on the character of each of them. Yet another strategy is primitivization: "Instead of giving a definition . . . , I prefer to define them [concepts] implicitly through a discussion of how to construct them. This is roughly analogous to geometric primitives like point and line which are defined via theorems about them."[16]

Couldn't social scientists learn how to use the word 'concept' from philosophers, often billed as conceptual analysis professionals? Why not ask them?

---

12. Wittgenstein 1978, 412, 433.
13. Newton (1968) 1971, 3.
14. Machery 2010, 401.
15. Weiskopf 2009, 146.
16. Goertz 2006, 1.

First, because the 'concept' of philosophers isn't the 'concept' of social scientists.[17] Second, because philosophy isn't in better shape than social science. Even 'conceptual engineers' have reservations about concepts.[18]

Ryle illustrates the point from his (non-gaseous) ordinary language perspective:

> Sometimes philosophers say that they are analysing or clarifying the 'concepts' which are embodied in the 'judgments' of the plain man or of the scientist, historian, artist or who-not. But this seems to be only a gaseous way of saying that they are trying to discover what is meant by the general terms contained in the sentences which they pronounce or write. For, as we shall see, 'x is a concept' and 'y is a judgment' are themselves systematically misleading expressions. [. . .] [I]t is not true in any natural sense that "there are concepts."[19]

Another complication is that concepts "tend to be associated with individual words in natural language." BURRITO is associated with 'burrito.' HEALTH is associated with 'health.' Is there a limit to the number of words with which a concept can be associated? Margolis and Laurence speak of "manifestly complex concepts like NOCTURNAL ANIMALS THAT LIVE IN TREES or TO WALK AIMLESSLY ON A NEWLY PAVED ROAD."[20] Can you always increase the complexity of a concept, or at some point it'd stop being a concept and become something else?

One more complication is that you've got on the one hand the 'concepts' in the research of social scientists, and on the other the 'concepts' in the lives of the people social scientists observe. The former occur in works on methodology and logic of inquiry, but also in papers' discussions of their data and methods, operationalization, measurement, and validity. 'Concept formation' refers to concepts that social scientists have reason to work with.[21]

The latter are objects of social science research. Investigated experimentally, ethnographically, and historically and genealogically. By psychology, cognitive science, anthropology, history, and sociology. The way psychologists and cognitive scientists look at it, individuals 'have' and 'acquire' concepts. The way anthropologists, historians, and sociologists look at it, societies have sets of concepts or conceptual repertoires. In some of these contexts, 'concept' may

---

17. Machery 2009.
18. Cappelen 2018; M. Isaac, forthcoming; Koch 2021a; Sawyer 2020a, b.
19. Ryle 1932,139, 141; see also W. James 1890, 461.
20. Margolis and Laurence 2019.
21. Bevir and Kedar 2008; Gerring 1999, 2012.

be replaced or supplemented by 'category,' and 'categorization' and 'classification' processes may be foregrounded.

Nowhere to be found: consensuses on what concepts are or what the word 'concept' refers to.

———

While consensuses are lacking, there are overlaps, which specialized dictionaries aim to concisely represent, for the sake of possibly mystified readers. Per *A Dictionary of Sociology*: "concepts. The terminological means by which social scientists seek to analyse social phenomena, to classify the objects of the observed world, impart meaning through explanation to these phenomena, and formulate higher-level propositions on the basis of these observations."[22] Per *A Dictionary of Psychology*: "concept. A mental representation, idea, or thought corresponding to a specific entity or class of entities, or the defining or prototypical features of the entity or class, which may be either concrete or abstract. The traditional psychological definition is a category that divides some domain into positive and negative instances."[23] (Contrasting the sociology and psychology dictionaries underscores one of the abovementioned complications.)

In linguistics, it's common to embed 'concept' in Ogden and Richards's semiotic or semantic triangle.[24] Per *The Concise Oxford Dictionary of Linguistics*: "concept. A construct mediating between a word and whatever it is used to refer to: e.g., a concept 'dog', as mediating, in the minds of speakers, between the word *dog* and the set of animals identified by it. Hence as a construct across languages: thus 'dog' might be seen as common to both English *dog* and *chien* in French, *Hund* in German, etc."[25]

Per *The Oxford Dictionary of Philosophy*: "concept. A concept is that which is understood by a term, particularly a predicate. To possess a concept is to be able to deploy a term expressing it in making judgements: the ability connects with such things as recognizing when the term applies, and being able to understand the consequences of its application. The term 'idea' was formerly used in the same way, but is avoided because of its associations with subjective mental imagery, which may be irrelevant to the possession of a concept."[26]

---

22. Scott 2014, s.v. "concepts."

23. Colman 2015, s.v. "concept.".

24. Ogden and Richards (1923) 1930.

25. Matthews 2014, s.v. "concept." But what is a 'construct' (more on this below)?

26. Blackburn 2016, s.v. "concept." See also Margolis and Laurence (2019): "Concepts are the building blocks of thoughts."

Ontologically, "there are two dominant frameworks in contemporary philosophy": concepts are taken to be either abstract objects or mental representations.[27]

There are overlaps within and across disciplines. And yet, regardless of which dictionary you prefer, 'concept' or CONCEPT means trouble. It's divisive. Some scholars are unhappy with it, while others argue it's an asset and even that it's indispensable.

What's the case against concepts?

The ambiguity and vagueness of 'concept' have negative effects, and are at the root of miscommunication, just like the ambiguity and vagueness of 'neoliberalism,' 'empathy,' 'depression,' and 'happiness.'[28] Weitz's observation is as applicable to the social sciences as to philosophy, as applicable at present as it was in his time:

> Concepts have been construed as universals, images, thoughts, meanings, abstract objects, and as habits, skills or dispositions. Many philosophers have distinguished radically between concepts and language. Others, more recently, reduce talk about concepts to talk about language. Some even reject concepts altogether, regarding them as misleading and misguided ontological projections of certain ordinary uses of language. The concept of concept, as its vast history makes abundantly clear, is a family of concepts.[29]

It's hard to tell what people mean by 'concept.' In spite of this, one objection has been raised time and again: a concept can't be empirically apprehended. It consists in an individual's mental state and, as far as science is concerned, that's unknowable. It's not suitable for social science research.[30]

Take linguists' triangle as a starting point: the concept BATHTUB, the word 'bathtub' (or 'Badewanne,' 'bañera,' etc.), and actual bathtubs (like Archimedes of Syracuse's). You might be interested in the relationships between 'bathtub' and BATHTUB, 'bathtub' and bathtubs, or BATHTUB and bathtubs. You might ask what represents what (refers to, stands for, picks out) and how this is accomplished. But here's the thing. Bathtubs and utterances of 'bathtub' exist in a way that

---

27. Margolis and Laurence 2007, 561.

28. Adcock 2005; Slaney and Racine 2011.

29. Weitz 1972, 86.

30. More broadly, some traditions dislike the mind/mental/cognitive character of CONCEPT.

BATHTUB doesn't. You can't have independent access to BATHTUB, except as mediated by 'bathtub.' Even if BATHTUB had neural substrates or underpinnings (as opposed to the neural substrates of the use of 'bathtub'), the concept wouldn't be endowed with the sort of existence bathtubs and utterances of 'bathtub' have.[31] 'Concept' turns out to be "vacuous" and "redundant":

> [Linguist John Lyons] argues that the use of the term ['concepts'] in semantic theory is essentially vacuous. Suppose I say that in order to use the word *table* correctly (i.e., of tables), a person needs to 'have the concept' of table. The evidence that a person does have the concept can only be the person's ability to use the word appropriately. But if I am capable of judging whether or not a person does use the word appropriately, there is no need for me to bring in the concept as a criterion for correct use. Concepts become redundant.[32]

Concepts are charged with ontological mysteriousness, empirical inaccessibility, and vacuousness and redundancy. Identifying concept possession and use results in circular reasoning, or unwittingly switching to word and language use. Individuating c is an unsolvable problem. There's no empirical way forward. No data can establish that something is one distinct concept. Nor that these are two instances of one concept. Nor that these are two concepts, but they're identical. Therefore, concepts have no place in empirical science.

What's the case for concepts?

The distinction between words and concepts does have something going for it. Concepts do have something going for them. Gervasio says: '*sería útil tener una mesa.*' Hildegard says: '*es wäre hilfreich, einen Tisch zu haben.*' While their utterances sound quite different, they're making the same assertion: it'd be helpful to have a table. They aren't referring to any particular table, or set of tables, such as all of the tables they've seen, read about, imagined, dreamt about, or hallucinated in their lives in Montevideo and Berlin. Nor all of the tables they'll see, read about, imagine, dream about, and hallucinate in the future. What they're talking about isn't tangible or imaginary tables. It's not Spanish or German lexical items either. Which is why an additional entity, TABLE, a concept, seems to be needed.

---

31. I'll leave it at that, so I'm not driven far afield by concept nativism and the 'language of thought hypothesis,' cognitive ontologies, and Chomsky and universal grammar (Borghi et al. 2018; Carey 2009; Fodor 1975; Janssen, Klein, and Slors 2017; Laurence and Margolis 2002).

32. J. Taylor 2001, 6.

Jones says 'car,' James says 'automobile.' Jones says 'taxi,' James says 'cab.' They're uttering different words, but they seem to be talking about the same thing. Not any particular collection of cars (or automobiles), but CAR (or AUTOMOBILE). Not any particular collection of taxis (or cabs), but TAXI (or CAB).

What of the special case of natural kinds? On the one hand, there's gold, the material stuff, whose atomic number is 79. On the other hand, there are natural language words, like 'gold,' 'oro,' and 'Gold.' Whether you happen to say 'gold' or 'oro' is inessential; they're merely symbols, signs, representations. All these words are expressing or representing the same non-linguistic thing. And what is *this*? This would seem to be GOLD (not gold).

Defenders of the word/concept distinction affirm that you can't make do without it. 'You'd be screwed without BATHTUB. Without CULTURE, WELFARE STATE, and ETHNICITY. Without TIME and TABLE.' One word may express or represent many concepts. One concept may be expressed or represented by many words. Across natural languages, but also within one natural language. There are glossaries and there are dictionaries. Glossaries don't start with words but with concepts. Then, they look for all the words that represent this concept (and in more than one language, if written for international audiences). Natural language dictionaries start with a word. Then, they elucidate which concepts it represents.

The case for concepts is shored up by bringing history and diachronic change into the picture. First, it's been argued that without concepts you couldn't make sense of the relationship between changes in meaning and in subject matter.[33] In Sawyer's words: "Words change meaning over time. Some meaning shift is accompanied by a corresponding change in subject matter; some meaning shift is not. [...] I argue that an account of linguistic meaning can accommodate the first kind of case, but that a theory of concepts is required to accommodate the second."[34]

One of Sawyer's examples is the English word 'meat,' which "used to mean food in general, and used to have a correspondingly broader extension than it has today." So, both meaning and subject matter have changed over time. By contrast, 'whale' and 'atom' "are associated with distinct theories of the same subject matter at different times." Likewise, 'consent' and 'rape' "are also underwritten by different understandings of the same subject matter at different times."[35] These are dual phenomena and so should their explanations be.

33. Strawson 1963.
34. Sawyer 2018, 127.
35. Sawyer 2018, 128.

Sawyer claims that "where there is stability of subject matter through linguistic change . . . it is concepts that explain the stability."[36] Without concepts, there couldn't be genuine disagreements about whales, atoms, and rape, and relativism couldn't be staved off. One thing is a theory of meaning, another thing is a theory of concepts. One thing is language, another thing is thought.[37]

Second, it's been argued that a concept can exist prior to any word expressing it. For obvious reasons, this argument is up historians' alley. Skinner denies that "possessing a concept is equivalently a matter of knowing the meaning of a word":

> To argue for any such equivalence is undoubtedly a mistake. First of all, it cannot be a necessary condition of my possessing a concept that I need to understand the correct application of a corresponding term. Suppose, for example, that I am studying Milton's thought, and want to know whether Milton considered it important that a poet should display a high degree of originality. The answer seems to be that he felt it to be of the greatest importance. [. . .] But I could never have arrived at this conclusion by examining Milton's use of the word *originality*. For while the concept is clearly central to his thought, the word did not enter the language until a century or more after his death. Although a history of the word *originality* and its various uses could undoubtedly be written, such a survey would by no means be the same as a history of the concept of originality—a consideration often ignored in practice by historians of ideas.[38]

Skinner's point about Milton generalizes. In this or that epoch, in this or that place, people wanted to do something nobody had done before. But their language didn't have a word for it. That's a great idea, to be original, but 'original' wasn't available to them. People do, want, and imagine things the names for which they aren't aware of. It's a rare word or their vocabulary isn't all that wide.

You may agree with Skinner, but doubt that he needs the word 'concept' to refer to that. I, for one, don't think he does. What Skinner has in mind, in his own words, is distinctions and classifications: "if we wish to grasp how someone sees the world—what distinctions he draws, what classifications he accepts—what we need to know is not what words he uses but rather what concepts he possesses."[39] I'd suggest calling them 'distinctions' and 'classifications.'

36. Sawyer 2018, 129.

37. Sawyer 2020a, b.

38. Q. Skinner 1989, 8–9; see also Q. Skinner 1979, 206.

39. Q. Skinner 1989, 7.

What's the bottom line?

The philosophical literature on concepts must struggle with the preceding arguments and counterarguments. Those of concept-friends and concept-foes. The literature is extensive and intricate. Fortunately, I don't have to. In accordance with my general tactic, my toolkit should be lean. I want to survey the land, assess my options, and clarify potential confusions.

I believe I can skip the extra dimensions and complications that CONCEPT introduces. My arguments will be about words. Social science communities' key words: how they're used, how they should be used, how to make decisions about uses. To be sure, this isn't separable from words' functions, what they're for, and other dangerous philosophical things. If reference or representation is part of what they do, what is this reference to or representation of? Philosophical puzzles are hardly ever far removed from my arguments. But they're never my focus.

You could object by pointing to my arguments' philosophical leanings and what they're more and less compatible with. 'Philosophically speaking, your approach harmonizes with Wittgensteinian sensibilities. Wittgensteinians sympathize with your looking at words rather than concepts, word uses rather than meanings, and word uses in specific languages and language communities. And with your aversion to Socrates-type "what-is-*F*?" inquiries and metaphysical essences.' Maybe so—in these respects. I see harmonies, but also disharmonies.[40] Either way, I'll continue to insist that I'm not speaking philosophically. Philosophers' stance diverges from mine. My job description is pragmatic and doesn't mention the philosophical foundations of concepts, language, and representation. Thank goodness.

Why don't you reconceptualize CONCEPT, or adopt a particular CONCEPT, or a particular conception of CONCEPT, or redefine the word 'concept,' so that it means to draw distinctions? Can't you stipulate the meaning of this 'technical term' in your work?

Cool reflexive question: whether I can do that is one question I'm asking in this book.

Suppose I tried out your suggestion. I'd stipulate that my use of the word 'concept' deviates from the norm in social science. By 'concept' I don't mean an abstract or mental entity. Rather, I mean an activity, a way of acting. Or an institutionalized cultural practice, or a habitual way of lumping certain things

---

40. M. Bennett and Hacker 2003; Gunnell 2020; Pardo and Patterson 2013; Racine and Slaney 2013; Slaney and Racine 2011.

together, consciously or unconsciously. Demarcating the boundaries of the set, so A and B are in it, but C and D aren't. Highlighting and becoming attuned to certain similarities and dissimilarities, on the basis of which things are split and lumped. Treating certain things as being alike.

Alternatively, by 'concept' I could mean a disposition to act in certain ways. Being disposed to make certain distinctions in certain situations. Being disposed to understand, perceive, treat, and react to things in certain ways—namely, things of this sort in this way, things of that sort in that way. As Gunnell observes: "MacIntyre . . . claimed that possessing a concept amounts to behaving, or being able to behave, in a certain way and that conceptual change entails changes in behavior. . . . We might very well conclude from this sort of definition that a concept is not so much a kind of thing at all but rather, as Ryle at times claimed, a dispositional or functional category."[41]

In this thought experiment, my uses of 'concept' wouldn't refer to entities, but to practices of classification or categorization. These practices are observable. If you say that POPULISM exists in our society, you mean you've observed a social, institutionalized distinction, such that objects having properties P_1, P_2, and P_3 are reliably grouped together. The English word 'populism' and the Spanish word '*populismo*' are used to refer to this set. You might add that this society 'has a concept,' it 'has POPULISM.' But it wouldn't actually possess anything. Social actors would make, or be disposed to make, a particular distinction. 'To have' is a way of speaking.

Opting for this stipulation of 'concept' would have implications for the character of conceptual change. GENDER, SANDWICH, and DIGNITY have changed. But there's no tangible thing that undergoes changes, as my bike or the Ship of Theseus have. Nor an intangible thing, like the rules of soccer in 1990 or Uruguay's mortality rate in the last three decades. There's no thing. No thing whose properties might be like this today and like that tomorrow. The claim isn't that *it*, SANDWICH, a concept, has changed. Instead, what's changed is a practice: the practice of lumping certain food items together. That's conceptual change. That GENDER, SANDWICH, or DIGNITY have changed is a way of speaking.

You're right: this stipulation could be designed to suit my aims. But why use the word 'concept' for this job? What reason do I have, seeing as I'd need to carry out several operations to 'reconceptualize' or 'redefine' it? I don't know what's the benefit vis-à-vis sticking to 'drawing distinctions.' I'm not sure who'd benefit from this move.

There's a sense of 'can' in which I can do this. But I don't think I should.

41. Gunnell 2011, 133.

4.3 FAQs about words and meaning

I concede that CONCEPT *or 'concept' might be troublesome. But isn't* WORD *or 'word' troublesome as well?*

Yes, it is. Wordhood is no walk in the park.[42] Just like concepts, it's controversial how to individuate words, how to tell what is and isn't a word. Their character and properties are hard to pin down. There are many accounts of words or lexical items, what they are, what they do, and how they relate to meanings and to the world.

That being said, 'word'/WORD seems to me to beat 'concept'/CONCEPT. It's a bit less problematic, a bit easier to get ahold of and work with, at least for my purposes. It's more parsimonious and empirically tractable.

What exactly do you mean by 'word'? Linguists, lexicographers, and lexicologists talk about words, terms, word-forms, lexemes, morphemes, lexical units, lexical entries, and lexical items. Distinctions between word types and tokens. Lexemes and lemmas. Phonological, prosodic, orthographic, morphological, and syntactic words. This is all quite confusing.

It *is* confusing. 'Word' is a common word, which is ambiguous in several ways. An important one is that there are types, occurrences, and tokens:

> In ordinary parlance 'word' is ambiguous between a type-level reading (as in "*Color* and *colour* are spellings of the same word"), an occurrence-level reading (as in "there are thirteen words in the tongue-twister *How much wood would a woodchuck chuck if a woodchuck could chuck wood?*"), and a token-level reading (as in "John erased the last two words on the blackboard").[43]

The list of difficulties for 'word' is long. There are highbrow scholarly concerns, but also hands-on challenges for lexicographers and others who work with words, such as how to treat clitics, contractions, logograms, and initialisms and acronyms.[44]

In some fields and contexts, it's sensible to try and dispense with 'word' altogether. For lexicographers and lexicologists, "the familiar term 'word' is both too broad and too narrow; one would not want to consider *goes* as a lexical unit, although it is a word, whereas expressions such as *(to) cut up* or *red herring* are lexical units but consist of several words."[45] 'Lexical unit' or 'lexeme' is preferable, as

---

42. Bauer 1983; Cappelen 1999; Di Sciullo and Williams 1987; Gasparri 2021; Irmak 2019; D. Kaplan 1990, 2011; M. Murphy 2010; Plag 2003; J. Taylor 2015, 2017; Thomasson, forthcoming.

43. Gasparri and Marconi 2019.

44. Trask 2004.

45. Klein 2001, 8764–65; see also Cruse 1986.

it includes "simple words . . . such as *cup*," "bound morphemes, like *un-* as in *un-happy*," "morphologically complex words . . . like *greenhouse*," and "set phrases whose meaning is not compositional, such as phrasal verbs like *throw up*."[46]

In this book, however, I'm going to stick with 'word.' My arguments are about social scientists' words (and, less frequently, two-word expressions). For instance: psychologists disagree about the correct uses of the word 'intelligence'; political scientists use the word 'state' in multiple ways; the word 'gender' is disputed in gender studies and the sociology of gender. 'Intelligence,' 'state,' and 'gender' are 'orthographic words'—that is, "an uninterrupted string of letters which is preceded by a blank space and followed either by a blank space or a punctuation mark."[47]

This is a rough-and-ready policy, susceptible to objections. What if a language doesn't have blank spaces? Why should written languages be the model? Admittedly, I'm speaking somewhat loosely. But my arguments don't need more precision and fine-grained distinctions in this domain, unlike work on lexical meaning and lexicographic conventions.

If 'word' makes you nervous, a fine alternative would be 'lexical item' or 'lexical unit.'

You privilege word use over meaning. Why is that?

Meaning is a hornet's nest in philosophy and linguistics. To say anything meaningful about lexical meaning, or the meaning of words and expressions, I'd have to walk through those minefields and emerge unscathed. Which seems to me avoidable for my arguments about the practice of social science.

Meaning is presumably abstract and unobservable, while use is presumably concrete and perceptible.[48] Meaning implicates inaccessible mental states, at least on some views. (On other views, "'meanings' just ain't in the head.")[49] It requires commitments in semantic theory. Taking sides on the relations between semantic content and context, semantics and pragmatics; and on the relations between extension and intension, reference and sense.[50]

Meanwhile, skeptics deny that there's such a thing as word meaning at all. Perhaps "the phrase 'the meaning of a word' is . . . a dangerous nonsense-phrase";

---

46. M. Murphy 2010, 7–8.

47. Plag 2003, 4; see also Trask 2004.

48. Not so fast. What word is being used? What exactly can you perceive? You can hear a string of sounds and you can observe ink marks on a piece of paper. But claims about word use necessitate inferences and auxiliary premises.

49. Putnam 1975a, 144.

50. Frege 1892; Horwich 2005; Putnam 1973, 1975a; Strawson 1950.

"there is *no* simple and handy appendage of a word called 'the meaning of (the word) "x".""[51] It's an "illusion" that "words have fixed and stable meanings."[52]

I realize that word use isn't a picnic. The semantic issues won't magically disappear. I'll be lucky if they leave me alone for a while, but they'll reappear, be it through the front door or the back door. Still, use does seem to fare better than meaning. It's more capable of evading heavy-duty metaphysics. Above all, I believe use is fitting and sufficient for this book's arguments. I'll look at the use of social science words, such as 'capitalism' or 'empathy.' I'll discuss how words should be used and how to decide how words should be used—taking their semantic properties into account, alongside other considerations.

In these regards, my arguments have affinities with approaches that emphasize language use, such as Wittgenstein's, speech act theory, and pragmatics.[53] For a variety of reasons, many other philosophers and linguists privilege use, substitute use for meaning, reduce meaning to use, and are suspicious of meaning.[54] As per usual policy, though, I don't claim to know what meaning is, nor how meaning and use relate to each other.[55] This book is about social science research, and I'm driven by expediency and practicality.

In a nutshell: given what I'm up to, use beats meaning. It may help me decrease my minefield walks to a minimum. Surely not to zero.

4.4 FAQs about other words and expressions

Besides 'to define' and 'to conceptualize,' social scientists often say they 'understand X as Y,' 'construe X as Y,' and 'view X as Y.' Also: 'X is best understood as Y' or 'X is most usefully understood as Y.' Anything wrong with that?

In contemporary social science, these expressions are roughly equivalent.[56] They work in the same way. 'X' stands for an English word and 'Y' stands for a characterization of it, which varies in character, features, and length.

---

51. Austin 1961, 24, 30.

52. J. Taylor 2017, 256.

53. Wittgenstein (1953) 2009, § 43: "For a *large* class of cases of the employment of the word 'meaning'—though not for *all*—this word can be explained in this way: the meaning of a word is its use in the language." "Can be explained" improves on "can be defined" in Anscombe's translation (Stern 2004, xii). The German verb is '*erklären.*'

54. Stroud 2017.

55. Horwich 2005.

56. Rarer are 'to analyze *X*,' 'to construe *X* as *Y*,' and 'to explicate *X*' (Carnap [1950] 1962).

For my money, they give social scientists too much leeway: a lot of things can count as 'understanding X as Y,' and a lot of outcomes can count as having succeeded at it and being best at it. (Then there's usefulness, as in 'most usefully understood'—to be continued . . .) It's nebulous what these verbs mean and what procedures they call for. Whether social scientists write 'to define' or 'to understand' doesn't appear to be a well-considered choice. Their unsystematic use of quotation marks is also a bad sign. Understanding altruism or understanding 'altruism.' Defining altruism and defining 'altruism.' Which is it and why?

Similarly, social scientists liberally use the nouns 'understanding' and 'view.' You have a novel understanding of X or a novel view of X. In this literature, there are numerous understandings or views of X (also numerous 'conceptions' of X—on which more below). Yet, it's underspecified what an understanding or view must consist in. For example, 'understanding' and 'view' are ambiguous between: (1) defining the word 'racism'/giving an account of the concept RACISM/saying what racism is, and (2) making empirical claims about racism, its characteristics, causes, and effects.

Besides 'words' and 'concepts,' social scientists often talk about 'terms' and 'notions.' Anything wrong with that? And what's up with 'construct'?

Social scientists aren't careful with 'term' and 'notion' either. 'Term' is ordinarily taken to be a language item, something like a word. Sometimes 'term' and 'word' strike me as synonymous. The distinction between mention and use can get lost. Social scientists are less likely than linguists and philosophers to graphically indicate they're mentioning a term, whether it's with quotation marks, italics, or another typographic marking (as in 'the term "gender" has two vowels' or 'the term *gender* has two vowels').

In more careful social science, uses of 'term' are closer to the fields of terminography and terminology.[57] 'Term' means "a word or expression that has a precise meaning in some uses or is peculiar to a science, art, profession, or subject."[58] Not any word or expression. This meaning is similar to the technical term 'technical term' ('*terminus technicus*') or 'term of art' ('*vocabulum artis*').

By 'notion' social scientists seem to mean something like "concept" or "idea." Like ordinary English speakers do. In particular, these two senses of

57. Bergenholtz 1995; Humbley 1997.

58. *Merriam-Webster.com Dictionary*, s.v. "term," accessed September 15, 2022, https://www.merriam-webster.com/dictionary/term.

'notion': "conception or impression of something known, experienced, or imagined" and "an inclusive general concept."[59]

My policy is to avoid both 'term' and 'notion.' They invite misunderstandings, as they aren't used consistently and precisely. Neither serves a function that couldn't be taken over by other words and expressions.

'Construct' originates and has been most frequent in psychology, starting in the mid-twentieth century.[60] I quote again Colman's *Dictionary of Psychology*: "A model based on observation guided by a theoretical framework. In psychometrics, a psychological attribute, such as intelligence or extraversion, on which people differ from one another; more generally any complex concept synthesized from simpler concepts. Also called a latent variable."[61]

Constructs have been expected to help on many fronts: measuring phenomena, apprehending and accounting for unobservable entities, organizing and representing data, synthesizing several concepts or variables. At the same time, there are plenty of worries about constructs, their ambiguity, and what their distinctive contributions are. Which partly overlap with worries about concepts.[62] Arguably, "the 'construct' concept . . . was recruited more for ideological reasons than valid logical ones."[63] There isn't "a clear or consistent definition of the term."[64] I'll pass.

Social scientists' disputes are neither about concepts nor about words. They're about conceptions of a concept; say, conflicting conceptions of GENDER *or* WELFARE STATE. *What's your beef with this?*

In *A Theory of Justice*, Rawls writes: "it seems natural to think of the concept of justice as distinct from the various conceptions of justice and as being specified by the role which these different sets of principles, these different conceptions, have in common."[65] In *Power: A Radical View*, Lukes's "distinction between 'concept' and 'view' is closely parallel to that drawn by John Rawls between 'concept' and 'conception.'"[66] There is one POWER concept. There are several

59. *Merriam-Webster.com Dictionary*, s.v. "notion," accessed September 15, 2022, https://www.merriam-webster.com/dictionary/notion.

60. Cronbach and Meehl 1955; MacCorquodale and Meehl 1948.

61. Colman 2015, s.v. "construct."

62. Lovasz and Slaney 2013; Slaney and Garcia 2015.

63. Michell 2013, 20.

64. Slaney and Racine 2013, 4.

65. J. Rawls 1971, 5.

66. Lukes 1974a, 27.

views or conceptions of it. It's an essentially contested concept, in Gallie's sense.[67] But different conceptions must share a "common core."[68]

In "Constitutional Cases," chapter 5 of *Taking Rights Seriously*, Dworkin calls it a "crucial distinction": "When I appeal to the concept of fairness I appeal to what fairness means, and I give my view on that issue no special standing. When I lay down a conception of fairness, I lay down what I mean by fairness, and my view is therefore the heart of the matter." Dworkin also points out that "the difference is a difference not just in the *detail* of the instructions given but in the *kind* of instructions given."[69]

The distinction between concept and conception does solve some problems. It's been used as a matter of course in many arguments and literatures, though more often used than meticulously analyzed.[70] Unfortunately, it doesn't supply what I'd need. What I'd need to be ready to forge ahead. It doesn't help with the individuation of concepts. You need concept C in order to look at conceptions of it, rather than conceptions of other concepts. Lukes disagrees with Dahl's one-dimensional view (or conception) of power and with Bachrach and Baratz's two-dimensional view (or conception) of power. But what makes it the case that they're having a disagreement about POWER, the concept? What is it to be a concept, or a component of the concept, as opposed to a component of the conception of the concept? There are better and worse answers to these questions, but, from my point of view, we're back where we started. The difficulties occasioned by CONCEPT are still with us.

Working with words and their uses remains preferable.

Take social science research on altruism, which aims to describe and explain it. It's true that one lab's altruistic behavior can differ from another's. So, the issue is what altruism really is (neither a word, 'altruism,' nor a concept, ALTRUISM). Isn't this an empirical question, like what manganese is?

Socrates and his interlocutors sparred over 'what-is-F?' questions, also referred to as 'what-is-X?' or 'what-is-F-ness?' questions.[71] Although he claimed to know nothing, he did seem to know how not to tackle them. Neither a large collection of examples nor facts about lexical meaning would do. You have to

67. Gallie 1956.

68. Lukes 1974b, 187.

69 . R. Dworkin 1977, 134–35. An earlier version had appeared in the *New York Review of Books* in 1972 (Burley 2004, 402).

70. Criley 2007; Ezcurdia 1998; Flew 1985; Higginbotham 1998; Swanton 1985.

71. H. Benson 1990a; J. Clark 2018; R. Robinson 1941, 1950; Wolfsdorf 2003a, b.

find out not what 'justice' means, but what justice is. Not what 'courage' means, but what courage is. Likewise, Aristotle endeavored to discover the nature or essence of a thing: what it really is.[72]

In some places and times, statements about what F is have gone by the name of 'real definitions.' Not only in Hellenic places and ancient times:

> when we [contemporary analytic philosophers] ask what it is for a thing to be a person or for a creature to be conscious or for a fact to be a law of nature or for two expressions to be synonymous or for an object to be colored or for an action to be free or for an artifact to be an artwork, we are best understood as seeking real definitions of the properties, kinds, and relations that figure in our questions, rather than semantic or conceptual equivalents, even when the correctness of the account is meant to be recognizable a priori.[73]

The expression 'real definition' has had many detractors, on the grounds that 'definitions' are about language; definienda must be language items. Irrespective of what you call them, though, these have always been archetypically philosophical questions. What is justice? What is consciousness? What is a person? What is art? One part of philosophy, one of its most recognizable parts, is 'metaphysical' or 'ontological' problems.[74] Metaphysicians make 'to be F is to be G' claims and 'just is' statements.[75] Not what F appears to be. Nor how F appears to people to be (that'd be sociology of knowledge). Nor the observable causes and consequences of F (that'd be neurobiology, political science, engineering, rehabilitation science, etc.).

What should social scientists do about 'what-is-F?' questions? I'm afraid I'll have to get a bit metaphysical myself (more on this below). I believe social science is better off without them. Are you asking what's altruism, empathy, power, gender, neoliberalism? Bad idea! Bad question! One reason is social scientists' unfavorable disposition to natures or essences, in a metaphysically realist sense, in Plato's or Aristotle's sense, or in the natural kinds and natural kindness sense. They'd find it implausible. Few would agree that altruism, empathy, and neoliberalism are essentially like manganese (see chapter 7).

I'm talking about social scientists' work and the phenomena they empirically investigate. I'm not weighing in on the proper place of 'what-is-F?'

---

72. So did al-Kindī, al-Fārābī, and Ibn Sīnā. See Adamson 2016; Kennedy-Day 2003.

73. Rosen 2015, 189; see also Correia 2017; K. Fine 1995.

74. Varzi 2011.

75. Dorr 2016; Rayo 2013.

questions, 'what-*F*-is' claims, and 'real definitions' in philosophy, or for that matter elsewhere. But philosophers' reactions can nonetheless be telling:

> A very large part of the cause of the birth and long life of this confused concept, real definition, is surely the occurrence in language, or at least in Indo-European languages, of the question-form: 'What is *x*?' Real definition first appears in literature as the answer to questions put by Socrates having the form 'What is *x*?' And the confusedness of the concept of real definition is an effect of the vagueness of the formula 'What is *x*?' For it is the vaguest of all forms of question except an inarticulate grunt. Real definition flourishes because the question-form 'What-is-*x*?' flourishes; and this question-form flourishes precisely because it is vague. It saves us the trouble of thinking out and saying exactly what it is that we want to know about *x*. By saying 'What is *x*?' we can leave to our answerer the task of discovering what particular information about *x* we want. We can also use this question-form to express a general desire to be given any useful information about *x* of any sort.[76]

'What-is-*F*?' is a sensitive question for contemporary analytic philosophers' identities and self-understandings. It uncomfortably interrogates philosophy's relationships to science, and the changing fortunes of metaphysics within it.[77] Luckily, my claims focus on the practice of social science, what's beneficial to it, and doable. That said, they aren't free from metaphysics, as they reject certain pictures of the social world. I can't say I have no horse in that metaphysical race.

Do you take issue with the expressions X 'counts' or 'qualifies' as a Y?

I take no issue with 'to count as' and 'to qualify as' to report findings about how things are classified, picked out, defined, and identified. In Uruguay, chess doesn't qualify as a sport, while in Paraguay it does. It's an interesting finding for the sociology of knowledge or sociology of cognition. However, to make methodological or ontological claims yourself, there are better ways of speaking. For realists (and the like) about sport, I'd suggest sticking to the verb 'to be': chess is a sport. For conventionalists (and the like), I'd suggest highlighting that it's their choice, or their community's classificatory scheme. In it, chess doesn't belong in the same group as basketball and tennis. In these contexts, 'to count as' and 'to qualify as' are prone to being misunderstood.

But I may be nitpicking.

---

76. R. Robinson 1950, 190.
77. Hempel 1952, 2–20.

Activity DF consists in social scientists drawing distinctions and assessing which distinctions are worth drawing. Do you take drawing distinctions to be the same as classifying and categorizing?

Yes. Or two aspects of one activity.

If you will, you can say that classifying and categorizing objects necessitates having made a distinction according to which to classify and categorize them. A sociologist of religion, or the sociology-of-religion community, makes a distinction between religions and non-religions. Or between religions, sects, cults, spiritual movements, and magic. Moral psychologists make a distinction between morality, altruism, and pro-social behavior. Or between empathy, sympathy, and theory of mind. Democratic and non-democratic regimes. Developed, underdeveloped, and developing countries.

What these social scientists are doing might be called 'drawing distinctions,' 'classifying,' or 'categorizing.' 'Drawing boundaries,' 'taxonomizing,' or 'typifying.' They're creating 'taxonomies' or 'typologies.' For my purposes, these formulations can be treated together—for mine, but not for everyone's.[78]

If you will, you can say that drawing a distinction makes no sense unless you're already classifying or categorizing things according to it. There can be no abstract distinction, pure reason distinction, apart from what's being distinguished. Perhaps to draw a distinction and to classify are two aspects of the process.

There are loads of names for the products of this activity: 'classes,' 'categories,' 'kinds,' 'types,' 'taxa,' 'clusters,' 'sets,' and 'groups.' Names that have more than one meaning.[79] Taken together, they make up a classification system, typology, or taxonomy. A planet is a type of celestial object. The Iranian Revolution of 1979 is a member of the set of social revolutions.[80] Animals may be classified into three categories: carnivores, herbivores, and omnivores.

'Kind' must be handled with care. Metaphysicians and philosophers of science fight over natural kinds' magical power to 'carve nature at its joints' (*Phaedrus* 265d–266a). Philosophers of biology fight over natural kinds in relation to species, taxa, and taxonomic principles and methods.[81] Human kinds, or interactive kinds, are equally contentious: "kinds of people, their behaviour,

---

78. Bokulich 2020; Marradi 1990.

79. Bokulich 2020; Daston 2004b; Farber 1976; Stinchcombe 1968; Witteveen 2016. A famous type of type is Weber's 'ideal type'—on which see Aronovitch (2012), Eliaeson (1990), Swedberg (2018a), and Weber (1904).

80. Skocpol 1982. See also Foran 2005; Goodwin 2001.

81. Brigandt 2009; Dupré 1981; Ereshefsky and Reydon 2015; R. Wilson, Barker, and Brigandt 2007.

their condition, kinds of action, kinds of temperament or tendency, kinds of emotion, and kinds of experience."[82]

Objections to natural kinds and human kinds are of many kinds. For instance, Hacking recounts that both the left and the right got mad at him:

> When I have tried to indicate that there are interesting differences between 'human kinds'—kinds of people and their behaviour—and what are commonly called natural kinds, I found myself assaulted from left and right. The nominalist 'left' says that all kinds are human, or at any rate, there are no kinds in nature. The realist 'right' says that there are indeed natural kinds, and that human kinds—at any rate those susceptible of systematic study— are among them.[83]

If I could skirt the philosophy of kinds and go about my business, I gladly would. But I can't. Suppose that, against all odds, neoliberalism turns out to be a natural kind like nitrogen. (I can't believe this, but it's a supposition.) Then, political scientists' distinctions between neoliberal and non-neoliberal policies would be looking to correspond to nature, carve nature at its joints, like distinctions between chemical elements in the periodic table.[84] Suppose psychopathological classifications carved nature at its joints.[85] Their success would have to be judged accordingly. Nature, the structure of reality, would be the final arbiter. Quite another story if human kinds are conventional, 'socially constructed,' or something along these lines.

So, I'll have to return to these issues and how they affect my arguments. Concerning nomenclature, I'm wary of 'kind' getting thrown around and getting out of hand. Otherwise, I'm OK with all the other options, both for the activity and for the products. 'To draw a distinction' is my favorite.

Do distinctions or classifications need to be explicit?

I don't think so. You can explicitly propose a distinction or classification by writing a paper about it, or by telling an audience about it. Another option is that practices, actions, institutions, ideas, bureaucracies, and spaces are based on it, without its having been stated discursively. The former: someone draws an explicit distinction between dogs and non-dogs, or a scale of degrees of

---

82. Hacking 1995, 351–52. See S. Allen 2021; Rachel Cooper 2004; Hacking 1991, 1995, 1999, 2002, 2007a, b; Khalidi 2013.

83. Hacking 1991, 109.

84. J. Campbell, O'Rourke, and Slater 2011.

85. Kincaid and Sullivan 2014.

dogness. The latter: what people do and say are based on a particular way of classifying four-legged animals, which helps them get things done, express ideas, communicate, solve problems, and cope with the world.

No doubt, this is too quick. For starters, 'based on' is imprecise, possibly too permissive. And are non-explicit distinctions the same as dispositions (see above)?

4.5 FAQs about sources

I understand you're trying to get us out of here and move on with your arguments. But I'd like to learn more about this sort of stuff and its history. Who's written about it? Who's helped you?

A massive book could be devoted to reviewing scholarship on "this sort of stuff." It'd have to encompass the history of philosophy, linguistics, lexicography and lexicology, and the social sciences. Only occasionally have these discussions been in touch with one another. Their arguments and nomenclatures rarely overlap. So much for interdisciplinarity and multidisciplinarity.

That could be a fascinating book. But this book isn't that book. Instead, I'll succinctly introduce the bodies of work from which I've learned the most and on which my arguments draw.

SOCIOLOGICAL METHODOLOGY AND LOGIC OF INQUIRY

Methodology in the sense not of techniques but their foundations: in virtue of what a method delivers on its promises, what the logic behind methodological tools is, and what inferences they license. Also known as 'meta-methodology.'[86] The goal is to assist practitioners. Assist empirical sociologists to do research well; develop satisfactory observation, operationalization, and measurement practices; and put forward sound arguments.[87]

Deeper issues are waiting in the wings: the relationships between observations and the phenomena they're observations of; what is and isn't comparable; where concepts come from; and how concepts, dimensions, and indicators relate to one another. For instance, you might try to distinguish: a thing/phenomenon, call it 'A'; one of the dimensions or aspects of A; an indicator of this dimension or aspect of A; and another thing/phenomenon, call it 'B,' whose occurrence is correlated with A's occurrence, perhaps caused by A. Yet, B is

---

86. Marsden 2019.
87. Mohr et al. 2020.

distinct from *A*, ontologically distinct, like the mercury in your thermometer is distinct from your body temperature. Where does a concept end? "Which indicators are considered 'part of' the concept, and which are considered independent of or external to it?"[88] Which symptoms are indicators of a disease rather than part of it?

None of this is straightforward.[89] In the twentieth century, influential scholarship on the logic of inquiry and foundations of methodology was published by Blalock, Blumer, Cicourel, Lieberson, Lundberg, Merton, Stinchcombe, and many others.[90] Fast-forward to the twenty-first century, and sociologists have never stopped working in this area. It's an intellectually exciting and creative one, though quite small. These works overlap with sociological theory and philosophy of social science, because people who are into the logic of inquiry tend to be into sociological theory and philosophy of social science, too.[91] Foci and emphases have predictably changed. Recent US sociology has spent more time on causation, explanation, and generalization than on concepts, words, and definitions. One exception is Swedberg.[92]

I'm sorry these remarks about sociology are parochially 'American.' I'm aware that other sociological traditions exist, I'm aware that languages other than English exist, but the preceding paragraphs shamelessly ignore them anyway.[93]

88. Lazarsfeld 1958, 103; see also L. Hu and Kohler-Hausmann 2020.

89. Alexandrova 2017; Alexandrova and Haybron 2016; Cartwright and Runhardt 2014; H. Chang 2004; Holzhauser and Eggert 2019; Michell 1999, 2005; Tal 2013, 2019; Vessonen 2017. Some view these issues as prerequisites for objective, systematic, formal, commensurable, generalizable, and scientific knowledge, which quantification would be the royal road to. Cf. Espeland and Sauder 2016; Espeland and Stevens 1998, 2008; Mennicken and Espeland 2019; Nirenberg and Nirenberg 2021; Porter 1995.

90. Blalock 1982; Blumer 1931, 1940, 1954, 1957; Cicourel 1964; Duncan 1984; Homans 1967; Lazarsfeld 1993; Lieberson 1985; Lundberg 1939, 1942; Merton 1968b; Stinchcombe 1968; W. Wallace 1971; Zetterberg (1954) 1965.

91. A. Abbott 2001, 2004, 2016; Adams, Clemens, and Orloff 2005; Becker 2014, 2017; Biernacki 2012; Elman, Gerring, and Mahoney 2020; Ermakoff 2014; Gorski 2004; Gross 2018a, b; Kohler-Hausmann 2019; Krause 2021a, b; Lieberson and Lynn 2002; Little 2016; Luker 2008; Mahoney 2021; Martin 2011; Mohr et al. 2020; S. Morgan and Winship 2012; Pacewicz 2022; Porpora 2015; Prasad 2021b; Reed 2011; Riley, Ahmed, and Emigh 2021; Silver 2020; Small 2009, 2013; Stinchcombe 2005; Tavory and Timmermans 2014; Thacher 2006; Tilly 2008; Timmermans and Tavory 2022; Zerubavel 2020.

92. Swedberg 2016, 2018b, 2020a, b, 2021.

93. Abend 2006.

COMPARATIVE POLITICS

Political scientists have reflected on concepts and conceptualization practices more than other social scientists. The subfield of comparative politics led the way, because comparative research throws these issues into sharp relief.[94] In the 1970s and 1980s, Sartori's "Concept Misformation in Comparative Politics"; Sartori, Riggs, and Teune's *Tower of Babel*; and Sartori's edited volume *Social Science Concepts* laid the groundwork for this literature.[95] The "tradition of Giovanni Sartori" has had champions and critics.[96] Both have encouraged political scientists never to take their concepts for granted.

Collier has looked at conceptual stretching, conceptual innovation, and essentially contested concepts. Concepts and concept formation have also been scrutinized by Gerring, Goertz, and Goertz and Mahoney. Critical voices, such as Bevir and Kedar, have objected to Sartori's and Collier's approaches. Bevir and Blakely propose an interpretive, anti-naturalist alternative. Gunnell proposes a Wittgenstein-inspired alternative. Schaffer's alternative is interpretivist elucidation. Simmons and Smith urge the field to rethink comparison. An older dissenting voice is Connolly's.[97]

Political scientists speak of 'concept formation,' particularly when they get less epistemological and more methodologically applied. This expression has a distinguished career in German philosophy and social science, with noteworthy interventions by Kant, Rickert, and Weber.[98] What does it refer to in contemporary, empirically oriented political science? Gerring says it encompasses "three aspects of a concept": "'Concept formation' conventionally refers to three aspects of a concept: (a) the events or phenomena to be defined (the extension, denotation, or definiendum), (b) the properties or attributes that define them (the intension, connotation, definiens, or definition), and (c) a label covering both *a* and *b* (the term). Concept formation is thus a triangular operation; good concepts attain a proper alignment between *a*, *b*, and *c*."[99]

94. Przeworski and Teune 1970.

95. Sartori 1970, 1984; Sartori, Riggs, and Teune 1975. These ideas transcended the ivory tower (Riggs 1979, 1981). As in the abovementioned UNESCO program Interconcept, the aim was standardization and commensurability in international communities.

96. Collier and Gerring 2009.

97. Bevir and Blakely 2018; Bevir and Kedar 2008; Collier, Hidalgo, and Maciuceanu 2006; Collier and Levitsky 1997; Collier and Mahon 1993; Connolly (1974) 1983; Gallie 1956; Gerring 1999, 2012; Goertz 2006, 2008; Goertz and Mahoney 2012; Gunnell 1998, 2011, 2017, 2020; Schaffer 2016; E. Simmons and Smith 2021.

98. Oppenheimer 1925; Rickert (1902) 1913; see Outhwaite 1983.

99. Gerring 1999, 357–58. These three aspects became four elements in Gerring's 2012 book.

Political scientists have to form or formulate concepts. This is a task, a choice, comparable to other methodological tasks necessitated by their research projects. Political science methodologists ask on which grounds to make these choices; what makes a concept good.[100]

One among many difficulties is how to distinguish between a concept itself, POPULISM or WELFARE STATE, and what it's associated with: phenomena it causes or is caused by, or attributes or occurrences it's seen together with. Compare to the traditional view of natural kind concepts. The atomic number of GOLD belongs to its nature. It's an essential property. It's not something associated with GOLD, not something that frequently co-occurs with it, not even something that co-occurs with it without exception. To have atomic number 79 is to be gold. By contrast, that wealthy people's necklaces are made out of gold is inessential. It's inessential even if every one of them were made out of gold. But how to make this distinction if you're instead considering POPULISM or WELFARE STATE? EMPATHY, PLANET, or SANDWICH?

FOUCAULDIAN GENEALOGIES, HISTORICAL EPISTEMOLOGY AND ONTOLOGY

After archaeology, there was genealogy. Influenced by Bachelard, Canguilhem, and Nietzsche, Foucault became a genealogist. Concepts, conceptual systems, and conceptual practices should be historically analyzed. You shouldn't neglect how concepts come into being and their trajectories over time. Ahistorical social science and philosophy are myopic.[101]

This French tradition was formative for Hacking, who's studied concepts as "historical entities":[102] "Philosophical analysis is the analysis of concepts. Concepts are words in their sites. Sites include sentences, uttered or transcribed, always in a larger site of neighborhood, institution, authority, language. If one took seriously the project of philosophical analysis, one would require a history of the words in their sites, in order to comprehend what the concept was."[103] That "concepts are words in their sites" is a suggestive statement, but not self-explanatory. Nor does it suffice to individuate concepts. Anyway, the

---

100. Gerring 1999.

101. Bevir 2008; Bitbol and Gayon 2015; Braunstein 2002; Dews 1992; Lecourt 2002; Méthot 2013; Saar 2008, 2009.

102. Hacking 1990b, 358.

103. Hacking 1990b, 359; cf. Martínez Rodríguez 2016, 2021. In *The Taming of Chance*, Hacking (1990a, 7) underlines institutions as sites: "Philosophical analysis is the analysis of concepts. Concepts are words in their sites. Their sites are sentences and institutions. I regret that I have said too little about institutions, and too much about sentences and how they are arranged."

larger project has been pursued by many scholars on both sides of the Atlantic, following in the footsteps of Foucault, Hacking, or both. 'Historical ontology' and 'historical epistemology' have become interdisciplinary research areas.[104] In sociology, Somers has proposed a "historical sociology of concept formation."[105]

These historical endeavors don't belong to the fields of methodology and logic of inquiry. They aren't akin to political scientists' and sociologists' 'concept formation.' Instead, they produce accounts of societies, institutions, and social processes by means of conceptual genealogies. They've been especially interested in the history of science. For example, the emergence, transformation, and nasty uses of scientific concepts in psychology and psychiatry. Psychology and psychiatry are the subject matter. No methodological contributions are made to them.

HISTORICAL DICTIONARIES AND ENCYCLOPEDIAS; GERMAN AND BRITISH HISTORIANS

Dictionaries and encyclopedias must be mindful of the nature of their units. Not only how to pick them, but also what they consist in and how to recognize one when you see it. Historical dictionaries and encyclopedias take it up a notch. A classic is Raymond Williams's *Keywords: A Vocabulary of Culture and Society*. Its 'keywords' are "significant, binding words in certain activities and their interpretation," and "significant, indicative words in certain forms of thought."[106] "Political concepts" is in the title or subtitle of Calise and Lowi's *Hyperpolitics*; *Political Concepts*, edited by Bellamy and Mason; and *Political Concepts: A Critical Lexicon*, edited by Bernstein, Ophir, and Stoler (a New School for Social Research online journal and later book).[107] *Words and Worlds*, edited by Das and Fassin, is a "political lexicon," each of whose chapters is "organized around a term": toleration, power, war, revolution, corruption, and so on.[108] The history of philosophical concepts is dealt with, one at a time, in the series Oxford Philosophical Concepts: SPACE, EVIL, DIGNITY, HEALTH, PLEASURE, . . .

104. Daston and Galison 2007; Feest and Sturm 2011; Gingras 2010; Hacking 2002; Kusch 2010; Rheinberger 2007.

105. Somers 1995a, b; see also Djelic and Bothello 2013; Strand and Lizardo 2022.

106. R. Williams 1976, 13; see also (1958) 1960.

107. Bellamy and Mason 2003; Bernstein, Ophir, and Stoler 2018; Calise and Lowi 2010; "Editorial Statement," Political Concepts, accessed May 24, 2015, http://www.politicalconcepts .org/editorial-statement/.

108. Das and Fassin 2021, 2.

Another twentieth-century classic is Otto Brunner, Werner Conze, Reinhart Koselleck, and their collaborators' *Geschichtliche Grundbegriffe: Historisches Lexikon zur politisch-sozialen Sprache in Deutschland*. Its eight volumes were published between 1972 and 1997. This isn't the place to examine the German school of conceptual history (*Begriffsgeschichte*), and its methodological principles and development.[109] Same goes for the Cambridge School of intellectual history and history of political thought: Pocock, Dunn, Skinner, and others. There's been a lot of commentary on both approaches, as well as compare-and-contrast exercises.

I'll just say a word about Skinner. Building on Wittgenstein and Austin, he maintains that "speech is also action" and "'words are also deeds.'"[110] One of his central claims is,

> in Wittgenstein's phrase, that concepts are tools. To understand a concept, it is necessary to grasp not merely the meanings of the terms used to express it, but also the range of things that can be done with it. This is why, in spite of the long continuities that have undoubtedly marked our inherited patterns of thought, I remain unrepentant in my belief that there can be no histories of concepts as such; there can only be histories of their uses in argument.[111]

Skinner believes that a concept is distinct from "the terms used to express it." He's not talking about doing things with words, but doing things with concepts. He underscores "the range of things that can be done with it." With it. With a concept. For researchers on the ground, the pesky problem remains how to pick it out.

CONCEPTUAL ENGINEERING IN ANALYTIC PHILOSOPHY

In September 2018, New York University hosted a conference titled "The Foundations of Conceptual Engineering." It was jointly organized by NYU's New York Institute of Philosophy and ConceptLab in Oslo. The topic of the conference was summarized thus: "One dimension of cognitive success is getting it right, i.e. gaining knowledge of facts. Another dimension of cognitive success is using the right concepts, i.e. framing a topic in the right way. This

---

109. In English, see Richter (1987, 1993, 1995) and Palonen (1997, 2002).

110. Q. Skinner 1988, 260. "Words are also deeds" comes from Wittgenstein's ([1953] 2009, § 546) *Philosophical Investigations*. "Words are deeds" comes from *Culture and Value* (*Vermischte Bemerkungen*). It's the epigraph of the 1988 book I'm quoting, *Meaning and Context: Quentin Skinner and His Critics*, edited by Tully. On '*Worte sind Taten*,' see Gorlée 2012, 107–10.

111. Q. Skinner 1988, 283.

view, if correct, tasks inquirers with critically examining the concepts they are using and perhaps replacing those concepts with new and better ones. This task is often known as 'conceptual engineering.'"[112] The adverb "often" was probably an exaggeration at that time. Yet, since then, conceptual engineering has indeed become an up-and-coming intellectual social movement.[113] A milestone was the publication of Cappelen's *Fixing Language*.[114] It sparked animated discussions, and stimulated further work on both individual concepts and on challenges to the whole enterprise. Conceptual engineers build on neighboring themes in analytic philosophy, such as verbal disputes, meta-linguistic negotiation, whether GENDER and RACE can be reformed, and whether Carnap's explication changes the subject.[115] In addition, Cappelen's conceptual engineering joined forces with Burgess and Plunkett's 'conceptual ethics.'[116] The resulting volume, *Conceptual Engineering and Conceptual Ethics*, consolidated the field and its most salient preoccupations.[117]

In Cappelen's words, conceptual engineering is "*the project of assessing and developing improvements of our representational devices*."[118] Notably, he speaks of 'representational devices,' not 'concepts,' because "it's unclear and contro-versial what concepts are (and whether there are any)." 'Representational de-vices engineering' would be more accurate, but this expression "doesn't roll off the tongue in the way 'conceptual engineering' does."[119] Style and prosody aside, there's no consensus on Cappelen's elimination of concepts, nor on what it is that engineers engineer.[120]

Representational devices might have "a variety of defects": "cognitive de-fects (that undermine our ability to reason properly), moral or political defects

---

112. "The Foundations of Conceptual Engineering," NYU Arts & Science, Department of Philosophy, https://as.nyu.edu/content/nyu-as/as/departments/philosophy/events/fall-2018 /conceptual-engineering.html.

113. Frickel and Gross 2005.

114. Cappelen 2018.

115. Carnap (1950) 1962; Chalmers 2011; Haslanger 2000, 2006; Pinder 2020; Plunkett 2015; Plunkett and Sundell 2013; Saul 2006; Strawson 1963.

116. Burgess and Plunkett 2013a, b.

117. Burgess, Cappelen, and Plunkett 2020; see also Burgess and Plunkett 2020.

118. Cappelen 2020, 132.

119. Cappelen and Plunkett 2020, 3. Cappelen (2018, 199): "Calling the topic of this book 'conceptual engineering' wasn't an easy choice and arguably it wasn't a good one. At the end of the day—looking at the positive proposal as a whole—there aren't any concepts involved and there's hardly any engineering."

120. Flocke 2021; M. Isaac, forthcoming; Koch 2021a; Sawyer 2020a, b; Thomasson, forthcoming.

(that undermine moral or political values of various sorts), theoretical defects (that undermine progress within some theoretical field), or semantic defects (where the semantic value is incoherent, incomplete, or missing)."[121] Conceptual engineers' plan is to revise and ameliorate defective representational devices.[122]

You might contend that conceptual engineering is old wine in a new bottle. The history of philosophy is full of it, except for the label. As MacIntyre observed in *A Short History of Ethics*, "philosophical inquiry itself plays a part in changing moral concepts":

> To analyze a concept philosophically may often be to assist in its transformation by suggesting that it needs revision, or that it is discredited in some way, or that it has a certain kind of prestige. Philosophy leaves everything as it is—except concepts. And since to possess a concept involves behaving or being able to behave in certain ways in certain circumstances, to alter concepts, whether by modifying existing concepts or by making new concepts available or by destroying old ones, is to alter behavior.[123]

Present-day conceptual engineers can reply that they aren't duty bound to demonstrate their originality. Novel or not, they're engineering a solid approach, working out the tasks it involves, what it can and can't accomplish, and meeting objections to it. For this, they've built on the latest advances in philosophy of language and metaphilosophy. Some conceptual engineers have taken up socially, morally, and politically important representational devices, like RACE, WOMAN, and RAPE. Consistent with these concepts' social and political import, and with the spirit of the times, they've spawned bitter exchanges. In scholarly journals, but also on the internet and social media.[124]

It's an open question among philosophers where they can make a social and political difference, if anywhere.[125] For whatever it's worth, I find it significant that RACE, WOMAN, and RAPE are on the table. It's indicative of the concerns

121. Cappelen and Plunkett 2020, 3.

122. The expression 'conceptual engineering' was used by Blackburn (1999) and by Brandom (2001, 587). It was subsequently borrowed by Scharp (2013, 2020) and Eklund (2015).

123. MacIntyre 1966, 2–3.

124. A. Byrne 2020; Dembroff 2021; Weinberg 2020.

125. You can conceptually engineer any representational device, whether or not it's socially, morally, and politically important. Cappelen (2018, 118): "There are connections here to some of the literature on so-called 'essentially contested concepts.' . . . [H]owever, there's nothing in principle distinctive about 'rape' compared to, say, 'salad': these processes are all contested." Cappelen agrees with Väyrynen's (2014) critique of essentially contested concepts. 'Salad' is Dorr and Hawthorne's (2014) example.

and dispositions of newer generations of analytic philosophers vis-à-vis their predecessors.

This book draws on conceptual engineers and their search for a "method for normative conceptual work."[126] One of their lessons is that representational devices can fail communities in several ways, including morally and politically.

4.6 Concluding FAQs

Why do you stress that your arguments are addressed to social science researchers?

I do insist that I'm tackling obstacles to the practice of social science research. I'm not defending any approach to social or political theory. Nor any sociological tradition. Nor did I set out to contribute to metaphysics, metaethics, philosophy of science, epistemology, or philosophy of language. Ideally, regardless of your views in these domains, you'd be able to buy my arguments. These should be as orthogonal to your commitments as possible; cut across cleavages in philosophy and social and political theory as much as possible.

'As much as possible,' because nobody can be wholly above the fray, wholly non-committal and aperspectival, in an 'Archimedean' fashion.[127] At some points, my arguments have to take philosophical sides. At times, I need auxiliary tools on which philosophers, political theorists, or linguists don't agree. One example: I'll rely on the view that it's preferable to solve collective problems democratically than autocratically (all other things equal). Another example: I'll rely on the view that Platonism is wrong and there aren't any Forms. If you sympathize with Platonism and autocracy, I may have to lose you. So be it.

I say 'rely' advisedly. I won't attack autocratic decision-making, or defend democratic processes and communities, as political theorists and political philosophers do. I won't engage metaphysical arguments about Platonism. I'll give reasons for relying on those views, but they're specific to the issues I'm dealing with, the situation social science communities find themselves in, and facts about social scientists' inclinations and practices.

Mainstream social scientists have always tried to break free from philosophy, in particular from ethics and metaphysics. They've painstakingly performed boundary work to demarcate the social sciences, qua sciences, from philosophical inquiry. Insofar as the desired endpoint is absolute "[independence]

---

126. Thomasson 2020, forthcoming.
127. R. Dworkin 1996; Midgley 1974.

of any philosophy," it's never been attained and it never will.[128] This doesn't entail, however, that social scientists are undercover philosophers or closet ethicists.[129] Not all philosophical assumptions and commitments are alike. Some are conducive to the aims of empirical research projects. Others not so much or not at all.

All in all, my argument should be capacious. Its premises should be acceptable to most people, despite dissimilar convictions in philosophy and social and political theory. And yet, even a big tent won't have room for everyone.

Isn't your toolkit simplistic? Doesn't it miss a lot of things? Aren't the relations between language, concepts, and the world "more complicated than that"?

I do want my toolkit to be lean, pared down, simple. Clear and unambiguous. I don't like multifunction tools: I prefer to do one task at a time. I like to travel light, so my luggage doesn't get me bogged down.

I don't like multifunction words either. Nor words whose meaning is constantly being debated, and can create confusion and miscommunication. I prefer to avoid words that carry heavy historical loads, and are associated with particular traditions and schools of thought, so mentioning them triggers emotions, allegiances, yays and boos. True, any word can do that. But some more than others. True, all toolkits have built-in substantive, 'theoretical,' or conceptual leanings. But I trust mine will have few.

Few and not decisive. A leaning or commitment shouldn't turn into full-fledged partiality, bias, and irreparably loaded dice. This isn't an all-or-nothing affair. Toolkits load the dice to different degrees and in different ways—more and less substantively consequential. There are degrees to which researchers and audiences might be aware of what's built into a toolkit and its effects. So, my toolkit should try and be a good guy. No trespassing. Whether my arguments succeed or fail is a separate question.

My toolkit does miss lots of things, like any toolkit, standpoint, map, or abstraction. As the Healy theorem goes, "things in the world are always 'more complicated than that'—for any value of 'that.'"[130] Many things must be out of sight and out of focus for you to be able to focus on what you want to. Your gaze can't be all-encompassing. If it were, you wouldn't like it. Like Lewis Carroll's map:

---

128. Durkheim 1895, 172. Cf. Hollis 1977; Karsenti 2013; Lemieux 2012.
129. Abend 2008b.
130. Healy 2017, 123.

'What do you consider the *largest* map that would be really useful?'

'About six inches to the mile.'

'Only *six inches!*' exclaimed Mein Herr. 'We very soon got to six *yards* to the mile. Then we tried a *hundred* yards to the mile. And then came the grandest idea of all! We actually made a map of the country, on the scale of *a mile to the mile!*'

'Have you used it much?' I enquired.

'It has never been spread out, yet,' said Mein Herr: 'the farmers objected: they said it would cover the whole country, and shut out the sunlight! So we now use the country itself, as its own map, and I assure you it does nearly as well.'[131]

Why did you write this chapter as FAQs?

Why not?

131. Carroll 1893, 168; see also Borges (1946) 1960; Eco 1994.

5

Two activities

Anything is in some way like anything else. [...] [S]imilarity tends under analysis either to vanish entirely or to require for its explanation just what it purports to explain.

—GOODMAN (1972)[1]

5.1 Introduction

I've argued that social science communities are uncertain about the relationships between their objects of inquiry, their words, and their knowledge claims. The problem is hardly new. In the 1930s, Lundberg complained: "I have said that the first requirement of a sound scientific theory is a clear definition of terms." "That sociologists exhibit only slight agreement even in the use of the most common terms is a matter of common knowledge. The same sociologist frequently uses the same term in various senses in the same article."[2] Lundberg's complaint was hardly new. In the 1890s, in one of sociology's founding documents, *The Rules of Sociological Method*, Durkheim observed:

> In our present state of knowledge we do not know exactly what the state is, nor sovereignty, political freedom, democracy, socialism, communism, etc. Thus our method should make us forswear any use of these concepts so long as they have not been scientifically worked out [*constitués*]. Yet the words that express them recur continually in the discussions of sociologists. They are commonly used with assurance, as if they corresponded to things well known and well defined, while in fact they evoke in us only confused notions, an amalgam of vague impressions, prejudices and passions. Today

1. Goodman 1972, 440, 446.
2. Lundberg 1936, 709; 1939, 58.

we mock at the strange ratiocinations that the doctors of the Middle Ages constructed from their notions of heat and cold, humidity and dryness, etc. Yet we do not perceive that we continue to apply the selfsame method to an order of phenomena which is even less appropriate for it than any other, on account of its extreme complexity.[3]

"As if they corresponded to things well known and well defined." "An amalgam of vague impressions." Durkheim's observations about "our present state of knowledge" turned out not to be specific to his present. They've lingered on. Social scientists have continued to make comparable observations ever since.

Fields, subfields, and literatures are uncertain about how to use their key words and what they refer to. The identity of their objects of inquiry is forever controversial. Social scientists do research and make claims about creativity, happiness, family, and gender. Art, capitalism, diversity, and work. But what are these things? Innumerable 'definitions,' 'conceptions,' 'concepts,' 'understandings,' and 'views' of each of them coexist, but their coexistence is neither harmonious nor peaceful. Innumerable ways to distinguish work from non-work, art from non-art, capitalism from non-capitalism, family from non-family.

As a result, some of social scientists' claims are incommensurable. Sometimes they talk past one another and have 'merely verbal disputes' (more on this below). Some seemingly empirical discrepancies, seemingly about the world, are actually due to their word uses. Peer review processes and recruitment committee meetings are encumbered by 'what-is-F?' issues. Time-consuming, inefficient, and vexing discussions ensue. Dead ends and deadlocks.

I've argued that social science communities don't know how to deal with these issues. How to tell if someone's way of using or defining word 'w' is preferable to someone else's. What makes one answer better than another. What it is to get it right. Who or what is in a position to decide what it is to get it right, if anybody or anything. Whether it makes sense to ask what it is to get it right. Whether community members can be prohibited from using words however they please, and if so, on which grounds.

What a mess. Perhaps we can leave it at that and get on with our research? Wash our hands of the matter, like Pontius Pilate? No, we can't. The problem does have philosophical and metaphysical aspects, and multiple connections to the history of philosophy, and to the history of social and political thought. Yet, for empirical social scientists, the problem is as practical as they come. This is because of the key roles played by the key words at stake.

---

3. Durkheim (1895) 2013, 33–34; see also Durkheim 1897, 1–2.

One of their roles is to mediate between a slice of the empirical world and social scientists' observations and measurements of it, their claims and theories about it, and their recommendations for policy and law. Empirical social science needs these words. It needs these words to perform well, to do a good job of it.

What is to be done? If you set out to tackle a problem, you obviously need to understand it well: grasp what sort of problem you're confronting, why exactly it's a problem, whom it's a problem for, why it can't be ignored, whether it's been fittingly articulated, and what parts it might have. What proposals have been previously advanced to solve it? Which ones turn out, on closer inspection, to be misguided? What's possible and impossible to accomplish—so you don't end up being disappointed, owing to badly calibrated ambitions?

In this chapter I argue that the problem should be broken down into two. Social science communities typically conflate two activities whose starting points and objectives are dissimilar. Consequently, neither has been adequately analyzed and tackled. For things to move along, these two activities need to be disentangled, and their nuts and bolts need to be separately dissected.

5.2 Words and distinctions

I'd like to distinguish two activities. One of them I'll call 'word goes first!' Henceforth 'Activity WF.' The other I'll call 'distinction goes first!' Henceforth 'Activity DF.' Both activities are undertaken by social scientists in their work, but they've been commonly run together. I'll argue that each has its own aims, methods, and standards of success. Distinct aims, methods, and standards. To which social scientists' disputes over words are usually blind. While I present Activity WF and Activity DF as different undertakings, I'll also expound their relationships and overlaps. In both activities, the community is the ultimate decision-maker and arbiter.

What follows is a brief introduction to Activity WF and a longer introduction to Activity DF. In subsequent chapters I'll examine both in more detail.

Activity WF: word goes first!

The starting point of Activity WF is a word, 'w,' which is typically common and important. Common and important in a scientific discipline or subdiscipline. It may also be common and important in social life, public policy, the law, education, or popular culture. Or all of the above. For instance, 'populism,' 'terrorism,' 'gender,' and 'art.' 'Race,' 'family,' 'theater,' 'depression,' and 'happiness.' These words are central in contemporary social science, but also in politics and society. (Instead of one word, the starting point could be a two-word expression, or a small group of related words. For the sake of simplicity, I prefer one-word illustrations.)

The question is how 'w' should be used. Alternative, functionally equivalent formulations: what 'w' should mean, what the extension of 'w' should be, and what to use 'w' for. Practitioners of *Activity WF* advance proposals, for which they provide reasons. They make arguments as to why 'w' should be used in the ways they say it should be used (as the plural indicates, it's not assumed that there's one best use). Why are their proposed uses better than others? Better in which ways? Why is their 'better' better than others? If they're suggesting to revise a widespread use of 'w,' why their revisions would improve on current practices.

Activity WF is a normative endeavor. Members of social science communities will argue for this use (or these uses) of 'w,' as opposed to another, or as opposed to any other. They'll supply reasons. But what sorts of reasons? Whatever they are, they'll be publicly scrutinized. Individuals make proposals and suggestions, but this is a collective activity. Normative authority doesn't lie with individual community members: it lies with the community as a whole. The community will decide, on the basis of what's good for it, useful to it, consistent with its aims, or whatever (on which more below). It'll decide what sorts of reasons can be supplied, and what sorts of reasons are beside the point.

Additionally, *Activity WF* concerns whether the community should use 'w' at all. Whether there are any acceptable uses of it, given its possible functions and effects, epistemic pros and cons, ethical pros and cons, inside and outside the community. In some cases, there'll be none. For example, slurs and lexical items that regularly contribute to pejorative speech acts. They're morally unwanted around here.[4] In short, which words should and shouldn't be used in our community? The sought-after result is a good lexicon for our language.

Activity WF should enable you to tell 'w'-things from non-'w'-things. Given a thing before you, the question is whether it's a 'case' of 'w,' subsumable under it, falling within its extension, a data point in general descriptions and explanations of 'w.' In 1904, there arose an armed conflict in Uruguay between *colorados*, led by President José Batlle y Ordóñez, and *blancos*, led by Aparicio Saravia.[5] Does it fall under 'revolution' and hence can add to sociologists' and political scientists' causal theories of revolution? Or does it fall under 'civil war' and hence

---

4. But see section 2.3 on moratoriums and the temptation of fresh starts.

5. Barrán and Nahum 1972; Mena Segarra 1977.

can add to sociologists' and political scientists' causal theories of civil war? To both? To neither? I'm assuming a simple opposition, 'w' and non-'w,' and things falling on one or the other side of the line. But 'w' may be represented as a continuum or as a more complex structure.

Given several things before you, the question is whether they're all instances, variants, or types of 'w.' "Are slavery in Attica in the fifth century B.C., in Ireland in the ninth century A.D., and in Virginia in the nineteenth century A.D. variants of the same institution?"[6] Knowing how to use 'w' implies mastering this distinction. It implies you can differentiate its extension from everything else, from the rest of the world, and proceed accordingly. Under this description, *Activity WF* approaches *Activity DF*. Except that the latter starts with and focuses on drawing a distinction.

Activity DF: *distinction goes first!*

Forget about words that are common and important in your field, public policy, the law, and social life. Put aside words and language altogether. Instead, make a distinction. Come up with a classificatory system and classificatory criteria, through which objects are sorted into classes. Put differently, carve reality however you wish. Given a set of objects, split and lump them as you see fit. Create groups, kinds, or categories. Then give each one a name. Any name. Literally any name. Call them what you want.

You can draw distinctions among people according to their age, genitalia, or hair color. According to their soccer skills or the length of their pinky fingers. You can group together twins and triplets, or group together twins and birds, because they "are both associated with Spirit."[7] Both are permissible.

As far as *Activity DF* is concerned, there's so much pointless talk out there about what makes a sandwich a sandwich; the true, essential difference between sandwiches and burritos; and the true, essential difference between sandwiches and hot dogs. Baloney! You decided to put together sandwiches, burritos, and hot dogs, and call them 'sanbuhots.' The three usual categories compose a broader one. A larger set of things. Which makes sense, since you're planning on opening a sanbuhots restaurant next month in your hometown. Just like there are numerous types of salads and numerous types of noodles, there are numerous types of sanbuhots, which your menu invitingly depicts. Their ingredients are diverse. Some have baloney, others bologna, others wieners, others hummus, and yet others guacamole. In some of them, what sandwiches

6. MacIntyre 1973, 1.
7. Evans-Pritchard 1954, 31.

the sandwiched ingredients is ciabatta bread, in others it's a hot dog bun, in others it's corn tortillas.

It's your choice, too, whether to be a splitter or a lumper: "Splitters make very small units—their opponents say that if they can tell two animals apart, they place them in different genera, and if they cannot tell them apart, they place them in different species. Lumpers make large units—their opponents say that if a carnivore is neither a dog nor a bear they call it a cat."[8] If a country is neither in North America (meaning the United States and Canada) nor in Western Europe, many Global North lumpers will call it 'underdeveloped.' Being a lumper about something doesn't commit you to being a lumper about everything, but there are temperamental propensities and path dependencies. Lumpers enjoy lumping and splitters enjoy splitting.

Distinction d is up to you. Your groups or sets are up to you: their members, their boundaries, their shape, the classificatory rules to be followed. You decide what will be distinguished from what and how. Whether d produces a dichotomy, a trichotomy, a continuum, or a multidimensional space. Relying on necessary and sufficient conditions or on degrees of membership, fuzzy sets, and prototypes. Based on one property or on a configuration of properties. How does your classification classify things and how does your distinction distinguish among things? What do your groups look like? A few illustrations:

- Per my d, there are two kinds of thing in the universe: there are sandwiches, there are non-sandwiches, and there are necessary and sufficient conditions for belonging to one or the other.
- Per my d, there are sandwiches, there are non-sandwiches, and there are, irreducibly, borderline cases, which are neither one nor the other. Like some people are neither bald nor non-bald. Baldness and sandwichness are vague. However, I'm not forced to and I won't give up the dichotomy between sandwiches and non-sandwiches.
- Per my d, there are sandwiches, there are non-sandwiches, and there are things outside the domain of d. Beyond its 'universe of discourse,' the set over which it ranges, its scope, or something like that.[9] It'd make no sense to apply d to these things, or classify them using d.
- Per my d, there are degrees of sandwichness: a continuum, from 1 to 10, so a food item can be more or less of a sandwich. A BLT has higher sandwichness than falafel sandwiches and ice cream sandwiches.
- Per my d, there are five kinds: cold sandwiches, hot sandwiches, open sandwiches, burritos (a type of sandwich), and non-sandwiches.

8. Simpson 1945, 23.
9. Boole 1854, 42.

- Per my *d*, there are five kinds. Within some of them, you've got continua; for example, having more or less burritoness.

––––––––

Distinction *d* is up to you. There are no intrinsic constraints, residing in things themselves: anything may be grouped together with anything else. Any two things are similar and different to each other in an infinite number of ways. My bass and the Eiffel Tower. There's an infinite number of properties they share and an infinite number of properties they don't share. Then, as a practitioner of *Activity DF*, you're free to highlight one (or more) among the former or one (or more) among the latter. Pick your preferred sameness or difference.[10] I hate to have to come down on *Sesame Street*, but the foundations of "one of these things is not like the others" are shaky:

> Similarity, unlike motion, cannot be salvaged merely by recognizing its relativity. When to the statement that a thing moves we add a specification of the frame of reference, we remove an ambiguity and complete our initial statement. But when to the statement that two things are similar we add a specification of the property they have in common, we again remove an ambiguity; but rather than supplementing our initial statement, we render it superfluous. For . . . to say that two things are similar in having a specified property in common is to say nothing more than that they have that property in common.[11]

Social scientists' projects won't be metaphysical. *Activity DF* compels you neither to endorse nor to reject philosophers' joint-carving inquiries, Goodman's nominalism, Putnam's "cookie cutter" objection to realism, or Varzi's "metaphysical desert."[12] A desert where there are "no natural boundaries": "All the boundaries we find are lines we have drawn, artificial fencings that merely reflect of our own demarcations, our classifications, our organizing activity. We may have the feeling that in some cases such demarcations are grounded on natural discontinuities in the underlying reality. But look closely and you'll see that there are no discontinuities. It's just sand, and sand, and sand . . ."[13]

---

10. Nirenberg and Nirenberg 2021.

11. Goodman 1972, 444–45; see also Enflo 2020; Goodman (1951) 1977; Morreau 2010.

12. Campbell, O'Rourke, and Slater 2011; Putnam 1987, 1988; Sider 2011; Varzi 2014.

13. Varzi 2014, 19–20. "In the desert there are dogs and cats, and trees and flowers. It's just that those are not different kinds of thing, each with its own essence and persistence conditions. Simply, some portions of reality strike us as dogging while others as catting, or treeing, or flowering" (26).

To be sure, your social science research will have metaphysical presuppositions. It'll be inconsistent with some views about the nature and structure of reality. Nonetheless, your ambitions and aims lie elsewhere. Metaphysics isn't your line of business.

Nice division of labor! Except if natural kinds get in social scientists' way. Natural kinds, like einsteinium or *Panthera leo*, are said to carve nature at its joints. They aren't constructed, but discovered. While particulars have particularities, these are superficial, inessential. Not only the particularities of Cecil, Simba, the Metro-Goldwyn-Mayer lion, and the Cowardly Lion, but also of chemical elements' isotopes. A natural kind-based classification is "able to cut up each kind according to its species along its natural joints, and . . . not to splinter any part, as a bad butcher might do" (*Phaedrus* 265e). Hence, they threaten the autonomy of *Activity DF*. If there are natural kinds in a domain, it seems they must be sovereign. They must fully determine the conduct of *Activity DF*. Scientists' distinctions and classifications would be obligated to fall in line.

Natural kinds would make demands on *Activity WF* as well. Asking what capitalism is would be no different from asking what einsteinium is. The right use of the word 'capitalism' would come down to its successfully referring to capitalism, the natural kind. You'd get your distinctions and classifications right, as well as your essences and real definitions right, as an upshot of getting your natural kinds right.

The million-dollar question is whether there are natural kinds in the social world. The sixty-four-thousand-dollar question is whether social science, and in particular *Activity DF*, can operate independently of them, independently of whether they turn out to exist. I'll return to natural kinds in due course. For now, I'll make three remarks:

(1) I want to take into account social scientists' views about natural kinds. Knowing whether social scientists believe there are natural kinds in the social world isn't the same as knowing whether there are natural kinds in the social world. Yet, thinking pragmatically, it does make a difference. I don't have data to back this up, but I suspect that few social scientists see themselves as looking for natural taxonomies, over and above conventional social taxonomies. Few of them have intuitions about the social world that could accommodate natural kinds as traditionally understood, ontologically essential, hardcore and heavy-duty. Most will deny that their classifications and categories are joint-carving.[14]

14. Dupré 2002.

(2) Instead, social scientists are likely to say that being Hispanic, being a woman, being beautiful, and being a gifted child are 'socially constructed' categories. I know, I know: it's easier to utter the expression 'socially constructed' than to be clear about it.[15] It's very easy if your audience is favorably predisposed to it, because of its progressive political overtones. Few social scientists appear to have thought through the nitty-gritty of their social constructionist talk. Few seem to be familiar with recent philosophical work on kinds, which looks at actual scientific practice and grapples with actual cases, hard cases, falling somewhere in between arbitrary collections and nature's alleged joints.[16] There aren't two distinct kinds of kinds. To express it nostalgically, natural kinds aren't what they used to be: unambiguous and safe havens in an ambiguous and dangerous world. Robust. Natural.

Importantly, while social scientists aren't metaphysicians, they are taking metaphysical sides. Whether they reject natural kindness explicitly and reflectively, or rather implicitly and intuitively, they're taking sides. This is a substantive view about the metaphysics of the social world.

(3) Be that as it may, I think social science communities have a passable way out of this quagmire. *Activity DF* needn't commit to any ontology. It needn't be guided by metaphysics. It might, but it doesn't need to. Its position and tasks remain safe without having to go there. Even if Goodman's and Goodman-type views turned out to be metaphysical bunk. Even if it turned out that there are natural kinds in the social world, or other classes of things somehow grounded in nature or reality, or Platonic Forms, they wouldn't be mandatory for the practice of *Activity DF*.[17] They'd surely be good candidates to base your *d* on. They'd be ex hypothesi explanatorily and predictively powerful, and explanation and prediction are at the top of many social scientists' lists.

Nevertheless, you'd still be free to and might have reason to classify things in other ways. The world might put pressure on you, but at the end of the day you continue to have choices. You might classify

---

15. Berger and Luckman 1966; Hacking 1999; Spector and Kitsuse 1977.

16. Brigandt forthcoming; Ereshefsky and Reydon 2015; Franklin-Hall 2015; Godman 2018, 2021; Khalidi 2013; Magnus 2018; Ruphy 2010; Slater 2015; R. Wilson, Barker, and Brigandt 2007.

17. On how they might be "grounded in nature or reality," see Carey 2009; Fodor 1975; Millikan 2010, 2017.

TABLE 5.1. Contrasting *Activity DF* and *Activity WF*

	General issue	Specific case	Natural language (e.g., English)	Examples
Activity WF	• What words it'd be good for us (a social science community) to use • How it'd be good for us (a social science community) to use particular words • Why? On which grounds?	• Whether word '*w*' should be used • How word '*w*' should be used	• Starting point is natural language uses • Natural language shapes practice and outcomes	• 'Race' • 'Health' • 'Mental health' • 'Colonialism' • 'Institution' • 'Work'
Activity DF	• What distinctions it'd be good for us (a social science community) to draw and accept • Why? On which grounds?	• Whether distinction *d* should be drawn or accepted	• Logically independent from natural language • Call it what you want • But there's a 'but'	• Tripartite (and exhaustive) distinction among developed, developing, and underdeveloped countries • Quinquepartite (and exhaustive) distinction among gay, straight, bisexual, heteroflexible, and homoflexible people

Uruguay together with Senegal and Ghana, or together with Costa Rica and Argentina. Whale together with dolphin, gibbon, and platypus, or together with dolphin, shark, and trout. Einsteinium together with fermium, nobelium, and mendelevium, or together with elephant, eggplant, and emoji. Your choice.

5.3 The catch

Distinction d is up to you. But there's a catch. It must deliver good epistemic things. It must be epistemically fecund and valuable in some way. Good for social science knowledge; good for social science communities insofar as they're producers of knowledge, of empirical accounts, of well-founded understandings about social phenomena and processes.

I suppose someone could set out to produce bad epistemic things. They'd have, as an individual, such a desire and intention. For whatever crazy or sane reason: I'm not going to psychoanalyze them. But the community won't be interested in their pointless and senseless work. It sets the standards. There are incentives, disincentives, rewards, and constraints on *Activity DF* entailed by doing social science within communities. A genuine Robinson Crusoe wouldn't have to justify their weird, capricious, self-interested, or self-indulgent behavior. They wouldn't be accountable to the rest of us. Their social science, their scientific distinctions and classifications, would be none of our business. Nobody would ever hear about them. So, they could do whatever they felt like. But we, social science communities, can't.

To forge ahead, our community will have to figure out what these epistemic goods are, and how to figure out if something is an epistemic good. If it is an epistemic good, whether it's a worthwhile one, worth our time and effort, and worth our time and effort more than others. Whether it's something important to us. Furthermore, we'll have to assess if d can deliver other things, good non-epistemic things. I'm going to argue that its social and moral consequences should be part of the equation—apart from its good or bad consequences for scientific knowledge.

I'll return to these issues in due course. For now, I'll highlight two more moving parts. First, the attempt to tell apart epistemic and non-epistemic goods may fail. Either empirically or in principle. Second, epistemic goods aren't set in stone. Not even within a scientific field. They can and do vary across communities, time periods, and disciplines. Take mainstream social science, as practiced in the United States and Western Europe today, and published mostly in English. Obvious candidates for goods pursued by social scientists are correct descriptions, causal explanations, and predictions of social phenomena. Policy implications concerning poverty, inequality, and discrimination are also very welcome. Less standard goods are understanding and perspicuous interpretation. Shedding light on social phenomena, stimulating people's imagination, and fostering their ability to come up with novel, lucid, and interesting insights.[18] "Thinking up . . . new aims, new words, or new disciplines" and "[reinterpreting] our familiar surroundings in the unfamiliar terms of our new inventions."[19]

Your grounds for d might lie elsewhere. If you're a social scientist who's seeking unusual and creative epistemic goods, go ahead and argue for them. Alternatively, your social science endeavors might be patterned after a natural science discipline of which you're a fan. Physics or biology.[20] You might be a champion of natural kinds in the social world, unlike most of your colleagues at your sociology department. You argue that d carves nature at its joints, or it has an evolutionary explanation, or it's based on human nature. You may give support to your d in these and other ways. (Naturally, this doesn't mean your arguments are good arguments and your grounds should be accepted.)

Distinction d is up to you, but it should pay off. It should contribute to or be useful for valuable aims. Epistemic ones for sure, yet not only epistemic ones. '"Be useful," I hear you say? Didn't you have qualms about usefulness? Wasn't usefulness insufficient?' Yes, that's right. We'll need to reexamine the 'argument from usefulness' and my response to it (chapter 3). Social science projects have an obligation to clearly specify useful for what and for whom. What goals can d help bring about? What goals it'll detract from? What are its costs and who'll pay the bills? In which ways is d better than other distinctions that could be drawn? The community will scrutinize these considerations and their value. It'll give a thumbs-up to d, if it's beneficial not only to you but to all of us (more on this in chapter 9).

For example, your project may draw a distinction between people who own the means of production and everyone else. People who identify themselves as 'straight,' 'gay,' 'bisexual,' 'asexual,' 'pansexual,' or 'questioning.' Actions deemed to violate etiquette norms and actions deemed to violate moral norms. The domain of morality and the domain of ethics. Modern, early modern, and premodern societies.[21] Societies where apples are eaten for breakfast,

18. Abend 2006; Abend, Petre, and Sauder 2013; Glaeser 2014; C. Taylor 1971.

19. Rorty 1979, 360.

20. Lieberson and Lynn 2002.

21. Historians' periodization is a form of *Activity DF* (Le Goff 2014). It checks all the boxes. Truth claims about a historical period are a function of its boundaries, but there's no fact of the

societies where they're eaten for dessert, and societies where they aren't eaten at all. This seems prima facie an arbitrary, random, pointless distinction. However, if it delivers desirable goods, then you're good. That's all *Activity DF* asks from you.

You may decide to group together Judaism, Buddhism, Confucianism, Children of God, Haitian Vodou, Santería, and Umbanda. Then, you'll give this group a name of your choosing, which facilitates referring to it. A label or shorthand. You can pick an English word or coin a new word: it's pure stipulation. You aren't fettered by 'religion,' 'sect,' 'cult,' and 'spiritual tradition,' neither to their uses in standard English nor to their uses in anthropology, sociology, and theology. Your distinction *d* needn't map onto an already existing one. It might, but it doesn't need to.

Activity DF doesn't require you to pay attention to natural language words, nor to distinctions and groupings that exist in society. Yet, your *d* may correspond to a socially recognizable one, or to the ordinary meaning of English words (or whatever language you're writing in). If that's the case, you can use this preexisting distinction or meaning to your advantage. Piggyback on it. These familiar classes can pay off epistemically. You'll show how. You wouldn't be elucidating what 'w' really means, or what it should mean, but bringing out the benefits of distinguishing between 'w'-things and other things. Under this description, *Activity DF* approaches *Activity WF*.

What's the rationale for this piggybacking move? There are two. One appeals to collective intelligence, swarm intelligence, crowdsourcing, the wisdom of crowds, or the wisdom of the multitude.[22] The other appeals to communities' practices and traditions, including conceptual and linguistic ones, as reflecting historically accumulated knowledge and experience. In *Constructing Social Theories*, Stinchcombe makes this point with methodological intentions: "a science starts off with its variables defined by common sense, by the distinctions that people make in daily life. Because people, in order to live efficiently, have to take account of the causal forces at work in the world, they make distinctions which are institutionalized in the language they speak."[23] For Austin, too, ordinary language outdoes the armchair:

---

matter about when it starts and ends. Boundaries are the subject of disputes. Usefulness criteria aren't clear . . .

22. Waldron 1995.

23. Stinchcombe 1968, 41.

Our common stock of words embodies all the distinctions men have found worth drawing, and the connexions they have found worth marking, in the lifetimes of many generations: these surely are likely to be more numerous, more sound, since they have stood up to the long test of the survival of the fittest, and more subtle, at least in all ordinary and reasonably practical matters, than any that you or I are likely to think up in our armchairs of an afternoon—the most favoured alternative method.[24]

The payoffs of *Activity DF* are relative (different communities appreciate different things) and come in degrees (they're appreciated more or less). Some epistemic goods are widely coveted and esteemed. Others are local: they're esteemed only within a tradition, school, or paradigm. The weights attributed to competing epistemic goods, their priority and importance, are also local. In this respect, the 'argument from theoretical vocabularies' sheds light on the workings of *Activity DF* (chapter 3). The success of *Activity DF* projects isn't up to you, it's not subjective or arbitrary, but it is relative to their social and institutional contexts.

There's one more difficulty, to which I'll also return: the foregoing depiction of *Activity DF* assumes that objects (entities, things) can be unproblematically individuated. Here's one pencil, there's another pencil. This is one sandwich I'm eating. A second sandwich is over there. This isn't one sandwich, but half.

But that's a troublesome assumption, in social science as much as in natural science.[25] Actually, *Activity DF* comprises a prior step. You might have to come up with individuation criteria, with which to decide what makes a thing be a thing. One thing, as opposed to two things or one part of a larger thing. *Activity DF* has no prescription for you: you can do it as you wish; it's got nothing to do with words or language. Given a chunk of social stuff, a chunk of the social world, a dataset, go ahead and slice and dice it as you want. But don't take a victory lap just yet. Not just anything goes here either. The community will again be the arbiter.

Intuitively, this might look like a temporal sequence. First, you have a set of individual objects in front of you (organizations, phenomena, processes, societies, countries). Then, you go on to classify them. Once you know what constitutes *one* religion, as opposed to more or less than one, you can sort religions into categories. Once you know what's one war, one political ideology, one

---

24. Austin 1957, 8.
25. A. Abbott 1995; Bueno, Chen, and Fagan 2018.

emotion, one mode of production . . . In reality, however, these pursuits are interdependent.

5.4 Moving forward: pragmatically

Activity WF and *Activity DF* are two ways in which social scientists establish relationships between their objects of inquiry, their words, and the world. Via key words (or sets of key words) and distinctions (or sets of distinctions). They're distinct activities, but not exclusive.

The point isn't just about social science. Take astronomy. It has good reason to work on *Activity WF*: start with the word 'planet,' and ask how to use it and what it should refer to (see the appendix). 'Planet' has been a major player in the history of astronomers' practices and theories. Implicated in museums, education, popular culture, and the media. Given these historical legacies, and its contemporary social and cultural entanglements, astronomers can't throw away the question of how 'planet' should be used. To be precise: they could throw away this question, but I think they shouldn't.

One group of astronomers will work on and struggle with *Activity WF*, which has a conspicuous public side. Meanwhile, another group of astronomers will prefer projects that involve *Activity DF*, but no *Activity WF* at all. Another group or the same group at other times of the day, other days of the week, or other points in their careers. For some groups and scientists, it'll make sense to work on both activities simultaneously.

Activity DF puts to one side the word 'planet,' the history of astronomy, and the goals of museums and planetariums. It doesn't care about societies' reactions, the brouhahas around the International Astronomical Union (IAU) demoting Pluto in 2006, and the "letters from children and parents" requesting that planetariums "put Pluto back on display."[26] Instead, *Activity DF*'s design is to make a good distinction. Or more than one. Good *how*? Good for what and for whom? That's itself to be determined, communally determined. Spoiler alert: it's not circumscribed to epistemic or scientific goodness.

You may end up with two classes of celestial bodies, and Pluto, Eris, Ceres, and Jupiter being in the same one. Or with two classes, but Pluto and Jupiter not being together. Or you may end up with five classes. In any of these cases, to avoid confusion, and anger, you might opt for avoiding the word 'planet' and the expression 'dwarf planet.' As you intended, your contribution will make sense and have a point only to your peers, who share your epistemic aims, or can sympathize with them. To most others, it'll seem meaningless and

---

26. Messeri 2010, 197.

pointless. *Activity DF* is fine with that. Your attitude has downsides, but *Activity DF* is fine with it.

––––––––

To say that *Activity WF* and *Activity DF* are distinct, or can be analytically distinguished, isn't to say that they're unconnected. Word goes first: establishing the correct uses of 'planet,' 'democracy,' or 'love' in a community entails distinctions between what does and doesn't fall under their extension. Or, if you like, it entails an account of how things fall to a greater or lesser degree under the extension of 'w.' For instance, assume the psychological literature on love were of one mind regarding the right use of 'love.' This common use entails a distinction between loving someone, liking them, liking them a lot, being sexually attracted to them, liking them a lot and being sexually attracted to them, and being infatuated with them. Psychologists' experiments must recruit participants who are in love specifically in this sense of the word 'love.'

Distinction goes first: unlike *Activity WF*, engaging in *Activity DF* can be orthogonal to communities' word uses. You can call your categories what you want, and you can even make up words to refer to them. And yet, as a matter of fact, the practice of *Activity DF* may wind up turning to natural language words, as an additional, logically independent step. Imagine a practitioner of *Activity DF* who came up with a good distinction or classificatory system. Next, they may turn to *Activity WF* in order to adopt certain common words. Having argued that Perón doesn't belong with Orbán, Trump, Bolsonaro, Modi, and Le Pen, you could stop there. Or you could go on to argue that the word 'populist' should be used to refer to this category, because of these or those reasons. Reasons that will be subjected to public scrutiny.

According to my account, *Activity WF* and *Activity DF* are distinct undertakings. Success and failure at them are to be assessed accordingly.

––––––––

My attitude toward *Activity WF* and *Activity DF* is pragmatic. I say 'pragmatic,' not 'practical,' as the latter is already working overtime for me. Worry not: "when I make a word do a lot of work like that . . . I always pay it extra."[27]

27. Carroll 1911, 221. Maybe you'd describe my attitude as pragmatist, as in the American pragmatism of James, Peirce, Dewey, and Jane Addams? Maybe it's both pragmatic and pragmatist? I leave these exegetical issues open.

What does my pragmatic attitude amount to? My chief goal is to make something—a process, an organization, a mechanism, a machine, a body organ—work better. There's no time to waste, because it's always in operation, always running, even while it's being examined and repaired. Neurath's boat–like: "There is no *tabula rasa*. We are like sailors who have to rebuild their ship on the open sea, without ever being able to dismantle it in dry-dock and re-construct it from the best components."[28] What I'm after at the moment isn't knowledge in and of itself. I'm not looking for abstract or philosophical knowl-edge, nor attempting to solve a theoretical or intellectual puzzle.

Since I'm after the adequate functioning of something in the real world, you could compare my attitude to that of bike mechanics, plumbers, and ship-wrights. Physicians, dentists, organizational consultants, and wedding plan-ners. Unlike bike mechanics and plumbers, though, our problem is such that adequate functioning isn't limited to technical and mechanical elements. Eth-ics and politics have to be in the mix, too. They aren't separate factors, but constitutive of good functioning.

We have a problem. I'm trying to find a way out of it, or a way to cope with it. At least a partial one. At least for the time being. It should take into account the circumstances in which social science is conducted, and hopefully it'll lead to practices' being reformed and enhanced. It needn't be perfect, it can't be perfect, but it does need to be acceptable. Whom it should be acceptable to and what acceptability consists in are themselves significant questions. We're a diverse group. Something is hampering our interactions and collaborations, precluding us from realizing our full collective potential. As it turns out, it's something to do with our words and distinctions.

As I see things, the goal is an arrangement that's superior to the status quo. A good arrangement would be nice; an excellent arrangement would be excel-lent. But I'd rather be modest: relative superiority—superiority to what we now have—is good enough. Social scientists are already acting in the world. Their practices have consequences. Can these practices be reformed, such that these consequences are better? What is it for them to be better?

We won't solve the problem in a definitive manner, once and for all. That's either impossible or unrealistic, as bike mechanics, plumbers, and dentists can testify. Instead, I propose to work toward achievable objectives. Improve on what we have, improve on how we're doing things at present. That'd be a good outcome.

My pragmatic attitude toward *Activity WF* and *Activity DF* means that we, the community, are in a peculiar position. It's the same position ethics and

---

28. Neurath 1983, 92; see also Neurath 1944, 47.

politics are in. Your life is continuously going on. Not acting isn't an option. You might not know what's right and wrong, good and bad, you might hesitate about your own convictions, you might feel confused, but you must do something anyway.

You have to act. Abstract reflection and skeptical doubt are significant components of the life of the mind. They shine at university seminar rooms, libraries, and long walks. Yet, when you have to act, they won't help. They come across as frivolous, even ridiculous. Last Thursday you attended a lecture by an eminent moral philosopher. She convincingly showed that actions and policies can't ever be justified. (Or she was unable to make up her mind, so she suggested suspending judgment on the matter.)

Can her brilliant lecture speak to your life? Right now, a few meters away from you, someone is beating their small child. A large corporation is exploiting its workers. A totalitarian regime is torturing its citizens. Either you'll do something about it, or you won't. You have to choose a career path. You have to vote. You'll continue to eat meat, you'll become a vegetarian, or you'll become a vegan. Every single day. What to believe about these things can wait; what to do about them can't. You must lead your life: there's no Pause button, there's no detached agnosticism.

This immediacy is at the heart of my approach. We all have to keep doing our research day in and day out; the tenure clock doesn't have a Pause button either. I'm asking what social scientists are to do, given that their research must go on tomorrow. Tomorrow morning.

A pragmatic attitude doesn't imply that practicalities—immediacies, urgencies, deadlines—give you carte blanche. Nor do they excuse hasty research, thinking, and writing. But still.

———

The aims of *Activity WF* and *Activity DF* are different. Being aware of this difference is a step forward. Not mixing them up. It is a step forward. But it raises further questions. One follow-up is whether the social sciences should pursue primarily, or even exclusively, *Activity WF* (and ditch *DF*). Or, rather, they should pursue primarily, or even exclusively, *Activity DF* (and ditch *WF*). Or both.

I believe both *Activity WF* and *Activity DF* should be pursued. Each contributes to the development of the social sciences, to their diverse intellectual and material goals. Which include discovering and communicating more true things about the social world, getting more people to listen to more true things about the social world, and getting more resources to be able to discover and communicate more true things about the social world. Money for scientists to be able to carry out their research, but also money for scientists to be able to buy groceries and pay rent to be able to work. Capitalism makes no exceptions.

It is tempting to try and ditch *Activity WF*. It doesn't harmonize with a popular account of what science is and what scientists do. It's another old story. Social scientists who hope to mirror natural scientists who hope to mirror nature. For them, science is indifferent to language; it's indifferent to what things are called and how words are used. The world and its laws, regularities, and mechanics remain the same regardless. Thus, *Activity WF* seems to jeopardize the scientific status of social science.

I'll argue that this temptation should be resisted. I get why it's tempting and how it can be beneficial. But its costs outweigh its benefits. I believe social scientists should work on both *Activity WF* and *Activity DF*. Unfortunately, this catholic belief can only take us so far. Time and effort are scarce resources. Research grants are scarce as well. How are they to be allocated? Which projects should be prioritized?

I'll argue that this is a practical reason issue. A practical reason issue for a collectivity or community. For this reason, I alone can't settle it.

6

Practical reason activities

6.1 The basic idea

Social science needs both *Activity WF* (word first) and *Activity DF* (distinction first) to advance its projects and make good on its promises: investigate and provide accounts of the social world. How should these two activities be practiced and evaluated? Their success must be evaluated with adequate standards, yardsticks, criteria. Anyone who embarks on *Activity WF* or *Activity DF* has to understand what an erroneous or otherwise bad result would be. This has to be clear to them and to everyone else (as in any scientific enterprise). Researchers, audiences, and journal reviewers should be cognizant of what it'd be to get it wrong, and how they'll know someone got it wrong.

Suppose two social scientists disagree about a distinction, a classification system, or how to define and use a key word. One sociologist thinks distinction *d* is a good one and should be used; another sociologist thinks the opposite. One political science team thinks these four countries and these three organizations fall under the extension of word 'w'; another political science team thinks they don't. How to determine who's in the right? And not just who's in the right in this particular situation, but what procedures to employ in any disagreement about a contested word use or distinction.

I argue that this is a practical reason issue. A practical reason issue for a collectivity or community. For this reason, I alone can't settle it. In this book or anywhere else. Nobody can. You can't settle it by yourself, no matter how hard you reflect on it or how smart you are, never mind how much authority and power you have. Instead, it must be addressed with the help of practical reason mechanisms. What you can do, as an individual community member, is to put forward arguments, make proposals, get conversations started, and get balls rolling. You can extend invitations to others to join you, to work and reason together, to assess your and their reasons. You can accept their invitations. This must be a collective discussion, a communal praxis, a joint effort, a public process.[1]

Eventually, collective decisions can emerge and be adopted in the practice of social science. They won't be good forever, but good enough for now, good enough to work with in your lab or field site tomorrow morning. You, an individual, are expected to make contributions to this process. You can and should keep making contributions. But they'll have to be engaged and assessed by your fellow community members.

———

The following fourteen points characterize *Activity WF* and *Activity DF* as practical reason problems. They provide a sketch, somewhat rough around the edges. They're meant to apply mutatis mutandis to both activities: our scientific community might be considering how word 'w' should be used or whether distinction *d* should be accepted. The specificities of each activity will be taken up later on.

(1) NO TRUTH-APTNESS

The problem isn't truth-apt. It won't have true answers or solutions, which a conscientious scientist could discover, if they worked and thought hard enough, and if they were clever and ingenious enough. There's no fact of the matter about it.

This is unlike standard factual questions; say, what the capital of Uruguay is, or how many Paraguayan citizens are taller than 205 centimeters. It's also unlike scientists' empirical questions; say, what the melting point of gold is, or whether the divorce rate in 2007 was higher in Germany or in France. It's certainly unlike mathematical and logical questions; say, what the smallest prime number greater than 1,000 is.

Admittedly, truth-aptness is a can of worms. You might prefer to say 'no objective truth,' but 'objectivity' is another can of worms. Even more wormy. I hope you get my drift nonetheless.[2]

---

1. Cf. Kitcher 2011.

2. I may be trying to pull myself out of the fire too quickly. My excuse is the usual. I need to move on, there's a huge literature on this, I must stay focused. This is sometimes a lame excuse, a cop-out, but I hope not in this case. (But then, everyone hopes not in their case. I may be again trying to pull myself out of the fire too quickly.) On why objectivity is a can of worms, see Alexandrova 2018; Daston and Galison 2007; H. Douglas 2004; Freese and Peterson 2018; Harding

(2) PRACTICAL: ACTION, NOT BELIEF

The problem is practical. It's a problem about what to do, not what to believe. It's about good actions—and true beliefs insofar as they're instrumental in discerning and bringing about good actions. In this sense, it's comparable to asking what we should we cook for dinner tonight, or to which organizations we should make donations this year. It's comparable to a referendum that a country's citizens are going to vote on: whether to abolish public radio and television fees, whether to deport foreign criminals, or whether to enshrine cycling and cycling infrastructure in the constitution.

We're making a collective decision, which will affect all of us. The agent or decision-maker is a 'we.' See point (4).

(3) PRACTICAL: NOT TECHNICAL, NO ALGORITHM

The problem is practical but not technical. It can't be outsourced to a team of engineers, policy sociologists, applied economists, or to a supercomputer, superintelligence, AI (artificial intelligence), or algorithm.

Technicians and AIs are provided with an end, and they work out the best means to attain it. Similarly, given X, Y, and Z, technicians and AIs can calculate how maximize X, how to minimize Y, and how to carry out Z in the most time- and cost-effective fashion.

By contrast, our problem involves figuring out what the ends should be in this situation, what goods we're after, how to weigh them, what and who matter, what's worth caring about and pursuing, and what we don't give a damn about.[3] Algorithms can't take care of this. There's no method, in the sense of an explicit and unambiguous series of steps, specified a priori, that community members can follow and obtain a solution at the end.

(4) COLLECTIVE

The problem is collective. It's a problem about what a community or collectivity should do, not what an individual should do. It's about what's good for us, not for me alone. What's good for you guys, not for you alone. That something works for you, your experiments, and your models isn't a good enough reason, because we're all in it together.

It's a problem both about and for a group.

1995; Janack 2002; Lloyd 1995; Lloyd and Schweizer 2014; Longino 1990; Megill 1994; Novick 1988; Porter 1995.

3. Haugeland 1979.

What's the community? A first response: whoever and whatever might make use of 'w' or d. A broader response: whoever and whatever might make use of 'w' or d, as well as whoever and whatever might be affected by them, whoever and whatever might have a stake (the stakeholders). A scientific discipline, a subdiscipline, a small research network, a large interdisciplinary or transdisciplinary network, the entire scientific community, . . . [4] The state, society at large, industry and commerce, future generations, non-human animals, . . .

(5) BETTER AND WORSE SOLUTIONS

The preceding points, particularly (1) and (3), don't entail skepticism, subjectivism, or nihilism about the problem. There are better and worse solutions to it. Demonstrably better and worse, demonstrably good and bad. ('Demonstrably' is doing the heavy lifting in the previous sentence, so it'll have to be unpacked.)

Solution S_1 is superior to solution S_2. Whether a solution is good isn't a matter of opinion. It's not the case that any solution is as good as any other. And it's not merely that most people happen to believe S_1 to be superior to S_2: it actually is. Contrast to: most people happen to find bananas to be more delicious than endives. Are bananas more delicious than endives? No. It's a matter of taste. Deliciousness is in the taste buds of the eater.

It doesn't follow that, given a proposed solution, it can always be determined whether it's good or bad. Nor can it always be ranked relative to other solutions.

It's a separate question how to obtain good solutions, how to ensure they're actually good, how to certify their goodness. But this much is clear: it's not like textbook examples of verifying a statement's truth. Unlike 'the square root of 225 is 15,' you can't do the math. Unlike 'the capital of Uruguay is Asunción,' you can't look it up in an atlas or on DuckDuckGo.

(6) WHAT'S AT STAKE

Resources, careers, status, power, money, recognition, prestige, and honor are at stake.

Solutions are about word uses (*Activity WF*) and distinctions (*Activity DF*). They have consequences for research, science, and knowledge. They also differentially affect community members' standing and reputation. They may increase your odds of getting a job, tenure, a Nobel Prize. They partly determine whether your research has implications for public policy and whether you're going to be deemed a cutting-edge social scientist (or, rather, your

---

4. Ankeny and Leonelli 2016; Koskinen 2017.

claims are going to be deemed unimportant, uninteresting, or batshit crazy). They also differentially affect various stakeholders.

(7) INITIAL CONDITIONS

The problem has initial conditions, which a satisfactory solution has to take into account. These conditions can be empirically discovered. They're social facts. For example, a community's structural, organizational, and cultural arrangements. The distribution of material resources, status, and power. The circumstances and situation of whomever and whatever are affected by 'w' or d. People's and organizations' interests, goals, preferences. How they use language. Inequalities of diverse sorts.

Comparing communities, diachronically and synchronically, will show diverse initial conditions. Good solutions will vary accordingly.

(8) COMMUNITY MEMBERS' INPUT

A satisfactory solution needs the input of community members. (This is unlike factual and technical questions—see (1) and (3) above.)

Part of this input is information about them. Another part of this input is their preferences, what they want. The former, information, doesn't necessitate participants' input, but asking them would be easy and effective. Caveat: Stasi officers and surveillance capitalists beg to differ.[5] The latter, preferences, does necessitate participants' inputs. Caveat: except if you believe that individuals misapprehend or are deluded about their own preferences. Better to infer them, fans of psychoanalysis and false consciousness would contend.

Individuals' preferences get a say, but they aren't the only game in town and they don't have the last word. Merely aggregating individual preferences isn't the solution. How to aggregate preferences isn't self-evident either.

(9) COMMUNITY MEMBERS' PARTICIPATION: COLLECTIVE PROCESS

A satisfactory solution requires community members' participation. (This is unlike factual and technical questions—see (1) and (3) above.)

My point is about the nature of the task at hand. Only a collective, participatory process can deliver the goods. It's up to the community to establish the

5. Zuboff 2019.

best way for it to go, all things considered, how it collectively wishes to proceed, what's good for it.

This can't be established from the outside. Not by a top-down ruling. Not by an authoritarian ruler. Not by an enlightened despot. Not by a well-intentioned, rational, and intelligent observer. Not by hard-working researchers and scientists. Not by a council of the world's finest scientists and philosophers. A fortiori, not by some guy, like me.

That said, expert advisors can be of help. Social scientists—for instance, to tell people about the consequences of policies they're slated to vote on. Philosophers—for instance, to detect fallacies and ambiguities and clear up muddles. Whether some guy can be of help remains to be seen.

This process involves collective discussion, reasoning, and reason-giving. Working together. It's a public process, so it's transparent and open to participation at any time. While not any process would fit the bill, there are many options as to what it should look like. Hence, the community will have to select one (or a combination) of them. See points (10) and (14).

(10) COMMUNITY MEMBERS' PARTICIPATION: DEMOCRATIC PROCESS

A satisfactory solution requires community members' participation in a democratic manner. Only a collective, participatory, and democratic process can deliver the goods. Weaker version: a collective, participatory, and democratic process will best deliver the goods.

For the process to be democratic, participation ought to be protected from relations of domination. Participants ought not to be coerced, directly or indirectly. Power, status, and money ought not to be mobilized to shape the collective outcome.[6] Just like any other democratic process.

Admittedly, what it is to be democratic is a can of worms. I hope you get my drift nonetheless.[7]

(11) COMMUNITY MEMBERS' PARTICIPATION: ENACTMENT OR PERFORMANCE

Activity WF is about words and *Activity DF* is about distinctions or classifications. In both cases, they have to be enacted or performed. This means that community members adequately use 'w' and d in their ordinary practices. It's not that

---

6. Lukes 2021a, b.

7. I may be trying to pull myself out of the fire too quickly, etc.

they pen thoughtful treatises on 'w' and d ('theoretical,' 'meta-theoretical,' or higher-order treatises), but that 'w' and d figure in their research in the right way.

I speak of communities' decisions and agreements, and procedures to reach them. However, I'm not imagining an official written document in which an agreement or decision is recorded and then people sign off on it. In fact, these decisions and agreements would be worthless if they weren't performed or enacted. (You could argue, more radically, that they only exist insofar as they're performed or enacted.) Performance and enactment through scientific practices: using a word or making and using a distinction in scientific work, which is then published, read, cited, commented on, built on, criticized, refuted. 'W' or d playing a role in researchers' observations, inferences, and claims, and in the community's organizational structures, routines, and symbolic goods and values.

Speakers of a social science language, members of a social science community, implement the results of Activity WF and Activity DF by doing the things they normally do. They teach and advise students, award doctorates and fellowships, publish papers, review manuscripts, write op-eds, and talk to journalists and podcasters. They react positively to appropriate 'w' and d practices. They react negatively to inappropriate 'w' and d practices. Their reactions fit the degree of appropriateness or inappropriateness. (It's up to the community whether to set up implementation agencies and communication initiatives.)

I speak of communities' reaching agreements and making decisions, but the process never comes to an end. It has no end point, but it's incessantly going on. It's incessantly being revised, enacted, performed. The results of Activity WF and Activity DF can and will be revised. Yet, community members justifiably rely on them for the time being. Besides being ever-changing, these results needn't be fully precise. (You could argue, more radically, that they can't be.) Their level of detail may vary. Indeed, their form is itself to be communally discussed.

(12) REASONS

Giving and assessing reasons is the name of the game. A satisfactory solution will be supported by good reasons (as far as it can be told, as far as we can see, etc.). For instance, the reasons that support S_1 show it to be better than S_2.

Social life is replete with reason-giving. Everywhere.[8] But scholarly communities are exceptionally attuned to this practice. One of their foundations is that scholarship gives reasons to believe p (or not to). Well-thought-out, public reasons. Specious, capricious, and sloppily crafted ones won't make it in this business: scholars are trained to catch and refute them.

8. Tilly 2006.

I'm intentionally speaking of 'reasons' in general. Point (12) doesn't place constraints on what kind of reasons are acceptable. There are many. Some are referred to as 'arguments,' 'results,' 'tests,' and 'proofs,' which are mobilized to warrant belief in *p*.

(13) EVIDENCE AND FACTS

Good and bad in point (4) and reasons in point (12) are responsive to evidence and facts. In spite of (1), evidence and facts are part of the package. A good solution must take them into account in various ways. But this is only one part.

(14) LEVELS

Besides its democratic character, there's a lot more to decide about the process. At least two levels must be distinguished. Consider these four issues:

TABLE 6.1. Levels

	Particular	General
First order	(A) How the community should use this particular 'w' or whether this particular *d* should be accepted	(B) How the community should use any given 'w' or whether any given *d* should be accepted
Second order	(A′) How the community should determine how the community should use this particular 'w' or whether this particular *d* should be accepted	(B′) How the community should determine how the community should use any given 'w' or whether any given *d* should be accepted

The difference between (A) and (B) is one of generality. (A′) and (B′) bring another level into the picture. This structural feature can be found in many political, social, and organizational contexts. A community is going to have a discussion about (A) or (B). It aims to establish criteria for collective practices. In the case under scrutiny, they have to do with word uses and distinctions, but they could be about anything else. With a little luck, the community comes to realize that there are many ways in which these discussions could be regulated: what its rules are, what success in it is, what moves are valid, what's beside the point, and who gets to be heard. Therefore, the community needs a second-order discussion about the first-order discussion. It aims to establish criteria to establish criteria for collective agreements and decisions about (A) and (B).

This second-order discussion is also a practical reason, collective one. There's no truth to be obtained, but there are good and bad, better and worse solutions. Its outcome will decisively shape (A) and (B), just like in political and social decision-making processes.

We're dealing with two levels. At least two levels. I'll have more to say about them and the threat of an infinite regress.

6.2 Dinnertime

Practical reason? As Hintikka puts it, this is "reason in so far as it is occupied with human action, human doing and making, and with the results of such action."[9] In Wallace's words, practical reason "is the general human capacity for resolving, through reflection, the question of what one is to do. Deliberation of this kind is practical in at least two senses. First, it is practical in its subject matter, insofar as it is concerned with action. But it is also practical in its consequences or its issue, insofar as reflection about action itself directly moves people to act."[10]

Where I say a 'practical reason problem,' others would prefer a 'political problem.' The latter is common in much of the humanities and social sciences. The former is typical in analytic philosophy and political theory. The contrast between theoretical and practical reason is a staple of the history of philosophy, harking back to Aristotle's 'phronēsis,' and especially since Kant. It has long structured the division of philosophical labor. Research and teaching. Fellowships, professorships, library sections, subject headings, and other organizational structures bear the name 'practical reason' ('praktische Vernunft,' 'raison pratique,' etc.).[11]

I have misgivings about the polysemy and ubiquity of the word 'political.' Its constant presence in scholarship, society, and politics. People mix up its functions as 'category of practice' and 'category of analysis.'[12] Its meanings differ across disciplines. I fear it'll cause misunderstandings about what I'm trying to do. In addition, 'political' may call to mind actual politics or Realpolitik. Ruthless fights, unfairness, and corruption. Politicians obsessed with their careers, popularity, campaign finances, and reelection. Particularistic interests prevailing over the common good. Lies and bullshit. Lots of ugliness,

9. Hintikka 1974, 83.
10. R. Wallace 2020.
11. R. Chang and Sylvan 2021.
12. Brubaker and Cooper 2000.

egoism, and narcissism. Mitch McConnell. That's all descriptively true about politics, but it's not what I intend to talk about. If I'd chosen to use the word 'political' in 'a political problem,' it wouldn't be as a description of actual politics, but as a kind of consideration or perspective.

I think 'practical reason' is less prone to confusion. It's also fittingly broader: political considerations are encompassed by practical reason. Granted, 'political' would have had some advantageous associations. It would have underscored interests, resources, and power, which my account does underscore. I guess you can't have it all.

———

There's nothing mysterious about the practical reason picture I'm outlining. It's a familiar one, recognizable in everyday social life.

Saturday afternoon. A bunch of friends are hanging out at the apartment of one of them. It's about 4 p.m. and their plan is to cook and eat dinner together around 8 p.m. 'What should we cook for dinner?' 'What would be a good idea for us to cook for dinner?' There are better and worse answers to these questions. For instance, two people are vegetarian, so roasted chicken would be a bad idea. Undoubtedly, objectively bad. They don't have much time to go grocery shopping and cook, so cholent would be a bad suggestion, as it must be cooked overnight. Undoubtedly, objectively bad. Note that there can be many good answers and there needn't be one best answer (two or more options can be tied for the first place).

An individual can't answer these questions by themselves, in isolation, be they a member of the group of friends or somebody else. You can't individually establish, or find out, what they/we should cook for dinner. Why not? For one, you must learn about group members' desires, wants, and preferences: what kind of food, or what specific dish, each person feels like eating tonight. How hungry they think they'll be, so how much food, and how many courses, they think they'll want to eat. How much effort they'd like to expend in the preparation, cooking, and serving. And so on. People have to express these desires and preferences.

Additionally, you've got to collect various facts about group members. Their cooking skills. Medical dietary restrictions and allergies. Religious dietary restrictions. Their views about food and about animal ethics. Their broader ethical outlooks. More generally, what it'd be good for a participant to eat for dinner (aside from what they want to eat for dinner). Hence, people must share these facts with one another, or must have shared them in the past, such that they're already known. Or else, a third party should collect them. A private detective. Facebook, Google, and Alexa.

More facts to be collected: what ingredients can be purchased in the area, and at what time grocery stores close. Whether anybody drove their car or everyone rode their bike or the bus, in order to assess grocery shopping feasibility. What equipment, utensils, and pots there are in the kitchen. (These facts can be found out by an individual, like ordinary factual inquiries.)

On top of all that, this group of friends needs to decide how to aggregate its members' preferences and desires. There isn't an incontrovertible aggregation method. It's not incontrovertible what and how to count. Two of them have been going through a lot lately, and they're in financial dire straits, so their enjoyment could be argued to take precedence. 'Ida and Circe get to say what we'll cook for dinner!' Yielding to them is the least truly supportive friends could do. But wait: Ida's and Circe's food preferences are unlikely to coincide, so it'll be aggregation time again. Speaking of calculations, the dinner has to be paid for. Should people chip in in proportion to their income or wealth? To each according to their needs, from each according to their abilities? But wait: wealth and income diverge enormously. In proportion to the former, to the latter, or to a composite measure?

Crucially, people don't have a piece of paper in a drawer where their dinner preference or desire is written. They can't open the drawer and read it out loud. Nor is this preference stored somewhere in their brain, or on their iPhone/ extended mind, from which it could be retrieved.[13] Nor is it an inference from what each person preferred, desired, liked, and chose in similar circumstances in the past, so as to guess—to 'predict'—what they'll do or want in the future (assuming 'similar circumstances' were unproblematic). The group isn't trying to find something out, and then making sure it's true. Instead, it's trying to come to agree and decide on a good course of action.

In fact, an individual's preference may not exist as such before they start thinking about it, seeking to figure out or bring out what they want and what they'd be satisfied with. At this point, there's a more moderate and a more extreme way for the argument to go. The former is that this task can be accomplished by an individual by themselves. No dialogue, discussion, or other people are necessary. The latter is that an individual's preference comes out only as a consequence of the collective discussion. Things would be different if you were at home, planning on cooking dinner for yourself, so you'd introspectively bring out your preference, what you're hungry for. But this is a group dinner.

Individuals' desires and preferences might be dependent on one another. And in a recursive fashion. Loving one's friends means being happy when they're happy, enjoying their enjoyment, taking pleasure in their pleasure. What I prefer

13. A. Clark and Chalmers 1998.

to have for dinner is shaped by my friends' preferences. To some extent, my preference will take their preference into account. To be sure, if a friend feels like eating something I profoundly dislike, or I'm ethically opposed to, I can't go with their preference. But even in this case, I'll take it into account. (To what extent should I take it into account, though? How much should your preference influence mine? We might need to collectively discuss these questions, too.)

I'm lucky to have good friends who feel the same way toward me.[14] Just as what I want is dynamically sensitive to what they want, so what each of them wants is dynamically sensitive to what I want (and to what others want as well). Desires and preferences, what people want, might change as we go along. They adjust themselves as the interactive process—our conversation about what to cook for dinner—unfolds. Group members don't have fixed, frozen preferences about dinner, which could be represented as exogenous utility functions and indifference curves.[15]

I've been talking about a bunch of friends' plans for dinner. I've referred to them as a group. Many social scientists and philosophers of social science argue that you can, and sometimes you should, attribute properties to groups as such.[16] That's the best way to give accounts of their character, workings, and relations (the most informative, illuminating, economical, accurate, explanatorily powerful way). The collective is more than the sum of its parts. Its preferences aren't the sum of individuals' preferences. What's best for it isn't the sum of what's best for each individual. Its agency is irreducible to its members' agency, taken together. From this perspective, what's obtained at the end of the process is a new thing. It's an emergent property. An attribute of the group, which couldn't possibly have existed before. The process brought it into existence.

All in all, a group of friends' collective discussion about what to cook for dinner isn't an exchange of information. Nor is it an attempt to discover a truth. Rather, it's a collective quest. It's a process through which they'll come to see what the best thing to do for the group is, all things considered. It's a construction of sorts. Yet, that the outcome is constructed means neither that it's made up nor that anything goes.

The best answer doesn't preexist and isn't independent from their discussions and interactions, as a standard factual answer would.[17] Neither the

14. Sauder 2020.

15. Besbris 2020.

16. Durkheim (1912) 1968; Effingham 2010; B. Epstein 2019; M. Gilbert 1989, 1990; List and Pettit 2011; Ritchie 2013, 2015, 2020; Tuomela 2007, 2013.

17. What sorts of answers preexist discussions about them and the processes through which they're obtained? Whether this is so in morality and politics pits realism against constructivism (on which more below).

smartest and best-informed individual nor the fanciest algorithm can tell the group what to cook this evening. On the plus side, they'd be able to rule out menu options, on the basis of the information collected and deductive logic. 'It's impossible for you guys to cook this appetizer, because an essential ingredient can't be bought anywhere in town; no grocery store or market has it.' 'This entrée would be lethal to a group member, because of a rare medical condition, and a rule that has strict priority over anything else is: the food shouldn't kill anybody.' An individual or algorithm can get these eliminations right.

A bunch of friends have a plan: to cook and eat dinner together at around 8 p.m. They don't know what yet, but something will have to be cooked and eaten. They must act.

6.3 Collective

Am I sure there isn't a way for *Activity WF* and *Activity DF* to be up to individual social scientists? Up to individual social science labs or teams? It doesn't seem to be a crazy expectation. In your work, you expect to be able to freely decide what to investigate and how. Likewise, you may expect to be able to freely decide how to use word 'w,' and how to classify things and draw distinctions among kinds of things. A free, autonomous, agile, and flexible decision-maker. Not reliant on slow-moving and tiresome communities.

It is an alluring prospect. When an individual has a problem, the problem might be hard, but at least they can address it however they please. Following their own inclinations, desires, and preferences. Collectivities add extra layers of problems to a problem. Everyone must deal with a lot of other people, and must take into account both their opinions and what's good for them. And their schedules, if meetings need to be held. People stand in relations to one another, as network analysts show; collectivities have structures and histories. As it happens, some of these people misunderstand you. Some of them strike you as confused, stupid, or morally shady. After a bad day at work, you just can't stand them.[18] Setting aside any judgment about these people's intellectual and moral qualities, some of their goals and interests will conflict with yours. Not to mention that the whole thing is too time-consuming and too much effort, meetings are boring, and Zoom meetings are extra boring.

'Tough cookies,' I say. *Activity WF* and *Activity DF* are to be tackled by a community. Despite the costs we'll incur, it's the only way. There aren't any

18. D. Wallace 2009.

"shortcuts."[19] The problem is a collective problem, a problem for a community. This is both because of its intrinsic nature and because of broader moral and scientific norms, which social scientists are likely to accept. They're as a matter of fact likely to accept them, I think, but in any event they ought to.

My argument here has two components. The first is a reprise of my response to 'the argument from stipulative freedom' (chapter 3). Proponents of stipulative freedom maintain that you, a social scientist, can decide on your own how to use words and what signs refer to in your work. Just like in mathematics, logic, and constructed languages, it's your free stipulation. The only requirement is that you announce how you decided to define and use word 'w.' Henceforth I'll use 'digitalization' to refer to "treating one or more members of a specified group unfairly as compared with other people."

As I showed, the argument from stipulative freedom isn't convincing. It doesn't pass the Humpty Dumpty test. No social science community will greenlight the preceding definition of 'digitalization.' It doesn't pass the cumulation test. Stipulative freedom would impair literatures' joint work. Individuals' uses and definitions of 'w' would diverge. Without coordination, they wouldn't be working together toward describing and explaining and understanding a social phenomenon.

That's about *Activity WF*, but what about *Activity DF*, which does give you, an individual, total freedom to draw a distinction? The second response applies. Cumulation would be impaired if every project could pick its own set of distinctions. There need to be communal standards to discriminate among distinctions. Not any distinction will be acceptable.

The second component has to do with the conflict between your self-interest and everybody else's—a paramount theme in social and political theory. Suppose *Activity WF* and *Activity DF* were individual activities, and individuals weren't constrained by the community's good, norms, and institutions. Social scientist Marosa can use word 'w' and make distinction *d* thinking exclusively of her data, models, and claims. She does whatever works best for her, regardless of whether it works for other people. So, Marosa's 'w' and *d* maximize the attention afforded to her scholarship. The attention of her discipline, funding agencies, policy makers, and the media. Of her university's deans, vice deans, senior associate deans, assistant vice deans, and other permutations of these job titles. All of which is obviously profitable for Marosa, for her status and reputation. She'll get promotions, interviews, and grants. Job talks and invitations to deliver keynote speeches.

19. Lafont 2020.

While Marosa is ecstatic, her self-interest isn't aligned with the community's interests. A social science community wants the benefits of *Activity WF* and *Activity DF* to accrue to it, to its status and objectives. Objectives such the advancement of social science knowledge, policy impact, the reputation of social scientists' research, and funding for its material prerequisites: jobs, careers, salaries, and grants. Interactions among social scientists should be epistemically fruitful and morally appropriate. Epistemically fruitful and morally appropriate interactions have in turn organizational and cultural enablers. Arguments should be intelligible and communication shouldn't be hampered. Not to pick on Marosa, but the community isn't partial. We don't care about her objectives and status. Not any more than we care about anybody else's. Because there's no invisible hand to turn 'private vices' into 'publick benefits,' letting individualism loose would be ill-advised.[20]

Perhaps it's in every social scientist's self-interest to do whatever they feel like with their words and distinctions. However, the community will suffer—as it does in any collective action problem and tragedy of the commons. I'd like to underscore one unwelcome effect of individual social scientists' self-interest; one among several unwelcome effects it can have. It's the overextension, overuse, or stretching of key words.[21]

Marosa is dead set on expanding the scope of her claims about 'w.' Expand it as much as possible. Both how many phenomena they apply to (neighboring areas and disciplines included) and how many cultures and societies they apply in (they're also true in Uruguay and Paraguay). The more general her claims are, the more they'll be germane to other social scientists and to journalists, and the more they'll be quoted and discussed. Their importance would increase concomitantly with the increase in the extension of 'w.' Since Marosa is ex hypothesi wholly self-interested, she gives no weight to anything or anybody else. She doesn't care in the least about the community.

But we do. Overextension leads to emptiness. If a word can be applied to everything, or almost everything, it'd be empty, or almost empty. It'd fail to pick out anything particular; it'd fail to draw any interesting distinctions. Being a 'fascist,' being a 'socialist,' having been 'sexually harassed,' or being 'in love': uttering these words implies understanding that in certain circumstances it'd be a mistake to use them, because that would *not* be a case of fascism, socialism,

20. Mandeville 1705, (1714) 1725.

21. Abend 2018a; Collier and Mahon 1993; Sartori 1970. Münch (1991, 103–8; 1995, 93–101, 160–61) talks about 'inflation' of words and language.

sexual harassment, or love. The right-wing politician ruling my country is terrible, but he isn't a fascist. My friend likes her new girlfriend a lot, she loves
having sex with her, but she's not in love with her.

These circumstances aren't immutable. They may justifiably expand or contract, in accordance with changes in culture, language, human interests, and
communities' trajectories. Yet, at any given point, there must be a non-
arbitrary way to tell use from misuse and overuse—even if imperfectly,
roughly, imprecisely, vaguely. The use of 'w' has to have limits, so we don't
wind up with a vacuous word. With apologies for the self-quotation: "You do
not want every attempt at making art to get called 'art,' or else the concept of
art would become empty. You do not want too many political systems to get
called 'democratic,' like East Germany and North Korea, or else the concept
of democracy would not serve you well."[22]

Overextension risks confusion and miscommunication within social science communities. We aren't sure what you're claiming anymore, because
'w' applies to pretty much anything. The uses of a word multiply, which en-
courages further overextensions, individuals' being individualistic, and potentially a free-for-all. Merely verbal disputes become more common. Review
articles and conferences try to make sense of the situation and bring it under
control. Instead of parsimony and economy, permissiveness reigns, which
"leads to vagueness and miscommunication, at least most times. Writing or
saying ['w'] has costs."[23]

Overextension risks confusion and miscommunication outside the ivory
tower, insofar as social science is received and put to work in society, organizations, and public policy. For example, scientists have been using the words
'decision' and 'choice' more and more profusely—and society and the media
have followed in their footsteps. These days neurons, bees, plants, heroin addicts, corporations, AIs, and driverless cars are described as decision-makers.
A mosquito decided to bite you and a self-driving car chose to turn left.

At first, this might seem harmless. Harmless literal or metaphorical talk.
Even good. Suggestive and heuristically fruitful experimentation with the limits of words. But it may have

> undesirable moral, legal, and political consequences. Social and political
> actors may struggle to draw boundaries between decision and non-decision,
> between entities that can and cannot make choices. Get confused and
> caught up in pointless debates. Fetishize decision-making moments, ne-
> glecting what led to and enabled them. Misdirect blame, praise, punishment,

22. Abend 2018a, 835.
23. Abend 2018a, 835.

resources, and policies. Unethical people may profit from these confusions, and get away with it by hiding behind choices allegedly made by machines, algorithms, Facebook, corporations, organizations, rules, protocols, and brains.[24]

Not only a person's every action and bodily movement but also their inaction gets represented as the product of implicit decision-making processes. Which muddies up the difference between decision and action. Decision is basically equated with action. At the same time, the language of decision-making and choices may encroach on outcomes, phenomena, and processes that were previously considered social structural, causally attributable to social structural forces. All of this bodes ill for societies where 'choice' is a value-laden word, and ascribing legal and moral responsibility has been a perpetual headache.[25]

I've been speaking of individual scientists' selfish motives. Individuals whose word uses and distinctions are calculated to serve their interests. Fellow community members don't figure in their calculations. Hopefully this isn't statistically representative of scientists. Not even of economists.[26] But there's still reason to worry in the absence of such intentions. Insufficient carefulness (hastiness, thoughtlessness, recklessness) can be just as bad. Suppose a social scientist uses words and draws distinctions however suits their fancy, in ways that sound intuitively OK to them, without much or any reflection. They don't stop to consider their costs, their effects on others, on the literature, on the community, its practices, and its language. The common good doesn't appear in their thinking. Were harmful effects to materialize, this social scientist wouldn't be off the hook because they had no morally questionable intent, no intent to profit from 'w' or d at the expense of others, no mens rea.

Social science is a communal project. It takes place within epistemic communities and their attendant organizations. Fleck's thought communities or Kuhn's paradigms.[27] Communities of inquiry, à la Peirce and Dewey.[28] Disciplines, fields, literatures. As a community member, you have obligations to it—the community in which you operate, to which you contribute, with which you're in dialogue, and outside of which you'd be talking nonsense. It

24. Abend 2018a, 833.

25. Brandmayr 2021a, 2021b.

26. Gerlach 2017; Marglin 2008; Marwell and Ames 1981.

27. L. Fleck (1935) 2019; Kuhn (1962) 1970.

28. Peirce 1868, 1878. Thanks to Albert Atkin and Tullio Viola for their comments on pragmatism.

welcomes neither selfish nor reckless behavior. It demands that everyone be responsible and do their part. It's only fair.

6.4 The good and the true

A community is facing a practical reason problem. Whether it's about a word (*Activity WF*) or about a distinction or classification (*Activity DF*), there are no true answers. Rather, the community will be looking for good solutions or outcomes—for the attainment of which it'll need good procedures and practices. That answers aren't truth-apt doesn't entail that whatever a community member says is good (or is good for them) will ipso facto be good (or be good for them). It doesn't entail either that truth and other customary scientific goals and principles are immaterial. However, the community must elucidate their proper place and role.

Scientists are in the business of making true claims about the world. Descriptions, explanations, predictions, generalizations, among many others. This is one of the main things they're in the business of—whatever else they hope to do and deliver, too, from technologies to public policies to revolutions. The institutions and practices of science ought to be designed with this aim in view. *Activity WF* and *Activity DF* don't make such claims, but they have to help with this. In this sense, they're auxiliary. *Activity WF*, whereby a community makes decisions about the uses of word 'w,' should bolster the community's capacity to make true claims about the world. *Activity DF*, whereby a community makes decisions about acceptable distinctions and classifications, should bolster the community's capacity to make true claims about the world.

Yet, 'making true claims about the world' is incomplete. Scientific research aims at many desiderata, which may be in competition with one another, and may be incompatible with one another (see chapter 9). These aims aren't uniform, they aren't the same across the board, but specific to different parts of science and of social science. To different times and places. Scientific communities must make choices on the basis of various epistemic values: there's no single objective, no single formula. What they do have are general parameters and constraints: a basic idea of what scientists are after, what science is all about, what wouldn't be scientific research and argument, but poetry, soccer, or tarot-card reading (no doubt, the more detailed this idea, the less consensual it gets). Still, my point is that science doesn't demand one unique thing.

I start with a simple, simplified outline. On the one hand, there are scientific objectives and goods ('the true'). On the other, there are moral/practical objectives and goods ('the good'). *Activity WF* and *Activity DF* should contribute to classic scientific objectives, like offering accurate descriptions of phenomena, and explanations that connect causes and effects. But not solely. Scientific objectives underdetermine the outcomes of *Activity WF* and *Activity DF*. Even if you supposed, for the sake of argument, that they weren't themselves multifarious. In other words, they're consistent with many outcomes of *Activity WF* and *Activity DF*. Not any communal decision about 'w' or *d* will be consistent with what scientific research is trying to accomplish—scientific research *stricto sensu*; for example, your survey experiments and statistical models. But many will.

I argue that the success of *Activity WF* and *Activity DF* should be appraised in light of contributions to both scientific and moral/practical goods. Although we're doing science, moral/practical reasons will have to be listened to. Lo and behold, new hurdles await: how to balance the two, which practical/moral objectives are desirable, and how to decide which practical/moral objectives are desirable. Going deeper: how to protect science from bias and ideology, and how to make sure it's trustworthy.[29] These are very contemporary quandaries. STS has been grappling with them, because of its apparently debunking implications. As far as I can see, acknowledging that science isn't pristine, and there's more to science than scientific goals, doesn't force you to conclude that science is just politics. Nor that it's politics by other means.[30] The reason why contemporary societies are disappointed in science might be that their expectations were off to begin with. STS has shown what they shouldn't expect.

Instead of fantasizing about what science would look like if it were conducted by incorporeal and perfect deities, we're better off improving science as conducted by corporeal and imperfect humans, against the backdrop of varying cultural and organizational configurations. Scientific norms should be addressed to real-life scientific practices and institutions. This is my plan for *Activity WF* and *Activity DF*.

6.5 Deliberative democracy and constructivism

I'm not keen on attaching famous labels to my characterization of *Activity WF* and *Activity DF*. A label can trigger positive or negative emotional responses to it, to the school it stands for, and to the authors associated with it. 'I don't like hanging out with those folks!' 'I'm a sucker for them!' My arguments should stand or fall on their own merits. This isn't to say they don't stand on

---

29. Oreskes 2019.

30. Latour's (1984, 257) sentence—"La science, c'est la politique continuée par d'autres moyens"—has taken on a life of its own, beyond its original context. "Science is not politics. It is politics by other means. But people object that 'science does not reduce to power.' Precisely. It does not reduce to power. It offers *other means*" (Latour [1984] 1988, 229).

the shoulders of giants. How could they not? I've learned from present and past scholarship as much as the next guy. For example, I'm indebted to political theorists' and political philosophers' work on democratic theory, the general will, theories of justice, practical reason, and normativity.

My characterization of *Activity WF* and *Activity DF* draws on the literatures on deliberative democracy and constructivism. However, I have a minimalist, selective relationship to them. I've borrowed some ideas and tools, but not the whole shebang. These tools serve clear-cut functions and aren't too heavy. I won't advance any arguments about deliberative democracy and constructivism per se, as my concern is social scientists' *Activity WF* and *Activity DF*, and how to conduct them well. Scientific communities, disciplines, and languages have many peculiarities. So, I'm not implying any generalizations or extrapolations to other social and political communities.[31]

Deliberative Democracy

While "the idea of deliberative democracy and its practical implementation are as old as democracy itself," its contemporary "revival" has been remarkable.[32] Gutmann and Thompson "define [it] as a form of government in which free and equal citizens (and their representatives), justify decisions in a process in which they give one another reasons that are mutually acceptable and generally accessible, with the aim of reaching conclusions that are binding in the present on all citizens but open to challenge in the future." Along similar lines, Bächtiger et al. argue that "deliberative democracy is grounded in an ideal in which people come together on the basis of equal status and mutual respect, to discuss the political issues they face and, on the basis of those discussions, decide on the policies that will then affect their lives."[33]

Political scientists are predominantly thinking of citizens in contemporary polities, but any community can benefit from deliberative democratic arrangements. Any community that must make decisions, come to agree on norms

---

31. I'm also indebted to pragmatist ideas as regards the community of inquiry or inquirers, stakeholders, and laypeople taking part in it, and the connections between getting it right in science, in morals, and elsewhere. On pragmatism, deliberative democracy, constructivism, and their interrelationships, see Bohman (2004), Dryzek (2004), Festenstein (2004), Fuerstein (2021), Kadlec (2008), Lever (2021), Misak (2004, 2013), Misak and Talisse (2021), Ogien (2015), and Talisse (2007, 2011, 2014).

32. Elster 1998, 1. See, e.g., Bächtiger et al. 2018; Dryzek et al. 2019; Gutmann and Thompson 2004; Parkinson and Mansbridge 2012.

33. Bächtiger et al. 2018, 2; Gutmann and Thompson 2004, 7.

and institutions, figure out the best way to go. To achieve this, counting votes won't cut it. Certainly not by itself. People have to come together, discuss diverse proposals and arguments, come up with original ones, and collectively reflect on what to do. They have to deliberate. But what is this? For Fishkin and Mansbridge, for instance, "the root notion is that deliberation requires 'weighing' competing arguments for policies or candidates in a context of mutually civil and diverse discussion in which people can decide on the merits of arguments with good information."[34]

Community members should engage one another, consider their mutual concerns, give reasons to one another, as a mechanism or procedure to make decisions that have an impact on the community as a whole. Were it not for communal deliberation, outcomes, decisions, and policies wouldn't be justified:

> The conception of justification that provides the core of the ideal of deliberative democracy can be captured in an ideal procedure of political deliberation. In such a procedure participants regard one another as equals; they aim to defend and criticize institutions and programs in terms of considerations that others have reason to accept, given the fact of reasonable pluralism and the assumption that those others are reasonable; and they are prepared to cooperate in accordance with the results of such discussion, treating those results as authoritative.[35]

Of course, actual political life is nothing like that. Money and power are on average more efficacious than reason-giving. Emotion trumps reason. People don't regard one another as equals and discussions aren't civil. Sophistry and demagoguery get you more social media followers than being well-informed, measured, and well-meaning. Like Trump in the United States and Waldo in the British series *Black Mirror*.[36]

Of course, advocates of deliberative democracy are familiar with actual political life. Their account of democracy isn't descriptive, but normative. Ideally, what should carry the day is "the unforced force of the better argument."[37] People should see through deceptive rhetoric, sophistry, and demagoguery. Ideally, self-dealing bigots who "grab [women] by the pussy" would never get elected.

34. Fishkin and Mansbridge 2017, 8.

35. J. Cohen (1996) 1997, 413.

36. "The Waldo Moment," *Black Mirror* series 2, episode 3, directed by Bryn Higgins (Endemol, 2013).

37. Habermas (1992) 1996, 306.

Deliberative democracy has struggled with the relationships between the normative and the empirical.[38] Whether deliberative democracy is a normative ideal, an aspiration to strive toward, an 'ideal theory.' Or, rather, it's a feasible proposal to tackle concrete political issues in concrete settings. Objections have been raised on both counts. Regarding the former: it's not an ideal worth striving to, but actually detrimental to democracy. At least, it's worse than other democratic frameworks, varieties, and models. Regarding the latter: it's got no use, it's a mere thought experiment that can't aid real-world politics and decision-making. In a non-ideal world, like ours, "the deliberative ideal cannot easily be institutionalized—and perhaps cannot be institutionalized at all."[39]

Scholarship on deliberative democracy is rich and diverse. There are Habermasian and critical theory strands. Rawlsian and liberal strands. Socialist and Marxist strands. Plus, there are by now three generations of it.[40] What are their commonalities, then? Elster, editor of the volume *Deliberative Democracy*, responds: "All agree . . . that the notion [of deliberative democracy] includes collective decision making with the participation of all who will be affected by the decision or their representatives: this is the democratic part. Also, all agree that it includes decision making by means of arguments offered *by* and *to* participants who are committed to the values of rationality and impartiality: this is the deliberative part."[41]

The conduct of *Activity WF* and *Activity DF* might be informed by these ideas. The virtues of deliberative democracy are inseparable from its downsides, though, so it won't be a free lunch (on which more below).

Constructivism

My approach also draws on constructivism. To prevent misunderstandings: constructivism isn't the social construction thesis, which sociologists and STS scholars are fond of. It's a thesis about normativity, the bases of normativity, especially in ethics and politics. One thesis or several theses.[42]

Constructivists argue that the best or right answer to questions of kind Q is that produced by procedure P. Then, they go on to describe P. To take Rawls's 'theory of justice' as an example:

38. Bohman 1998; Steiner 2012.

39. Shapiro 2017, 78.

40. Elstub 2010.

41. Elster 1998, 8.

42. Forst 2007; Korsgaard 1996, 2003; O'Neill 1989; J. Rawls 1971, 1980.

In Rawls's famous original position 'procedure,' parties described as free, equal, and rational select principles of justice from behind a "veil of ignorance." [. . .] [W]hereas a non-constructivist might regard the original position procedure as a means of discovering principles of justice whose truth is independent of that procedure, the constructivist holds, in contrast, that there is no truth about justice independent of the procedure; the truth of the principles consists in the fact that they are the ones that would be selected by the parties in the original position.[43]

Similarly, Habermas argues that "discursive agreement among all those possibly affected by a norm is not just the most reliable indicator of the justice or moral rightness of a norm. Instead, this is what the moral rightness of a norm consists in. Such agreement is thus a sufficient condition for moral rightness."[44] In Korsgaard's words, "there are answers to moral questions *because* there are correct procedures for arriving at them." For realists it's the other way around: "there are correct procedures for answering moral questions *because* there are moral truths or facts which exist independently of these procedures, and which those procedures track."[45]

Originally inspired by Kant, constructivism has now Humean, Aristotelian, and Nietzschean flavors as well.[46] Its classic proponents, Rawls, Habermas, and Korsgaard, remain as significant as ever. But constructivism has traveled a long and fruitful road since their seminal works. Positions have diversified and complexified.[47] Yet, an ambition shared by constructivists of all stripes is to ground norms and values (moral or otherwise), without recourse to suspect metaphysics and ontologically mysterious facts. Unlike realism, constructivism aims neither at representation of external reality nor at correspondence with normative facts.[48] Its aim isn't to discern what the world is like. Grounding or validation is internal; it's a function of the procedure, argumentation, deliberation, and agreement themselves. As Rawls says about justice, "apart from the procedure of constructing the principles of justice, there are no moral facts."[49]

It's not all roses, mind you. Getting constructivism off the ground is already hard work. Additional difficulties arise as soon as you start to fill in the details.

---

43. Street 2010, 365.

44. Lafont 2012, 288.

45. Korsgaard 1996, 36–37.

46. LeBar 2008; Lenman 2010; Silk 2015.

47. Bagnoli 2013, 2017; Lenman and Shemmer 2012; Street 2010.

48. Brink 1989; Enoch 2011; Sayre-McCord 1988.

49. Rawls 1980, 519.

For example, whether constructivism is an ethical or metaethical view, whether it's a distinct metaethical view, under which conditions the very distinction between ethics and metaethics breaks down, and whether the best account of constructivism is a 'proceduralist' or a 'practical standpoint' one.[50] What kind of rightness, truth, or validity should a constructivist take to be their goal?[51] Is constructivism undermined by Plato's 'Euthyphro Dilemma'?[52] How can constructivists demonstrate that a particular procedure is good, the best, or at least superior to its competitors?

Evidently, this last question is a deal-breaker. If the community went with a wrong procedure, then the outcome would be wrong as well. So, the issue is what kind of argument or justification can be satisfactory here. On this, Enoch is worth quoting at length:

> Suppose we are about to start our weekly tennis match, and we are trying to decide who should serve first. We decide to flip a coin and you win. This settles things—you should now serve first. Why is it that this is so? In particular, what is the relation between the correctness or justification of the relevant result . . . and the procedure that got us there . . . ? Sometimes, procedures are justified because they are the best (or at least a pretty good) way of getting to what is independently a justified or correct outcome. Think, for instance, of dividing a cake utilizing the you-cut-I-choose method: assuming it's fair to divide the cake roughly equally (the independently justified result), the you-cut-I-choose procedure is justified because it is likely to lead to this division. But this is not right for the case of the coin toss. It's not as if there is an independently justified or correct result (that you serve first), and the coin toss procedure is justified because likely to lead to this result. Rather, the order is reversed: The procedure is justified independently of the result (perhaps because we should both be given equal chance to serve first), and the result (that you should serve first) derives its justification from that of the procedure it is the result of. Constructivism can be seen as an attempt to generalize from the coin toss example and the model of pure procedural justice of which it is an example.[53]

As is my wont in this book, I bracket philosophers' controversies over constructivism, and sidestep metaethics and the distinction between normative

---

50. Enoch 2009; Street 2008, 2010, 2016. Street argues for the 'practical standpoint characterization' of constructivism (against the standard, 'proceduralist' one).

51. Nino 1996, 112–13.

52. Street 2010; Walden 2015.

53. Enoch 2009, 319.

and metaethical constructivism.[54] I'll just borrow two constructivist elements and bring them to bear on *Activity WF* and *Activity DF*. First: due to the kind of activities they are and the goals they pursue, the way to find the best answers is the sort of community process I've begun to sketch out. Second: this procedure isn't warranted because of convenience or effectiveness, but because of its ability to determine answers' goodness. In these domains and situations, the best answer just is what's obtained by following the correct procedure. That it can be inconvenient and ineffective is an ineludible side effect. Flipping a coin would be so much smoother.

Many ordinary tasks are such that a particular process, a series of steps, is necessary to achieve what you want to achieve. A more highbrow illustration is the 'dialectical method' in the history of philosophy and social theory. Only a dialectical process of thought and argumentation can get you to the right concept or idea.[55] You won't get there unless you go through the process. Every step is essential, time and history are essential, there are no shorter or faster routes.

Alternatively, I could argue that this process is one of collective action or practice, and that it's got enabling powers. The community's engagement in this process enables the achievement of the best answer. Our participating, our acting together, our discussing the problem is what opens up paths that will allow us to perceive and arrive at the best answer. Another alternative argument builds on illocutionary acts: in participating we're ensuring the solution will be the right solution. The very act of participating accomplishes that.

———

Just when I was rubbing my hands at the thought of moving on, I hear you have more obstacles for me in store? New batches of critics? Putting all labels and philosophy aside, they oppose the elements I've associated with the literatures on deliberative democracy and constructivism. Either they oppose these elements as such, anywhere, or as applied to *Activity WF* and *Activity DF*.

There are critics who have a beef with the entire constructivist project. They are of two kinds, supported by opposite rationales. First: any answer to *Activity WF* and *Activity DF* is as good as any other ('skepticism' or 'subjectivism'). Second: there are objective facts about them, which should be treated like any other fact ('realism' or 'robust realism').

54. Bagnoli 2017.
55. Forster 1993; Wong 2006.

There are critics who have a beef with my deliberative democracy leanings. They deny that collective processes in social science communities should be deliberative. Voting is preferable to talking. Deliberation is no guarantee of anything. It's slow-moving and byzantine. It neither elicits individuals' true preferences nor ushers in the good of the community. In fact, "deliberation may lead people to hold beliefs that are not in their best interest."[56] They insist that we do have alternatives. Deliberative democracy fares worse than other models of democracy, be they more adversarial, elitist, participatory, communitarian, pragmatist, or something else. Maybe we should go with radical and agonistic approaches.[57] Or with Schumpeterian democracy.[58] Or with sortition or lottocracy.[59]

There are critics who condemn not just deliberative democracy, but democracy tout court. 'Democracy is intrinsically defective, as we've known since Plato!' Or, more conservatively (no pun intended), they partly approve of democracy, with the proviso that it be "used only where it is in place," as Weber said.[60]

Their mistrust of democracy may originate in Plato's *Republic* and philosopher-king arguments. There are many people who'd rule better than the people. There's noocracy, technocracy, gerontocracy, aristocracy, plutocracy, and epistocracy.[61] More liberally (no pun intended), they may support paternalism in any of its versions. 'Fuck Mill and Kant! We always cheer for the "interference by some outside agent in a person's freedom for the latter's own good."'[62] In medical ethics, for example, the conflict is between physicians' allegedly paternalist decisions and patients' autonomy and consent. In public health debates, 'nanny states' are accused of interfering with individual citizens' choices. Anti-paternalists argue that the state shouldn't trample on people's liberty to choose to smoke tobacco, shoot up heroin, drink sugary beverages, refuse vaccination for themselves and their children, not wear a seat belt, or not wear a face mask during a pandemic.

In the case of *Activity WF* and *Activity DF*, my critics claim that members of social science communities aren't capable of regulating these activities, due

---

56. Przeworski 1998, 140–41.

57. Mouffe 1999, 2000, 2005; Selg 2013; Van Bouwel 2015; Van Bouwel and Van Oudheusden 2017.

58. Posner 2005.

59. Guerrero 2014.

60. Weber (1919) 1946, 134.

61. Brennan 2016; Estlund 2003; Méndez 2022; Reiss 2019.

62. Le Grand and New 2015, 7; see also Coons and Weber 2013; Dworkin 1972, 65.

to incompetence and apathy, intellectual and moral shortcomings, or other failings. Who should be in charge, then? This is a job for a leader or select elite, not the whole community. A rational, intelligent, well-intentioned, and enlightened agent, which isn't necessarily a community member. A father or a state. A sage, spiritual leader, or Nobel Prize laureate. Epistemically qualified professionals, technicians, or intellectuals. An organization, an algorithm, or a god.

How am I to respond to these three lines of criticism? Are some of their points compatible, or can they be made compatible, with my overall picture? If this were so, I could replace parts of the machinery to attain superior functioning. I'm not committed to the specifics of my proposal, as there's surely much room for improvement—though, as more and more Ship of Theseus parts get replaced, it'll make less and less sense to speak of 'my overall picture.'

Other objectors are recalcitrant, however. It's either their or my views. Philosophy will be back at the table, despite my efforts to kick it out (or brush it under the carpet). The situation is, again, that you gainsay my premises, I can't persuade you to change your mind, and you can't persuade me to change my mind either. We'll have extensive conversations before we give up and accept this unfortunate outcome, but, at some point, there'll be nothing more we can do about it.

I won't go there at the present time. But let me suggest why I'm unconvinced by paternalism in the settings I'm thinking of. It's not because of paternalists' potentially authoritarian or totalitarian tendencies. Nor because of unethical or incompetent governments that claim to know what's good for the people better than the people themselves. These are separate issues. Nor is it about the wisdom of the crowds, large groups' capacity to discover the truth, or crowdsourcing's accuracy and reliability surpassing any individual.[63] These are separate issues as well.

Rather, I'm unconvinced due to my understanding of *Activity WF* and *Activity DF*. There's no true answer to be discovered. It's a different ball game, where collective processes are necessary to obtain good arrangements, to

---

63. Does this encompass epistemic democracy? It depends on whether it's expected to excel at truth-tracking or at other epistemic undertakings. On epistemic democracy, "Condorcet's jury theorem," and whether diversity trumps ability, see Anderson (2006), J. Cohen (1986), Estlund (2008), Goodin and Spiekermann (2018), Hong and Page (2004), Landemore (2012), Landemore and Elster (2012), List and Goodin (2001), Singer (2019), and Thompson (2014). For a review, see Schwartzberg (2015). On Dewey's "epistemic democracy without truth," see Fuerstein (2021).

make decisions that are good for the community and beyond. For this reason, *Activity WF* and *Activity DF* aren't jobs for paternalism, whether or not it holds water elsewhere.

6.6 'Practical'

In this book, I'm assigning a lot of work to the expression 'practical reason,' as well as to the words 'practical' and 'moral.' I do thank them for their service. They're serving in two distinct areas, though.

First, there's my depiction of *Activity WF* and *Activity DF* qua activities. Social science communities should have processes in place to make collective decisions about word uses (*Activity WF*) and distinctions and classifications (*Activity DF*). Which processes would fit the bill? This depends on the character of the problem the community has in its hands. I argue that it's a practical reason problem, which should be addressed by means of practical reason mechanisms. Answers can't be true, the final criterion isn't truth, because the question isn't factual, truth-apt, or otherwise externally decidable.

Rather, answers can be good; the final criterion is goodness, practically speaking. It's about the goodness of communities' decisions about word uses and distinctions. Compare: a process to establish what the fertility rate in Uruguay is (outcome is true or false) versus a process to establish whether our organization, company, or institute should have gender-neutral restrooms (outcome is good or bad). Analogously: what empathy really is (outcome is true or false) versus how our community should use the word 'empathy' (outcome is good or bad).

Second, there are the objectives that *Activity WF* and *Activity DF* are driven by, or oriented toward, insofar as they're social science activities. What makes an answer good depends on what sort of thing the community is up to—whether it's a community of theater actors, Scrabble players, or sociologists of religion. This statement strikes me as obvious. It applies to *Activity WF* and *Activity DF*, and to all aspects of social science and social scientists' work, from developing methodological tools to teaching undergraduate students.

In this respect, I argue that the objectives of much social science should be both epistemic/scientific and practical/moral. I say 'much,' because a sweeping generalization would probably be false. Social science is a large and heterogeneous collection of disciplines, each of which is a large and heterogeneous collection of people, projects, topics, tools, and objects. Compare: the reason to prefer my answer is epistemic/scientific (practical/moral stuff doesn't count) versus the reason to prefer my answer is partly epistemic/scientific and partly practical/moral. Compare: using 'empathy' in this fashion will bring about epistemic goods (more knowledge) versus using 'empathy' in this fashion will bring about both epistemic and moral goods (more knowledge, more equality within the community, desirable effects on society).

In sum, one thing is the character of the problem a community is facing and the process it calls for. Another thing is the community's objectives, and hence what it is that the process should help accomplish, and what sorts of reasons will be pertinent. How should social science communities conduct *Activity WF* and *Activity DF*? What processes are good and bad, better and worse? I argue that there are better and worse answers. The trick is how to cash out goodness and how it'll capture the objectives of social science communities. Which, if I'm right, should be both epistemic/scientific and practical/moral.

These two areas are distinct, but not independent. Besides this distinction, I portrayed my attitude as pragmatic. While I avoided the word 'practical,' there are overlaps between a pragmatic attitude and practical reason problems (first area) and practical/moral goals and reasons (second area). I won't spell out all the relationships between these three elements, as doing so might itself belie my pragmatic attitude. I've got other fish to fry now. I daresay bigger fish to fry, but you be the judge.

6.7 The plan

Communities of social scientists will work together and make collective decisions about their words, distinctions, and classifications. Community members will give reasons to one another. Deliberate. Consider objections and implications. For all of this, they have to acquire empirical information, be it through consulting secondary sources or doing new research. The community has to come to shared understandings, decisions, and agreements that it's OK with, even though they aren't universally agreed upon and they aren't expected to last forever.

In practice, communities' work needn't look like the meetings of legislative and other deliberative political bodies, or the higher-ups of corporations and other organizations (more on this below). People may physically congregate in a room, but they don't need to. Communities' decisions won't be formally recorded and announced, at a specific point in time, as the product of the deliberations, and coming into force next month. These might seem to be natural models, suggested by certain modern imaginaries and customs. But social science communities can use more imagination and creativity in these regards. The form and mechanics of their joint work is up to them. These aren't superficial aesthetic details: creative, innovative forms can go a long way. Either way, there need to be acceptable procedures, which sanction acceptable

and unacceptable moves; acceptable and unacceptable reasons, considerations, and goals. At a higher-order level, social scientists have to give reasons
to one another about these procedures, too.

What's a good answer to communities' normative questions about words
(*Activity WF*) or distinctions (*Activity DF*)? What would make a good solution good? Goodness according to which principles, aims, interests, norms,
and understandings? What criteria and methods to employ? How to go about
adjudicating disagreements about particular words and distinctions? Communities' discussions will take up these questions. Answers must emerge from
adequate processes. Interactive processes that unfold over time. While I'm
stressing their collective nature, I don't mean to deny that human beings exist.
It's human beings, not society or the community, who move about, speak,
think. Fight, eat, shit, and chop off the heads of kings. Individual community
members participate in and contribute to the processes through which *Activity
WF* and *Activity DF* are conducted. I, for one, am going to go ahead and share
some thoughts, make some proposals, and run some ideas by you guys. I'll
elaborate on my claims about moral/practical goals. I'll argue for justice/fair-
ness in certain places, in scientific places, in methodologically vital and exact-
ing places, where they're often deemed extraneous.

How to use 'w'? Should *d* be accepted? A social science community is after
word- and distinction-related norms, manifested or embodied in concrete criteria. Norms and criteria should be guided, among other things, by their social
effects. Their effects on resources, material and symbolic. The practice of *Activity WF* and *Activity DF* should contemplate who'll win and who'll lose, what
they'll win and what they'll lose, inside and outside the community. Suppose
our field were considering a certain criterion to evaluate words or distinctions.
If accepted, it'd harm disadvantaged community members, the 1 percent
would profit, and inequality would grow. Therefore, we have a pro tanto reason
to reject it. It's our responsibility to find an alternative and put it into place.

There's a further twist to the story. I've argued that *Activity WF* and *Activity
DF* have to attend to two kinds of objectives. On the one hand, there are epis-
temic/scientific objectives, which are what scientists normally think of when
they make decisions about their research. They're thinking of the success
of experiments, fieldwork, data collection and analysis, and models. On the
other hand, there are moral/practical objectives, which scientists seldom
think of when they make decisions about their research. Not explicitly anyway.
For example, equality and justice in their community.

And here's the twist: what is it for experiments, fieldwork, and models to
succeed—to succeed within science, scientifically speaking, qua pieces of scientific work? It turns out that their success isn't accountable to one standard

only, but to many. Science isn't monistic. There are competing desiderata that scientific communities seek, value, and reward. Which ones to prioritize? How much weight is each to be afforded? Narrowly epistemic/scientific criteria can't answer these questions. Moral/practical considerations are needed, even within the realm I referred to as 'epistemic' or 'scientific.' It's not purely epistemic/scientific after all.

Second Act

7

Word first

O Menexenus and Lysis, how ridiculous that you two boys, and I, an old
boy . . . should imagine ourselves to be friends—this is what the by-standers
will go away and say—and as yet we have not been able to discover what is a
friend!

—PLATO, *LYSIS* 223B[1]

Words . . . are of no importance whatever to us; they are mere labels for
keeping track of things. So we say, 'Such and such a thing we are going to
call *A*.' . . . We do not say—an entirely different matter—'Such and such a
thing is *A*.'

—PARETO (1916)[2]

7.1 Words

Activity WF is about words. How words should be used. Key words for a social
science community, like 'ethnicity,' 'inequality,' and 'poverty.' Expressions consisting of more than one word, like 'civil war,' 'welfare state,' 'artificial intelligence,' and 'mental health.' The community will decide which uses of 'w' are
acceptable around here. It'll also decide how many acceptable uses 'w' has. It
needn't be one and it shouldn't be too many. The goal is practical: to improve
communities' practices, their language use and its worldly consequences. To

---

1. This is Benjamin Jowett's nineteenth-century translation. In Stanley Lombardo's rendition,
Socrates says they've "made fools of [themselves]," as "what a friend is, we have not yet been
able to find out."

2. Pareto (1916) 1935, § 119. Thanks to Federico Brandmayr for suggesting that quoting this
Pareto passage is Pareto optimal.

use words better. To decide which words to use and to forgo, thus improving their lexicons.

My account of *Activity WF* is about how to do things with words. Key words are my focus, my unit of analysis—as opposed to larger chunks of language and language use, or a more holistic account of language practices, language games, and forms of life.[3] Needless to say, word uses have semantic, pragmatic, and social contexts. Words aren't self-standing. They exist within networks and ecologies. They're part of social processes and practices. There are reasons why they're there: they're doing something, which someone wanted them to do. Word meanings and uses are relational, indexical, contextual. Without such backgrounds and relations, what comes out of people's mouths wouldn't be intelligible. Arguably, it wouldn't be language at all. By spotlighting and discussing a word, one word at a time, I'm not signaling a commitment in the philosophy of language. It's an expository shorthand.

I argue that *Activity WF* isn't truth-apt: there are no true answers, but good results. Good for what? Good for whom? Hold your horses for a bit.

————

Chapter 1 showed that 'sandwich,' 'bread,' and 'meat' can't be defined and used in a non-committal manner. Nor can social scientists' key words, like 'technology,' 'work,' 'bureaucracy,' 'communication,' or 'institution.' Deciding how it'd be good to use 'w' is a normative pursuit. Goods and values will be front and center.

My point is about any key word in social science research, not just the special case of 'thick' ones, which are simultaneously descriptive and evaluative.[4] To speak of a 'terrorist,' 'racist,' or 'Islamophobic' group is to describe it and to censure it. To say that a regime was a 'democracy,' comparable to other 'democracies,' is both to describe it and to praise it. Your policy is 'discriminatory.' That's a case of 'genocide.' These people are 'artists' and these works are 'creative.'[5] Social scientists use thick words in their research projects, hypotheses, comparisons, and generalizations. They figure in explananda and explanantia. Thick words' participation isn't flagged as irregular, but their normativity doesn't vanish. The positive or negative evaluation can't be peeled off.[6]

3. Moyal-Sharrock 2015; Wittgenstein (1953) 2009.

4. Abend 2019; D. Roberts 2013; Väyrynen 2013; B. Williams 1985. Kindred ideas are 'appraisive concepts' and 'dual character concepts' (Gallie 1956; Reuter 2019).

5. Sánchez-Dorado 2020.

6. C. Taylor 2003, 306.

Thick words are visibly normative. But I'm talking about any key word. 'Bureaucracy' as much as 'democracy,' 'communication' as much as 'terrorism,' 'institution' as much as 'intelligence.' Measurements of and claims about 'w' can't be above the normative fray. Including economists' key words, despite their self-understanding as more scientific, objective, and value-free than the rest of social science.[7] As Dupré argues, the "value-laden nature of the terms in which we talk about ourselves and our social existence" is "inescapable." Evolutionary psychologists' 'rape' and macroeconomists' 'inflation' and 'work' are cases in point:

> [Inflation] is seen as the sort of thing that can be described and theorized without regard to its goodness or badness. The problem here is somewhat different from that for rape. The normative judgment is fundamental to the meaning of rape and therefore fundamental to negotiations about what should and should not count as rape. With inflation, normativity comes in a little later. The primary problem . . . is that there is no unequivocal way of measuring this economic property. It would be easy enough if everything changed in price by identical percentages, but of course that does not happen. How should we balance a rise in the price of staple foods, say, against a fall in the price of air travel? The immediately obvious reply is that we should weight different items in proportion to the amount spent on them. The problem, then, is that not all goods are equally consumed by all people or even by all groups of people. It is quite commonly the case that luxury goods fall in price while basic necessities rise. It might be that these cancel out under the suggested weighting, so that there is no measured inflation. But for those too poor to afford luxury goods, there has manifestly been an increase in the price level.[8]

From the point of view of research ethics, one fear is that a dishonest evolutionary psychologist gerrymanders the extension of 'rape' and a dishonest economist gerrymanders the extension of 'inflation' and 'work,' so the data support their preconceptions. However, from the point of view of *Activity WF*, what matters is that nobody can use words non-committally. That's not an option, no matter how well-intentioned, judicious, and fair you are.

So, how should social scientists use 'inflation,' 'work,' 'religion,' and 'neoliberalism' in their research?

———

7. Dupré 2007; Putnam and Walsh 2012; Reiss 2017.
8. Dupré 2007, 37–38.

'Wait there a second!' a linguist or lexicographer might demur:

Asking how a word should be used is a non-starter. You can describe the use of words and expressions, but nobody can prescribe how they should be used. The way you hear native speakers speak Spanish, that's how Spanish is spoken, and that's the right way to speak it. Mistakes are only made by foreigners, toddlers, and preschoolers. How do you plan on judging words and expressions as being used well or badly, correctly or incorrectly, better or worse? Based off of what?

This linguist or lexicographer is right about natural languages. Lexical meaning, grammar, and all their aspects. Researchers don't get to decide what's correct and incorrect. Their commission is to observe and describe how language is used, what for, and by whom. Observe ordinary people and organizations. Observe newspaper articles, social media posts, internet forums, and text messages.[9] Their commission isn't to dictate norms and promulgate prescriptions.[10] Linguists and lexicographers have a point about natural languages, but it doesn't comprise social science languages. Or so I wish to suggest. You can evaluate the uses of key social science words and try to improve them. To be more accurate, it's not you, but we. The community. I argue that this is a practical reason problem for a community. It must legislate for itself and set up appropriate legislative mechanisms.

If I'm seeing things right, something isn't quite right with 'w.' In many social science communities, 'w' use is inconsistent and confusing. It's been so for a long time. Discussions about it are unproductive, opening the door to objectionable moves, whereby power and seniority beat reason and fairness. They've been so for a long time. The community would be better off if it got more clearheaded about the use of 'w' and about arguments about the use of 'w,' if it better understood what's at stake, and if it had more-or-less shared understandings about it. Not necessarily precise ones. It can be enough to have a rough sense of what's OK and what's completely off. Not necessarily explicit ones, lists of rules posted on people's pinboards or saved on their desktops. It can be enough for them to be manifested in and enforced through ordinary practices, institutions, norms, and dispositions.

---

9. Crystal 2009.

10. Language users' attitudes can be normative. Pragmatics and the sociology of language examine people's normative reactions to and prescriptive judgments about words that seem inappropriate and offensive, and sentences that sound ungrammatical. Young people's speech is ugly. Their grammar is wrong. There are natural and contrived expressions. Fitting and unfitting tones. Uses, misuses, and slightly odd uses of words. Not only foreigners and toddlers are disapproved of.

The languages of social science communities are liable to normative evaluation. Community members are the evaluators. We aren't external observers, but participants. We can judge them as good or bad. We may desire change, and sometimes we ought to desire change. We aren't imprisoned by extant norms and practices any more than gender activists are imprisoned by extant gender norms and practices. They are constraining, yes. They shape us, yes. And yet, a better world is possible.

7.2 Words, words, words

I've described *Activity WF* as being about words. Word goes first. However, this isn't how social scientists construe their arguments and discussions about their objects of inquiry. Rarely are they said to be about lexical semantics. Instead, social scientists express themselves in ontological terms. They aren't talking about the meaning of words, but about the nature of social things. What is culture? What is capitalism? What is ethnicity? What is intelligence? What is artificial intelligence? What is empathy? What is language? What is religion? What is terrorism? What is *F*? This is the form of the questions social scientists ask, answer, and have disputes over. It's the form of many titles of conference sessions, panels, and colloquia. Of many articles and special journal issues.

Social scientists want to know what *F* is, as their research is (or is going to be) about *F*. Their empirical claims are about *F*, a thing, and its properties, causes and effects, and history. What are the main characteristics of populism? What features do all religions have? How has neoliberalism changed from the 1990s to the present? How and why did capitalism come into being? The plan is: you've got a topic, and then select a narrower object or phenomenon within it. Next, you go on to investigate something about it. You ask what it's like, what it's caused by, or how it's changed. (This isn't an empirical account of researchers' steps, nor a temporal sequence, but an idealized reconstruction.)

Per this strategy, social scientists' things are like other things in the world, whose existence isn't in doubt, and which can be identified, picked out, and referred to. They are things out there, like the International Monetary Fund (IMF), Paris's tenth arrondissement (administrative district), or Antarctica. You can investigate how they've changed over time. Likewise, you can investigate how sets of things have changed, like US airports since the 1980s or the measles morbillivirus since Thomas Peebles isolated it in the 1950s. Being able to pick it or them out is necessary for your research project to work out. As long as you're able to identify Antarctica and the tenth arrondissement, you can test claims about them—for example, about the former's shrinking and the latter's gentrification over the past decades.

It's suggestive how social scientists express their commitment to the existence of F and to F's being what they believe it to be. Ontological claims are oftentimes uttered as if they had an exclamation mark. 'That's not a terrorist group!' (It lacks these two essential properties.) 'That isn't a case of capitalism! Not an example of a capitalist society!' (It's only a proto-capitalist one.) Equally suggestive are insertions of the adverbs 'really' and 'truly,' habitually italicized or prosodically stressed. 'My research demonstrates what empathy *really* is.' 'As my paper shows, this is what capitalism *truly* is.' Both social scientists and philosophers perform this "desk-thumping, foot-stamping shout of 'Really!'"[11] When it comes to interrogatives, the stress is placed on the word 'is': "it is as if one can hear the stamping of feet upon utterance of the word 'is' when we ask, what *is* a species?, what *is* an organism?, or what *is* a gene?"[12] These rhetorical emphases betoken emotions. Perhaps anxiety and persuasive intent.[13] Conviction that there are such objects or entities out there.

Are these social scientists making ontological arguments? They don't describe themselves as pursuing ontological inquiries, but as advancing scientific methodology, social theory, or substantive social science. Yet, wittingly or unwittingly, their concern is hands-down ontological. The ontology of the social world: what there is, what things there are, and what these things are like. The conclusion of this inquiry will tell us what F is. This is what F is. That's what F is not. Or, which is similar but not identical: what it is to be F. In virtue of what something is F.[14] When social scientists disagree about what F is, as they often do, they're having an ontological disagreement.

This is all very Socratic of social scientists. And Platonist and Aristotelian. As the founding fathers of Western philosophy did, they're asking what's the real nature or true essence of F, also known as '*to ti esti*' or '*ti esti*' questions.[15]

---

11. Fine 1986, 129.

12. Waters 2018, 91.

13. Stevenson (1938, 331; see also 1944): "A 'PERSUASIVE' definition is one which gives a new conceptual meaning to a [familiar] word without substantially changing its emotive meaning, and which is used with the conscious or unconscious purpose of changing, by this means, the direction of people's interests."

14. Berker 2018; Dorr 2016; Correia 2017; Rayo 2013.

15. Charles 2010b; Politis 2015. On Aristotle on definition ('*horismos*') and essence, see Angioni (2014), Charles (2000, 2010a), Chiba (2010), Demoss and Devereux (1988), Modrak (2010), and Whitaker (1996). The Greek expression '*to ti esti*' means something like "the what-it-is"; that which makes a thing the kind of thing it is. A similar expression is '*to ti ēn einai*,' which has been rendered as "the what-it-was-to-be," "what it is to be something," and "what it is to be it" (Aubenque 1962; Burger 1987; P. Byrne 1997, 247 and passim; Courtine and Rijksbaron [2004] 2014). In Latin, they became '*essentia*' and '*quidditas*.' Things are complicated by the

They're asking 'what-is-X?' questions, also known as 'what-is-F?' or 'what-is-F-ness?' questions.[16] Also known as 'real definitions,' too.[17]

This is what Socrates and his companions were up to. In the *Meno*, they wanted to find out what virtue is. In the *Hippias Major*, what beauty or fineness ('*kalon*') is. Love ('*eros*') and friendship ('*philia*') in the *Symposium, Lysis*, and *Phaedrus*. Justice in the *Republic*, courage in the *Laches*, sophistry in the *Sophist*, piety or holiness ('*hosion*') in the *Euthyphro*, knowledge ('*epistēmē*') in the *Theaetetus*, and temperance or moderation ('*sōphrosunē*') in the *Charmides*. Mere examples of just, virtuous, or pious actions wouldn't satisfy them. Nor would language and lexicography settle it—that is, what the meanings of the Greek words '*dikaiosunē*,' '*aretē*,' or '*hosion*' were, or how Greek speakers used them. Their interest was ontological: what justice, virtue, and piety are. Justice, Virtue, and Piety. In the Islamic world, al-Kindī (ca. 800–870), al-Fārābī (ca. 870–950 or 951), and Ibn Sīnā (ca. 970–1037) followed suit.[18]

Social scientists' questions about capitalism, neoliberalism, culture, class, the welfare state, terrorism, power, and religion are similarly Socratic. 'What is F?' isn't to do with the meaning of English words or English speakers' uses of words, let alone with French or Arabic. Rather, the underlying assumption is that there's something for capitalism, neoliberalism, culture, depression, and religion to be. For it to really be. Like water is H_2O and clay is "earth mixed up with any fluid" (*Theaetetus* 147c). What is water? H_2O.

Social scientists' job is to find out what F is, and consequently what it's not and shouldn't be included in their explanandum or dependent variable. A concept or definition must capture F, the object. Of course, you may be wrong about it. You may claim that the literature on capitalism is totally wrong about what capitalism is and the literature on neoliberalism is only partly right about what neoliberalism is (it's missed an essential part of it). From this Socratic or ontological perspective, the function of words (or concepts) is instrumental: they are tools to track down, correspond to, and stand for these objects out there. Capitalism, the thing, which the word 'capitalism' refers to. Terrorism, the thing. Religion, the thing.

Scholastics' distinction between '*quidditas*,' a thing's whatness, and '*haecceitas*,' a thing's thisness. "So, an object such as Bucephalus possesses a *quidditas*, in this case *horse*. . . . To know the *quidditas* of a given object is to know its sortal essence. In addition to his *quidditas*, Bucephalus would also be said to possess an *haecceitas*, a thisness or individual essence that makes him the particular horse that he is. Together, the *quidditas* and *haecceitas* of an individual object provide the Scholastic definition for that object" (D. Smith 2016, 237–38).

16. H. Benson 1990a; J. Clark 2018; R. Robinson 1941, 1950; Wolfsdorf 2003a, b.

17. Rosen 2015.

18. Adamson 2016; Kennedy-Day 2003.

But here's the thing. These social scientists don't realize that 'what-is-*F*?' questions aren't gratis. You've got to pay metaphysical taxes, so to speak. Five interrelated metaphysical theses are required. (You could argue, more moderately, that a lower tax is due: some combination of them, but not all of them.) Alternative formulations: these are implicit assumptions, presuppositions, or ontological or metaphysical commitments of social scientists' 'what-is-*F*?' approach. A 'what-is-*F*?' approach needs them. Only if these theses are true, can a 'what-is-*F*?' approach work, be it in the social sciences or elsewhere.

In broad brush strokes, the five theses are as follows:

THESIS 1: ABSTRACT OBJECTS

Social scientists make claims about 'abstract objects,' or abstract entities, such as love, intelligence, addiction, diversity, and neoliberalism.[19] These abstract objects exist, even though they're immaterial and you can't point to them. Like concrete objects, abstract objects have properties: tables have properties P_1 and P_2, planets have properties P_3 and P_4, the moon has properties P_5 and P_6, and capitalism has properties P_7 and P_8. They can be the subject of sentences. The moon is smaller than Venus. The moon is made of blue cheese. Neoliberalism is expanding across the world.

Platonists are more demanding. Their abstract objects are Plato's "Forms" or "Ideas." They're unchanging, exist outside space and time, and don't causally interact with the world. But this is a higher bar, which social scientists don't need.

THESIS 2: METAPHYSICAL REALISM

Nominalism argues that the social world is a collection of particulars. Societies group these particulars in various ways. These are conventions, inventions, constructions. By contrast, realism argues that some groupings are real. They exist independently of us. There are objective similarities among their members. A historically prominent variant of realism is that some groupings are natural. They carve social reality at its joints, like the natural kinds of chemistry and physics.

19. Metaphysicians' standard examples of abstract objects are numbers, sets, lines, triangles, properties, and propositions. Much of the discussion is about mathematics (Balaguer 1998; Benacerraf, 1965, 1973; Frege 1884). So, my abstract objects may not be considered bona fide. Not that metaphysicians agree on what it is to be abstract and what it is to be an object.

Realists say: it's not up to you to decide what is and isn't a populist regime, a capitalist system, a civil war, an altruistic action, or a mentally healthy person. This is to be discovered. The social world has an objective structure, according to which things fall into classes, groupings, or kinds. Particulars (a particular civil war, a particular altruistic action) instantiate or exemplify these groupings.

THESIS 3: ESSENTIAL PROPERTIES

Membership in groupings, categories, classes, or kinds is determined by essential properties (as opposed to accidental ones). Capitalism must have properties P_7 and P_8. If something doesn't have these properties, then it's not an instance of capitalism. Populism must have properties P_9 and P_{10}. If something doesn't have these properties, then it's not an instance of populism. Social scientists have to discover what these essential properties are. What's essential and what's accidental isn't a convention, invention, or construction. More broadly, social things, categories, and phenomena have essences.

An amended version of this thesis is that essential properties aren't binary. A thing is essentially a particular kind of thing insofar as it reaches a certain level of this property. The variable or measurement instrument isn't categorical, but continuous.

THESIS 4: UNIVERSALITY

Groupings, categories, classes, or kinds are universal. As a matter of sociological fact, they vary across societies. ('They' is problematic: what exactly is it that varies?)[20] But this is due to metaphysical errors. Some societies fail to grasp the true metaphysical structure of the social world, so they get their categories wrong. If you ask 'what is mental illness?' 'what is altruism?' or 'what is populism?' you're trying to get at their nature or essence. Which is universal and orthogonal to what it's taken to be in contemporary US society, Uruguay, or Paraguay—an interesting project for sociologists of knowledge, historians of ideas, linguists, anthropologists, and ethnobiologists, but ontologically beside the point.[21] Imagine a society in which whales are said to be a

---

20. Uruguayans and Paraguayans dissimilarly categorize armed conflicts as civil wars ('*guerras civiles*'). Some members of the category are the same, but not all. The category has dissimilar members in the United States as well. Might the translation be at fault? What guarantees that '*guerra civil*' and 'civil war' are synonymous, not false friends?

21. Begossi et al. 2008; B. Berlin 1992; Ellen 2006; Hunn 2007; Ludwig 2017, 2018.

type of fish. Its taxonomies, 'folk categories,' ichthyology textbooks, and wild-life documentaries are good data for sociologists and historians. Yet, they're mistaken about reality.

THESIS 5: LANGUAGE AND REALITY

There are abstract objects, such as capitalism, terrorism, and empathy. They are prior to and independent of language. Social scientists should track them down. Dedicated lexical items should pick them out. The essence or nature of F remains unaffected. It makes no difference whether the one-humped ungulate gets called 'dromedary' or 'Arabian camel'; whether gold gets called 'gold' or '*oro*'; and whether populism gets called 'populism' or 'פופוליזם.' The referent is the same thing.

Therefore, you're correctly using the word 'populism' if and only if you're using it to refer to populism, the abstract object whose essential properties are P_9 and P_{10}. If you use the word 'populism' to refer to anything but this one object, you'd be making an error.

The point holds even if it's not yet known what this object is—social scientists are still working on it. Before Cavendish, Watt, and Lavoisier, chemists didn't yet know that water was H_2O.[22]

———

Social scientists do not put forward these theses in their writings, presentations, and lectures. Nor would they explicitly endorse them. For the most part, I believe social scientists don't appreciate them properly. They aren't fully aware of their tacit assumptions or commitments, what's demanded by 'what-is-F?' questions and 'what-F-is' claims, what they're getting themselves into. I'll suggest that most social scientists would, upon reflection, reject these theses.

7.3 Dump ontology

I argue that social scientists should jettison 'what-is-F?' questions. Bad kind of question to invest their time and effort in. *Activity WF* is about language use. It's not an ontological inquiry. Dump ontology!

I can think of three tactics to support this recommendation. First, I could offer metaphysical reasons. Reasons why the preceding five theses are false, or

---

22. Putnam 1973, 1975a.

at least hard to believe. Why there's no there there. Second, I could invoke social scientists' understandings of the ontology of the social world. What their largely unarticulated inclinations, assumptions, or intuitions are. Third, I could support it in a pragmatic fashion, in light of empirical facts about social scientists, social science, and the aims and drivers of social science research.

I'm not going to go down the first road. Proponents of these theses—realists, essentialists, Platonists, Aristotelians—have their reasons. Thousands of years' worth of reasons. There's no knock-down, apodictic argument to show them wrong and convince them to change their minds. I'd have an easier time of it if I could report metaphysical truths and get back to my claims about social science. But I can't.[23]

Am I therefore forced to place my metaphysical bets, despite Durkheim's view that "sociology doesn't need to take sides between the great hypotheses that divide metaphysicians"?[24] I already conceded that I am. And I'm not going to be betting on those five theses.[25] Qua theses about the nature of the social world, they strike me as implausible. (They strike me as implausible about the natural world, too, but that's another story.)[26] One day a metaphysician may conclusively refute one of them, or show it to be meaningless. Perhaps the opposite comes to pass: one of them is conclusively proven to be true. You never know. I'll keep my ears open, as I may have to adjust my arguments accordingly. Or abandon them altogether.

While I can't abstain, I can keep trying to minimize my philosophical engagements and commitments. To state the obvious, I'm no metaphysician. The best reasons *I* can offer aren't metaphysical. So, I'll try a combination of the second and third lines of argument. Neither is a clincher, but, taken together, they make a good case against ontology.

The second argument factors in social scientists' ontological understandings of the social world. More precisely, what social scientists' beliefs would

---

23. Metaphysicians' controversies over realism, nominalism, conceptualism, and their many ramifications are alive and well. As per Bourget and Chalmers's (2014, 493) survey of philosophers, 39.3% endorse Platonism about abstract objects, 37.7% endorse nominalism, and 23.0% fall under "other." Nor could I report agreed-upon truths about what a property is, a sparse property (Lewis 1983), to share a property, degrees of similarity, overall similarity, and resemblance.

24. Durkheim (1895) 2013, 172–73.

25. Cf. A. Abbott 2016; Mahoney 2021. Abbott champions a processual sociology. Mahoney's (2021, 1) "set-theoretic social science" combats "essentialism": "an innate bias in which human beings understand the world as consisting of entities that possess inner essences, which endow the entity with an identity and a certain nature."

26. Dupré 2012; Dupré and Leonelli 2022.

be, if they were presented with these issues and were asked to reflect on them. (A counterfactual, since normally they're tacit.) Pending data collection, I'm going to venture a guess about their modal beliefs. Social science research is about entities and phenomena the reality of which isn't in doubt. There's no doubt that civil war, poverty, terrorism, and gender discrimination exist. They exist and they cause a lot of suffering. Moreover, if you do your methodological homework, you can obtain scientific knowledge about them. Social science advances and tests propositions about civil war, poverty, terrorism, and gender discrimination. To some degree, "epistemic objectivity" can be achieved.[27]

At the same time, social scientists would say that the mode of existence of these entities and phenomena is distinctive. It's dependent on societies, on institutions and language, on classificatory practices. It's dependent on us. Natural kindness doesn't fit with social scientists' intuitive inclinations or dispositions. Their objects of inquiry don't have natural kind status; they're 'socially constructed.'

My guess is that, if social scientists are openly and articulately asked about metaphysical realism, most would repudiate it. Few would be down with theses 1 through 5. Fewer would be down with Plato. Social scientists do ask 'what-is-F?' questions and make 'what-F-is' statements in their work. But they aren't fully clear about their ontological commitments—that is, things the existence of which they're committing themselves to by virtue of having asked that question or made that statement. Nor are they fully clear about their meta-ontological commitments—that is, views about ontology and ontological inquiry they're committing themselves to. For understandable reasons, few social scientists analyze what their question or statement entails about the nature of the social world. Yet, once they see what their endeavors require, once they realize the metaphysical taxes they'd be charged, they probably wouldn't want to pay them. So, by these social scientists' own lights, 'what is F?' should be abandoned.

As I said, I don't have representative data on social scientists' beliefs. Instead, I'm tapping my experience. My membership in social science communities and my participation in social science practices. Besides, I'm suggesting that these beliefs and intuitions are widespread, not universal, yet I can't quantify this. In my defense, I think well-informed informants would share my assessment. Knowledgeable community members' estimates are likely to be similar to mine. But this is itself a guess.

Third line of argument: in social science literatures, 'what is F?' confronts serious methodological obstacles. When two 'what-F-is' claims are at odds

27. Searle 1995.

with each other, social scientists aren't equipped to resolve disagreements whose core isn't empirical but ontological. True, they can appeal to facts about the social world—for example, whether neoliberal policies intensify inequalities, where religious participation is growing, how diverse French firms are, and whether contemporary civil wars are deadlier than their modern counterparts. (They may appeal to facts about language use, too, as demanded by some approaches to language and ontology.) Whatever you do with these facts, though, they won't tell you what neoliberalism, religion, civil war, and diversity are, and thus what they're instantiated by. They can't decide whether Menem's administration in Argentina was neoliberal and whether Umbanda is a religion.

Social scientists lack methods or techniques to answer 'what-is-*F*?' questions. Their arguments and discussions are methodologically at a loss, as attested by countless articles, special issues of journals, and conferences. Confusion and standoffs are recurrent. By contrast, for philosophers, especially metaphysicians, it's normal working conditions to wrestle with questions nobody has a clue how to go about answering. Absence of definite, predetermined methods is business as usual. They won't be daunted or disheartened.

Indeed, philosophy has been characterized as the investigation of problems for which there aren't such methods, and/or problems whose formulation isn't clear yet. Philosophers may begin a project not knowing for sure what it is they're trying to find out, never mind how. Once problems get well formulated and suitable methods are developed, they're ipso facto forwarded on: from the desks of philosophers to the desks of scientists. To each their own! Philosophers do talk about 'method' and 'philosophical methodology,' but in a broader sense than scientists.[28] Philosophical methodology is about how to do philosophy well. It's not looking to devise codified techniques. Mechanical formulas or recipes are out of the question. (But then, maybe scientific methodology isn't or shouldn't be any different?)[29]

'What-is-*F*?' questions put social science in a place that it's seldom in. A place where social scientists aren't trained to be. Metaphysics is a specialized field of inquiry. It can be done well or badly. But that's not taught in social science graduate programs. A place that's probably strange and awkward for social scientists to be in, because the scientific method isn't king, and the empirical world isn't the final arbiter. Worse, experiments become thought experiments, speculation and uncertainty are unavoidable, and intuitions and congruence with common sense might be decisive. Not to mention that philosophers'

---

28. Cappelen, Gendler, and Hawthorne 2016; D'Oro and Ovegaard 2017; Haug 2014.
29. Cf. A. Kaplan 1964, 406–10.

pronouns 'we,' 'our,' and 'us' can make social scientists uncomfortable. 'What seems to us plausible or reasonable.' 'What makes sense to us.' The worry is that 'we' actually refers to the author, their friends, colleagues, and students. Social scientists are generalization and sampling experts, so they suspect a more representative 'we' wouldn't be homogeneous and wouldn't share the author's intuitions and feelings.[30]

If a social scientist wishes to address ontological questions about the nature of F, they're free to do so. At the time of this writing, this is still a free country. But they'd be doing metaphysics, engaging metaphysicians' scholarship, following the rules of that game—which are unlike the rules of sociology, history, political science, and psychology.[31] In this game, other moves are permitted and forbidden, admired and scorned. Other metrics determine who wins. They'd succeed or fail qua metaphysicians. Good luck with that.

———

Social scientists aren't methodologically qualified to address 'what-is-F?' questions. Their motivation is empirical and their resources, equipment, and training are tailored accordingly. It's not a good idea for them to get involved in ontology. At least, my argument shifts the burden of proof. So you wanna make a strong statement about what F really is? What's the true nature of capitalism, religion, populism, altruism, artificial intelligence, mental health, or gender? So you wanna criticize other people's 'concept' or 'definition' of it: it's wrong, false, that's not what F really is? Then you must be able to explain how such questions can be addressed in social science, by social scientists: what exactly they get at, what it is to get them right, and how to adjudicate disagreements. I don't know that you can pull it off, but either way it's your responsibility to try and justify the point of your inquiry.

At first glance, 'what is F?' seems like a natural question. It resonates with a natural account of social scientists' work. Experts on F know what it is. It resonates with Western societies' tacit metaphysical picture, in which independently existing objects have properties and essences.[32] Objects are something like substances, which persist in time, despite undergoing change. If you

———

30. This worry doesn't entail cognitive relativism or subjectivism, or skepticism about rationality and reasonableness. But these views have been attractive to sociologists, anthropologists, and historians, who study variation in epistemic norms and in standards of truth and rationality. See Abend 2008b; Gellner 1985; Hollis and Lukes 1982; Jarvie 1984; Lukes 1967, 2008.

31. Brick et al. 2022.

32. Cf. O. Abbott 2020; Emirbayer 1997; Powell and Dépelteau 2013; Priest 2009; Westerhoff 2007.

start with a thing, it makes sense to ask what this thing is. Culturally, it makes total sense to ask what love is, what multiculturalism is, what socialism is, or what art is. Magazines, podcasts, art exhibits, movies, and friends at bars and cafés talk about the nature of friendship, intelligence, and trust. They discuss what F is. Ontology at the bar.

I've argued that 'what is F?' is a deficient question for social scientists. It's repeatedly led them to blind alleys. This isn't the sort of thing they'll benefit from exploring. Nor are they well prepared to take it up. My intention isn't to substitute a preferable ontology, but to pack up and leave this sphere. Turn from ontology to semantics/language use. My take will better fit social scientists' objectives, interests, and abilities. Their own beliefs, too.

7.4 Descriptively and normatively

The words 'theory,' 'theoretical,' and 'theorize' have lots of uses. Compare the journals *Political Theory* and *Journal of Economic Theory*: political theorists are Hobbes and Rousseau virtuosi; economic theorists are math wizards. Enter literary theorists, sociological theorists, social theorists, comparative and historical sociologists, demographers, and ethnographers. They all produce 'theory,' they all 'theorize,' but not in the same sense of the word. These words have positive valence. 'Theoretically informed' is a compliment, while 'atheoretical' and 'undertheorized' are reproaches. In some disciplines, 'atheoretical' papers shall not be published.

In my article "The Meaning of 'Theory,'" I zeroed in on sociology. I argued that it's an error to believe "that theory is an object out there that our concepts or language can track down." It's erroneous to suppose "that there is something—indeed, one thing—out there for the word 'theory' to really correspond to. Then, if one used the word to refer to anything but *that* object, whatever it turned out to be, one would be mistaken."[33] Therefore, I urged sociologists to replace 'what is theory?' with 'how is "theory" used?' and 'how should "theory" be used?' While I've changed my mind about some aspects of this article, I think the basic arguments are on target and aren't limited to 'theory.'

Activity WF doesn't concern itself with objects in the world, but with words and expressions in a language, such as the language of a social science community. It asks what they should mean or how they should be used ('semantics: normatively'). However, a prior issue is what they actually mean or how they're actually used ('semantics: descriptively'). There's no conflict between the

---

33. Abend 2008a, 176, 182.

former and the latter, but cooperation. Cooperation, but not as equals: there's a hierarchy as far as *Activity WF* is concerned. By the 'priority' of descriptive semantics I don't mean it's fundamental, but propaedeutic. The bigger challenge is normative.

Semantics: descriptively

The goal of a descriptive semantics approach is to find out how a word (or expression) is used in a social science community, by speakers of a social science language. Typically, you'll examine a word that's central in a literature or field, but appears to be polysemous, so elucidating its meanings and uses is profitable. You'll have to specify a time frame, too. You're interested in German political scientists' uses of the word '*Kapitalismus*' since the 1960s. What is meant by 'theory' in contemporary sociology, management and organization studies, higher education research, archaeology, or biology.[34] You set out to examine 'race' in anthropology and biology. The "travels and adventures" of 'serendipity.' The meanings of 'diversity,' 'racism,' 'social class,' 'method,' or 'mechanism' in recent US sociology, or in sociology elsewhere.[35]

In short, you'll empirically investigate the uses of a social science word. Your investigation is about lexical semantics. It's like writing an entry for a dictionary of a language, which happens to be the specialized language of a community of social scientists. It's a specialized dictionary, a terminological dictionary or glossary. The community in question might be a discipline, institutionalized in universities and associations, such as sociology or political science. Or it might be a thematic literature, disciplinary or interdisciplinary, such as the literature on happiness, empathy, or power.

The real pros are lexicologists and lexicographers. This is what they do for a living.[36] 'Lexicology' might be defined as "the scientific investigation of the lexicon."[37] Lexicography is expressly about dictionaries. A *Dictionary of Lexicography* defines it as "the professional activity and academic field concerned with DICTIONARIES and other REFERENCE WORKS. It has two basic

---

34. Abend 2008a; Bargheer 2017; Hamann and Kosmützky 2021; Levine 1997; Marradi 1989; Pigliucci, Sterelny, and Callebaut 2013; Rapoport 1958; Sandberg and Alvesson 2021; M. Smith 2011.

35. Aviles and Reed 2017; Knight and Reed 2019; Merton and Barber 2004; Morning 2011; Shiao and Woody 2021; Swedberg 2021.

36. Atkins and Rundell 2008; Durkin 2016; Fuertes-Olivera 2018; Landau 2001; Svensén 2009; Tarp 2008.

37. Klein 2001, 8764.

divisions: lexicographic practice, or DICTIONARY-MAKING, and lexico-graphic theory, or DICTIONARY RESEARCH."[38]

These fields produce, revise, and analyze natural language dictionaries; they focus on natural language words. In addition, there's the neighboring field of terminology, also known as terminology science. And the neighboring field of terminography, also known as terminological lexicography, special or specialized lexicography, or language-for-specific-purposes (LSP) lexicography.[39] These fields produce, revise, and analyze terminological dictionaries; they focus on domain-specific technical terms. Terminography and terminology are sometimes depicted as subdivisions of, respectively, lexicography and lexicology. But caveat emptor: these fields' names haven't been terminologically stable, which doesn't bode well for the rest of us, mere mortals. If *they* can't stabilize their own names . . .

The practice of lexicography is a good model for *Activity WF*'s descriptive step. Social scientists can learn from lexicographic approaches and best practices, which have been tested in many languages and over the course of millennia. Lexicographers' inquiries into the meaning of words and expressions are descriptive, not prescriptive. Like regular empirical science. They observe people's behavior and groups' norms. They gather and analyze data, such as language corpora. They make generalizations based on samples, which further evidence may confirm, disprove, or qualify.

For example, lexicographers may investigate what '*zapatilla*' means in Peninsular, Argentine, and Uruguayan Spanish. What the norms and practices of speech communities are, such that, in certain contexts, if you uttered '*zapatilla*' you wouldn't be understood. Even more, you'd be presumed to be a gringo or *guiri*, as the case may be. Lexicography furnishes descriptions of language behavior that are taken to be correct (natural, effective, felicitous) in a community. In turn, these descriptions may come in handy if you'd like to communicate in Spanish and not come across as a gringo (or *guiri*). Purchasing a dictionary will help you communicate in Montevideo and will help lexicographers make a living.

Lexicographers don't decide what '*zapatilla*' ought to mean, and then enforce their decree in Madrid, Buenos Aires, or Montevideo. They don't make the rules in their offices and meeting rooms, but record what people say and do. They're like Anscombe's detective, who records if a person buys butter or margarine:

38. R. Hartmann and James 1998, 85. See also Cruse 2001; Geeraerts 2016; Klein 2001.

39. Bergenholtz 1995; Humbley 1997. See also Hartmann and James 1998, 139–40. On Eugen Wüster and terminology, see Campo (2012) and Felber (1980).

Let us consider a man going round a town with a shopping list in his hand. Now it is clear that the relation of this list to the things he actually buys is one and the same whether his wife gave him the list or it is his own list; and that there is a different relation where a list is made by a detective following him about. [...] [I]f the list and the things that the man actually buys do not agree ... then the mistake is not in the list but in the man's performance ... ; whereas if the detective's record and what the man actually buys do not agree, then the mistake is in the record.[40]

Admittedly, these issues are trickier than I've made them out to be up to now. Both the supposed dichotomy between description and prescription, and dictionaries' supposed commitment to descriptivism.[41] For one, there's no dichotomy:

Descriptive and prescriptive can co-exist within a single work (and, indeed, at times within a single entry). The precise point at which descriptivism shades into prescriptivism can at times be difficult to locate. [...] While a general trajectory from prescriptive to descriptive can be identified in the history of dictionary-making, even this exhibits unexpected configurations, especially if agendas of moral and cultural prescriptivism are brought into consideration.[42]

Dictionaries make normatively difficult decisions and have normatively contentious policies, such as labeling a lexical item 'informal,' 'colloquial,' 'slang,' 'non-standard,' 'dialect,' 'obsolete,' 'old-fashioned,' 'dated,' 'archaic,' 'offensive,' 'derogatory,' or 'vulgar'; whether to include or exclude a lexical item in the first place; and how to define socially and politically sensitive lexical items.[43] What are their rationales? Some dictionaries consult experts, who make authoritative expert judgments on rightness and wrongness, correctness and incorrectness. For example, the usage panels of *American Heritage Dictionary, Harper Dictionary of Contemporary Usage,* and the national academy model, like the *Académie française* (est. 1635) and the *Real Academia Española* (est. 1713). A dictionary's staff may have a larger impact on the final product than its committee of experts, notables, and 'immortals.' But the point is their institutionalized existence and its prescriptivist implications.

---

40. Anscombe (1963) 2000, 56.

41. Ottenhoff 1996; D. Skinner 2012; Wells 1973.

42. Mugglestone 2016, 546–47.

43. Balteiro 2011; P. Benson 2001; Brewer 2016; Graham (1973) 1974; Moon 1989; M. Murphy 1991; Norri 2000; Russell 2018a, b, 2021.

Whatever the intentions and beliefs of their authors were, dictionaries go on to play social and cultural roles. They become tools and sources of reasons. They're employed to police language use and discipline offenders—among whom disadvantaged ethnic minorities, immigrants, the poor, colonies, and 'the provinces' are significantly overrepresented. Dictionaries' authority and power are put to various uses. Lexicographers and linguists present the results of empirical research, but social actors can turn their descriptions into prescriptions. Like teachers who turn descriptive into normative semantics. You just have to add one more premise to transform what the case is (or is generally the case, or has been generally the case) into what is right.

These complications notwithstanding, social scientists' descriptive semantics can still follow the basic practices and orientation of lexicographic research. No, there isn't a stark dichotomy between description and prescription. Yes, there are different approaches to lexicographic work. However, lexicographers' basic assignment remains to describe language use. Language as it's spoken and written today.

For the practice of *Activity WF*, descriptive semantics is valuable as far as it goes. It's important to know how 'w' is used in a community. You may find various senses of 'w.' It's a polysemous word (homonymy is less likely).[44] Its senses are related to one another and are difficult to disentangle. You may find semantic confusions and ambiguous uses, which call for disambiguation. You can make a contribution to a social science literature by showing that key word 'w' is ambiguous, and then spelling out its various meanings, senses, or uses. Of this ambiguity people aren't aware, and hence they talk past one another. Alternatively, your contribution can be to show that 'w' is perniciously vague—that is, it has borderline cases and it's uncertain what its extension comprises. Of this vagueness people aren't aware, and hence their claims are imprecise.

All good things. But that's how far the descriptive approach can take you. Suppose you find that sociologists define and use the word 'populism' in three divergent ways. You label them 'populism$_1$,' 'populism$_2$,' and 'populism$_3$.' They don't refer to the same set of political phenomena, regimes, and leaders. They aren't completely different, but still, they produce different results, coefficients, and predictions. As per one sociologist, 'populism' applies to Andrés Manuel López Obrador (AMLO) and Cristina Fernández de Kirchner. That's how they use the word in their research. A second sociologist maintains that

44. Homonyms are etymologically unrelated, like 'bat$_1$' (flying mammal) and 'bat$_2$' (baseball club), or 'mole$_1$' (burrowing rodent) and 'mole$_2$' (naevus). Polysemes have common etymologies and are the product of metaphorical usage.

AMLO and Cristina aren't populists. Neither belongs to the category. As per a third sociologist, AMLO is a populist, but Cristina isn't.

What to do? Is only one of these sociologists right or can they all be right at the same time? The overarching conundrum, which keeps getting in the way, is how the sociological literature on populism should use the word 'populism.' Lexicography can't tell you. *Activity WF* needs normative semantics.

Semantics: normatively

Special issue of the prestigious *Uruguayan Journal of Sociology* (*UJS*) on populism. You'd submitted a paper, but, much to your chagrin, it wasn't accepted for publication. An anonymous referee claimed that some of your 'cases' weren't instances of populism at all. 'It's wrong to lump together Perón, Trump, Orbán, Modi, and Erdoğan,' they wrote in their review.[45] As a result, your data analyses explain not the phenomenon of populism but something else. They didn't say what.

The special issue's lead article isn't empirical. Rather, the author frames it as having 'conceptual' aims. It proposes a novel 'definition' of 'populism,' which greatly enlarges its extension. So much so that Gétulio Vargas, Lula, Bolsonaro, Evo Morales, Chávez, AMLO, Cristina, Macri, Pacheco, and Pepe Mujica all fall under it. The author argues that populism exists in Europe, the Americas, Africa, and Asia. It's more than two millennia old: the Roman *populares* were populists. It can be right-wing, left-wing, or neither. An enormous group. As a counterbalance, the *UJS* editors decided to publish a response article, contending that "this far-reaching definition is a step backward for the field. These are extremely different politicians and political parties, which don't belong together. For many years, scholars have been doing careful empirical work, so that good, empirically based discriminations can be made. But this author's undiscriminating definition throws everything overboard."

One fine sociologist says it's a good definition of 'populism.' Another fine sociologist says it's terrible. These judgments of goodness and badness aren't based on the same criteria of goodness and badness. No wonder there's no consensus.

At this point, things will need to get normative. Normative means being in the 'should,' 'right,' and 'good' business. Being normative about language means prescribing and proscribing, like language teachers, usage guides, and style manuals.[46] As regards ordinary language, this is what 'language mavens' do. Linguists are descriptivists—and conspicuously proud of their descriptivism.

---

45. Cf. Tuğal 2021.
46. Van Ostade 2017, 2019.

Language mavens are prescriptivists.[47] This is "a traditional binary in modern linguistics":

> The descriptive linguist standing in opposition to the prescriptive pundit or 'grammarian.' Descriptive linguists study language change as a natural and inevitable part of any living language. Prescriptive commentators and scholars react to language change, typically with a desire to 'fix' the language: both *fix* in the sense of hold stable (i.e., fix in time) and *fix* in the sense of improve. [...] In linguistics, prescriptivism often serves as a foil: the linguistic 'bad guy,' so to speak.[48]

Language mavens lament the sorry state of the English, Arabic, or French language of their day, which isn't what it used to be. They belong to an age-old "complaint tradition."[49] They make "proposal[s] for correcting... the English tongue."[50] They urge their fellow speakers to speak well, grammatically and semantically. They're passionate about it.

Simple contrasts between good and bad guys are too simple. So are blanket censures of prescriptivism.[51] But linguists are right to point out that language mavens' prescriptivist arguments, their correctness and incorrectness verdicts, aren't well grounded. They misconstrue natural language, how it works, and how it changes. Since language is constantly changing, there's no fixed yardstick and standpoint from which to judge people's speech and writing, and rule that they're in the wrong. To judge that people's acceptable isn't truly acceptable. They aren't speaking 'proper English.'[52] In fact, no individual, no elite committee, no VIP summit can legitimately make such pronouncements.

Can this objection to language mavens be brought to bear on social science communities? I think not. How should 'populism,' 'power,' or 'culture' be used? Which criteria should be used to determine how 'populism,' 'power,' or 'culture' should be used? Which goodness and badness criteria are good and bad? Natural language isn't receptive to these normative questions and regulation prospects. Social scientists' specialized languages might be.

---

47. Newman 1974; Safire 1990; Truss 2003. Cf. Cameron 1995; Crystal 2006; Pinker 1994.

48. Curzan 2014:1, 12.

49. Milroy and Milroy 1999; Watts 2011.

50. Swift 1712.

51. Barber and Stainton (2021, 63): "'linguistic prescriptivist' seems to be a loaded label for which no neutral characterization is possible," so "we propose dropping the label... and talking instead of 'language norming,' by which we mean to include *any attempt to evaluate language use on normative grounds.*"

52. Crowley 1991.

———

Language mavens' prescriptivism isn't top-shelf. Unlike them, conceptual engineers have a sophisticated grasp of language, reference, and representation.[53] Their intent is to ameliorate English words, especially morally, with their cutting-edge philosophical tools. On the other hand, they're less empirically well versed about societies, social structures, and institutions. There's much sociological scholarship that speaks to their ambitions of "implementation" and "activism"; how to make an actual difference and actually change word uses.[54] Scholarship on social, cultural, and institutional change, its explanation, and challenges to it. On social conflict. On the role of organizations and social movements. Trained as analytic philosophers, conceptual engineers are strong on the nature of language, but they're rarely conversant with social science research. This is a pity. While their projects are about words, or representational devices, they necessitate looking at actual social and political conditions, organizations, power, economic interests, and all the usual suspects. Empirical stuff, which varies across time and place. Uruguayan Spanish. Montevideo. 2022.

———

My project isn't about natural languages and causing English or German to change (on which more below). Instead, it's about normatively intervening in the languages of social science communities. These interventions require goodness and badness criteria. 'That's a bad way of using "culture"!' At present, communities' criteria are undetermined and unclear. So are the aims they should serve and their point. For these are conditional normative statements. If you wish to attain this and that, you should use word 'w' according to these three criteria. What goals do they—sociologists of populism, the editors and editorial board of *UJS*, the sociological community at large—wish to attain?

It's equally difficult to locate rights and responsibilities to tackle the uses of 'w.' Where do they lie? Who or what is entitled to take up these tasks? Who or what is organizationally or morally obligated to take them up? Not only are these inclusions and exclusions tricky but, as ever, they can get fishy. You might argue the sociological community is responsible, or the community of speakers of the sociological language. But this seems worrisomely vague. Pinning it down may lead you down a rabbit hole. Maybe it should be up to a smaller

53. Burgess, Cappelen, and Plunkett 2020; Cappelen 2018; Haslanger 2000, 2006.

54. Cantalamessa 2021; Decock 2021; Deutsch 2020; Jorem 2021; Koch 2021b; Pollock 2019; Queloz and Bieber 2022.

community: a more specialized, integrated, organizationally anchored collective entity. Better delimited and more aware of itself as a community. Like the International Astronomical Union (IAU), which was thought to be responsible for 'planet.' Maybe a subfield or subdiscipline (sociology of morality, political sociology, Egyptology), or a smaller interdisciplinary network.

There are other ways of delimiting the community and language; more or less usual, more or less intuitively plausible. Speakers not of the sociological language but only of English-language sociology. To be honest, French and German sociologists make things too messy. Or speakers of American English–language sociology only. British sociologists make things too messy. And don't get me started on Australian, Nigerian, and Jamaican sociologists.

————

As I see things, there are four basic features of a normative semantics approach for social science communities.

First, it tries to make headway in situations like my 'populism' example. Together with descriptive semantics, it hopes to lead to better communication and fewer misunderstandings. To prevent social scientists' semantic muddles. Yet, understanding what someone else said, understanding what everyone says, isn't enough. It may turn out that there's something wrong with someone's using 'w' in that way and for that purpose. The community has to institute good norms (rules, directives, instructions, principles, criteria) for the use of 'w.' Good (satisfactory, acceptable, appropriate, sensible, reasonable) arrangements. How to cash out 'good' is of substantial substantive significance. The devil is in the details.

Second, like methodology, it's about what should be done. What to do, so that scientific research goes well, is well grounded, produces good results, or something along these lines. How to cash out 'goes well' or 'well grounded' is of substantial substantive significance. The devil is in the details.

Third, normative semantics will draw on descriptive semantics. One premise of your normative argument about 'w' is a description of the ways in which the community uses 'w,' in which contexts, and what for. Plus, a description of the ways in which it's been used in the past. Their history or genealogy.[55]

55. You might counter that your view about the practice of normative semantics determines its relationship to descriptive semantics. Point well taken. For you, how 'w' should be used is orthogonal to how 'w' is presently used. If you advance this proposal, the community will consider it. Reasons for and against it will be supplied, including the objections to the argument from stipulation. I'm not in a position to reject it out of hand (though these objections seem to me fatal).

Fourth, it isn't humble about its reach. On the contrary, it claims to be inescapable. Even the view that everyone is free to use 'w' however they wish is a normative semantics proposal. Even the view that nothing should be done about semantic muddles is a normative semantics proposal. For instance, you say that there are three ways of using 'populism' in sociology, but nothing can or should be done about it. Or, nothing can or should be done about it, except making people aware of this semantic fact. Neither of these statements is neutral. Differently put: one person claims that nothing can or should be done about the multiple uses or meanings of 'populism'; another person claims that 'populism$_2$' can and should be favored. The former isn't impartial agnosticism. It isn't 'Archimedean.'[56] Both claims are taking sides. Both are participants in the same realm, sometimes called 'metasemantic.'

As I see things, *Activity WF* is a particular kind of normative semantics endeavor. 'W' is a key word in a social science field or literature. How should it be used? This is a practical reason question for a community. It should be answered through a good collective process. This collective process will serve social science research; it'll help social science communities do their job.

Normativity can be variously grounded; normative considerations are diverse. I claim that morality should be part of the package. Semantic/language use practices ought (in this regard) to be partly guided by moral stuff. Scientific practices ought (in this regard) to be partly guided by moral stuff.

———

I argue that an individual can't establish or decide how to use 'w,' how 'w' is correctly and incorrectly used. I'm an individual, therefore I can't establish or decide this. However, it doesn't follow that I'm condemned to inaction. Collective processes comprise individuals' actions, many individuals' actions, even if the whole ends up being more than the sum of its parts. Collective processes must somehow get started, too. An individual may extend an invitation to others. A first move or step, which other people can respond to. A conversation starter.

56. R. Dworkin 1996.

8

Activity WF and its discontents

What's in a name? That which we call a rose
By any other name would smell as sweet

—SHAKESPEARE, ROMEO AND JULIET, ACT 2, SCENE 2

None of you, facing a text or seated at a play, can resist the temptation of
saying, 'This is THEATRE,' or, 'This is not THEATRE.'

—PASOLINI (1968)[1]

8.1 Trouble

Like civilization, gentrification, and globalization, *Activity WF* has its fair share
of discontents. *Activity DF* devotees envisage a future in which social science
ditches *Activity WF* and we all live happily ever after. They say:

> *Activity WF* is empirically undecidable and speculative. Doesn't it belong
> in philosophy or somewhere in the humanities? I'm a social scientist. My
> job is to discover patterns in the social world. I'm interested in my hypoth-
> eses and models, whether my empirical claims are true, and whether my
> predictions will turn out to be true. I did duly provide my definition of 'w'
> (not its dictionary definition) in my grant proposals, journal articles, and
> conference presentations. But this is a formal accessory, which isn't empiri-
> cally testable. What matters is that my project has delivered novel causal
> explanations, supported by rigorous statistical analyses. Scientists don't
> need *Activity WF* in the least. Only *Activity DF*.

---

1. Pasolini (1968) 2007.

My initial reply is: 'I hear you. I see where you're coming from.' *Activity DF* has much to recommend it. Besides your preferred epistemic payoffs, it promises asepsis and freedom. It seems to allow you to do your own thing, and stay away from messy stuff, like language, 'theoretical' frameworks, conceptual schemes, and never-ending disputes over words.

Except that it doesn't. It won't make you free. It's not free from trouble. One sort of trouble pertains to commensurability, cumulation, and collaboration (see chapter 3). Insofar as researchers' definitions, distinctions, and classifications are stipulations, which each one chooses at will, results won't be commensurable. Collaboration will be burdensome. Outside the ivory tower, society will have no use for findings about your favorite arbitrary class of things, statistically impeccable though they might be. They'll be considered futile exercises. *Activity DF* isn't heaven. *Activity WF* isn't hell.

Activity WF has its fair share of discontents. At the end of the day, I don't think their discontent is defensible. I don't think they're adequately weighing what *Activity WF* does bring to the table. I see why you might prefer to spend your time on *Activity DF* rather than *Activity WF*. Yet, while *Activity DF* spares *you* many difficulties, someone else will have to deal with the difficulties you're conveniently evading. Who wants to be a nimby?

———

Activity WF isn't everyone's cup of tea. Hard-nosed social scientists, hard-working empirical workers, may instinctively find it uninviting. 'That's what theorists spend their time on. Social theorists, political theorists, cultural theorists. Bespectacled, pipe-smoking individuals, who enjoy writing nuanced essays and dropping French and German words at every turn. Not my thing.'

It's true that much 'theory' asks what *F* really is, what a given social thing is, what its essence is. (Less frequently, what the word 'w' means or how it should be used.) Plenty of 'theorists' do pepper their texts with French and German words. But there's another side to the story. Whether it's bespectacled individuals who self-identify as 'theorists' or individuals who don't fit this description, *Activity WF* practitioners are rendering a service for all of social science.

Activity WF serves run-of-the-mill, meat-and-potatoes social science research. It's necessary for empirical research to actually be about the world—and specifically about the phenomena it's intended to be about. For it to reach beyond academic conversations, and fancy-schmancy conferences and journals. To contribute to public policy, by making recommendations about education, immigration, gender, diversity, religion, race and ethnicity, and mental health. Recommendations to international organizations about sustainability, sustainable development goals, corporate social responsibility, and multiculturalism. To be relevant to societies and polities, and consequently merit their financial support. To speak to various publics: the media, civil society, NGOs, business, political activists, and undergraduate students. For public sociology.[2]

Your colleagues in your small subdiscipline yearn for asepsis and freedom. But the rest of the world cares about terrorism, civil war, inequality, religion, and social movements. Nobody cares about 'terrorism$_{SG}$,' 'civil war$_{SG}$,' 'inequality$_{SG}$,' 'religion$_{SG}$,' and 'social movements$_{SG}$.' That is, 'SG,' as some guy stipulatively defined it, in a journal article that only specialists will read. If social science were thus regulated by and oriented toward its internal conventions, it'd become a self-referential game. It'd compromise its raison d'être, its *Daseinszweck*. (I say, while puffing on my pipe.)

I agree that *Activity WF* means trouble. Baleful and recalcitrant kinds of trouble. The very kinds of trouble that motivate this very book. Wars over words won't leave social science alone. They're saddled by dead ends and confusions. Persistent confusions that motivate this very book. So, I can sympathize with *Activity WF*'s discontents. All things considered, though, the call to ditch it isn't persuasive. Social science needs *Activity WF*. My question is how to amend it so that troubles are overcome and stop being disrupting, how it can best serve communities' goal of advancing social science knowledge, producing true knowledge claims about social phenomena. Not merely about 'social phenomena.'

8.2 Merely

> How many Disputes there are in all Arts and Sciences merely about Words.
>
> —WERENFELS (1702)[3]

Some social scientists will balk at *Activity WF* on the grounds that it's merely about words. They won't buy my earlier defense of a semantic approach:

> You reject 'what-is-*F*?' questions, you deny that *F* is a thing that exists out there in the social world, you deny that these are ontological matters. As a consequence, we're left with nothing but mere words and language use. *Activity WF* claims are merely verbal claims. *Activity WF* disputes are merely verbal disputes. No substantive, real, important issue is at stake. That which we call a 'rose' by any other name would smell as sweet.

2. Burawoy 2005.
3. Werenfels (1702) 1711, ix.

Is this line of attack cogent? I don't think so. *Activity WF* is indeed about words. It's about words, but it isn't merely about words.

Is a football spherical? Landon is sure: 'no, it's not!' Marcus is just as certain: 'yes, it is!' Predictable answers, since Landon is American and Marcus is British. They're simply using the word 'football' differently. They both know that the object with which Manchester United and Tottenham Hotspur play is spherical, whereas the object with which the Green Bay Packers and the New York Giants play is oval-shaped. Unfortunately, their heated dispute goes on and on, until the wee hours of the night, as neither realizes where they're going astray—possibly due to their substantial beverage intake at the bar (or pub).

Sometimes disputes are merely about words. Sometimes disputants don't realize that their dispute is merely about words. "Parties A and B are having a merely verbal dispute if and only if they are engaged in a sincere prima facie dispute D, but do not disagree over the subject matter(s) of D, and merely present the appearance of doing so owing to their divergent uses of some relevant portion of language," writes Jenkins.[4] "A merely verbal dispute is one in which the two parties to the dispute don't disagree about any non-verbal facts and only seem to disagree because they mean different things by their words," writes Balaguer.[5]

That 'the whole thing is merely a verbal dispute' is a usual critique in philosophy, the social sciences, and the humanities. Mere 'logomachy,' as people used to say.[6] Much of metaphysics, for instance, has had to deal with it.[7] Does God exist? Do composite objects (i.e., objects that have parts) exist? How about numbers? Holes? Does society exist? When metaphysicians disagree about what does and doesn't exist, one possible explanation is semantic: they don't mean the same thing by 'God,' 'object,' 'numbers,' 'holes,' or 'society.'

Another semantic explanation: they don't mean the same thing by 'to exist' or 'to be.' For "being is said in many ways," as Aristotle said in *Metaphysics* Γ.2.[8] You believe in the 'existence' of societies, a party's vibe, a company's

4. Jenkins 2014b, 456.

5. Balaguer 2020, 1181.

6. Cicero's ([55 BCE] 1942) *On the Orator* I.xi.47: "controversy about a word has long tormented those Greeklings, fonder as they are of argument than of truth." See also Burke 2018; Kivistö 2014; Werenfels (1702) 1711; 1 Timothy 6:4; 2 Timothy 2:14. Logomachy could be compounded by logodaedaly—i.e., "verbal legerdemain" (Bailey 1826, 73).

7. Balaguer 2020; Carnap 1950; E. Hirsch 2005.

8. On Aristotle on being and existence, senses of 'being' vs. kinds of being, and the Greek verb 'to be' ('*einai*'), see Adamson and Galluzzo (forthcoming), Brakas (2011), L. Brown (1994), Hintikka (2004), Kahn (1966), Knuuttila and Hintikka (1986), and Kung (1986).

culture, and individuals' motives—in your sense of 'to exist' or 'to be.' I don't. I believe there 'are' no such things—in my sense of the word. They're just metaphors or ways of speaking.

Take mereology (the philosophical study of parts and wholes). Mereologists like to ask whether the Eiffel Tower has parts, whether a hole has parts, whether objects have both spatial and temporal parts, and whether a bikini, a five-piece rock band, or a multivolume encyclopedia is one thing, appearances to the contrary.[9] They like sandwiches, too.[10] Critics of mereology can paraphrase Aristotle and point out that 'object' and 'part' are also "said in many ways." These semantic facts are to blame for allegedly substantive mereological conflicts between allegedly substantive mereological arguments.

Take epistemology. Epistemologists' foremost problem, ever since Plato's *Theaetetus*, has been what knowledge is and what it is to know something. Their foremost problem, or, less charitably, an obsession they can't let go of. Despite innumerable clever arguments and clever Gettier and Shmgettier cases, they don't seem to have nailed it.[11] Why is that? Critics would argue that these disputes aren't substantive. They boil down to "divergent uses of some relevant portion of language"—namely, the verb 'to know.' I say 'I know that *p*' in my idiolect; Shmgettier says 'I know that *p*' in his. Everyone sticks to their idiolect, so the dispute doesn't get anywhere.

———

A timeless comparison raises analogous concerns: whether non-human animals are essentially different, or essentially similar, to human animals. More and more facts are continuously being discovered, data and analyses become more and more sophisticated, but the basic question keeps arising in the same form. Apparently, human animals can't help but wonder whether (some) non-human animals have morality, language, culture, politics, and agency. Whether (some) non-human animals are intelligent, can learn, grieve, love, and play.[12]

One side says that humans aren't truly unique: there's no difference in kind between human and non-human animals.[13] It's only that humans' language,

9. Casati and Varzi 1994; Van Inwagen 1981; Varzi 2000.

10. K. Fine 1999; Koslicki 2007.

11. Gettier 1963; E. Hirsch 2011, 118.

12. Bekoff and Pierce 2009; Boesch 2012; De Waal 2000; Flack and De Waal 2000; Langlitz 2020; Lents 2016. On the "discontinuities" between human and non-human animals, see, e.g., Penn et al. (2008); Povinelli (2004).

13. Darwin (1871) 1874, 126; cf. M. Boyle 2017.

morality, and politics are much more developed and complex. The other side says that non-human animals are being misleadingly anthropomorphized. Either side may say, if the dispute turns sour, that its antagonists are ideologically biased. They're biased by religion, atheism, evolutionary theory, scientism, politics, or what have you. These are classic controversies in scientific, philosophical, and public forums.[14] Yet, at least sometimes, everyone seems to agree on the facts, so the disagreement is about the correct use of the words 'intelligence,' 'politics,' 'grieve,' or 'play.'

Ethologists have shown that conspecifics cooperate with and help one another. Should these cooperative and helping behaviors be called 'moral'? And if so, 'moral' behaviors or moral behaviors? With or without quotation marks—the former indicating a lesser status than full-fledged morality, you're not speaking literally, it's a metaphorical analogy?[15] Nobody doubts that non-human animals communicate through sounds and movements. Nor that they don't speak any English. Should the word 'language' be used for waggle dances and alarm signals? Should birds and chimpanzees be described as exhibiting 'language' behavior? Their communication would be achieved through a much more rudimentary 'language' than English. But the difference would be one of degree, not of kind.

As divisive as the comparison between human and non-human animals is the comparison between human animals and machines.[16] One side says that AIs are intelligent and are able to think, and algorithms are capable of making moral and immoral decisions. Opponents of these claims cry: 'No, they aren't!' One side says that robots and AIs can truly understand you, in the same way human beings can. Perhaps they don't truly understand you yet; Siri and Alexa aren't technologically there yet. But one day they will. Opponents cry: 'No, they can't and never will! They'll never be able to go beyond responding to inputs as though they understood. This is imitation. It's not the real thing.'

For your part, looking at these controversies from the outside, you wonder: are we sure they don't reside exclusively (or primarily) in the meaning of 'intelligence,' 'to think,' 'morality,' and 'to understand'?

In contemporary scholarship, capacities for agency, decision-making, cognition, and morality show up in even less expected sites. Not only are they attributed to non-human animals and AIs. Ordinary objects, artifacts, and

14. Daston and Mitman 2005; Fitzpatrick 2017; Kennedy 1992; Monsó and Andrews, 2022; Pearson 2017; Rowlands 2012.

15. Figdor 2018; Masserman, Wechkin, and Terris 1964; Quervel-Chaumette et al. 2016; Silberberg et al. 2014.

16. Collins 2018; Dreyfus 1972; Haugeland 1979; Searle 1980; Turing 1950.

scientific instruments may be agents.[17] Plants are believed to make decisions, communicate, remember, and act intelligently.[18] Even a door closer may turn out to be a "highly moral, highly social actor."[19] The ideas of 'material agency' and 'non-human agency' have been gaining currency in anthropology, archaeology, sociology, STS, political theory, the humanities, and (in its own way) plant science. Bolstered by the work of Latour, Callon, Bennett, and Deleuze and Guattari (in their own way).[20] Opponents of these ideas cry: 'that's false!' Angrier opponents cry: 'this is nuts!'

Again, are we sure these controversies don't reside exclusively (or primarily) in the meaning of 'decision,' 'to think,' 'to remember,' 'intelligence,' 'to act,' 'moral actor,' and 'social actor'? Plant scientists do a great job of explaining plants' responses to environmental stimuli, the effects of their competition for light, breaking seed dormancy, and selective seed abortion.[21] Does it matter if the words 'intelligence' and 'decision-making' get used to describe these responses? Can't these disputes be chalked up to your having chosen a peculiar stipulative definition of 'actor'—say, Latour's "any thing that [modifies] a state of affairs by making a difference is an actor"?[22]

Whether a dispute is verbal or substantive may not be obvious. Pinning down what verbalness and substantiveness consist in, and how to tell them apart, is challenging.[23] At any rate, 'mere verbality' works in practice as an accusation, a dismissal, an objection. 'Your claims and disputes are misconceived. You're all wasting your time with issues that turn solely on dissimilar terminologies and uses of language. Go back to work on substantive, important stuff!'

In the social sciences, this accusation can be directed at *Activity WF*. 'It's pointless. It's just about English words, not social reality. Mere terminological matters. Matters of definition. Science is about real things; scientists' objects

17. J. Bennett 2010; Connolly 2013; A. Jones and Boivin 2010; Kohn 2013; Pickering 1993.

18. Calvo et al. 2020; Figdor 2018; Gruntman et al. 2017; Karban 2015; Karban and Orrock 2018; Mancuso and Viola (2013) 2015; Trewavas 2016.

19. Johnson 1988, 198. On microbes' agency, see Latour ([1984] 1988). On actor-network theory's actors, networks, actants, and assemblages, see Latour (2005); Muniesa (2015); and Blok, Farías, and Roberts (2020).

20. Related bodies of work are 'the material turn' or 'the materiality turn,' 'the new materialism,' and 'the ontological turn' in anthropology and STS.

21. Meyer et al. 2014; Topham et al. 2017.

22. Latour 2005, 71. Cf. De Laet and Mol 2000; Law and Mol 2008. That you 'choose' your definition is how Latour puts it.

23. Balaguer 2020; Balcerak Jackson 2013, 2014; Belleri 2018; Chalmers 2011; D. Greco 2015; Jenkins 2014a, b; Vermeulen 2018.

of inquiry are real things. What causes terrorism and civil war, the properties of neoliberalism and creativity, ongoing changes in family structures. But you're merely talking about talk, speaking about speech. Stop talking about that.'

8.3 Verbal and merely verbal

The 'mere verbality!' objection does have much going for it. It can do good by calling attention to "the traps that language sets us."[24] It can prevent confusions caused by "divergent uses of some relevant portion of language."[25] Verbal issues must be straightened out so that substantive issues can be well construed. Check whether people are using 'liberalism' to refer to different things or are applying 'poverty' differently in borderline cases. Whether their key words are ambiguous or vague. Whether their idiolects diverge in more intricate ways. Subsequently, you can assess if the substantive issue, or a part thereof, remains.

At a basic level, this is good old clearing the ground. It's getting irrelevant stuff out of the way, and dissolving spurious problems. Also: sharpening the question under consideration, what exactly you're asking, what's worth attending to and focusing on. Consider the abortion and euthanasia controversies. A usual word is 'life.' Its role in the discussion, however, may be misunderstood.

Lexicographers and language teachers are interested in 'life' in and of itself. The former in ordinary uses of it. The latter in their students' mistakes. Elsewhere, lexicographers and language teachers are interested in '*Leben*,' '*vida*,' or '*vita*.' By contrast, what societies are agonizing over isn't language. What they must address and come to agree on, what makes people distressed and uncertain, what morality and the law must regulate, isn't language. Rather, it's the conditions under which ending a pregnancy is permissible, and the conditions under which switching off a ventilator, withdrawing medical treatment, or withdrawing artificial hydration and nutrition is permissible—whatever 'life' might mean. In this sense, the word 'life' is a mere instrument, a means to an end. This instrument may be used or misused. You may have moral and political reasons to prefer this or that use. A society or community has reason to use 'life'—and encourage the use of 'life'—in such a way that its norms are upheld and its ends are furthered. But these norms and ends aren't semantic. In this sense, that which we call a 'burrito' by another other name would taste as delicious.

---

24. Austin 1957, 7–8.
25. Jenkins 2014b, 456.

The 'mere verbality!' objection can do a great deal of good by exposing sophistry, demagogy, and doublespeak. People who take advantage of the rhetorical, emotional capacities of language to advance reprehensible particularistic interests, sell you stuff you don't want or need, keep you watching or scrolling down, and other morally shady ends. Surely no decent person would want to be (and be seen as being) against 'life.' Surely no US person would want to be (and be seen as being) against 'choice.' Words' positive or negative connotations can be exploited by psychological techniques, which advertising, marketing, and public relations professionals excel at. They become an obstacle to rationality, a wrong turn. Because of effective rhetoric and persuasion, the real issue gets out of sight.[26]

The 'mere verbality!' objection can do a great deal of good, too, where disputants don't realize that their dispute is merely verbal. As in Landon's 'football$_{\text{American English}}$' and Marcus's 'football$_{\text{British English}}$.' Such oversights also happen in loftier locales than bars (or pubs). They do happen in social science seminar rooms, conferences, committee meetings, books, and journals. (Whether these locales are loftier than bars you can decide for yourself; beware of merely verbal disputes caused by 'lofty.')

To detect verbalness, Chalmers recommends the "method of elimination":

> When faced with a dispute that is potentially verbal with respect to a term *T*, one can simply ask the parties: can you state what you are disagreeing about without using (or mentioning) *T*? Or can you at least state some part of the debate this way? If the parties can do this, and if the resulting debate is nonverbal, this is strong evidence that the original dispute had substantive elements. If they cannot, then it is evidence that the original debate was wholly verbal.[27]

If Landon and Marcus tried to state their disagreement without the word 'football,' they'd realize they agree about the shape of footballs. Call it what you want. Whatever you call them, this object over here (worshipped by US people) is oval-shaped, whereas that object over there (worshipped by people all over the world) is spherical. Chalmers's method would quickly set things straight.

Yet, as Chalmers observes, "verbal issues often have serious practical import." In these situations, the method of elimination isn't apt, because "term *T*" is at the heart of the issue. *T* itself. *Its* extension. The set of things *it* refers to. Therefore, *T* can't be replaced:

---

26. Bolinger 1980; Herman and Chomsky 1988; Lutz 1989; Stanley 2015.
27. Chalmers 2011, 529.

Sometimes words matter. Disputes over words are sometimes important disputes, when something important rests on matters of linguistic usage. [...] What counts as 'torture' or as 'terrorism' might be, at one level, a verbal issue that a philosopher can resolve by distinguishing senses. But in a rhetorical or political context, words have power that transcends these distinctions. If the community counts an act as falling into the extension of 'torture' or 'terrorism,' this may make a grave difference to our attitudes toward that act. As such, there may be a serious practical question about what we *ought* to count as falling into the extension of these terms.[28]

The legal and political histories of 'torture,' 'terrorism,' and 'marriage' are good illustrations. The law is a good source of illustrations, because of its evident lexical semantic bases. They're dramatically evident where verdicts and sentences hinge on what word 'w' is taken to refer to, and the "Courts ... act as an animated and authoritative dictionary."[29] But the point isn't about the law. It's about the whole of communities' social and political life. Their organizational and economic arrangements. Their social practices and political institutions. Natural language words matter and have effects in and of themselves. Linguistic usage matters and has effects in and of itself. People, groups, and organizations have reason to care about words' meanings and uses in and of themselves.[30] Social science does, too.

———

Social relations, practices, norms, and institutions are dependent on language use. 'Dependent' is a catchall word in this context, which encompasses diverse relationships—as diverse as the uses and functions of language themselves are. To get a feel for this diversity, think of what sociolects, jargons, polite speech, gendered and gender-inclusive language, and formal and informal registers can do. Think of poems, puns, word play, and humor. Baby talk, euphemisms, and nonsense. Doublespeak. 'Empty signifiers' and 'floating signifiers.'[31] Labeling and looping effects—where the exact words with which you get labeled and categorized, and then recognize and identify yourself as, make a major difference.[32] Think of the role of language in social processes such as in-group/out-group distinctions, identity claims, solidarity, and nationalism.

28. Chalmers 2011, 516–17.
29. Macmillan 1937, 163.
30. Bolinger 1980; McConnell-Ginet 2008, 2020.
31. Laclau 1996, 2005; Lévi-Strauss 1950.
32. Hacking 1995, 1999.

Status distinctions, discrimination, cultural capital, and symbolic violence. Collective memory and emotions.

Language can be put to work in many ways.[33] There are many things you can do with words. Everyday things, like smooth social interactions, without embarrassment, without embarrassment over embarrassment.[34] Performative things, like illocutionary acts, if you utter the right words in the right place at the right time.[35] Say 'I'm sorry about that' and you'll have apologized. Say 'I bet you 50 bucks Uruguay will defeat Paraguay tomorrow' and you'll have made a bet. Say 'I do,' both of you, and you guys will be married. Say 'I name this ship "the Queen Elizabeth,"' "as uttered when smashing the bottle against the stem," and a ship will ipso facto be called 'the Queen Elizabeth.'[36]

These themes are explored day in and day out in the fields of pragmatics, sociolinguistics, conversation analysis, ethnomethodology, rhetoric, literary and cultural studies, and a good deal of ethnographic research in anthropology and sociology. The take-home point for my argument is that linguistic usage is crucial, and specifically the precise combinations of words and expressions used. Only some of them will do the trick, work interactionally and conversationally, provided their delivery is satisfactory.[37] Only some will be felicitous, given the relevant felicity/social/cultural conditions.

The use of word 'w' makes a difference, above and beyond its semantic content and function.[38] Its very utterance, since 'w' has intrinsic effects. Various factors and mechanisms may be at play: a word-form's having specific properties in a language, connotations, genealogy and etymology, aesthetic and phonetic features, and its triggering emotions and associations. Word-forms have histories, which are known to language users, or are otherwise psychologically present. They're embedded in institutions and practices. 'W' can be any kind of word. An illustrative kind (though atypically extreme) is slurs and taboo words. They're intrinsically offensive or cringeworthy, like the n-word.[39]

---

33. Jakobson 1960; Nuyts 1989, 1993; Searle 1995, 2010. Classifications of the functions of language rely on accounts of its nature and origins, but that's a story for another occasion.

34. Goffman (1955) 1967.

35. Austin 1962; Heffern 2008; Langton 1993; Medina 2022; Searle 1989. See also Faraone 1995; Martín Hernández and Torallas Tovar 2014; Tambiah 1968.

36. Austin 1962, 5.

37. Goffman (1974) 1986, 1981; Grice 1989.

38. Per chapter 4, I'm using 'word' as a rough-and-ready tool, disregarding its ambiguities. It can be a string of letters, string of sounds, word-form, lexeme, or lexical item or unit; it can be a type or a token.

39. Allan and Burridge 2006; Díaz-Legaspe 2020; Hom 2010; Jay 2009; Jeshion 2021.

Such 'lexical effects' are widespread, as Cappelen points out: "Expressions have effects beyond what philosophers and linguists classify as their semantic and pragmatic effects. An expression can have cognitive and emotive effects over and beyond (and in some sense independently of) any of its semantic and pragmatic properties." His examples include 'marriage,' 'rape,' 'organic,' 'hacker,' 'refugee,' and 'combatant.'[40] They're well chosen to underscore the intertwinement between language, organizations, and the law. These are noteworthy intertwinements, but the bottom line is that lexical effects are all around us.

8.4 Struggles

An important property of natural language is that it's not up to any individual.

It's not up to you how 'cool,' 'friend,' or 'queer' can be used in American English today. There are conditions under which uttering 'that's a cool thing,' 'they're friends,' or 'I'm queer' wouldn't be adequate. You wouldn't be understood. You'd be thought to be a foreigner or a crazy person. These conditions have social consequences. There are conditions under which certain words and expressions would convey undesired emotions, spark undesired feelings. You don't need to be talking about sensitive political or moral problems. People feel strongly about the extension of 'world music,' 'opera,' 'sport,' and 'sandwich,' irrespective of how they affect the law and the finances of Panera Bread and Qdoba Mexican Grill.

In addition, everyday discourse differs from philosophically curated discourse. Philosophers evaluate the effects of problematic words by means of rational analysis. They disambiguate ambiguous words, and consider eliminating them for the sake of argument. They take their time. In everyday conversations, people can't interject commentaries on method and logic, employ elaborate analytical techniques, and thus sidestep mere verbality. This isn't an option in social interactions and social life. Language can't be put to one side. The reason is twofold.

First, right now you aren't in a philosophy or linguistics seminar room. Nobody's heard of David Chalmers. People are trying to put a substantive point across, get something done, perform a social action. They want their speech act to succeed. They have no time or patience for meta- and meta-meta-points. The topic of the conversation isn't language, lexicology, or semantics. Never mind metasemantics.

Second, 'w' can't be analytically separated from the problem. In social life, the correctness of uses of 'queer,' 'slut,' 'populist,' or 'terrorist' is precisely what

40. Cappelen 2018, 123, 128.

the fight is about—even if people don't put it this way and aren't clear about it. There are different ways of using 'w,' and what's contested is which one or ones to favor. People are committed to 'w' itself, their way of using it, and the ends and values 'w'—their way of using 'w'—helps realize. Explicitly or more often implicitly, lexical semantics is driven by such forces and motives. Social, psychological, cultural, political forces.

You're committed to this use of 'queer,' because it helps accomplish progressive ideas and gender policies, advocated by your organization. You're committed to this use of 'terrorism,' in whose extension falls a group you despise: Antifa, Proud Boys, PLO, or Irgun. You'll defend these uses in the public sphere, in a courtroom, on social media, at the café and at the bar. This is normal social life. People don't have to be aware of the relationships between word uses and their moral and political values.

—————

An important property of natural language is that it's not up to any individual.

Dystopian dictators, totalitarian regimes, and Big Brothers have a dream: they dream of controlling language and meaning at will. This would give them a lot of power. Power over legal and political issues, but also socially and culturally, which can consolidate their domination in a profound manner.[41] They could make inconvenient words and expressions disappear. Systematically equivocate. Deploy their absolute semantic powers to obfuscate inconvenient issues. Manipulate people's beliefs about reality through strategic manipulation of meaning.[42]

Had these strategies been effective, it'd be widely believed that the Democratic People's Republic of Korea is democratic and the German Democratic Republic was democratic. When the United States supports brutal tyrants, it'd be believed to be promoting democracy and freedom. 'Concentration camps,' 'rightsizing,' and 'enhanced interrogation techniques' would succeed at concealing what they really stand for.[43] Trump would have gotten away with his statement in June 2020 that 'tear gas' wasn't used on crowds of protesters. War would be peace and freedom would be slavery. It'd be a dreamland for winners of the Doublespeak Award.[44]

41. Lukes 2021a, b.

42. Klemperer (1947) 1995; Lutz 1989; Orwell (1949) 1984.

43. Beard and Cerf 2015.

44. "The Doublespeak Award," National Council of Teachers of English, n.d., https://ncte.org/awards/doublespeak-award/.

Fortunately, this is only a dream/nightmare. In fact, natural languages can't be controlled and steered in the total fashion totalitarian dictators wish. Natural language is to a large degree autonomous, immune to top-down commands, undisciplined and ungovernable. Meanings and uses are dynamic. They're collective. They diffuse spontaneously throughout society. Expressions' acceptance and spread are social processes, for which no underground organizations and leaders are responsible. Hence, there's nobody for dictators to censor and torture (to subject to 'enhanced interrogation techniques').

I did say "to a large degree." Sometimes it *is* possible to have some effect on language use, and thereby boost your political ambitions and weaken your enemies. Sociolinguists and sociologists of language investigate language policies, management, planning, engineering, and regulation—of which national standardization, the production of one language for the nation, is a prototypical example. These policies are designed to serve the interests of the state.[45] But other actors may also endeavor to bring about language change. Social movements, political groups, business gurus, public intellectuals, and activists. Advertising agencies, television and movie stars, hip hop artists, and influencers. They can introduce neologisms and try to get others to use them. Try to stigmatize words and expressions they deem harmful. Condemn slurs and ill-intentioned euphemisms. If they're lucky, and skillful, and have prestige and resources, they may influence others. To some degree. Their efforts may have an impact on natural language.

What of dystopian dictators, who have total power over society, schools, and the media, and no discernible integrity or scruples? Assuming they're more or less competent, their language edicts and policies can be backed up by effective communication and indoctrination mechanisms, along with effective surveillance, repression, and punishment. In the long run, they may indeed increase the frequency of desired expressions and decrease the frequency of undesired ones. However, not even Big Brother is able to fully control natural language. Official edicts won't change what words mean. Totalitarian dictators aren't in a position to accomplish that, their totalitarianism notwithstanding. They don't have the means or authority for that, their abundant means and absolute authority notwithstanding. That's the nature of meaning and meaning change, and its capacity to go its own way—compare with dictators' ability to declare wars and name battleships. A fortiori, it's a long shot for movie stars and influencers to influence words' meanings and uses. There's only so much you can do.

There's only so much you can do, but you can do something. Plus, people may overestimate the degree to which something can be done. Either way,

---

45. Robert Cooper 1989; Spolsky 2004, 2009, 2012; Weng 2018, 2020.

some people do try and do something. In many historical contexts, language becomes the object of social and political struggles (besides being a tool to carry out social and political projects, and an expression or reflection of social processes). These struggles aren't only about semantics, but also involve grammar, spelling, pronunciation, and style.[46] They might concern the legitimacy of a language or 'dialect,' their appropriateness for a given purpose, and whether what you're speaking is a language or dialect to begin with. As the 'Weinreich witticism' has it, a language is a dialect with an army and a navy.[47] Tough luck if you lack an army, you're an underprivileged minority, or you "are the border."[48]

As with any social struggle, there are many interested parties: organizations, groups, and individuals; political groups, religious groups, and social movements; educators and lexicographers; politicians, judges, and professional associations. They all have interests in how things turn out—language things, and in particular semantic things. But they haven't necessarily articulated their interests (as political parties' demands, programs, and promises). Parties' starting points are unequal. Resources are at stake.[49]

The outcomes of these struggles, as with any social struggle, are contingent. They can be partly accounted for by contending actors' power, status, position, capital. Some people and organizations are more successful than others. Yet, this process is unlike a political revolution and subsequent regime change, where a king is overthrown and a republic is founded soon thereafter. Language

46. Bourdieu 1991; Boutet 2016; Cameron 1995; García, Flores, and Spotti 2017.

47. In fact, the witticism is due to "a Bronx high school teacher," who told Weinreich in Yiddish: "A shprakh iz a dialect mit an armey un flot." Weinreich recorded it in a 1945 article (Maxwell 2018, 264).

48. Severo 2010, 2019. Severo's poem "Sixty," originally in Portuñol, was translated by Laura Cesarco Eglin and Jesse Lee Kercheval in the *New Yorker* (Severo 2019). On African-American Vernacular English (AAVE), or 'ebonics,' see "LSA Resolution on the Oakland 'Ebonics' Issue," drafted by John R. Rickford, Linguistic Society of America, January 1997, https://www.linguisticsociety.org/resource/lsa-resolution-oakland-ebonics-issue.

49. Sociologists and linguists do research on social actors' fights over language, and how it reflects social realities and inequalities. Ever the combat sportsman, Bourdieu (1991, 44, 37) finds fault with linguists who "merely incorporate into their theory a pre-constructed object, ignoring its *social laws of construction* and masking its social genesis." Saussure "treats language as an object for contemplation rather than an as instrument of action and power. [...] [O]ne must not forget that the relations of communication *par excellence*—linguistic exchanges—are also relations of symbolic power in which the power relations between speakers or their respective groups are actualized." Speech act theory gets a more sympathetic treatment, but doesn't emerge unscathed either (see also Rosaldo 1982).

change is slow and it's controllable only to a limited extent. Social actors' actions and intentions have limited efficacy.

8.5 Social science

Social science fields use specialized languages: the language of comparative politics, demography, moral psychology, or economic sociology. But these are largely intelligible to English speakers—as long as they can get past the technical terms and jargon, "verbal false limbs" and "pretentious diction."[50] The similarities between social science languages and English invite epistemological doubts and self-consciousness. You may doubt whether they're distinct languages at all, as opposed to English supplemented with a few neologisms, Latinisms, or mathematical symbols, as the case may be. At this juncture, scientism and physics envy tend to kick in. Particle physics and molecular biology aren't believed to be substantively reliant on English. The social sciences are, which discredits their scientific credentials and legitimacy.[51]

Simplifying quite a bit, I imagine 'the sociological language' to be the language used by sociologists to express and communicate their work. The language of their scholarly articles, books, and presentations. There's a community, the sociological community, that speaks this language. 'The anthropological language' refers to the language of anthropologists' work. There's 'the conversation analysis language,' 'the comparative politics language,' 'the empathy research language,' and so on. I'm not saying I have a method to individuate these languages and communities. There's not one sociological community and one sociological language, but many overlapping communities and subcommunities. Each of them could be argued to have a language. Their boundaries are fuzzy. There are organizationally recognized subdisciplines, but not all subdisciplines have organizational recognition. There are interdisciplinary communities. There are sociologists writing sociology in English in the United States, in English in the United Kingdom, in English in Australia, in French in France, in French in Canada, in Hebrew, in Spanish.

Moreover, sociologists aren't speaking the sociological language all the time. They don't speak to their families and to baristas in it. What language are they speaking to undergraduate students, deans, podcasters, journalists, and

---

50. Orwell (1946) 1968, 130, 131; see also Andreski 1972; Sorokin 1956.

51. According to this line of thinking, scientific propositions necessitate their own language. Natural languages are defective. They're fine for ordinary communication, poetry, and humor, but not for science. While the theories of true sciences are formal and mathematically expressed, the social sciences are overdependent on natural language.

policy makers? How can you tell? Do interdisciplinary and multidisciplinary teams have their own language? And then there's the challenge of determining who counts as a sociologist in the first place, and the politics of community membership (more on this below).

This is all quite hard to sort out and far from innocuous. It probably can't be settled to everyone's satisfaction. In any event, *Activity WF* is about these specialized languages. It's about key words for social science fields or communities. While 'w' is also an English word, like 'diversity' or 'race,' the issue is how to use it in social science language *L*. The following are typical characteristics of 'w' in language *L* and community *C* (or typical initial conditions):

(1) 'W' has a long historical trajectory in *L*, in the social sciences more generally, and even earlier, in philosophy and social thought. The history of the field is full of theories of and claims about 'w.'

(2) The meanings and uses of 'w' have been controversial in *C*. Community members use it in divergent ways. There are also explicit disputes over it: how to correctly use 'w,' or what it means, or how to define it. However, these disputes are couched in ontological language, as being about what *F* is (the thing 'w' is supposed to refer to).

(3) 'W' has a long historical trajectory in society at large, too.

(4) The meanings and uses of 'w' have been controversial in society. Policy makers, politicians, journalists, and organizations use it in divergent ways. There are also explicit disputes over it: how to correctly use 'w,' or what it means, or how to define it. However, these disputes are couched in ontological language, as being about what *F* is (the thing 'w' is supposed to refer to).

(5) Social scientists intend their claims about 'w' to have implications beyond the ivory tower. Your immediate audiences are scholars, members of *C*, who read scholarly journals and attend scholarly conferences. But you hope that policy makers, educators, therapists, the business world, judges, lawmakers, the media, and social media will eventually take note.

(6) 'W' plays important institutional and cultural roles in *C*, and sometimes in other social science communities as well. It occurs in the names of subfields, journals, endowed chairs, and awards. Literatures may be organized around it and job ads may use it: our department is looking for someone who does research on 'w,' or someone who specializes in the sociology of 'w.'

(7) 'W' plays important roles in society at large, too. Policy makers, NGOs, judges, the media, and various publics ask for knowledge about 'w.' 'W' is routinely used in organizational, legal, and cultural contexts.

(8) As a result of the preceding points, 'w' (the word-form itself) triggers emotions and associations. It has positive and negative connotations.

(9) Aside from the preceding points, 'w' (the word-form itself) may have lexical effects in *L*, by virtue of its lexical effects in English (or whatever natural language it's taken from).

(10) 'W' may be both descriptive and evaluative. Put differently, 'w' may have evaluative elements built into it. In saying that something is an instance of or falls under the extension of 'w,' you aren't only describing it but also evaluating it. Examples of positive evaluation: 'democracy,' 'freedom,' 'art,' and 'intelligence.' Examples of negative evaluation: 'inequality,' 'populism,' 'neoliberalism,' and 'terrorism.' In this regard, 'w' works like 'thick ethical concepts' and 'appraisive concepts.'[52]

The situation calls for *C* to undertake *Activity WF*. 'W' and the use of 'w' are themselves important. Chalmers's method of elimination can't dissolve the issue.

The importance of 'w' for *C* is based on this community's characteristics and the situation it finds itself in. This isn't the same as the importance 'w' might have outside of scholarship: in society, politics, and the law. In other words, there are reasons specific to *C* such that it should discuss, assess, and make decisions about acceptable uses of 'w.' These reasons may have relations to and be influenced by the broader society, but they aren't reducible to it.

It's a further question how social science communities' *Activity WF* may have an impact on the use of 'w' in a natural language and society at large, and the conditions under which scientific uses may 'trickle down' to society. What seems to me indubitable is that, if *C* knew to have an impact on society, it'd have additional reasons to take *Activity WF* seriously. Sadly, there are way too many sexist and homophobic assholes out there.[53] The correct use of 'gender,' 'woman,' 'queer,' 'sexuality,' and 'perversion' shouldn't be up to them. To the extent that it can, *C* should help weaken and delegitimize their interventions. Sadly, there are way too many racist and xenophobic assholes out there. The correct use of 'race,' 'ethnicity,' 'nation,' and demonyms or gentilics ('American,' 'Swiss,' 'German') shouldn't be up to them. To the extent that it can, *C* should help weaken and delegitimize their interventions.[54]

52. Gallie 1956; B. Williams 1985. One critique of (10) is that no concepts are thick in this sense. Another critique is that all concepts are thick in this sense. For my argument, (10) is optional.

53. A. James 2012; Nunberg 2012.

54. A. Byrne 2020; Dembroff 2021; Díaz-León 2016; Haslanger 2000, 2006; Saul 2006; Simion 2018; Spender 1980; Tirrell 1993.

8.6 Against

You'd have grounds to object to the significance of *Activity WF* if words didn't have lexical effects within scientific communities, disciplines, and fields. But they do. Despite their scientific standing, language *L* and community *C* aren't free from them.

As in many other respects, scientific communities resemble other communities. Their social and political dynamics aren't unique. As for their languages:

> It would be an absurd prejudice to assume that those engaged in 'serious' theorizing are immune to lexical effects. They are obviously not. How we label our views and the choice of central theoretical terms can have all kinds of noncognitive effects that scholars often exploit (for the most part without being aware of doing it). The use of a particular term can be a way to indicate allegiances, trigger associations, make appeal to authority . . . , and sometimes just to show off. [. . .] Roughly, the idea is: *show me which words you use, and I'll tell you who your friends are (or who you want your friends to be)*. We can imagine a (I would say) defective intellectual discipline or practice where the primary goal was to choose grammatical combinations of lexical items *with the right lexical effects*—i.e., the primary goal of writing was to exploit lexical effects.[55]

At times, scholars do seem to intentionally try and make such lexical effects work to their advantage. Other times their words have desirable lexical effects even though they didn't consciously reflect on their word choices. Imagine you're writing a paper, you're in the flow, and you don't stop to assess the consequences, advantages, and disadvantages of using 'w' in your next sentence. You just keep writing.

Although you didn't reflect on your word choice, it'll still have effects, and it can still be sociologically and social psychologically accounted for. Through socialization processes, community members have acquired dispositions to use language in particular ways. They have acquired intuitive, tacit, automatic ways of referring to and talking about things. These practices are neither calculating nor calculated, but their effects are likely to benefit you, your colleagues, friends, and students. Your uses of 'w' are biased in your favor.[56]

Which means inequality—one of sociologists' favorite topics. What benefits Rodríguez might not benefit Fernández. Even more, something may benefit

---

55. Cappelen 2018, 128–29; see also Cappelen 2020, 144. Objection: if someone isn't aware of these "non-cognitive effects," they aren't exploiting them. 'To exploit' requires conscious intention. But perhaps this is a merely verbal dispute.

56. Bourdieu 1984.

Rodríguez because it doesn't benefit Fernández. Rodríguez and Fernández disagree as to how 'w' should be used. As it happens, Rodríguez's view would redound to her benefit. Fernández's view would redound to her benefit. A way forward is needed that isn't partial to either. This is where *Activity WF* comes in.

———

You'd have grounds to object to the significance of *Activity WF* if the social sciences were self-standing systems, whose symbols referred only to its own, internal entities. But they aren't. Lexical effects are of singular import for social science, owing to the intended relationship between social science research and actual social phenomena and processes. (This is an elaboration of characteristics (5) and (9) above.)

Social scientists' claims are typically meant to hook up to the real world. Their research isn't supposed to be about 'democracy,' 'gender fluidity,' and 'digitalization,' but about democracy, gender fluidity, and digitalization. Political scientists hope to make contributions to real-life political processes, advise officeholders and candidates, and shape public policy. The research of public health scholars, social psychologists, and sociologists of education is funded by public agencies and private foundations. Why? Because they help address social problems. Whatever words social scientists might use, their point is to get at real social problems.

These words don't come alone, but with a heavy natural language and social baggage. 'W' is the object of social scientists' claims, theories, and policy implications. This is purposely the very 'w' that plays important roles and has an important historical trajectory in society. Policy makers devote much effort to 'w,' which they hope to influence, change, stimulate, or combat. Politicians give speeches about the current state of 'w.' Journalists and pundits have strong opinions about 'w.' Organizations have rules that involve 'w.' 'W' sparks emotions and memories. It's associated with certain people, groups, and stories.

None of this would be the case if 'w' were a made-up technical term, a scientific neologism, a stipulation. Sticking to stipulated neologisms would make social scientists' life easier. And yet, this isn't what you find in most social scientists' presentations and writings, let alone in their grant proposals and on their websites. One reason is that invented, artificial languages wouldn't fly with social and political actors, such as governments, policy makers, think tanks, and funding agencies. Nor with universities, students, and the media. Another reason is that, for the most part, social scientists don't see themselves as playing clever self-referential games with words and numbers, but referring to significant social phenomena and processes. Phenomena that societies recognize, thematize, agonize over, and need help with. Which is why they listen to and pay for social science research.

There are reasonable objections to *Activity WF*, its practice and its point. Nevertheless, all things considered, social science communities are better off with than without it.

8.7 For

How should 'w' be used in social science community C? I argue that this is an important question for C, because of two kinds of reasons. First, speaking prudentially: if C doesn't address this question and remains content with the status quo, 'w' use will be afflicted by misunderstandings, miscommunication, and inefficiency. These consequences can be observed in much of social science. They've always been there. Due to a bad state of semantic affairs, C's epistemic aims are undermined. To make things worse, its communication with society is impaired. Teaching, advising, and sharing findings and ideas are impaired. Second, speaking morally: if C doesn't address this question and remains content with the status quo, it can expect unequal and unjust outcomes. Unfair distribution of resources. Power and status carrying the day. Therefore, there are both prudential and moral warrants for *Activity WF*.

As is well known, the duty of every well-trained and well-socialized social scientist is to get papers published in highly cited peer-reviewed journals. Having conducted state-of-the-art statistical analyses, Rodríguez offers an explanation of worldwide trends in happiness. Unfortunately for her, the editor rejects her manuscript, because Reviewer #2 rejects her definition of 'happiness.' If it picked out what it should pick out, Rodríguez's explanantia wouldn't account for much of the variance of the dependent variable.

Fernández's submission is about the educational policies of neoliberal regimes, and how they constitute self-interested subjects and *homines economici*. These claims are based on systematic data collection and research on five neoliberal regimes. Unfortunately for her, the editor rejects her manuscript, because Reviewer B rejects her definition of 'neoliberal.' The expression 'neoliberal regime' doesn't apply to one of the regimes Fernández studied, so her paper's chief conclusions are inaccurate or false.

Words' extensions encroach on social scientists' research and careers. Reviewers are precluding the publication of Rodríguez's and Fernández's papers by means of lexical semantics decrees. This is so even if, upon being challenged, they'd speak in ontological, not semantic, terms. They'd claim to have highlighted authors' errors about, respectively, what happiness is and what neoliberalism is. In either case, reviewers' decisions have real-world effects. Peer-reviewed journals are loci where both ideas and interests clash. Top journals' reviewers and editors are gatekeepers. As it happens, Rodríguez's paper undercuts Reviewer #2's own published work. An ethical reviewer would try to set their self-interested biases aside, but not everyone's intentions are ethical. And not everyone whose intentions are ethical can bring themselves, psychologically, to set their self-interested biases aside.

Journal reviewers are in a powerful position. The legitimate sources of their gatekeeping powers are epistemic: their knowledge of political science, sociology, history, psychology, or anthropology. They can legitimately evaluate submissions in their areas of expertise. But their authority isn't semantic. Their substantive knowledge doesn't bestow such abilities on them. It shouldn't be up to them how 'w' can and can't be used. Rather, this authority should reside with community C. Not only Rodríguez and Fernández but the entire community is harmed by reviewers' acting as though they were licensed to establish the correct extension of 'happiness' and 'neoliberal.'

Suppose you're the chair of a committee that will award a high-status honor in your field: the famous 'so-and-so best article award in the sociology of culture,' or the even more famous 'such-and-such best article award in psychological research on morality.' Famous and endowed with a sizable monetary prize. You're yourself a high-status scholar in this field, holding an endowed professorship at a top department and university, and a much-cited and award-winning author. That's why you were invited to chair the committee. Alternatively, suppose you've been appointed chair of your department's recruitment committee. Your department intends to hire a sociologist who specializes in the study of religion, or a sociologist of race and ethnicity, or an anthropologist who specializes in the study of ritual and magic. That's how the jobs were advertised.[57]

Whether it's the award committee scenario or the recruitment committee scenario, you open the first meeting with these remarks:

> I'm the chair of this committee, I call the shots here, so I'm going to define 'w' as follows: "xyz."
>
> [Award committee scenario:] If an article doesn't present research and findings about *that*, it's not about culture and therefore it's not eligible for the award.
>
> [Recruitment committee scenario:] If a scholar doesn't do research and publish on *that*, they don't qualify for our job.
>
> Case closed. Let's now move on . . .

57. On 'qualitative sociology,' see Aspers and Corte (2019, 2021), Brown-Saracino (2021), and Small (2021). The word 'qualitative' doesn't refer to a social phenomenon, but it shapes the distribution of methodological capital, it's in journals' names, researchers may identify with it, etc.

My thought experiment dramatizes, for effect, the committee's meeting and the chair's sociopathy. Exhibiting such behavior overtly would be frowned upon. But subtler behaviors can amount to roughly the same thing. High-status people are structurally able to determine, or decisively shape, what 'culture,' 'morality,' or 'religion' do and don't apply to. Their lexical semantics moves will determine, or decisively shape, the outcome: who'll get jobs and awards. Their top-down semantic stipulations will be decisive.

It goes without saying (I hope) that this picture is indefensible. It brings out what (I hope) no community and no community member can approve of. That you have status and power in the field of the sociology of culture shouldn't entitle you to issue decrees about the right use of 'culture.' Nor to load the semantic dice or otherwise behave like a semantic dictator. As I've argued, it's not as if you can discover the truth about the meaning of 'culture.' There is no truth. What community C is after isn't truth but goodness. A good answer and a good procedure to arrive at that answer. Affording autocratic semantic powers to high-status members of C would be a bad policy. It'd rest on a mistake about key word 'w' (e.g., 'culture'). Its effects would be morally defective. Unjust and unequal.

My argument about moral acceptability doesn't target individuals' motives. If a renowned committee chair happens to be unscrupulous, they'll manipulate the outcome to give jobs, grants, fellowships, and awards to their cronies. Hopefully this is seldom the case. But my argument works without vile intentions and sketchy morals. A committee chair's remarks, their definition of 'w,' might be a well-meaning attempt at clarification. It might stem from their sincere belief that stipulation is all we need. Still, it's a bad thing for the community. Bad for equality. The chair's thinking is still faulty.

A special case of the committee scenario foregrounds scholarly disciplines' boundary work.[58] 'W' is the name of a discipline, such as 'sociology,' 'anthropology,' 'political science,' or 'psychology.' A department's recruitment committee is discussing an applicant's merits. Their work is praised by some members of the committee, but another member yells (as they pound the table): 'This is not sociology!' 'This is not philosophy!' 'This is not political science!' These exclamations are prima facie ontological. But they can be rephrased to be about lexical semantics. This angry committee member was saying: 'The word "sociology" shouldn't be used to refer to this guy's work!' Or: 'This guy's work is in certain respects too different from the work of A, B, or C—work to which the word "sociology" undoubtedly applies!'

Scientific disciplines demarcate themselves from neighboring disciplines, so their singularity and significance are appreciated—and hence their budgets don't

58. Gieryn 1983; Lamont and Molnár 2002.

get cut, and student applications, grants, and public attention don't decline. Boundaries must be drawn between sociology and non-sociology (social psychology, anthropology, philosophy). Between political science and non-political-science (political philosophy, political sociology, political psychology). And so on.

Scientific disciplines also demarcate themselves from non-science.[59] Astronomers aren't astrologers, chemists aren't alchemists, psychiatrists aren't psychoanalysts. Historically, this is a sore spot for social scientists. Which explains their pounding the table particularly hard when they yell, 'this is not science!' ('It's rather essayistic, speculative, unfalsifiable work. It's got no methodology. It's the work of a humanities scholar, a journalist, a writer. A bad fit for the job.') Sometimes followed up by pointing to an exemplar: 'See, *that* is real science!'

In sum, three criticisms may torpedo a candidate for the job, grant, or award. They're not doing sociological research on *neoliberalism*. They're not doing *sociological* research on neoliberalism. Or they're not doing *scientific* research on neoliberalism. Whichever it is, 'we wish you good luck in your future endeavors.' Whichever it is, I believe there's no justification for semantic autocrats.

Once again, science and universities aren't extraordinary. 'This is not poetry!' 'This is not dance!' 'This is not theater!'[60] And the most general and notorious: 'This is not art!' In the arts, this isn't merely a verbal issue either. We're talking about status, power, money, recognition, and honor as well. Spots at celebrated museums and theaters, world-famous awards, write-ups in prominent newspapers and magazines. Book and ticket sales. Social media likes and YouTube and Vimeo views. Invitations to swanky parties and events.

As Stevenson remarked in his 1944 *Ethics and Language*:

> In the nineteenth century, for instance, critics sometimes remarked that Alexander Pope was 'not a poet.' The foolish reply would be, 'It's a mere matter of definition.' It is indeed a matter of definition, but not a 'mere' one. The word 'poet' was used in an extremely narrow sense. This, so far from being idle, had important consequences; it enabled the critics to deny to Pope a laudatory name, and so to induce people to disregard him.[61]

8.8 How words matter

Hiring faculty members, reviewing journal submissions, and reviewing grant submissions are central to the functioning of social science communities. They're central from an organizational point of view, and they also instantiate

---

59. Gieryn 1983; Laudan 1983; Popper (1935) 2002, (1963) 2002.

60. Pasolini 1968, (1968) 2007.

61. Stevenson 1944, 213.

and enact a constitutive question for social science disciplines: what good social science is. *Activity WF* isn't an abstract, philosophical exercise. These evaluations allocate resources, making a big difference to people's, organizations', and fields' destinies. As per usual in social and political life, there are interests and biases. Networks and structural constraints. Stratification and inequality.[62]

I've argued that a widespread practice is objectionable. Community members make, as a matter of course, lexical semantic moves that shape scholarly situations and outcomes—whether relatively stable or one-off situations, like reviewing a paper or grant proposal. The absence of clear, public, and well-founded rules and procedures is advantageous to high-status and powerful community members. Imagine you make a claim about the extension of 'w' in a discussion or evaluation meeting. The more status and power you have, the more likely your claim is to work. To be taken as legitimate and prevail. But this outcome is wrong. It's mistaken about the lexical semantics of social science languages. It's got neither epistemic nor moral warrant. What does and doesn't fall under 'w' shouldn't be at an individual's discretion. Nor should it be at the discretion of a small group of individuals. Or so I argue in this book.

Activity WF offers an alternative path, whereby the community relies on adequate processes to establish how 'w' should be used. Collective processes, in which nobody occupies a privileged position. Nobody's got a megaphone. The challenge is how to spell out goodness, goodness principles and criteria, and how to ensure that they'll guide communal practices and institutions. In my account of *Activity WF*, good outcomes are good in virtue of both epistemic and moral goods. In virtue of both epistemic and moral virtues. 'W' is a tool to do social science: pick out objects of inquiry and explananda, measure, compare, generalize, and set scope conditions. 'W' is a scientific tool, but social science communities' choices about it can and should have positive effects on justice/fairness.

———

In the early eighteenth century, Samuel Werenfels, a professor of rhetoric and theology at Universität Basel, reprobated "the Evil of Contending about Words":

> My Design in this Essay is to apply a Remedy to a most pernicious Distemper, which has long afflicted the Learned World. Tho a perfect Cure is rather to be desir'd than expected, yet if I can give any check to it, I shall not think my Labour lost: For it's next to impossible to tell how much contending

62. Brankovic, Ringel, and Werron 2018; Espeland and Sauder 2016; Hamann 2016, 2019; Hirschauer 2010, 2015; Lamont 2009; Teplitskiy 2016.

merely about Words there is almost in every Point, in which learned Men are divided; and how many Quarrels and wrangling Disputes, with which Learning is so miserably pester'd, wou'd immediately vanish, cou'd we but once distinguish Verbal Differences from Real.[63]

Werenfels had reason to reprobate this "most pernicious Distemper" and to look for a remedy. But his diagnosis isn't always valid. Yes, some "wrangling Disputes" may "immediately vanish," but not all of them will. You can't always "distinguish Verbal Differences from Real."

Our social science community keeps disagreeing about how to use 'w.' Is this a merely verbal dispute? It needn't be and in this case it's not. It's verbal, but not merely so. It can't be dissolved by putting 'w' to one side. The dispute is about words, and it doesn't disown being about words. It's not ashamed of it, because these words have momentous consequences. Momentous consequences for the community, and possibly for larger social and political processes.

Words, words, words. What do you read, my lord? What are you guys trying to figure out? We can respond unapologetically. Word uses in our community. Words, words, words.

63. Werenfels (1702) 1711, 1.

9

Distinction first

I have noted the arbitrariness of Wilkins, of the unknown (or apocryphal) Chinese encyclopedist, and of the Bibliographical Institute of Brussels; obviously there is no classification of the universe that is not arbitrary and conjectural.

—BORGES (1952)[1]

A class is a group of things; and things do not present themselves to observation grouped in such a way.

—DURKHEIM AND MAUSS (1901–2)[2]

9.1 Distinctions and classifications

Activity DF is about social scientists' distinctions. Their classifications or categorizations. It's about how to carve up social reality. How to group, cluster, or taxonomize things. Splitting and lumping.[3] Appropriating Putnam's metaphor for the sake of social science, reality is "a piece of dough . . . which we can slice into pieces in different ways."[4] The question is which cookie cutters to use, when, and where. Unlike Putnam and his interlocutors, social scientists' intent isn't metaphysical, but empirical. 'My findings and claims are about *X*, not about *Y* or *Z*. This is how to distinguish between *X* and non-*X* . . .' 'I've found a relationship between two sets of social things, *A* and *B*. This thing is a member of *A*; that thing isn't. And that other thing is a borderline case, or is partly a member of *A*. Here's how to tell what goes with what . . .'

---

1. Borges (1952) 1960, 134–35.
2. Durkheim and Mauss 1901–2, 7–8.
3. Simpson 1945, 22–24.
4. Putnam 1987, 19; see also 1988.

By means of such distinctions and classifications, social scientists fashion their objects of inquiry, the phenomena they describe and explain, and their limits. Methodologically, distinctions and classifications are fundamental. Methods and measurement instruments demand multiple categorization choices. From the design of questionnaires, vignettes, and experiments to statistical analyses. 'My independent variable, education, is ordinal, and it consists of five categories (completed primary school, completed secondary school, some undergraduate education, undergraduate degree, graduate degree).' 'For these analyses, I turned an interval variable into an ordinal one; the cut-off points are 50, 100, 150, and 225. My rationale is . . .' As a demography team, you could delimit age groups, cohorts, and generations in various ways, with implications for your statistical results, and the presentation of findings and conclusions. Or you could choose not to create any age groups. Data on people's sex/gender might be sorted into two, or three, or four, or nine groups . . .

How should distinctions be drawn in social science projects, data collection, statistical analyses, and arguments? What reasons do social scientists have for going one way rather than another? I argue that the community is the arbiter. Very well, but on which grounds should *it* accept or reject a distinction, a classification system, a way of grouping things? Why consent to these categorizations, but not to those? Additionally, to what extent and why do communities have normative authority over individual social scientists (so these aren't autonomous decision-makers maximizing their expected utility)?

I've shown that *Activity WF* is constrained by the nature of the beast. Individual social scientists aren't free to use 'w' however they please. *Activity DF* appears to permit more individual freedom. After all, I said that *d* was up to you. Distinctions and classifications ought to serve your social science research. They aren't language items, so are unaccountable to lexical semantics. They aren't collective in the sense language is. And yet, I'll argue that *Activity DF* has its own way of limiting your freedom. The community isn't there in the first instance, but it'll soon make its presence felt. It'll impose constraints and get its normative demands heard.

Like *Activity WF*, *Activity DF* isn't truth-apt: there are no true answers, but good results. Good for what? Good for whom? Scientifically good, morally good, in some other way, all of the above?

One premise is clear. You can't draw distinctions and classify things noncommittally. Classifications and distinctions shape your perspective, what your work is compatible with (claims, theories, approaches, datasets), which scholarly and policy projects you're able to speak to, what's salient and significant. They may provide "a grand vision guiding research," which won't be up some people's alley and whose payoffs won't be egalitarian.[5] They may confer value on things, because of associations with other things, being together in a group, or because of an object's location in classificatory networks and sets of distinctions. Indeed, value because of the very fact of something counting, of being counted, being noticed, being individuated.

Like *Activity WF*, *Activity DF* is a problem for a community. It's unlike a math problem, which a skilled individual can crack; which it'd be possible for a Robinson Crusoe to solve by themselves. Like *Activity WF*, *Activity DF* doesn't admit of correct or true solutions, but of good outcomes. Or better outcomes than the alternatives. These outcomes can't be discovered, but must be arrived at. They must be arrived at by the community as a whole.

So, practical reason is again with us. I'm sorry to upset its fans, but *Activity DF* will end up resembling *Activity WF* more than they would have hoped.

9.2 Research on classification

Sociologists have done a whole lot of research on classification or categorization: how societies split and lump things, what distinctions they do and don't draw, how they get this work done, culturally and organizationally. A whole lot of things must be classified. For example, societies and states make distinctions among people according to their gender, sexual orientation, religion, and race and/or ethnicity. Whence these categories? How do they deal with ambiguous cases? This is going on everywhere all the time. Professions and jobs, crimes, diseases, and monies. Works of art and art forms, non-human animals, and time and space. You name it: the social world is shot through with practices of classification, splitting and lumping, drawing distinctions and boundaries. They're ubiquitous and unavoidable.

Sociological studies of classification emphasize two aspects of it. On the one hand, classifications appear to be social, in the way sociologists like it.[6] They're based on cognitive processes that appear to be shared or collective. As such, they've been a core theme in the sociology of knowledge—the subfield that harks back to Marx and Engels's *The German Ideology*, Durkheim and Mauss's *Primitive Classification*, Durkheim's *Elementary Forms of Religious Life*, and Mannheim's *Ideology and Utopia*.

On the other hand, sociologists stress that classifications aren't just mental states. Perhaps they aren't mental states at all. More conservatively, they aren't imprisoned in minds. Rather, they're used, implemented, and negotiated in

---

5. Leonelli 2016, 133.
6. A. Rawls 1996.

social life, organizations, politics, and the economy. They're materially and technologically embodied. To observe classifications, you have to observe them in action, as they're fought over, and as they interact with organizational and cultural arrangements. Don't overlook their effects on material resources, status, power, and other unequally distributed social and political goods.[7] Discriminations among people and groups can help discriminate against some of them.

Classificatory practices and systems are a staple of sociological research. Of anthropological and historical research, too. The data show how they vary across time and place. The salience of similarities and dissimilarities varies across societies, but also within a society: individuals don't see eye to eye; groups don't see eye to eye either. The salience of boundaries varies. Sociologists ask what accounts for these variations. What accounts for divergent ways of "distinguishing like from unlike; deciding what is to count as likeness or unlikeness"?[8]

Given these distinctions' tangible and tangibly unequal effects, classification struggles are likely. What differentiates these struggles from other struggles ('ma nishtana')? How do they play out? Besides classification systems' social consequences, they also have social causes or origins. For instance, Durkheim and Mauss argued that "the classification of things reproduces [the] classification of people."[9] Therefore, your account of a society and culture shouldn't neglect the classifications at work in it, what the classes are, how they were created, and the circumstances under which they're resisted. Ritvo says it well: "the classification of animals, like that of any group of significant objects, is apt to tell as much about the classifiers as about the classified."[10]

Classification and categorization have been investigated by sociologists of culture, morality, organizations, knowledge, inequality, and stratification, among other subfields.[11] By STS scholars, like Bowker and Star, for whom classifications are "powerful technologies" and a "significant site of political and ethical work."[12] By intellectual and conceptual historians. Social and cultural anthropologists (another branch of Durkheim's family).[13] Linguists,

---

7. Hacking 1995, 1999; Lamont and Fournier 1992; Steensland 2006.

8. Bloor 1982, 267.

9. Durkheim and Mauss 1901–2, 8 (my translation).

10. Ritvo 1997, xii.

11. Bourdieu 1979, 2015; DiMaggio 1987; Durand and Paolella 2013; Fourcade 2012; Fourcade and Healy 2013; Hannan et al. 2019; Nippert-Eng 1996; Steensland 2006; Strand 2011; Zerubavel 1991, 1996.

12. Bowker and Star 1999, 319.

13. M. Douglas 1966.

psychologists, and cognitive scientists, with their distinct starting points and foci—for example, the psychological and neural underpinnings of categorization, and whether there are any universal categories, such as basic colors.[14]

Sociologists do empirical research on classification systems and practices. Their findings are about distinctions that people, organizations, and societies draw: what they are, how they vary, and why they're drawn. 'Folk' ones, if you wish. Folk categories, concepts, taxonomies, or classifications.[15] At the same time, sociologists need their own classification systems in order to depict and represent the social world, including the classification systems they find in the social world. What's the relationship between these two classification systems?

It's an old question. Easy to notice, but hard to answer. In response, two camps have often come about. The first camp says: they should strategically collaborate. They can work together. Sociologists may benefit from classifications and categories encountered in their research. Proponents of this view privilege understanding over explanation, and are fond of ethnographic methods. Their typical aim is to understand social phenomena, interactions, or cultural processes, which necessarily involve subjectivities. Ordinary people's concepts, or folk categories, are argued to be indispensable to empathetically understand culturally specific meanings and experiences. If you look at society from the outside, through your scientific conceptual lenses or meta-language, you won't be able to apprehend the meanings people attach to things and events. You'll miss their interpretations of and feelings about their worlds, how social life is experienced, what it is like to do something, go through something, or be something. Their first-personal character, qualia, phenomenological experience will fly under your radar.

Ethnographers are concerned with empathetic and phenomenological understandings, but most sociological research isn't. Yet, you don't have to do ethnography to claim that the best analytical categories emerge from the people you're studying, or from interactions with them. Interaction as opposed to, for example, getting your categories from a sociological school, a well-regarded author, or your own thoughts and impressions. This first camp also comprises:

- The argument that societies' classifications and distinctions are sociologically profitable, because of their explanatory power. They've been durable

14. Barsalou 1983; Lakoff 1987; Medin 1989; Medin and Smith 1984; Miller et al. 2003; Roberson, Davies, and Davidoff 2000; Rosch 1973.

15. B. Berlin 1973; B. Berlin, Breedlove, and Raven 1966; Rosaldo 1972.

in society for a reason. It's not merely tradition and inertia, but time-tested epistemic payoffs.[16]

- Experimental philosophy (hip people call it 'x-phi'). Experimental philosophers design studies to listen to and learn from ordinary people's ('the folk') understandings, judgments, concepts, and intuitions.[17] Their empirical findings have philosophical significance; they impinge on the truth or falsity of philosophical theories. An argument about what knowledge is and isn't must accommodate what people say knowledge is and isn't. Thus, experimental philosophers are unlike (1) traditional philosophers who consult their own intuitions while sitting in their armchairs in Oxford or Cambridge, and unlike (2) social scientists who report third-personally what people believe, judge, or intuit, as if it were in quotation marks.

The second camp says: these two classification systems—sociologists' and folk ones—should be independent. It's a methodological error to conflate folk concepts and analytical concepts. This response is most persuasive where classifications are expected to track natural kinds. Some of physics and chemistry. Maybe some of biology. Folk biological taxonomies have anthropological and historical interest, but aren't germane to present-day biology. Biologists' taxonomies ought to carve nature at its joints. At its most scientistic, this camp is a form of 'eliminative materialism,' which scraps the whole of folk psychology and ordinary people's views about thought, cognitive processes, and the mind. All of it is "radically false" and "fundamentally defective," as neuroscience shows. Shows, or could in principle show, or will one day show.[18]

This camp has been charged with moral failings. Being guilty of "epistemic injustice" and "hermeneutical marginalization."[19] Its accounts and explanations ethnocentrically bring 'our' concepts to bear on 'unfamiliar' societies, groups, practices, and ideas. They snub 'local knowledge' and sources of evidence. Centers can afford to ignore peripheries' distinctions and typologies, but not vice versa. The Global North has systematically ignored epistemic communities in the Global South. Not cool.[20]

16. Austin 1957, 8; Stinchcombe 1968, 41.

17. Knobe and Nichols 2008.

18. Paul Churchland 1981, 67; see also Patricia Churchland 1986.

19. Fricker 2007.

20. Alatas and Sinha 2017; Batthyány and Caetano 2018; Beigel 2013; Bourdieu and Wacquant 1998; Connell 2006; Go 2020; Gutiérrez Rodríguez, Boatcă, and Sérgio Costa 2010; Hughes 1961; Rodriguez Medina 2014; Steinmetz 2013; Torres 2020, 2021; Wallerstein 2007.

What are the lessons for the practice of *Activity DF*?

First, social science communities shouldn't confuse *Activity DF* and empirical research on classification, categories, and distinctions. They're logically independent. They're logically independent whether or not their interaction is desirable. It's a separate question whether *Activity DF* should take into account actually existing classification systems and common 'folk' distinctions. And if so, how. It strikes me as a case-by-case question. A question about this instance of *Activity DF*, the distinction you'd like to make at this point in time, for these purposes. Whether it should take into account actually existing classification systems and common 'folk' distinctions. And if so, how.

Second, recall my response to argument (iii), 'they'll tell you!' (chapter 3). Does it also block the relationship between folk and social scientists' distinctions? According to this argument, research on religion in Uruguay or art in Paraguay should rely on Uruguayans' own definition of 'religion' and Paraguayans' own definition of 'art.' Your project will use these words in whichever ways they use them. My response showed why this argument fails. Not any definition of 'religion' and 'art' will work. You can't be tolerant all the way. Now, both the argument and my counterargument are about words. Word definitions or uses. The stuff of *Activity WF*. But *Activity DF* starts with distinctions. These distinctions needn't correspond to natural language words or sociological language words. Therefore, my counterargument doesn't apply. There's no requirement that your research be about religion or art. Nobody will be checking sameness of topic across cultures and languages. In fact, any distinction drawn in Uruguay or Paraguay could be acceptable in your social science community, bizarre though it might seem.

And yet, your distinction will have to prove its worth in specific ways—just like any other. Any of their distinctions could be acceptable, but not any will. Reliably discriminating between acceptable and unacceptable is the community's job. For the moment, here's an advantage of a folk Uruguayan distinction. If your social science project follows it, your findings will make sense to Uruguayan people, organizations, and media. Your claims can be integrated into Uruguayan institutions and practices, from policy making to education. This is a good thing.

Third, societies contain all sorts of folk classifications and distinctions. Classification practices occur in many settings. Classifiers range from formal organizations to ordinary people in their day-to-day life, from states to informal groups. All of this might be empirically investigated by sociologists of classification. What about sociologists' own classification practices and systems? Sociology is a community or group, which can be studied like any other. These studies belong to the sociology of sociology or the sociology of social science.[21]

If sociologists are themselves your subjects, your folk, how do *these* folk distinctions relate to the conduct of *Activity DF*? Why pay attention to them? One reason is that you intend your results to contribute to this community— say, sociology of art or sociology of morality. Whether you like it or not, ignoring its practices and traditions might mean they'll ignore your results. As ever, you won't be heard by a group of people or organizations if you don't speak their language and mention their points of reference. Another reason is that this is a community of experts. You observed expert observers. Hence, you can expect them to have developed, over the years, epistemically good distinctions. As ever, provided you largely share their aims and outlook, it makes sense to build on their work.

9.3 Good news and bad news

I've got some good news and some bad news for practitioners of *Activity DF*. The good news is, the world is open to you. You have no constraints, neither from natural language nor from ontology. Neither English nor the structure of reality will dictate how to draw your distinctions, how to classify things, what groups you'll end up with, and how to delineate their borders. In this sense, you're free. Your project's distinctions and classification systems are up to you. To you and your collaborators.

The bad news is, you aren't really free. Not anything goes. Normative assessments are around the corner. Their degree of formalization and institutionalization varies, but they're nonetheless there. You make a move in or contribution to science, and it'll be valid (or not), acceptable (or not), in light of communal validity or acceptability criteria. I'm talking neither about methodological nor about logical validity, but something like fit with the goals, rules, and spirit of the game (which includes but isn't limited to methodology and logic). In social science research, examining witchcraft substance isn't valid, idiosyncratic anecdotes and personal experiences can't be validly generalized, and non sequiturs are a no-go.[22] Moreover, valid moves and

21. Abend 2006; Abend, Petre, and Sauder 2013; Bourdieu 1984, 2001; Camic, Gross, and Lamont 2011; Fassin and Steinmetz, forthcoming; C. Fleck 2007; Franzen et al. 2019; Gouldner 1970; Heilbron, Guilhot, and Jeanpierre 2008; Mayrl and Wilson 2020; Steinmetz 2005, 2013; Turner and Turner 1990.

22. Evans-Pritchard (1937) 1976, 15–17.

contributions vary in their quality. What you did is excellent, in light of communal goodness criteria. Your idea, paper, or invention is outstanding and deserves an award.

Social science communities will judge the practice and results of *Activity DF*. Outcomes will be judged better or worse. Ideally, most community members understand, in advance, how their work will be evaluated, with which tools, along which dimensions. Graduate students are taught just that. Otherwise, you'd be unsure as to what's worth your time and effort—whether you're a social scientist, engineer, manager, or dancer. For sure, there are the norms of idealized science, and there are the norms of actual science.[23] All I'm saying is that the latter exist, whatever they are.

In one sense, you're free to pursue *Activity DF* as you wish. As far as language and ontology are concerned, your distinctions are up to you. Go ahead and draw and use them in your social science research. Happy classifying and sorting things out! But persuading the scientific community is a whole new ball game. Your results may be considered terrible and your paper won't get published. Your distinction *d* may be judged senseless, pointless, unmotivated, capricious. Just bad. In this sense, you aren't free. This freedom isn't worth its salt.

Unless you do have good reasons to draw the distinction you drew and to classify things the way you did. What makes these reasons good reasons? They aren't good in virtue of your preferences and desires (of which you're evidently the source: they are *your* preferences and desires), as an eggplant parmigiana is delicious in virtue of your taste (of which you're evidently the source: it is *your* taste). In this respect, your reasons can't be individual, like '*d* works for my article and that's that.' They can't be private and stipulative. On the contrary, they'll be assessed by communal criteria of validity and goodness, which aren't up to you. They'll determine if your reasons pass muster.

What should these communal criteria for *Activity DF* be?

———

This is where the abovementioned 'argument from usefulness' comes in (chapter 3). My response to it wasn't enthusiastic. However, it's not so much wrong as incomplete. It must be developed. It's now time to see how.

The thrust of the argument is this. A social scientist can draw whatever distinctions are useful to them and their project. Per distinction *d*, they'll have

23. Hagstrom 1965; Merton 1973; Turner 2007.

certain sets of objects, entities, phenomena, organizations, or whatever. For some projects and aims, it's useful to group together al-Qaeda, Islamic State (IS), Hamas, Nationalsozialistische Untergrund (NSU), and Combat 18. For other projects and aims, it's useful to add to this group Befreiungsausschuss Südtirol, KKK, Euskadi Ta Askatasuna (ETA), Montoneros, Tupamaros, and Fuerzas Armadas Revolucionarias de Colombia (FARC). For yet other projects and aims, it's most useful to have three groups: Montoneros, Tupamaros, and FARC; al-Qaeda, IS, and Hamas; and NSU, Combat 18, and KKK.

These projects aren't making ontological claims. They aren't appealing to natural kinds or essentialisms. Nor to universals or realisms.[24] Nobody is claiming to know what a terrorist group is, let alone what terrorism really or truly is. Nor what's the difference between a terrorist group, a liberation movement, and a criminal organization. Nor are these projects making normative semantic claims about the correct uses of the word 'terrorism.' Indeed, the word 'terrorism' needn't figure in their work at all. It's simply that categorizing things in this or that fashion increases certain payoffs. It helps you with what you wanted to accomplish. It is useful.

Say you're an ethologist. For some projects and aims, it's useful to group together *Felis catus*, *Felis silvestris*, and *Felis lybica*. For other projects and aims, it's more useful to draw a distinction between domestic cats and wildcats. It's beside the point what is and isn't a natural kind, whether a species can be a natural kind, and what it'd be for a classification, taxonomy, and homology to be natural and objective.[25] In *The Origin of Species*, Darwin wrote that species were "merely artificial combinations made for convenience" and scientists should abandon "the vain search for the undiscovered and undiscoverable essence of the term species":

> From these remarks it will be seen that I look at the term species as one arbitrarily given, for the sake of convenience, to a set of individuals closely resembling each other. [...] In short, we shall have to treat species in the same manner as those naturalists treat genera, who admit that genera are merely artificial combinations made for convenience. This may not be a cheering prospect; but we shall at least be freed from the vain search for the undiscovered and undiscoverable essence of the term species.[26]

24. Libera 1996.

25. Brigandt 2009; Reydon 2003; Rieppel 2007; Ruse 1987; Wilkins and Ebach 2014; D. Williams and Ebach 2018; R. Wilson, Barker, and Brigandt 2007.

26. Darwin (1859) 1909, 69, 525.

Ever since Darwin, there have been multiple concerns about species, as a kind of thing. Species 'concepts' and 'definitions' have multiplied.[27] 'Taxonomic inflation' has been decried.[28] The "so-called 'species problem' has plagued evolutionary biology."[29] For the sake of argument, though, suppose these concerns turned out to be unfounded. Natural kinds, or natural classifications of some sort, would be able to govern the classification of animals, including your felines. In spite of that, an alternative grouping might be preferable on this occasion, given your project's character and aims.

These examples show the freedom at the heart of *Activity DF*. Not even natural kinds would be able to dictate your scientific work's classificatory practices. However, such individual freedom is only one aspect of *Activity DF*; it'll soon meet unfreedoms or collective constraints. It's not unfreedom as if you were enslaved, incarcerated, or a loaded gun were pointed at you. But the community does have strong demands and there are strong incentives for you to comply with them. It won't do to say 'it is useful to do this' and move on.

As my response to the 'argument from usefulness' pointed out, usefulness is elliptical. It doesn't say enough; it doesn't suffice to justify your research design and methodological choices. It shouldn't be allowed to function as a blank check, such that 'it's useful to draw this distinction' is a polite way of saying 'I want to draw this distinction, so I'll do it.' What's useful to you isn't irrelevant, but it's not a justificatory argument either. The real question is useful for what and for whom, relative to what, compared to what.

A scientific community can break down the question into two steps. Call 'Z' what something is useful for. First, how is the community to make well-grounded decisions about diverse Zs? How can it tell if a given Z is OK, legitimate, acceptable, something we want to go for, or something like that? For example, useful to impress your romantic partner and useful to help you cook a delicious dinner aren't going to fly. They aren't goals of our scientific community at all. Second, among the Zs that are deemed OK or legitimate, among legitimate useful-for-Z claims, comparative judgments of worth must be made. They'll have to be weighed and traded off against one another. Time and resources are scarce: how should the community invest them? What's most important for scientific projects in our community to accomplish?

Communal assessments of usefulness—and of the usefulness of particular distinctions—must be aware of numerous kinds of legitimate goals. All of

27. De Queiroz 2007; Dupré 2002; Ereshefsky 1998; Pigliucci 2003; Richards 2010; Wilkins 2003, 2009a, b.

28. N. Isaac, Mallet, and Mace 2004.

29. Pigliucci 2003, 596.

them can warrant usefulness claims. Despite their popularity, explanation and prediction are two among many. Social science is a large category and scientific projects are a diverse bunch. They set out to accomplish a variety of things. There's variation in projects' aims: what they're explicitly up to, the goods and payoffs they hope to achieve. This is patent (in written form) in the first section of articles and grant proposals, or (in oral form) in meetings where experiments and surveys are designed. There's also variation in the epistemic values and 'theoretical virtues' projects are driven by, and according to which their results can be assessed. In addition, non-epistemic values play legitimate roles in scientists' work, their aims, and their choices—assuming you can and should separate out epistemic and non-epistemic values.[30]

Traditional philosophies of science weren't kind to values. Values were regarded as pollutants, regrettably ubiquitous pollutants, to be avoided at all costs. They were confined to the 'context of discovery.' Philosophers of science used to be hung up on demarcation: what differentiates science from non-science, essentially, once and for all.[31] Science was regarded as a pure and clean pursuit of objective knowledge. A *sacred* pursuit—sociologists and anthropologists might critically interject. It should be demarcated from anything social, cultural, normative. Oddly, from anything human.

Those philosophies of science have been rightfully discredited. To make a long story short, their weaknesses have been laid bare by two types of scholarship. First, empirical research on scientific practices and institutions, done by sociologists, anthropologists, historians, and STS scholars. Second, more discerning philosophical accounts of science, which aren't averse to society, morality, and culture.[32] Values are part and parcel of scientific work. The social dimensions of knowledge aren't embarrassing. They aren't brushed under the carpet, but incorporated into the account—as feminist philosophers, communitarian epistemologists, and social epistemologists have. So are the virtues—as virtue epistemologists have.

---

30. H. Douglas 2009; Elliott and McKaughan 2014; Lacey 2004, 2017; Longino 1995, 1996, 2004; Rooney 1992. I'll continue to use the adjectives 'epistemic' and 'non-epistemic,' even though the distinction can be criticized.

31. Laudan 1983; Pigliucci and Boudry 2013; Popper (1935) 2002, (1963) 2002.

32. Alexandrova 2017, 2018; H. Douglas 2004, 2009; Harding 1991; Hicks 2014; Kincaid, Dupré, and Wylie 2007; Kourany 2010; Lacey 2013; Longino 1990, 2002, 2004, 2013. For pragmatist accounts, see Dewey (1929), Putnam (2002), and Rorty (1991). My expression 'more discerning philosophical accounts of science' paints with a broad brush. It encompasses a lot of views, which might only share their rejection of 'traditional philosophies of science' (an expression that paints with a broad brush as well).

Much progress has been made on the character of epistemic value, the distinction (or alleged distinction) between epistemic and non-epistemic values, their direct and indirect roles, and the ways in which they're ineluctable.[33] The interconnections between values and science have been looked at closely, in specific conjunctures, so as to make out what they're doing and what to do about them, if anything. Further, the goalposts are now better set: science is admitted to be an imperfect human and social endeavor. For good or ill, it can't but be a human and social endeavor; we've got to work with what we've got.

Patently, moral convictions and cultural values can harm science. They may damage scientific research and results, and their uptake in society. Unprincipled actors are ready to take advantage of porous boundaries between science and morality, put scientific findings to awful political uses, and sow doubt about scientists' research and its applications. Climate change deniers, gender and racial discrimination deniers, and anti-vaxxers' conspiracy theories spring to mind. Most obviously, what a scientist wishes to be the case shouldn't influence what they see and what they come to believe is the case. Nor what they say and publish. What the government, a funding agency, a corporation, or the Pope wishes to be the case shouldn't influence what a scientist comes to believe is the case. Nor what they say and publish. Unfortunately, sometimes they do.[34]

These perversions come in more and less conscious varieties. One thing is scientists' deliberately fabricating data or concealing results, so their conclusions wind up being consistent with their values and worldviews. Or consistent with the interests of corporations or governments that sponsored the research. Plain evil. Another thing is values' unconsciously influencing how scientists see the world, design their studies, assess and interpret the evidence, and advance their arguments, so their conclusions wind up being substandard or false. 'Biased,' as they say. It's a more complex defect. Here scientists' vices are insufficient open-mindedness, fair-mindedness, cognitive flexibility, and ability to see things afresh and change their minds. In turn, these vices can be fostered by communities' socialization practices, and formal and informal incentives to conform—the end of the continuum being groupthink. Scientific communities have better built-in defenses than other social and political groups, but they're far from being immune.

33. H. Douglas 2000, 2009; Elliott 2011; Elliott and McKaughan 2014; Hicks 2014; Intemann 2001, 2005; Pritchard 2007; Putnam 2002; Reydon and Ereshefsky 2022; Steel 2010, 2013.

34. Krimsky 2013; Legg, Hatchard, and Gilmore 2021; Sacks et al. 2020; Wilholt 2009.

Values don't need to harm science. They may, but they don't need to. What's more, under certain conditions, for certain purposes, they may be good for the community. If well understood and used, some values can make positive contributions to scientific work.

9.4 Desiderata

Scientific projects are a diverse bunch. They have diverse goals, seek diverse goods, and are guided by diverse values and virtues. Taken together, I'll refer to scientific projects' goals, goods, values, and virtues as 'desiderata.'[35]

The multiplicity of desiderata is challenging for scientific communities, which must make judgments about them, along with the distinctions and categories that serve them. But how? Not only are there multiple desiderata, but also multiple sorts of desiderata. They don't seem to be commensurable. Scientific communities need to order them, systematize them, and bring them into a sound arrangement that enables comparative judgments. But how?

Enter Kuhn. Whether or not Kuhn's arguments are right, accurate, and consistent, they do excel at fruitfulness. He had a knack for it. In "Objectivity, Value Judgment, and Theory Choice," a lecture delivered in 1973, he suggested five "characteristics of a good scientific theory":

> First, a theory should be accurate: within its domain, that is, consequences deducible from a theory should be in demonstrated agreement with the results of existing experiments and observations. Second, a theory should be consistent, not only internally or with itself, but also with other currently accepted theories applicable to related aspects of nature. Third, it should have broad scope: in particular, a theory's consequences should extend far beyond the particular observations, laws, or subtheories it was initially designed to explain. Fourth, and closely related, it should be simple, bringing order to phenomena that in its absence would be individually isolated and, as a set, confused. Fifth—a somewhat less standard item, but one of special importance to actual scientific decisions—a theory should be fruitful of new research findings: it should, that is, disclose new phenomena or previously unnoted relationships among those already known. These five characteristics—accuracy, consistency, scope, simplicity, and fruitfulness—are all standard criteria for evaluating the adequacy of a theory.[36]

35. This is sufficient for my purposes, but it'd be too imprecise for other. Cf. Keas 2018; Potochnik 2015; Pritchard 2007, 2021; Schindler 2018.

36. Kuhn 1977, 321–22.

You may disagree with the fundamentality of these five "characteristics" in natural science or social science. Still, assume they guide your social science project. Accuracy, consistency, scope, simplicity, and fruitfulness are in your sights. This is why you draw distinction *d*: because it helps make your project virtuous in these respects. It's useful for that. This is how you cash out the 'argument from usefulness.'

The thing is that Kuhn proposed five desiderata, so judgments about their relative importance must be made. Choices must be made. They have to be made by individual scientists, as they design and conduct their research, as they collect and analyze their data. But they won't be making discretionary decisions. Importance judgements have to be made by the communities in which their work is carried out, and to which their work is addressed. These are the highest courts of scientific worth.[37] No one can serve so many masters.

How many masters? Kuhn didn't mean to be exhaustive: his five goods were only a sample.[38] I want to lay a more extensive list on the table, because its sheer extensiveness is a defining feature of the challenge confronted by scientific communities. Trade-offs between five desiderata could have been manageable. Even more manageable would have been five desiderata of a theory, in fields whose theories' point and form are more or less standard. There you'd start with considerable common ground already. Yet, this is a limiting case. For most scientific communities and projects, it's a much larger and messier world. The limiting case of classical mechanics is more straightforward than relativity theory, too.

My list of desiderata doesn't require a radical philosophy of science or a drastic departure from scientists' conventional self-understandings. Later on, I'll relinquish this moderate stance by bringing morality to the fore. Note that philosophers and methodologists normally speak of the desiderata of scientific *theories*. I speak of the desiderata of scientific *projects*, which comprise many stages and parts. One of them is theories. Not that I'm at ease with the polysemy of the word 'theory,' within and across disciplines.[39]

My list is based on two types of sources. First, empirical data, observed facts about scientific practice, drawn from the sociology of science and STS. They tell us what scientists' actual desiderata are. Second, normative arguments in the philosophy of science, logic of inquiry, and social science methodology. They tell us what scientists' desiderata ought to be.

37. There's some room for individual preferences and styles, but how much room? You aren't a simplicity kind of guy. Your colleagues' theories are simpler than yours, but you can't disregard simplicity altogether.

38. Kuhn 1977, 321.

39. Abend 2008a; Krause 2016; Lizardo 2014.

TABLE 9.1. Desiderata of scientific projects

Group		Desideratum	Notes or examples
Description	1	Accurate description	Of a phenomenon, and, more broadly, of reality
	2	Fine-grained description	Of a phenomenon, and, more broadly, of reality
	3	Parsimonious, economical description	Of a phenomenon, and, more broadly, of reality
	4	Orderly description, reality well ordered, well organized	E.g., through classifications, taxonomies, or typologies
	5	"Problematizing redescription"[a]	
Explanation	6	Powerful explanation	
	7	Explanatory/causal laws	
	8	Causal explanation of an event	Or of an instance, case, phenomenon, process, change, trend
	9	Causal mechanisms	
	10	Functional explanation, functional account of a system	
Generalization	11	Generality, generalizability, scope, comprehensiveness	Possibly universality, universalizability
	12	General laws, no ad hoc clauses	Possibly universal laws
	13	Clear scope conditions	E.g., only in WEIRD countries, or planet Earth, or the Milky Way, only in the eighteenth century in Europe
Prediction	14	Quantity of predictions	
	15	Breadth of predictions	
	16	Accuracy of predictions	

Category	#	Description	Note
Understanding, vision	17	Understanding of, insight into, perspicuous interpretation of a phenomenon; making it intelligible, shedding light on it	As opposed to explanation
	18	Heuristic gains	
	19	Ability to see what couldn't be seen before	E.g, as if you supplied a microscope or telescope
	20	Ability to see further and deeper[b]	
	21	Attention to and focus on what's key about a phenomenon, process, situation	And disregard of what isn't key
Tractability, doability	22	Empirically tractable questions, doable empirical research	Given your methods: experiment, randomized controlled trial, statistical in general, statistical for your specific technique and model, etc.
	23	Manageability of data	As opposed to drowning in data
	24	Measurability of properties	Be it quantitatively or qualitatively
	25	Potential for quantification, formalization, and modeling	
General scientific virtues	26	Simplicity and parsimony of approach, assumptions, and models	Also known as Occam's razor
	27	Beauty, elegance, and other aesthetic qualities	
	28	Novelty, originality	
	29	Potential for unification of scientific theories	
	30	Potential for unification of scientific disciplines	

Continued on next page

TABLE 9.1. (*continued*)

Group		Desideratum	Notes or examples
	31	Fruitfulness, fecundity, generativity	Leading to more work on the subject; excitement about it; new ideas, hypotheses, research questions, approaches, paradigms, ways of thinking, etc.
	32	Testability, falsifiability, refutability	
	33	Replicability, reproducibility[c]	
	34	Openness, open science	
	35	Potential for data standardization and sharing	Within fields and with other actors and organizations
	36	Certainty, confidence in truth of results and claims	
	37	Truth	
	38	Interestingness for a scientific community; being stimulating, intriguing, exciting to it	
Consistency, coherence	39	Internal consistency (or coherence)[d]	
	40	Consistency (or coherence) with what's well established in the field	
	41	Consistency (or coherence) with broader facts	
	42	Consistency/compatibility with prior expectations	Results/claims make sense, are plausible, are believable, fit with common sense, seem like they could be true, don't seem fanciful or crazy
	43	Inconsistency/incompatibility with prior expectations	Results/claims are surprising, at odds with common sense, at odds with extant work/theory, groundbreaking, unexpected findings, unexpected implications

Social and political implications, applications, interventions	44	Desirable consequences for society and social life	E.g., preventing suffering, saving lives, helping people
	45	Other desirable real-world consequences	
	46	Policy implications and recommendations in general, applicable to many comparable situations, present and future, capacity to shape policy in general	
	47	Policy implications and recommendations for this particular place, time, situation	Given initial conditions, descriptive statistics, distribution of crucial variables
	48	Policy readiness in general, straightforward application, few and clear steps from scientific claims in a paper to practical use	
	49	Communicability of results outside scientific field, intelligibility to diverse publics/ translatability into accounts intelligible to diverse publics	
	50	Interestingness for society at large; being stimulating, intriguing, exciting to it	

[a] See Longo and Zacka 2019; Shapiro 2002.

[b] Lukes (2021b, 106): "I introduced 'dimensions' into this debate as what was, I confess, something of a rhetorical trick, although I was not conscious of this at the time. For, first, who would want a one- or two-dimensional view of something if you could see it in three. But, more trickily, talk of 'dimensions' rather than 'faces' suggests that what you see three-dimensionally you see in greater depth and more realistically."

[c] See Cartwright 1991; H. M. Collins 1985, 1991; Fidler and Wilcox 2021; Nichols et al. 2021

[d] Coherence is generally taken to be more encompassing than consistency (Haack 2004; J. Young 2018). H. Chang's (2017, 111) "operational coherence" is a different beast.

This is a long and heterogeneous list, which gives a flavor of the range of desiderata that have been pursued and defended. Less charitably: it's a bit of a hodgepodge. Its items seem to belong to different levels. They're properties of different parts of a scientific project and/or of the project, the whole thing. Furthermore, I don't expect everyone to endorse all of them. It's inconsequential whether my fifty desiderata are too many or too few; what I failed to include and what I shouldn't have included. Some people are convinced that good science is one thing, and its products' good social, political, or moral effects is another. Welcome byproducts, or not unwelcome byproducts, if you will, but not desiderata of science itself. Not what science itself is seeking. To others, heuristic gains, perspicuous interpretation, communicability, or beauty are overrated. Actually, they don't belong in the list at all. Yet others say that interestingness is subjective, or supervenient on other items, or both.[40]

That'd be all alright with me.

Some people will argue that my list is omitting one vital desideratum. Or that truth is the one fundamental desideratum, the ultimate standard, the boss of all things epistemic.[41] That'd be alright with me, too.[42] The specifics can be argued over. But there's a less demanding benchmark, a lowest common denominator, which I'm counting on. These items shouldn't strike you as having nothing to do with science, not in the ballpark, totally nuts.

I classify desiderata into nine groups, but they could be reorganized in many other ways. For example, Keas claims that the virtues of scientific theories "are best classified into four classes: evidential, coherential, aesthetic, and diachronic."[43] Douglas says that "there are four groups into which we can divide the cognitive value terrain: *Groups 1 and 2*: Values that are minimal criteria for adequate science, applied to the theory per se (group 1) or the theory in relation to evidence (group 2). [...] *Group 3*: Values that are desiderata when applied to theories per se. [...] *Group 4*: Values that are desiderata when applied to theories in relation to evidence."[44]

I'm not committed to my ninefold classification. Nothing much hangs on it.

40. Davis 1971.

41. Ahlstrom-Vij and Grimm 2013; Pritchard 2021; Sylvan 2018.

42. You could normatively argue that truth is the only desideratum, period. Nothing else matters. I'm not sure how I'd like to react to that.

43. Keas 2018, 2761.

44. H. Douglas 2013, 799–800.

Putting specifics to one side, it's uncontroversial that scientific projects face trade-offs.[45] Yes, some desiderata might go together and reinforce one another. Maximizing one can help maximize others. Yet, this positive-sum game doesn't always obtain. At the very least, there are desiderata that can't be concurrently maximized. They pull you in different directions. They call for different research approaches and thus distinctions and classifications. Even truth and explanation might do so.[46]

One issue is scarce time and energy and opportunity costs. Another issue is desiderata that are intrinsically in conflict with one another. Realizing this desideratum implies that others will worsen. Necessarily. For instance, the simpler and more parsimonious your account, the less it can accomplish descriptive, explanatory, and understanding goals that require, by their very nature, more extensive discussions and complex analyses. There's a conflict between the value of surprise, unexpectedness, and inconsistency with extant work and common sense on the one hand, and on the other hand the value of plausibility, believability, and consistency with extant work and common sense. The compliment 'wow, that's groundbreaking; it's unbelievable!' coexists with the critical remark 'that's implausible and just hard to believe.'

Like elsewhere in life, setting priorities is taxing. Ranking items. Giving weights. What to prioritize? When, where, under what conditions? How does this vary across disciplines and projects? Some desiderata could be necessary: not only desirable, but sine qua non for something to be considered science. Some desiderata could be out of place: not a matter of preferences, interests, taste, style, perspective, or values, but downright out of place.

To grapple with these questions, more encompassing understandings of science, scientific arguments, and scientific research will have to come into play. Understandings of what science is all about, what it should be all about, what scientists want it to be all about, or what scientists should want it to be all about. What its point is. What a science must do and have and what's optional. Whether it makes sense to speak of 'science,' in the singular, and its objectives and point—of theoretical physics and sociology of gender, of evolutionary biology and microeconomics.

My list of desiderata is long and heterogeneous. It's primarily epistemic, like Kuhn's. However, some items are partly aesthetic and moral, or have aesthetic

---

45. On model building, see Levins (1966), Matthewson and Weisberg (2009), and Weisberg (2003, 2006).

46. Cartwright 1983.

and moral aspects. Which is the direction toward which I'm going, particularly morality. You hope to deliver true and accurate scientific results about a phenomenon. But you might also hope that these results be good, morally speaking. Where is this moral goodness going to come from? If you hope to deliver good results aesthetically speaking, where is this aesthetic goodness going to come from? Isn't beauty in the eye of the beholder and aren't 'style' choices idiosyncratic?[47]

Epistemic goodness is already multisided and messy, even if restricted to science (as opposed to other sorts of knowledge and understanding), even if restricted to textbook natural science (as opposed to scientific practice). But it pales in comparison to goodness, values, and desiderata in ethics and aesthetics.[48] In these realms, the options on the market are overwhelmingly numerous. To expect consensuses seems optimistic, if not wishful thinking.

———

In your scientific project, you chose to sort things into certain categories; you chose to draw certain distinctions. These are well suited to help you achieve desiderata #8, #16, and #31. Or to help you realize desiderata #3 and #30. Put differently, *Activity DF* will be useful for those purposes. But which of these purposes should be pursued?

You can't determine alone which desiderata are most important and valuable. There's no correct answer to this question, no correct solution, in the sense that empirical science, mathematics, and logic might attain. No truth to be discovered.

You could tell us about importance, value, or usefulness to you. To you only. You could share your private preferences or desires with us. But we're talking about a project, move, or contribution within a communal practice, within an institutional and cultural framework. The practice, culture, and institutions of a scientific discipline. A scholarly literature or network. As I see things, the comparative importance of desiderata is a practical reason problem, on which *Activity DF* directly depends. It's a practical reason problem for the community.

47. Fleck (1935) 2019; Gayon 1996; Hacking 1992; Ording 2019; Queneau 1947.

48. Breitenbach 2013; Ivanova 2017; Ivanova and French 2020. Perhaps there are intrinsic connections between epistemic, ethical, and aesthetic values; between the true, the good, and the beautiful. Perhaps these aren't independent terms, so choosing well in one pays off in all of them. Keep your fingers crossed.

We, the community, will accept some usefulness-for-Z claims, while reject-
ing others. Among the former, some may eventually be revised and specified.
Others may be overturned, either because the community and its institutions
have changed, or because they had been misjudged. Considerations and reasons
will have to be presented. Exchanged, reflected on, and publicly examined.
They'll help assess desiderata, alongside their specifications (for example,
the conditions under which they are and aren't a priority, or the places
where they are and aren't desirable). We'll have to make decisions about
particular desiderata. We accept Z and rank it highly. Although we might
be assisted by rules of thumb and general principles, these aren't algorithms
or formulas. They won't produce answers for us. *We* have to produce the answers. What should we cook for dinner tonight? Which desiderata should we
be guided by?

We have to make collective decisions. I believe some of our reasons and
considerations should have to do with morality. With what's right and good,
fair and just. The moral good of our scientific community, our stakeholders,
society at large. Distinction d is accountable to scientific and epistemic objectives.
It'll have to perform well scientifically and epistemically (whatever that's taken
to be and however it's measured). But it's also accountable to moral objectives.
It'll have to perform well morally (whatever that's taken to be and however it's
measured).

At this point, three objections are brewing. First, the preceding can't be
affirmed in the abstract, as if it applied to any situation, community, time,
and place. Second, an objector can point out, no doubt accurately, that I'm
just some guy. Didn't I say that the decision-maker must be the community?
Who am I to affirm that morality should or shouldn't be taken into account?
Third, prediction is king. In science, prediction is the utmost desideratum.
Always. Come what may. Period. It trumps everything else. Scientists are in
the predictive business, either because predicting and controlling nature and
society is science's function, or because correct prediction is a proxy for
truth. So, the right way to classify things and draw distinctions is this: whatever augments your project's predictive power. Do Hamas and Montoneros
belong in the same group? If predictive power is increased, they do. If it isn't,
they don't.

A variant of this objection substitutes 'explanation' for 'prediction' (and
assumes they're symmetrical anyway).[49] Stinchcombe:

> It is, of course, possible for any moderately ingenious man to multiply dis-
> tinctions and develop concepts. But to be useful a conceptual scheme must

49. Hempel 1942, 1958.

be informed by an idea of the motors of social action; the *only justification* for classifying two phenomena together and distinguishing them from others is that we think the two phenomena classed together play the same role in a scheme of explanation, that their differences are irrelevant and their similarities crucial.[50]

My reply is that there's nothing wrong with being a fan of prediction and explanation. They've got tons of fans. For many scientific disciplines and projects, they're an understandable, defensible, and commendable desire. What's missing is an argument demonstrating that prediction, or explanation, is the one most important desideratum. The "only justification," as Stinchcombe suggests. An argument that doesn't beg the question. (That the goal of science is to control nature can't be a premise.) Prediction and explanation are popular, but they aren't everyone's ambition. Not in sociology, not in astronomy, and not in physics. How will you persuade someone who isn't already persuaded?

But there's more. Typically, scientists who believe prediction (or explanation) is an important desideratum don't believe it's the one and only one. So, they face the usual obstacles: how much weight each desideratum should be allocated, how important predictive (or explanatory) power is, and how to measure and implement relative importance.

9.5 Individuation

Up to now, I've presented *Activity DF* as consisting of three steps. First, there's a set of elements (objects, things, entities) before you. Second, there are many ways to split and lump them; you go ahead and choose one of them. Step three, you have your groups, the product of your classification. With them, you can conduct your investigation and analyses—provided they're communally acceptable.

These three steps gloss over the individuation of the elements you started out with. Sometimes it's unclear what one object is. One thing, distinct from its environment, not two or more things, not one part of a thing. An individual—that is, "a particular which . . . is separable, countable, has acceptably clear-cut spatial boundaries, and exhibits transtemporal identity."[51] As Dupré puts it:

50. Stinchcombe 1964, 679 (emphasis added).
51. Pradeu 2010, 247.

A final problem with scientific classification . . . is that 'things' are often distinguishable only after classification, rather than presenting themselves to be classified in full-fledged thingness. So, for example, it is obvious to common sense that a tree is an individual thing. But from one biological perspective a copse of elm trees, all suckers from the same root system, should be seen as a single individual. A more interesting example is the recent development of the concept of a gene. The more science finds out about the workings of DNA inside living cells, the harder it is to find principled ways of dividing the DNA into components suitable for classification into anything related to the historical meaning of 'gene.'[52]

For much biological work to work, you need distinct, recognizable individuals. Whether it's arguments about populations, reproduction, or evolution; whether it's taxonomies, comparisons, or theories. This is a cat. That's another cat. There's a third cat. One organism. One microorganism. One cell. Yet, the animal world and especially the plant world aren't always ontologically docile.[53] They may conflict with ordinary perception and understanding. It may not be plain what an organism is, where its boundaries are, and how growth differs from reproduction.

Think of quaking aspens, such as Pando in Utah (not to be confused with Pando in Canelones). It looks like many trees, but they're all part of the same root system. Siphonophores, which are colonies of zooids. Corals, which are composed of polyps and zooxanthellae. Certain fungi.[54] Symbionts and holobionts.[55] Even human beings, since a human body is "populated by bacteria, archaea and fungi . . . [and] also by viruses."[56] There's no unique way to distinguish one of it. Where and when does it end? What's part of it and what's not, but something else?

This isn't news. In the nineteenth century, Huxley and Spencer realized that biological individuation is a minefield.[57] More than two millennia earlier, Heraclitus already had (*Cratylus* 402a). Present-day biologists and philosophers of biology are still looking for a way out. It might be advisable to distinguish between two kinds of individuals, physiological and evolutionary ones, and to deny that "the notions of *organism* and *biological individual* [can] be used

---

52. Dupré 2006, 31.
53. Clarke 2012; Janzen 1977; White 1979.
54. Molter 2017, 2019.
55. Doolittle and Booth 2017; S. Gilbert, Sapp, and Tauber 2012; Skillings 2016.
56. Dupré and Guttinger 2016, 110.
57. Lidgard and Nyhart 2017.

interchangeably."[58] Maybe "collective individuals" have to be admitted to the club.[59] Maybe traditional metaphysical frameworks are unfit for the task, and the only viable tactic to accommodate biological phenomena is to ditch substances and turn to processual ontologies.[60]

The lesson for *Activity DF* is that there's no fact of the matter about individuation. An untrained eye sees a jellyfish over there and a tree over here. It sees nothing to quarrel about. But this eye has myopia and astigmatism. The world can't tell you what one thing is, how to distinguish an entity from its environment and from other entities. Picking out individuals necessitates making choices, much like you have choices when you classify and make distinctions among things. Who has to make choices, again? As I've been arguing, it's not you, but we, the community.

'Hang on,' you reprovingly interrupt. 'Not so fast.' You believe in metaphysical substances. You don't make much of the fact that scientists aren't sure, in some plant and animal cases, what counts as one of them. They aren't good enough biologists, or not good enough at biological individuation. Not yet anyway. Nature's joints aren't a matter of opinion, whether you're identifying kinds of things or you're individuating things.

This is another juncture at which philosophical divergences may carry the day, since my arguments are incompatible with essentialisms. We'll have to sit down together, and look closely at your objection and its intended reach. Can I do something about it without abandoning my plan? Our discussion isn't guaranteed to bear fruit. If it doesn't, we'll have to part ways. Irreconcilable metaphysical differences.

———

Biological individuation is elusive. A fortiori (I think), individuation is more elusive in the social world. It bedevils social scientists. They're hard-pressed to say what's one institution, one action, one interaction, one belief. One psychological state, one practice, one policy. One phenomenon, one culture, one ideology, one society. Picking out one organization (the McDonald's Corporation, NYU) and one person (Lady Gaga, Emilio Frugoni) seem less tricky, because their commonsense and legal individuation can be good

58. Pradeu 2016b, 797; cf. DiFrisco 2019.

59. Bouchard and Huneman 2013.

60. Bueno, Chen, and Fagan 2018; Dupré 2012; Dupré and Guttinger 2016; Dupré and Leonelli 2022; Ereshefsky and Pedroso 2013, 2015; S. Gilbert, Sapp, and Tauber 2012; S. Gilbert and Tauber 2016; Guay and Pradeu 2016; Hull 1978; Pradeu 2016a; J. Wilson 1999.

FIGURE 9.1. Pando: how many trees is that? Photo: J Zapell. This image is a work of the Forest Service of the United States Department of Agriculture. Public domain photo.

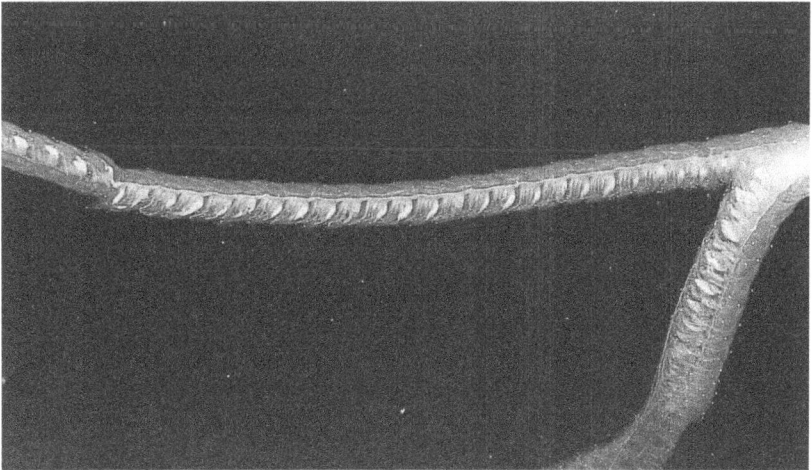

FIGURE 9.2. Siphonophore: how many animals is that? NOAA Office of Ocean Exploration and Research. Public domain photo. https://oceanexplorer.noaa.gov/image-gallery/.

FIGURE 9.3. Dandelion siphonophore: how many animals is that? NOAA Office of Ocean Exploration and Research. Public domain photo.

enough for social science research. Except where diachronic change makes it tricky again. Except where mereology gets tricky—say, what is and isn't a part of an organization.

You have to distinguish a thing from other things. You have to deal with its boundaries: this society is distinct from that society, this action is distinct from that action (rather than being the same action, or two parts of a larger action). And you have to deal with continuity/identity over time: in virtue of what is this institution the same institution it was last year, last month, ten minutes ago. Which lands social scientists with philosophers who've asked what it is to be the same person as last month, and to be the same ship as twenty years ago. What makes B the true successor of A, what makes C and D belong to the same tradition, and what warrants the diachronic identity of a concept at time t_1 and time t_2.[61]

If my account is on the right track, two things are up in the air. One is what the objects are: what's to be taken as one object, or one unit or individual. The other is how to classify these objects, what distinctions to make among them. (They're in fact interwoven, but can be analytically isolated.) In both cases, decisions will have to be good and useful from a communal perspective. Useful to attain goals our community is after, and sees as worth being after. In both

---

61. On individuation in the history of metaphysics and theology, see Gracia (1994); Lukasiewicz, Anscombe, and Popper (1953); and Whiting (1986). An influential 'continental' work is Simondon ([1964] 1995). On succession and tradition, see Gallie (1956) and Ruben (2010).

cases, the basic question is which desiderata apply and to what degree. If I'm right, none of this is up to individual scientists.

9.6 How to choose

Social scientists and philosophers have converged on a picture of science that neither romanticizes nor trivializes it. Scientific knowledge isn't what it used to be thought to be. Textbooks tell fairy tales. There are no such things as pure sense perception and pure data. No view from nowhere, no God's eye view. Facts won't speak for themselves. The evidence is always consistent with more than one theory. The world won't tell us, by itself, which claims, hypotheses, models, or theories are correct. While it doesn't remain silent, judgments and decisions have to be made. By us. Knowledge and science are social products. They're produced by human beings in their social and material contexts, with particular tools and devices. They're embodied, they're practical accomplishments, they're socially and organizationally embedded. However, these realizations don't entail that knowledge and science are reducible to ideology, subjective opinions and preferences, and politics.

Within this picture, values and virtues have been assigned preeminent roles. Initially, the conversation centered on cognitive or epistemic values.[62] Cognitive, epistemic, or intellectual virtues and vices. Eventually, they were joined by non-epistemic or non-cognitive values, despite (or because of) the complications they bring along.[63] At the same time, the distinction between the epistemic and the non-epistemic, cognitive and non-cognitive values, has come under attack.[64]

Epistemic values are a much easier sell than non-epistemic ones. The former, like simplicity and coherence, can be argued to be extra-scientific in some sense. But this is only a limited sense. The latter, especially moral values, are hard to square with many scientists' self-understanding, with the public understanding

62. Pritchard 2007.

63. 'This picture' groups together a lot of stuff. Lumping mode. Work on epistemic injustice (Fricker 2007), pragmatic encroachment in epistemology (Kim and McGrath 2019; Moss 2018; Stanley 2005), and inductive risk in the philosophy of science (H. Douglas 2000; Elliott and Richards 2017; Steel 2010, 2013). Foucault (1975) on power/knowledge, Habermas (1968a) on knowledge and interests, and the whole pragmatist tradition. Virtue epistemology (Alfano 2013b; Axtell 1997; J. Greco 2012). Traditional views of science and knowledge have been also chastised by feminist and standpoint epistemologists (Code 1991; Haraway 1988; Harding 1991; Wylie 2012), communitarian epistemologists (Kusch 2002), and (two kinds of) social epistemologists (Collin 2013; Fuller 1988, Goldman 1999).

64. Lacey 2004, 2017; Longino 2004; Rooney 1992.

of science, and with many scientific organizations' 'frontstage.'[65] Unsurprisingly, they're often met with skepticism. It's been difficult to justify why non-epistemic considerations should play a role in epistemic pursuits and scientific knowledge, and to specify just what roles and where.

One well-established path for bringing non-epistemic values into the picture is 'inductive risk' arguments.[66] Rudner's "The Scientist qua Scientist Makes Value Judgments" presented the crux of the argument:

> Now I take it that no analysis of what constitutes the method of science would be satisfactory unless it comprised some assertion to the effect that the scientist as scientist accepts or rejects hypotheses. But if this is so then clearly the scientist as scientist does make value judgments. For, since no scientific hypothesis is ever completely verified, in accepting a hypothesis the scientist must make the decision that the evidence is sufficiently strong or that the probability is sufficiently high to warrant the acceptance of the hypothesis. Obviously our decision regarding the evidence and respecting how strong is "strong enough," is going to be a function of the importance, in the typically ethical sense, of making a mistake in accepting or rejecting the hypothesis.[67]

You have to decide whether the evidence is sufficiently strong. You have to make a judgment. You can't be certain, but only more or less confident in a claim. So, importance "in the typically ethical sense" influences which risks you're willing to take, when you're ready to stand behind a claim, how you weigh the costs and benefits of competing options. Moral considerations must figure in your acceptance or rejection of hypotheses—and the real-life practices, institutions, and technologies based on them: vaccines and AIs; reforming education and regulating industry and business. In science, but also elsewhere. Whether you're a physician, a journalist, a cook, or talking to your neighbor. Indeed, you might be a statistician who's assessing the costs of making an error. Pissing off your spouse or boss can be very costly, as Blalock pointed out:

> The decision as to the significance level selected depends on the relative costs of making the one or the other type of error [type I or type II] and should be evaluated accordingly. . . . In the coin-flipping example, suppose that the decision involved refusing to continue gambling with a coin the honesty of which were in doubt. If a male gambler were faced with the prospects of a nagging wife should he return home with empty

65. Goffman 1956, 78.
66. H. Douglas 2000; Elliott and Richards 2017; Hempel 1965; Steel 2010, 2013.
67. Rudner 1953, 2.

pockets, he would do well to quit the game if there were even a reasonable doubt about the coin. In such a case he would select a large critical region since the penalty for making a type II error (i.e., staying in the game when the coin is actually dishonest) would be quite large. On the other hand, if he were to run the risk of insulting his boss if he claimed that the coin was dishonest, he would want to be very sure of this fact before he made his decision. In the latter case he should select a very small critical region, thereby minimizing the risk of a type I error.[68]

The basic point has been known for long.[69] But recent philosophy of science has dug deeper into it. Going "beyond inductive risk," Brigandt argues that "social values . . . may determine a theory's condition of adequacy, which among other things can include considerations about what makes a scientific account unbiased and complete."[70] For their part, Elliott and McKaughan argue that "nonepistemic values can . . . override epistemic considerations in assessing scientific representations for practical purposes."[71]

In any of these versions, scientific communities' recognizing non-epistemic values shapes their picture of science, what scientists are considered to be doing, and what successful work is. Add the feminist tradition in the philosophy of science, including standpoint epistemology, which has long argued that social and political values can be good for science—provided they're selected and used well.[72] In Longino's terms, "objectivity" doesn't amount to the "absence of social values," but their good "management."[73] While this feminist tradition doesn't speak with a unified voice (duh!), stressing moral desiderata is one of its hallmarks. Moral criteria, principles, and aims are required to carry out and judge scientific work.

A case in point is Kourany's *Philosophy of Science after Feminism.* Her "ideal of socially responsible science" "recognizes" that "social values inevitably enter into science [and] we, as a society, have a definite say—through funding priorities and restrictions, for example—as to what these social values will be";[74]

---

68. Blalock 1979b, 160.

69. Churchman 1948.

70. Brigandt 2015, 326.

71. Elliott and McKaughan 2014, 1.

72. Anderson 2014; De Melo-Martín and Intemann 2016; Intemann 2015, 2017; Kourany 2010; Longino 1990, 1995, 2002, 2004, 2013.

73. Longino 2002, 50; cf. Rolin 2017.

74. "Indeed, given that science is both a profound shaper of society and a profound beneficiary of society, these social values should be chosen so as to meet the needs of society, including the justice-related needs of society."

"sexism and androcentrism must be rooted out of science"; "rooting sexism and androcentrism out of science is tantamount to implanting egalitarian social values into science"; "scientific rationality must be defined in terms of scientific success"; and "scientific success must be defined in terms of social success—human flourishing, what makes for a good society—as well as empirical success."[75] Differently put, Kourany's "ideal of socially responsible science permits only those social values in science that make for a good society, only those social values that can be morally justified."[76] Her account of science puts morality front and center. Equality and the good society aren't an afterthought, a byproduct, a kind lagniappe.

Attempts at building values into the practice of science are divisive. Moral values are most treacherous. They can be appropriated by critics of science and expertise, who wish to undermine their legitimacy in the public sphere. 'Scientists are as partial as politicians and activists.' 'The theories of science are on a par with the theories of other groups and organizations.' 'Scientists provide only one side of the story.' Critics equate values with subjectivity and bias. Science isn't special. In the offing: conspiracy theories and bullshit, which social media companies will hasten to amplify for profit.

Social scientists or philosophers who see the force of arguments about non-epistemic values may not be prepared to go moral all the way. Their refusal can itself have moral grounds. The eventuality of undermining science and expertise would be morally perilous, irresponsible, irresponsibly enabling groups that trade on irrationality and antidemocratic sentiments. Happily, it's not an all-or-nothing choice. For example, a researcher can stick to epistemic values only, and then piggyback on Putnam's tripartite argument. First, "science . . . presupposes values"; second, "*epistemic* values (coherence, simplicity, and the like) are values, too"; and third, epistemic values are "in the same boat as ethical values with respect to objectivity."[77] A third way of sorts. There are others.

––––––––

Suppose it's been agreed that the list of desiderata for scientific projects should transcend the epistemic domain. It's been also agreed that moral ends and values should be somehow in the mix. How should they be in the mix?

75. Kourany 2010, 68.

76. Kourany 2010, 79.

77. Putnam 2002, 4.

Which moral ends and values? Won't there be never-ending disagreements about these?

Scientists' distinctions will be acceptable insofar as they serve communal moral ends and advance communal moral values (all other things being equal). They'll be preferable insofar as they better serve those moral ends (all other things being equal). In practice, there'll be disagreements. Moral disputes within scientific communities are sure to arise. For instance, fighting against sexism and androcentrism won't seem to everyone equally important. Some will say that the importance of this moral fight can't be overstated, but science isn't responsible for it. What then?

It's not the happiest prospect for a scientific community. It'll take up considerable time and effort, and it'll try the patience of many community members. It'll involve laborious moral thinking and argumentation, possibly deadlocks and frustration, while people are anxious to go back to their research, articles, and grant proposals. But I'm afraid they have to live with it. Arguments about morality and values are a prerequisite for the assessment of scientific distinctions and classifications. A scientific community isn't in a position to properly judge *Activity DF* without a moral compass, a moral outlook, a sense of what its work is for. A sense of what it's up to, ethically speaking. You don't leave your house without a moral outlook either.

On the plus side, it doesn't need to be a full-fledged or precise ethical account, nor a perfectly consensual one. That'd be too much to ask—and I'm already asking a lot. What this scientific community does need is some sense of good and bad, of the goods to be pursued, and of the wrongs and horrors to be avoided. If you're a social scientist who has sexist and racist goals, your *Activity DF* will be bad. Inasmuch as it helps your project achieve those desiderata, it's pro tanto a bad scientific distinction.

Imagine a totalitarian regime, whose leader and their aides and sycophants fabricate scientific results. They censor articles, and they control what does and doesn't get published in the journals. A few years later, giving in to international pressure, the regime stops imposing such overt policies. Its renewed strategy is to mandate the use of certain distinctions and ban others. Scientific projects must classify things as the regime dictates: ethnicities, countries, organizations, genders, sexual orientations, political ideas, revolutions (or not), terrorist groups (or not), religions, social classes. These mandates and bans were devised to favor the leader's interests, their worldview, their bogus statements about unprecedented economic and social development, and the domination and exploitation of the people. My point is that the resulting research would be terrible in virtue of its morally terrible distinctions, irrespective of any other accomplishments: descriptive accuracy, meticulousness, methodological sophistication, statistically significant results, or generalizability. It'd be terrible qua scientific research.

I've been underlining the immediate, real-world implications of social scientists' classifications, distinctions, and word uses. Immediate as in tomorrow morning. As a community, we have options among values and desiderata, some of which are in competition with one another. We must select, reject, combine, and weigh them. To do this, we could really use well-thought-out ideas, which can orient our discussions and practices.

Some philosophers say something in the vicinity of 'it depends on your goals' or 'it depends on our goals,' and leave it at that, without addressing the relativist elephant in the room. They're right, but not helpful, because the concern is precisely what our goals should be and how to prevent their being determined in an unfair/unjust and unequal fashion. Other philosophers take it for granted that there'll be a consensus, a rational consensus, and leave it at that. Or that a rational consensus is in principle possible. It may be, yes, but they aren't very helpful either.

Some philosophers use the pronoun 'we' and make claims about 'us,' even though their evidence is anecdotal. Their default setting is that 'we' means our society, located in North America (excepting Mexico) or Western Europe (mostly the United Kingdom, France, Germany, and the Nordic countries). Our society is the United States ($p \leq .05$). 'We' can more narrowly refer to our scientific community, or to well-thinking scientists or philosophers, provided they do think well. Instead of referring to actual people, 'we' is an abstract ideal of reason. It papers over that social groups have disagreements, conflicts, and multifarious ends. There are many differences among 'us.' In fact, had it not been for these disagreements, 'we' wouldn't have raised the question in the first place.

For better assistance, communities may turn to scholarship that's mindful of the practical challenges involved, and of the social character of the processes through which research gets conducted, and knowledge gets produced, validated, and communicated. Empirically minded philosophers of science who do provide good sociological and historical accounts, in which social circumstances and institutional mechanisms have been thought through.[78] Social scientists who've examined how communities, scientific or otherwise, succeed at being democratic and participatory. They've inquired into the tools, practices, incentives, and structures that are conducive to morally good outcomes (on which more below).

---

78. Alexandrova and Fabian 2022; Longino 2002; M. Sample 2022.

Next up: get more concrete about the practice of *Activity DF*—and also of *Activity WF*. That's the next step for us, the community. Get together, think together, work together. Give reasons to one another. Think hard about *Activity DF* and *Activity WF* as they are and will be conducted on the ground, along with communities' assessments of their worth, and conflicts about them. Work out what to do, taking into account organizational and social factors, stratification and status dynamics, and the discrepancies between individual and collective interests. Try things out.

The goal is to improve communities' understanding and practice of *Activity DF* and *Activity WF*. Getting them to work better, from both an epistemic and a moral viewpoint. Communities have to get clear on the nature of the problem, how to judge distinctions and word uses, applicable criteria and metacriteria. For all of this, there's no alternative but to get everyone involved. It's a long-term participatory undertaking.

9.7 A Chinese encyclopedia

Scientific communities aren't going to greenlight any distinction or classification. The classification of animals that Borges attributes to "a certain Chinese encyclopedia" hasn't gained any traction among zoologists and ethologists.[79] Many other proposals haven't and won't either. How to determine which ones are acceptable and desirable? You can rephrase the question in terms of 'usefulness,' the usefulness of distinctions and classifications, keeping in mind that this is neither a free pass nor a trump card. For what and whom is *d* useful? For what and whom it's not useful? For what and whom it's harmful? How does *d* compare to possible alternatives? The community will pose these questions to judge *d*'s acceptability and desirability.

I've argued that the usefulness of distinctions and classifications is a collective problem. It's up to all of us, not you. Usefulness for you and your project can be a consideration. What makes your life easier isn't off the table, but it doesn't call the shots. In this respect, and appearances to the contrary, individual scientists don't have discretion and autonomy. While you can try to do whatever you feel like, the arbiter will be the community. It won't be cool with selfish behavior, whose sole end is to advance your career and get your papers published, no matter what. For instance, the community might be represented by the reviewers of your manuscript, your dissertation committee, your fellow graduate students, and your job talk audiences. You might try, but a well-functioning

79. Borges (1952) 1960, 134.

scientific community won't allow utter selfishness. It'll be organizationally and culturally prepared to detect unacceptable desiderata, and the distinctions based on them. Just like it'll be prepared to arrest unacceptable word uses, be they due to selfishness or craziness. Due to confusion, ignorance, or someone who's performing a Humpty Dumpty impression.

This is what I have in mind. Scientists make *Activity DF* proposals within scientific communities, which aim at scores of desiderata. The community has procedures to evaluate them, their arrangement, and how much a distinction helps achieve them. Procedures that are institutionalized, organizationally embedded, functional, legitimate, and have teeth. Procedures, criteria, principles, methods—more or less formal, more or less standardized, more or less general, more or less flexible. Good science uses morally good distinctions and classifications. These are selected through collective procedures that must themselves pass moral tests. Non-epistemic considerations matter to both what we're after and how we decide what we're after.

Evaluating desiderata and distinctions isn't straightforward, particularly since morality has been invited to the party. The community will probably encounter undecidable instances, either in principle or in practice. As a matter of fact, there are obstacles galore—for *Activity DF* as much as for *Activity WF*. There are detrimental organizational structures and incentives. Detrimental psychological tendencies and cognitive biases. And there's the plain fact of disagreement in communities, groups, and societies. Whatever the subject matter, people have divergent views about it, and their coming to agree is the exception, not the norm. Neither agreeing substantively, nor agreeing as to where they're happy to disagree. Not even how to disagree about how to disagree.[80] Working together and making collective decisions is difficult. Difficult in many ways and for many reasons.

Noticing that it'll be a rough going for any scientific community, critics smell blood and pounce: 'It's quixotic to aim for epistemically and morally good outcomes, rational resolution of disputes, fair/just and efficient procedures, and agreed-upon practices. Are you fucking serious?'

I see what they're saying. Yet, their point is general and it'd prove too much. It might well merit a companions-in-guilt response.[81] Or it might merit the response, and temperament, of unwavering political activists and social movements. 'We aren't intimidated by ideals whose realization is uncertain and far off. We're up for difficult tasks, and we won't give up because they're difficult.

---

80. Christensen and Lackey 2013; Feldman and Warfield 2010; Grundmann 2019; Machuca 2017. Thanks to Sebastian Kohl for his comments on this topic.

81. Clipsham 2019; Cowie 2018; Lillehammer 2007.

The effort seems quixotic to many. Some mornings it seems quixotic to us. But we'll continue to struggle for change nonetheless.'

———

I argue that an individual can't establish by themselves the criteria to tell apart good from bad distinctions, good from bad classifications, more and less important desiderata. I'm an individual, therefore I can't establish this. However, collective processes must somehow get started. An individual may extend an invitation to others. A first move or step, which other people can respond to. A conversation starter.

10

Conversation starters (fragments, sketches, suggestions, doubts)

MENO: Can you tell me, Socrates, whether virtue is teachable? Or is it not teachable, but attainable by practice? Or is it attainable neither by practice nor by learning, and do people instead acquire it by nature, or in some other way?

. . .

SOCRATES: How could I know what *sort* of thing something is, when I don't know *what* it is? Or do you think that, if someone doesn't know at all who Meno is, it is possible for him to know whether Meno is beautiful or rich or even of good birth, or, as it may be, the opposites of these? Do you think that possible?

—PLATO, MENO 70A–71B[1]

10.1 Hey!

Hey! Let's get together and think together about *Activity WF* and *Activity DF*. How should we use word 'w'? How should we establish how we should use word 'w'? How should we establish how we should establish how we should use word 'w'? And so on . . . (Also: how to deal with this infinite regress, or whether we're OK with turtles all the way down.)

Which distinctions are acceptable and unacceptable around here? How should we establish which distinctions are acceptable and unacceptable around here? How should we establish how we should establish which distinctions are acceptable and unacceptable around here? And so on . . . (Also: how to deal with this infinite regress, or whether we're OK with turtles all the way down.)

---

1. This is Alex Long's translation (*Plato: Meno and Phaedo*, edited by David Sedley, published by Cambridge University Press).

Our collective answers to these questions should lead to collective action, organizational reforms, cultural and educational initiatives. We may decide to try out this well-founded initiative, see how it does, amend it, amend it again, and so on. It'll be a ceaseless collaborative project: thought and discussion, design and redesign, trial and error, better and worse results. We want to make a difference to our social science communities' practices, grounded in solid understandings of their circumstances, tools, methods, and aspirations. What we're after is improvements on the status quo. Action.

———

In chapter 2, I introduced a problem and ominously called it 'the problem.' It turned out not to be 'a' or 'the,' but more than one. I'm dissatisfied with the logic underlying social scientists' uses of key words and distinctions, with prevalent procedures, criteria, and reasons (or lack thereof). Are my misgivings warranted? I've done my best to explain why I think they are. Obviously, I may be mistaken, and I'd be happy to be shown to be mistaken. Happy twice over. Happy because a mistake would have been found and corrected, so we'd be all better off. Happy because not having a problem is better than having it. Tell me where I went wrong!

Identifying a problem isn't to be able to solve it. 'The problem' can't be solved by an individual. Yet, being unable to solve a problem isn't to have nothing to contribute to its solution.

———

Hey, you guys, let's get together! Let's *all* get together: no member of the community should be excluded.

Uh-oh, I hear you say this is too quick and vague? I hear you have qualms about 'all'—namely, whether literally all of us ought to be there?

You also have qualms about one other infinite regress, which my call to get together gives rise to. Who gets to participate in a discussion about 'w' or d? Who gets to participate in a discussion about who gets to participate in a discussion about 'w' or d? Who gets to participate in a discussion ... ?

I hear you. Hold your horses for a bit.

———

I've drawn my examples of words and distinctions mostly from sociology, and occasionally from political science, anthropology, and history. I've spoken somewhat imprecisely of 'social science communities,' and problems for 'the social sciences.' In many cases, I could have included 'the humanities,' humanities scholars, regardless of their stance vis-à-vis scientific methods. I also inspected biological individuation arguments, and in the appendix I'll inspect planetary scientists' disputes over the extension of 'planet,' and how they resemble disputes over the extension of 'populism' or 'diversity.'

Assume I'm right that something isn't quite right about key words and distinctions in empirical research. Which disciplines and projects have to confront these issues, and which ones remain untouched by them? Well-trodden dichotomies between *Naturwissenschaften* and *Geisteswissenschaften*, between causal explanation and empathetic understanding, can't cut it. Pluto, Venus, and Jupiter are chunks of matter (rock, gas, ice). They don't have consciousness, language, and intentions. There aren't subjective meanings for planetary scientists to understand and interpret. Nevertheless, naming and classifying these celestial objects can be as contentious as naming and classifying Buddhism, Confucianism, and Umbanda. Biologists' individuation of an organism can be as problematic as sociologists' individuation of a culture, an action, or an institution. The source of these difficulties lies with us, researchers and research communities, not with them, our objects of inquiry.

The word 'planet' matters to several institutions. The distinction between planets and dwarf planets matters to schools, teachers, children, and the media. Most projects in biology, physics, chemistry, and astronomy aren't like that. They aren't close enough to societal concerns, so they can remain esoteric. But this isn't a law of nature: a biologist's or a physicist's research may be of interest to society, public policy, and the law. Public opinion and the media may get turned on to it. Insofar as such social connections obtain, these projects will be in the same boat as anthropological accounts of religion, the sociology of gender and race inequalities, and political scientists' findings about the causes of populism.

There's no dichotomy between two kinds of disciplines, and attendant kinds of endeavors, to which my concerns respectively do and don't apply. To be sure, they're more likely to apply in what's conventionally called 'social sciences' and 'humanities,' but that's all, a higher probability. Further, they apply to different degrees to different projects. There's variation within the social sciences and humanities: *Activity WF* and *Activity DF* are more or less problematic, more or less saliently problematic, depending on the specifics. Economists' projects are more likely to be able to remain esoteric about their words and distinctions than sociologists' projects, but that's all, a higher probability.

————

First things first. I've been talking about and I'll continue to talk about morality. I want to make room for moral reasons, moral considerations, moral norms. I argue for a logic of research that contemplates how to be just/fair, how to offset inequalities, and how to discourage selfishness. To prevent misunderstandings: I believe it's uncontroversial that social science communities are in the knowledge production business. Whatever else they might set out to accomplish, whatever else they might be driven by or make decisions on the basis of, obtaining social science knowledge isn't optional. Else, they'd stop being social science communities. There are many things a cook can do qua cook. But if their activity didn't have anything to do with preparing food, they wouldn't be doing it qua cook. 'Social science' is a capacious expression and hopefully your community is diverse and pluralist about what it does. But its capacity and pluralism can't be infinite.

The devil is in the details: what a community accepts as social science knowledge, and how this relates to morality, justice/fairness, inequality, and non-selfishness. But first things first. We're in the social science business. My arguments are about communities that observe, analyze, and make claims about the social world. Their sights are set on empirical truth.

10.2 Are some animals more equal than others?

Discussions about words and distinctions are primarily discussions about particular words and particular distinctions. This 'w' or this d. One community will reflect on and make decisions about the uses of 'happiness.' Another discussion will be about 'corruption.' Others about 'artificial intelligence,' 'globalization,' and 'technology.' A conversation might be about the distinction between trust and trustworthiness, between empathy and sympathy, between profession and occupation, or the classification of ethnicities or genders. Economic and social historians will discuss the distinction between capitalism and proto-capitalism, since they hope to account for the rise of capitalism, while historians of political violence try to distinguish among wars, civil wars, riots, and a few skirmishes. Sociologists and psychologists who study 'altruism' and 'selfishness' will get together. Sociologists and anthropologists who study religious practices and phenomena will get together.

The way I envision these discussions, stakeholders will also participate. If there are meetings, they'll be in attendance. Stakeholders are someway affected by 'w' or d, by research that uses 'w' or d, even though they aren't academics or academic organizations. They'll express their views and give reasons, as other participants do.

To get these conversations started, we have to get specific. We may talk about 'altruism,' its current uses, their effects, how it's been translated, how it's been used elsewhere, and which English words are similar to and are used interchangeably with 'altruism.' We may need a fine-grained history of distinctions between Christianity and Judaism on the one hand, and, on the other, spiritual practices and institutions originating outside the Global North. The history of the distinction between Christianity and Judaism on the one hand, and beliefs and practices that don't involve monotheism and an omniscient and omnipotent deity on the other. And so on.

This book isn't the place to start any of these conversations. My conversation starters are about all of them, or at least many of them. It's an open question if their generality is a kiss of death.

————

Academic elites. Holders of endowed chairs. Chairs of recruitment committees, chairs of best book and best article prizes, chairs of university departments, chairs of funding panels. Journal editors. Fancy-pants professors at top universities, influential scholars, presidents of professional associations and scientific academies, deans, and other higher-ups. These people are social science communities' elites—I mean no demeaning connotation. Oftentimes they decide how word 'w' should and shouldn't be used, and whether distinction d is or isn't acceptable (see chapter 2 and chapter 8). It's an exclusive, VIP club. Most scholars of 'w' and d can't get into it.

I'm unhappy with this arrangement. I'd like us to consider how to change it. I invite you, fellow community members, to think and talk about it together. Carefully, critically, fair-mindedly. 'Us' being the communities of which I'm a member, comprising more junior and more senior people, neophytes and higher-ups. Hence the first-person-plural pronoun. But I'm also reaching out to communities my research is unrelated to. This 'we' wouldn't be literal; it'd refer to any community of researchers. Let's consider how to change this arrangement.

Wherever meritocratic systems are operational, academic elites should have superior scholarly qualifications and abilities. (This idealization of meritocracy needn't be empirically interrogated or contested at this time. Bear with me.) They're excellently prepared to do scientific research on 'w'- and d-related things. Current practices and institutions assume that, therefore, they're the best *Activity WF* and *Activity DF* decision-makers. They're justifiably in charge of 'w' and d. They're in charge for the same reason they're in the best position to judge knowledge claims in their areas of expertise. An experienced professor, who's published outstanding research on 'w' and has read extensively in this area, can review a manuscript on 'w' more proficiently than a first-year graduate student.

I've argued against this rationale. But I have to tread cautiously and fine-tune my argument, since *Activity WF* and *Activity DF* can use this professor's help in some ways—practical reason activities though they are. The following three paragraphs offer a progressively better account of the situation.

(1) To a first approximation: I've shown that *Activity WF* and *Activity DF* aren't your archetypical scientific activity and outcome. They're a different kettle of fish. The desired end result isn't true claims and correct theories, but good collective arrangements and decisions. A dinner with which everyone is content. With the food, with its preparation, with its financing. So, all community members are equal, in that we all get a say, we all get equal participation, rights, and decision-making powers. No VIP privileges for anybody. Famous professors and committee chairs aren't more competent than Jane Doe and John Doe, because practical reason and morality aren't scientific and intellectual aptitude, nor scholarly experience and accomplishments. In democratic elections, politicians' and political experts' votes don't count more, do they? All animals are equal. No animals are more equal than others.[1]

(2) Paragraph #1 is, however, importantly incomplete. *Activity WF* and *Activity DF* encompass moral/practical stuff and epistemic/scientific stuff. Moral goods, goals, projects, values, hopes, ways of life. And epistemic goods, knowledge, facts, scientific laws, understanding. But here's the thing. To obtain the latter, knowledge and expertise are advantageous. They're necessary. As a community, we're looking to predict how this 'w' or *d* will achieve these scientific desiderata, given multifaceted initial conditions, epistemic and social. What's more, we'd prefer words and distinctions that resonate with societies' concerns, people can make sense of, and policy makers can work with. Decision-making about 'w' and *d* will be enhanced by under-standing what's at stake and by being well-informed about their history, too. Who can assess these factors effectively and reliably? Assuming again a functioning meritocracy, elites are likely to have the wherewithal to be helpful. On average, they're more likely to be able to help than younger and greener community members (no offense to our students, no adultism). Some animals are more equal than others after all?

1. Orwell (1945) 1964, 83.

(3) Paragraph #2 is, however, importantly incomplete. It says that knowledge and expertise are advantageous, and that they're necessary. True. Yet, as I argued earlier, they aren't sufficient. The epistemic/scientific realm isn't exclusively epistemic and scientific. Values and the community come into play in various forms, at various points, not least in choosing and ranking desiderata. There are more and less radical variants of this argument, but they all weaken academic elites' position, as I presented them in paragraph #2. Yes, there are community members who can uniquely contribute to *Activity WF* and *Activity DF*, in virtue of their knowledge and expertise. They can tell us important things about 'w' and *d* that most of us are unaware of. However, they don't get to make decisions autonomously. Not even about epistemic/scientific goods. *Activity WF* and *Activity DF* are communal jobs, in which everyone can and should get involved.

To support this last point, you may prefer a Weberian take: knowledge and expertise are brought to bear on means, but not on ends. Academic elites can be recruited as technicians. Ends are above their pay grade, be they epistemic or moral.[2] The community retains its sovereignty and ultimate decision-making authority.

———

Summing up, *Activity WF* and *Activity DF* can be represented as containing two elements, whose modi operandi are dissimilar. Concerning the moral/practical side of things, nothing trumps equality, equal participation, equal rights. Just like the principle of 'one person, one vote' in democratic elections, nobody can be excluded. Not irresponsible, immoral, and apathetic individuals. Not assholes. More and less intelligent people, wiser and less wise, well-informed and uninformed: everyone gets one vote (more on this below). Concerning the epistemic/scientific side of things, abilities are unequally distributed. To the extent that they're necessary for the good practice of *Activity WF* and *Activity DF*, communities will have to consider how to articulate the two elements. To make things more complicated, this question itself reproduces the tension between equal democratic participation and unequal epistemic endowments and capacities.

Companions-in-guilt reminder, if it makes you feel better: *Activity WF* and *Activity DF* are in good company. Their quandaries are analogous to well-known tensions between democracy and science, democratic institutions and

2. Weber (1919) 1946.

technocratic doctrines, citizens and experts (more on this below).[3] What's to be judged and decided by citizens directly, by their elected representatives, and by unelected experts? Where to trust science and expertise as advisors (scientists on tap, but not on top)? Where to fully outsource a decision or policy to them, because it's about scientific truths and calculations, not citizens' desires, understandings, and agreements? A usual follow-up is suggestions to replace the people with a select few, or with a select one, like a philosopher-king or scientist-king. To replace democratic decision-making with the rule of the wise, epistocracy, or technocracy. You know how it goes.

Tough issues for a social science community. It'll be challenging to articulate moral/practical and epistemic/scientific goods, egalitarian and inegalitarian dimensions of *Activity WF* and *Activity DF*, participation and knowledge. Not to mention that distinguishing between moral/practical and epistemic/scientific 'elements' is easier on paper than in actuality. For good or bad, these challenges aren't abstract. They'll require hands-on work, tailored to this community, these circumstances, and this instance of 'w' or *d*. Establishing and running concrete policies and offices, organizations and organizational processes, implementation mechanisms, institutional and educational initiatives. Proposals must be applied and pragmatic.

Challenging though these challenges are, the alternative would be tantamount to burying our head in the sand. Communities are diverse. People are diverse; they have diverse talents and skills. You and your research team can see, find out, and understand many things that my research team and I can't. We don't want to forgo talented and skillful people's contributions to our collective goals, to the goals we have as a social science community. It'd be a loss. At the end of the day, though, the collectivity will decide what we should cook for dinner tonight.

———

What should not happen, I think, is what often happens in present-day social science. Elites are known to know more. They're considered to be more epistemically able. Hence, they wind up in social structural and organizational positions from which they rule on a variety of disputes, be they over empirical accounts, statistical analyses, the state of the art, or word uses and distinctions. As if the last item were analogous to the other three. They have de facto powers

---

3. Mark Brown 2009; Callon, Lascoumes, and Barthe 2001; Collins and Evans 2007; Dewey 1927; H. Douglas 2005; Eyal 2019; Feyerabend 1978, 1980; Habermas 1968b; Jasanoff 2003; Kitcher 2001, 2011; Lane 2014; Oreskes 2019; Pamuk 2021; Schudson 2006.

to pronounce judgments about word misuses and unacceptable distinctions, qua committee chairs, professors, advisors, and journal editors. Your 'w' is wrong! Your d is bad!

Elites' intentions might be irreproachable. They're genuinely convinced that their authority is legitimate, they're in the right, their definition or distinction is the best. At least, it's as good as it can be in light of very real pressures, like a 5:30 p.m. flight.[4] In spite of irreproachable intentions, their policies and rulings can still be reproachable. The semantic dice are now loaded in their favor. Favoring research they're sympathetic to, including their own. Their de facto authority results in inequalities and injustices.

The community seems to play along. Why is that? Perhaps elites' control over 'w' and d passes unnoticed. These processes are opaque to most community members. People misjudge the situation: 'Decisions are being made by our most knowledgeable peers, which is how it should be. So, these are the best decisions.' Our most knowledgeable peers may themselves misjudge the situation.

Community members may suppose that currently accepted word uses and distinctions were arrived at naturally, or democratically, or consensually. Or they fail to see that *Activity WF* and *Activity DF* don't admit of correctness, so a knowledgeable person can't find out and know their solution. Or they fail to see that existing practices don't serve everyone's interests. They believe there's never been a problem to begin with.[5]

I've argued that this whole set-up rests on a mistake. It's blind to the other side of the equation. To this side I'm calling you guys' attention.

10.3 Moral goodness

> This community . . . must not be limited, but must extend to all races of beings
> with whom we can come into immediate or mediate intellectual relation. It
> must reach, however vaguely, beyond this geological epoch, beyond all bounds.
>
> —PEIRCE (1878)[6]

Hey, folks, fellow community members! Let's talk about moral goodness in *Activity DF* and *Activity WF*. What sorts of moral goodness? How to attain them? With which moral criteria will these activities be judged?

---

4. Lamont 2009, 155.

5. The sociology of knowledge and agnotology ask why people have false beliefs. If false consciousness and elites' intentions are your cup of tea, you might hypothesize that they're hiding the fact that the dice are semantically loaded (see chapter 3).

6. Peirce 1878, 610–11.

To get the ball rolling, I'm going to submit a few proposals for your consideration. For us to think about and discuss, assess their implications and how they might work in practice, specify their scope, weigh up pros and cons. As far as I can see, these are good proposals. But I might be missing or misjudging something. Maybe I'm morally narrow-minded and politically one-sided and deluding myself about it. Insufficiently imaginative and daring. Reasoning badly. Even if I'm not, I'm just one guy. That's where you—you guys—come in.

Justice/fairness

Social science communities should strive toward *Activity WF* and *Activity DF* outcomes that are just/fair.[7] Besides a collective decision's usefulness for Z, where Z is an epistemic good the community is after, it'll be accountable to moral fairness/justice standards. Suppose the community has decided how the word 'w' may be used. Its decision has scientific payoffs. It's good for data collection and analysis; for description, explanation, and generalizability. Now, is it fair to everyone? To everyone who participated in the deliberative process and everyone on whom it'll have an impact? Communities will have to have plans for trade-offs between usefulness to attain epistemic goods and usefulness to attain moral goods, and plans to deal with incompatibilities between them.

That's about outcomes, such as communities' acceptance of certain word uses and distinctions. In addition, the practice of *Activity WF* and the practice of *Activity DF* will be accountable to moral standards, and specifically justice/fairness standards. No doubt, these activities must produce outcomes that serve social science research, social scientists' analyses and writings, communities' communication and evaluation practices. *Activity WF* and *Activity DF* have to accomplish that, and be effective and efficient at it, or else they'd be remiss. However, it's not effectiveness and efficiency at any cost. Absolute monarchs and dictators can get stuff done quickly, since they don't have to consult anyone. They don't have to follow any rules, and nobody can confront them and oppose their plans. But they're blatantly unjust. Their 'justice' is Thrasymachus's (*Republic* 338c).

I believe social science communities' procedures should be guided, in part, by justice/fairness considerations. This is quite abstract and what it entails is

---

7. I'm using 'justice' and 'fairness' roughly, as non-technical English words. That's also why I write 'just/fair' and 'fairness/justice' with a slash. I think/hope getting more precise isn't necessary here. I think/hope the preceding thought/hope isn't just self-serving.

debatable. So, consider an illustration you're unlikely to find dubious: procedures should try and mitigate structural inequalities. Disadvantaged people, groups, and organizations are taken less seriously, given less time to express themselves and make their case, and paid less attention to. This is no good. Procedures should mitigate disadvantages on the basis of gender, race and ethnicity, class, and disability, as well as disadvantages that are less politically and culturally prominent.

Why? What's the argument for this policy? In our communities, we all have a right to make contributions to *Activity WF* and *Activity DF*. In fact, everyone needs everyone else's contributions. The best solution will take into account everyone's interests, goals, views, and ideas. If it doesn't, it wouldn't be the best solution. On this account, then, morality would be intrinsically valuable and also the best policy.

Material and economic inequalities

What's the significance of material and economic factors for the just/fair practice of *Activity WF* and *Activity DF*? It's got two aspects. First, community members' starting points are unequal, which hinders the proper conduct of these activities. Second, collective decisions about words and distinctions can have unequal material consequences, within and outside the community. There'll be winners and losers. Having won in the past is a good predictor of winning again in the future. In economic, political, and social life, in science, and elsewhere: the rich tend to become richer, and the poor tend to become poorer.[8]

Both inequalities, that of starting points and that of consequences, ought to be recognized and attenuated by the community. Let's talk about how, drawing on the large sociological literature on inequality. Our community is likely to agree that inequality, material and otherwise, is a bad thing. We'd like our community processes not to be determined by unequal relationships and situations. That 'w' and d can diminish inequalities is one reason for us to approve of them and use them.

If you're into fundamentals and into ethics, you might probe my rejection of inequality, and what it's justified by. Some fellow community members believe that inequality is good. It incentivizes individuals to work hard and to try to get to the top. It's healthy. It's natural. The rich deserve to be rich. What am I to say to them?

In any event, it's not embarrassing to acknowledge that social science communities' decisions about words and distinctions take material factors and

---

8. Merton 1968a.

inequalities into account. They're taken into account in order to make things better—as opposed to pretending they don't exist or assuming they won't make a difference for the worse. Scientific communities' self-understandings ought to be perceptive and honest—as opposed to the fiction of science as a pure, sacred endeavor, and contexts of justification as free from social, cultural, and economic contamination.[9]

Democracy

'Democracy' is a notoriously overused and abused word, but I'm going to go ahead and say it anyway: *Activity DF* and *Activity WF* should be democratic.[10] Democratic in some sense of the word 'democracy.' Democratic and inclusive, in some sense of the word 'inclusion.' Everyone should get invited. Participation should be universal. On the face of it, this sounds nice, but familiar troubles surface right away.

First, aren't there any grounds whatsoever to prohibit someone from participating in these activities? Their being ten months old? Utterly shitfaced? Lest Godwin's law be used against me, I'm going to leave it at that. You get my drift.

Second, suppose you insisted that women (or for that matter men), by virtue of being women, shouldn't be permitted to participate. You felt that Uruguayans (or for that matter Paraguayans), by virtue of being Uruguayan, shouldn't be permitted to participate. You'd exclaim, being an anti-Uruguayan activist: 'fuck those fuckers!' Or suppose you insisted that bunioned people shouldn't get invited.[11] How's the community to react to your proposal? I, for one, am ready to argue that you're wrong. I have very good arguments to that effect. I bet others will join in. We'll show why it's morally indefensible to exclude women, Uruguayans, and bunioned people; why your position is discriminatory, sexist, and xenophobic. Yet, if you stick to your guns, we'll have to part ways. Irreconcilable moral differences.

Third, how are we going to individuate the community? How to determine who's a member of the community in the first place? You've probably seen this Trojan horse before. A community looks inclusive and democratic and participatory and lovely, because it disguises prior exclusions, "prior ring-fencing,"

9. On the 'purity of science,' its functions, and its critics, see Kale Lostuvali (2015), Latour (1999), Merton (1938), Panofsky (2010), and Shapin (2010).

10. Collier, Hidalgo, and Maciuceanu 2006; Collier and Levitsky 1997; Gagnon 2018; Gallie 1956.

11. Kohler-Hausmann 2019.

its well-compensated and shredded bouncers.[12] It disguises the prior constitution of the social and political body. Undesirables and undocumented persons weren't let in.[13] Community membership is itself a practical reason problem, which will evidently shape the outcome of *Activity WF* and *Activity DF* (and any other community process). Besides asking how we're going to determine who's a community member, we have to ask how we're going to determine how we're going to determine who's a community member, and so on (and how to deal with this infinite regress).

By the way: by speaking of 'we,' I'm counting myself as a member. But who said I was? Being the owner of this quill, and of this soapbox and bullhorn, isn't enough of a reason.

Fourth, the community, even a broad and inclusive community, may not be broad and inclusive enough. Social scientists' *Activity WF* and *Activity DF* can affect many other people, organizations, the environment, future generations. These are rightfully interested parties or stakeholders. So, they should get to participate somehow. The challenge is how. Word uses, distinctions, knowledge, and understanding should be 'co-produced' with them. The challenge is how.[14]

At the 2006 General Assembly of the International Astronomical Union (IAU), the disputes over the definition of 'planet' and the status of Pluto came to a head (see the appendix). One view was that planetary scientists are sovereign, because of their scientific expertise and knowledge. A more convincing view was that this semantic question shouldn't be answered by scientists alone. It matters what other people and organizations say. There isn't a property, an essential property, which scientists could identify in their labs, offices, or conferences. You can't discover the nature of planethood. By the same token, both psychiatrists and patients should have a say in the classification of mental health conditions. Patients, along with their loved ones, their families and friends.[15] Participation and collaboration are hard, they aren't guaranteed to function well, but ignoring patients is a mistake. A mistake due to many psychiatrists' and psychiatric organizations' misconceptions about *Activity DF*.

---

12. Misak 2013, 37. Peirce "thought that truth was a matter for the community of inquirers—not for this or that individual inquirer. [. . .] With [Chauncey] Wright, Peirce thinks that inquiry must be a democratic, community project, with no prior ring-fencing of what counts as the community."

13. "Manu Chao—Clandestino (Official Music Video)," YouTube, September 12, 2019, https://youtu.be/7AzimrAgWbA.

14. Alexandrova and Fabian 2022; Filipe, Renedo, and Marston 2017; Norström et al. 2020.

15. Bueter 2019, 2021; Gagné-Julien 2021; Gureje and Stein 2012; Sadler and Fulford 2004; Schnittker 2017; Whooley 2010.

They misconstrue it as a solely scientific activity, whose success consists in correspondence with reality.

The extension of 'disability' shouldn't be up to scientists and experts alone, ignoring the people who potentially fall within it. A cue can be taken from inclusive research in disability studies, which has moved "away from research *on* people," replacing it with "research *with* them."[16] Mutatis mutandis, this applies to *Activity WF* and how to use the word 'disability.' Don't impose it on people from the outside, but work things out with them. It also applies to *Activity DF*: distinctions among kinds of disability, among more and less severe disabilities, and, last but not least, the distinction between ability and disability, abled and disabled people, people with and without a disability. Do we want to draw this distinction in our community at all? To what extent is it good for all of us, for science and for society, and for institutions and organizations that have to do with disability? Who's harmed by it? On the whole, does it alleviate or exacerbate suffering?

'Disability' is a thick ethical term or thick ethical concept.[17] Like 'cruelty,' 'exploitation,' 'integrity,' and 'ostentatiousness,' it's at once descriptive and evaluative. The uses of any word can have moral implications, whether or not it's transparently evaluative. However, thick words add an immediate moral dimension, built into their very meaning or their very use. In the case of 'disability' in contemporary societies, the effects of its built-in evaluations are hefty. All the more reason to work collaboratively on it.

———

Stakeholders can be diverse and numerous, depending on the word or distinction under consideration. They include communities and groups where social science knowledge is going to be employed. Policy makers and the state. NGOs and intergovernmental organizations. The media, markets, corporations, and the law. Producers of technologies. Schools, museums, and religious groups and organizations. Professions, trade associations, ordinary citizens, and the environment. The list can go on and on: any social, political, or economic actor may have a stake.

This means trouble. Stakeholders introduce many thorny questions, which this book won't get to conscientiously address. I'll mention six of them. They're challenges for us, the community. Please help!

16. Catala 2020; Nind 2017, 278; Walmsley 2001; Walmsley and Johnson 2003. Thanks to Edurne García Iriarte for her comments on these issues.

17. Abend 2019; D. Roberts 2013; Väyrynen 2013; B. Williams 1985.

First, my arguments focus on social science communities whose work is about 'w' or *d*. They undertake *Activity WF* and *Activity DF* with a view to advancing their goals. Then, I come along and say: 'don't neglect how external actors will fare; they also have a horse in this race, and a major one at that.' To which you could reply that I'm getting things upside down. Social science isn't in a position to magnanimously invite stakeholders to talk and express their preferences. *They* run the show. 'W' and *d* are established far away from social science communities and research. Economic interests and political forces establish how to classify things, how to split and lump things, what classes of things are called, and words' extensions—which go on to be legally sanctioned. Large corporations, states, the law, and other mighty actors couldn't care less about social science scholarship and they're seldom affected by it. It's social scientists who must adapt their work, words, and distinctions to these sturdy and indifferent realities.

Second, stakeholders' participation in *Activity WF* and *Activity DF* is reminiscent of the relationships between scientists' and laypeople's epistemic authority, or between experts and citizens in democratic societies. Much has been written about the democratization of science and the varieties of 'democratized science,' 'citizen science,' 'crowd science,' 'participatory science,' 'participatory research,' 'inclusive research,' 'co-production,' and 'co-creation.'[18] While these expressions comprise multiple ideas and heterogeneous undertakings, three positions can be distinguished. You can argue for the participation of people/non-experts in:

- Selecting societies' research priorities, funding priorities, and thereby where and how science is significant in society, culture, and politics
- Observation and data collection
- Data analysis, and judgments about the truth and worth of propositions and theories; as an imprecise shortcut, you could say participation in 'internal' tasks; internal to the substance of science[19]

---

18. Alexandrova and Fabian 2022; Mark Brown 2015; H. Douglas 2009; S. Epstein 1996, 2007; Filipe, Renedo, and Marston 2017; Heigl et al. 2019; Herzog and Lepenies, forthcoming; Irwin 1995; Kasperowski and Hillman 2018; Kelty and Panofsky 2014; Kleinman 1998; Koskinen 2017; Kullenberg and Kasperowski 2016; Macq, Tancoigne, and Strasser 2020; Moore 2017, 2018; Norström et al. 2020; Rolin 2009; Schrögel and Kolleck 2019; Van Bouwel 2009. On the varieties of online participation, see Fish et al. (2011), Kelty et al. (2015), and Kelty and Erickson (2018).

19. Shapin 1992, 1995. An imprecise shortcut, which has fallen out of favor. Internalism is said to respect science too much, as sociologists and philosophers of science used to. Further, the distinction between internal and external factors has allegedly collapsed: nothing is external.

Activity WF and *Activity DF* belong to the last category. Yet, words and distinctions are narrower than scientific propositions and theories. In which respects does the analogy hold water? Which similarities and which differences matter?

Third, it's one thing to assert that stakeholders should participate in *Activity WF* and *Activity DF*, although these activities are scientific instruments, means to scientific ends, and normally within professionals' jurisdiction. Making this assertion is free, and you'll make friends in some necks of the academic woods. It's another thing to buckle down and work out who'll get to participate, how they'll participate, and how their perspectives and interests will be integrated with those of scientific communities and researchers. Differences between scientists and stakeholders might recommend different forms of participation—unlike citizens' voting in elections and referendums in contemporary democracies. There's much to learn from the history of democratized science and inclusive research, their practice, felicitous and infelicitous attempts, and scholarship and participants' reflections on them.

Fourth, being affected by 'w' or *d* isn't specific enough. No matter how 'to affect' is specified, though, it's probably a matter of degree. Different stakeholders will be affected to different degrees. Does it follow that the more affected you are, the more you should get to shape the outcome? Can this be squared with equality principles, or, rather, are equality principles limited to community members?

Fifth, stakeholders can be diverse and numerous. Some will present the community with distinct puzzles. Should AIs participate in conversations about the extension of 'AI'? Better said: prima facie AIs, or presumed AIs, because their status is precisely the issue, so circularity is unavoidable. Imagine 'w' is 'terrorism,' and you invite Hamas and NSU to sit at the table. Do you expect them to show up and engage your community, a politically toothless group of academics, and nerds to boot?

Sixth, how can the environment, non-human animals, and future generations be represented in a collective conversation? The good news is, future generations will have access to time machines, or have access to time machines, so they don't need proxies and delegates in the 2020s. They can time travel and physically join their ancestors at the meeting. Paradoxes may ensue, but killing your great-grandparents will fail.[20]

———

There are similar concerns about content vs. context and epistemic vs. non-epistemic. See also Kitcher's (2011, 91) quadripartite schema.

20. Lewis 1976, 150.

An inclusive policy will extend invitations to everyone. See you all at 6 p.m. in the agora! Good, but insufficient. An effective inclusive policy must anticipate obstacles to participation and lessen their effects. Some people have to be at work till 11 p.m. or have to take care of their children. Some aren't fluent in English (or the natural language we'll be speaking). For people whose salaries are low and who barely make ends meet, public transport is a non-negligible expense.

———

My proposal is that *Activity DF* and *Activity WF* should be democratic in some sense of the word 'democracy.' In which sense, exactly? Shouldn't this be up to the community? Arguably so.

What I've been describing might be likened to deliberative democracies of one kind or another (chapter 6). However, I've deliberately not indicated which kind, and I've only associated myself with the overarching orientation of this approach. While I find deliberative democracy a good framework for social science communities' decisions about 'w' and *d*, this isn't a deal-breaker. I'd argue that, at least, it's a good general, revisable, and potentially self-correcting framework to kick things off, given the character of these communities and their members. But many arrangements and political philosophies are compatible with my outlook. Not any, of course, but many.

Perhaps our community ends up concluding that something else would be better for us. For your money, or for you guys' money, I might have overvalued deliberation (too slow, cautious, and conservative!), and overvalued reasons and arguments. My sources on deliberative democracy are dated or partial accounts. I've undervalued dissent and conflict, and failed to give agonistic pluralism its due. Maybe I didn't give pragmatism or critical theory their due, or I overlooked other important traditions and ideas.[21] I've certainly overlooked ideas that originate in faraway places with strange-sounding names, and whose originators haven't had the decency to express them in English.

We can talk about all of this. Indeed, we should. In any case, our community's openness to difference, tolerance, and pluralism must bottom out somewhere. There are premises and building blocks we've collectively come to see as non-negotiable (or, counterfactually, we'd assent to and defend, if opposition arose). Either because they're morally non-negotiable, or because they're

———

21. Azmanova 2012; Dewey 1927, 2021; Fung and Wright 2001; Lafont 2020; Mouffe 1999, 2000, 2005; Prasad 2021a, b; L. Sanders 1997; Selg 2013; Van Bouwel 2015; Van Bouwel and Van Oudheusden 2017; I. Young 2000.

enablers of the intended practice, institution, or discussion. It'd be impossible without them. In the social science communities I've been thinking about and I'm well acquainted with, one building block is as follows. Community members endorse democratic norms and values, and prefer democratic to non-democratic ideals and principles. Predictably, we can't agree on the meaning of 'democracy' and its implementation. But most of us agree that our community and organizations should operate democratically, in the sense that we govern ourselves, make decisions, and participate in one way or another. It'd be wrong for anyone to be slighted or silenced. No dictators, autocrats, or juntas among us.

Our community shall democratically run *Activity WF* and *Activity DF*, as well as meta-level discussions about their good practice. Here we dig in our heels: an individual (or a small group) shouldn't be allowed to unilaterally establish outcomes in a top-down manner. 'Let's find a wise leader, to whom the community can entrust all decisions about words and distinctions' is a non-starter around here.[22]

Crucially, principles aren't behaviors and norms aren't practices. I'm not assessing the degree to which scientists and scientific organizations act in accordance with democratic values. Divergences between norms and practices, divergences between moral convictions and quotidian organizational processes and social interactions: that's another story. A story at the root of this book.

Selfishness

Don't be selfish![23] Be a public-spirited fellow! Don't think only of yourself, your research, experiments, and papers. Your career and your students. Our communities' decisions about the practice of *Activity WF* and *Activity DF* should be driven by the common good.

You shouldn't favor policies, decisions, and answers just because they're advantageous to you, because your arguments will be more general and more significant, or because your models and figures will be neater, more beautiful, and more powerful. It's in your self-interest to increase your citations and

22. While my firsthand observations are for the most part in North America and Western Europe, probably any scientific community would concur with these norms. Scientists anywhere will OK their thrust. (Present-day scientific communities. Might the past be a foreign country?)

23. Same as above. Like 'justice' and 'fairness,' the words 'selfish,' 'egoistic,' and 'self-interested' have had countless uses in the history of thought. 'Interest' and 'self-interest' alone are semantic Pandora's boxes (Hirschman 1986; Mansbridge 1990; Swedberg 2005). I use 'selfishness' as an ordinary English word, despite its vagueness and ambiguity.

h-index. The interests of the community include no such thing: you aren't special that way.[24] Instead, we want word uses and distinctions to be advantageous to all of us, the community as a whole, and beyond. To society and the world. So, we ask everyone to favor what favors the common good.

You might retort that regrettably you can't. Self-interest is psychologically potent. We're all vulnerable to biases. We all rationalize and unconsciously deceive ourselves. Even where we see what's the altruistic thing to do, weakness of the will gets the upper hand. Hashtag *akrasia*.

I say: point well taken. The community must counterbalance these all-too-human inclinations and weaknesses. It must ask which tools can be effective, from socialization and education to organizational design and institutionalized incentives and disincentives. Selfishness leads to antisocial and unethical behavior, so counterbalancing and managing it is standard fare for any community. It's one of the functions of graduate school socialization, face-to-face events, and peer review systems. Referees and editors represent the community, its shared epistemic-cum-moral norms, the common good. Interacting with professors, advisors, fellow graduate students, and colleagues is a reminder that that we're all together in this. Calls for replicability, transparency, and preregistration of studies are recent attempts to keep up with such inclinations and weaknesses. The community is there, checking on you, actually or potentially, while you're gathering and analyzing your data, while you're putting together your arguments.[25]

Activity WF and *Activity DF* can take further steps in this direction, adapted to their needs. Scholarship on organizational behavior may suggest tools and techniques, honed in its studies of capitalist firms, where selfishness isn't in short supply. Moral and political philosophers' arguments may be turned into applied devices. Veils of ignorance and ideal speech situations were conceived of as thought experiments. Yet, we might adopt them in the real world, in our real-world discussions.[26] Imperfect approximations to the ideal, but better than nothing, and perfectible over time.

If you're into fundamentals and into ethics, you might probe my rejection of selfishness, and what it's justified by. One of our fellow community members could be Gyges in book 2 of Plato's *Republic*, or Hobbes's "Foole" in chapter 15 of *Leviathan*: "The Foole hath sayd in his heart, there is no such thing as Justice"; "there could be no reason, why every man might not do what he

24. Abend 2018a.

25. Atmanspacher and Maasen 2016; Cartwright 1991; Collins 1985, 1991; Freese and King 2018; Freese and Peterson 2017; Nosek et al. 2018.

26. Frohlich, Oppenheimer, and Eavey 1987; Huang, Greene, and Bazerman 2019.

thought conduced thereunto: and therefore also to make, or not make; keep, or not keep Covenants, was not against Reason, when it conduced to [one's] benefit."[27] A community member could argue that selfishness is morally good.[28] It's virtuous. Altruism and cooperation aren't. What if she's Ayn Rand? Part of the community might uphold the *Fable of the Bees* dictum, "private vices, publick benefits."[29] Individuals' self-interest brings about communal good. What am I to say to them?

Amoralists, moral skeptics, and defenders of selfishness are tough nuts to crack. Demonstrating that they're wrong isn't easy, as the history of ideas easily demonstrates. They deny tenets we thought everyone was on board with. Fortunately, my arguments don't need to refute these views as such, as general ethical and/or metaethical ones. It suffices to show they're implausible regarding the practice of social science research, its communication and application in society, and in particular *Activity WF* and *Activity DF*.

Certain moral duties and non-selfishness are part and parcel of these endeavors. They were mentioned in the job description, when you applied for the position. Or, they're a consequence of the necessarily communal character of research, and the communal character of word uses and distinctions. They'd be meaningless were it not for the collective. To be sure, it's you who did the research and it's you who proposed a distinction in your paper. But they ultimately belong to the community. These things aren't yours, but ours.

If a private language were possible, you'd be free to do with yours as you pleased.[30] In the privacy of your home or office. It'd be like living outside of society, alone, on a remote island, instead of your apartment in Brooklyn. But this isn't the situation you're in. Private languages are impossible and you're not living on a remote island. Rather, you're doing research within a community, presenting your results to a community, attending its conferences, serving on its committees, announcing your pathbreaking contributions to its edifice of knowledge, accepting its honors and awards, and training or being trained by other community members. Being a community member entails moral obligations. You owe something to it. You also have moral obligations to fellow community members.

An objector might push back against this purported entailment, which I expressed as "being a consequence of":

27. Hobbes 1651, 72.
28. Galbraith 1964, 16.
29. Mandeville (1714) 1725.
30. Wittgenstein (1953) 2009, §§ 244–71.

You're forgetting a contractualist premise, without which your argument founders. Something like, 'we've all agreed to this.' But I don't accept this premise. Nor do I buy transcendental tacks, for which the community is a precondition or enabler, and which focus on the conditions of possibility of speech, rational discourse, and communication.[31]

I'm sorry to give this objector short shrift, but I think I have a simple reply. Even conceding that it's not an entailment, even without the contractualist premise, the community would still have legitimate demands on each of us—by virtue of our participating in it, being members of it, and benefiting from it.

Description

For social science communities to make decisions about words and distinctions, they have to grasp their initial conditions. This task is empirical, but it's also moral.

It's a prevailing assumption in social research that description and evaluation are separate, successive steps. First, we have to describe our community, our goals and interests, research projects, word uses and distinctions, and stakeholders. Then, with these facts under our belt, we'll turn to moral evaluation. We'll collectively establish what's good for us, what goods we should be after, which our decisions about 'w' and *d* will be based on.

But that's a faulty separation. Descriptions of social phenomena and processes are already morally evaluative in several ways.[32] They're perspectival. They can't be exhaustive, so we have to decide what to leave out. We have to look at the right things in the right way. Attentively, discerningly, charitably, and perhaps lovingly. Maybe our vision is clouded. Something is blocking our view. And how are we going to tell, narrate, arrange what we saw? Maybe we suck at it. Our accounts may be distorted by self-interest, biases, and fantasy.

10.4 Conditional

For both *Activity WF* and *Activity DF*, the best way to go depends on what our goals are, what we're trying to do, what we're up to. Normative statements about them are conditional. If we want this, then we should do that. *Activity WF*: if we want to attain Z_1 and Z_2, this is a good/the best way to use 'w.' *Activity DF*: if we want to attain Z_3 and Z_4, *d* is a good/the best distinction to draw.

---

31. E.g., Apel 1973a, b, 1976.
32. Murdoch 1956; (1970) 2014; 1998, 73; Putnam 2002.

There's no such thing as the best or right use of a word or definition, period. Nor the best or right distinction or classification, period. Rather, it's all about what we want to do and which tools can help us with that. It's useful for Z. In both activities, desiderata are a function of communities' broader goals. 'W' and d are useful (or not) in relation to our desiderata and broader goals.

You can put the point in pragmatist terms. In terms of 'practical consequences,' 'practical difference,' and 'effects of a practical kind.' Hat tip to James, Dewey, and Peirce. Jane Addams. Rorty and Putnam. You can, but you don't have to. (I won't, because I've been overusing the word 'practical,' and I prefer my argument not to commit to any school and its terminology.) In either case, the chief question becomes what broader goals our community ought to pursue.

What should we want to do and accomplish? What should our priorities be? What should we use 'w' and d for? This means we'll have to consider what the point of social science is, why doing social science is worth our while. Needless to say, these are difficult and controversial foundational problems. There's no fact of the matter about them. Plus, communities have a hard time constraining their goals and ambitions, since there are too many things it'd be nice to accomplish. No wonder they may find themselves deadlocked.

But they don't always find themselves deadlocked. There are better and worse answers, clearly legitimate and important goals, and clearly illegitimate and unimportant ones. Sensible and crazy. Possibly realizable and possibly utopian. With effort and a little luck, thoughtful and well-meaning community members are able to tell the difference. Needless to say, communities' foundational problems don't have to be resolved for *Activity WF* and *Activity DF* to be undertaken and keep going. Good enough is good enough. We all have to keep going. You can put the point in pragmatist terms, too.

This 'w' and this d will have practical consequences of various kinds. Not only for our social science community's production of knowledge, but also social and political. Take 'civil war.'[33] You might propose to define 'civil war' in such a way that Syria is at civil war. This definition seems to you good for Syria and the Syrian people, politically and legally, encouraging international attention and aid. So, you argue that, ceteris paribus, our community has reason to go for it. We might only make a tiny difference in the real world, because we lack real power, because we're mere academics somewhere in the Midwest, in Central Switzerland, or in southern Uruguay. But who knows? We may get more people to adopt our word uses and definitions. We can speak to the

---

33. Armitage 2017; Cartwright and Runhardt 2014; Gersovitz and Kriger 2013.

media, professional associations, and students, and may catch the attention of social movements, international aid organizations, and politicians.

Similarly, you might propose a distinction among armed conflicts based on three properties: P_1, P_2, and P_3. A classification of armed conflicts that groups together Syria since 2011, the Spanish war of succession upon Carlos II's death (1701–14), and Uruguay's Guerra Grande (1839–51). By contrast, World War II and the US war between northern and southern states (1861–65) aren't in the set, since they don't meet one of the three criteria.

As a scholar of armed conflicts, you advocate this classification because it seems to you to benefit your research community. Its explanations and predictions, for sure. But it'd also benefit community coordination and cooperation, cordiality and collegiality, and community members' importance in the public sphere. These benefits don't accrue to scientific work itself (its content, if you will), but to the conditions under which it's produced (its contexts, if you will). Furthermore, your classification can help achieve goals that are downright social and political. For instance, people in your country are familiar with X, which is widely believed to be a bad thing, which caused much suffering and should have been prevented (say, Uruguay's Guerra Grande). But they aren't too familiar with Y (say, Syria today). By associating X and Y, by putting them in the same category, by saying they're analogous, you'd be helping raise consciousness about Y and motivating people to act.

Per my account of *Activity DF*, you aren't obligated to give a name to this group. Yet, because you'd like to have social and political effects, you have an incentive to use English to your advantage. So, go ahead and call it something that people feel strongly about. Like 'civil war.' As regards natural language, you'd be striking a balance. Your classification partly overlaps with everyday use, but not completely. For example, the US 'civil war' isn't in the group. Consistency with everyday use wasn't one of your three criteria, it wasn't a decisive factor, but you didn't discount it either.

Your proposal is on the table. It's now the community's turn.

10.5 Natural language

You guys! We'll have to talk about a classic theme, as it pertains to *Activity WF* and *Activity DF*. What are the relationships between social science and natural language? What are the relationships between natural language and *Activity WF* and *Activity DF*, their good practice and outcomes? To get us started, this is my suggestion: natural language should be an anchor, a reference point. Ordinary language should have some normative authority in social science. Ordinary language, as used on the streets of New York, Berlin, or Montevideo; in newspapers and magazines; on the internet, podcasts, and television shows. Which raises the question of how much authority is some authority. And the question of how to proceed empirically, since natural language is a moving target. What does *it* tell us? Where does *it* make its pronouncements?

My tentative response is that our best bet is dictionaries. They're imperfect indicators of language use and they're indicators of only one facet of language use. They record and document people's uses of words and expressions, what their meanings seem to be, as far as lexicographers can determine. Still, I think dictionaries are good enough. They sum up a great deal of information about the streets of New York, Berlin, and Montevideo, and their online counterparts. Other options would be too time-consuming, complex, and expensive. So, dictionaries' definitions of words and expressions should have some normative authority in social science.

Activity WF concerns itself with specialized social science languages, what you hear at conferences and read in journals. According to a commonly held view, social science languages borrow natural language words, but they aren't governed by natural language rules and conventions. Social scientists aren't forced to use 'sustainability,' 'sexuality,' 'diversity,' 'capitalism,' and 'intelligence' as speakers of American English would. I don't deny that. On the other hand, I believe social science shouldn't deviate too much from natural language, from lexical semantics, from lexicographers' findings. To some extent, social science communities are accountable to English, Arabic, or Spanish. They aren't fully free and autonomous to establish how to use 'w.' There's a golden mean to be aimed at.

My rationale isn't rocket science. Natural language is a bulwark against a free-for-all, where social science words could refer to anything, social scientists' stipulations could get batshit crazy, and batshit crazy would have to be legit and kosher—Humpty Dumpty style.[34] That's not the promised land: our kashruth laws know better. Psychologists' claims about intelligence, political scientists' claims about civil war, and sociologists' claims about poverty have to have something to do with 'intelligence,' 'civil war,' and 'poverty.' That is, with the English words, as they're defined in *Webster's Third* or the *Oxford English Dictionary* or some such (more on this below). The social sciences aren't formal disciplines, producing closed systems of truths and relations among symbols. Instead, their work tries to hook up to the world. It's intended to be about actual social phenomena and refer to actual social processes. Ideally, it'll have implications for public policy, and it'll help people understand themselves, their historical circumstances, and their social structural constraints.

34. Carroll 1911, 220–21.

Natural language is a sensible way to align social scientists' claims with social reality, shared social reality, built into ordinary practices and institutions. Natural language meanings/uses can be our default guides, our default mediators, as they are in social life. This tactic could be defended pragmatically or metaphysically. What social science expressions refer to will be based on what ordinary language directs us toward. Roughly based. The semantic authority of natural language isn't total. It's not total in our social lives, much less in social science. It can and should be amended, if it's morally or logically defective. If it's problematic, confusing, or outdated. If it disappoints us or fails us in other ways. Either way, dictionary definitions of 'intelligence,' 'work,' or 'diversity' should play a role in social science research on intelligence, work, and diversity. For the practice of *Activity WF*, straying from them is a minus. One desideratum is not to stray from them.

In a nutshell, the acceptable uses of 'w' in social science ought to be sensitive to the acceptable uses of 'w' in English. Much hangs on how to cash out 'sensitive to,' though. I'm not sure. What do you say?

———

Once again, an inconvenient fact rears its inconvenient head. Which dictionary or dictionaries are supposed to stand in for natural language?

There are many English dictionaries. Appealing to "the UAD: the Unidentified Authorizing Dictionary, usually referred to as 'the dictionary'" is a legerdemain.[35] I've just mentioned *Webster's Third* and the *Oxford English Dictionary*. But you could also look up the definition of 'w' in *Webster's New World Dictionary*, or in *Random House Webster's Unabridged Dictionary*, or in the *American Heritage Dictionary of the English Language*. Their depictions of English won't exactly coincide. You may pick one dictionary, or you may create a composite measure. But a composite measure of which ones?

While we're at it: there isn't only one English language or dialect. Assuming the individuation of a dialect isn't itself a mess (which it is), for each purported dialect there might be more than one dictionary.

Besides the wealth of dialects and dictionaries, anyone who's ever consulted a dictionary knows that words may have more than one sense. As the social and legal disputes over burritos' sandwichness illustrate (chapter 1), you can go dictionary shopping and you can go within-dictionary definition shopping. Which sense of the word is supposed to be our anchor or reference point?

35. Moon 1989, 63.

What's more, you might worry about the inherent drawbacks of dictionary definitions. They're formal statements that can sound artificial and be difficult to understand. They endeavor to elucidate, classify, state, communicate the meanings and uses of a lexical item. But semantic and pragmatic contexts are indispensable to do a good job of this. Dictionaries can't supply them, except for example sentences.[36] Dictionary definitions can't succeed at elucidating a word's meanings, because meaning is always meaning-in-context, meaning is always indexical, meaning is use, and semantics is powerless without pragmatics. A word isn't the right unit of analysis; a word doesn't *have* meanings; "you shall know a word by the company it keeps."[37]

Do these worries have merit? If they did, dictionaries wouldn't be suitable tools for the practice of *Activity WF* and *Activity DF*.[38] Natural language wouldn't be well represented by dictionaries, so we'd have to look for a plan B.

———

Once again, another inconvenient fact rears its inconvenient head. English isn't the only natural language game in town. To rephrase, then: in a nutshell, the acceptable uses of 'w' in social science ought to be sensitive to the acceptable uses of 'w' in L (where L is the natural language used by social scientists in their research and writing). But this isn't a free lunch. In fact, it risks getting quite pricey. If 'w' is specific to L, and a dictionary of L provides a test or evidence, how do research projects across natural languages relate to one another?

The fear is that social science work on 'power' in American English and on '*Macht*' in Standard German couldn't be said to be about the same thing. Looking them up in dictionaries of American English and Standard German, you realize that 'power' and '*Macht*' aren't exact synonyms. '*Pouvoir*' and '*puissance*' in French French would add fuel to the fire.[39] That'd be a bitter pill to swallow.

36. Heid, Prinsloo, and Bothma 2012; Heuberger 2016; Stamper 2017. Technological developments, the internet, online dictionaries and corpora, etc., can go some way toward remedying this, but not all the way. See Frankenberg-Garcia 2012, 2014; Fuertes-Olivera 2012; Hargraves 2018; Ooi 2018; Tarp and Fuertes-Olivera 2016.

37. Firth 1968, 179. I'm thinking of a word's 'company' more comprehensively than Firth's (1957, 1968) collocations. See also Firth's (1957, 190–215) "Modes of Meaning."

38. Another objection to dictionaries as proxies: word uses and meanings are never independent from people's mental states, the intentions of a language user, what they thought they were trying to communicate or do. Each time. For every utterance.

39. Aron 1964, 32. Thanks to Steven Lukes for bringing Aron's paper to my attention and for his comments on these issues.

As I discussed above (chapter 4), a popular strategy is to postulate a concept, POWER, which transcends natural languages. 'Power' and '*Macht*' aren't synonymous, their denotations and connotations diverge, but both US and German journals are publishing novel findings about POWER. Unfortunately, this is also a bitter pill to swallow. Whence this additional entity, concept C? What sort of thing is it? What makes it the case, in a non-circular fashion, that words across languages are instances of C?

It is a dilemma. There are defensible responses to both horns, but none of them will let you off scot-free. Sticking to words strikes me, all things considered, as preferable to postulating concepts. But you might disagree. For you, insofar as social science communities are international, intelligibility across languages has to have precedence. And not just intelligibility, but collaboration, researchers' working together, exchanging ideas, feeding off one another, their findings' cumulating—despite the fact that we're writing in Spanish and you guys are writing in Arabic. Not only have my arguments imagined monolingual social science communities, but they've also taken words to be English words. Some of you might protest against my monolingual and English-centric policy. It's at best an unrealistic simplification and at worst a serious flaw. I'd join your protest myself.

What are my options now? One option is to say that multilingual communities' substantive overlaps don't require postulating metaphysically spooky entities. The object of inquiry of our international community isn't picked out by 'w,' the English word, but by the conjunction of several semantically related words in various languages, including 'w.' 'W' is one among several. It'd be like a mereological sum that recognizes their slightly different extensions and intensions, shades of meaning, related or unrelated etymologies, and most frequent uses in their respective languages. Admittedly, 'semantically related words' isn't a clear criterion. Vagueness is sure to be a headache. Moreover, words can be semantically related in an infinite number of respects. Which ones do and don't count? The thing is, criteria for a word to gain entry to the multilingual set won't be neutral. They won't be neutral among natural languages, which was the impetus for the whole reorganization to begin with.

Notwithstanding these stumbling blocks, the conjunction move may be workable. We've got 'power' and '*Macht*' and '*pouvoir*' and '*puissance*' and '*poder*.' Do you feel compelled to add that this conjunction is a concept, C, or that henceforth it's going to be referred to as 'concept C'? Well, you could suggest this terminological convention, and perhaps your community will embrace it. Personally, looking at the history and polysemy of the word 'concept,' I wouldn't recommend it.

———

My ideas about natural language and lexical semantics are directly relevant to *Activity WF*. Though less directly, they're also relevant to *Activity DF*. Logically, distinctions can keep their distance from language. But here's the thing: distinctions are means. They're tools for social science research, and social science research isn't addressed only to a narrow circle of specialists, even if these are responsible for a first round of quality control. Outside this narrow circle, your sets and groups can't be arbitrarily named anymore. You'll have to explain what the distinction between '*gavagai*' and '*havagai*' has to do with the real world. Policy makers will ask how your distinctions help reform institutions, laws, regulations, and practices. You'll be asked if you're making a distinction between 'religions' and 'sects,' or between 'planets' and 'dwarf planets.' Then, my proposal—natural language as anchor—will knock on your door, too.

———

Activity WF isn't independent from natural language. 'W' is a social science word and it's also an English word: the former shouldn't disregard the latter. *Activity WF* isn't independent either from the history of uses of 'w' in the community. 'W' has long been used by our organizations, by our journals, by our teachers, and by our teachers' teachers. Previous generations don't get the last semantic word. Nor do we want to commit etymological fallacies. However, we do exist within a tradition. Within multiple traditions. We come from somewhere, and it'd be ill-advised to disregard what's been done before our time: semantically as much as socially and politically.

In these regards, both *Activity WF* and *Activity DF* have obligations to the genealogies of our practices, to our histories and traditions. What distinctions our community is going to accept will partly depend on their contributions to what matters to us. What matters to us partly depends on what has mattered to our predecessors. Indeed, you don't need to be a communitarian to recognize this: what makes sense to you makes sense to you because of traditions within which you exist. It follows that social science communities should study their histories. In particular, the histories of words-things-distinctions relationships, what things have gotten called, how things have gotten classified, and what classes have gotten called.

We're not historically curious for its own sake, but to better understand what we've come to find interesting, important, and meaningful. Historical, genealogical research can benefit our future-oriented and action-oriented conversations, providing them with both empirical and normative inputs.

The pendulum shouldn't swing too far in this direction, or else we wouldn't be able to go beyond our predecessors. Tradition would become a prison.

Many people in many societies and historical periods have been prisoners of tradition. Many people still are. Tradition undercuts their interests; their intellectual and moral lives are truncated; the ruling classes slyly instrumentalize time-honored beliefs and practices, so they become fetters. These fetters have to be burst asunder.

We're not historically curious for its own sake, but to better understand what we've come to find interesting, important, and meaningful. To better grasp the ideas, reasons, and assumptions that we've inherited and seem to us self-evident. To spot the corrupt and self-serving ones, distance ourselves from them, and correspondingly reform our traditions, institutions, and practices.

You can't change your past. You'll remain a descendant of traditions you've come to censure. That's where you come from. These structures, histories, problems, and injustices were there already. But you can change your future.

10.6 Differences and diversities

Our social science communities are diverse. Our diversities are manifold. We're diverse with respect to culture, race and ethnicity, gender, sexual orientation, socioeconomic status, age, ability, and national origin, and also epistemologically and morally. Practitioners of *Activity WF* and *Activity DF* will have dissimilar views about 'w' and *d*. This can be partly accounted for by their epistemological, methodological, ontological, and theoretical diversities; the diversity of their epistemic pursuits; the diversity of their tools and technologies; as well as the distinct moral and political perspectives from which they come at 'w' and *d*.[40]

This is a terrific asset. *Vive la différence.* In the communities I'm a member of, we welcome these diversities, we're enriched by them, even though they're sometimes a pain in the ass. We are, or ought to aspire to be, a pluralist community in this regard. Or so I'm prepared to argue in our discussions. (But I wouldn't foreground the word 'pluralism,' because it's a troublemaker and can get us off track.)

However, I don't believe any difference whatsoever is welcome. There are limits beyond which our community won't go. Moral limits. Limits set by the character of social science research, the plans we have, what we're up to. Or by the subject matters we work on. Or by natural language. Flexible and change-able limits, yes, but limits nonetheless.

Practitioners of *Activity WF* and *Activity DF* may have diverse intuitions about natural language. Different people find different dictionaries to be more

40. Ruphy 2015.

descriptively accurate, better reflecting their uses of words and expressions. Language is fluid and variegated. In our community, we welcome these diversities, we're enriched by them, even though they're sometimes a pain in the ass. They leave us with a conundrum: how natural language can be an anchor, if it's not one thing, but a multiplicity.

There are limits to language diversities, too. Flexible and changeable limits, yes, but at some point you won't be speaking English anymore. At some point, you won't be speaking a language anymore, but making random noises. We aren't going to accommodate private dictionaries and Humpty Dumpty's stipulations. While there's no such thing as *the* dictionary, there are tomes we can reasonably view as *a* dictionary, and our selection of a set of dictionaries can be more or less reasonable (though it's never neutral and it's always contestable). We'll be using our dictionaries' definitions—that is, English language dictionaries, not Uqbar language dictionaries (see chapter 3). Otherwise, we couldn't claim to be doing research on religion, art, altruism, sport, creativity, or happiness. We'd be changing the subject.[41]

The way I envision them, *Activity WF* and *Activity DF* are participatory and democratic. Participants work together to arrive at good arrangements. They make and evaluate arguments, and analyze possible regulation and implementation policies, deliberating about their form, features, consequences, strengths, and weaknesses. Responsible, thoughtful, and engaged participation is highly desired. Decisions shouldn't be a reflection of participants' unconsidered preferences and immediate reactions, nor of their natural language intuitions. It's not a referendum in which you vote, pressing a button on your phone, to communicate your stance or preference, as if you were communicating a piece of information about yourself ('I feel like eating tacos for dinner'). Good deliberation and collective work are decisive; voting is one mechanism among others. The community has a practical reason problem, and practical reason problems aren't solved by adding up subjective preferences, utilities, and tastes.

You and I started out having different viewpoints. We were at odds about 'w' and d, about criteria to assess 'w' and d options, and about criteria to assess criteria to assess 'w' and d options. We started out being very epistemologically and morally different to each other. It's possible that I (and/or you) change in the course of our collective activities. Not necessary, but possible. Our collective activities may change me (and/or you). It's possible, too, that we come to agree about 'w' and d decisions, even though our epistemological and moral rationales differ.[42] Not necessary, but possible.

41. Belleri, forthcoming; Cappelen 2018; Strawson 1963; Sundell 2020.
42. Abend 2014; C. Taylor 1999.

Differences and diversities are valuable for the community, for our scholarship, for its policy implications, for our lives. But they aren't exogenous and fixed, unmovable, beyond interrogation and transformation. Differences and diversities aren't conversation killers. Rather than blindly obeyed, they are to be appreciated and taken into account. At times they *are* fundamental, and insurmountable, but we'll have to see when and where.

10.7 Levels

You guys! We'll have to talk about a thorn in our side, which has kept coming up in this book. It's got to do with levels or orders. Do you recall our group of friends planning on cooking dinner tonight? They've narrowed down their entrée options to two: eggplant parmigiana or cauliflower gratin. To decide whether to cook the former or the latter, they've narrowed it down to either voting or flipping a coin. To decide whether to vote or flip a coin, they've narrowed it down to either using whichever is faster or using whichever is a better fit with the spirit of their friendship . . .

A social science community will be having discussions about word 'w' or distinction *d*. It'll be looking to make collective decisions about them, looking to establish what we qua community are and aren't down with. For instance, 'terrorism' is at present being used in certain ways. Are they more-or-less good? What reasons do we have to go for these uses (rather than those)? On the one hand, our immediate questions are about 'terrorism' and its relationships to social science research on terrorism. The research of political scientists, sociologists, and historians, either as three separate communities or as one interdisciplinary community. On the other hand, we have to figure out what procedures are good procedures; that is, procedures to present, discuss, and evaluate arguments and reasons—and, at a higher level, procedures to present, discuss, and evaluate procedures. This isn't about 'terrorism' per se, although not orthogonal to it. The best procedure might depend on the content of what we're trying to solve, the specific words and topics we're dealing with.

These are well-traveled roads. We'll meet pesky procedural quandaries, as democratic theory and democratic practice incessantly have:

- What should and shouldn't be voted on?
- When should we stop deliberating and move on—whether it's to vote, or flip a coin, or give up and turn to something else?
- How are votes to be counted?
- Which issues require unanimity or special majorities?

- When are committees to be set up?
- What can be decided by elected representatives?

And again: who's a community member and who gets to participate in the first place?

And again: what's the procedure to select a procedure? Given any level or order, you can logically ask a higher-level or higher-order question. Is this infinite regress destructive? Can social scientists acknowledge the logical point without being undermined or paralyzed by it—pragmatically put it aside and be able to move forward?

––––––

ARGLE: What's a good solution to our problem?

BARGLE: Well, my dear Argle, we want to be systematic about this. So, we need a good method and approach to answer what's a good solution to our problem.

ARGLE: OK. What's a good method and approach to answer what's a good solution to our problem?

BARGLE: Well, my dear Argle, we want to be systematic about this as well. So, we need a good method and approach to answer what's a good method and approach to answer what's a good solution to our problem.

ARGLE: *Gai kaken oifen yam*, Bargle![43]

––––––

The foregoing twofold distinction is fine as a first pass, I think, its virtues being simplicity and comprehensibility. It could be rendered as a distinction between substance and procedure, as it's drawn in jurisprudence.[44] However, a closer look suggests other classificatory possibilities. I'd like to suggest the following five categories to classify the tasks of social science communities with regards to *Activity WF* and *Activity DF* (I'll use only the former as my illustration):

43. Yiddish for 'go shit in the sea' or 'go shit in the ocean.'

44. Ailes 1941; J. Cohen (1996) 1997; Malcai and Levine-Schnur 2014, 2017; Ribeiro 2021; Risinger 1982; Solum 2004. As in jurisprudence, you can object that procedures can't be kept solely procedural, free from substance.

(1) BASIC ISSUE

The basic issue is how to use 'w', which uses are good and bad, what the best option is. (Others would say 'how to define "w"' or 'what the meanings of "w" are'.)

(2) GROUNDS

In arguments about how to use 'w', addressed to our community: what kinds of grounds are acceptable; what sorts of reasons are good sorts of reasons; what kind of evidence is and isn't apropos; what desiderata we're after.

(3) FORM

What kind of answer we're looking for; of which form. For example: a rule, a list of necessary and sufficient conditions, a paradigmatic instance, a prototype. Which in turn depends on whether we're talking about a word, 'w', as I prefer, or rather a concept, a thing, or something else. If it's a concept, whether a concept is a container or set, in the mind or head, or rather a disposition.[45] Or whether there are no limitations: any form can in principle work.

(4) PROCEDURES, RULES OF THE GAME, WHAT MAKES A PROCESS A GOOD ONE (DISCUSSION)

Specifically, procedures to present proposals, speak, discuss, deliberate, exchange ideas, give reasons, advance arguments, evaluate them, persuade one another, listen to one another, attend to one another.

(5) PROCEDURES, RULES OF THE GAME, WHAT MAKES A PROCESS A GOOD ONE (DECISION)

Specifically, procedures to make collective decisions about 'w', to arrive at collective agreements (for the time being), to establish how 'w' is to be used (until we revise our policy).

As ever, once you examine procedures in more depth, further procedural questions arise. The implementation of procedures requires additional choices of procedure. Democracy, sure thing, but how? Making sure everyone is well informed, sure, but how? Giving everyone a chance to speak, sure, but how

45. Gunnell 2017.

exactly? Voting, sure thing, but how? Where and at what time? What's a foul? Online voting, sure thing, but how?

The community will also encounter difficulties of the application-on-the-ground variety, once neat abstractions encounter messy realities—as any abstraction, rule, map, representation, proposition, and generalization must. What to do if this exception comes to pass or if this ambiguous case transpires? These are all applied choices. They can't be confidently foreseen. They have to be made all the way down the line, and might not be minor technical details. Choices about procedures shape the outcome, the quality of the outcome, its effectiveness and fairness, and the extent to which a practice actually does what it's meant to do, actually expresses the principles it's supposed to express. As ever, there are procedural tricks to corrupt practices and manipulate outcomes, which communities need to detect and thwart.

10.8 Envoi

This is my invitation. It's a series of conversation starters. They'll succeed if the conversation does start, if social science communities do find these issues to be worth their time and effort, and start working on them. They'll pass with flying colors if communities' conversations are clear, procedurally satisfactory, thoughtful, and animated. Bonus points if they're friendly and funny. Extra bonus points if there is free food.

11

As a matter of fact

cómo voy a creer / dijo el fulano
que la utopía ya no existe

—BENEDETTI (2000)[1]

11.1 Dude!

'Dude, you're so naive! Social scientists won't ever follow your suggestions. Let me take that back. *Of course*, social scientists won't ever follow your suggestions. Most people's priority is their careers. Asking them to do what's good for the community, at a cost to themselves, is utopian. It won't work in the real world.

'Plus, it's preposterous to imagine that social science communities will actually get together, deliberate, and work together on *Activity WF* and *Activity DF*. Pre-pos-ter-ous. It'd be too laborious to organize these meetings, even if they were virtual. Organizations have no incentives to do it. Community members have no time to spare. Let alone time to devote to the common good. Did I mention that their priority is career advancement? They also have partners, children, parents, and pets. They need to walk their dogs, work out, go to the movies, and go on vacations.

'Social scientists will never engage in the discussions you're imagining, through which communities cooperatively and public-spiritedly establish uses of words and distinctions. A veil of ignorance? The unforced force of the better argument? These are philosophers' wacko fantasies. In less fantastical places, it's all about interests and power. They'll willy-nilly continue to carry the day. Angry disputes won't come to an end, and privileged community members

---

1. Benedetti 2000, 132.

won't give up their privileges. Professors at top US universities would rather be autonomous decision-makers about 'w' or d than listen to the community. Listen to students and independent scholars; in Missoula, Montana, and Ibadan, Nigeria.

'Dude. Abide. Get real. You're naive about morality as motivation, and your suggestions are wildly unrealistic. As a matter of fact, your whole analysis and your conversation starters are pointless. Stop dreaming and accept reality.'

———

'Dude, you yourself brought up apt business and legal analogies. The production and sale of bread are slated to get a new tax break. Obviously, producers of matzo, crackers, rye bread, naan, cloud bread, banana bread, brioche, tsoureki, challah, and pretzels will swear that their product is a type of bread. They'll swear to God, Demeter, Empanda, and Fornax. As *Sabritas v. United States* shows, producers of wheat tortillas, corn tortillas, and taco shells will try and jump on the bread bandwagon, too.[2] They'll argue their case, lobby, and go to court if need be.

'You yourself insightfully likened science to business. You underscored that power and interests aren't absent from scientific research and organizations. Word uses, definitions, distinctions, and classifications have material consequences and unequal effects. You're right about all of this. But your conclusions are baloney. Social scientists are *homines economici* who behave just like businesspeople and their lawyers. They'll do whatever is in their self-interest, regarding words, distinctions, or anything else. Much like litigation in court, they'll say whatever increases the likelihood of their coming out on top. It's capitalism, stupid!'

———

'Dude. Let me give you one piece of advice. I know "realism" has a bad rap: such a killjoy. But the side of realism is the side your arguments always want to be on. Problem-solving must be anchored in reality. Your ideas must accord with empirical facts. I shouldn't have to say this to you, a card-carrying scientist.

'"Idealism" is at best a distraction, like a viral TikTok video. A distraction that young people, dreamers, and a few stubborn philosophers are keen on. At worst, it's a mechanism to disseminate and buttress false consciousness, so that

---

2. Sabritas v. United States, 998 F. Supp. 1123 (Ct. Int'l Trade 1998).

the ruling class can safeguard its undeserved prerogatives. As for moral reasons and goals, come on! Morality reeks of moralism, as it always has, in its secular and religious incarnations. Get real!'

11.2 Real life

Do these critics sound familiar?

These are common tropes in the history of social and political life, and in the history of social and political thought. Accusations of naivete, wishful thinking, romanticism, excessive optimism, and Panglossian outlooks. Being 'divorced from reality,' especially dreamy academics, whose heads are in the clouds. Oppositions between doable (good) and undoable (bad) ideas, realistic (good) and unrealistic (bad) social and political theories. Methodological and epistemological objections to thought experiments, fictional scenarios, assumptions, and models. Skepticism about ideals and utopias. You must pay tribute to reality and realities, to viability and feasibility. Social and political critiques must be empirical. Where are your data on actual practices, structures, and organizations? Your data on people and on human nature? Remember that ought implies can!

Fifty years of controversies over 'ideal theory' and 'non-ideal theory,' since Rawls's *A Theory of Justice*, may spring to mind.[3] Machiavelli may also spring to mind, complaining five hundred years ago that "many have imagined republics and principalities that have never been seen or known to exist in truth."[4] Yes, many have done so. Many have, on the other hand, deplored utopias and fictions, Plato's Kallipolis, Moore's *Utopia*, 'states of nature,' and other imaginary worlds.[5] Similar criticisms have been recurrently leveled at socialists— all of them, not only 'utopian' ones, like Saint-Simon and Fourier. They say they want a revolution. They say the point isn't to interpret the world, but to change it. Are they sure a better world is actually possible? Aren't the expressions "real utopia"[6] and "realistic utopia"[7] self-contradictory?

3. J. Rawls 1971.

4. Machiavelli (1532) 1998, 61.

5. Cozzaglio and Favara 2021; Erman and Möller 2020; Estlund 2020; Galston 2010; Geuss 2008; Horton 2017; Jubb 2012; McKean 2016; Mouffe 2005; Sen 2009; A. Simmons 2010; Valentini 2012; B. Williams 2005. The clashes between 'ideal' and 'non-ideal' theories sometimes conflate more than one issue. Diverse uses of 'ideal,' 'non-ideal,' and 'realism' have to be disentangled, too.

6. Wright 2010.

7. J. Rawls 1999.

We're a group of friends, roommates, or coworkers. A research team, family, rock band, or jazz septet. If you suggest a plan for us for tomorrow, or a task for us to complete by next Friday, you normally intend it to be doable. Unfeasibility would normally kill it. You can't make a feasible proposal without knowledge about the group, its capacities, situation, and constraints. The data won't necessarily be systematic, as in a scientific project, but you do need realistic guesses or assumptions. By 2:30 p.m. we can't clean the house spotless. (It's 1:15 p.m. and we live in the Château de Versailles.) By next Friday we can't compose a dozen tunes, rehearse them, record them, and mix and master the album.

Under which circumstances is feasibility decisive? It depends on the feasibility of what, what this thing is, and what it's for. Social and political theories don't have to look like the plan to record our next album by next Friday. Your theory isn't a plan. Or your theory was designed to be performative. What it says about the world is false at this time, but it'll become true as an effect of its use.[8]

More frequently, proposals bring something about by encouraging people to care about it and work toward it. Through perlocution rather than illocution. Their grammatical mood is hortative. Let's do it! They offer an ideal to be striven toward. Even if not reached, even if not reachable, it can function as a guide. An ideal that can be approximated, like religious holiness, spiritual perfection, and Messi's skill and vision.[9] A standard to gauge our progress. A model or yardstick to which reality can be compared, as ruler-and-compass circles and squares can be compared to geometrical circles and squares (*Republic* 510d–e).

———

I'm not getting off the hook easily here. I don't know if political and social theory are, but I am not. I did set out to address an actual problem, which social science communities are afflicted by. My hope is to make things better for social science research. Help social scientists improve their word uses and distinctions, improve the quality of their arguments, and get away from confused and fruitless disputes. When all is said and done, I hope to support the production of good social science knowledge, attained through morally and epistemically good procedures, and whose effects are morally and epistemically good.

8. Healy 2015; MacKenzie 2006; MacKenzie, Muniesa, and Siu 2007.
9. Galeano 1993, 230.

It's only fair for a critic to press me on real life, on what will happen in the real world. I did say my proposals weren't meant as philosophical disquisitions, but as calls to get moving, didn't I? They're addressed to actual social scientists. They should be implemented in actual social science communities and organizations.

I see where this critic is coming from, and why they suspect my proposal and invitation stand no chance. They believe I'm making an empirical error. I'm mistaken about what social science communities are like, what my colleagues and graduate students are like, and what our organizations and culture are like. I do recognize that there's something going for their concern. Surely there's something going for the spirit of their concern. However, I don't think they're calibrating well their analysis, nor the categories into which they sort approaches and proposals. Let me explain.

––––––––

I agree: you can't count on community members' acting morally, altruistically, and caring about the well-being of others. You can't count on their sidelining self-interest; what will bring them money, status, power, recognition, and honor. No sensible observer of society and history would make such a generalization. But no sensible observer thinks either that this is a black-or-white matter. Instead, it's a distribution, where some people act morally, more or less morally, some of the time.

Say you measure altruism in one or several communities. To be methodologically expedient, you break down practices and institutions into sets of individual actions, so your data are a finite number of instances. Each can be either altruistic or selfish. Better yet, you use a continuum, ranging from totally altruistic to totally selfish. Once all the measurements are in, you'll report means and standard deviations. Variation will be the name of the game.

I agree: you can't count on community members' being reliably thoughtful in discussions about words and distinctions. You can't count on their being level-headed, careful, logical, sensible, and judicious. But this isn't a black-or-white matter either. Instead, there's a distribution. In any community, people differ in their thoughtfulness, level-headedness, and judiciousness. Nor do people exhibit these virtues (or vices) consistently. Individuals may fluctuate, so things also change over time, across moments and situations.[10]

––––

10. This is a modest empirical claim. It doesn't imply that the causal master is always situational, individuals' behavior exhibits no consistency or patterns, and virtues and character are imaginary. My argument has no dog in these fights (Alfano 2013a; Doris 2002).

What we'll definitely see is variation, as we would anywhere else. The incidence of altruistic actions varies within groups and societies, across groups and societies, and over time. Variables vary: it's a case-by-case empirical question how they do. In some communities, places, and times, my proposals will fail. Nothing good will come about. Confusions about words, distinctions, and the adjudication of disputes will live on, or for the most part live on. The powerful will continue to call the shots and exploit the powerless, using *Activity WF* and *Activity DF* to advance their self-regarding aims. I don't close my eyes to the possibility of this upshot any more than to the actuality of Trump's and Bolsonaro's electoral victories. They were democratically elected by their respective political communities in 2016 and in 2018. Sadly, it can and it does get even worse. In many countries, democratic procedures are bypassed, and tyrants oppress their peoples at will, while paying lip service to democracy, justice, and morality.

But this isn't proof that I'm naive or utopian about social science communities, nor that their collective problems, their problems of the commons, can't ever get better, so we must throw our hands up in the air. It's no proof that human beings are essentially and immutably racist, sexist, xenophobic, and homophobic. Some people are, some people aren't. Some people sometimes are, but not all the time. Being more or less aware of it, more or less prepared to openly defend their attitudes, more or less ashamed of them. Situations, interactions, relations, and moods matter. There are many shades of gray. Further, people can change their mind about things, and as a result they can change their practices. Not everyone, but some people do. People, including social scientists, are responsive to reasons. Not always, but sometimes they are.

The conclusion isn't exhilarating. Yet, I suppose it's pretty much common sense. We have to keep working to get increasingly closer to the good, if we can. Try and do away with the structural causes and enablers of racism, sexism, xenophobia, and homophobia. Deploy cultural and institutional devices to expand thoughtful and level-headed participation, and reduce selfishness, immorality, and apathy. If our community got a D last time, work hard to get a C. If we got a B, try to get an A or A+. The usual stuff.

———

Feasibility isn't a binary variable. My proposals' real-world success isn't a binary variable either. Nor is it unidimensional, since there are many ways for things to get better.

One way to make progress is through increased awareness and understanding. Our community will be better off to the extent that we're aware of the distinction between *Activity WF* and *Activity DF*, we don't run them together, and we're aware of their practical reason character. To the extent that we understand the problems we have and how to address them. 'No, no, no. That's a non-answer.' 'That'd be a dead end, a waste of time. Here's why.' If I'm right, telling your friends and colleagues would be a step forward. At conferences, in the hallways, online, and in your writings and presentations. Understanding can also be promoted through community members' teaching, supervising PhD candidates, serving on committees and as referees, and collaborating with peers. If things go well, communication will improve and misunderstandings will dwindle.

Tell your friends and colleagues! Assuming my account does increase awareness and understanding, how to diffuse them throughout social science communities? Organizational and structural changes are key, because of their reach and robustness. Especially organizations that are seen as representing the community as such, as the source of symbolically central and official representations. Let's get them on board: professional associations, university departments and faculties, journals, and public and private research foundations. Meanwhile, individuals can do their part as individuals, despite the limited influence any one can have. Their arguments can make a difference. In scholarly communities, people are used to arguments and are open to them. People may be convinced by arguments. In the longer run, a substantial crowd can have effects on cultural and institutional arrangements, habitual practices, accepted norms, and organizations' rules and regulations.

Were awareness and understanding to become widespread in a community, its public opinion would be receptive to policies to improve *Activity WF* and *Activity DF*. Its climate would be ripe for them. They'd be viewed as worthy of attention, time, and resources.

———

Size matters. The social science communities I've been thinking of are relatively small. They aren't as small as a group of friends who are hanging out at the apartment of one of them. But still. Small communities are more likely to be persuaded by my views about morality, the common good, and practical reason in the logic of scientific research. Meetings, discussions, and collective decisions are more likely to come about. New policies and organizational reforms can be more easily executed. Small communities are more likely to be well predisposed and receptive to my proposals.

———

Activity WF and *Activity DF* require community processes. Much work is needed to get them started, actually started and moving, and to keep them up and running over time. The results of this work aren't either/or: either success or failure. There are degrees of success. Degrees of progress. If a critic claims that there'll never ever be any progress anywhere, perhaps it's they who are misjudging empirical reality. Get real!

11.3 Here and now

'Hi there! We buy your arguments. We're on the same page about *Activity WF* and *Activity DF*. We agree that they're practical reason problems, and it'd be good for our community to engage in collective work, deliberation, and decision-making in one way or another. So far, so good. We'd now like to know, very concretely, how to make this happen. Here and now. The sooner we can get down to work, the better. We'd like to know what concrete actions you recommend to get things going; how to begin to change our practices, organizations, and culture; which causes can be manipulated to bring about the wished-for results. We realize that nobody can tell our community where to go. But can't you give us narrowly technical, means-to-ends advice?'

––––––––

Maybe this strikes you as a cop-out, as if I were kicking the can down the road, but I don't know how much I'll be able to help. For one, the purview of technical advice—narrowly technical, merely technical—isn't an innocuous matter. The danger is trespassing. Encroaching on what a community itself, together with its stakeholders, must decide. It's the old story of technocrats encroaching on democracies.

Setting that aside, your questions can't be answered on the fly. There's a lot of scholarship in social science and philosophy to study and draw on. A lot. In addition, what your community is looking for isn't general statements, which abstract away from its peculiarities. Answers have to be a function of the particulars: social, political, and organizational initial conditions; how economic and cultural resources are distributed; the history of the community; its epistemic aspirations; and much more. What is to be done here and now isn't what is to be done there and then. Your community needs actionable proposals to set things in motion. Actionable proposals supported by good arguments. They have to fit your community's circumstances.

For any value of 'here and now,' these proposals will be hard to put together and defend. Linking the general and the particular can get knotty, too. For any value of 'here and now,' data on the community have to be conscientiously collected and analyzed, which is an arduous project in its own right. Arguments about means, ostensibly technical, proudly introduced as wholly technical, will blend into arguments about ends. (Also, is the boundary between means and ends itself local? Is it up to us?) The distinction between consultants' technical calculations and communities' procedural choices will get fuzzy.

Lots of challenges. Will you guys pick up where I must leave off? Maybe this strikes you as a cop-out, but I'll look forward to seeing your results.

———

That being said, I can offer a couple of conversation starters, for whatever they're worth.

Specific instances of *Activity WF* and *Activity DF* will be about specific words and distinctions. To carry them out, we'll need to find good sites and design good formats. Forums created and optimized for our purposes. Tools, technologies, and infrastructures tailored to the tasks before us. In spaces that provide the requisite affordances or enablers.[11] What should these sites and formats look like? What would suit the aims of the activities we'll be undertaking and the procedures we'll be following? How many formats would it be optimal to have in our repertoire and what would each be used for?

A natural initial thought is that we want to talk to one another, we want to get together. This means we want to hold meetings, like the meetings of legislatures, committees, and scientific associations. Not so much one-off meetings, but regular get-togethers, where we work together, deliberate, and make collective decisions over the course of a certain period. How are we going to conduct and organize them? Will they be in the flesh, virtual, or hybrid? In this conjuncture, do the pros of physical co-presence outweigh its cons? Et cetera.

Social science communities have the capacity to think imaginatively and boldly about sites and formats. They have the capacity and determination to be innovative, organizationally and technologically. To transcend and outdo the standard meeting format. Additionally, conversations about 'w' or *d* might be construed out of individual contributions made at various times and places. If these contributions are oriented toward the community, as proposals or

---

11. Abend 2022; Barlösius 2019; Bell and Zacka 2020; Gibson 1979; Gieryn 2000, 2002; Keane 2016; Klinenberg 2018; Larkin 2013; Star 1999; Star and Ruhleder 1996.

suggestions, they could be conceived of as diachronic participation in a collective project. Along the same lines, past arguments could be brought to bear on our present discussions.

At this abstract level, there isn't a lot to say. To assess the worth of sites and formats, you have to inspect their actual instantiations. Actual buildings and rooms, technologies and software, guidelines for deliberation. Seating arrangements, their effects, and complaints about them. Actual shapes and textures. Et cetera.

What do you guys think? Will you concretize, elaborate, or rebuff my conversation starters?

———

Whatever site and format a community opts for, it'll have to ensure that adequate epistemic and moral conditions obtain. Conditions for the conduct of *Activity WF* and *Activity DF*, and conditions for the conduct of discussions about conditions for the conduct of *Activity WF* and *Activity DF*.

In practice, how can communities institute adequate conditions? I don't have anything original to say about this. One vital aspect is to reform organizational structures, so that they're well aligned with the goals of communal discussions and work. Organizations can enable and constrain, incentivize and disincentivize. Organizational behavior scholarship should be of help, furnishing empirically substantiated generalizations, causal mechanisms, and good and bad models. Another vital aspect is money, money, money. I'm afraid that in capitalist societies you won't get anywhere without financial support. Communities' initiatives must be paid for. Economic inequalities threaten to foil *Activity WF* and *Activity DF*, as they foil other collective epistemic endeavors and efforts at understanding. Which means communities' discussions need a whole new chapter on their funding options, economic interests, and evil economic interests. Science in capitalist societies.

Besides financial assistance, we can use social scientific and philosophical assistance as well. Our community must take advantage of both. The former: sociologists' and political scientists' empirical research, in particular if it's led (more or less cogently) to normative proposals. The latter: philosophers' and political theorists' normative proposals, if they're based (more or less systematically) on empirical research.

Democratic and participatory practices have been studied by sociologists of social movements, political sociologists, and organizational sociologists, often by means of ethnographic research. Whether their data are about organizations, associations, political communities, or social movements, these studies have examined the nuts and bolts of participation, deliberation, and self-government.[12] Their organizational, cultural, and economic foundations. Participants' accounts. The instruments, tools, and rhetorical and cultural devices they avail themselves of. The hurdles they face. Their effectiveness— for example, the conditions under which massive participation and equality are realizable, and the causal mechanisms that produce good outcomes. These bodies of research can be serviceable to *Activity WF* and *Activity DF*, provided social science communities' shared objectives include deepening participatory democratic practices and reducing inequality. As I think they should.

Philosophers are most helpful to social science communities' *Activity WF* and *Activity DF* if they've looked closely at empirical realities, processes, possibilities, and constraints. For instance, philosopher of science Longino, who underscores what communities' "discursive interactions" require. She argues that "an adequate normative theory of knowledge must then be a normative theory of social knowledge, a theory whose norms apply to social practices and processes of cognition." She goes on to indicate "the criteria I take to be necessary to assure the effectiveness of discursive interactions": venues, uptake, public standards, and tempered equality.[13]

Or take Alexandrova and Fabian's 2022 article on "participatory approaches to science" and the co-production of scientific knowledge. Instead of staying in their offices and university libraries, the authors are "informed by our experiences collaborating with Turn2us, a national anti-poverty charity in the UK."[14] They focus on knowledge about people's well-being and thriving, but I paraphrase to fit my argument: communities' discussions about distinctions and word uses should "ensure healthy power dynamics." By "providing payments," the effects of economic inequalities can be lessened, and more representative participation can be achieved, of both community members and stakeholders.

Similarly situated, at the intersection between philosophy and empirical research, is Serrano Zamora and Herzog's 2022 article "A Realist Epistemic Utopia?" Their point of departure isn't in philosophy of science, but in political philosophy. Yet, it's political philosophy concerned with the relationships between politics and epistemic practices. Through an ethnography of a 2019 climate camp in Germany, Serrano Zamora and Herzog look at

---

12. Baiocchi 2005; Baiocchi and Ganuza 2016; Chen 2016; Eliasoph 2014; C. Lee 2015; C. Lee, McQuarrie, and Walker 2015; Polletta 2002, 2014; Polletta and Gardner 2018; Schneiderhan and Khan 2008. See also Fishkin 1995, 2009; Luskin, Fishkin, and Jowell 2002.

13. Longino 2002, 129.

14. Alexandrova and Fabian 2022, 15.

how social actors dealt with two different tensions: the pre-existence of difference in knowledge and their tension with ideals of horizontality and inclusion on the one hand, and the tension between these ideals and the efficiency of the camp's organization on the other. [...] We have identified epistemic mechanisms such as an experimental attitude, the avoiding of specialization and the redistributions of knowledge, and epistemic humility, which, together, were able to avoid hierarchization and exclusion.[15]

These philosophical projects aren't about social science communities, nor about words and distinctions. Yet, *Activity WF* and *Activity DF* can learn from them. Alexandrova and Fabian and Serrano Zamora and Herzog collected firsthand evidence on practices and institutions. They used social science approaches and methods to observe the social world. This isn't typical for philosophers' work on democratic and participatory practices. In philosophy, normative arguments about epistemic goods, values, and virtues may have empirical underpinnings, they may have implications for practice, but these needn't be methodically worked out. The data aren't first-rate. Seldom do philosophers get their hands dirty, real dirty, and ethnographically investigate cultural and organizational conditions, actual social interactions, and implementation opportunities and difficulties—and how all of this varies.[16]

We've seen that there are exceptions. *Activity WF* and *Activity DF* should enlist their help.

———

I've argued that procedures should be established through adequate community processes. Community members have to give reasons and make decisions about them. Therefore, I'm unable to say anything about the content of the rules of the game. I'm not a member of your community. I haven't even met you guys. So, I'm ineligible to participate. Is that all there is to it, though? Maybe an outsider can make good suggestions from the outside, on the basis of the character of the problem and situation, which the community will then democratically consider. Maybe some procedures are sensible and

15. Serrano Zamora and Herzog 2022, 53–54.

16. I'm not blaming them. The division of scholarly labor shapes aptitudes and specialties. Understandably, philosophers' forte isn't organizational design, nor qualitative and quantitative social science methods. Their professional training doesn't comprise cultural challenges to change, and cultural differences across scientific communities (comparative politics vs. economic sociology; US vs. French sociology).

effective in many places, despite the specifics of specific communities, words, and distinctions.

I've insisted that you can't discover how to use 'w.' There's no fact of the matter about it. In light of this fact, here's a proscription for social science communities to consider: no turning down manuscripts or dismissing applications and candidates on semantic grounds, by making top-down semantic claims. It's a foul. Fancy people, committee chairs, university deans, and winners of prestigious awards in 'w' aren't excepted. Nobody gets special semantic privileges.

In the thought experiment I'm concocting, this rule goes on to be communally accepted, and is now well known. Journals, book publishers, hiring committees, and funding agencies endorse it. It's organizationally enforced and culturally reinforced. It's underlined in guidelines given to reviewers, editorial boards, and members of committees and panels, when they set about their assignments. For example, the following two judgments, if uttered, would be disqualified. 'This manuscript isn't making a theoretical contribution, per this definition of "theoretical," which is the way to correctly use the word. Here it is . . .' 'This manuscript isn't making a contribution to the literature on religion, per this definition of "religion," which is the way to correctly use the word. Here it is . . .'

To be precise, these judgments would be disqualified as long as one more condition obtains. No one can make exclusionary semantic claims if they're speaking for themselves, making semantic claims by themselves, qua individual. By contrast, you may be legitimately speaking on behalf of the community, reporting a collective, democratic decision that the community had previously made. The community decided what's the 'way to correctly use the word'—that is, 'theory' or 'religion.' These uses would indeed be correct, but not because you said so or thought so. You're simply representing the community; you're a spokesperson for it.

Some rules of the game follow from the basic goals of communities' collective discussions, insofar as these are assented to. The conditions under which discussions are conducted should enable deliberation and argumentation. Should or must. It's debatable which modal verb to use, whether the weaker 'should' or the stronger 'must,' indicating a transcendental argument or making-it-possible claim.[17] In either case, the function of these conditions is to facilitate joint reflection and work. Prevent biases. Ensure that there's no place for intimidation and fear. Ensure that a high-status community member can't harm the career chances of someone whose opinions they dislike (unlike

17. Abend 2022.

ordinary boss-employee relations; unlike faculty meetings where assistant professors don't dare to contradict their tenured colleagues).

Everyone has to be free to think and to speak their mind. A gun isn't being held to your head. Your economic subsistence doesn't hang in the balance.

———————

My proposals for social science are based on moral foundations and arguments. If I'm right, social science communities have moral goods at their heart in a twofold fashion. Both in terms of what they should be after and in terms of how they should conduct their business. Of course, I may turn out to be mistaken about the good and about which things are morally good and bad. I may be making dim-witted assumptions about morality. After all, my field isn't normative ethics, and this isn't a book about normative ethics. But if I'm right about the big picture, we can make warranted moral demands on one another. Demands on community members' actions, goals, and motivations. The more moral, the better. The more people are more moral, the better.

Are there any proven methods to strengthen the morality of social science communities—their moral practices, behaviors, norms, character, dispositions? People's education and upbringing can probably help. Sanctions can probably help as well. Neither is a silver bullet, but their average effects are usually positive. No news there. Societies rely on these positive effects to become more decent and happier places. To make more people more likely to flourish and lead well-lived lives. Education will take you only so far, but it's not worthless. Communities sensibly put much effort into training, socializing, and professionalizing future members.

As you yourself might have experienced, or might be now experiencing, the education of young social scientists isn't solely about methods, literatures, theories, and how to get published in *American Journal of Sociology* or *American Sociological Review*. Much of it is about moral stuff, whether explicitly or implicitly. I think it should be more explicitly, self-consciously, self-assuredly, and clearly geared toward fostering moral goods, as opposed to circuitous and guarded about it.[18] This includes the standard moral goods I'd like to incorporate into the logic of social science research, such as justice, equality, and non-selfishness. It may also include the virtues of civility, open-mindedness, and humility. Increasing their prevalence will enhance social scientists' substantive exchanges about their objects of inquiry, and their conversations and decisions

---

18. But wait. Young social scientists might already be too old. University students might be too old to acquire certain moral dispositions and to be spontaneously moved by them.

about 'w' and *d*. Journal reviewers' reports would better accomplish what they're expected to. *Activity WF* and *Activity DF* would get better, and so would communal life.[19]

Sanctions can be more or less formal. There are informal social norms, like the interactional norms that microsociologists dissect.[20] Being frowned on and looked down on. Eyebrows being raised and interactions being awkward. I wouldn't underestimate the muscle of informal norms in scholarly communities, which tend to be small, tight, and share morally laden narratives and genealogies. However, formal rules are also needed, like the abovementioned proscription. Backed up by rewards and penalties, incentives and disincentives, along with enforcement systems. Communities' central organizations should stand behind them and make it known that they stand behind them.

I've been talking about moral goods and requirements that are of necessity general, and hence imprecise. In real life, many goods will be community-specific, specific to particular places and times. They'll be collectively established by each of them. Consequently, the substance of moral education and sanctions has to be community-specific as well. Putting specificities to one side, though, the structure of incentives should be conducive to communities' moral objectives. Presently, they're geared toward scientific and career rewards. Changing this will take much work. Much luck. And telling apart what's structural from what's superficial.

Activity DF and *Activity WF* are communal problems. We need to figure out, together, what to do and how to increase the probability that it gets done. We need to select and design good tools and mechanisms. As I've argued, it's not a job for individuals. It's not for them to discern the right way forward and act in the right way. Much less to instruct, discipline, and regulate themselves, govern themselves, as discrete entities, each in the privacy of their home or office. Instead, all of these responsibilities lie with the community. The buck stops with the community.

It'd be a smoother ride if people could be trusted to do the right thing as soon as they were asked to do the right thing, or as soon as they realized what the right thing was. It'd be easier to give people a few lectures, post some signs around town or around the office, and run some online ads concerning the importance of morality. Offer workshops about altruism and selfishness, and about morally inappropriate and insensitive language. At the end of which participants would take a multiple-choice test. People who acquired correct

---

19. Why these virtues? You could argue that it's up to the community whether humility and civility are good, and also how pluralist (or relativist) it wishes to be.

20. Garfinkel 1967; Goffman 1963; Scheff 1990.

moral understandings would be motivated by them, as 'moral internalism' maintains. Leave them alone and they'll take it from there.

I don't think these strategies can deliver the goods. Durable policies for the good practice of *Activity DF* and *Activity WF* have to be social and structural. Unwanted outcomes should be structurally blocked, rendered impossible, or rendered very difficult and costly. To this end, the community sits in the driver's seat. It has to arrive at legitimate policy decisions, and it'll probably need many kinds of measures—financial, organizational, cultural, educational, and technological. These measures should act in concert. They can shape individuals' outlooks and practices, one at a time, but they'll also begin to effect structural changes.

————

This is an open-ended book. It ends with an ellipsis.

Some important questions are left unanswered. Some weren't even broached. In several areas, I just began to scratch the surface. There's a lot to think through and work out. Charitably, you might chalk this up to this book's character. It's an invitation, which aims to encourage people to join in. It's a call to work together. Addressed to you. To you guys. This is consistent with my arguments about the powers of individuals and of communities. I've said a lot. It's high time I shut up and let others speak.

Less charitably, I'm kicking the can down the road. Shirking my duties. I'm dodging problems and challenges I'd be obligated to deal with.

Either way, this is an unfinished work.

11.4 Critical FAQs

As a matter of fact, harmonious consensuses are never achieved. Indeed, they're impossible. Is that your aim for Activity WF *and* Activity DF? *Are you looking to eradicate conflict and disagreement?*

No, I'm not. No, we're not.

Conflict isn't a bogeyperson. Nor is disagreement in and of itself. I'm not suggesting that communities try and prevent conflicts about words, distinctions, and classifications at all costs. Nor that they try and make conflict disappear, so they're in a state of perfect, harmonious consensus. That'd be foolish. For one, conflict and disagreement aren't necessarily bad for a community. They can, but needn't be. Some are, but not all. Some are good, productive, and serve desirable functions. Moreover, there are conflicts that won't go away, whether you like it or not. They're inherent in social interaction, organization, and structure. Rooted in people's dissimilar goals and interests, diverse perspectives, and legitimate divergences. Legitimate and at times commendable divergences, both epistemically and morally advantageous.[21]

Our communities' aims vis-à-vis conflict and disagreement have to be subtle and discriminating. We want to make good collective decisions about words and distinctions, which we're going to be using as we do our research, teach, read other people's ideas and arguments, and informally and formally evaluate them. These undertakings are disrupted by some kinds of disagreements, but not by all. We must look closely into each of them. Some sources of conflict can be safely put aside or bracketed. People can be on board with this arrangement, or with this step, as a pragmatic way to collectively move forward. They can be on board despite deeper disagreements with someone else's viewpoint, metaphysical premises, or "moral background" assumptions.[22] It can be a compromise, even if it's not their top preference, it's not what they'd go for if they were deciding by themselves.

Keep in mind that *Activity WF* and *Activity DF* aren't trying to get to the bottom of the issue, philosophically speaking. Instead, they're practical assistants. Social science communities must do research, make knowledge claims, exchange ideas, collaborate, and communicate with society. Advisors must advise advisees and funding organizations must grant grants. Without wasting time on irresolvable questions and merely verbal disputes. It's a lower practical standard.

Sometimes community members won't see eye to eye at all. No acceptable compromises can be reached, regardless of the quality of deliberations and the thoughtfulness, selflessness, and public-spiritedness of participants. Not even reluctant compromises as to how to tolerate one another, coexist with one another, and where to agree to disagree. The possibility of this outcome has to be reckoned with. Still, research and evaluation must go on. No matter how *Activity WF* and *Activity DF* shake out, whatever decision-making procedures end up being employed, some people will be majorly dissatisfied. If the majority rule is employed, for example, the minority may be majorly dissatisfied.

So be it. Under certain circumstances, I don't know that there's a better alternative. All democracies and democratic theories are familiar and have to live with these eventualities—stemming from the diversity of worldviews and ways of life in a community, political and value pluralism, and clashing interests.[23]

21. Coser 1956; Dahrendorf 1959; Maynard 1985; Mouffe 2005; Simmel 1908.

22. Abend 2014; C. Taylor 1999.

23. Outside my jurisdiction: what deliberation is capable of; which disagreements and conflicts are impervious to it; under which conditions (if any) people would come to see eye to eye eventually, provided everyone were clearheaded and well-meaning; and whether 'people' is too general.

As a matter of fact, people get pissed off when they don't get their way and when they're forced to make compromises. Are you imagining friendly, peaceful, and all-around cooperative discussions? Are you imagining idyllic communities engaging in joint work and having calm conversations over tea?

No, I'm not.

I'd rather do without suppositions about discussions' peacefulness and people's tranquility. Now, it's Social Psychology 101 that real-world interactions involve real-world emotions, emotions can cloud people's judgment, and discussions can devolve into brawls. Furthermore, as sociological and psychological facts, people' emotions, sympathies, and animosities have lives of their own. Their causal origins may have nothing to do with the issues at stake— namely, social science research, words and distinctions, knowledge and truth. Those guys just rub you the wrong way.

At any rate, the big challenge remains the contradictions between communities' and community members' goals. Their incongruent interests, which can bring about anger, bitterness, and hostilities. It's the usual challenge: how to get more people to be more committed to the common good. How to build societies and cultures where people are fulfilled by collective accomplishments, and find that the collectivity's demands on them are justified. 'Given what our community is up to and how it operates, pervasive selfishness would be bad. We get it. We're also happy to pay our taxes and be truthful.'

It's notoriously hard to make headway toward this state of affairs. The real world doesn't like it, so to speak. Entrenched capitalist institutions don't like it either. But I wouldn't be defeatist about it. Scientific communities' built-in objectives and starting points are such that, I think, there's reason to have some hope.

As a matter of fact, solutions can't ever be stable and final. It's impossible for a community to attain everlasting solutions to anything. Is that your aim for Activity WF *and* Activity DF?

No, it's not.

I concur: solutions are temporary; they're always works in progress. What our community has collectively established looks good now. But soon it won't anymore. Soon it'll meet new trials and there'll be new options available to us. Thus, the outcomes of *Activity WF* and *Activity DF* are good only for the time being. One level up, our procedures and criteria are good only for the time being. Till we have to revise our policies. (I'm assuming again a simplified picture, consisting of only two levels.) In this regard, a community might long for immovable foundations, an eternal constitution, infinite regress no more. But immovability is a temptation to be resisted. Restricted movement and limited adaptability would be major handicaps.

The revisability of *Activity WF* and *Activity DF* checks out. So does the perpetual need for reassessment and readjustment. Everything is constantly changing in the world: communities' composition, structure, and goals; organizations' interests; people's desires and abilities; social, economic, technological, and political conditions; communities' stakeholders and where they stand; the rivers into which you step. Language, knowledge, and values won't sit still either. Nothing is frozen in time. That's our condition, as temporal beings, beings who exist in time. Hence, *Activity WF* and *Activity DF* must keep up with these changes. Communities' practices—solutions, answers, outcomes, arrangements, criteria—will lag somewhat behind. But they should remain timely.

That's all alright with us. Nothing lasts forever anyway (except for true love). In the meantime, the community can work with its temporary arrangements. We can go on with our research tomorrow. Tomorrow morning.

You're neglecting holism. Words are inextricably intertwined with other words. Distinctions are inextricably intertwined with other distinctions. Do you take Activity WF *and* Activity DF *to be about isolated words and distinctions?*

To make their analyses and discussions more manageable, social science communities may zero in on 'w' as an isolated word and d as an isolated distinction. Taking up words and distinctions one at a time is like taking up causal factors or variables one at a time, even though everything is connected with everything else. Communities typically have disputes over individual, separate items. One 'w' or one d. But there are also disputes over sets or networks of interrelated items, which is a good thing. Their uses are interrelated in a research area. They may belong to one 'theory,' 'theoretical approach,' school of thought, with its perspective and terminology (e.g., postmodern theory, Marxist theory, feminist theory, rational choice theory, or systems theory). Its key words and distinctions are meant to stand or fall together. Whatever virtues they have, whatever goods they help attain, they do so jointly.[24]

My arguments can accommodate one lexical item or a network, one distinction or several. In both cases, *Activity WF* and *Activity DF* shouldn't lose sight of words' and distinctions' relations. Their contexts and backgrounds,

---

24. Abend 2008a; Fuhse 2022.

semantic and social. However, I concede that I'm not in the clear if you're a fundamental holist.[25]

General propositions ('for all x') don't do justice to the real world, suffused as it is with exceptions, contingencies, special cases, and unique combinations of factors. What sort of generality are you aiming for?

We shouldn't aim for *Activity WF* or *Activity DF* solutions that work across the board. There aren't any universal principles.[26] The best outcome regarding a particular word (or interrelated words) or a particular distinction (or inter-related distinctions) in a social science community is a case-by-case issue.

I'm not ruling out well-delimited generalizations, nor general rules of thumb, like my own procedural suggestions. Yet, while such generalizations aren't empty, they won't produce answers to concrete instances of *Activity WF* and *Activity DF*. No principle could cover the enormous variety of communities, 'w' and *d* challenges, their initial conditions, their institutional and cultural backdrops. All the context-dependent factors, interests, and objectives that bear on the two activities.

Crucially, what a community will be talking about is specific desiderata, con-flicts, and social inequalities. Tangible institutions and practices rather than ab-stract ideas. We'll scrutinize these museums, these schools and teachers, these extant laws, these possible economic consequences, given this political system, in a community that speaks this language, and so on. Given all of that, we've concluded that we should use the word 'capitalism' or the word 'planet' to ...

There can't be a methodological formula for social science communities to conduct Activity WF *and* Activity DF. *Is this what you're proposing?*

No, it's not.

To ensure this isn't a merely verbal dispute: you can use the word 'formula' to mean a fixed, preordained series of steps. In this sense, a methodological formula is rigid, and it'll algorithmically produce an output. In this sense, I agree, there aren't any formulas a community can follow to make decisions about its words, distinctions, and classifications. Indeed, I see no formulas in scientific practice at all.

By 'methodological formula' you might instead be referring to some collec-tive, public guidelines, some sense of where to go and where not to, how to

---

25. On holism, see Dresner (2012) and Quine (1951).
26. Cf. Dancy 2004; G. Dworkin 1995.

proceed and how not to, what to be guided by and what not to. Then, yes, this is what I have in mind. That's the whole point. (But your use of 'formula' is odd.) These general guidelines must go hand in hand with individualized evaluations and judgments. You won't get anywhere without discernment and understanding of particular configurations, payoffs, and trade-offs.

That a community thinks through and works together to establish procedures leaves a lot open about them, including what they'll look like, their form, and the character of the demands they'll make. What's certain is that procedures won't resemble a calculator or machine. They aren't sets of inflexible and uniform rules, nor step-by-step instructions. They can't mechanically settle disputes over 'w' or d. They won't deliver the best solution to a community, but they'll help it reach good outcomes.

Communities' criteria for *Activity WF* and *Activity DF* will reflect some articulation of their goals, values, interests, and desiderata, as per their deliberative processes. These criteria aren't ready-made, ready to be applied. In fact, it's impossible for them to be ready to be applied. Their application can't be formalized ex ante, but necessitates the exercise of judgment at every turn. There's no option but to collectively discuss these judgments as well.

When a disagreement about word 'w' or distinction d arises, you should let people fight it out each time, freely and spontaneously. There's nothing to prearrange or regulate. Won't Reason prevail?

It won't, if the conditions aren't right: socially, organizationally, spatially, politically, economically, and epistemically.

Observing the practice and history of social science, I've concluded that something is amiss with its words, distinctions, and classifications; with how acceptability gets determined, who has a say, and who doesn't; and how these choices are argued for, when they are. In these respects, social science communities aren't functioning well. Non-interventionism or quietism would be a bad policy. It's an implausible expectation that a community can work things out, each time, without any guidelines or guidance at all. Without any orientation and directions as to how to assess arguments, weigh considerations, and rank kinds of reasons. Without spelling out anything procedural, and without making provisions for people who have less status and capital and are in the periphery, literally or figuratively. Currently, social science communities are far from pulling this off.

In a small PhD seminar you're teaching this semester, the basic norms of truth and argument are largely uncontroversial, and face-to-face interaction supports the practice of good argumentation, and bolsters trust and ethical behavior. Not even in these nicely curated forums can Reason be sure to prevail. For social science communities, non-interventionism is hopeless. A hopeless hope. Ordinary social processes are at work: ordinary social institutions, norms, and structures. There's power and self-interest and inequality. Power, self-interest, and inequality should be formally curtailed, or else they'll reign untrammeled. People's intentions are sometimes good and altruistic, sometimes bad and selfish. Regardless of intentions, human beings have epistemic and moral limitations.

Epistemically and morally good outcomes won't naturally come about. There's no 'start impeccable reason-giving process' button to press. Rather, social science communities need to work on adequate frameworks for the practice of *Activity WF* and *Activity DF*—which they have to construct, select, and put in place. They need legitimate procedures and normative guidelines. Effective organizational mechanisms must be set up, and social inequalities must be counteracted. Where good conditions, procedures, and guidelines are in place, then yes, people will give reasons and make arguments about the case at hand. The discussion will be specific to 'w' or *d*, along with the structure of the community, distribution of resources, probable winners and losers, stakeholders, and the whole social and political enchilada.

In your account, moral/practical goods are central. Are you thereby subsuming social science under ethics and turning social scientists into social justice warriors in disguise?

No, I'm not.

Only Twitter thinkers think that either a person is a morality-free, value-free, objective scientist or they're a social justice warrior. This isn't a dichotomous variable. It's neither a dichotomy nor only one variable, but a multidimensional space of continuous variables. There are lots of values on lots of variables. We're seeking good combinations of good values, or good combinations of golden means.

That an activity involves moral (or political) stuff doesn't mean it 'just is' morality (or politics). Unlike social movements and applied ethicists, social science is in the business of producing good social science knowledge. At first, this seems a straightforwardly epistemic task. On closer inspection, it isn't. Producing good social science knowledge involves moral/practical goods and aims. This involvement can take various forms, which can be beneficial or deleterious to social science communities in various ways.

My arguments aren't about social science in its entirety, but about *Activity WF* and *Activity DF*. I've argued that they aren't truth-apt. Unlike empirical research, their results aren't truth claims. Truth isn't the judge. You could metaphorically say that moral/practical goods pick up part of the tab. Not a totally clear metaphor, but being intriguing and thought-provoking picks up part of the tab.

As a matter of fact, social science communities are having Activity WF *and* Activity DF *conversations already. They've been having them all along. Someone proposes d, or certain uses for 'w.' Fellow community members respond. Reasons are exchanged. Sometimes the proposal is accepted by the community. These processes go on and on. Aren't you asking us to do what we're already doing?*

There are many arguments and conversations that could and should be recast, with a few adjustments, as contributions to *Activity WF* and *Activity DF*. Present and past. On the minus side, these imputations will have a wobbly leg: participants' understandings have often been deficient. Social science communities should have a good grasp of what they're doing and what's going on. This time, knowledge about the anatomy of your legs may help you to walk.[27]

For a community to practice *Activity WF* and *Activity DF* well and effectively, it should be able to think clearly about:

(1) Their overarching logic and mechanics
(2) Technical tools (words vs. concepts, single quotation marks, definitions)
(3) What's wrong with 'what-is-F?' questions
(4) Starting with a word vs. starting by making a distinction
(5) What makes *Activity WF* and *Activity DF* practical reason activities
(6) What makes one proposal and argument better than another
(7) What the competing desiderata are, how to compare their value, and, if needed, how to bring them under one roof[28]
(8) Who gets to participate and how
(9) A proposal's payoffs: who/what would profit and who/what wouldn't (or worse)
(10) Proposals' payoffs: who/what should profit and who/what shouldn't (or worse)
(11) How to adjudicate disputes over word uses and distinctions

At present, clearheadedness isn't prevalent. Even if a few people have it, the community doesn't—neither its membership quantitatively speaking, nor its norms and institutions. It is a tall order. Moreover, people's arguments have been overwhelmingly about scientific and epistemic gains, and

---

27. Weber 1922, 217.
28. Some sense of what to do, since there can't be an algorithm.

overwhelmingly about scientific and epistemic gains for themselves, for the benefit of authors' arguments, models, or papers (mostly couched in terms of usefulness). I've argued that this is wrong. We're a community, and what drives us isn't what's good for you but the common good, what's good for us all, taken together. The moral and communal implications of going for distinction *d*, or going for these uses of word 'w,' aren't sufficiently recognized. They aren't sufficiently recognized for what they are: methodologically and epistemologically valid grounds.

Granted, I might be misjudging communities' degree of clarity. My appraisals might be inaccurate and overgeneralize. These are empirical questions, so please go ahead and prove me wrong!

Your arguments are about social science communities. What's a community? As a matter of fact, it's always controversial who is and isn't a community member. Isn't that a piece of trickery on your part?

I'm guilty as charged. I talk about *Activity WF* and *Activity DF* as practiced by a community, but this is no reliable bedrock. It's an imprecise and contestable analytical construction. There's no easy way to individuate a community. No easy answer to what makes a community a community, whom and what to leave out, and why. Neither easy nor neutral, as many (many, many) people have shown.

I've put forward arguments about social science communities' practices, languages, interests, and aims. One of my building blocks is the community. A community. This community. I've made claims about what's good for it, its good, what it's after, its members. How is *this* community, which my claims refer to, to be identified? Delimiting a community can't be done impartially, non-committally. It's impossible, much like you can't define 'terrorism' or 'meat' in a value-free, objective, unbiased, or disinterested manner. Add ugly motives to the mix, and outcomes can be manipulated through strategic changes in membership requirements and strategic redrawing of boundaries. Gerrymandering, exclusion, and "prior ring-fencing."

This is a serious objection. I don't know to what degree it undercuts my arguments. I guess one possible reply is that individuating the community is a separate problem. A problem that numerous social science and philosophy projects must face up to: the community is a ubiquitous building block and starting point. (Cowardly kicking the can down the road? Cowardly hiding behind, once again, companions in guilt?)

Another possible reply is that the pertinent community needn't be identified precisely. My claims do refer to a community, but they can make do with a rough idea of what it is, of where its boundaries lie. The sociology of education community. The interdisciplinary social science community that investigates morality, which comprises psychologists, anthropologists, and sociologists. Demography. These people and organizations. Sort of. There are borderline cases, but also definite ones. Unfortunately, if I so argued, I'd deserve a taste of my own medicine: my counterargument to 'that's too static!' (see chapter 3).

I can think of other replies, but they aren't knockdown arguments either. I've got to get going now, though, so I'll leave the matter open.

Are you sure about your overall account?

No, I'm not.

Not to mention the abovementioned unanswered questions and unresolved problems. Sending out an SOS.

11.5 Coda

Inaction isn't an option. This has been my baseline: the show must go on. Research won't stop any more than life will stop, so we can make ourselves a tea, or a *mate*, and ponder our deepest ethical conundrums. We must act now, always, all the time.

Social science communities are conducting, applying, and evaluating research now, always, all the time. Social scientists are busy drawing distinctions, individuating entities, and classifying them. Referring to social phenomena and processes by means of key words. Describing and explaining 'w,' finding its historical origins, examining its different parts and different forms, and comparing cases of it. They're routinely sought out, as experts on 'w,' by the media and policy makers. If tomorrow is a bit better than today, epistemically and morally, that's already something.

A bit more moral goodness, justice, and equality would be good news. A lot more moral goodness, justice, and equality, all over the world, in every social science community, would be amazing. But this isn't the benchmark I'm recommending. If I were, I could be justifiably accused of naivete, wishful thinking, and utopianism. Luckily, I don't have to promise any level of success, more or less optimistically. I won't make any forecasts. (I'm not in that line of business.) As long as it's possible for things to improve, we have to do our best, and we'll see how well we do. It is possible. I'll see you guys soon.

EPILOGUE (SO, WILL SOCIAL SCIENTISTS' NEVER-ENDING DISPUTES OVER WORDS EVER END?)

NO, THEY WON'T.

Nor should they.

But they should be well understood, and well set up, in order for something good to come out of them.

Well set up analytically or conceptually. Well 'framed,' some people would say (I'm not a fan). Well set up organizationally, materially, and socially, well organized and prepared, in order for the community to get the job done. It's a hands-on job; a continuing, never-ending hands-on job.

———

I've argued that social science communities' having disputes over words isn't equivalent to their having merely verbal disputes. That a dispute is about a word, or involves a word, doesn't entail that it's unimportant, superficial, not substantive. Social scientists can separate the wheat from the chaff.

I've argued that disputes over words tend to conflate two activities. One I called 'word goes first!' or *Activity WF*. It concerns social scientists' word uses and how to appraise them. The other I called 'distinction goes first!' or *Activity DF*. It concerns social scientists' distinctions and classifications and how to appraise them. For each activity, social science communities should get clear on what to do, what to circumvent, and what's at stake.

I've argued that they're both practical reason activities. Their outcomes can't be true or false, but they'll be good or bad, better or worse, in light of a community's characteristics, practices, and goals. The community is looking for a good way to go, good standards and procedures, a good arrangement. Good for now. It's good enough at this time, but it'll have to be revamped or replaced at a later point.

Social science projects can have many aims. What they intend to offer can be diverse. Hence, there are many things the practice of *Activity WF* and *Activity DF* could help with. Which means trade-offs. Communities have to make choices about goods and values, both epistemic and non-epistemic. There are plenty of them. They range from standard scientific desiderata (e.g., explanatory power, generality, and simplicity) to standard moral goods (e.g., justice/fairness and equality). Communities will have to set priorities. The point of setting priorities isn't philosophical, but to provide social scientists with tools that are ready to hand, as they design and conduct their research— research that eventually will be communally scrutinized. Should we prioritize shooting for this or that good? Will our literature be in better shape if we do this or that?

Communities need well-thought-out criteria and procedures. Not uninformative generalities, where conflicts over words and distinctions aren't anticipated, and their practical reason character isn't noticed. Not appeals to usefulness without filling in the blanks: for what and whom something is useful, useless, and actively harmful. Not individuals' ad hoc decisions and self-regarding methodological tactics, so 'w' and d work for your research. It works for you. End of story.

Communities need well-thought-out criteria to assess word uses, distinctions, and classifications: on which grounds is one to be preferred to another? Procedures through which to establish these criteria. Procedures to work together, exchange reasons, and come to conclusions. To adjudicate disagreements among community members, be they explicit disputes or discrepant practices. To come to see which disagreements are generative as they are, and which ones don't call for adjudication but only for disambiguation. To come to see which disagreements are bad but irresolvable, so it's pointless to go on, and it'd be wiser to focus instead on how conflicting views and diverging practices can coexist (hopefully). Communities need well-thought-out procedures for deliberation and communication. Plus higher-order procedures to establish these procedures.

Who should decide these things? Not the people who normally do, by default, as a matter of course. I've argued that it's not high-status community members, like full professors, holders of endowed chairs, and editors of top journals, but the community as a whole. Everybody should be there and everybody's interests should be taken into account. The conditions under which Activity WF and Activity DF are practiced should be such that everybody gets a say, and nobody is halfheartedly listened to or made light of.

Not that 'everybody' is self-explanatory. Nor is 'the community.' My arguments have liberally referred to the community, despite its fuzziness and well-established shaky standing. The constitution of the community is as big a mess as the uses of key words and distinctions. Further, I've claimed that everybody in the community doesn't include everybody who's entitled to being included. When a social science community embarks on deliberation and decision-making processes about 'w' or d, it shouldn't forget its stakeholders, the class of stakeholders, despite its fuzziness and well-established shaky standing.

Activity WF and *Activity DF* will have consequences for them, too, so they should be invited to participate. They'll present their reasons and work together with community members. Not that the distinction between stakeholders and community members is self-explanatory.

Interests can be wide-ranging. Various kinds of interests should figure in collective discussions about words and distinctions. The good of various kinds of entities can and should be factored in. Various groups, associations, and organizations. Institutions, states, cultural practices, and traditions. The environment. Future generations . . .

––––––

At the beginning of this book, I highlighted a few similarities among social scientists, Panera Bread's lawyers, and meat and dairy lobbies. Foregrounding these similarities suggests a hazard for social science communities, which they're well advised to build defenses against and alternatives to. A lawyer is hell-bent on winning the case for their client, as a manager is hell-bent on increasing their corporation's profits and a lobbyist won't exhibit equanimity and fair-mindedness.

How do they feel about the well-being, desires, and interests of other people, the community, society, the environment? 'Not our fucking problem!' 'Not what we get paid for!' These are accepted practices and attitudes in large swaths of contemporary societies, embedded in longstanding organizational and legal structures. Culturally, no red flag is raised. It's OK. This is what lawyers, managers, and lobbyists do in their work. They have to. They're obligated to. Business is business. Fiduciary duties. Enter your favorite morally putrid excuse here.

Irrespective of what lawyers, managers, and lobbyists should and shouldn't do, this isn't what social scientists should do. It's not the right approach to their work qua knowledge producers, and it's not the right relationship between individuals and collectivities.[1] Communities' aims, even their more narrowly epistemic aims, aren't always consistent with individuals' aims. Nor with the sum of individuals' aims. Social scientists shouldn't be licensed to act as autonomous decision-makers, who can do with their words and distinctions as they please, whose word uses and distinctions can be designed to serve their

––––––

1. Knowledge producers as opposed to overt moral agents, overtly setting out to make the world a better place. It's a separate question if they should set out to do this. There are independent moral and epistemic reasons for social scientists not to emulate lobbyists, lawyers, and managers, but I'm now putting them to one side.

own interests, if they so wish. According to my account, the common good gets the last word. The common good, epistemically and morally. The community holds the reins. As we've learned over and over again, science and knowledge go adrift without ethics. Scientific and epistemological norms wish they were supreme, but they aren't. They ought to be ethically grounded.

Social science communities will have to work hard, culturally and organizationally, toward putting good arrangements in place. What will they be looking to facilitate and accomplish? Fruitful collective discussions and work on instances of *Activity WF* and *Activity DF*. Collective decisions about word uses, distinctions, and classifications that are governed by good criteria, and that are arrived at in good ways. Collective decisions about criteria that are governed by good higher-order criteria, and that are also arrived at in good ways. In addition, communities will have to engineer structures and enablers, so as to approximate the conditions—social, political, economic—under which the two activities can be practiced well, and inequalities' pernicious effects are minimized.

Clashes driven exclusively, and evidently, by the contending parties' self-interest don't make for good social science. *Activity WF* and *Activity DF* have broader horizons than the pecuniary interests of two restaurant chains, which happen to be causally dependent on the extension of the word 'sandwich.' I'd say broader and nobler horizons.

———

'Real scientists don't have disputes over words and distinctions, let alone never-ending ones.'

'Disputes over words are stupid.'

'Definitions, distinctions, and classifications are entirely up to you.'

'Don't make such a big fuss over this stuff. We're all well aware that our empirical research is based on key concepts or key words, and we know how to deal with them.'

'Everyone's wasting their time and should instead go back to their labs, computers, field sites, or archives, and carry on with their empirical research. Stop talking and get your hands dirty right now!'

'There's only one way forward: "w" should be banned from our social science field. To talk about these issues, new words are needed. We have to leave this mess behind and start afresh.'

Do you still hear these critical voices? Perhaps a book can't assuage them. It might need to be supplemented with another sort of understanding, acquired through and enacted in collective, real-world practices. Acquired and developed through interaction, dialogue, discussion; through well-set-up disputes and deliberative processes. Perhaps this understanding can't be reached without listening to many people's voices. Their ideas, questions, grievances—in their own words and voices. Without listening to them attentively.[2] I'm not sure. But I see how reading a book may fall short. Or writing one, for that matter.

———

Colleagues and friends!
Fellows and comrades!
I've argued that the whole thing is a job for communities.
I'm just one guy.
Whether my suggestions are perspicacious or asinine, sensible or nonsensical, they don't enjoy a special status. They're just one guy's suggestions.
So, here's my invitation:

———

2. Bommarito 2013; Daston 2004a; Debus 2015; Ganeri 2017; Murdoch (1970) 2014; S. Panizza 2015; Pedersen, Albris, and Seaver 2021; J. Williams 2018. See also *Phaedrus* 274b–277a. Thanks to Nuno Ramos for his thoughts on these issues.

Make Pluto Great Again

As citizen Tyson, I feel compelled to defend Pluto's honor. It lives deeply in our twentieth-century culture and consciousness.... Nearly every school child thinks of Pluto as an old friend. [...] As professor Tyson, however, I must vote—with a heavy heart—for demotion.

—NEIL DEGRASSE TYSON (1999)[1]

Children say, 'Did they forget about Pluto?' Some even say, 'Did you forget my friend Pluto?'

—*NEW YORK TIMES* (2001)[2]

A.1 Planethood wars

In 2004, Mike Brown (California Institute of Technology), Chad Trujillo (Gemini Observatory), and David Rabinowitz (Yale University) reported the "discovery of a candidate inner Oort cloud planetoid." It "has received the permanent designation (90377) Sedna."[3] In 2005, the same team reported the "discovery of a planetary-sized object in the scattered Kuiper belt."[4] Provisionally referred to as '2003 UB313' and nicknamed 'Xena.' The following year, the International Astronomical Union (IAU) announced that it had been christened 'Eris.'[5] Its size was at the time estimated to exceed Pluto's.

---

1. Tyson 1999.

2. K. Chang 2001.

3. Michael Brown, Trujillo, and Rabinowitz 2004, 645.

4. Michael Brown, Trujillo, and Rabinowitz 2005.

5. "IAU Names Dwarf Planet Eris," Press Release iau0605, IAU, September 14, 2006, Munich, https://www.iau.org/news/pressreleases/detail/iau0605/.

The discoveries of Eris and Sedna meant trouble for Pluto. Especially Eris. If Pluto was a planet, then Eris had to be a planet as well. If Pluto and Eris were planets, then Sedna, Ceres, Haumea, Makemake, Gonggong, Quaoar, Orcus, Salacia, 2002 MS$_4$, and other yet-undiscovered trans-Neptunian objects might have to be planets as well. By contrast, if Eris wasn't a planet, then Pluto couldn't be said to be a planet either. Instead of nine planets, the solar system would have only eight. Forget what you learned in school; rectify astronomy textbooks and planetarium shows. It was a dilemma for astronomers and planetary scientists: neither substantially expanding the set of planets nor kicking out Pluto was an attractive option.[6]

Ceres (discovered in 1801), Pluto (discovered in 1930), and trans-Neptunian objects like 15760 Albion (discovered in 1992) had long provoked classification and definition difficulties. So had Pallas, Juno, Vesta, and asteroids in general.[7] These were sometimes publicly debated, particularly the "arguments for and against demoting Pluto."[8] For instance, in 2001, "news that astrophysicists at the American Museum of Natural History do not consider Pluto a planet spurred more than 100 e-mail messages, some critical, some supportive, to Dr. Neil de Grasse Tyson, director of the museum's Hayden Planetarium."[9]

Eris and Sedna made these difficulties more urgent. Inescapable. Now the fundamental questions had to be faced head-on. What is a planet? What is planethood? Is Pluto a planet? It seemed like a job for the IAU, the association founded in 1919 "to promote and safeguard the science of astronomy in all its aspects."[10] Iwan Williams, of Queen Mary and president of Division III (Planetary Systems Sciences), "was charged with establishing what defines a planet." His committee was set up in 2004. It "discussed the problem by email for 18 months or so. It became clear that the committee was not coming round to a unanimous view." Instead, it presented "three definitions," along "with an indication of the level of support for each."[11]

At that point, the IAU's Executive Committee "decided to establish a new and smaller Planet Definition Committee . . . to take things forward."[12]

6. Planetary science is a multidisciplinary field, comprising research in astronomy, geology, meteorology, chemistry, and biology. Sometimes it's categorized as a branch or subfield of astronomy (Cruikshank and Chamberlain 1999).

7. Metzger et al. 2019.

8. Freedman 1998.

9. "Icy Pluto's Fall from the Planetary Ranks," *New York Times*, February 13, 2001, F2; see also K. Chang 2001; Tyson 1999, 2009.

10. "About the IAU," IAU, n.d., https://www.iau.org/administration/about/.

11. I. Williams and Bell Burnell 2006, 5.16.

12. I. Williams and Bell Burnell 2006, 5.16.

Williams was a member of it. The other members were Richard Binzel (MIT), André Brahic (Paris VII), Catherine Cesarsky (IAU's president-elect), Dava Sobel (popular science writer), Junichi Watanabe (National Observatory of Japan's director of outreach), and its chair, Owen Gingerich (Harvard-Smithsonian Center for Astrophysics). Make a mental note of this: the Planet Definition Committee was specifically asked to "discuss the broader social implications of any new definition of a planet and recommend a course of action which balances the scientific facts with the need for social acceptance of any change," and to "[include] emphasis on history, outreach, writing and education."[13] Its proposals were to be considered at the upcoming 2006 General Assembly, in Prague, Czech Republic, between August 14 and 25.[14]

The media and the general public loved the topic. They always have: before, during, and after Prague.[15] A widespread assumption—shared by scientists, the public, and the media—was that 'what is a planet?' and 'how to define "planet"?' were interchangeable, getting at the same thing. Nobody fretted over what it is to define something. It was also assumed that the word 'planet' and the concept PLANET were interchangeable, getting at the same thing, too. These assumptions opened the door to imprecise discussions, which quarrels about planets and Pluto are as prone to as quarrels about sandwiches and burritos and quarrels about empathy and neoliberalism.

A widespread expectation was that astronomers needed to know what a planet was, it'd be scandalous if astronomers didn't know that, and possessing such knowledge would allow astronomers to settle any particular instance: is *this* a planet? Settle any instance once and for all. The status of Pluto, Eris, Ceres, and any other celestial body. "Some people think that the astronomers will look stupid if we can't agree on a definition or if we don't even know what a planet is," wrote astronomer Jay Pasachoff from Prague, as IAU members were in the midst of the debate.[16] As Gibor Basri (University of California at Berkeley) had said a few years earlier: "It's something of an embarrassment that we

13. Ekers 2019, 52.

14. "Scientific Program," Astronomy 2006, n.d., https://www.astronomy2006.com/scientific-program.html.

I can't delve into the whole story of the 2006 conference and its prequels and sequels, nor into the longer history of 'planet' definitions (A. Boyle 2010; Michael Brown 2010; Ekers 2019; Marschall and Maran 2009; Tancredi 2006, 2007; Van der Hucht 2008; Weintraub 2006). One precedent worth mentioning, though, is the definition of the IAU's Working Group on Extrasolar Planets, chaired by Alan Boss (Boss et al. 2007; IAU 2004; I. Williams et al. 2007).

15. K. Chang 2022.

16. Quoted in Overbye 2006.

currently have no definition of what a planet is. [...] We live on a planet; it would be nice to know what that was."[17]

In preparation for the General Assembly, the Planet Definition Committee "met in Paris in June and came up with a compromise."[18] It recommended "a new definition of a planet: any body in orbit around a star that is not a star itself nor in orbit around a much larger planet, and that is massive enough for gravity to have squished it into an approximately spherical shape."[19] So, the solar system was to have twelve planets: Mercury, Venus, Earth, Mars, Ceres, Jupiter, Saturn, Uranus, Neptune, Pluto, Charon, and Eris (still called '2003 UB_{313}' at the time). This definition was in for a rough ride.

———

The Prague conference began on August 14. The committee's proposal was publicized on August 16, and critical responses arose straightaway. The next day, a *Nature* editorial, "Round Objects," backed the new definition, while acknowledging that there were reasonable objections to it: "we understand and, to some extent, sympathize." However, "we would suggest that . . . [astronomers] acquiesce in the new definition. [...] They should do this for two reasons: it is not a bad definition; and it will at least stop the rumbling debate over the status of Pluto."[20]

The adverbial phrase "at least" and the litotes "not a bad definition" sound lukewarm—consistent with the editorial's sympathizing with the objectors. How it rejected convenience wasn't a game changer either: "It has been convenient to have a small and easily memorized number of planets in the Solar System, but convenience is not the only thing that counts."[21] At any rate, *Nature* did end up throwing its weight behind the committee, and thus urged "IAU members to accept the proposal."

Nature, shmature, the Planet Definition Committee's recommendations weren't going to fly. As a member of the Resolutions Committee recounted, the proposal "was not at all acceptable to the body of IAU members—so much so that it provoked a near-riot!"[22] Science journalist Daniel Fischer witnessed the August 18 business meeting of IAU's Division III (Planetary Systems Sciences). He observed:

17. Quoted in R. Sanders 2003.
18. I. Williams and Bell Burnell 2006, 5.16.
19. Hogan 2006a.
20. *Nature* 2006.
21. *Nature* 2006.
22. I. Williams and Bell Burnell 2006, 5.17.

It immediately became clear that a majority of the planetary astronomers present saw things quite differently from the Planetary Definition Committee. [. . .] Suddenly a draft for a very different resolution on defining a planet appeared on the projection screen, already carrying the signatures of several astronomers. According to that text a planet "is by far the largest object in its local population." . . . The original draft . . . was dead on that day, and indeed it lost in another straw poll on August 22 when the EC [Executive Committee] tried one last time to sell it (with slight modifications) to the assembled astronomers, this time in a plenary session. [. . .] By the morning of August 24 the EC had come up with a totally new text that was basically yielding to the demands of the assembly.[23]

The alternative proposal was presented by Uruguayan astronomers Gonzalo Tancredi (who wrote the first draft and circulated it) and Julio Fernández.[24] Other early advocates were Brian Mardsen, Mark Bailey, Alan Boss, Daniela Lazzaro, Javier Licandro, and Alessandro Morbidelli. While Mike Brown wasn't a member of IAU and was "vacationing half a world away from where the astronomical action was," he sent a supportive email.[25]

A lot transpired in Prague between August 18 and 24: discussions, emails, meetings, negotiations, amendments, and rewrites.[26] Nothing unusual here. These are normal social and political processes within scientific communities, as STS has repeatedly shown. To make a long story short, the IAU membership eventually approved the basic elements of Tancredi et al.'s proposal.[27]

At the closing ceremony of the General Assembly, on August 24, a majority of members voted in favor of Resolution 5A ("Definition of 'Planet'") and Resolution 6A ("Definition of Pluto-Class Objects").[28] The former "was not counted but was passed with a great majority," whereas the latter "was passed with 237 votes in favour, 157 against and 17 abstentions."[29] In the IAU's press release, Resolution 5A was given three very similar titles, yet not exactly alike. First: "Definition

23. Fischer 2006.

24. Fienberg 2006.

25. Michael Brown 2010, 205–6; Tancredi 2006. Nevertheless, in a *New York Times* op-ed, published on August 16, Brown (2006) wrote: "I hope the union . . . simply declares 2003 UB313 our 10th, full-fledged planet."

26. Ekers 2019; Haberkorn 2007; Tancredi 2006.

27. Thanks to Gonzalo Tancredi for information and documents concerning the 2006 IAU General Assembly.

28. See also "XXVIth IAU General Assembly (2006)—Session II" (video), IAU, February 11, 2011, https://www.iau.org/public/videos/detail/iau2006session2/.

29. "IAU 2006 General Assembly: Result of the IAU Resolution Votes," Press Release iau0603, IAU, August 24, 2006, Prague, https://www.iau.org/news/pressreleases/detail/iau0603/.

of 'planet.'" Then: "Definition of Planet." The former is about a word, in quotation marks, and the latter about a thing. Third: "Definition of a 'Planet' in the Solar System," where the scope condition, the solar system, isn't a trivial detail.

Whatever the right title was, the resolution read:

> The IAU therefore resolves that planets and other bodies in our Solar System, except satellites, be defined into three distinct categories in the following way:
>
> (1) A "planet" is a celestial body that (a) is in orbit around the Sun, (b) has sufficient mass for its self-gravity to overcome rigid body forces so that it assumes a hydrostatic equilibrium (nearly round) shape, and (c) has cleared the neighbourhood around its orbit.
>
> (2) A "dwarf planet" is a celestial body that (a) is in orbit around the Sun, (b) has sufficient mass for its self-gravity to overcome rigid body forces so that it assumes a hydrostatic equilibrium (nearly round) shape, (c) has not cleared the neighbourhood around its orbit, and (d) is not a satellite.
>
> (3) All other objects, except satellites, orbiting the Sun shall be referred to collectively as "Small Solar System Bodies."[30]

Resolution 6A was that "Pluto is a 'dwarf planet' by the above definition and is recognized as the prototype of a new category of trans-Neptunian objects." Cold-bloodedly killing Pluto's planethood! How dared they! It was plain to everyone that Pluto fans weren't going to appreciate the news. Owen Gingerich said it in so many words: "There is a large Pluto fan club out there that is going to be incensed by our actions."[31] While the social reaction was predictable, I don't know that anybody predicted its intensity. So intense as to bring about demonstrations to "save Pluto."

Resolution 5A was preceded by a preamble, which gives reasons for the need for new definitions:

> Contemporary observations are changing our understanding of planetary systems, and it is important that our nomenclature for objects reflect our current understanding. This applies, in particular, to the designation "planets." The word "planet" originally described "wanderers" that were known only as moving lights in the sky. Recent discoveries lead us to create a new definition, which we can make using currently available scientific information.[32]

---

30. "IAU 2006 General Assembly: Result of the IAU Resolution Votes". Note that the definienda aren't words, but things, and the peculiar use of 'to define.'

31. Quoted in Hogan 2006b.

32. "IAU 2006 General Assembly: Result of the IAU Resolution Votes".

A Classification Problem

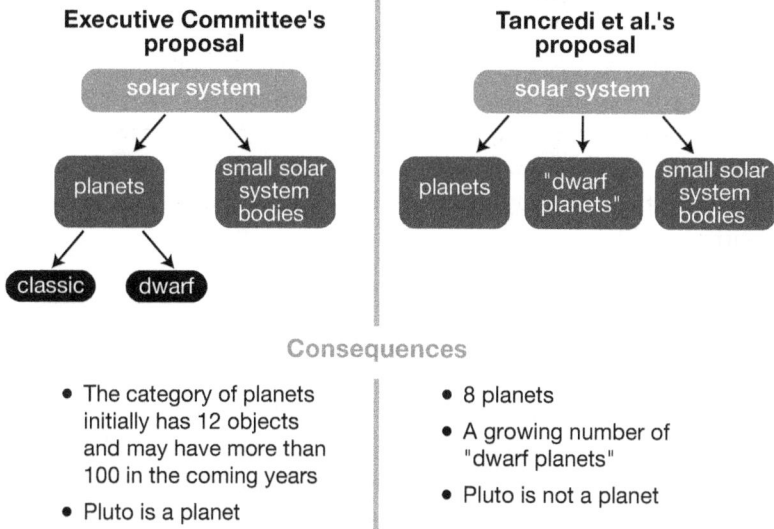

Executive Committee's proposal

```
        solar system
         ↙        ↘
                small solar
   planets       system
                bodies
   ↙      ↘
classic   dwarf
```

Tancredi et al.'s proposal

```
            solar system
        ↙        ↓        ↘
                "dwarf"   small solar
   planets      planets"  system
                          bodies
```

Consequences

- The category of planets initially has 12 objects and may have more than 100 in the coming years

- Pluto is a planet

- 8 planets
- A growing number of "dwarf planets"
- Pluto is not a planet

FIGURE A.1. Competing proposals at the IAU's 2006 General Assembly. Diagrams by Gonzalo Tancredi (my translation). http://www.astronomia.edu .uy/Charlas/Definicion_planeta/Definicion%20planeta_archivos/frame.htm.

The IAU's definition was stipulative. As the IAU's then-outgoing president Ronald Ekers retrospectively put it, "at 15:34 CEST 24 Aug 2006 Pluto ceased to be a planet as defined by IAU resolutions." What IAU members did was to "create a new definition."[33] They started out with a definiendum, 'planet,' they discussed possible definientia, and they collectively chose one of them. Then, the IAU announced its "resolution" about the correct use of this word.

Astronomers had to distinguish good from bad, acceptable from unacceptable definientia. Individually and collectively. They had to assess definitions that seemed plausible, compare their merits and demerits, and go for the best one. I'd like to examine their grounds, which considerations and criteria were (and weren't) used, and which ones were argued for and against. You could additionally examine how considerations and criteria varied across individuals, groups, and networks; whether proponents of competing definitions of 'planet' appealed to competing criteria to assess competing definitions of 'planet'; and to what extent and to whom this distinction (definitions vs. criteria to assess definitions) was manifest.

33. Ekers 2019, 55.

Ever since August 2006, the genre of commentary on the IAU's resolutions has thrived. Positive and negative, sympathetic and unsympathetic, thoughtful and flippant. Not only astronomers and planetary scientists but also other social actors, the media, and the general public have weighed in. Celebrating the change. Condemning it. Proposing amendments, major or minor. Through careful essays and careless tweets. Much of the public controversy has revolved around the impact of 'planet' definitions on Pluto. We can all sympathize. Nobody likes to be demoted and nobody likes to be called a 'dwarf planet.'[34]

A.2 Pluto killers

"Astronomers expel Pluto from the planetary club. [. . .] Controversy as textbooks face urgent rewrite," read the *Guardian*'s title and subtitle on August 25. "Pluto loses planet status. Tense debate ends with a definition of 'planet,'" read *Nature*'s news report. "Pluto gets the boot as the planet count drops" and "New planet definition sparks furore" were the titles chosen by the magazine *New Scientist*.[35]

Status was unmistakably at stake—the status of having planet status. From a traditional perspective on the nature and workings of scientific research, this fact is perplexing. As per this perspective, scientists sort objects into classes and types, but these classifications aren't status hierarchies. No class is superior in terms of status, prestige, or value. Scientists are identifying objective similarities and differences, not giving Grammy awards. As far as science is concerned, protons aren't more valuable than neutrons. Lead doesn't have a lower status than gold (chemistry isn't jewelry). Yet, as a matter of fact, planets were recurrently depicted as being at the top of a status hierarchy. Pluto was "demoted" and "downgraded." It should be "re-elevated." There was a "club," from which it was expelled. Its VIP card and privileges were terminated.

Criticisms of the IAU's resolutions weren't temperate. One of *New Scientist*'s interviewees was Alan Stern, of the Southwest Research Institute. Stern was (and still is) the principal investigator of NASA's New Horizons mission to Pluto and the Kuiper Belt, which had been launched in January 2006. He wasn't pleased: "The definition introduced is fundamentally flawed. . . . As a scientist, I'm embarrassed."[36] In Stern's view, the new definition entails that Mars, Jupiter, Neptune, and the Earth aren't planets, because they haven't cleared the

---

34. Yuhas 2015.

35. In the order I quote them: I. Sample 2006; Hogan 2006b; Battersby 2006; Shiga 2006.

36. Shiga 2006.

neighborhood around their orbit. On September 6, he declared war on the IAU. The New Horizons project, "like a growing number of the public, and many hundreds if not thousands of professional research astronomers and planetary scientists, will not recognize the IAU's planet definition resolution of Aug. 24, 2006."[37] In addition, Stern and Mark Sykes (Planetary Science Institute and University of Arizona) initiated a petition, "Protest the IAU Planet Definition": "We, as planetary scientists and astronomers, do not agree with the IAU's definition of a planet, nor will we use it. A better definition is needed."[38] The petition soon collected more than two hundred signatures. It's still accessible online, and, as of this writing, it's got more than four hundred.[39]

Critics also had harsh words for the class of dwarf planets. Oddly, it was at odds with the rules of hyponymy.[40] "Pluto is one of a new category of object to be known as 'dwarf planets' (which, not to be confusing, don't fall under an umbrella term of 'planets,' and must, by definition, be written with single quote marks)."[41] The chair of the Planet Definition Committee, Owen Gingerich, was reported to have protested: "Pluto is a dwarf planet, but we are now faced with the absurdity that a dwarf planet is not a planet. . . . Is a human dwarf not a human?"[42]

Boos to the IAU originated inside and outside the academic community. Some people expressed disappointment, sadness, or anger. Others went for satire: "Astronomers Declare February No Longer a Month." Fortunately, while February "does not belong in the same classification as the eleven 'true' months," it was "granted the newly created status of 'dwarf month.'"[43] As usual, anger vastly outnumbered satire.

Political actors and political interests played a role in the story. Very seriously and very non-satirically (appearances to the contrary), the US states of New Mexico and Illinois resolved that the IAU was mistaken. The New Mexico Legislature, underlining that New Mexico was "the longtime home of Clyde Tombaugh, discoverer of Pluto," "resolved . . . that [Pluto] be declared

---

37. "Unabashedly Onward to the Ninth Planet," New Horizons, September 6, 2006, http:// pluto.jhuapl.edu/News-Center/PI-Perspectives.php?page=piPerspective_09_06_2006.

38. Quoted in Hogan 2006c.

39. Mark Sykes, "Protest the IAU Planet Definition," iPetitions, n.d., https://www.ipetitions .com/petition/planetprotest/; The editors of Sky & Telescope, "The Fight for Pluto Rages On," Sky & Telescope, September 1, 2006, https://skyandtelescope.org/astronomy-news/the-fight-for -pluto-rages-on/.

40. Zimmer 2006a, b.

41. Hogan 2006b

42. Vedantam 2006.

43. Haber 2009.

a planet."[44] It's as if New Mexico legislators had read Austin and Searle, and took their planet declaration to be performative, like declaring a war. Likewise, the Illinois Senate "reestablished . . . full planetary status" to Pluto. The bill noted that "Clyde Tombaugh, discoverer of the planet Pluto, was born on a farm near the Illinois community of Streator," and pointed out that "Pluto was unfairly downgraded to a 'dwarf' planet." Therefore: "RESOLVED, BY THE SENATE OF THE NINETY-SIXTH GENERAL ASSEMBLY OF THE STATE OF ILLINOIS, that as Pluto passes overhead through Illinois' night skies, that it be reestablished with full planetary status, and that March 13, 2009 be declared 'Pluto Day.'"[45]

Pluto was treated unfairly! Never mind what astronomers say, in New Mexico and Illinois Pluto is a planet. Period.

Illinois and New Mexico legislators aren't representative of Illinois and New Mexico opinion, much less of US opinion. But it's arguable that nationalism influences some Americans' opinions about planets, as it influenced these state legislators who made Pluto great again. Maybe it influenced Jim Bridenstine (Republican Congressman and NASA administrator during the Trump presidency), who in 2019 "declared Pluto a planet once again."[46] To their credit, none of these politicians accused the IAU of having a socialist bent, supporting terrorism, or being controlled by China or Venezuela. Jewish space lasers didn't come up either.

Either way, many condemnations of the IAU's new definition did arise in the United States. Allegedly, in the United States more than elsewhere.[47] On

44. "A Joint Memorial Declaring Pluto a Planet and Declaring March 13, 2007, 'Pluto Planet Day' at the Legislature," House Joint Memorial 54, 48th Legislature—State of New Mexico—First Session, 2007, https://www.nmlegis.gov/Sessions/07%20Regular/memorials/house/HJM054.html.

45. Illinois Senate Resolution SR0046, 96th General Assembly (2009), https://www.ilga.gov/legislation/96/SR/PDF/09600SR0046lv.pdf. See also the resolution of the Illinois House of Representatives in 2015: "RESOLVED, BY THE HOUSE OF REPRESENTATIVES OF THE NINETY-NINTH GENERAL ASSEMBLY OF THE STATE OF ILLINOIS, that we urge the International Astronomical Union to restore Pluto to full planetary status." "RESOLVED, That we declare 2015 as 'The Year of Pluto'" (Illinois House Resolution HR0225, 99th General Assembly [2015], https://www.ilga.gov/legislation/99/HR/PDF/09900HR0225lv.pdf).

46. Quoted in Starr 2019.

47. I haven't quantitatively corroborated this frequent frequency claim. Nor a common perception that Neil deGrasse Tyson exemplifies: "If you go to Europe and talk about Pluto they look at you like, 'Yeah, it's that little thing out there.' You come to America, it's 'Pluto—that's my favourite planet!'" (Shiga 2008). I'm not trying to account for the 2006 outcomes and subsequent reactions to them, but I think they aren't reducible to nationalist ideologies and pro- and anti-US sentiments. That'd be too facile (A. Boyle 2010, 114–15; see also Sykes 2008).

September 1, 2006, "defenders of Pluto as a planet rallied at New Mexico State University . . . , joined by the wife and son of Pluto's discoverer, Clyde Tombaugh." There, "astronomer Bernie McNamara [spoke] to a high-spirited group of Pluto supporters outside the university's Zuhl Library."[48]

US discontents formed associations and groups, like the Society for the Preservation of Pluto as a Planet. Based in Brookline, Massachusetts and Brooklyn, New York, its mission statement states that "members of the Society . . . are dedicated to the proposition that Pluto has been and always should be considered a planet."[49] Or like Save Pluto, whose online store sells "Save Pluto Gear" (t-shirts, buttons, mugs). It doesn't mince its words: "rogue scientists [railroaded] vote to demote Pluto," "the vote was hijacked," "the IAU President and a small committee clandestinely and materially changed the naming resolution, kept it secret from dissenting members and the press . . . and concluded with a show of hands without an official count."[50]

Mike Brown—the Caltech astronomer who co-discovered Eris and in 2010 published the book *How I Killed Pluto and Why It Had It Coming*—has reported getting hate mail, "obscene messages on my office line,"[51] and even death threats.[52] In his estimation, "astronomers who question Pluto's status come across as bullies trying to kick everyone's favorite cosmic underdog out of the club."[53] Brown's Twitter handle is @plutokiller.

Another prominent Pluto killer is Neil deGrasse Tyson. He got a lot of flak in 2001 when Hayden Planetarium demoted Pluto. Hate mail. Written by children. On the bright side, outrage and indignation could be cute: "Dear Mr. Tyson, I think Pluto is a planet. Why do you think Pluto is no longer a planet? I do not like your anser!!! Pluto is my faveret planet!!! You are going to have to take all of the books away and change them. Pluto is a planet!!!!!!! Your friend, Emerson York."[54]

48. David 2006.

49. "Pluto Is a Planet!," Society for the Preservation of Pluto as a Planet, n.d., www .plutoisaplanet.org.

50. SavePluto.com, n.d., www.savepluto.com.

51. "Mike Brown: The Astronomer Who Slayed Planet Pluto," *Independent*, January 7, 2011, https://www.independent.co.uk/news/science/mike-brown-the-astronomer-who-slayed -planet-pluto-2177993.html.

52. Tehelka TV, "Michael Brown, Pluto Killer at THiNK 2011," YouTube, November 18, 2011, https://youtu.be/9uDNK_Qm5oI.

53. Michael Brown 2006.

54. Lucas Reilly, "6 Angry Letters Kids Sent Neil deGrasse Tyson about Pluto," Mental Floss, August 4, 2013, https://www.mentalfloss.com/article/52042/6-angry-letters-kids-sent-neil -degrasse-tyson-about-pluto.

Pluto's demotion even had lexical consequences in American English. In 2006 "the American Dialect Society voted 'plutoed' as the word of the year." "To *pluto* is to demote or devalue someone or something."[55]

More than fifteen years after Prague, on January 18, 2022, the *New York Times* ran a story titled "Is Pluto a Planet? What's a Planet, Anyway?"[56] On the nytimes.com website, it got 533 comments within two days (the comments section was subsequently closed). It also asked readers to vote on Pluto's planethood: yes or no. As of February 9, more than two hundred thousand people had volunteered a response. Can you guess the results of the poll?

Do you think Pluto should be considered a planet?

Yes.	70%
No.	30%

This reflects the opinions of 200,170 New York Times readers.

FIGURE A.2. *New York Times* poll, January 18, 2022 (results as of February 9, 2022).

———

It was a tall order to consensually define 'planet.' Hurdles abounded. The sources of these hurdles were reflected and dramatically performed throughout the IAU's General Assembly in Prague, and in its reception and ramifications. The Prague resolutions were supposed to close the matter, but they didn't come close to it. Neither the astronomy and planetary science community nor the general public turned over the page. The definition of 'planet' and the status of Pluto have continued to resurface. Discontents have never given up. Emotions have continued to run high.

In August 2008, a scientific conference and educator workshop was held at the Johns Hopkins University Applied Physics Laboratory in Laurel, Maryland. The name says it all: "The Great Planet Debate."[57] On the first day of the

55. "'Plutoed' Voted 2006 Word of the Year," American Dialect Society, January 5, 2007, https://www.americandialect.org/plutoed_voted_2006_word_of_the_year; Zimmer 2007.

56. K. Chang 2022.

57. "Conference to Grapple with Planet Definitions," press release, Johns Hopkins University Applied Physics Laboratory, May 15, 2008, https://www.jhuapl.edu/PressRelease/080515.

conference, August 14, there was a special event: a debate between Neil de-Grasse Tyson and Mark Sykes, moderated by Ira Flatow (host of *Science Friday* on National Public Radio). Tyson: the Pluto killer. Sykes: foe of the IAU's definition and advocate of using "roundness alone as the distinguishing feature of a planet." The Great Planet Debate didn't have a winner, however. It was reported that it "[ended] in stalemate."[58] "Scientists . . . [agreed] to disagree."[59]

In July 2015, the New Horizons probe's flyby of Pluto was big news. It took amazing and gorgeous pictures. And it predictably reignited the controversy.[60] A new petition, "Declare Pluto a Planet," was signed by more than 6,600 people. The authors of the petition were smart to underscore definitions' real-world effects. Millions of dollars were claimed to be on the line: "this is about much more than planetary definitions. When bureaucratic bodies with little expertise in planetary science choose to create inaccurate definitions of planets, they threaten to suppress millions of dollars in funding for future generations of space exploration."[61]

In 2017, Runyon, Stern, and colleagues proposed a "geophysical definition of a planet for use by educators, scientists, students, and the public: A planet is a sub-stellar mass body that has never undergone nuclear fusion and that has sufficient self-gravitation to assume a spheroidal shape adequately described by a triaxial ellipsoid regardless of its orbital parameters." Per this definition, there'd be planets galore (more than 110 known planets at that time), which they viewed favorably.[62]

Runyon et al. sought to neutralize "a common question we receive": "Why did you send New Horizons to Pluto if it's not a planet anymore?"[63] As in the

---

58. Shiga 2008.

59. "Scientists Debate Planet Definition and Agree to Disagree," Planetary Science Institute, September 19, 2008, https://www.psi.edu/news/press-releases/2008/scientists-debate-planet -definition-and-agree-disagree.

60. LaFrance 2015.

61. Other Space on Yahoo, "Declare Pluto a Planet #PlutoFlyby," Change.org, n.d., https://www.change.org/p/international-astronomical-union-declare-pluto-a-planet -plutoflyby.

62. "A simple paraphrase of our planet definition—especially suitable for elementary school students—could be, 'round objects in space that are smaller than stars'" (Runyon et al. 2017).

63. "Many members of the public, in our experience, assume that alleged 'non-planets' cease to be interesting enough to warrant scientific exploration. . . . To wit: a common question we receive is, 'Why did you send New Horizons to Pluto if it's not a planet anymore?' To mitigate this unfortunate perception, we propose a new definition of planet, which has historical precedence" (Runyon et al. 2017).

2015 petition, they brought up financial considerations: "This definition high-lights to the general public and policymakers the many fascinating worlds in our Solar System that remain unexplored and are worthy of our exploration, along with the necessary budgets." On an internet forum, someone italicized "along with the necessary budgets" and commented: "Now we're getting closer to the real, underlying reasons for this proposal!" The comment ended with a smiley.[64]

Alan Stern has tirelessly defended this geophysical definition. "Yes, Pluto Is a Planet"—insisted his 2018 *Washington Post* editorial, written together with David Grinspoon.[65] On April 29, 2019, PSW Science (formerly known as the Philosophical Society of Washington) hosted "A Planet Definition Debate." The event took place in the Powell Auditorium of the Cosmos Club, in Washing-ton, DC, and it was livestreamed on the web. Stern was pitted against Ronald Ekers, former IAU president, who argued for the IAU definition. As recorded in the minutes, "following the robust question and answer period, [PSW Science] President Millstein invited audience members to vote on the PSW website in favor of either the IAU definition or the GPD [geophysical planet definition]. When voting closed, the IAU definition received 33 votes and the GPD re-ceived 175 votes."[66]

This electoral landslide notwithstanding, there's no scarcity of detractors of the New Horizons team's definition. They say it's substantively substan-dard and it lacks impartiality. Jean-Luc Margot (UCLA) has suggested, if somewhat obliquely, that the team has an illegitimate interest in the debate. "Almost all planetary scientists have moved on." Yet, "there are a few people, primarily and perhaps not coincidentally associated with the New Horizons mission to Pluto, who apparently cannot accept a universe where Pluto is not classified as a planet." For Carolyn Porco (Space Science Institute), the GPD would "hijack the word planet." It "would serve no purpose at all, except to make the people who study small-bodies feel more important."[67]

Tombaugh was born in Illinois. He lived in New Mexico and taught at New Mexico State University. Illinois, New Mexico, and New Mexico State Univer-sity had an axe to grind. So does New Horizons. They aren't discussing what the best definition of 'planet' is, or how to best use the word, from a detached,

64. CuddlyRocket, March 6, 2017, comment on Pluto-Planet Debate Discussions, forum, NASA Space Flight, https://forum.nasaspaceflight.com/index.php?topic=37818.480.

65. Grinspoon and Stern 2008.

66. "A Planet Definition Debate: Alan Stern (PI New Horizons Mission) & Ron Ekers (Past President IAU," PSWScience, n.d., https://pswscience.org/meeting/is-pluto-a-planet/.

67. Quoted in Mack 2017.

impartial position: the outcome will affect their standing. The status of Plato will affect their status. I'm not making conjectures about motives and mental states. It's in their interest that Pluto be a planet, where interest isn't necessarily or directly material, but it can be.

To whom does the preceding not apply, though? Who can cast the first stone? A community must decide (establish, agree on) how to use 'w' or whether to accept distinction *d*. As a community member, you've been thinking about it, listening to other people's ideas, and asking them questions. You look forward to discussing your thoughts and conclusions with others. Could a person or organization impartially undertake these tasks? Part of the problem is how to cash out 'detached,' 'impartial,' and 'having an axe to grind.' 'Interested perspective,' 'disinterested,' and 'having a stake.' Yet, roughly speaking, you could endorse weaker or stronger theses:

(1.1) It's typical for community members to have an interested (epistemic) perspective.

(1.2) It's typical for them to have an axe to grind.

(2.1) It's necessary for community members to have an interested (epistemic) perspective.

(2.2) It's necessary for them to have an axe to grind.

These theses need unpacking, but I can go straight to my point. Any of them would put planetary scientists' disputes over 'planet' in the same boat as social scientists' disputes over 'intelligence,' 'gender,' or 'globalization.' In this respect, they'd resemble political and legal disputes over 'marriage,' 'rape,' and 'refugee'; over 'sandwich,' 'burrito,' and 'cheese' (see chapter 1).

It wouldn't follow that skeptics (or nihilists) have won the day. For them, any interest is legitimate. Anything goes. There aren't better and worse ways to evaluate word uses as better or worse, as 'better' and 'worse' are just reflections of individual desires and rationalizations of preferences. But this doesn't follow. The challenge for scientific communities is how to move from particularistic, self-regarding interests to an expanded circle, where multiple perspectives and interests are taken into account. How to deliver outcomes that further everyone's good rather than the good of one party or another. How to achieve solutions that are good: good for everyone and everything involved and good simpliciter.

A.3 Criteria

Like the clashes of sandwichness warriors, the clashes of planethood warriors are hindered by the absence of clear criteria. By 'criterion' I mean a standard according to which definitions of 'planet' are evaluated, compared, and ranked (definitions or, as I'd prefer, proposals as to how 'planet' should be used). That

FIGURE A.3. Not a planet. Photo: NASA/Johns Hopkins University Applied Physics Laboratory/Southwest Research Institute/Alex Parker. Public domain photo.

which makes good definitions of 'planet' good and bad definitions of 'planet' bad. Given a definition or usage proposal, which reasons can support it. On which grounds you might positively or negatively assess it, accept or reject it. In virtue of what one definition, or one proposal, is better than another.

As before, I'm drawing a distinction between orders or levels. A first-order argument (or disagreement) is about 'planet' definitions. A second-order, meta-level, or second-level argument (or disagreement) is about criteria to judge 'planet' definitions. The distinction is analytical. In reality, the two arguments are typically offered together. Needless to add, the latter has a direct impact on the former. You believe that criteria C_1 and C_2 are most appropriate, so your definition will aim to satisfy them, not C_3 or C_4. Many scientists' defenses of a second-order criterion are intertwined with their case for a first-order definition. But this needn't disqualify a second-order argument.[68]

Criteria can be explicit or implicit. They might be written down in codes, books, and textbooks, or embedded in communities' routines and practices, taken for granted, and only thematized if controversies or revolutions arise. Criteria can be about different aspects of a definition. A salient distinction is content (internal features; properties of the definition itself) on the one hand, and how it was arrived at and validated (external features; properties of the process, method, or procedure) on the other. Other criteria are about definitions' form or structure. For instance, whether the definiens must provide necessary and sufficient conditions to discriminate what does and doesn't fall under the extension of 'planet,' or rather planethood is a continuous variable, a matter of degree. Whether to go for the former or the latter might be a function of scientific, empirical, or metaphysical convictions, convictions about what the world is like, but also of what the definition is for.

I'm interested in the criteria planetary scientists do and don't appeal to, which criteria are deemed irrelevant, and whether their irrelevance is asserted or it's so evident that nobody needs to bother. No astronomer ventured a Thrasymachus-like defense of their definition of 'planet': 'it's the best because I'm the strongest person at this conference' (*Republic* 338c). Nobody appealed to the beauty of definientia either. Moreover, I'm interested in how criteria are weighed and combined, since I don't expect any criterion to single-handedly do the trick. A bit more of this, a bit less of that. Trade-offs. Not 30 percent, but 25 percent. *X* ought to trump *Y*.

More generally, planetary scientists may express views about the nature of their arguments about criteria. Marosa claims that any criterion is as good as any other. Or that it's impossible to adjudicate disagreements about criteria, and then she explains why that's the case. Ida's view about reality is such that the worth of criteria is unknowable. Circe's view about language is such that defining 'planet' is impossible, word definitions are nonsense, or word meanings can't be stipulated or legislated. Or she thinks astronomers' disputes are merely verbal. Completely pointless. All of these would be third-order or third-level views— comparable to philosophers' views in metaethics, metasemantics, or metaphilosophy.[69] They do crop up from time to time, but not too often, because

---

68. Not without additional premises or facts. It'd be uncharitable to accuse astronomers of arguing for second-order criteria only insofar as they'll produce the first-order results they already espouse. What of the second-order arguments of politicians and attorneys?

69. Third-order claims are about second-order claims, but they also affect first-order claims. If there's no right answer to your question about criteria to assess definitions of 'planet,' there might be no right answer to your question about the definition of 'planet' either.

they're further removed from planetary scientists' immediate concerns (and those of the media and the public): what a planet is and how to define 'planet.'

In what follows, I outline some of the criteria apparent in the planethood wars. I group them into eleven clusters:

(1) Who gets to define 'planet'/society and culture

'Who are you to say what *F* is or how to define "*w*"? Who's to say this? You aren't in a position to determine it!' This complaint is heard in many areas of life. At times, it's a knee-jerk reaction, seeking to challenge and delegitimize opponents. But it can stem from reasonable epistemological misgivings.

As applied to 'planet,' the complaint goes like this. Why does the IAU get to define 'planet'? What grants it the authority to do so? A different organization of astronomers should have been in charge. The American Astronomical Society. The Sociedad Uruguaya de Astronomía. Or a more comprehensive scientific organization, so that a large array of disciplines can participate in the process. That might still be too narrow. The definition of 'planet' has social effects, so professional scientific organizations should join forces with social, cultural, educational, and political organizations.

At the beginning of September 2006, *Sky & Telescope,* a magazine based in Cambridge, Massachusetts, reported that "it's not over yet." "The fight for Pluto rages on":

> Other battle lines are being drawn as some scientists are questioning the IAU's authority in this matter altogether. The director of the Center for Space Exploration Policy Research, Mark Bullock, released the following statement: "A key public-policy question is who has the social mandate to alter the definition of something as fundamental as a planet. Scientists have in the past vested the IAU with authority to name asteroids and other planetary objects. However, the word 'planet' has cultural, historical, and social meaning and as such requires much broader discussion and consensus than those required for the naming of astronomical bodies."[70]

Bullock speaks of a "social mandate" and a word's "cultural, historical, and social meaning." Therefore, the IAU doesn't have sufficient authority to make this decision. A "broader consensus" is required. In fact, this point hadn't escaped the IAU's Executive Committee's attention. When they formed the Planet Definition Committee, they explicitly mentioned "the need for social acceptance of any change," as well as "history, outreach, writing and education." Two out of seven committee members represented popular science and outreach.

70. Editors of *Sky & Telescope* 2006.

At the 2006 General Assembly, outgoing IAU president Ronald Ekers (Australia Telescope National Facility and Australian National University) said this wasn't a question for "science alone." On August 22, he

> reminded his colleagues that the planethood question was too big to decide by science alone. "This is not just a scientific issue of what is correct," he said. "There is no correct answer to this question. The question is, what is a sensible compromise that will work? And not just work for the profession-als in the field, but work for everybody who is interested in the skies, the planets, is curious, is educating, and so on."[71]

Ekers's position was inclusive, even though taking someone into consideration doesn't imply letting them speak, let alone vote. At the same time, he was ad-vancing a third-order argument: the definition of 'planet' isn't the sort of question that can be answered correctly or incorrectly. It's not truth-apt. The commu-nity of astronomers wasn't after correctness, but a "compromise that will work"—a suggestion that has a pragmatist ring to it. Ekers analyzed the nature of the problem, and how it can and can't be resolved, as a philosopher might do.[72] In light of its nature, the IAU shouldn't neglect what would "work" for teachers and curious people.

Planetary scientists summoned diverse social and cultural considerations and their corresponding rationales. Money! Astronomy is materially dependent on public support, so it should be responsive to society. Owen Gingerich, chair of the Planet Definition Committee, "who is also a historian, said astronomers had blown it by ignoring public sentiment and the historical significance of Pluto: 'We are an expensive science, and if we don't have public support, we are not going to be able to do our work.'"[73]

Children! Will your 'planet' definition be acceptable to them? Will it hurt their education or their feelings? They shouldn't be disenfranchised, seeing as their friend Pluto is feeling blue.[74] Prestigious scientific magazines quoted children verbatim: "'Please don't turn Pluto into a dwarf planet because that makes me sad. I'll miss Pluto a lot.' Daniel Dauber, aged six, on Nature's Newsblog."[75]

Runyon, Stern, and colleagues' "geophysical planet definition" "would ex-pand the number of planets from eight to approximately 110."[76] It's "part of the appeal of the new definition, Runyon says. He says he would like to see the

71. A. Boyle 2010, 124.

72. Bokulich 2014; Égré and O'Madagain 2019.

73. Vedantam 2006.

74. Messeri 2010.

75. Hogan 2006c, 966.

76. Runyon et al. 2017.

public more engaged in solar system exploration. As the very word 'planet' seems to carry a 'psychological weight,' he figures that more planets could encourage that public interest."[77] To evaluate definitions of 'planet,' one criterion is their effects on public interest. Word-forms aren't neutral signs; they can be psychologically mighty. However, as regards teachers and "planetary pedagogy," Runyon, Stern, and colleagues concede that their GPD has a downside. "Certainly 110 planets is more than students should be expected to memorize, and indeed they ought not. Instead, students should learn only a few (9? 12? 25?) planets of interest." The number of planets shouldn't be excessively large; it's not a "No Ice Ball Left Behind" policy.[78]

Teachers, students, textbooks, and planetariums represent social factors and cultural expectations. Some planetary scientists argue they're valid, defensible criteria in discussions about 'planet.'

(2) Fit with ordinary language and 'the dictionary'; fit with common sense

It's an old Pandora's box: the relations between scientific research and ordinary language (see chapter 10). One standpoint is that never the twain shall meet. In his book *Is Pluto a Planet?*, Weintraub rehearses it: "I, for one, am very dissatisfied when I read the *OED* definitions. I hope you are similarly bothered. Because the dictionary definition of *planet* is essentially worthless, scientifically, we have to probe much deeper into astronomy in order to answer what initially appeared to be a simple question."[79]

Weintraub, an astronomy professor at Vanderbilt University, disapproves of this criterion, as many natural scientists and social scientists have. But this is a divisive issue. In parts of the social sciences, ordinary language has played important roles, even in definitions of key words and 'technical terms.' This line of thought can be bolstered by casting a wider net: lexical meaning, or dictionary definition, gets transformed into common sense, or people's "intuition."[80] Should scientists' definitions be in sync with them? In an *Annual Review of Earth and Planetary Sciences* piece, Basri and Brown say 'yes':

> There is another characteristic of a good definition that, although much less objective, also seems to be a major factor. The definition should have 'cultural support,' by which we mean that it cannot violate any strong

77. A. Hirsch 2017.
78. Michael Brown 2006.
79. Weintraub 2006.
80. Runyon et al. 2017.

preconceptions held by a large number of people. The word planet has been around for a long time, and scientists need to take care not to try to change too much the meaning of a word that everyone already knows and uses.[81]

If you violate people's "strong preconceptions" more profoundly, you'll meet another version of this criterion. That's crazy! That's ridiculous! In scientific communities, philosophical communities, and social life alike, some statements come across as crazy. Results and theories may come across as unreasonable, very unreasonable, or downright ridiculous. They're at odds with scientists' intuitions or with scientific common sense. 'Your theory is crazy' or 'your theory has a crazy implication' is an objection to it. 'This *just can't* be true!' These objections are methodologically and epistemologically contentious, though, because novel scientific claims and discoveries can be at odds with widely held intuitions. There's a tension between a claim being believable (yet possibly not novel) and being hard to believe (yet potentially a breakthrough) (see chapter 9).

Craziness and ridiculousness judgments may be made about scientists' word uses and definitions. Take Stern's criticism of "dynamically based definitions." They "are deeply flawed because they do not take into account any physical properties of the body in question, and give ridiculous results, for example classifying identical large objects in different orbits differently—so that even Earths are not always planets, which is crazy."[82]

(3) Scientific knowledge

'Planet' isn't an ordinary word. It belongs to a special class: scientific words, words that help do science, words with which scientific things get done. Should scientific knowledge and facts impinge on their definitions and uses? What aspect of scientific knowledge and facts? Just how should they affect 'planet,' 'altruism,' 'inequality,' or 'religion'?

Promoters of this criterion believe that scientific knowledge can shape—translate into, be incorporated into—words' definitions and uses. Then, they have to say how. They have to deal with the worry that scientific knowledge is compatible with many definientia, so it underdetermines how a word should be defined. One possible response: this criterion is necessary, but not sufficient.

The preamble to the IAU's definition invoked scientific knowledge. Nomenclature should "reflect" understanding, recent discoveries, and available scientific information. Recent discoveries "led" astronomers to new definitions. The meanings of astronomers' words shouldn't be dictated by etymology, by what a

81. Basri and Brown 2006, 195.
82. "Scientists Debate Planet Definition" 2008.

word "originally described," but by science. However, the IAU explained neither what sort of scientific information leads to the best semantic choices nor what to do if scientific information is consistent with more than one definiens.

(4) Intrinsic, relational, and processual properties

Scientific classifications might be based on different kinds of properties. Weintraub distinguishes two: an object's location and its intrinsic properties. The former "shouldn't matter" to arguments about planethood. The latter "should matter more": "Some planetary astronomers would argue that were the Earth placed in the Kuiper Belt, it would not be able to clear its neighborhood and thus would not be considered, by the IAU definition, a planet; apparently location matters. Here a planet, there not a planet. I'd argue that location shouldn't matter; instead, the intrinsic properties of the objects themselves should matter more."[83]

Similarly, Stern draws a distinction between classification by an object's properties and classification by what an object is near to: "he says the issue is not really Pluto's status so much as the idea of putting objects in orbital contexts. 'We do not classify objects in astronomy by what they are near,' he says. 'We classify them by their properties.'"[84]

The more general cleavage at play is between dynamicists and geophysicists. Boyle argues that these are "two different ways of seeing the solar system":

> One way focuses on the dynamics of a planetary system: How are things moving around, and how do those things affect one another? If a celestial body doesn't have much of a gravitational effect on other bodies, that object is hard to detect and hard to track. If lots of celestial bodies are in similar orbits, they all tend to blur together. [...] Another way of looking at a celestial body would be to look at it rather than around it. What's it made of? What kinds of geological processes are at work? Does it have a crust and a core? Is there an atmosphere, and weather? Are there volcanoes, and if so, what are they spewing out? Water? Sulfur? Methane?[85]

Alternatively, you could distinguish three kinds of properties. First, intrinsic ones. What an object intrinsically is and what it intrinsically has. Second, processual or historical ones. An object's origin, how it came about, how it was formed, and how it changed over time. In planetary science, this is cosmogony. Third, relational ones. An object's relations to other objects, to groups, to populations.

---

83. Weintraub 2015.
84. Hogan 2006c. He meant intrinsic properties.
85. A. Boyle 2010, 115–16; see also Bokulich 2014; Brusse 2016.

Scientific communities may use any of these properties to pick out and describe objects. They're all qualified to figure in words' definientia and to become criteria to judge competing 'planet' definitions. There's no predetermined hierarchy.

(5) Generality

Is a definition of 'planet' preferable if it applies to other planetary systems? To as many as possible? To any conceivable one? Or should it only apply to the solar system? Put differently, are exoplanets planets?

Lack of generality is one reason Philip Metzger (University of Central Florida) opposes the IAU's definition and Pluto's demotion: "So far we have studied only one solar system in great depth, so our dynamical definitions are based on a sample of one. It's unlikely that a sample of one oddball solar system is giving us an adequate picture."[86]

(6) Formalization and quantification

Is a definition of 'planet' preferable if it can be formalized and quantified?[87] According to champions of this stance, the more formalizable and quantifiable, the better (all other things equal). Science seeks accuracy, reliability, and objectivity, which are best attained through formalization and quantification. As they say, when you cannot express it in numbers, your definition is of a meager (or meagre) and unsatisfactory kind.[88]

(7) Vagueness

Words or predicates are vague if they have borderline cases. Textbook examples are 'tall,' 'old,' and 'bald.' Some people are neither clearly tall, nor clearly not tall. Neither clearly old, nor clearly not old, but somewhere in between. Somewhere-in-between regions are themselves vague. 'Borderline case' has borderline cases, and 'vague' is vague. As Williamson writes: "The phenomenon of vagueness is deep as well as broad. It would be shallow if it could be adequately described in precise terms. That is not generally possible. [...] The limits of vagueness are themselves vague."[89]

---

86. Metzger 2015.

87. See, e.g., Margot 2015.

88. Espeland and Stevens 2008; Kuhn 1977:178; Merton et al. 1984; Wirth 1940.

89. Williamson 1994, 2. On higher-order vagueness's problems and discontents, see Dietz and Moruzzi (2010), I. Hu (2017), Hyde (1994), Sainsbury (1991), and Sorensen (1985).

For some scientists, that a definiens doesn't produce vagueness is a most desirable feature, because it'll spare you troubles down the line. Others dissent. It's not desirable, because it doesn't do justice to the definiendum, to the word being defined, and to the things it refers to. The price to pay is too high.

Jack Lissauer (NASA's Ames Research Center) finds it desirable. Roundness is hence subpar, for how round is round enough? Where's the cut-off?

> The proposed 'geophysical' definition of planethood based upon roundness uses a poor criterion because there is no good dividing line. Indeed, there are likely to be more intermediate solar system objects that are in the fuzzy 'roundish' area than there are objects that are clearly round. In contrast, the eight planets recognized by the IAU are significantly different from the numerous small objects that are classified as 'minor planets' (asteroids).[90]

(8) Parsimony/simplicity

"We think that the definition should be kept as simple as possible."[91] "A good definition . . . should be succinct and easily understood by the public."[92]

Parsimony, or simplicity, is a traditional criterion in science and philosophy. Also known as Occam's razor. 'Nature is pleased with simplicity.' It's pleased with simple laws and with simple definitions. According to champions of this stance, the simpler, the better (all other things equal). Which isn't to say they agree on what should be simple/parsimonious and what simplicity/parsimony consists in.[93]

(9) Usefulness

"Definitions and classification schemes . . . are evaluated by their usefulness."[94] What makes a definition of 'planet' scientifically useful, useful for planetary science, useful for science? How to compare definitions' degree of usefulness? (And what makes a classification scheme scientifically useful, useful for planetary science, etc.?)

---

90. "Scientists Debate Planet Definition" 2008.

91. Tancredi et al. 2006.

92. Basri and Brown 2006, 195.

93. Baker 2007; Barnes 2000; Rudner 1961; Sober 1981.

94. Sykes 2008.

As we've seen, usefulness is a wide-ranging, multifaceted, and malleable idea (chapter 3 and chapter 9). It's ubiquitous in both natural science and social science. Usefulness proposals diverge. Some are about accomplishing or satisfying *X*, while others are about accomplishing or satisfying *Y*. So, the claim that a definition or classification is useful pushes the question one step back. Useful for what and for whom? As compared to what? Is each person free to choose their favorite usefulness criterion?

(10) Procedure and implementation

The goodness of a 'planet' definition is a function of the goodness of the way in which it was arrived at, the procedure of which it's a product, the method on which it's based (as constructivism claims—see chapter 6). It's a function of how planetary scientists went about defining 'planet,' individually or collectively. Procedures embody principles, values, and objectives. They should embody good ones.

Some of scientific communities' decisions are made democratically. They democratically elect the presidents of professional associations. But the accuracy of measurements and the truth of knowledge claims are established through other mechanisms. Should their semantic and classificatory decisions result from democratic procedures? Strongly democratic, in that everyone has the right to participate and vote? Does 'everyone' mean literally everyone?

Next, you can distinguish procedures as guidelines, principles, or norms, and their on-the-ground implementation. The IAU is a professional, scientific, expert body. Suppose members have agreed to carry out a democratic vote at its triannual assembly. Should it be a show of hands or secret ballot? What quorum is needed? Are absent members allowed to vote?

In 2015, looking retrospectively at the 2006 events, Weintraub wrote:

> The efforts of a very small clique of Pluto-haters within the International Astronomical Union (IAU) plutoed Pluto in 2006. Of the approximately 10,000 internationally registered members of the IAU in 2006, only 237 voted in favor of the resolution redefining Pluto as a "dwarf planet" while 157 voted against; the other 9,500 members were not present at the closing session of the IAU General Assembly in Prague at which the vote to demote Pluto was taken. Yet Pluto's official planetary status was snatched away.[95]

In this passage, Weintraub's concern is implementation. Had more members voted, the IAU's plutoing Pluto would have been OK. His point is about

95. Weintraub 2015.

quorum. Likewise, Alan Stern said at the time: "I am just disgusted by the way the IAU, which is meant to represent the best in science, handled this matter."[96] Inadequate implementation: "Stern is . . . critical of the fact that only astronomers present for the vote, which occurred at the end of the two-week meeting, were allowed to have their say on the matter. No email voting was allowed for the decision—it was made by a show of hands—and that meant that less than 5% of the nearly 9000 IAU members actually voted."[97] Here Stern isn't objecting to the democratic principle the IAU relied on, a vote by the membership of an international scientific association, but to its execution.

However, Stern and his colleagues haven't stopped there. They've also objected to the very idea of voting to make this decision: "Should we really define a word by voting?" "For instance, as far as I (Kirby [Runyon]) know as a planetary geologist, no one has ever voted on the definition for a barchan sand dune."[98] Indeed, it introduces biases and unfreedom: "Voting on key taxonomical terminology and the relationships between taxa is anathema in science (see e.g., Ride, et al., 2012) and is contrary to the traditions evolved over many centuries to reduce social, political and personal cognitive biases in science. It injects unhelpful dynamics and social pressures into science and impinges on individual scientists' taxonomical freedom."[99]

Writing in *Science*, Mark Sykes lamented "the unfortunate impression that science is done by vote in a conference hall."[100] That science is done by vote is one concern. That science is done by vote in a conference hall is another concern. Maybe a democratic vote was the way to go, but not the way the IAU did it. Giving the impression that science is done by vote in a conference hall is yet another concern. It doesn't refer to what was done, but what will be thought of it.

Unlike Runyon and Stern, Tancredi applauded the IAU for making its collective decision democratically. One virtue of the IAU's definition was being the product of a democratic process. A definition is better and preferable because of its genealogy, how it was produced, how it came to be accepted, how agreements about it came about—independently of its intrinsic virtues. Tancredi wasn't shy about deploying political ideas, specifically "the rich Latin American traditions of popular participation":

> What seemed impossible at the beginning of the Assembly, to change the initial proposal of the EC, was achieved in a vote in which more than 75%

96. Quoted in Hogan 2006c.
97. Shiga 2006.
98. Runyon and Stern 2018.
99. Metzger et al. 2019, 30.
100. Sykes 2008, 1765.

of the participants approved the proposal of the 8 planets promoted by us. [...] [It] is important to emphasize that this fact represents a lesson in democracy that recovers [*rescata*] the rich Latin American traditions of popular participation.[101]

Naturally, the IAU stands behind the principle at stake: it favors democratic decision-making in cases like the definition of 'planet.' Individual members might take issue with this, but my point is about the organization. It makes important decisions by means of democratic votes, and thereby it periodically reaffirms, performatively, its democratic convictions. Each time the IAU calls its members to participate and commits to their democratic choice, it's voting with its feet (sort of).

At the 2006 General Assembly, the IAU could have gone for another approach and different criteria. It could have relied on a dictionary or several dictionaries, in several languages, being an international organization. Or the definition could have been up to the Planet Definition Committee alone. Or the Executive Committee could have met behind closed doors and eventually would have announced what 'planet' thenceforward referred to. Or the IAU could have flipped a coin. But it didn't.

(11) Method and intuition

"I know a planet when I see it and there are eight of them." Thus spoke Richard Conn Henry (Johns Hopkins University), an IAU member who was "pleased with the outcome."[102] Henry's method mirrors Justice Potter Stewart's in *Jacobellis v. Ohio*.[103] I don't know how to define it, but I know obscenity, and a planet, when I see it. Stern is of the same methodological mind. As he said in a 2011 interview, "it shouldn't be so difficult to determine what a planet is. When you're watching a science fiction show like 'Star Trek' and they show up at some object in space and turn on the viewfinder, the audience and the people in the show know immediately whether it's a planet, or a star, or a comet or an asteroid."[104] Elsewhere, Stern refers to this as "the Star Trek test for planethood."[105]

101. Tancredi 2007, 76 (my translation).

102. Quoted in Shiga 2006.

103. Jacobellis v. Ohio, 378 U.S. 184 (1964). Cf. Gewirtz 1996.

104. Wall 2011.

105. "The Starship Enterprise shows up at a given body, they turn on the cameras on the bridge and they see it. Captain Kirk and Spock could look at it and they could say, 'That's a star, that's a planet, that's a comet.' They could tell the difference" (A. Boyle 2010, 117).

Captain Kirk, Spock, Henry, and Stern can be associated with intuitionism. With the moral intuitionism of Sidgwick, Moore, Ross, or Prichard. "The view that we can know or justifiably believe some . . . facts directly, without inferring them from other evidence or proof."[106] Captain Kirk et al. don't have to provide definitions, reasons, and arguments. Their intuition simply tells them what a planet is. In fact, it doesn't *tell* them anything; it's an immediate perception, as if it were a special sense. They can perceive these facts, realities, or self-evident truths.

Intuitionism isn't the go-to approach if you're looking for criteria to evaluate word definitions and uses, and you'll have to adjudicate disagreements. Much like in ethics, political philosophy, and the law, people's intuitions may conflict with one another. Planetary scientists' intuitions did conflict with one another. If they hadn't, there wouldn't have been such a planethood brouhaha in the first place.

On the plus side, moral intuitionism is a rich and resourceful tradition, which could help planethood intuitionism overcome standard epistemological objections. Moreover, it might well be that some people have the right intuitions about objects in space, they're intuiting how things really are, whereas other people's intuitive sense is malfunctioning. Even so, dealing with disagreements and conflicts isn't intuitionists' forte.

A.4 Prejudice

I could go on. I could identify more criteria in the planethood wars. But the previous eleven clusters suffice as illustrations. Many kinds of reasons have been offered. Many kinds of criteria have been brought to bear. This partly accounts for the persistence of disagreements. Disputes over the adequate use and definition of 'planet' have been persistent. Within the astronomy and planetary science community, but also in public forums and the media. Second-order criteria tend to be implicit. If you tease them out, they often come across as ad hoc. Spontaneous reactions and proclivities rather than well-developed positions. The rationales for definitional criteria may be mentioned, but not methodically argued for. Sometimes lexical semantics and ontology get fused, and first-order and second-order claims get mixed up.

Sometimes. There are astronomers who do see things more discerningly, including the abovementioned Ekers and Mike Brown. Brown claims that "some astronomers" were "disingenuous or . . . simply not very thoughtful. Or perhaps both." In a 2008 blog post, he offers a third-order analysis, an analysis of "the bigger questions," as Ekers did as well. It considers what the 'planet'

106. Tropman 2014, 177.

disputes were and weren't about, and the relationship between classification, scientific knowledge, word use, and definition. "Does it matter? Is it all just semantics? What's in a name, anyway?"[107]

As Brown sees it, astronomers proposed two classification schemes. First: round objects versus non-round objects. Second: large solitary objects versus collections of small objects. Both schemes can be "useful."

> All that is left to decide is who now gets to use the magical word "planet." There is absolutely no scientific argument that anyone could possibly make to prefer one over the other. That would be akin to asking which one is correct. The answer is that they are both correct, and both useful. Even most astronomers have missed this point. Some astronomers continue to attack and defend the planet definition on scientific grounds. They tend to try to obscure what they are really doing, which is trying to argue that one of the two classification schemes is better and the other flawed. Astronomers making such arguments are either being disingenuous or are simply not very thoughtful. Or perhaps both. There is even a conference being held this summer to discuss the "scientifically correct" definition of "planet" which is about the most nonsensical conference topic I can image.[108]

Like Ekers, Brown argues that correctness judgements are out of place.[109] Neither about the two classification schemes, nor about dissimilar ways of using or defining 'planet.' Furthermore, attacking and defending definitions isn't a job for science, but a job for "culture": "Claiming that there are *scientific reasons* why any one of them deserves to be the category of 'planet' should disqualify you from further discussion on the grounds that you are conflating the job of science and the job of culture."[110]

What is "culture" to do? If there are "cultural (educational, emotional, etc.) pros and cons of the word 'planet' being applied to different classification systems," how should "culture" go about making a decision? Brown broaches reasonable questions about the suitability of criteria and procedures. The public would have to decide. Astronomers can participate, of course, but they'd be participating qua members of the public.

I think Brown has a peculiar understanding of the epistemological bases of "cultural" arguments—advanced in the public sphere, in the agora, by the

107. Michael Brown 2008b.

108. Michael Brown 2008b.

109. He shouldn't have written "they are both correct," but I may be nitpicking.

110. Michael Brown 2008a.

public, by social actors. Our community has agreed that, for the time being, scientific reasons are out of the picture. Science can't solve the issue. Then, what we're left with are "prejudices." Yours, mine, Mike Brown's:

> If the public is to have just one definition with which to try to understand the solar system, which is the best one to use? Which best captures the richness and complexity of the solar system? Which tells them the most about [the] universe around them with just a simple word? I have my own prejudice on what the right answer is here, but it is simply that: a prejudice. You can have a different one. Then, when it comes time to do the science, we can all revert to whatever classification is most useful for the problems we want to address.[111]

I beg to differ with Brown's self-analysis. I don't believe he has a "prejudice" about the definition of 'planet.' While his preferred definition isn't entailed by his scientific research and knowledge of astronomy, that's not tantamount to being prejudiced. However, he does seem to have a prejudice about non-scientific reasons: how they work and what they can do.

111. Michael Brown 2008b.

ACKNOWLEDGMENTS

THE PUBLIC PERFORMANCE of gratitude undermines genuine gratitude. Acknowledgment sections are front regions.[1] In thanking a fancy scholar for their feedback, I'm making it known that I have a relationship with them and they're interested in my work. In thanking a fancy organization, I'm making it known that I was awarded one of its coveted fellowships or grants.

Acknowledging acknowledgment sections' perverse qualities and effects doesn't annul them. Saying that you're genuinely grateful doesn't make your gratitude genuine. If anything, the adverb 'genuinely' is a suspicious word choice.

———

I'm genuinely grateful to Anna Alexandrova, Patrik Aspers, Adrian Favell, Ilya Kliger, Issa Kohler-Hausmann, Monika Krause, Clemens Kroneberg, Martin Kusch, Sabina Leonelli, Steven Lukes, James Mahoney, Sanyu Mojola, David Nirenberg, Fran Osrecki, Anthony Ossa-Richardson, Nigel Pleasants, Daniel Schönpflug, Barbara Stollberg-Rilinger, Richard Swedberg, Sofía Torallas Tovar, Tobias Werron, Bernardo Zacka, and the reviewers for Princeton University Press for their feedback. Michael Sauder, "on the other hand, did not help" at all.[2]

At Princeton University Press, Meagan Levinson was a perceptive and supportive editor. She went above and beyond. Assistant editor Erik Beranek and production editor Jenny Wolkowicki were terrific, too. It was a pleasure to work with Maia Vaswani, an extraordinary copyeditor. (Will she copyedit the word 'copyeditor,' and 'copyedit,' or perhaps copy-edit or copy edit them?) I also thank Katie Osborne for the cover design and Virginia Ling for preparing the index.

1. Goffman 1956.
2. Goffman (1974) 1986, 18.

I got comments and suggestions from Fabien Accominotti, Mohammad Al Attar, Fabian Anicker, Albert Atkin, Lars Behrisch, Kathi Beier, Federico Brandmayr, Jennifer Brichzin, Weitseng Chen, Christian Dayé, Matías Dewey, Christopher Faraone, Uljana Feest, Juan Fernández, Robert Fishman, Sabine Frerichs, Edurne García Iriarte, Luca Giuliani, Federica Gregoratto, Eduardo Halfon, Eddie Hartmann, Heiko Hecht, Lisa Herzog, Henning Hillmann, Nicole Holzhauser, Eva Horn, Stephen John, Deborah Jones, Christian Joppke, Webb Keane, Christopher Kelty, Sebastian Kohl, Inkeri Koskinen, Hannah Landecker, Hallvard Lillehammer, Christopher McCrudden, Patrick McGovern, Martin Mulsow, Sascha Münnich, Axel Paul, Andreas Pettenkofer, Katha Pollitt, Monica Prasad, Nuno Ramos, Agustín Rayo, Matthias Roick, Sophie Roux, Ulinka Rublack, Wolfgang Schluchter, Tanja Schneider, Anna Schriefl, Michael Seewald, Kathia Serrano Velarde, Kathleen Slaney, Devin Terhune, Guy Tillim, Achille Varzi, Elina Vessonen, Tullio Viola, Alexandre Werneck, Petri Ylikoski, Enrica Zanin, and Bénédicte Zimmermann. I chipped my penalty at Sebastián Abreu's suggestion.

Peter Adamson, Justina Díaz Legaspe, Karen Edwards and Mark Fernando (at the American Sociological Association), James Lenman, Susana Monsó, Nick Seaver, Alan Sica, and Gonzalo Tancredi shared or helped me track down primary and secondary sources, including forthcoming papers and unpublished documents. Thanks to Annika Henrizi at Zentral- und Hochschulbibliothek Luzern, and to Anja Brockmann, Stefan Gellner, Kirsten Graupner, Dominik Hagel, and the whole team at the Wissenschaftskolleg zu Berlin library.

While colleagues' and reviewers' comments make your life harder, librarians make your life much easier. Gratitude to the latter might be more genuine than to the former.

———

In a book's acknowledgments, authors are required to say (to confess, to admit, more or less apologetically) that their book has been long in the making. This book has been long in the making. I started out in the aughts by looking at the word 'theory'; eventually, I came to realize that the magic words are 'sandwich' and 'burrito.' In my defense, it could have taken longer. I didn't subject the manuscript to the "gnawing criticism of the mice,"[3] nor have I waited till "the ninth ripening Year mature [its] Worth."[4] I'm indebted to

3. Marx 1980, 102.

4. Horace 1749, 477. Thanks to Anthony Ossa-Richardson for pointing me to this passage.

Northwestern University, New York University, Universität Luzern, Lichtenberg Kolleg, Max-Weber-Kolleg, and Institut d'études avancées de Paris for their support, collegiality, and free office supplies. I completed the manuscript at, and due to, the wonderful Wissenschaftskolleg zu Berlin. Despite these organizations' materially safeguarding my livelihood, my debt to them is moral; it's not financial, I don't think.

At the very early stages of the project, I was lucky to get to run my thoughts by Charles Camic, Carol Heimer, and Arthur Stinchcombe, and thus to benefit from "the unique contributions of art."[5] Thanks to my colleagues, friends, and students at New York University and Universität Luzern: Christine Abbt, Delia Baldasarri, Max Besbris, Joachim Blatter, Craig Calhoun, Rainer Diaz-Bone, Paula England, David Garland, Valentin Groebner, Martin Hartmann, Raimund Hasse, Christoph Hoffmann, Michael Hout, Jennifer Jennings, Colin Jerolmack, Eric Klinenberg, Jeff Manza, Gerald Marwell, Ann Morning, Vanessa Müller, Sophie Mützel, Caitlin Petre, Sonia Prelat, Gaetano Romano, Arvi Särkelä, Patrick Sharkey, Iddo Tavory, Florencia Torche, Adaner Usmani, Giovanni Ventimiglia, and Lawrence Wu. At Luzern, I was lucky to get to run my thoughts by Lukas Posselt and Patrick Schenk. Cornelia Sidler provided invaluable administrative assistance, and so did Daniel Arold, Sina Conrad, Heike Griebel, Tobias König, Alexandra Kratzer, and Fabian Zoller.

Audiences at the London School of Economics, University of Cambridge, Universidad Carlos III, Universität Luzern, Universität St. Gallen, Universität Bern, Graduate Institute of International and Development Studies, Wissenschaftskolleg zu Berlin, Max-Weber-Kolleg, École des hautes études en sciences sociales, Université de Strasbourg, Wirtschaftsuniversität Wien, Zentrum für interdisziplinäre Forschung at Universität Bielefeld, Technische Universität Braunschweig, Universität Heidelberg, Universität Göttingen, Universität Bremen, and Universität Mannheim listened to my blah-blah-blah and didn't throw rotten tomatoes at me.

During the recent pandemic, giving a presentation meant giving an online presentation, where communication is somewhat impaired, but, on the plus side, rotten tomatoes aren't an occupational hazard. There's a possible world in which these presentations took place at Umeå Universitet, Sapienza—Università di Roma, Universität Hannover, Universität der Bundeswehr München, and Universidade Federal do Rio de Janeiro. It's a happy counterfactual world. Virtual attendees' questions were helpful nonetheless.

---

5. Sauder 2019, 4.

I thank Felicitas, Alma, and Emilio for their comments on virtue epistemology, applied ethics, and deliberative democracy. They've also contributed to our understanding of the point of this book. What might it be? Could a "tally of a person" grasp it (*Symposium* 191d)? Love is the answer. *Je mehr ich gebe, Je mehr auch hab' ich: beides ist unendlich.*

———

That's about it.

I believe this book doesn't contain any errors.[6] If it did, though, I alone wouldn't be responsible for them.[7]

6. Makinson 1965.

7. I'm paraphrasing Goffman (1981, 5). Again (Abend 2014, 388).

REFERENCES

Abbott, Andrew. 1988. *The System of Professions*. University of Chicago Press.

———. 1995. "Things of Boundaries." *Social Research* 62:857–82.

———. 2001. *Time Matters*. University of Chicago Press.

———. 2004. *Methods of Discovery*. W. W. Norton.

———. 2016. *Processual Sociology*. University of Chicago Press.

Abbott, Owen. 2020. *The Self, Relational Sociology, and Morality in Practice*. Palgrave Macmillan.

Abend, Gabriel. 2006. "Styles of Sociological Thought." *Sociological Theory* 24:1–41.

———. 2008a. "The Meaning of 'Theory.'" *Sociological Theory* 26:173–99.

———. 2008b. "Two Main Problems in the Sociology of Morality." *Theory and Society* 37:87–125.

———. 2014. *The Moral Background*. Princeton University Press.

———. 2017. "What Are Neural Correlates Neural Correlates Of?" *BioSocieties* 12:415–38.

———. 2018a. "The Limits of Decision and Choice." *Theory and Society* 47:805–41.

———. 2018b. "The Love of Neuroscience." *Sociological Theory* 36:88–116.

———. 2019. "Thick Concepts and Sociological Research." *Sociological Theory* 37:209–33.

———. 2022. "Making Things Possible." *Sociological Methods & Research* 51:68–107.

Abend, Gabriel, Caitlin Petre, and Michael Sauder. 2013. "Styles of Causal Thought." *American Journal of Sociology* 119:602–54.

Achinstein, Peter. 1965. "The Problem of Theoretical Terms." *American Philosophical Quarterly* 2:193–203.

Adams, Julia, Elisabeth S. Clemens, and Ann Shola Orloff, eds. 2005. *Remaking Modernity*. Duke University Press.

Adamson, Peter. 2016. *Philosophy in the Islamic World*. Oxford University Press.

Adamson, Peter, and Gabriele Galluzzo. Forthcoming. "Being as Existence." In *Being*, edited by N. Germann and P. Porro. Brepols.

Adcock, Robert. 2005. "What Is a Concept?" *Political Concepts*, Committee on Concepts and Methods Working Paper Series.

Adler, Franz. 1947. "Operational Definitions in Sociology." *American Journal of Sociology* 52:438–44.

Adorno, Theodor W. 1970. *Ästhetische Theorie*. Suhrkamp.

Ahlstrom-Vij, Kristoffer, and Stephen R. Grimm. 2013. "Getting It Right." *Philosophical Studies* 166:329–47.

Ailes, Edgar H. 1941. "Substance and Procedure in the Conflict of Laws." *Michigan Law Review* 39:392–418.

Alatas, Syed Farid, and Vineeta Sinha. 2017. *Sociological Theory beyond the Canon.* Palgrave Macmillan.

Alexander, Jeffrey. 1991. "Understanding Social Science." *Perspectives* 14 (1): 2–3.

———. 2002. "On the Social Construction of Moral Universals." *European Journal of Social Theory* 5:5–85.

Alexander, Larry, and Saikrishna Prakash. 2004. "'Is That English You're Speaking?'" *San Diego Law Review* 41:967–95.

Alexandrova, Anna. 2017. *A Philosophy for the Science of Well-Being.* Oxford University Press.

———. 2018. "Can the Science of Well-Being Be Objective?" *British Journal for the Philosophy of Science* 69:421–45.

Alexandrova, Anna, and Mark Fabian. 2022. "Democratising Measurement." *European Journal for Philosophy of Science* 12:7.

Alexandrova, Anna, and Daniel Haybron. 2016. "Is Construct Validation Valid?" *Philosophy of Science* 83:1098–109.

Alfano, Mark. 2013a. *Character as Moral Fiction.* Cambridge University Press.

———. 2013b. "The Most Agreeable of All Vices." *British Journal for the History of Philosophy* 21:767–90.

Allan, Keith, and Kate Burridge. 2006. *Forbidden Words.* Cambridge University Press.

Allcock, J. B. 1971. "'Populism': A Brief Biography." *Sociology* 5:371–87.

Allen, Sophie R. 2021. "Kinds Behaving Badly." *Synthese* 198:S2927–56.

Allen, Woody. 1966. "Yes, but Can the Steam Engine Do This?" *New Yorker*, October 8, 1966.

Alpert, Harry. 1938. "Operational Definitions in Sociology." *American Sociological Review* 3:855–61.

Alpi, Amadeo, Nikolaus Amrhein, Adam Bertl, Michael R. Blatt, Eduardo Blumwald, Felice Cervone, Jack Dainty, et al. 2007. "Plant Neurobiology: No Brain, No Gain?" *Trends in Plant Science* 12:135–36.

Anderson, Elizabeth. 2006. "The Epistemology of Democracy." *Episteme* 3:8–22.

———. 2014. "Uses of Value Judgments in Science." *Hypatia* 19:1–24.

Andreski, Stanislav. 1972. *Social Sciences as Sorcery.* André Deutsch.

Angioni, Lucas. 2014. "Definition and Essence in Aristotle's *Metaphysics* vii 4." *Ancient Philosophy* 34:75–100.

Ankeny, Rachel A., and Sabina Leonelli. 2016. "Repertoires." *Studies in History and Philosophy of Science* 60:18–28.

Anscombe, G.E.M. (1963) 2000. *Intention.* 2nd ed. Harvard University Press.

Apel, Karl-Otto. 1973a. *Transformation der Philosophie.* Vol. 1. Suhrkamp.

———. 1973b. *Transformation der Philosophie.* Vol. 2. Suhrkamp.

———, ed. 1976. *Sprachpragmatik und Philosophie.* Suhrkamp.

Aprill, Ellen P. 1998. "The Law of the Word." *Arizona State Law Journal* 30:275–336.

Arendt, Hannah. 1961. *Between Past and Future.* Viking.

Aridi, Rasha. 2020. "In a Global First, Lab-Grown Chicken Nuggets Will Soon Be on the Menu in Singapore." *Smithsonian Magazine*, December 4, 2020. https://www.smithsonianmag.com/smart-news/lab-grown-meat-earns-approval-be-sold-first-time-ever-180976460/.

Armitage, David. 2017. *Civil Wars*. Yale University Press.

Aron, Raymond. 1964. "*Macht, Power,* Puissance: Prose démocratique ou poésie démoniaque?" *European Journal of Sociology* 5:27–51.

Aronovitch, Hilliard. 2012. "Interpreting Weber's Ideal-Types." *Philosophy of the Social Sciences* 42:356–69.

Ashmore, Malcolm, Michael Mulkay, Trevor Pinch, and HESG (Health Economists' Study Group). 1989. "Definitional Work in Applied Social Science." *Knowledge and Society* 8:27–55.

Aspers, Patrik, and Ugo Corte. 2019. "What Is Qualitative in Qualitative Research." *Qualitative Sociology* 42:139–60.

———. 2021. "What Is Qualitative in Research." *Qualitative Sociology* 44:599–608.

Atkins, B. T. Sue, and Michael Rundell. 2008. *The Oxford Guide to Practical Lexicography*. Oxford University Press.

Atmanspacher, Harald, and Sabine Maasen, eds. 2016. *Reproducibility*. Wiley.

Aubenque, Pierre. 1962. *Le problème de l'être chez Aristote*. Presses universitaires de France.

Austin, J. L. 1957. "A Plea for Excuses." *Proceedings of the Aristotelian Society* 57:1–30.

———. 1961. "The Meaning of a Word." In *Philosophical Papers*, edited by J. O. Urmson and C. J. Warnock, 23–43. Clarendon.

———. 1962. *How to Do Things with Words*. Clarendon.

Aviles, Natalie B., and Isaac Ariail Reed. 2017. "*Ratio* via *Machina*." *Sociological Methods & Research* 46:715–38.

Axtell, Guy. 1997. "Recent Work in Virtue Epistemology." *American Philosophical Quarterly* 34:1–26.

Azmanova, Albena. 2012. *The Scandal of Reason*. Columbia University Press.

Babbie, Earl. 2013. *The Practice of Social Research*. 13th ed. Wadsworth.

Bächtiger, André, John S. Dryzek, Jane Mansbridge, and Mark E. Warren. 2018. "Deliberative Democracy: An Introduction." In *The Oxford Handbook of Deliberative Democracy*, edited by A. Bächtiger, J. S. Dryzek, J. Mansbridge, and M. Warren, 1–31. Oxford University Press.

Bagnoli, Carla, ed. 2013. *Constructivism in Ethics*. Cambridge University Press.

———. 2017. "Constructivism in Metaethics." In *The Stanford Encyclopedia of Philosophy*, Winter 2017 ed., edited by E. N. Zalta. Metaphysics Research Lab, Center for the Study of Language and Information, Stanford University.

Baier, Annette. 1986. "Trust and Antitrust." *Ethics* 96:231–60.

———. 1992. "Trusting People." *Philosophical Perspectives* 6:137–53.

Bailey, Samuel. 1826. *A Letter to a Political Economist*. R. Hunter.

Baiocchi, Gianpaolo. 2005. *Militants and Citizens*. Stanford University Press.

Baiocchi, Gianpaolo, and Ernesto Ganuza. 2016. *Popular Democracy*. Stanford University Press.

Baker, A. 2007. "Occam's Razor in Science." *Biology & Philosophy* 22:193–215.

Balaguer, Mark. 1998. *Platonism and Anti-Platonism in Mathematics*. Oxford University Press.

———. 2020. "Why Metaphysical Debates Are Not Merely Verbal." *Synthese* 197:1181–201.

Balcerak Jackson, Brendan. 2013. "Metaphysics, Verbal Disputes and the Limits of Charity." *Philosophy and Phenomenological Research* 86:412–34.

———. 2014. "Verbal Disputes and Substantiveness." *Erkenntnis* 79:31–54.

Ball, Derek. 2020. "Metasemantic Ethics." *Ratio* 33:206–19.

———. 2021. "An Invitation to Social and Political Metasemantics." In *The Routledge Handbook of Social and Political Philosophy of Language*, edited by J. Khoo and R. K. Sterken, 42–55. Routledge.

Balteiro, Isabel. 2011. "Prescriptivism and Descriptivism in the Treatment of Anglicisms in a Series of Bilingual Spanish-English Dictionaries." *International Journal of Lexicography* 24:277–305.

Baluška, František, and Stefano Mancuso. 2020. "Plants, Climate and Humans." *EMBO Reports* 21:e50109.

Bannister, Robert C. 1987. *Sociology and Scientism*. University of North Carolina Press.

Barber, Alex, and Robert J. Stainton. 2021. "Linguistic Prescriptivism." In *The Routledge Handbook of Social and Political Philosophy of Language*, edited by J. Khoo and R. K. Sterken, 56–69. Routledge.

Bargheer, Stefan. 2017. "The Invention of Theory." *Theory and Society* 46:497–541.

Barlösius, Eva. 2019. *Infrastrukturen als soziale Ordnungsdienste*. Campus Verlag.

Barnes, E. C. 2000. "Ockham's Razor and the Anti-superfluity Principle." *Erkenntnis* 53:353–74.

Barney, Rachel. 1998. "Socrates Agonistes." *Oxford Studies in Ancient Philosophy* 16:63–98.

———, Rachel. 2001. *Names and Nature in Plato's "Cratylus."* Routledge.

Barrán, José Pedro, and Benjamín Nahum. 1972. *Historia social de las revoluciones de 1897 y 1904*. Banda Oriental.

Barsalou, Lawrence W. 1983. "Ad Hoc Categories." *Memory & Cognition* 11:211–27.

Bartels, Andreas, and Semir Zeki. 2000. "The Neural Basis of Romantic Love." *NeuroReport* 11:3829–34.

Barton, Carlin A., and Daniel Boyarin. 2016. *Imagine No Religion*. Fordham University Press.

Basri, Gibor, and Michael E. Brown. 2006. "Planetesimals to Brown Dwarfs: What Is a Planet?" *Annual Review of Earth and Planetary Sciences* 34:193–216.

Battersby, Stephen. 2006. "Pluto Gets the Boot as the Planet Count Drops." *New Scientist*, August 24, 2006. https://www.newscientist.com/article/dn9824-pluto-gets-the-boot-as-the-planet-count-drops/.

Batthyány, Karina, and Gerardo Caetano, eds. 2018. *Antología del pensamiento crítico uruguayo contemporáneo*. CLACSO (Latin American Council of Social Sciences).

Bauer, Laurie. 1983. *English Word-Formation*. Cambridge University Press.

Beaney, Michael. 2013. "What Is Analytic Philosophy?" In *The Oxford Handbook of the History of Analytic Philosophy*, edited by Beaney, 3–29. Oxford University Press.

Beard, Henry, and Christopher Cerf. 2015. *Spinglish*. Blue Rider.

Becker, Howard S. 1998. *Tricks of the Trade*. University of Chicago Press.

———. 2014. *What about Mozart? What about Murder?* University of Chicago Press.

———. 2017. *Evidence*. University of Chicago Press.

Begossi, A., M. Clauzet, J. L. Figueiredo, L. Garuana, R. V. Lima, P. F. Lopes, M. Ramires, A. L. Silva, and R.A.M. Silvano. 2008. "Are Biological Species and Higher-Ranking Categories Real?" *Current Anthropology* 49:291–306.

Beigel, Fernanda. 2013. "Centros y periferias en la circulación internacional del conocimiento." *Nueva sociedad* 245:110–23.

Bekoff, Marc, and Jessica Pierce. 2009. *Wild Justice*. University of Chicago Press.

Bell, Duncan, and Bernardo Zacka, eds. 2020. *Political Theory and Architecture*. Bloomsbury.

Bellamy, Richard, and Andrew Mason, eds. 2003. *Political Concepts*. Manchester University Press.

Belleri, Delia. 2018. "Two Species of Merely Verbal Disputes." *Metaphilosophy* 49:691–710.

———. Forthcoming. "Downplaying the Change of Subject Objection to Conceptual Engineering." *Inquiry*.

Belnap, Nuel. 1993. "On Rigorous Definitions." *Philosophical Studies* 72:115–46.

Benacerraf, Paul. 1965. "What Numbers Could Not Be." *Philosophical Review* 74:47–73.

———. 1973. "Mathematical Truth." *Journal of Philosophy* 70:661–79.

Benardete, José A. 1993. "Real Definitions: Quine and Aristotle." *Philosophical Studies* 72:265–82.

Benedetti, Mario. 2000. *El amor, las mujeres y la vida*. Editorial Sudamericana.

Bennett, Jane. 2010. *Vibrant Matter*. Duke University Press.

Bennett, M. R., and P.M.S. Hacker. 2003. *Philosophical Foundations of Neuroscience*. Blackwell.

Benson, C. Randolph. 1971. "Problems in Terminology, Concept Formation, and Theory Construction." *Sociological Focus* 4:107–25.

Benson, Hugh H. 1990a. "Misunderstanding the 'What-Is-F-ness?' Question." *Archiv für Geschichte der Philosophie* 72:125–42.

———. 1990b. "The Priority of Definition and the Socratic Elenchus." *Oxford Studies in Ancient Philosophy* 8:19–65.

———. 2013. "The Priority of Definition." In *The Bloomsbury Companion to Socrates*, edited by J. Bussanich and N. Smith, 136–55. Bloomsbury.

Benson, Phil. 2001. *Ethnocentrism and the English Dictionary*. Routledge.

Berg, Gabriele, Daria Rybakova, Doreen Fischer, Tomislav Cernava, Marie-Christine Champomier Vergès, Trevor Charles, Xiaoyulong Chen, et al. 2020. "Microbiome Definition Revisited." *Microbiome* 8:103.

Bergelson, Vera. 2014. "The Meaning of Consent." *Ohio State Journal of Criminal Law* 12:171–80.

Bergenholtz, Henning. 1995. "Wodurch unterscheidet sich Fachlexikographie von Terminographie?" *Lexicographica* 11:50–59.

Berger, Peter L., and Thomas Luckmann. 1966. *The Social Construction of Reality*. Doubleday.

Berker, Selim. 2018. "The Unity of Grounding." *Mind* 127:729–77.

Berlin, Brent. 1973. "Folk Systematics in Relation to Biological Classification and Nomenclature." *Annual Review of Ecology and Systematics* 4:259–71.

———. 1992. *Ethnobiological Classification*. Princeton University Press.

Berlin, Brent, Dennis E. Breedlove, and Peter H. Raven. 1966. "Folk Taxonomies and Biological Classification." *Science* 154:273–75.

Berlin, Isaiah, Richard Hofstadter, Donald MacRae, Leonard Schapiro, Hugh Seton-Watson, Alain Touraine, F. Venturi, Andrzej Walicki, and Peter Worsley. 1968. "To Define Populism." *Government and Opposition* 3:137–79.

Bernard, L. L. 1941. "The Definition of Definition." *Social Forces* 19:500–510.

Bernstein, J. M., Adi Ophir, and Ann Laura Stoler, eds. 2018. *Political Concepts: A Critical Lexicon*. Fordham University Press.

Besbris, Max. 2020. *Upsold*. University of Chicago Press.

Beurton, Peter, Raphael Falk, and Hans-Jörg Rheinberger, eds. 2000. *The Concept of the Gene in Development and Evolution*. Cambridge University Press.

Beversluis, John. 1987. "Does Socrates Commit the Socratic Fallacy?" *American Philosophical Quarterly* 24:211–23.

Bevir, Mark. 2008. "What Is Genealogy?" *Journal of the Philosophy of History* 2:263–75.

Bevir, Mark, and Jason Blakely. 2018. *Interpretive Social Science*. Oxford University Press.

Bevir, Mark, and Asaf Kedar. 2008. "Concept Formation in Political Science." *Perspectives on Politics* 6:502–17.

Biernacki, Richard. 2012. *Reinventing Evidence in Social Inquiry*. Palgrave Macmillan.

Bierstedt, Robert. 1959. "Nominal and Real Definitions in Sociological Theory." In *Symposium on Sociological Theory*, edited by L. Gross, 121–44. Harper and Row.

Bitbol, Michel, and Jean Gayon, eds. 2015. *L'épistémologie française, 1830–1970*. 2nd ed. Éditions Matériologiques.

Blackburn, Simon. 1999. *Think*. Oxford University Press.

———. 2016. *The Oxford Dictionary of Philosophy*. 3rd ed. Oxford University Press.

Blalock, Hubert M. 1969. *Theory Construction*. Prentice-Hall.

———. 1979a. "Measurement and Conceptualization Problems." *American Sociological Review* 44:881–94.

———. 1979b. *Social Statistics*. 2nd ed. McGraw-Hill.

———. 1982. *Conceptualization and Measurement in the Social Sciences*. Sage.

———. 1986. "Multiple Causation, Indirect Measurement and Generalizability in the Social Sciences." *Synthese* 68:13–36.

Bloch, Marc. 1928. "Pour une histoire comparée des sociétés européennes." *Revue de synthèse historique* 46:15–50.

Blok, Anders, Ignacio Farías, and Celia Roberts, eds. 2020. *The Routledge Companion to Actor-Network Theory*. Routledge.

Bloor, David. 1982. "Durkheim and Mauss Revisited." *Studies in History and Philosophy of Science Part A* 13:267–97.

Blumenthal, Albert. 1940. Letter to the editor. *American Journal of Sociology* 45:918.

———. 1954. "An Inductive Study of the Nature of Culture." *Social Forces* 33:113–21.

Blumer, Herbert. 1931. "Science without Concepts." *American Journal of Sociology* 36:515–33.

———. 1940a. "The Problem of the Concept in Social Psychology." *American Journal of Sociology* 45:707–19.

———. 1940b. Letter to the editor. *American Journal of Sociology* 45:918.

———. 1954. "What Is Wrong with Social Theory?" *American Sociological Review* 19:3–10.

———. 1957. "Sociological Analysis and the 'Variable.'" *American Sociological Review* 21:683–90.

———. *Symbolic Interactionism*. Prentice-Hall.

Boesch, Christophe. 2012. *Wild Cultures*. Cambridge University Press.

Bohman, James. 1998. "The Coming of Age of Deliberative Democracy." *Journal of Political Philosophy* 6:400–425.

———. 2004. "Realizing Deliberative Democracy as a Mode of Inquiry." *Journal of Speculative Philosophy* 18:23–43.

Bokulich, Alisa. 2014. "Pluto and the 'Planet Problem.'" *Perspectives on Science* 22:464–90.

————, Alisa. 2020. "Understanding Scientific Types." *Biology & Philosophy* 35:54.

Bolinger, Dwight. 1980. *Language, the Loaded Weapon*. Longman.

Bommarito, Nicolas. 2013. "Modesty as a Virtue of Attention." *Philosophical Review* 122:93–117.

Boole, George. 1854. *An Investigation of the Laws of Thought, on Which Are Founded the Mathematical Theories of Logic and Probabilities*. Walton and Maberly.

Borges, Jorge Luis. (1946) 1960. "Del rigor en la ciencia." In *El hacedor*, 103. Emecé.

————. (1952) 1960. "El idioma analítico de John Wilkins." In *Otras inquisiciones*, 131–36. Emecé. (Originally published in *La nación*, February 8, 1942.)

————. (1977) 1989. "Tigres azules." In *Obras completas, 1975–1985*, 381–88. Emecé.

Borghi, A. M., L. Barca, F. Binkofski, and L. Tummolini. 2018. "Varieties of Abstract Concepts." *Philosophical Transactions of the Royal Society B* 373:20170121.

Boring, Edwin G. 1923. "Intelligence as the Tests Test It." *New Republic* 36:35–37.

————. 1945. "The Use of Operational Definitions in Science." *Psychological Review* 52:243–45.

Boss, Alan P., R. Paul Butler, William B. Hubbard, Philip A. Ianna, Martin Kürster, Jack J. Lissauer, Michel Mayor, et al. 2007. "Working Group on Extrasolar Planets." In *Reports on Astronomy 2002–2005: Proceedings IAU Symposium No. XXVIA, 2006*, edited by O. Engvold, 183–86. Cambridge University Press.

Bouchard, Frédéric, and Philippe Huneman, eds. 2013. *From Groups to Individuals*. MIT Press.

Boudry, Maarten, and Massimo Pigliucci, eds. 2017. *Science Unlimited?* University of Chicago Press.

Bourdieu, Pierre. 1979. *La distinction: Critique sociale du jugement*. Minuit.

————. 1984. *Homo academicus*. Minuit.

————. 1991. *Language and Symbolic Power*. Translated by Gino Raymond and Matthew Adamson. Polity.

————. 2001. *Science de la science et réflexivité*. Raisons d'agir.

————. 2015. *Sociologie générale*. Vol. 1. Raisons d'agir and Seuil.

Bourdieu, Pierre, Jean-Claude Chamboredon, and Jean-Claude Passeron. 1968. *Le métier de sociologue*. Mouton and Bordas.

Bourdieu Pierre, and Loïc Wacquant. 1998. "Sur les ruses de la raison impérialiste." *Actes de la recherche en sciences sociales* 121–22:109–18.

Bourget, David, and David J. Chalmers. 2014. "What Do Philosophers Believe?" *Philosophical Studies* 170:465–500.

Boutet, Josiane. 2016. *Le pouvoir des mots*. La Dispute.

Bowen, Sarah. 2015. *Divided Spirits*. California.

Bowker, Geoffrey C., and Susan Leigh Star. 1999. *Sorting Things Out*. MIT Press.

Boyd, Richard. 1999. "Homeostasis, Species, and Higher Taxa." In *Species*, edited by R. A. Wilson, 141–85. MIT.

Boyle, Alan. 2010. *The Case for Pluto*. John Wiley.

Boyle, Matthew. 2017. "A Different Kind of Mind?" In *The Routledge Handbook of Philosophy of Animal Minds*, edited by K. Andrews and J. Beck, 109–18. Routledge.

Brakas, Jurgis (George). 2011. "Aristotle's 'Is Said in Many Ways' and Its Relationship to His Homonyms." *Journal of the History of Philosophy* 49:135–59.

Brandmayr, Federico. 2021a. "Explanations and Excuses in French Sociology." *European Journal of Social Theory* 24:374–93.

———. 2021b. "Social Science as Apologia." *European Journal of Social Theory* 24:319–37.

Brandom, Robert. 2001. "Modality, Normativity, and Intentionality." *Philosophy and Phenomenological Research* 63:587–609.

Brankovic, Jelena, Leopold Ringel, and Tobias Werron. 2018. "How Rankings Produce Competition." *Zeitschrift für Soziologie* 47:270–88.

Braunstein, Jean-François. 2002. "Bachelard, Canguilhem, Foucault: Le 'style français' en épistémologie." In *Les philosophes et la science*, edited by P. Wagner, 920–63. Gallimard.

Breitenbach, Angela. 2013. "Aesthetics in Science." *Proceedings of the Aristotelian Society* 113:83–100.

Brennan, Jason. 2016. *Against Democracy*. Princeton University Press.

Brenner, Eric D., Rainer Stahlberg, Stefano Mancuso, and František Baluška. 2007. "Plant Neurobiology: The Gain Is More Than the Name." *Trends in Plant Science* 12:285–86.

Brentano, Franz. 1874. *Psychologie vom empirischen Standpunkte*. 2 vols. Duncker und Humblot.

Brewer, Charlotte. 2016. "Labelling and Metalanguage." In *Oxford Handbook of Lexicography*, edited by P. Durkin, 488–500. Oxford University Press.

Brick, C., B. Hood, V. Ekroll, and L. de-Wit. 2022. "Illusory Essences." *Perspectives on Psychological Science* 17:491–506.

Bridgman, P. W. 1927. *The Logic of Modern Physics*. Macmillan.

———. 1938. "Operational Analysis." *Philosophy of Science* 5:114–31.

Brigandt, Ingo. 2009. "Natural Kinds in Evolution and Systematics." *Acta biotheoretica* 57:77–97.

———. 2015. "Social Values Influence the Adequacy Conditions of Scientific Theories." *Canadian Journal of Philosophy* 45:326–56.

———. Forthcoming. "How to Philosophically Tackle Kinds without Talking about 'Natural Kinds.'" *Canadian Journal of Philosophy*.

Brink, David O. 1989. *Moral Realism and the Foundations of Ethics*. Cambridge University Press.

Brown, James Cooke. 1960. "Loglan." *Scientific American* 202:53–63.

Brown, Leslie. 1994. "The Verb 'to Be' in Greek Philosophy." In *Language*, edited by S. Everson, 212–36. Cambridge University Press.

Brown, Mark B. 2009. *Science in Democracy*. MIT Press.

———. 2015. "Politicizing Science." *Social Studies of Science* 45:3–30.

Brown, Michael E. 2006. "War of the Worlds." *New York Times*, August 16, 2006.

———. 2008a. "What's in a Name?" Mike Brown's Planets, June 22, 2008. http://www.mikebrownsplanets.com/2008/06/whats-in-name.html

———. 2008b. "Ground Rules for Debating the Definition of 'Planet.'" Mike Brown's Planets, June 29, 2008. http://www.mikebrownsplanets.com/2008/06/ground-rules-for-debating-definiton-of.html.

———. 2010. *How I Killed Pluto and Why It Had It Coming*. Spiegel und Grau.

Brown, Michael E., Chadwick Trujillo, and David Rabinowitz. 2004. "Discovery of a Candidate Inner Oort Cloud Planetoid." *Astrophysical Journal* 617:645–49.

———. 2005. "Discovery of a Planetary-Sized Object in the Scattered Kuiper Belt." *Astrophysical Journal* 635:L97–100.

Brown-Saracino, Japonica. 2021. "Unsettling Definitions of Qualitative Research." *Qualitative Sociology* 44:591–97.

Brownstein, Michael. 2018. *The Implicit Mind*. Oxford University Press.

Brubaker, Rogers, and Frederick Cooper. 2000. "Beyond 'Identity.'" *Theory and Society* 29:1–47.

Brusse, Carl. 2016. "Planets, Pluralism, and Conceptual Lineage." *Studies in History and Philosophy of Modern Physics* 53:93–106.

Bueno, Otávio, Ruey-Lin Chen, and Melinda Bonnie Fagan, eds. 2018. *Individuation, Process, and Scientific Practices*. Oxford University Press.

Bueter, Anke. 2019. "Epistemic Injustice and Psychiatric Classification." *Philosophy of Science* 86:1064–74.

———. 2021. "Public Epistemic Trustworthiness and the Integration of Patients in Psychiatric Classification." *Synthese* 198:4711–29.

Burawoy, Michael. 2005. "For Public Sociology." *American Sociological Review* 70:4–28.

Burger, Ronna. 1987. "Is Each Thing the Same as Its Essence?" *Review of Metaphysics* 41:53–76.

Burgess, Alexis, Herman Cappelen, and David Plunkett, eds. 2020. *Conceptual Engineering and Conceptual Ethics*. Oxford University Press.

Burgess, Alexis, and David Plunkett. 2013a. "Conceptual Ethics I." *Philosophy Compass* 8:1091–101.

———. 2013b. "Conceptual Ethics II." *Philosophy Compass* 8:1102–10.

———. 2020. "On the Relation between Conceptual Engineering and Conceptual Ethics." *Ratio* 33:281–94.

Burgess, Alexis, and Brett Sherman, eds. 2014. *Metasemantics*. Oxford University Press.

Burke, Kenneth. 2018. *The War of Words*. Edited by A. Burke, K. Jensen, and J. Selzer. University of California Press.

Burley, Justine, ed. 2004. *Dworkin and His Critics*. Blackwell.

Byrne, Alex. 2020. "Are Women Adult Human Females?" *Philosophical Studies* 177:3783–803.

Byrne, Patrick H. 1997. *Analysis and Science in Aristotle*. State University of New York.

Calise, Mauro, and Theodore J. Lowi. 2010. *Hyperpolitics*. University of Chicago Press.

Callon, Michel, Pierre Lascoumes, and Yannick Barthe. 2001. *Agir dans un monde incertain*. Seuil.

Calvo, Paco, Monica Gagliano, Gustavo M. Souza, and Anthony Trewavas. 2020. "Plants Are Intelligent, Here's How." *Annals of Botany* 125:11–28.

Cameron, Deborah. 1995. *Verbal Hygiene*. Routledge.

Camic, Charles, Neil Gross, and Michèle Lamont, eds. 2011. *Social Science in the Making*. University of Chicago Press.

Campbell, George. (1776) 1823. *The Philosophy of Rhetoric*. 7th ed. William Baynes.

Campbell, Joseph Keim, Michael O'Rourke, and Matthew H. Slater, eds. 2011. *Carving Nature at Its Joints*. MIT Press.

Campo, Ángela. 2012. "The Reception of Eugen Wüster's Work and the Development of Terminology." PhD dissertation. Université de Montréal.

Canovan, Margaret. 1981. *Populism*. Harcourt Brace Jovanovich.

Cantalamessa, Elizabeth Amber. 2021. "Disability studies, conceptual engineering, and conceptual activism." *Inquiry* 64:46–75.

Cappelen, Herman. 1999. "Intentions in Words." *Noûs* 33:92–102.

———. 2018. *Fixing Language*. Oxford University Press.

———. 2020. "Conceptual Engineering: The Master Argument." In *Conceptual Engineering and Conceptual Ethics*, edited by A. Burgess, Cappelen, and D. Plunkett, 132–51. Oxford University Press.

Cappelen, Herman, Tamar Szabó Gendler, and John Hawthorne, eds. 2016. *The Oxford Handbook of Philosophical Methodology*. Oxford University Press.

Cappelen, Herman, and David Plunkett. 2020. Introduction to *Conceptual Engineering and Conceptual Ethics*, edited by A. Burgess, Cappelen, and D. Plunkett, 1–26. Oxford University Press.

Carey, Susan. 2009. *The Origin of Concepts*. Oxford University Press.

Carnap, Rudolf. 1950. "Empiricism, Semantics, and Ontology." *Revue internationale de philosophie* 4:20–40.

———. (1950) 1962. *Logical Foundations of Probability*. 2nd ed. University of Chicago Press.

Carroll, Lewis. 1893. *Sylvie and Bruno Concluded*. Macmillan.

———. 1911. *Alice's Adventures in Wonderland and Through the Looking-Glass and What Alice Found There*. Macmillan.

Cartwright, Nancy. 1983. *How the Laws of Physics Lie*. Oxford University Press.

———. 1991. "Replicability, Reproducibility, and Robustness: Comments on Harry Collins." *History of Political Economy* 23:143–55.

Cartwright, Nancy, Jordi Cat, Lola Fleck, and Thomas E. Uebel. 1996. *Otto Neurath*. Cambridge University Press.

Cartwright, Nancy, and Rosa Runhardt. 2014. "Measurement." In *Philosophy of Social Science*, edited by N. Cartwright and E. Montuschi, 265–87. Oxford University Press.

Casati, Roberto, and Achille C. Varzi. 1994. *Holes and Other Superficialities*. MIT Press.

Cassam, Quassim. 2019. *Vices of the Mind*. Oxford University Press.

Catala, Amandine. 2020. "Metaepistemic Injustice and Intellectual Disability." *Ethical Theory and Moral Practice* 23:755–76.

Chalmers, David. 2011. "Verbal Disputes." *Philosophical Review* 120:515–66.

Chambers, Chris. 2017. *The Seven Deadly Sins of Psychology*. Princeton University Press.

Chambers, Chris, Marcus Munafo, et al. 2013. "Trust in Science Would Be Improved by Study Pre-registration." Open letter. *Guardian*, June 5, 2013. https://www.theguardian.com/science/blog/2013/jun/05/trust-in-science-study-pre-registration.

Chang, Hasok. 2004. *Inventing Temperature*. Oxford University Press.

———. 2017. "Operational Coherence as the Source of Truth." *Proceedings of the Aristotelian Society* 117:102–22.

———. 2021. "Operationalism." In *The Stanford Encyclopedia of Philosophy*, Fall 2021 ed., edited by E. N. Zalta. Metaphysics Research Lab, Center for the Study of Language and Information, Stanford University.

Chang, Kenneth. 2001. "Pluto's Not a Planet? Only in New York." *New York Times*, January 22, 2001, A1.

———. 2022. "Is Pluto a Planet? What's a Planet, Anyway?" *New York Times*, January 18, 2022.

Chang, Ruth, and Kurt Sylvan, eds. 2021. *The Routledge Handbook of Practical Reason.* Routledge.

Chapin, F. Stuart. 1939. "Definition of Definitions of Concepts." *Social Forces* 18:153–60.

Charles, David. 2000. *Aristotle on Meaning and Essence.* Oxford University Press.

———. 2010a. "Definition and Explanation in the Posterior Analytics and Metaphysics." In *Definition in Greek Philosophy*, edited by Charles, 286–328. Oxford University Press.

———, ed. 2010b. *Definition in Greek Philosophy.* Oxford University Press.

Chen, Katherine C. 2016. "'Plan Your Burn, Burn Your Plan.'" *Sociological Quarterly* 57:71–97.

Chiba, Kei. 2010. "Aristotle on Essence and Defining-Phrase in His Dialectic." In *Definition in Greek Philosophy*, edited by D. Charles, 203–51. Oxford University Press.

Chouhy, Gabriel. 2021. "The Moral Life of Econometric Equations." *European Journal of Sociology* 62:141–82.

Christensen, David, and Jennifer Lackey, eds. 2013. *The Epistemology of Disagreement.* Oxford University Press.

Churchland, Patricia Smith. 1986. *Neurophilosophy.* MIT Press.

Churchland, Paul M. 1981. "Eliminative Materialism and the Propositional Attitudes." *Journal of Philosophy* 78:67–90.

Churchman, C. West. 1948. "Statistics, Pragmatics, Induction." *Philosophy of Science* 15:249–68.

Cicero, Marcus Tullius. (55 BC) 1942. *De Oratore: Books I, II.* Translated by E. W. Sutton. William Heinemann and Harvard University Press.

Cicourel, Aaron V. 1964. *Method and Measurement in Sociology.* Free Press of Glencoe.

Clark, Andy, and David Chalmers. 1998. "The Extended Mind." *Analysis* 58:7–19.

Clark, Justin C. 2018. "Socratic Inquiry and the 'What-Is-F?' Question." *European Journal of Philosophy* 26:1324–42.

———. Forthcoming. "Socrates, the 'What Is F-ness?' Question, and the Priority of Definition." *Archiv für Geschichte der Philosophie.*

Clarke, Ellen. 2012. "Plant Individuality." *Biology & Philosophy* 27:321–61.

Cleland, Carol E. 2012. "Life without Definitions." *Synthese* 185:125–44.

Clipsham, Patrick. 2019. "What's Left for the Companions in Guilt Argument?" *Ethical Theory and Moral Practice* 22:137–51.

Code, Lorraine. 1991. *What Can She Know?* Cornell University Press.

Cohen, Adam. 2009. "The Lord Justice Hath Rules." *New York Times,* May 31, 2009.

Cohen, Joshua. 1986. "An Epistemic Conception of Democracy." *Ethics* 97:26–38.

———. (1996) 1997. "Procedure and Substance in Deliberative Democracy." In *Deliberative Democracy*, edited by Bohman and Rehg, 407–37. MIT Press.

Cohen, Morris, and Ernest Nagel. 1934. *An Introduction to Logic and Scientific Method.* Routledge and Kegan Paul.

Collier, David, and John Gerring, eds. 2009. *Concepts and Method in Social Science.* Routledge.

Collier, David, Fernando Daniel Hidalgo, and Andra Olivia Maciuceanu. 2006. "Essentially Contested Concepts." *Journal of Political Ideologies* 11:211–46.

Collier, David, and Steven Levitsky. 1997. "Democracy with Adjectives." *World Politics* 49:430–51.

Collier, David, and James E. Mahon. 1993. "Conceptual 'Stretching' Revisited." *American Political Science Review* 87:845–55.

Collin, Finn. 2013. "Two Kinds of Social Epistemology." *Social Epistemology Review and Reply Collective* 2:79–104.

Collins, H. M. 1985. *Changing Order*. Sage.

———. 1991. "The Meaning of Replication and the Science of Economics." *History of Political Economy* 23:123–42.

Collins, Harry. 2018. *Artifictional Intelligence*. Polity.

Collins, Harry, and Robert Evans. 2007. *Rethinking Expertise*. University of Chicago Press.

Colman, Andrew M. 2015. *A Dictionary of Psychology*. 4th ed. Oxford University Press.

Comte, Auguste. (1830) 1934. *Cours de philosophie positive*. Vol. 1. Alfred Costes.

Connell, Raewyn. 2006. "Northern Theory." *Theory and Society* 35:237–64.

Connolly, William E. (1974) 1983. *The Terms of Political Discourse*. 2nd ed. Princeton University Press.

———. 2013. "The 'New Materialism' and the Fragility of Things." *Millennium* 41:399–412.

Coons, Christian, and Michael Weber, eds. 2013. *Paternalism*. Cambridge University Press.

Cooper, David E. 1972. "Definitions and 'Clusters.'" *Mind* 81:495–503.

Cooper, Rachel. 2004. "Why Hacking Is Wrong about Human Kinds." *British Journal for the Philosophy of Science* 55:73–85.

Cooper, Robert L. 1989. *Language Planning and Social Change*. Cambridge University Press.

Correia, Fabrice. 2017. "Real Definitions." *Philosophical Issues* 27:52–73.

Coser, Lewis A. 1956. *The Functions of Social Conflict*. Free Press.

Courtine, Jean-François, and Albert Rijksbaron. (2004) 2014. "To ti ên einai." In *Dictionary of Untranslatables: A Philosophical Lexicon*, edited by B. Cassin, 1133–39. Princeton University Press.

Cowie, Christopher. 2018. "Companions in Guilt Arguments." *Philosophy Compass* 13:e12528.

Cozzaglio, Ilaria, and Greta Favara. 2021. "Feasibility beyond Non-ideal Theory." *Ethical Theory and Moral Practice* 25:417–32.

Criley, Mark Edward. 2007. "Contested Concepts and Competing Conceptions." PhD dissertation, University of Pittsburgh.

Cronbach, Lee J., and Paul E. Meehl. 1955. "Construct Validity in Psychological Tests." *Psychological Bulletin* 52:281–302.

Crosbie, Thomas, and Jeffrey Guhin. 2019. "On the Ambivalence of the Aphorism in Sociological Theory." *Sociological Theory* 37:381–400.

Crowley, Tony, ed. 1991. *Proper English*. Routledge.

Cruikshank, Dale P., and Joseph W. Chamberlain. 1999. "The Beginnings of the Division for Planetary Sciences of the American Astronomical Society." In *The American Astronomical Society's First Century*, edited by D. DeVorkin, 252–68. American Astronomical Society.

Cruse, D. A. 1986. *Lexical Semantics*. Cambridge University Press.

———. 2001. "Lexical Semantics." In *International Encyclopedia of the Social & Behavioral Sciences*, edited by N. J. Smelser, P. B. Baltes, et al., 8758–64. Elsevier.

Crystal, David. 2006. *The Fight for English*. Oxford University Press.

———. 2009. *Txtng: The Gr8 Db8*. Oxford University Press.

"Current Items." 1939. *American Sociological Review* 4:709–19.

"Current Items." 1941. *American Sociological Review* 6:389–97.

Curzan, Anne. 2014. *Fixing English*. Cambridge University Press.

Dahrendorf, Ralf. 1959. *Class and Class Conflict in Industrial Society*. Stanford University Press.

Dancy, Jonathan. 2004. *Ethics without Principles*. Oxford University Press.

Danziger, Kurt. 1997. *Naming the Mind*. Sage.

Darwin, Charles. (1859) 1909. *The Origin of Species*. P. F. Collier.

———. (1871) 1874. *The Descent of Man, and Selection in Relation to Sex*. 2nd ed. John Murray.

Das, Veena, and Didier Fassin, eds. 2021. *Words and Worlds*. Duke University Press.

Daston, Lorraine. 2004a. "Attention and the Values of Nature in the Enlightenment." In *The Moral Authority of Nature*, edited by Daston and F. Vidal, 100–126. University of Chicago Press.

———. 2004b. "Type Specimens and Scientific Memory." *Critical Inquiry* 31:153–82.

Daston, Lorraine, and Peter Galison. 2007. *Objectivity*. Zone Books.

Daston, Lorraine, and Gregg Mitman, eds. 2005. *Thinking with Animals*. Columbia University Press.

David, Leonard. 2006. "Clyde Tombaugh's Family Joins Protest of Pluto's Downgrade." Space .com, September 5, 2006. https://www.space.com/2848-clyde-tombaugh-family-joins -protest-pluto-downgrade.html.

Davidson, Donald. 1963. "Actions, Reasons, and Causes." *Journal of Philosophy* 60:685–700.

———. 1984. *Inquiries into Truth and Interpretation*. Oxford University Press.

Davis, Murray S. 1971. "That's Interesting!" *Philosophy of the Social Sciences* 1:309–44.

Debus, Dorothea. 2015. "Losing Oneself (in a Good Way)." *European Journal of Philosophy* 23:1174–91.

Decock, Lieven. 2021. "Conceptual Change and Conceptual Engineering." *Inquiry* 64:168–85.

Deener, Andrew. 2017. "The Uses of Ambiguity in Sociological Theorizing." *Sociological Theory* 35:359–79.

De Ípola, Emilio. 2006. *Tristes tópicos de las ciencias sociales*. Ediciones de la Flor.

De Laet, Marianne, and Annemarie Mol. 2000. "The Zimbabwe Bush Pump." *Social Studies of Science* 30:225–63.

Dembroff, Robin. 2021. "Escaping the Natural Attitude about Gender." *Philosophical Studies* 178:983–1003.

Dembroff, Robin, Issa Kohler-Hausmann, and Elise Sugarman. 2020. "What Taylor Swift and Beyoncé Teach Us about Sex and Causes." *University of Pennsylvania Law Review Online* 169:1–12. https://scholarship.law.upenn.edu/penn_law_review_online/vol169/iss1/1.

De Melo-Martín, Inmaculada, and Kristen Intemann. 2016. "The Risk of Using Inductive Risk to Challenge the Value-Free Ideal." *Philosophy of Science* 83:500–520.

Demoss, David, and Daniel Devereux. 1988. "Essence, Existence, and Nominal Definition in Aristotle's *Posterior Analytics* II 8–10." *Phronesis* 33:133–54.

De Queiroz, Kevin. 2007. "Species Concepts and Species Delimitation." *Systematic Biology* 56:879–86.

Deutsch, Max. 2020. "Speaker's Reference, Stipulation, and a Dilemma for Conceptual Engineers." *Philosophical Studies* 177:3935–57.

De Waal, Frans. 2000. *Chimpanzee Politics*. Rev. ed. Johns Hopkins University Press.

Dewey, John. 1927. *The Public and Its Problems*. H. Holt.

———. 1929. *The Quest for Certainty*. Minton, Balch.

———. 2021. *America's Public Philosopher*. Columbia University Press.

Dews, Peter. 1992. "Foucault and the French Tradition of Historical Epistemology." *History of European Ideas* 14:347–63.

Díaz-Legaspe, Justina. 2020. "What Is a Slur?" *Philosophical Studies* 177:1399–422.

Díaz-León, E. 2016. "'Woman' as a Politically Significant Term." *Hypatia* 31:245–58.

Dietz, Richard, and Sebastiano Moruzzi, eds. 2010. *Cuts and Clouds*. Oxford University Press.

DiFrisco, James. 2019. "Kinds of Biological Individuals." *British Journal for the Philosophy of Science* 70:845–75.

DiMaggio, Paul. 1987. "Classification in Art." *American Sociological Review* 52:440–55.

Di Sciullo, Anna Maria, and Edwin Williams. 1987. *On the Definition of Word*. MIT Press.

Djelic, Marie-Laure, and Joel Bothello. 2013. "Limited Liability and Its Moral Hazard Implications." *Theory and Society* 42:589–615.

Dodd, Stuart C. 1951. "Scientific Methods in Human Relations." *American Journal of Economics and Sociology* 10:221–35.

Dodd, Stuart C., and Ethel Shanas. 1943. "Operational Definitions Operationally Defined." *American Journal of Sociology* 48:482–91.

Donne, John. 1624. *Devotions Vpon Emergent Occasions, and Seuerall Steps in My Sicknes*. A. M. for Thomas Iones.

Doolittle, W. Ford, and Austin Booth. 2017. "It's the Song, Not the Singer." *Biology & Philosophy* 32:5–24.

Doris, John M. 2002. *Lack of Character*. Cambridge University Press.

D'Oro, Giuseppina, and Søren Overgaard, eds. 2017. *The Cambridge Companion to Philosophical Methodology*. Cambridge University Press.

Dorr, Cian. 2016. "To Be F Is to Be G." *Philosophical Perspectives* 30:39–134.

Dorr, Cian, and John Hawthorne. 2014. "Semantic Plasticity and Speech Reports." *Philosophical Review* 123:281–338.

Douglas, Heather. 2000. "Inductive Risk and Values in Science." *Philosophy of Science* 67:559–79.

———. 2004. "The Irreducible Complexity of Objectivity." *Synthese* 138:453–73.

———. 2005. "Inserting the Public into Science." In *Democratization of Expertise?*, edited by S. Maasen and P. Weingart, 153–69. Springer.

———. 2009. *Science, Policy, and the Value-Free Ideal*. University of Pittsburgh Press.

———. 2013. "The Value of Cognitive Values." *Philosophy of Science* 80:796–806.

Douglas, Mary. 1966. *Purity and Danger*. Routledge and Kegan Paul.

Dresner, Eli. 2012. "Meaning Holism." *Philosophy Compass* 7:611–19.

Dreyfus, Hubert L. 1972. *What Computers Can't Do*. Harper and Row.

Dryzek, John S. 2004. "Pragmatism and Democracy." *Journal of Speculative Philosophy* 18:72–79.

Dryzek, John S., André Bächtiger, Simone Chambers, Joshua Cohen, James N. Druckman, Andrea Felicetti, James S. Fishkin, et al. 2019. "The Crisis of Democracy and the Science of Deliberation." *Science* 363:1144–46.

Duhem, Pierre. 1906. *La théorie physique: Son objet et sa structure*. Chevalier et Rivière.

Dumouchel, Paul. 2005. "Trust as an Action." *European Journal of Sociology* 46:417–28.

Duncan, Otis Dudley. 1984. *Notes on Social Measurement*. Russell Sage.

Dupré, John. 1981. "Natural Kinds and Biological Taxa." *Philosophical Review* 90:66–90.

———. 2002. "Is 'Natural Kind' a Natural Kind Term?" *Monist* 85:29–49.

———. 2006. "Scientific Classification." *Theory, Culture & Society* 23:30–32.

———. 2007. "Fact and Value." In *Value-Free Science?*, edited by H. Kincaid, J. Dupré, and A. Wylie, 27–41. Oxford University Press.

———. 2012. *Processes of Life*. Oxford University Press.

Dupré, John, and Stephan Guttinger. 2016. "Viruses as Living Processes." *Studies in History and Philosophy of Biological and Biomedical Sciences* 59:109–16.

Dupré, John, and Sabina Leonelli. 2022. "Process Epistemology in the COVID-19 Era." *European Journal for Philosophy of Science* 12:20.

Durand, Rodolphe, and Lionel Paolella. 2013. "Category Stretching." *Journal of Management Studies* 50:1100–1123.

Durkheim, Émile. 1895. *Les règles de la méthode sociologique*. Félix Alcan.

Durkheim Émile. (1895) 2013. *The Rules of Sociological Method*. Translated by W. D. Halls. Free Press.

Durkheim, Émile. 1897. *Le suicide*. Félix Alcan.

Durkheim, Émile. (1912) 1968. *Les formes élémentaires de la vie religieuse*. Presses universitaires de France.

Durkheim, Émile, and Marcel Mauss. 1901–2. "De quelques formes primitives de classification." *Année sociologique* 6:1–72.

Durkin, Philip, ed. 2016. *The Oxford Handbook of Lexicography*. Oxford University Press.

Dworkin, Gerald. 1972. "Paternalism." *Monist* 56:64–84.

———. 1995. "Unprincipled Ethics." *Midwest Studies in Philosophy* 20:224–39.

Dworkin, Ronald. 1977. *Taking Rights Seriously*. Harvard University Press.

———. 1996. "Objectivity and Truth." *Philosophy & Public Affairs* 25:87–139.

———. 2011. *Justice for Hedgehogs*. Belknap Press of Harvard University Press.

Eco, Umberto. 1994. "On the Impossibility of Drawing a Map of the Empire on a Scale of 1 to 1." In *"How to Travel with a Salmon" and Other Essays*, translated by William Weaver, 95–106. Harcourt, Brace.

Edmonds, David. 2017. "Cake or Biscuit?" *BBC News*, February 20, 2017. https://www.bbc.com/news/magazine-38985820.

Effingham, Nikk. 2010. "The Metaphysics of Groups." *Philosophical Studies* 149:251–67.

Égré, Paul, and Cathal O'Madagain. 2019. "Concept Utility." *Journal of Philosophy* 116:525–54.

Ekers, Ron. 2019. "The Prague IAU General Assembly, Pluto and the IAU Processes." In *Under One Sky: The IAU Centenary Symposium*, edited by C. Sterken, J. Hearnshaw, and D. Valls-Gabaud, 51–57. International Astronomical Union.

Eklund, Matti. 2015. "Intuitions, Conceptual Engineering, and Conceptual Fixed Points." In *The Palgrave Handbook of Philosophical Methods*, edited by C. Daly, 363–85. Palgrave Macmillan.

Eliaeson, Sven. 1990. "Influences on Max Weber's Methodology." *Acta sociologica* 33:15–30.

Eliasoph, Nina. 2014. "Measuring the Grassroots." *Sociological Quarterly* 55:467–92.

Ellen, Roy, ed. 2006. *Ethnobiology and the Science of Humankind*. Blackwell.

Elliott, Kevin C. 2011. "Direct and Indirect Roles for Values in Science." *Philosophy of Science* 78:303–24.

Elliott, Kevin C., and Daniel J. McKaughan. 2014. "Nonepistemic Values and the Multiple Goals of Science." *Philosophy of Science* 81:1–21.

Elliott, Kevin C., and Ted Richards, eds. 2017. *Exploring Inductive Risk*. Oxford University Press.

Ellwood, Charles A. 1931. "Scientific Method in Sociology." *Social Forces* 10:15–21.

Elman, Colin, John Gerring, and James Mahoney, eds. 2020. *The Production of Knowledge*. Cambridge University Press.

Elster, Jon 1998. Introduction to *Deliberative Democracy*, edited by Elster, 1–18. Cambridge University Press.

Elstub, Stephen. 2010. "The Third Generation of Deliberative Democracy." *Political Studies Review* 8:291–307.

Emirbayer, Mustafa. 1997. "Manifesto for a Relational Sociology." *American Journal of Sociology* 103:281–317.

Empson, William. (1930) 1949. *Seven Types of Ambiguity*. 2nd ed. Chatto and Windus.

Enflo, Karin. 2020. "Measures of Similarity." *Theoria* 86:73–99.

Enoch, David. 2009. "Can There Be a Global, Interesting, Coherent Constructivism about Practical Reason?" *Philosophical Explorations* 12:319–39.

———. 2011. *Taking Morality Seriously*. Oxford University Press.

Epstein, Brian. 2019. "What Are Social Groups?" *Synthese* 196:4899–932.

Epstein, Steven. 1996. *Impure Science*. University of California Press.

———. 2007. *Inclusion*. University of Chicago Press.

Ereshefsky, Marc. 1998. "Species Pluralism and Anti-realism." *Philosophy of Science* 65:103–20.

Ereshefsky, Marc, and Makmiller Pedroso. 2013. "Biological Individuality." *Biology & Philosophy* 28:331–49.

———. 2015. "Rethinking Evolutionary Individuality." *Proceedings of the National Academy of Sciences of the USA* 112:10126–32.

Ereshefsky, Marc, and Thomas A. C. Reydon. 2015. "Scientific Kinds." *Philosophical Studies* 172:969–86.

Ermakoff, Ivan. 2014. "Exceptional Cases." *European Journal of Sociology* 55:223–43.

Erman, Eva, and Niklas Möller. 2020. "A World of Possibilities." *Res publica* 26:1–23.

Espeland, Wendy Nelson, and Michael Sauder. 2016. *Engines of Anxiety*. Russell Sage.

Espeland, Wendy Nelson, and Mitchell L. Stevens. 1998. "Commensuration as a Social Process." *Annual Review of Sociology* 24:313–43.

———. 2008. "A Sociology of Quantification." *European Journal of Sociology* 49:401–36.

Estlund, David. 2003. "Why Not Epistocracy?" In *Desire, Identity and Existence*, edited by N. Reshotko, 53–69. Academic Printing and Publishing.

———. 2008. *Democratic Authority*. Princeton University Press.

———. 2020. *Utopophobia*. Princeton University Press.

Evans-Pritchard, E. E. (1937) 1976. *Witchcraft, Oracles, and Magic among the Azande*. Clarendon.

———. 1954. "A Problem of Nuer Religious Thought." *Sociologus* 4:23–42.

Ewegen, S. Montgomery. 2014. *Plato's "Cratylus."* Indiana University Press.

Eyal, Gil. 2019. *The Crisis of Expertise*. Polity.

Ezcurdia, Maite. 1998. "The Concept-Conception Distinction." *Philosophical Issues* 9:187–92.

Faia, Michael A. 1991. "Sociolog(omach)y." *Perspectives* 14 (3): 4–5.

Faraone, Christopher. 1995. "The 'Performative Future' in Three Hellenistic Incantations and Theocritus' Second *Idyll*." *Classical Philology* 90:1–15.

Farber, Paul Lawrence. 1976. "The Type-Concept in Zoology during the First Half of the Nineteenth Century." *Journal of the History of Biology* 9:93–119.

Farrer, Martin. 2007. "When Is a Biscuit a Teacake?" *Guardian*, December 14, 2007.

Fassin, Didier, and George Steinmetz, eds. Forthcoming. *The Social Sciences in the Looking-Glass*. Duke University Press.

Feest, Uljana. 2005. "Operationism in Psychology." *Journal of the History of the Behavioral Sciences* 41:131–49.

Feest, Uljana, and Thomas Sturm. 2011. "What (Good) Is Historical Epistemology?" *Erkenntnis* 75:285–302.

Felber, Helmut. 1977. "Developing an International Network for Conceptual Analysis in Social Sciences: The Interconcept Project of UNESCO." Meeting of Experts on "Interconcept" Principles and Strategies, Paris, UNESCO, May 9–11, 1977. SS/77/CONF.601/4.

———. 1980. "In Memory of Eugen Wüster, Founder of the General Theory of Terminology." *International Journal of the Sociology of Language* 23:7–14.

Feldman, Richard, and Ted A. Warfield, eds. 2010. *Disagreement*. Oxford University Press.

Festenstein, Matthew. 2004. "Deliberative Democracy and Two Models of Pragmatism." *European Journal of Social Theory* 7:291–306.

Feyerabend, Paul K. 1958. "An Attempt at a Realistic Interpretation of Experience." *Proceedings of the Aristotelian Society* 58:143–70.

———. 1978. *Science in a Free Society*. New Left Books.

———. 1980. "Democracy, Elitism, and Scientific Method." *Inquiry* 23:3–18.

———. 1981. *Realism, Rationalism and Scientific Method*. Cambridge University Press.

Fidler, Fiona, and John Wilcox. 2021. "Reproducibility of Scientific Results." In *The Stanford Encyclopedia of Philosophy*, Summer 2021 ed., edited by E. N. Zalta. Metaphysics Research Lab, Center for the Study of Language and Information, Stanford University.

Fienberg, Richard Tresch. 2006. "Planet Debate Heats Up." *Sky & Telescope*, August 18, 2006. https://skyandtelescope.org/astronomy-news/planet-debate-heats-up/.

Figdor, Carrie. 2018. *Pieces of Mind*. Oxford University Press.

Filipe, Angela, Alicia Renedo, and Cicely Marston. 2017. "The Co-production of What?" *PLoS Biology* 15:e2001403.

Fine, Arthur. 1986. *The Shaky Game*. University of Chicago Press.

Fine, Kit. 1995. "Ontological Dependence." *Proceedings of the Aristotelian Society* 95:269–90.

———. "Things and Their Parts." *Midwest Studies in Philosophy* 23:61–74.

Firebaugh, Glenn. 2008. *Seven Rules for Social Research*. Princeton University Press.

Firth, J. R. 1957. *Papers in Linguistics, 1934–1951*. Oxford University Press.

———. 1968. *Selected Papers of J. R. Firth, 1952–59*. Edited by F. R. Palmer. Indiana University Press.

Fischer, Daniel. 2006. "Inside the Planet Definition Process." *Space Review*, September 11, 2006. https://www.thespacereview.com/article/703/1.

Fish, Adam, Luis F. R. Murillo, Lilly Nguyen, Aaron Panofsky, and Christopher M. Kelty. 2011. "Birds of the Internet." *Journal of Cultural Economy* 4:157–87.

Fishkin, James S. 1995. *The Voice of the People*. Yale University Press.

———. 2009. *When the People Speak*. Oxford University Press.

Fishkin, James S., and Jane Mansbridge. 2017. Introduction to "The Prospects and Limits of Deliberative Democracy," edited by Fishkin and Mansbridge, special issue, *Daedalus* 146:6–13.

Fitzpatrick, Simon. 2017. "Animal Morality." *Biology & Philosophy* 32:1151–83.

Flack, Jessica, and Frans de Waal. 2000. "'Any Animal Whatever.'" *Journal of Consciousness Studies* 7:1–29.

Fleck, Christian. 2007. *Transatlantische Bereicherungen*. Suhrkamp.

Fleck, Ludwik. (1935) 2019. *Entstehung und Entwicklung einer wissenschaftlichen Tatsache*. Suhrkamp.

Flew, Antony. 1985. "The Concept, and Conception, of Justice." *Journal of Applied Philosophy* 2:191–96.

Flocke, Vera. 2021. "How to Engineer a Concept." *Philosophical Studies* 178:3069–83.

Florestal, Marjorie. 2008. "Is a Burrito a Sandwich?" *Michigan Journal of Race & Law* 14:1–59.

Fodor, Jerry. 1975. *The Language of Thought*. Crowell.

Foot, Philippa. 1995. "Does Moral Subjectivism Rest on a Mistake?" *Oxford Journal of Legal Studies* 15:1–14.

Foran, John. 2005. *Taking Power*. Cambridge University Press.

Forst, Rainer. 2007. *Das Recht auf Rechtfertigung*. Suhrkamp.

Forster, Michael. 1993. "Hegel's Dialectical Method." In *The Cambridge Companion to Hegel*, edited by F. Beiser, 130–70. Cambridge University Press.

Foucault, Michel. 1975. *Surveiller et punir*. Gallimard.

Fourcade, Marion. 2012. "The Vile and the Noble." *Sociological Quarterly* 53:524–45.

Fourcade, Marion, and Kieran Healy. 2013. "Classification Situations." *Accounting, Organizations and Society* 38:559–72.

Frankenberg-Garcia, Ana. 2012. "Learners' Use of Corpus Examples." *International Journal of Lexicography* 25:273–96.

———. 2014. "The Use of Corpus Examples for Language Comprehension and Production." *ReCALL* 26:128–46.

Franklin-Hall, Laura. 2015. "Natural Kinds as Categorical Bottlenecks." *Philosophical Studies* 172:925–48.

Franzen, Martina, Monika Krause, Christian Dayé, Verena Halsmayer, Julian Hamann, Nicole Holzhauser, Jasper Korte, Fran Osrecki, Andrea Ploder, and Barbara Sutter. 2019. "Das DFG-Netzwerk 'Soziologie soziologischen Wissens.'" *Soziologie* 48:293–308.

Freedman, David H. 1998. "When Is a Planet Not a Planet?" *Atlantic*, February 1998.

Freese, Jeremy, and Molly M. King. 2018. "Institutionalizing Transparency." *Socius* 4:1–7.

Freese, Jeremy, and David Peterson. 2017. "Replication in Social Science." *Annual Review of Sociology* 43:147–65.

———. 2018. "The Emergence of Statistical Objectivity." *Sociological Theory* 36:289–313.

Frege, Gottlob. 1884. *Die Grundlagen der Arithmetik*. Verlag von Wilhelm Koebner.

———. 1892. "Über Sinn und Bedeutung." *Zeitschrift für Philosophie und philosophische Kritik* 100:25–50.

Frickel, Scott, and Neil Gross. 2005. "A General Theory of Scientific/Intellectual Movements." *American Sociological Review* 70:204–32.

Fricker, Miranda. 2007. *Epistemic Injustice*. Oxford University Press.

Frohlich, Norman, Joe A. Oppenheimer, and Cheryl L. Eavey. 1987. "Laboratory Results on Rawls's Distributive Justice." *British Journal of Political Science* 17:1–21.

Fuerstein, Michael. 2021. "Epistemic Democracy without Truth." *Raisons politiques* 81:81–96.

Fuertes-Olivera, Pedro A. 2012. "Lexicography and the Internet as a (Re-)source." *Lexicographica* 28:49–70.

———, ed. 2018. *The Routledge Handbook of Lexicography*. Routledge.

Fuhse, Jan. 2022. "How Can Theories Represent Social Phenomena?" *Sociological Theory* 40:99–123.

Fuller, Steve. 1988. *Social Epistemology*. Indiana University Press.

Fung, Archon, and Erik Olin Wright. 2001. "Deepening Democracy." *Politics & Society* 29:5–41.

Futter, Dylan B. 2019. "The Socratic Fallacy Undone." *British Journal for the History of Philosophy* 27:1071–91.

Gagné-Julien, Anne-Marie. 2021. "Dysfunction and the Definition of Mental Disorder in the DSM." *Philosophy, Psychiatry, & Psychology* 28:353–70.

Gagnon, Jean-Paul. 2018. "2,234 Descriptions of Democracy." *Democratic Theory* 5:92–113.

Gagnon, Jean-Paul, Emily Beausoleil, Kyong-Min Son, Cleve Arguelles, Pierrick Chalaye, and Callum N. Johnston. 2018. "What Is Populism? Who Is the Populist?" Editorial. *Democratic Theory* 5:v–xxvi.

Galbraith, John Kenneth. 1964. "Let Us Begin." *Harper's*, March 1964:16–26.

Galeano, Eduardo. 1993. *Las palabras andantes*. Catálogos.

Gallie, W. B. 1956. "Essentially Contested Concepts." *Proceedings of the Aristotelian Society* 56:167–98.

Galston, William A. 2010. "Realism in Political Theory." *European Journal of Political Theory* 9:385–411.

Gambetta, Diego. 1988. "Can We Trust Trust?" In *Trust*, edited by Gambetta, 213–37. Basil Blackwell.

Ganeri, Jonardon. 2017. *Attention, Not Self*. Oxford University Press.

García, Ofelia, Nelson Flores, and Massimiliano Spotti, eds. 2017. *The Oxford Handbook of Language and Society*. Oxford University Press.

Garfinkel, Harold. 1967. *Studies in Ethnomethodology*. Prentice-Hall.

Gasking, Douglas. 1960. "Clusters." *Australasian Journal of Philosophy* 38:1–36.

Gasparri, Luca. 2021. "A Pluralistic Theory of Wordhood." *Mind & Language* 36:592–609.

Gasparri, Luca, and Diego Marconi. 2019. "Word Meaning." In *The Stanford Encyclopedia of Philosophy*, Fall 2019 ed., edited by E. N. Zalta. Metaphysics Research Lab, Center for the Study of Language and Information, Stanford University.

Gaut, Berys. 2000. "'Art' as a Cluster Concept." In *Theories of Art Today*, edited by Carroll, 25–44. University of Wisconsin Press.

———. 2005. "The Cluster Account of Art Defended." *British Journal of Aesthetics* 45:273–88.

Gayon, Jean. 1996. "De la catégorie de style en histoire des sciences." *Alliage* 26:13–25.

Geach, P. T. 1966. "Plato's *Euthyphro*." *Monist* 50:369–82.

Geeraerts, Dirk. 1989. "Introduction: Prospects and Problems of Prototype Theory." *Linguistics* 27:587–612.

———. 2016. "Lexicography and Theories of Lexical Semantics." In *The Oxford Handbook of Lexicography*, edited by P. Durkin, 425–38. Oxford University Press.

Gellner, Ernest. 1985. *Relativism and the Social Sciences*. Cambridge University Press.

Gerlach, Philipp. 2017. "The Games Economists Play." *PLoS ONE* 12:e0183814.

Gerring, John. 1999. "What Makes a Concept Good?" *Polity* 31:357–93.

———. 2012. *Social Science Methodology*. 2nd ed. Cambridge University Press.

Gersovitz, Mark, and Norma Kriger. 2013. "What Is a Civil War?" *World Bank Research Observer* 28:159–90.

Gettier, Edmund L. 1963. "Is Justified True Belief Knowledge?" *Analysis* 23:121–23.

Geuss, Raymond. 2008. *Philosophy and Real Politics*. Princeton University Press.

Gewirtz, Paul. 1996. "On 'I Know It When I See It.'" *Yale Law Journal* 105:1023–47.

Gibson, James J. 1979. *The Ecological Approach to Visual Perception*. Houghton Mifflin.

Gieryn, Thomas F. 1983. "Boundary-Work and the Demarcation of Science from Non-science." *American Sociological Review* 48:781–95.

———. 2000. "A Space for Place in Sociology." *Annual Review of Sociology* 26:463–96.

———. 2002. "What Buildings Do." *Theory and Society* 31:35–74.

Gilbert, Margaret. 1989. *On Social Facts*. Princeton University Press.

———. 1990. "Walking Together." *Midwest Studies in Philosophy* 15:1–14.

Gilbert, Scott F., Jan Sapp, and Alfred I. Tauber. 2012. "A Symbiotic View of Life." *Quarterly Review of Biology* 87:325–41.

Gilbert, Scott F., and Alfred I. Tauber. 2016. "Rethinking Individuality." *Biology & Philosophy* 31:839–53.

Gingras, Yves. 2010. "Naming without Necessity." *Revue de synthèse* 131:439–54.

Glaeser, Andreas. 2014. "Hermeneutic Institutionalism." *Qualitative Sociology* 37:207–41.

Go, Julian. 2020. "Race, Empire, and Epistemic Exclusion." *Sociological Theory* 38:79–100.

Godman, Marion. 2018. "Gender as a Historical Kind." *Biology & Philosophy* 33:21.

———. 2021. "Scientific Realism with Historical Essences." *Synthese* 198:S3041–57.

Goertz, Gary. 2006. *Social Science Concepts*. Princeton University Press.

———. 2008. "Concepts, Theories, and Numbers." In *The Oxford Handbook of Political Methodology*, edited by J. M. Box-Steffensmeier, H. E. Brady, and D. Collier, 97–118. Oxford University Press.

Goertz, Gary, and James Mahoney. 2012. "Concepts and Measurement." *Social Science Information* 51:205–16.

Goffman, Erving. (1955) 1967. "On Face-Work." In *Interaction Ritual*, 5–45. Penguin.

———. 1956. *The Presentation of Self in Everyday Life*. Edinburgh University Press.

———. 1963. *Behavior in Public Places*. Free Press.

———. (1974) 1986. *Frame Analysis*. Northeastern University Press.

———. 1981. *Forms of Talk*. University of Pennsylvania Press.

Goldman, Alvin I. 1999. *Knowledge in a Social World*. Oxford University Press.

Goodin, Robert E., and Kai Spiekermann. 2018. *An Epistemic Theory of Democracy*. Oxford University Press.

Goodman, Nelson. (1951) 1977. *The Structure of Appearance*. 3rd ed. D. Reidel.

———. 1961. "About." *Mind* 70:1–24.

———. 1972. "Seven Strictures on Similarity." In *Problems and Projects*, 437–46 Bobbs-Merrill.

Goodwin, Jeff. 2001. *No Other Way Out.* Cambridge University Press.

Gorlée, Dinda L. 2012. *Wittgenstein in Translation.* De Gruyter Mouton.

Gorski, Philip S. 2004. "The Poverty of Deductivism." *Sociological Methodology* 34:1–33.

Gould, Julius. 1977. "Interconcept: Selected Issues for Planning and Practice." Meeting of Experts on "Interconcept" Principles and Strategies, Paris, UNESCO, May 9–11, 1977. SS/77/ CONF.601/3.

Gould, Julius, and William L. Kolb, eds. 1964. *A Dictionary of the Social Sciences.* Free Press of Glencoe.

Gouldner, Alvin W. 1970. *The Coming Crisis of Western Sociology.* Basic Books.

Gracia, Jorge J. E., ed. 1994. *Individuation in Scholasticism.* State University of New York Press.

Graham, Alma. (1973) 1974. "The Making of a Nonsexist Dictionary." *ETC: A Review of General Semantics* 31:57–64.

Greco, Daniel. 2015. "Verbal Debates in Epistemology." *American Philosophical Quarterly* 52:41–55.

Greco, John. 2012. "A (Different) Virtue Epistemology." *Philosophy and Phenomenological Research* 85:1–26.

Green, Christopher D. 1992. "Of Immortal Mythological Beasts." *Theory & Psychology* 2:291–320.

Grice, Paul. 1989. *Studies in the Ways of Words.* Harvard University Press.

Grinspoon, David, and Alan Stern. 2018. "Yes, Pluto Is a Planet." *Washington Post*, May 7, 2018.

Grosley, Pierre-Jean. 1772. *A Tour to London; or, New Observations on England, and Its Inhabitants.* Translated by Thomas Nugent. Vol. 1. Lockyer Davis.

Gross, Neil. 2018a. "Pragmatism and the Study of Large-Scale Social Phenomena." *Theory and Society* 47:87–111.

———. 2018b. "The Structure of Causal Chains." *Sociological Theory* 36:343–67.

Grundmann, Thomas. 2019. "How to Respond Rationally to Peer Disagreement." *Philosophical Issues* 29:129–42.

Gruntman, Michal, Dorothee Groß, Maria Májeková, and Katja Tielbörger. 2017. "Decision-Making in Plants under Competition." *Nature Communications* 8:2235.

Guay, Alexandre, and Thomas Pradeu, eds. 2016. *Individuals across the Sciences.* Oxford University Press.

Guerrero, Alexander A. 2014. "Against Elections." *Philosophy & Public Affairs* 42:135–78.

Guhin, Jeffrey. 2014. "Religion as Site rather than Religion as Category." *Sociology of Religion* 75:579–93.

Gunnell, John G. 1998. "Time and Interpretation." *History of Political Thought* 19:641–58.

———. 2011. *Political Theory and Social Science.* Palgrave Macmillan.

———. 2017. *John. G. Gunnell.* Edited by C. Robinson. Routledge.

———. 2020. *Conventional Realism and Political Inquiry.* University of Chicago Press.

Gupta, Anil. 2019. "Definitions." In *The Stanford Encyclopedia of Philosophy*, Winter 2019 ed., edited by E. N. Zalta. Metaphysics Research Lab, Center for the Study of Language and Information, Stanford University.

Gureje, Oye, and Dan J. Stein. 2012. "Classification of Mental Disorders." *International Review of Psychiatry* 24:606–12.

Gutiérrez Rodríguez, Encarnación, Manuela Boatcă, and Sérgio Costa, eds. 2010. *Decolonizing European Sociology*. Ashgate.

Gutmann, Amy, and Dennis F. Thompson. 2004. *Why Deliberative Democracy?* Princeton University Press.

Haack, Susan. 2004. "Coherence, Consistency, Cogency, Congruity, Cohesiveness, &c." *New Literary History* 35:167–83.

Haber, Michael. 2009. "Astronomers Declare February No Longer a Month." GCFL.net, January 20, 2009. https://gcfl.net/archive.php?funny=4775.

Haberkorn, Leonardo. 2007. "El socialista que degradó a Plutón." *Gatopardo* 75:162–74.

Habermas, Jürgen. 1968a. *Erkenntnis und Interesse*. Suhrkamp.

———. 1968b. *Technik und Wissenschaft als Ideologie*. Suhrkamp.

———. (1992) 1996. *Between Facts and Norms*. Translated by William Rehg. MIT Press.

Hacking, Ian. 1990a. *The Taming of Chance*. Cambridge University Press.

———. 1990b. "Two Kinds of 'New Historicism' for Philosophers." *New Literary History* 21:343–64.

———. 1991. "A Tradition of Natural Kinds." *Philosophical Studies* 61:109–26.

———. 1992. "'Style' for Historians and Philosophers." *Studies in History and Philosophy of Science Part A* 23:1–20.

———. 1995. "The Looping Effects of Human Kinds." In *Causal Cognition*, edited by D. Sperber, D. Premack, and A. J. Premack, 351–83. Clarendon.

———. 1999. *The Social Construction of What?* Harvard University Press.

———. 2002. *Historical Ontology*. Harvard University Press.

———. 2007a. "Kinds of People: Moving Targets." *Proceedings of the British Academy* 151:285–318.

———. 2007b. "Natural Kinds: Rosy Dawn, Scholastic Twilight." *Royal Institute of Philosophy Supplements* 61:203–39.

Hagstrom, Warren O. 1965. *The Scientific Community*. Basic Books.

Hallen, Barry. 1995. "Indeterminacy, Ethnophilosophy, Linguistic Philosophy, African Philosophy." *Philosophy* 70:377–94.

Hamann, Julian. 2016. "Peer Review Post Mortem: Bewertungen in akademischen Nachrufen." *Berliner Journal für Soziologie* 26:433–57.

———. 2018. "Boundary Work between Two Cultures." *History of Humanities* 3:27–38.

———. 2019. "The Making of Professors." *Social Studies of Science* 49:919–41.

Hamann, Julian, and Anna Kosmützky. 2021. "Does Higher Education Research Have a Theory Deficit?" *European Journal of Higher Education* 11 (S1): 468–88.

Hanks, Patrick. 2016. "Definition." In *The Oxford Handbook of Lexicography*, edited by P. Durkin, 94–122. Oxford University Press.

Hannan, M., G. Le Mens, G. Hsu, B. Kovács, G. Negro, L. Pólos, E. Pontikes, and A. Sharkey. 2019. *Concepts and Categories*. Columbia University Press.

Hanson, Norwood Russell. 1958. *Patterns of Discovery*. Cambridge University Press.

Haraway, Donna. 1988. "Situated Knowledges." *Feminist Studies* 14:575–99.

Hardcastle, Gary L. 1995. "S. S. Stevens and the Origins of Operationism." *Philosophy of Science* 62:404–24.

Harding, Sandra. 1991. *Whose Science? Whose Knowledge?* Cornell University Press.

——. 1995. "'Strong Objectivity.'" *Synthese* 104:331–49.

Hargraves, Orin. 2018. "Information Retrieval for Lexicographic Purposes." In *The Routledge Handbook of Lexicography*, edited by P. A. Fuertes-Olivera, 701–14. Routledge.

Harris, Roy, and Christopher Hutton. 2007. *Definition in Theory and Practice*. Continuum.

Hart, H.L.A. (1953) 1983. "Definition and Theory in Jurisprudence." In *Essays in Jurisprudence and Philosophy*, 21–48. Clarendon.

Hart, Hornell. 1940. "Operationism Analysed Operationally." *Philosophy of Science* 7:288–313.

——. 1943. "Some Methods for Improving Sociological Definitions." *American Sociological Review* 8:333–42.

——. 1953. "Toward an Operational Definition of the Term 'Operation.'" *American Sociological Review* 18:612–17.

Hartmann, Martin. 2011. *Die Praxis des Vertrauens*. Suhrkamp.

——. 2020. *Vertrauen*. S. Fischer Verlag.

Hartmann, R.R.K., and Gregory James. 1998. *Dictionary of Lexicography*. Routledge.

Haskell, Thomas L. 1990. "Objectivity Is Not Neutrality." *History and Theory* 29:129–57.

Haslanger, Sally. 2000. "Gender and Race: (What) Are They? (What) Do We Want Them to Be?" *Noûs* 34:31–55.

——. 2006. "What Good Are Our Intuitions?" *Proceedings of the Aristotelian Society* 80:89–118.

Haug, Matthew C., ed. 2014. *Philosophical Methodology*. Routledge.

Haugeland, John. 1979. "Understanding Natural Language." *Journal of Philosophy* 76:619–32.

Hawley, Katherine. 2019. *How to Be Trustworthy*. Oxford University Press.

Hayek, F. A. 1952. *The Counter-Revolution of Science*. Free Press.

Healy, Kieran. 2015. "The Performativity of Networks." *European Journal of Sociology* 56:175–205.

——. 2017. "Fuck Nuance." *Sociological Theory* 35:118–27.

Hearnshaw, L. S. 1941. "Psychology and Operationism." *Australasian Journal of Psychology and Philosophy* 19:44–57.

Heffern, Rich. 2008. "Wrong Language Renders Baptism Null." *National Catholic Reporter*, March 21, 2008.

Heid, Ulrich, Daan J. Prinsloo, and Theo J.D. Bothma. 2012. "Dictionary and Corpus Data in a Common Portal." *Lexicographica* 28:269–92.

Heigl, F., B. Kieslinger, K. Paul, J. Uhlik, and D. Dörler. 2019. "Toward an International Definition of Citizen Science." *Proceedings of the National Academy of Sciences of the USA* 116:8089–92.

Heilbron, Johan, Nicolas Guilhot, and Laurent Jeanpierre. 2008. "Toward a Transnational History of the Social Sciences." *Journal of the History of the Behavioral Sciences* 44:146–60.

Hempel, Carl G. 1942. "The Function of General Laws in History." *Journal of Philosophy* 39:35–48.

——. 1952. *Fundamentals of Concept Formation in Empirical Science*. University of Chicago Press.

——. 1958. "The Theoretician's Dilemma." *Minnesota Studies in the Philosophy of Science* 2:37–98.

——. 1965. *Aspects of Scientific Explanation*. Free Press.

Herman, Edward S., and Noam Chomsky. 1988. *Manufacturing Consent*. Pantheon Books.

Herzog, Lisa, and Robert Lepenies. Forthcoming. "Citizen Science in Deliberative Systems." *Minerva*.

Heuberger, Reinhard. 2016. "Learners' Dictionaries." In *The Oxford Handbook of Lexicography*, edited by P. Durkin, 25–43. Oxford University Press.

Hicks, Daniel J. 2014. "A New Direction for Science and Values." *Synthese* 191:3271–95.

Higginbotham, James. 1998. "Conceptual Competence." *Philosophical Issues* 9:149–62.

Hill, Alette Olin, and Boyd H. Hill Jr. 1980. "Marc Bloch and Comparative History." *American Historical Review* 85:828–46.

Hintikka, Jaakko. 1974. "Practical vs. Theoretical Reason: An Ambiguous Legacy." In *Practical Reason*, edited by S. Körner, 83–102. Yale University Press.

———. 2004. *Analyses of Aristotle*. Kluwer.

Hirsch, Arthur. 2017. "Scientists Make the Case to Restore Pluto's Planet Status." *Hub*, March 16, 2017. https://hub.jhu.edu/2017/03/16/make-pluto-a-planet-again/.

Hirsch, Eli. 2005. "Physical-Object Ontology, Verbal Disputes, and Plain English." *Philosophy and Phenomenological Research* 70:67–97.

———. 2011. *Quantifier Variance and Realism*. Oxford University Press.

Hirschauer, Stefan. 2010. "Editorial Judgments." *Social Studies of Science* 40:71–103.

———. 2015. "How Editors Decide." *Human Studies* 38:37–55.

Hirschman, Albert O. 1986. *Rival Views of Market Society and Other Recent Essays*. Viking.

Hobbes, Thomas. 1651. *Leviathan, or The Matter, Forme, & Power of a Common-Wealth Ecclesiasticall and Civill*. Green Dragon in St. Pauls Church-yard, for Andrew Crooke.

Hodgman, John. 2020. "Judge John Hodgman on 'Sandwich-ness.'" *New York Times Magazine*, March 19, 2020. https://www.nytimes.com/2020/03/19/magazine/judge-john-hodgman-on-sandwich-ness.html.

Hoenig, Christina. 2019. "Notes on the Etymologies in Plato's *Cratylus*." *Classical Quarterly* 69:557–65.

Hogan, Jenny. 2006a. "Planets Are Round. Will That Do?" *Nature* 442:724–25.

———. 2006b. "Pluto Loses Planet Status." *Nature News*. Published August 24, 2006; last updated August 25, 2006. https://www.nature.com/news/2006/060821/full/news060821-11.html.

———. 2006c. "Pluto: The Backlash Begins." *Nature* 442:965–66.

Hogenboom, Melissa. 2013. "What Does a Stem Cell Burger Taste Like?" *BBC News*, August 5, 2013. https://www.bbc.com/news/science-environment-23529841.

Hollis, Martin. 1967. "The Limits of Irrationality." *European Journal of Sociology* 8:265–71.

———. 1977. *Models of Man*. Cambridge University Press.

Hollis, Martin, and Steven Lukes, eds. 1982. *Rationality and Relativism*. MIT Press.

Holmes, Oliver. 2020. "I Tried the World's First No-Kill, Lab-Grown Chicken Burger." *Guardian*, December 4, 2020.

Holzhauser, Nicole, and Frank Eggert. 2019. "The Role of Measurement in Theorising about the World." *Social Science Information* 58:301–26.

Hom, Christopher. 2010. "Pejoratives." *Philosophy Compass* 5:164–85.

Homans, George C. 1967. *The Nature of Social Science*. Harcourt, Brace and World.

Hong, Lu, and Scott E. Page. 2004. "Groups of Diverse Problem Solvers Can Outperform Groups of High-Ability Problem Solvers." *Proceedings of the National Academy of Sciences of the USA* 101:16385–89.

Horace [Quintus Horatius Flaccus]. 1749. *A Poetical Translation of the Works of Horace*. Translated by Philip Francis. Vol. 2. 3rd ed. A. Millar. (*Ars poetica* written about 19–18 BCE.)

Horton, John. 2017. "What Might It Mean for Political Theory to Be More 'Realistic'?" *Philosophia* 45:487–501.

Horwich, Paul. 2005. *Reflections on Meaning*. Oxford University Press.

Hoyningen-Huene, Paul. 1990. "Kuhn's Conception of Incommensurability." *Studies in History and Philosophy of Science* 21:481–92.

Hoyningen-Huene, Paul, and Howard Sankey, eds. 2001. *Incommensurability and Related Matters*. Kluwer.

Hu, Ivan. 2017. "'Vague' at Higher Orders." *Mind* 126:1189–216.

Hu, Lily, and Issa Kohler-Hausmann. 2020. "What's Sex Got to Do with Fair Machine Learning?" In *FAT* '20: Proceedings of the 2020 Conference on Fairness, Accountability, and Transparency*, 513. Association for Computing Machinery.

Huang, Karen, Joshua D. Greene, and Max Bazerman. 2019. "Veil-of-Ignorance Reasoning Favors the Greater Good." *Proceedings of the National Academy of Sciences of the USA* 116:23989–95.

Hughes, Everett C. 1961. "Ethnocentric Sociology." *Social Forces* 40:1–4.

Hull, David L. 1978. "A Matter of Individuality." *Philosophy of Science* 45:335–60.

Humbley, John. 1997. "Is Terminology Specialized Lexicography?" *Hermes* 18:13–31.

Hunn, Eugene. 2007. "Ethnobiology in Four Phases." *Journal of Ethnobiology* 27:1–10.

Hyde, Dominic. 1994. "Why Higher-Order Vagueness Is a Pseudo-Problem." *Mind* 103:35–41.

IAU (International Astronomical Union). 2004. Draft minutes of the Executive Committee 79th Meeting, May 24–26, 2004, UNAM, Mexico City.

Intemann, Kristen. 2001. "Science and Values." *Philosophy of Science* 68:S506–18.

———. 2005. "Feminism, Underdetermination, and Values in Science." *Philosophy of Science* 72:1001–12.

———. 2015. "Distinguishing between Legitimate and Illegitimate Values in Climate Modeling." *European Journal for Philosophy of Science* 5:217–32.

———. 2017. "Feminism, Values, and the Bias Paradox." In *Current Controversies in Values and Science*, edited by K. C. Elliott and D. Steel, 130–44. Routledge.

Ionescu, Ghiţa, and Ernest Gellner, eds. 1969. *Populism: Its Meanings and National Characteristics*. Weidenfeld and Nicolson.

Irmak, Nurbay. 2019. "An Ontology of Words." *Erkenntnis* 84:1139–58.

Irwin, Alan. 1995. *Citizen Science*. Routledge.

ISA (International Sociological Association). 1979. *ISA Bulletin*, no. 19 (Spring 1979).

Isaac, Joel. 2012. *Working Knowledge*. Harvard University Press.

Isaac, Manuel Gustavo. Forthcoming. "Which Concept of Concept for Conceptual Engineering?" *Erkenntnis*.

Isaac, Nick J. B., James Mallet, and Georgina M. Mace. 2004. "Taxonomic Inflation." *Trends in Ecology and Evolution* 19:464–69.

Ivanova, Milena. 2017. "Aesthetic Values in Science." *Philosophy Compass* 12:e12433.

Ivanova, Milena, and Steven French, eds. 2020. *The Aesthetics of Science*. Routledge.

Jakobson, Roman. 1960. "Linguistics and Poetics." In *Style in Language*, edited by T. A. Sebeok, 350–77. MIT Press.

James, Aaron. 2012. *Assholes: A Theory*. Doubleday.

James, William. 1890. *The Principles of Psychology*. Vol. 1. Henry Holt.

Janack, M. 2002. "Dilemmas of Objectivity." *Social Epistemology* 16:267–81.

Janssen, Annelli, Colin Klein, and Marc Slors. 2017. "What Is a Cognitive Ontology, Anyway?" *Philosophical Explorations* 20:123–28.

Janzen, Daniel H. 1977. "What Are Dandelions and Aphids?" *American Naturalist* 111:586–89.

Jarvie, I. C. 1984. *Rationality and Relativism*. Routledge.

Jasanoff, Sheila. 2003. "Technologies of Humility." *Minerva* 41:223–44.

Jay, Timothy. 2009. "The Utility and Ubiquity of Taboo Words." *Perspectives on Psychological Science* 4:153–61.

Jenkins, C.S.I. 2014a. "Merely Verbal Disputes." *Erkenntnis* 79 (Suppl. 1): 11–30.

———. 2014b. "Serious Verbal Disputes." *Journal of Philosophy* 111:454–69.

Jeshion, Robin. 2021. "Varieties of Pejoratives." In *The Routledge Handbook of Social and Political Philosophy of Language*, edited by J. Khoo and R. K. Sterken, 211–31. Routledge.

Johfre, Sasha Shen, and Jeremy Freese. 2021. "Reconsidering the Reference Category." *Sociological Methodology* 51:253–69.

Johnson, Jim [Bruno Latour]. 1988. "Mixing Humans and Nonhumans Together." *Social Problems* 35:298–310.

Jones, Andrew M., and Nicole Boivin. 2010. "The Malice of Inanimate Objects." In *The Oxford Handbook of Material Culture Studies*, edited by D. Hicks and M. C. Beaudry, 333–51. Oxford University Press.

Jones, Karen. 1996. "Trust as an Affective Attitude." *Ethics* 107:4–25.

Jorem, Sigurd. 2021. "Conceptual Engineering and the Implementation Problem." *Inquiry* 64:186–211.

Joseph, H.W.W.B. 1916. *An Introduction to Logic*. 2nd ed. Clarendon.

Jubb, Robert. 2012. "Tragedies of Non-ideal Theory." *European Journal of Political Theory* 11:229–46.

Jurca, Stephen M. 2013. "What's in a Name?" *Indiana Journal of Global Legal Studies* 20:1445–71.

Kadlec, Alison. 2008. "Critical Pragmatism and Deliberative Democracy." *Theoria* 117:54–80.

Kahn, Charles H. 1966. "The Greek Verb 'to Be' and the Concept of Being." *Foundations of Language* 2:245–65.

Kale Lostuvali, Elif. 2015. "Science and the Public Good in the American Research University." PhD dissertation, University of California, Berkeley.

Kaplan, Abraham. 1964. *The Conduct of Inquiry*. Chandler.

Kaplan, David. 1990. "Words." *Proceedings of the Aristotelian Society* 64:93–119.

———. 2011. "Words on Words." *Journal of Philosophy* 108:504–29.

Karban, Richard. 2015. *Plant Sensing and Communication*. University of Chicago Press.

Karban, Richard, and John L. Orrock. 2018. "A Judgment and Decision-Making Model for Plant Behavior." *Ecology* 99:1909–19.

Karsenti, Bruno. 2013. *D'une philosophie à l'autre*. Gallimard.

Kasperowski, Dick, and Thomas Hillman. 2018. "The Epistemic Culture in an Online Citizen Science Project." *Social Studies of Science* 48:564–88.

Kateman, Brian. 2019. "Non-dairy Milk Alternatives Are Experiencing a 'Holy Cow!' Moment." *Forbes*, August 19, 2019. https://www.forbes.com/sites/briankateman/2019/08/19/non-dairy-milk-alternatives-are-experiencing-a-holy-cow-moment/?sh=456ee71b4c44.

Kay, Richard S. 2009. "Original Intention and Public Meaning in Constitutional Interpretation." *Northwestern University Law Review* 103:703–26.

Keane, Webb. 2016. *Ethical Life*. Princeton University Press.

Keas, Michael N. 2018. "Systematizing the Theoretical Virtues." *Synthese* 195:2761–93.

Keil, Geert, Lara Keuck, and Rico Hauswald, eds. 2017. *Vagueness in Psychiatry*. Oxford University Press.

Keller, Simon. 2000. "An Interpretation of Plato's *Cratylus*." *Phronesis* 45:284–305.

Kelty, Christopher, and Seth Erickson. 2018. "Two Modes of Participation." *Information Society* 34:71–87.

Kelty, Christopher, and Aaron Panofsky. 2014. "Disentangling Public Participation in Science and Biomedicine." *Genome Medicine* 6:8.

Kelty, Christopher, Aaron Panofsky, Morgan Currie, Roderic Crooks, Seth Erickson, Patricia Garcia, Michael Wartenbe, and Stacy Wood. 2015. "Seven Dimensions of Contemporary Participation Disentangled." *Journal of the Association for Information Science and Technology* 66:474–88.

Kennedy, J. S. 1992. *The New Anthropomorphism*. Cambridge University Press.

Kennedy-Day, Kiki. 2003. *Books of Definition in Islamic Philosophy*. RoutledgeCurzon.

Kerlinger, Fred N. 1979. *Behavioral Research*. Holt, Rinehart and Winston.

Khalidi, Muhammad Ali. 2013. *Natural Categories and Human Kinds*. Cambridge University Press.

Kim, Brian, and Matthew McGrath, eds. 2019. *Pragmatic Encroachment in Epistemology*. Routledge.

Kincaid, Harold, John Dupré, and Alison Wylie, eds. 2007. *Value-Free Science?* Oxford University Press.

Kincaid, Harold, and Jacqueline A. Sullivan, eds. 2014. *Classifying Psychopathology*. MIT Press.

Kirchmeier, Jeffrey L., and Samuel A. Thumma. 2010. "Scaling the Lexicon Fortress." *Marquette Law Review* 94:77–259.

Kitcher, Philip. 2001. *Science, Truth, and Democracy*. Oxford University Press.

———. 2002. "On the Explanatory Role of Correspondence Truth." *Philosophy and Phenomenological Research* 64:346–64.

———. 2011. *Science in a Democratic Society*. Prometheus Books.

Kivistö, Sari. 2014. *The Vices of Learning*. Brill.

Klein, Wolfgang. 2001. "Lexicology and Lexicography." In *International Encyclopedia of the Social & Behavioral Sciences*, edited by N. J. Smelser, P. B. Baltes, et al., 8764–68. Elsevier.

Kleinman, Daniel Lee. 1998. "Beyond the Science Wars." *Politics and the Life Sciences* 17:133–45.

Klemperer, Victor. (1947) 1995. *LTI: Notizbuch eines Philologen*. Reclam.

Klinenberg, Eric. 2018. *Palaces for the People*. Crown.

Knight, Carly R., and Isaac Ariail Reed. 2019. "Meaning and Modularity." *Sociological Theory* 37:234–56.

Knobe, Joshua, and Shaun Nichols, eds. 2008. *Experimental Philosophy*. Oxford University Press.

Knuuttila, Simo, and Jaakko Hintikka, eds. 1986. *The Logic of Being*. D. Reidel.

Koch, Steffen. 2021a. "Engineering What?" *Synthese* 199:1955–75.

———. 2021b. "The Externalist Challenge to Conceptual Engineering." *Synthese* 198:327–48.

Kohler-Hausmann, Issa. 2019. "Eddie Murphy and the Dangers of Counterfactual Causal Thinking about Detecting Racial Discrimination." *Northwestern University Law Review* 113:1163–228.

Kohn, Eduardo. 2013. *How Forests Think*. University of California Press.

Korsgaard, Christine M. 1996. *The Sources of Normativity*. Cambridge University Press.

———. 2003. "Realism and Constructivism in Twentieth-Century Moral Philosophy." *Journal of Philosophical Research* 28:99–122.

Koskinen, Inkeri. 2017. "Where Is the Epistemic Community?" *Synthese* 194:4671–86.

Koslicki, Kathrin. 2007. "Towards a Neo-Aristotelian Mereology." *Dialectica* 61:127–59.

Kourany, Janet. 2010. *Philosophy of Science after Feminism*. Oxford University Press.

Krause, Monika. 2016. "The Meanings of Theorising." *British Journal of Sociology* 67:23–29.

———. 2021a. *Model Cases*. University of Chicago Press.

———. 2021b. "On Sociological Reflexivity." *Sociological Theory* 39:3–18.

Krimsky, Sheldon. 2013. "Do Financial Conflicts of Interest Bias Research?" *Science, Technology, & Human Values* 38:566–87.

Kuhn, Thomas S. (1962) 1970. *The Structure of Scientific Revolutions*. 2nd ed. University of Chicago Press.

———. 1977. *The Essential Tension*. University of Chicago Press.

Kullenberg, Christopher, and Dick Kasperowski. 2016. "What Is Citizen Science?" *PLoS ONE* 11:e0147152.

Kung, Joan. 1986. "Aristotle on 'Being Is Said in Many Ways.'" *History of Philosophy Quarterly* 3:3–18.

Kupferschmidt, Kai. 2018. "More and More Scientists Are Preregistering Their Studies. Should You?" *Science*, September 21, 2018.

Kusch, Martin. 2002. *Knowledge by Agreement*. Oxford University Press.

———. 2010. "Hacking's Historical Epistemology." *Studies in History and Philosophy of Science* 41:158–73.

Lacey, Hugh. 1999. *Is Science Value Free?* Routledge.

———. 2004. "Is There a Significant Distinction between Cognitive and Social Values?" In *Sciences, Values, and Objectivity*, edited by P. Machamer and G. Wolters, 24–51. University of Pittsburgh Press.

———. 2013. "Rehabilitating Neutrality." *Philosophical Studies* 163:77–83.

———. 2017. "Distinguishing between Cognitive and Social Values." In *Current Controversies in Values and Science*, edited by K. C. Elliott and D. Steel, 15–30. Routledge.

Laclau, Ernesto. 1996. *Emancipation(s)*. Verso.

———. 2005. *On Populist Reason*. Verso.

Lafont, Cristina. 2012. "Agreement and Consent in Kant and Habermas." *Philosophical Forum* 43:277–95.

———. 2020. *Democracy without Shortcuts*. Oxford University Press.

LaFrance, Adrienne. 2015. "What's So Great about Being a Planet?" *Atlantic*, July 14, 2015.

Lakoff, George. 1987. *Women, Fire, and Dangerous Things*. University of Chicago Press.

Lamont, Michèle. 2009. *How Professors Think*. Harvard University Press.

Lamont, Michèle, and Marcel Fournier, eds. 1992. *Symbolic Boundaries and the Making of Inequality*. University of Chicago Press.

Lamont, Michèle, and Virág Molnár. 2002. "The Study of Boundaries in the Social Sciences." *Annual Review of Sociology* 28:167–95.

Landau, Sidney I. 2001. *Dictionaries*. Cambridge University Press.

Landemore, Hélène. 2012. *Democratic Reason*. Princeton University Press.

Landemore, Hélène, and Jon Elster, eds. 2012. *Collective Wisdom*. Cambridge University Press.

Lane, Melissa. 2014. "When the Experts Are Uncertain." *Episteme* 11:97–118.

Langlitz, Nicolas. 2020. *Chimpanzee Culture Wars*. Princeton University Press.

Langton, Rae. 1993. "Speech Acts and Unspeakable Acts." *Philosophy & Public Affairs* 22:293–330.

Larkin, Brian. 2013. "The Politics and Poetics of Infrastructure." *Annual Review of Anthropology* 42:327–43.

Latour, Bruno. 1984. *Les microbes: Guerre et paix; suivi de, Irréductions*. Métailié.

———. (1984) 1988. *The Pasteurization of France*. Translated by Alan Sheridan and John Law. Harvard University Press.

———. 1999. *Pandora's Hope*. Harvard University Press.

———. 2005. *Reassembling the Social*. Oxford University Press.

Laudan, Larry. 1981. "A Confutation of Convergent Realism." *Philosophy of Science* 48:19–49.

———. 1983. "The Demise of the Demarcation Problem." In *Physics, Philosophy and Psychoanalysis*, edited by R. S. Cohen and L. Laudan, 111–27. D. Reidel.

Laurence, Stephen, and Eric Margolis. 2002. "Radical Concept Nativism." *Cognition* 86:25–55.

Law, John, and Annemarie Mol. 2008. "The Actor Enacted: Cumbria Sheep in 2001." In *Material Agency*, edited by C. Knappet and L. Malafouris, 57–77. Springer.

Lazarsfeld, Paul F. 1958. "Evidence and Inference in Social Research." *Daedalus* 87:99–130.

———. 1993. *On Social Research and Its Language*. University of Chicago Press.

LeBar, Mark. 2008. "Aristotelian Constructivism." *Social Philosophy and Policy* 25:182–213.

Lecourt, Dominique. 2002. *L'épistémologie historique de Gaston Bachelard*. J. Vrin.

Ledford, Heidi. 2008. "Disputed Definitions." *Nature* 455:1023–28.

Lee, Caroline W. 2015. "Participatory Practices in Organizations." *Sociology Compass* 9:272–88.

Lee, Caroline W., Michael McQuarrie, and Edward T. Walker, eds. 2015. *Democratizing Inequalities*. New York University Press.

Lee, Steven P. 2010. "The Moral Distinctiveness of Genocide." *Journal of Political Philosophy* 18:335–56.

Leeds, Stephen. 2007. "Correspondence Truth and Scientific Realism." *Synthese* 159:1–21.

Legg, Tess, Jenny Hatchard, and Anna B. Gilmore. 2021. "The Science for Profit Model." *PLoS ONE* 16:e0253272.

Le Goff, Jacques. 2014. *Faut-il vraiment découper l'histoire en tranches?* Seuil.

Le Grand, Julian, and Bill New. 2015. *Government Paternalism*. Princeton University Press.

Lemieux, Cyril. 2012. "Philosophie et sociologie: Le prix du passage." *Sociologie* 3:199–209.

Lemley, Mark A. 2020. "Chief Justice Webster." *Iowa Law Review* 106:299–323.

Lenman, James. 2010. "Humean Constructivism in Moral Theory." *Oxford Studies in Metaethics* 5:175–93.

Lenman, James, and Yonatan Shemmer, eds. 2012. *Constructivism in Practical Philosophy*. Oxford University Press.

Lents, Nathan H. 2016. *Not So Different*. Columbia University Press.

Leonelli, Sabina. 2016. *Data-centric Biology*. University of Chicago Press.

Lever, Annabelle. 2021. "Democracy and Truth." *Raisons politiques* 81:29–38.

Levine, Donald N. 1965. *Wax and Gold*. University of Chicago Press.

———. 1985. *The Flight from Ambiguity*. University of Chicago Press.

———. 1991. "On the Proposal to Standardize Sociological Concepts." *Perspectives* 14 (2): 6.

———. 1997. "Social Theory as a Vocation." *Perspectives* 19 (2): 1–8.

———. 2015. "Prologue: Social Theory as a Vocation." In *Social Theory as a Vocation*, xvii–xxix. Transaction.

Levins, Richard. 1966. "The Strategy of Model Building in Population Biology." *American Scientist* 54:421–31.

Lévi-Strauss, Claude. 1950. "Introduction à l'œuvre de Marcel Mauss." In *Sociologie et anthropologie* by Marcel Mauss, ix–lii. Presses universitaires de France.

Levy, Neil. 2015. "Neither Fish nor Fowl." *Noûs* 49:800–823.

Lewis, David. 1976. "The Paradoxes of Time Travel." *American Philosophical Quarterly* 13:145–52.

———. 1983. "New Work for a Theory of Universals." *Australasian Journal of Philosophy* 61:343–77.

Libera, Alain de. 1996. *La querelle des universaux*. Seuil.

Lidgard, Scott, and Lynn K. Nyhart, eds. 2017. *Biological Individuality*. University of Chicago Press.

Lieberson, Stanley. 1985. *Making it Count*. University of California Press.

Lieberson, Stanley, and Freda B. Lynn. 2002. "Barking up the Wrong Branch." *Annual Review of Sociology* 28:1–19.

Lillehammer, Hallvard. 2007. *Companions in Guilt*. Palgrave Macmillan.

List, Christian, and Robert E. Goodin. 2001. "Epistemic Democracy." *Journal of Political Philosophy* 9:277–306.

List, Christian, and Philip Pettit. 2011. *Group Agency*. Oxford University Press.

Little, Daniel. 2016. *New Directions in the Philosophy of Social Science*. Rowman and Littlefield.

Lizardo, Omar. 2014. "The End of Theorists." Lewis Coser Memorial Lecture, August 17, 2014.

Lloyd, Elisabeth A. 1995. "Objectivity and the Double Standard for Feminist Epistemologies." *Synthese* 104:351–81.

Lloyd, Elisabeth A., and Vanessa J. Schweizer. 2014. "Objectivity and a Comparison of Methodological Scenario Approaches for Climate Change Research." *Synthese* 191:2049–88.

Longino, Helen E. 1990. *Science as Social Knowledge*. Princeton University Press.

———. 1995. "Gender, Politics, and the Theoretical Virtues." *Synthese* 104:383–97.

———. 1996. "Cognitive and Non-cognitive Values in Science." In *Feminism, Science, and the Philosophy of Science*, edited by L. H. Nelson and J. Nelson, 39–58. Kluwer.

———. 2002. *The Fate of Knowledge*. Princeton University Press.

———. 2004. "How Values Can Be Good for Science." In *Science, Values, and Objectivity*, edited by P. Machamer and G. Wolters, 127–42. University of Pittsburgh Press.

———. 2013. *Studying Human Behavior*. University of Chicago Press.

Longo, Matthew, and Bernardo Zacka. 2019. "Political Theory in an Ethnographic Key." *American Political Science Review* 113:1066–70.

Lovasz, Nathalie, and Kathleen L. Slaney. 2013. "What Makes a Hypothetical Construct 'Hypo-thetical'?" *New Ideas in Psychology* 31:22–31.

Ludlow, Peter. 2014. *Living Words*. Oxford University Press.

Ludwig, David. 2017. "The Objectivity of Local Knowledge." *Synthese* 194:4705–20.

———. 2018. "Revamping the Metaphysics of Ethnobiological Classification." *Current Anthropology* 59:415–38.

Lukasiewicz, J., E. Anscombe, and K. Popper. 1953. "Symposium: The Principle of Individuation." *Aristotelian Society Supplementary Volume* 27:69–120.

Luker, Kristin. 2008. *Salsa Dancing into the Social Sciences*. Harvard University Press.

Lukes Steven. 1967. "Some Problems about Rationality." *European Journal of Sociology* 8:247–64.

———. 1974a. *Power*. Macmillan.

———. 1974b. "Relativism: Cognitive and Moral." *Proceedings of the Aristotelian Society* 48:165–89.

———. 2008. *Moral Relativism*. Picador.

———. 2021a. *Power*. 3rd ed. Red Globe.

———. 2021b. "Power and Domination." *Journal of Political Power* 14:97–108.

Lundberg, George A. 1936. "The Thoughtways of Contemporary Sociology." *American Sociological Review* 1:703–23.

———. 1939. *Foundations of Sociology*. Macmillan.

———. 1942. "Operational Definitions in the Social Sciences." *American Journal of Sociology* 47:727–45.

———. 1945. "The Growth of Scientific Method." *American Journal of Sociology* 50:502–13.

Luskin, Robert C., James S. Fishkin, and Roger Jowell. 2002. "Considered Opinions." *British Journal of Political Science* 32:455–87.

Lutz, William, ed. 1989. *Beyond Nineteen Eighty-Four*. National Council of Teachers of English.

Lyons, John. 1977. *Semantics*. Vol. 1. Cambridge University Press.

MacCorquodale, Kenneth, and Paul E. Meehl. 1948. "On a Distinction between Hypothetical Constructs and Intervening Variables." *Psychological Review* 55:95–107.

Machery, Édouard. 2009. *Doing without Concepts*. Oxford University Press.

———. 2010. "Précis of *Doing without Concepts*." *Philosophical Studies* 149:401–10.

Machiavelli, Niccolò. (1532) 1998. *The Prince*. Translated and with an introduction by Harvey C. Mansfield. University of Chicago Press.

Machuca, Diego E. 2017. "A Neo-Pyrrhonian Response to the Disagreeing about Disagreement Argument." *Synthese* 194:1663–80.

MacIntyre, Alasdair. 1966. *A Short History of Ethics*. Macmillan.

———. 1973. "The Essential Contestability of Some Social Concepts." *Ethics* 84:1–9.

MacIver, R. M. 1931. "Is Sociology a Natural Science?" In *Social Conflict: Papers Presented at the Twenty-Fifth Annual Meeting of the American Sociological Society, Held at Cleveland, Ohio, December29–31, 1930*, 25–35. University of Chicago Press.

———. 1942. *Social Causation*. Ginn.

Mack, Eric. 2017. "The Fight over Pluto Is Much Bigger than One (Dwarf) Planet." CNET, March 24, 2017. https://www.cnet.com/news/pluto-planet-new-horizons-alan-stern-iau-carolyn-porco/.

MacKenzie, Donald. 2006. *An Engine, Not a Camera*. MIT Press.

MacKenzie, Donald, Fabian Muniesa, and Lucia Siu, eds. 2007. *Do Economics Make Markets?* Princeton University Press.

Macmillan, Lord [Hugh Pattison]. 1937. *Law and Other Things*. Cambridge University Press.

Macq, Hadrien, Élise Tancoigne, and Bruno J. Strasser. 2020. "From Deliberation to Production." *Minerva* 58:489–512.

Macrae, Donald, Leonard Schapiro, F. W. Deakin, Hugh Seton-Watson, Peter Worsley, Ernest Gellner, and Isiah Berlin. 1967. *Conference on Populism: Verbatim Report*. London School of Economics.

Madison, Michael. 2006. "The Real McCoy, Sandwich Edition." Madisonian, November 16, 2006. http://madisonian.net/2006/11/16/the-real-mccoy-sandwich-edition/.

Magnus, P. D. 2018. "Taxonomy, Ontology, and Natural Kinds." *Synthese* 195:1427–39.

Mahoney, James. 2021. *The Logic of Social Science*. Princeton University Press.

Maines, David R. 1991. "On Collective Amnesia and the Concept." *Perspectives* 14 (3): 5.

Makinson, D. C. 1965. "The Paradox of the Preface." *Analysis* 25:205–7.

Malcai, Ofer, and Ronit Levine-Schnur. 2014. "Which Came First, the Procedure or the Substance?" *Oxford Journal of Legal Studies* 34:1–19.

———. 2017. "When Procedure Takes Priority." *Canadian Journal of Law & Jurisprudence* 30:187–213.

Mancuso, Stefano, and Alessandra Viola. (2013) 2015. *Brilliant Green*. Translated by Joan Benham. Island.

Mandeville, Bernard. 1705. *The Grumbling Hive: or, Knaves Turn'd Honest*. Sam Ballard.

———. (1714) 1725. *The Fable of the Bees: or, Private Vices, Publick Benefits*. 4th ed. J. Tonson.

Manning, John F. 2001. "Textualism and the Equity of the Statute." *Columbia Law Review* 101:1–127.

———. 2006. "What Divides Textualists from Purposivists?" *Columbia Law Review* 106:70–111.

Mansbridge, Jane. 1990. "Self-Interest in Political Life." *Political Theory* 18:132–53.

Marchesi, Julian R., and Jacques Ravel. 2015. "The Vocabulary of Microbiome Research." *Microbiome* 3:31.

Margalit, Avishai, and Gabriel Motzkin. 1996. "The Uniqueness of the Holocaust." *Philosophy & Public Affairs* 25:65–83.

Marglin, Stephen A. 2008. *The Dismal Science*. Harvard University Press.

Margolis, Eric, and Stephen Laurence. 2007. "The Ontology of Concepts: Abstract Objects or Mental Representations?" *Noûs* 41:561–93.

———. 2019. "Concepts." In *The Stanford Encyclopedia of Philosophy*, Summer 2019 ed., edited by E. N. Zalta. Metaphysics Research Lab, Center for the Study of Language and Information, Stanford University.

Margot, Jean-Luc. 2015. "A Quantitative Criterion for Defining Planets." *Astronomical Journal* 150:185.

Marradi, Alberto. 1989. "Teoría: Una tipología de sus significados." *Papers* 31:77–98.

———. 1990. "Classification, Typology, Taxonomy." *Quality & Quantity* 24:129–57.

Marschall, Laurence A., and Stephen P. Maran. 2009. *Pluto Confidential*. BenBella Books.

Marsden, Peter V. 2019. "Stanley Lieberson: Meta-methodologist Extraordinaire." *Sociological Methodology* 49:ix–xvii.

Martin, John Levi. 2011. *The Explanation of Social Action*. Oxford University Press.

Martín Hernández, Raquel, and Sofía Torallas Tovar. 2014. "A Magical Spell on an Ostracon at the Abbey of Montserrat." *Zeitschrift für Papyrologie und Epigraphik* 189:175–84.

Martínez Rodríguez, María Laura. 2016. "Foucauldian Imprints in the Early Works of Ian Hacking." *International Studies in the Philosophy of Science* 30:69–84.

———. 2021. *Texture in the Work of Ian Hacking*. Springer.

Marwell, Gerald, and Ruth E. Ames. 1981. "Economists Free Ride, Does Anyone Else?" *Journal of Public Economics* 15:295–310.

Marx, Karl. 1980. *Ökonomische Manuskripte und Schriften, 1858–1861*. *Text*. Dietz Verlag Berlin.

Maslíah, Leo. 1999. "La tragedia de ir a ver Titanic." In *Y pico*. World Music BA, compact disc.

Masserman, J., S. Wechkin, and W. Terris. 1964. "'Altruistic' Behavior in Rhesus Monkeys." *American Journal of Psychiatry* 121:584–85.

Matthews, P. H. 2014. *The Concise Oxford Dictionary of Linguistics*. 3rd ed. Oxford University Press.

Matthewson, John, and Michael Weisberg. 2009. "The Structure of Tradeoffs in Model Building." *Synthese* 170:169–90.

Mauss, Marcel. (1909) 1968. "La prière." In *Œuvres*, vol. 1, *Les fonctions sociales du sacré*, 357–477. Minuit.

Maxwell, Alexander. 2018. "When Theory Is a Joke: The Weinreich Witticism in Linguistics." *Beiträge zur Geschichte der Sprachwissenschaft* 28:263–92.

Maynard, Douglas W. 1985. "On the Functions of Social Conflict among Children." *American Sociological Review* 50:207–23.

Mayrl, Damon, and Nicholas Hoover Wilson. 2020. "What Do Historical Sociologists Do All Day?" *American Journal of Sociology* 125:1345–94.

McConnell-Ginet, Sally. 2008. "Words in the World." *Language* 84:497–527.

———. 2020. *Words Matter*. Cambridge University Press.

McGinnis, John O., and Michael B. Rappaport. 2019. "Unifying Original Intent and Original Public Meaning." *Northwestern University Law Review* 113:1371–418.

McKean, Benjamin L. 2016. "What Makes a Utopia Inconvenient?" *American Political Science Review* 110:876–88.

McKeon, Richard. 1998. *Selected Writings of Richard McKeon*. Vol. 1. University of Chicago Press.

———. 2005. *Selected Writings of Richard McKeon*. Vol. 2. University of Chicago Press.

Medin, Douglas L. 1989. "Concepts and Conceptual Structure." *American Psychologist* 44:1469–81.

Medin, Douglas L., and Edward E. Smith. 1984. "Concepts and Concept Formation." *Annual Review of Psychology* 35:113–38.

Medina, Eduardo. 2022. "Pastor Resigns after Incorrectly Performing Thousands of Baptisms." *New York Times*, February 14, 2022.

Megill, Allan, ed. 1994. *Rethinking Objectivity*. Duke University Press.

Mena Segarra, C. Enrique. 1977. *Aparicio Saravia: Las últimas patriadas*. Banda Oriental.

Méndez, María Pía. 2022. "An Epistemic Problem for Epistocracy." *Social Epistemology* 36:153–66.

Mennicken, Andrea, and Wendy Nelson Espeland. 2019. "What's New with Numbers?" *Annual Review of Sociology* 45:223–45.

Merrill, Thomas W. 1994. "Textualism and the Future of the *Chevron* Doctrine." *Washington University Law Quarterly* 72:351–77.

Merton, Robert K. 1938. "Science and the Social Order." *Philosophy of Science* 5:321–37.

———. 1968a. "The Matthew Effect in Science." *Science* 159:53–63.

———. 1968b. *Social Theory and Social Structure*. Free Press.

———. 1973. *The Sociology of Science*. University of Chicago Press.

Merton, Robert K., and Elinor Barber. 2004. *The Travels and Adventures of Serendipity*. Princeton University Press.

Merton, Robert K., David L. Sills, and Stephen M. Stigler. 1984. "The Kelvin Dictum and Social Science." *Journal of the History of the Behavioral Sciences* 20:319–31.

Mervis, Carolyn B., and Eleanor Rosch. 1981. "Categorization of Natural Objects." *Annual Review of Psychology* 31:89–115.

Messeri, Lisa R. 2010. "The Problem with Pluto." *Social Studies of Science* 40:187–214.

Méthot, Pierre-Oliver. 2013. "On the Genealogy of Concepts and Experimental Practices." *Studies in History and Philosophy of Science* 44:112–23.

Metzger, Philip T. 2015. "Nine Reasons Why Pluto Is a Planet." Philip Metzger's website, April 13, 2015. https://www.philipmetzger.com/nine-reasons-why-pluto-is-a-planet/.

Metzger, Philip T., M. V. Sykes, A. Stern, and K. Runyon. 2019. "The Reclassification of Asteroids from Planets to Non-planets." *Icarus* 319:21–32.

Meyer, Katrin, Leo L. Soldaat, Harald Auge, and Hans-Hermann Thulke. 2014. "Adaptive and Selective Seed Abortion Reveals Complex Conditional Decision Making in Plants." *American Naturalist* 183:376–83.

Michell, Joel. 1999. *Measurement in Psychology*. Cambridge University Press.

———. 2005. "The Logic of Measurement." *Measurement* 38:285–94.

———. 2013. "Constructs, Inferences, and Mental Measurement." *New Ideas in Psychology* 31:13–21.

———. 2020. "Thorndike's *Credo*." *Theory & Psychology* 30:309–28.

Midgley, Mary. 1974. "The Neutrality of the Moral Philosopher." *Proceedings of the Aristotelian Society* 74:211–29.

Miller, Earl K., Andreas Nieder, David J. Freedman, and Jonathan D. Wallis. 2003. "Neural Correlates of Categories and Concepts." *Current Opinion in Neurobiology* 13:198–203.

Millikan, Ruth G. 2010. *On Clear and Confused Ideas*. Cambridge University Press.

———. 2017. *Beyond Concepts*. Oxford University Press.

Milroy, James, and Lesley Milroy. 1999. *Authority in Language*. 3rd ed. Routledge.

Misak, Cheryl. 2004. "Making Disagreement Matter." *Journal of Speculative Philosophy* 18:9–22.

———. 2013. *The American Pragmatists*. Oxford University Press.

Misak, Cheryl, and Robert B. Talisse. 2021. "Pragmatism, Truth, and Democracy." *Raisons politiques* 81:11–27.

Modrak, Deborah. 2010. "Nominal Definition in Aristotle." In *Definition in Greek Philosophy*, edited by D. Charles, 252–85. Oxford University Press.

Mohr, John W., Christopher A. Bail, Margaret Frye, Jennifer C. Lena, Omar Lizardo, Terence E. McDonnell, Ann Mische, Iddo Tavory, and Frederick F. Wherry. 2020. *Measuring Culture*. Columbia University Press.

Molter, Dan. 2017. "On Mushroom Individuality." *Philosophy of Science* 84:1117–27.

———. 2019. "On Mycorrhizal Individuality." *Biology & Philosophy* 34:52.

Monsó, Susana, and Kristin Andrews. 2022. "Animal Moral Psychologies." In *The Oxford Handbook of Moral Psychology*, edited by M. Vargas and J. Doris, 388–420. Oxford University Press.

Moon, Rosamund. 1989. "Objective or Objectionable?" *English Language Research* 3:59–94.

Moore, Alfred. 2017. *Critical Elitism*. Cambridge University Press.

———. 2018. "Deliberative Democracy and Science." In *The Oxford Handbook of Deliberative Democracy*, edited by A. Bächtiger, J. S. Dryzek, J. Mansbridge, and M. Warren, 640–53. Oxford University Press.

Morgan, Mary S. 2020. "If *p*? Then What?" *History of the Human Sciences* 33:198–217.

Morgan, Stephen L., and Christopher Winship. 2012. "Bringing Context and Variability Back into Causal Analysis." In *The Oxford Handbook of Philosophy of Social Science*, edited by H. Kincaid, 319–54. Oxford University Press.

Morning, Ann. 2011. *The Nature of Race*. University of California Press.

Morreau, Michael. 2010. "It Simply Does Not Add Up." *Journal of Philosophy* 107:469–90.

Morton, Herbert C. 1994. *The Story of Webster's Third*. Cambridge University Press.

Moss, Sarah. 2018. "Moral Encroachment." *Proceedings of the Aristotelian Society* 118:177–205.

Mouffe, Chantal. 1999. "Deliberative Democracy or Agonistic Pluralism?" *Social Research* 66:745–58.

———. 2000. *The Democratic Paradox*. Verso.

———. 2005. *On the Political*. Routledge.

Moyal-Sharrock, Danièle. 2015. "Wittgenstein on Forms of Life, Patterns of Life, and Ways of Living." In "Wittgenstein and Forms of Life," edited by D. Moyal-Sharrock and P. Donatelli, special issue, *Nordic Wittgenstein Review*, October 2015: 21–42.

Mugglestone, Lynda. 2016. "Description and Prescription in Dictionaries." In *The Oxford Handbook of Lexicography*, edited by P. Durkin, 546–60. Oxford University Press.

Mulkay, Michael, Trevor Pinch, and Malcolm Ashmore. 1987. "Colonizing the Mind." *Social Studies of Science* 17:231–56.

Müller, Jan-Werner. 2016. *What Is Populism?* University of Pennsylvania Press.

Münch, Richard. 1991. *Dialektik der Kommunikationsgesellschaft*. Suhrkamp.

———. 1995. *Dynamik der Kommunikationsgesellschaft*. Suhrkamp.

Muniesa, Fabián. 2015. "Actor-Network Theory." In *International Encyclopedia of the Social & Behavioral Sciences*, 2nd ed., vol. 1, edited by J. D. Wright, 80–84. Elsevier.

Murdoch, Iris. 1956. "Vision and Choice in Morality." *Proceedings of the Aristotelian Society, Supplementary Volumes* 30:32–58.

———. (1970) 2014. *The Sovereignty of Good*. Routledge.

———. 1998. *Existentialists and Mystics*. Allen Lane.

Murphy, Kathryn, and Anita Traninger, eds. 2014. *The Emergence of Impartiality*. Brill.

Murphy, M. Lynne. 1991. "Defining Racial Labels." *Dictionaries* 13:43–64.

———. 2010. *Lexical Meaning*. Cambridge University Press.

National Cattlemen's Beef Association. 2019. *2019 Policy Book*. Washington, DC: National Cattlemen's Beef Association.

Nature. 2006. "Round Objects." 442 (7104): 719.

Needham, Rodney. 1975. "Polythetic Classification." *Man* 10:349–69.

Nehamas, Alexander. 1987. "Socratic Intellectualism." In *Proceedings of the Boston Area Colloquium in Ancient Philosophy*, edited by J. J. Cleary, 2: 275–316. University Press of America.

Nelson, Caleb. 2005. "What Is Textualism?" *Virginia Law Review* 91:347–418.

Neurath, Otto. 1944. *Foundations of the Social Sciences*. University of Chicago Press.

———. 1983. *Philosophical Papers, 1913–1946*. D. Reidel.

Newman, Edwin. 1974. *Strictly Speaking*. Bobbs-Merrill.

Newton, Richard F. (1968) 1971. "Concepts, Concepts, Concepts." In *Concepts in the Social Studies*, edited by B. K. Beyer and A. N. Penna, 3–5. National Council for the Social Studies.

Nichols, James D., Madan K. Oli, William L. Kendall, and G. Scott Boomer. 2021. "A Better Approach for Dealing with Reproducibility and Replicability in Science." *Proceedings of the National Academy of Sciences of the USA* 118:e2100769118.

Nind, Melanie. 2017. "The Practical Wisdom of Inclusive Research." *Qualitative Research* 17:278–88.

Nino, Carlos Santiago. 1996. *The Constitution of Deliberative Democracy*. Yale University Press.

Nippert-Eng, Christena. 1996. "Calendars and Keys." *Sociological Forum* 11:563–82.

Nirenberg, David, and Ricardo L. Nirenberg. 2021. *Uncountable*. University of Chicago Press.

Nongbri, Brent. 2013. *Before Religion*. Yale University Press.

Norri, Juhani. 2000. "Labelling of Derogatory Words in Some British and American Dictionaries." *International Journal of Lexicography* 13:71–106.

Norström, Albert V., Christopher Cvitanovic, Marie F. Löf, Simon West, Carina Wyborn, Patricia Balvanera, Angela T. Bednarek, et al. 2020. "Principles for Knowledge Co-production in Sustainability Research." *Nature Sustainability* 3:182–90.

Nosek, B., C. Ebersole, A. DeHaven, and D. Mellor. 2018. "The preregistration revolution." *Proceedings of the National Academy of Sciences of the USA* 115:2600–2606.

Novick, Peter. 1988. *That Noble Dream*. Cambridge University Press.

Nunberg, Geoffrey. 2012. *Ascent of the A-Word*. PublicAffairs.

Nuyts, Jan. 1989. "On the Functionality of Language." *Papers in Pragmatics* 3:88–129.

———. 1993. "On Determining the Functions of Language." *Semiotica* 94:201–32.

O'Connor, Anahad. 2019. "Fake Meat vs. Real Meat." *New York Times*, December 3, 2019.

Ogburn, William F. 1930. "The Folk-Ways of a Scientific Sociology." *Scientific Monthly* 30:300–306.

Ogden, C. K., and I. A. Richards. (1923) 1930. *The Meaning of Meaning*. 3rd ed. Kegan Paul.

Ogien, Albert. 2015. "Pragmatism's Legacy to Sociology Respecified." *European Journal of Pragmatism and American Philosophy* 7:1.

O'Neill, Onora. 1989. "Constructivisms in Ethics." *Proceedings of the Aristotelian Society* 89:1–17.

———. 2002. *A Question of Trust*. Cambridge University Press.

Ooi, Vincent. 2018. "Using the Web for Lexicographic Purposes." In *The Routledge Handbook of Lexicography*, edited by P. A. Fuertes-Olivera, 684–700. Routledge.

Oppenheimer, Hans. 1925. *Die Logik der soziologischen Begriffsbildung*. Verlag von J.C.B. Mohr (Paul Siebeck).

Ording, Philip. 2019. *99 Variations on a Proof*. Princeton University Press.

Oreskes, Naomi. 2019. *Why Trust Science*. Princeton University Press.

Orwell, George. (1945) 1964. *Animal Farm*. Longmans, Green.

———. (1946) 1968. "Politics and the English Language." In *The Collected Essays*, edited by S. Orwell and I. Angus, vol. 4, *In Front of Your Nose, 1945–1950*, 127–40. Secker and Warburg.

———. (1949) 1984. *Nineteen Eighty-Four*. Clarendon.

Osrecki, Fran. 2011. *Die Diagnosegesellschaft*. Transcript.

Ossa-Richardson, Anthony. 2019. *A History of Ambiguity*. Princeton University Press.

Ottenhoff, John. 1996. "The Perils of Prescriptivism." *American Speech* 71:272–84.

Outhwaite, William. 1983. *Concept Formation in Social Science*. Routledge.

Overbye, Dennis. 2006. "Pluto Seems Poised to Lose Its Planet Status." *New York Times*, August 22, 2006.

Pacewicz, Josh. 2022. "What Can You Do with a Single Case?" *Sociological Methods & Research* 51:931–62.

Palonen, Kari. 1997. "An Application of Conceptual History to Itself." *Finnish Yearbook of Political Thought* 1:39–69.

———. 2002. "The History of Concepts as a Style of Political Theorizing." *European Journal of Political Theory* 1:91–106.

Pamuk, Zeynep. 2021. *Politics and Expertise*. Princeton University Press.

Panizza, Francisco E., ed. 2005. *Populism and the Mirror of Democracy*. Verso.

Panizza, Silvia. 2015. "The Importance of Attention in Morality." PhD dissertation, University of East Anglia.

Panofsky, Aaron L. 2010. "A Critical Reconsideration of the Ethos and Autonomy of Science." In *Robert K. Merton*, edited by C. Calhoun, 140–63. Columbia University Press.

Pardo, Michael S., and Dennis Patterson. 2013. *Minds, Brains, and Law*. Oxford University Press.

Pareto, Vilfredo. (1916) 1935. *The Mind and Society*. Vol. 1, *Non-Logical Conduct*. Translated by Andrew Bongiorno and Arthur Livingston. Harcourt, Brace.

Park, Alexander. 2019. "Constructing the Sandwich." *Minnesota Law Review*, February 22, 2019. https://minnesotalawreview.org/2019/02/22/constructing-the-sandwich/.

Parkinson, John, and Jane Mansbridge, eds. 2012. *Deliberative Systems*. Cambridge University Press.

Parsons, Kathryn Pyne. 1973. "Three Concepts of Clusters." *Philosophy and Phenomenological Research* 33:514–23.

Pasolini, Pier Paolo. (1968) 2007. "Manifesto for a New Theatre." Translated by Thomas Simpson. *PAJ: A Journal of Performance and Art* 29:126–38.

Pasolini, Pier Paolo. 1968. "Manifesto per un nuovo teatro." *Nuovi argomenti*, new series, no. 9, January–March 1968.

Paxton, Pamela, and Jennifer L. Glanville. 2015. "Is Trust Rigid or Malleable?" *Social Psychology Quarterly* 78:194–204.

Pearson, Chris. 2017. "History and Animal Agencies." In *The Oxford Handbook of Animal Studies*, edited by L. Kalof, 240–57. Oxford University Press.

Pedersen, Morten Axel, Kristoffer Albris, and Nick Seaver. 2021. "The Political Economy of Attention." *Annual Review of Anthropology* 50:309–25.

Peirce, C. S. 1868. "Some Consequences of Four Incapacities." *Journal of Speculative Philosophy* 2:140–57.

———. 1878. "The Doctrine of Chances." *Popular Science Monthly* 12:604–15.

Penn, Derek, Keith Holyoak, and Daniel Povinelli. 2008. "Darwin's Mistake." *Behavioral and Brain Sciences* 31:109–78.

Pickering, Andrew. 1993. "The Mangle of Practice." *American Journal of Sociology* 99:559–89.

Pigliucci, Massimo. 2003. "Species as Family Resemblance Concepts." *BioEssays* 25:596–602.

Pigliucci, Massimo, and Maarten Boudry, eds. 2013. *Philosophy of Pseudoscience*. University of Chicago Press.

Pigliucci, Massimo, Kim Sterelny, and Werner Callebaut. 2013. "The Meaning of 'Theory' in Biology." *Biological Theory* 7:285–86.

Pinder, Mark. 2020. "On Strawson's Critique of Explication as a Method in Philosophy." *Synthese* 197:955–81.

Pinker, Steven. 1994. "Grammar Puss." *New Republic*, January 30, 1994.

Plag, Ingo. 2003. *Word-Formation in English*. Cambridge University Press.

Platt, Jennifer. 1996. *A History of Sociological Research Methods in America, 1920–1960*. Cambridge University Press.

Pleasants, Nigel. 2016. "The Question of the Holocaust's Uniqueness." *Journal of Applied Philosophy* 33:297–310.

Plunkett, David. 2015. "Which Concepts Should We Use?" *Inquiry* 58:828–75.

———. 2016. "Negotiating the Meaning of 'Law.'" *Legal Theory* 22:205–75.

Plunkett, David, and Tim Sundell. 2013. "Disagreement and the Semantics of Normative and Evaluative Terms." *Philosophers' Imprint* 13:1–37.

———. 2021. "Metalinguistic Negotiation and Speaker Error." *Inquiry* 64:142–67.

Poincaré, H. (1902) 1917. *La science et l'hypothèse*. Flammarion.

Politis, Vasilis. 2015. *The Structure of Enquiry in Plato's Early Dialogues*. Cambridge University Press.

Polletta, Francesca. 2002. *Freedom Is an Endless Meeting*. University of Chicago Press.

———. 2014. "Is Participation without Power Good Enough?" *Sociological Quarterly* 55:453–66.

Polletta, Francesca, and Beth Gardner. 2018. "The Forms of Deliberative Communication." In *The Oxford Handbook of Deliberative Democracy*, edited by A. Bächtiger, J. S. Dryzek, J. Mansbridge, and M. Warren, 70–85. Oxford University Press.

Pollock, Joey. 2019. "Conceptual Engineering and Semantic Deference." *Studia philosophica Estonica* 12:81–98.

Popper, Karl. (1935) 2002. *The Logic of Scientific Discovery*. Translated by the author, with Julius Freed and Lan Freed. Routledge.

———. (1963) 2002. *Conjectures and Refutations*. Routledge.

Porpora, Douglas V. 2015. *Reconstructing Sociology*. Cambridge University Press.

Porter, Theodore M. 1995. *Trust in Numbers*. Princeton University Press.

Posner, Richard A. 2005. *Law, Pragmatism, and Democracy*. Harvard University Press.

———. 2012. "The Incoherence of Antonin Scalia." *New Republic*, August 24, 2012.

Potochnik, Angela. 2015. "The Diverse Aims of Science." *Studies in History and Philosophy of Science* 53:71–80.

Povinelli, Daniel. 2004. "Behind the Ape's Appearance." *Daedalus* 133:29–41.

Powell, Christopher, and François Dépelteau, eds. 2013. *Conceptualizing Relational Sociology*. Palgrave Macmillan

Pradeu, Thomas. 2010. "What Is an Organism?" *History and Philosophy of the Life Sciences* 32:247–67.

———. 2016a. "The Many Faces of Biological Individuality." *Biology & Philosophy* 31:761–73.

———. 2016b. "Organisms or Biological Individuals?" *Biology & Philosophy* 31:797–817.

Prasad, Monica. 2021a. "Pragmatism as Problem Solving." *Socius* 7:1–13.

———. 2021b. *Problem-Solving Sociology*. Oxford University Press.

Prendergast, Chris. 1992. "Closing Credits from the (Out-Going) Editor." *Perspectives* 15 (4): 2.

Priest, Graham. 2009. "The Structure of Emptiness." *Philosophy East & West* 59:467–80.

Prior, William J. 1998. "Plato and the 'Socratic Fallacy.'" *Phronesis* 43:97–113.

Pritchard, Duncan. 2007. "Recent Work on Epistemic Value." *American Philosophical Quarterly* 44:85–110.

———. 2021. "Intellectual Virtues and the Epistemic Value of Truth." *Synthese* 198:5515–28.

Przeworski, Adam. 1998. "Deliberation and Ideological Domination." In *Deliberative Democracy*, edited by J. Elster, 140–60. Cambridge University Press.

Przeworski, Adam, and Henry Teune. 1970. *The Logic of Comparative Social Inquiry*. Krieger.

Putnam, Hilary. 1973. "Meaning and Reference." *Journal of Philosophy* 70:699–711.

———. 1975a. "The Meaning of 'Meaning.'" In *Language, Mind and Knowledge*, Minnesota Studies in the Philosophy of Science vol. 7, edited by K. Gunderson, 131–93. University of Minnesota Press.

———. 1975b. *Mind, Language and Reality*. Cambridge University Press.

———. 1981. *Reason, Truth, and History*. Cambridge University Press.

———. 1987. *The Many Faces of Realism*. Open Court.

———. 1988. *Representation and Reality*. MIT Press.

———. 2002. *The Collapse of the Fact/Value Dichotomy and Other Essays*. Harvard University Press.

Putnam, Hilary, and Vivian Walsh, eds. 2012. *The End of Value-Free Economics*. Routledge.

Queloz, Matthieu, and Friedemann Bieber. 2022. "Conceptual Engineering and the Politics of Implementation." *Pacific Philosophical Quarterly* 103:670–91.

Queneau, Raymond. 1947. *Exercises de style*. Gallimard.

Quervel-Chaumette, M., V. Faerber, T. Faragó, S. Marshall-Pescini, and F. Range. 2016. "Investigating Empathy-Like Responding to Conspecifics' Distress in Pet Dogs." *PLoS ONE* 11:e0152920.

Quine, Willard Van Orman. 1951. "Two Dogmas of Empiricism." *Philosophical Review* 60:20–43.

———. 1960. *Word and Object*. MIT Press.

———. 1975. "On Empirically Equivalent Systems of the World." *Erkenntnis* 9:313–28.

Racine, Timothy P., and Kathleen L. Slaney, eds. 2013. *A Wittgensteinian Perspective on the Use of Conceptual Analysis in Psychology*. Palgrave Macmillan.

Radomsky, Stephan. 2020. "Bundesfinanzhof stellt fest: Techno ist Musik." *Süddeutsche Zeitung*, October 29, 2020.

Ragin, Charles C. 2000. *Fuzzy-Set Social Science*. University of Chicago Press.

Ragin, Charles C., and Howard S. Becker, eds. 1992. *What Is a Case?* Cambridge University Press.

Rapoport, Anatol. 1958. "Various Meanings of 'Theory.'" *American Political Science Review* 52:972–88.

Rawls, Anne Warfield. 1996. "Durkheim's Epistemology." *American Journal of Sociology* 102:430–82.

Rawls, John. 1971. *A Theory of Justice*. Harvard University Press.

———. 1980. "Kantian Constructivism in Moral Theory." *Journal of Philosophy* 77:515–72.

———. 1999. *The Law of Peoples*. Harvard University Press.

Rayo, Agustín. 2013. *The Construction of Logical Space*. Oxford University Press.

Reed, Isaac. 2011. *Interpretation and Social Knowledge*. University of Chicago Press.

Reiss, Julian. 2017. "Fact-Value Entanglement in Positive Economics." *Journal of Economic Methodology* 24:134–49.

———. 2019. "Expertise, Agreement, and the Nature of Social Scientific Facts or: Against Epistocracy." *Social Epistemology* 33:183–92.

Reuter, Kevin. 2019. "Dual Character Concepts." *Philosophy Compass* 14:e12557.

Reydon, Thomas A. C. 2003. "Species Are Individuals—Or Are They?" *Philosophy of Science* 70:49–56.

Reydon, Thomas A. C., and Marc Ereshefsky. 2022. "How to Incorporate Non-epistemic Values into a Theory of Classification." *European Journal for Philosophy of Science* 12:4.

Rheinberger, Hans-Jörg. 2007. *Historische Epistemologie zur Einführung*. Junius Verlag.

Ribeiro, Gustavo. 2021. "Evidentiary Policies through Other Means." *Utah Law Review* 2021:441–78.

Richards, Richard A. 2010. *The Species Problem*. Cambridge University Press.

Richter, Melvin. 1987. "*Begriffsgeschichte* and the History of Ideas." *Journal of the History of Ideas* 48:247–63.

———. 1993. "Towards a Lexicon of European Political and Legal Concepts." *Critical Review of International Social and Political Philosophy* 6:91–120.

———. 1995. *The History of Political and Social Concepts*. Oxford University Press.

Rickert, Heinrich. (1902) 1913. *Die Grenzen der naturwissenschaftlichen Begriffsbildung*. J.C.B. Mohr.

Rieppel, Olivier. 2007. "Species." *Cladistics* 23:373–84.

Riggs, Fred W. 1979. "The Importance of Concepts." *American Sociologist* 14:172–85.

———. 1981. *Interconcept Report: A New Paradigm for Solving the Terminology Problems of the Social Sciences*. UNESCO.

———. 1986. *Help for Social Scientists: A New Kind of Reference Process*. UNESCO.

———. 1988. *The Intercocta Manual: Towards an International Encyclopedia of Social Science Terms*. UNESCO.

Riley, Dylan, Patricia Ahmed, and Rebecca Jean Emigh. 2021. "Getting Real." *Theory and Society* 50:315–56.

Risinger, D. Michael. 1982. "'Substance' and 'Procedure' Revisited with Some Afterthoughts on the Constitutional Problems of Irrebuttable Presumptions." *UCLA Law Review* 30:189–216.

"The Risk of Cyber War and Cyber Terrorism," 2017. Interview with Richard A. Clarke. *Journal of International Affairs*, June 1, 2017, https://jia.sipa.columbia.edu/risk-cyber-war-and-cyber-terrorism.

Ritchie, Katherine. 2013. "What Are Groups?" *Philosophical Studies* 166:257–72.

———. 2015. "The Metaphysics of Social Groups." *Philosophy Compass* 10:310–21.

———. 2020. "Social Structures and the Ontology of Social Groups." *Philosophy and Phenomenological Research* 100:402–24.

Ritvo, Harriet. 1997. *The Platypus and the Mermaid, and Other Figments of the Classifying Imagination.* Harvard University Press.

Robbins, Blaine G. 2016. "What Is Trust?" *Sociology Compass* 10:972–86.

Roberson, Debi, Ian Davies, and Jules Davidoff. 2000. "Color Categories Are Not Universal." *Journal of Experimental Psychology: General* 129:369–98.

Roberts, Debbie. 2013. "Thick Concepts." *Philosophy Compass* 8:677–88.

Roberts, Molly. 2018. "Big Dairy Is Going after Your Almond Milk." *Washington Post*, July 24, 2018.

Robinson, David G., Andreas Draguhn, and Lincoln Taiz. 2020. "Plant 'Intelligence' Changes Nothing." *EMBO Reports* 21:e50395.

Robinson, Richard. 1941. *Plato's Earlier Dialectic.* Cornell University Press.

———. 1950. *Definition.* Clarendon.

Rodriguez Medina, Leandro. 2014. *Centers and Peripheries in Knowledge Production.* Routledge.

Rolin, Kristina. 2009. "Scientific Knowledge." In *The Social Sciences and Democracy*, edited by J. Van Bouwel, 62–80. Palgrave Macmillan.

———. 2017. "Can Social Diversity Be Best Incorporated into Science by Adopting the Social Value Management Ideal?" In *Current Controversies in Values and Science*, edited by K. C. Elliott and D. Steel, 113–29. Routledge.

Rooney, Phyllis. 1992. "On Values in Science." *PSA: Proceedings of the Biennial Meeting of the Philosophy of Science Association* 1992:13–22.

Rorty, Richard. 1979. *Philosophy and the Mirror of Nature.* Princeton University Press.

———. 1991. *Objectivity, Relativism, and Truth.* Cambridge University Press.

Rosaldo, Michelle Zimbalist. 1972. "Metaphors and Folk Classification." *Southwestern Journal of Anthropology* 28:83–99.

———. 1982. "The Things We Do with Words." *Language in Society* 11:203–37.

Rosch, Eleanor H. 1973. "Natural Categories." *Cognitive Psychology* 4:328–50.

Rosen, Gideon. 2015. "Real Definition." *Analytic Philosophy* 56:189–209.

Rovira Kaltwasser, Cristóbal, Paul Taggart, Paulina Ochoa Espejo, and Pierre Ostiguy, eds. 2017. *The Oxford Handbook of Populism.* Oxford University Press.

Rowlands, Mark. 2012. *Can Animals Be Moral?* Oxford University Press.

Ruben, David-Hillel. 2010. "W. B. Gallie and Essentially Contested Concepts." *Philosophical Papers* 39:257–70.

Rudner, Richard. 1953. "The Scientist qua Scientist Makes Value Judgments." *Philosophy of Science* 20:1–6.

———. 1961. "An Introduction to Simplicity." *Philosophy of Science* 28:109–19.

Runyon, Kirby D., and S. Alan Stern. 2018. "An Organically Grown Planet Definition: Should We Really Define a Word by Voting?" *Astronomy*, May 2018. https://astronomy.com/magazine/2018/05/an-organically-grown-planet-definition.

Runyon, Kirby D., S. Alan Stern, T. R. Lauer, W. Grundy, M. E. Summers, and K. N. Singer. 2017. "A Geophysical Planet Definition." *Lunar and Planetary Science* 48:1448.

Ruphy, Stéphanie. 2010. "Are Stellar Kinds Natural Kinds?" *Philosophy of Science* 77:1109–20.

———. 2015. *Scientific Pluralism Reconsidered*. University of Pittsburgh Press.

Ruse, Michael. 1987. "Biological Species." *British Journal for the Philosophy of Science* 38:225–42.

Russell, Lindsay Rose. 2018a. "Toward a Feminist Historiography of Lexicography." *Dictionaries* 39:167–83.

———. 2018b. *Women and Dictionary Making*. Cambridge University Press.

———. 2021. "Dictionary Boycotts and the Power of Popular (Re)definition." *Dictionaries* 42:235–47.

Ryle, Gilbert. 1932. "Systematically Misleading Expressions." *Proceedings of the Aristotelian Society* 32:139–70.

———. 1933. "About." *Analysis* 1:10–12.

Saar, Martin. 2008. "Understanding Genealogy." *Journal of the Philosophy of History* 2:295–314.

———. 2009. *Genealogie als Kritik*. Campus Verlag.

Saatsi, Juha T. 2005. "On the Pessimistic Induction and Two Fallacies." *Philosophy of Science* 72:1088–98.

Sacks, Gary, Devorah Riesenberg, Melissa Mialon, Sarah Dean, and Adrian J. Cameron. 2020. "The Characteristics and Extent of Food Industry Involvement in Peer-Reviewed Research Articles from 10 Leading Nutrition-Related Journals in 2018." *PLoS ONE* 15:e0243144.

Sadler, John Z., and Bill Fulford. 2004. "Should Patients and Their Families Contribute to the *DSM-V* Process? *Psychiatric Services* 55:133–38.

Safire, William. 1990. *Language Maven Strikes Again*. Doubleday.

Sager, Juan C., ed. 2000. *Essays on Definition*. John Benjamins.

Sainsbury, R. Mark. (1990) 2002. "Concepts without Boundaries." In *Departing from Frege*, 71–84. Routledge.

———. 1991. "Is There Higher-Order Vagueness?" *Philosophical Quarterly* 41:167–82.

Salisbury, Tate J. 2020. "Labeling the New Meats." *Washington University Law Review* 97:1603–30.

Sample, Ian. 2006. "Astronomers Expel Pluto from the Planetary Club." *Guardian*, August 25, 2006. https://www.theguardian.com/science/2006/aug/25/starsgalaxiesandplanets.spaceexploration.

Sample, Matthew. 2022. "Science, Responsibility, and the Philosophical Imagination." *Synthese* 200:79.

Sánchez-Dorado, Julia. 2020. "Novel & Worthy." *European Journal for Philosophy of Science* 10:40.

Sandberg, Jörgen, and Mats Alvesson. 2021. "Meanings of Theory." *Journal of Management Studies* 58:487–516.

Sanders, Lynn M. 1997. "Against Deliberation." *Political Theory* 25:347–76.

Sanders, Robert. 2003. "An Orb by Any Other Name." *UC Berkeley News*, February 26, 2003. https://www.berkeley.edu/news/media/releases/2003/02/26_planet.shtml.

Sandis, Constantine. 2019. "No Use Crying over . . . ?" Vegan Society blog, June 14, 2019. https://www.vegansociety.com/news/blog/no-use-crying-over%E2%80%A6.

Sankey, Howard. 1993. "Kuhn's Changing Concept of Incommensurability." *British Journal for the Philosophy of Science* 44:759–74.

———. 1994. *The Incommensurability Thesis*. Ashgate.

Santas, Gerasimos. 1972. "The Socratic Fallacy." *Journal of the History of Philosophy* 10:127–41.

Sartori, Giovanni. 1970. "Concept Misformation in Comparative Politics." *American Political Science Review* 64:1033–53.

———, ed. 1984. *Social Science Concepts*. Sage.

Sartori, Giovanni, Fred Riggs, and Henry Teune. 1975. *Tower of Babel*. University of Pittsburgh Press.

Sauder, Michael. 2019. "The Art of Acknowledgments." *Contemporary Sociology* 48:1–4.

———. 2020. "A Sociology of Luck." *Sociological Theory* 38:193–216.

Saul, Jennifer. 2006. "Gender and Race." *Proceedings of the Aristotelian Society* 80:119–43.

Sawyer, Sarah. 2018. "The Importance of Concepts." *Proceedings of the Aristotelian Society* 118:127–47.

———. 2020a. "The Role of Concepts in *Fixing Language*." *Canadian Journal of Philosophy* 50:555–65.

———. 2020b. "Talk and Thought." In *Conceptual Engineering and Conceptual Ethics*, edited by A. Burgess, H. Cappelen, and D. Plunkett, 379–95. Oxford University Press.

Sayre-McCord, Geoffrey, ed. 1988. *Essays on Moral Realism*. Cornell University Press.

Scalia, Antonin. 1995. "Common-Law Courts in a Civil-Law System: The Role of United States Federal Courts in Interpreting the Constitution and Laws." Tanner Lectures on Human Values, Princeton University, March 8–9, 1995.

Scalia, Antonin, and Bryan A. Garner. 2012. *Reading Law*. Thomson/West.

Schaffer, Frederic Charles. 2016. *Elucidating Social Science Concepts*. Routledge.

Scharp, Kevin. 2013. *Replacing Truth*. Oxford University Press.

———. 2020. "Philosophy as the Study of Defective Concepts." In *Conceptual Engineering and Conceptual Ethics*, edited by A. Burgess, H. Cappelen, and D. Plunkett, 396–416. Oxford University Press.

Scheff, Thomas J. 1990. *Microsociology*. University of Chicago Press.

Schiappa, Edward. 1993. "Arguing about Definitions." *Argumentation* 7:403–17.

———. 2003. *Defining Reality*. Southern Illinois University Press.

Schindler, Samuel. 2018. *Theoretical Virtues in Science*. Cambridge University Press.

Schneiderhan, Erik. 2013. "Genocide Reconsidered." *Journal for the Theory of Social Behaviour* 43:280–300.

Schneiderhan, Erik, and Shamus Khan. 2008. "Reasons and Inclusion." *Sociological Theory* 26:1–24.

Schnittker, Jason. 2017. *The Diagnostic System*. Columbia University Press.

Schrögel, Philipp, and Alma Kolleck. 2019. "The Many Faces of Participation in Science." *Science & Technology Studies* 32:77–99.

Schudson, Michael. 2006. "The Trouble with Experts—and Why Democracies Need Them." *Theory and Society* 35:491–506.

Schwartzberg, Melissa. 2015. "Epistemic Democracy and Its Challenges." *Annual Review of Political Science* 18:187–203.

Scott, John. 2014. *A Dictionary of Sociology*. 4th ed. Oxford University Press.

Searle, John R. 1980. "Mind, Brains, and Programs." *Behavioral and Brain Sciences* 3:417–57.

———. 1983. *Intentionality*. Cambridge University Press.

———. 1989. "How Performatives Work." *Linguistics and Philosophy* 12:535–58.

———. 1995. *The Construction of Social Reality*. Free Press.

———. 2010. *Making the Social World*. Oxford University Press.

Sedley, David. 1998. "The Etymologies in Plato's *Cratylus*." *Journal of Hellenic Studies* 118:140–54.

———. 2003. *Plato's "Cratylus."* Cambridge University Press.

Selg, Peeter. 2013. "The Politics of Theory and the Constitution of Meaning." *Sociological Theory* 31:1–23.

Sen, Amartya. 2009. *The Idea of Justice*. Belknap Press of Harvard University Press.

Serrano Zamora, Justo, and Lisa Herzog. 2022. "A Realist Epistemic Utopia?" *Journal of Social Philosophy* 53:38–58.

Severo, Fabián. 2010. *Noite nu norte*. Ediciones del Rincón.

———. 2019. "Sixty." Translated by Laura Cesarco Eglin and Jesse Lee Kercheval. *New Yorker*, December 2, 2019. https://www.newyorker.com/magazine/2019/12/02/sixty.

Sewell, William H. Jr. 1967. "Marc Bloch and the Logic of Comparative History." *History and Theory* 6:208–18.

Shapin, Steven. 1992. "Discipline and Bounding." *History of Science* 30:333–69.

———. 1995. "Here and Everywhere." *Annual Review of Sociology* 21:289–321.

———. 2010. *Never Pure*. Johns Hopkins University Press.

Shapiro, Ian. 2002. "Problems, Methods, and Theories in the Study of Politics, or What's Wrong with Political Science and What to Do about It." *Political Theory* 30:596–619.

———. 2017. "Collusion in Restraint of Democracy." *Daedalus* 146:77–84.

Shiao, Jiannbin, and Ashley Woody. 2021. "The Meaning of 'Racism.'" *Sociological Perspectives* 64:497–517.

Shiga, David. 2006. "New Planet Definition Sparks Furore." *New Scientist*, August 25, 2006. https://www.newscientist.com/article/dn9846-new-planet-definition-sparks-furore/.

———. 2008. "Great Planet Debate Ends in Stalemate." *New Scientist*, August 15, 2008. https://www.newscientist.com/article/dn14540-great-planet-debate-ends-in-stalemate/.

Sider, Theodore. 2011. *Writing the Book of the World*. Oxford University Press.

Silberberg, A., C. Allouch, S. Sandfort, D. Kearns, H. Karpel, and B. Slotnick. 2014. "Desire for Social Contact, Not Empathy, May Explain 'Rescue' Behavior in Rats." *Animal Cognition* 17:609–18.

Silk, Alex. 2015. "Nietzschean Constructivism." *Inquiry* 58:244–80.

Silver, Daniel. 2020. "Figure It Out!" *Sociological Methods & Research* 49:868–905.

Simion, Mona. 2018. "Epistemic Trouble for Engineering 'Woman.'" *Logos & Episteme* 9:91–98.

Simko, Christina, and Jeffrey K. Olick. 2021. "What We Talk about When We Talk about Culture." *American Journal of Cultural Sociology* 9:431–59.

Simmel, Georg. 1908. *Soziologie*. Verlag von Duncker und Humblot.

Simmons, A. John. 2010. "Ideal and Nonideal Theory." *Philosophy & Public Affairs* 38:5–36.

Simmons, Erica S., and Nicholas Rush Smith, eds. 2021. *Rethinking Comparison*. Cambridge University Press.

Simmons, Joseph P., Leif D. Nelson, and Uri Simonsohn. 2011. "False-Positive Psychology." *Psychological Science* 22:1359–66.

Simondon, Gilbert. (1964) 1995. *L'Individu et sa genèse physico-biologique*. Jérôme Millon.

Simpson, George Gaylor. 1945. "The Principles of Classification and a Classification of Mammals." *Bulletin of the American Museum of Natural History* 85:1–350.

Singer, Daniel J. 2019. "Diversity, Not Randomness, Trumps Ability." *Philosophy of Science* 86:178–91.

Sinnott-Armstrong, Walter. 2005. "Word Meaning in Legal Interpretation." *San Diego Law Review* 42:465–92.

Skillings, Derek. 2016. "Holobionts and the Ecology of Organisms." *Biology & Philosophy* 31:875–92.

Skinner, David. 2012. *The Story of Ain't.* Harper.

Skinner, Quentin. 1979. "The Idea of a Cultural Lexicon." *Essays in Criticism* 29:205–24.

———. 1988. "A Reply to My Critics." In *Meaning and Context,* edited by J. Tully, 231–88. Princeton University Press.

———. 1989. "Language and Political Change." In *Political Innovation and Conceptual Change,* edited by T. Ball, J. Farr, and R. L. Hanson, 6–23. Cambridge University Press.

Skocpol, Theda. 1982. "Rentier State and Shi'a Islam in the Iranian Revolution." *Theory and Society* 11:265–83.

Slaney, Kathleen L., and Donald A. Garcia. 2015. "Constructing Psychological Objects." *Journal of Theoretical and Philosophical Psychology* 35:244–259.

Slaney, Kathleen L., and Timothy P. Racine. 2011. "On the Ambiguity of Concept Use in Psychology." *Journal of Theoretical and Philosophical Psychology* 31:73–89.

———. 2013. "What's in a Name?" *New Ideas in Psychology* 31:4–12.

Slater, Matthew H. 2015. "Natural Kindness." *British Journal for the Philosophy of Science* 66:375–411.

Slocum, Brian G. 2015. *Ordinary Meaning.* University of Chicago Press.

———, ed. 2017. *The Nature of Legal Interpretation.* University of Chicago Press.

Small, Mario Luis. 2009. "'How Many Cases Do I Need?'" *Ethnography* 10:5–38.

———. 2013. "Causal Thinking and Ethnographic Research." *American Journal of Sociology* 119:597–601.

———. 2021. "What Is 'Qualitative' in Qualitative Research?" *Qualitative Sociology* 44:567–74.

Smith, Adam Stuart. 2005. "The Affinities of Jaffa Cakes." *Null Hypothesis: The Journal of Unlikely Science* 1:2–6.

Smith, Deborah C. 2016. "Quid Quidditism est?" *Erkenntnis* 81:237–57.

Smith, Jonathan Z. 1998. "Religion, Religions, Religious." In *Critical Terms for Religious Studies,* edited by M. C. Taylor, 269–84. University of Chicago Press.

Smith, Michael E. 2011. "Empirical Urban Theory for Archaeologists." *Journal of Archaeological Method and Theory* 18:167–92.

Sober, Elliott. 1981. "The Principle of Parsimony." *British Journal for the Philosophy of Science* 32:145–56.

Solan, Lawrence M. 1993. *The Language of Judges.* University of Chicago Press.

Solan, Lawrence M., and Tammy Gales. 2016. "Finding Ordinary Meaning in Law." *International Journal of Legal Discourse* 1:253–76.

Solovey, Mark. 2020. *Social Science for What?* MIT Press.

Solum, Lawrence B. 2004. "Procedural Justice." *Southern California Law Review* 78:181–321.

Somers, Margaret R. 1995a. "Narrating and Naturalizing Civil Society and Citizenship Theory." *Sociological Theory* 13:229–74.

———. 1995b. "What's Political or Cultural about Political Culture and the Public Sphere?" *Sociological Theory* 13:114–44.

Sommers, Roseanna. 2020. "Commonsense Consent." *Yale Law Journal* 129:2232–324.

Sorensen, Roy A. 1985. "An Argument for the Vagueness of 'Vague.'" *Analysis* 45:134–37.

Sorokin, Pitirim A. 1956. *Fads and Foibles in Modern Sociology and Related Sciences.* Henry Regnery.

Spector, Malcolm, and John I. Kitsuse. 1977. *Constructing Social Problems.* Cummings.

Spender, Dale. 1980. *Man Made Language.* Routledge and Kegan Paul.

Spolsky, Bernard. 2004. *Language Policy.* Cambridge University Press.

———. 2009. *Language Management.* Cambridge University Press.

———, ed. 2012. *The Cambridge Handbook of Language Policy.* Cambridge University Press.

Stamper, Kory. 2017. *Word by Word.* Pantheon Books.

Stanley, Jason. 2005. *Knowledge and Practical Interests.* Oxford University Press.

———. 2015. *How Propaganda Works.* Princeton University Press.

Star, Susan Leigh. 1999. "The Ethnography of Infrastructure." *American Behavioral Scientist* 43:377–91.

Star, Susan Leigh, and Karen Ruhleder. 1996. "Steps Toward an Ecology of Infrastructure." *Information Systems Research* 7:111–34.

Starr, Michelle. 2019. "NASA Administrator Says Pluto Is Still a Planet, and Things Are Getting Heated." Science Alert, August 26, 2019. https://www.sciencealert.com/nasa-administrator -jim-bridenstine-says-pluto-is-a-planet.

Steel, Daniel. 2010. "Epistemic Values and the Argument from Inductive Risk." *Philosophy of Science* 77:14–34.

———. 2013. "Acceptance, Values, and Inductive Risk." *Philosophy of Science* 80:818–28.

Steensland, Brian. 2006. "Cultural Categories and the American Welfare State." *American Journal of Sociology* 111:1273–326.

Steiner, Jürg. 2012. *The Foundations of Deliberative Democracy.* Cambridge University Press.

Steinmetz, George, ed. 2005. *The Politics of Method in the Human Sciences.* Duke University Press.

———, ed. 2013. *Sociology & Empire.* Duke University Press.

———. 2020. "Historicism and Positivism in Sociology." In *Historicism,* edited by H. Paul and A. van Veldhuizen, 57–95. Bloomsbury.

Stern, David G. 2004. *Wittgenstein's "Philosophical Investigations."* Cambridge University Press.

Stevens, S. S. 1935a. "The Operational Basis of Psychology." *American Journal of Psychology* 47:323–30.

———. 1935b. "The Operational Definition of Psychological Concepts." *Psychological Review* 42:517–27.

———. 1946. "On the Theory of Scales of Measurement." *Science* 103:677–80.

Stevenson, Charles Leslie. 1938. "Persuasive Definitions." *Mind* 47:331–50.

———. 1944. *Ethics and Language.* Yale University Press.

Stinchcombe, Arthur L. 1964. Review of *Behavior in Public Places,* by Erving Goffman. *American Journal of Sociology* 69:679–80.

———. 1968. *Constructing Social Theories.* Harcourt, Brace and World.

———. 2005. *The Logic of Social Research.* University of Chicago Press.

Stotz, K., and P. Griffiths. 2004. "Genes." *History and Philosophy of the Life Sciences* 26:5–28.

Stotz, K., P. Griffiths, and R. Knight. 2004. "How Biologists Conceptualize Genes." *Studies in the History and Philosophy of Biological and Biomedical Sciences* 35:647–73.

Strand, Michael. 2011. "Where Do Classifications Come From?" *Theory and Society* 40:273–313.

Strand, Michael, and Omar Lizardo. 2022. "For a Probabilistic Sociology." *Theory and Society* 51:399–434.

Strawson, P. F. 1950. "On Referring." *Mind* 59:320–44.

———. 1963. "Carnap's Views on Constructed Systems versus Natural Languages in Analytic Philosophy." In *The Philosophy of Rudolf Carnap*, edited by P. A. Schilpp, 503–18. Open Court.

Street, Sharon. 2008. "Constructivism about Reasons." *Oxford Studies in Metaethics* 3:207–45.

———. 2010. "What Is Constructivism in Ethics and Metaethics?" *Philosophy Compass* 5:363–84.

———. 2016. "Constructivism in Ethics and the Problem of Attachment and Loss." *Aristotelian Society Supplementary Volume* 90:161–89.

Stroud, Barry. 2017. "Davidson and Wittgenstein on Meaning and Understanding." In *Wittgenstein and Davidson on Language, Thought, and Action*, edited by C. Verheggen, 123–38. Cambridge University Press.

Sundell, Timothy. 2020. "Changing the Subject." *Canadian Journal of Philosophy* 50:580–93.

Suppes, Patrick. 1957. *Introduction to Logic*. D. Van Nostrand.

Svensén, Bo. 2009. *A Handbook of Lexicography*. Cambridge University Press.

Swanton, Christine. 1985. "On the 'Essential Contestedness' of Political Concepts." *Ethics* 95:811–27.

Swedberg, Richard. 2005. *Interest*. Open University Press.

———. 2016. "On the Heuristic Role of Concepts in Theorizing." In *Theory in Action*, edited by P. Sohlberg and H. Leiulfsrud, 24–38. Brill.

———. 2018a. "How to Use Max Weber's Ideal Type in Sociological Analysis." *Journal of Classical Sociology* 18:181–96.

———. 2018b. "On the Near Disappearance of Concepts in Mainstream Sociology." In *Concepts in Action*, edited by H. Leiulfsrud and P. Sohlberg, 23–39. Brill.

———. 2020a. "On the Use of Abstractions in Sociology." *Journal of Classical Sociology* 20:257–80.

———. 2020b. "On the Use of Definitions in Sociology." *European Journal of Social Theory* 23:431–45.

———. 2021. "What Is a Method?" *Distinktion* 22:108–28.

Swift, J. 1712. *A Proposal for Correcting, Improving and Ascertaining the English Tongue*. Benj. Tooke.

Sykes, Mark V. 2008. "The Planet Debate Continues." *Science* 319:1765.

Sylvan, Kurt. 2018. "Veritism Unswamped." *Mind* 127:381–435.

Sztompka, Piotr. 1999. *Trust*. Cambridge University Press.

Tai, Steph. 2020. "Legalizing the Meaning of Meat." *Loyola University Chicago Law Journal* 51:743–89.

Taiz, Lincoln, Daniel Alkon, Andreas Draguhn, Angus Murphy, Michael Blatt, Chris Hawes, Gerhard Thiel, and David G. Robinson. 2019. "Plants Neither Possess Nor Require Consciousness." *Trends in Plant Science* 24:677–87.

Tal, Eran. 2013. "Old and New Problems in the Philosophy of Measurement." *Philosophy Compass* 8:1159–73.

———. 2019. "Individuating Quantities." *Philosophical Studies* 176:853–78.

Talisse, Robert B. 2007. *A Pragmatist Philosophy of Democracy*. Routledge.

———. 2011. "A Farewell to Deweyan Democracy." *Political Studies* 59:509–26.

———. 2014. "Pragmatist Political Philosophy." *Philosophy Compass* 9:123–30.

Tambiah, S. J. 1968. "The Magical Power of Words." *Man* 3:175–208.

Tancredi, Gonzalo. 2006. "Cronología de los hechos relativos a la Definición de Planeta adoptada por la Asamblea de la Unión Astronómica Internacional." Instituto de Física Facultad de Ciencias, n.d. http://www.fisica.edu.uy/~gonzalo/Diario_de_la_Asamblea_IAU_2006 .html.

———. 2007. "De 9 a 12 y finalmente 8." *Revista Latino-Americana de educação em astronomia* 4:69–77.

Tancredi, Gonzalo, Julio A. Fernández, Marcello Fulchignoni, Daniela Lazzaro, Alessandro Morbidelli, Mario Di Martino, Paolo Paolicchi, et al. 2006. "The Definition of a Planet." Unpublished MS. Text Document File.

Tarp, Sven. 2008. *Lexicography in the Borderland between Knowledge and Non-knowledge*. Max Niemeyer Verlag.

Tarp, Sven, and Pedro A. Fuertes-Olivera. 2016. "Advantages and Disadvantages in the Use of Internet as a Corpus." *Lexicos* 26:273–95.

Tavory, Iddo, and Stefan Timmermans. 2014. *Abductive Analysis*. University of Chicago Press.

Taylor, Charles. 1971. "Interpretation and the Sciences of Man." *Review of Metaphysics* 25:3–51.

———. 1999. "Conditions of an Unforced Consensus on Human Rights." In *The East Asian Challenge for Human Rights*, edited by J. R. Bauer and D. A. Bell, 124–44. Cambridge University Press.

———. 2003. "Ethics and Ontology." *Journal of Philosophy* 100:305–20.

———. 2016. *The Language Animal*. Belknap Press of Harvard University Press.

Taylor, John R. 2001. "Concepts, or: What Is It that a Word Designates?" *RASK* 15:3–26.

———, ed. 2015. *Oxford Handbook of the Word*. Oxford University Press.

———. 2017. "Lexical Semantics." In *The Cambridge Handbook of Cognitive Linguistics*, edited by B. Dancygier, 246–61. Cambridge University Press.

Teplitskiy, Misha. 2016. "Frame Search and Re-search." *American Sociologist* 47:264–88.

Thacher, David. 2006. "The Normative Case Study." *American Journal of Sociology* 111:1631–76.

"Theory Section News in Brief." 1991. *Perspectives* 14 (4): 3.

Thomasson, Amie L. 2020. "A Pragmatic Method for Normative Conceptual Work." In *Conceptual Engineering and Conceptual Ethics*, edited by A. Burgess, H. Cappelen, and D. Plunkett, 435–58. Oxford University Press.

———. Forthcoming. "Conceptual Engineering." *Inquiry*.

Thompson, Abigail. 2014. "Does Diversity Trump Ability?" *Notices of the American Mathematical Society* 61:1024–30.

Thumma, Samuel A., and Jeffrey L. Kirchmeier. 1999. "The Lexicon Has Become a Fortress." *Buffalo Law Review* 47:227–562.

Tilly, Charles. 2006. *Why?* Princeton University Press.

———. 2008. *Explaining Social Processes*. Routledge.

Timasheff, N. S. 1947. "Definitions in the Social Sciences." *American Journal of Sociology* 53:201–9.

———. 1952. "The Basic Concepts of Sociology." *American Journal of Sociology* 58:176–86.

Timmermans, Stefan, and Steven Epstein. 2010. "A World of Standards but Not a Standard World." *Annual Review of Sociology* 36:69–89.

Timmermans, Stefan, and Iddo Tavory. 2022. *Data Analysis in Qualitative Research*. University of Chicago Press.

Tirrell, Lynne. 1993. "Definition and Power." *Hypatia* 8:1–34.

Tobia, Kevin P. 2020. "Testing Ordinary Meaning." *Harvard Law Review* 134:726–806.

Topham, Alexander, Rachel Taylor, Dawei Yan, Eiji Nambara, Iain Johnson, and George Bassel. 2017. "Temperature variability Is Integrated by a Spatially Embedded Decision-Making Center to Break Dormancy in *Arabidopsis* Seeds." *Proceedings of the National Academy of Sciences of the USA* 114:6629–34.

Torres, Esteban, ed. 2020. *Hacia la renovación de la teoría social latinoamericana*. CLACSO.

———. 2021. *La gran transformación de la sociología*. Universidad Nacional de Córdoba and CLACSO.

Trask, R. L. 2004. "What Is a Word?" University of Sussex Working Papers in Linguistics 11/04.

Trewavas, Tony. 2016. "Plant Intelligence." *BioScience* 66:542–51.

Trivigno, Franco V. 2012. "Etymology and the Power of Names in Plato's *Cratylus*." *Ancient Philosophy* 32:35–75.

Tropman, Elizabeth. 2014. "Varieties of Moral Intuitionism." *Journal of Value Inquiry* 48:177–94.

Truss, Lynne. 2003. *Eats, Shoots & Leaves*. Profile Books.

Tuğal, Cihan. 2021. "Populism Studies." *Annual Review of Sociology* 47:327–47.

Tuomela, Raimo. 2007. *The Philosophy of Sociality*. Oxford University Press.

———. 2013. *Social Ontology*. Oxford University Press.

Turing, A. M. 1950. "Computing Machinery and Intelligence." *Mind* 59:433–60.

Turner, Stephen Park. 2007. "Merton's 'Norms' in Political and Intellectual Context." *Journal of Classical Sociology* 7:161–78.

Turner, Stephen Park, and Jonathan H. Turner. 1990. *The Impossible Science*. Sage.

Tyson, Neil deGrasse. 1999. "Pluto's Honor." *Natural History* 108:82.

———. 2009. *The Pluto Files*. Norton.

Uebel, Thomas. 2007. *Empiricism at the Crossroads*. Open Court.

UNESCO. 1956. "General Report of the Second Meeting of Experts on Social Science Terminology." *UNESCO International Social Science Bulletin* 8:519–24.

Urban, Hugh B. 2011. *The Church of Scientology*. Princeton University Press.

Valentini, Laura. 2012. "Ideal vs. Non-ideal Theory." *Philosophy Compass* 7:654–64.

Van Bouwel, Jeroen, ed. 2009. *The Social Sciences and Democracy*. Palgrave Macmillan.

———. 2015. "Towards Democratic Models of Science." *Perspectives on Science* 23:149–72.

Van Bouwel, Jeroen, and Michiel Van Oudheusden. 2017. "Participation beyond Consensus?" *Social Epistemology* 31:497–513.

Van der Hucht, Karel A., ed. 2008. *Proceedings of the Twenty Sixth General Assembly Prague 2006*. Transactions of the International Astronomical Union XXVIB. Cambridge University Press.

Van Inwagen, Peter. 1981. "The Doctrine of Arbitrary Undetached Parts." *Pacific Philosophical Quarterly* 62:123–37.

Van Ostade, Ingrid Tieken-Boon, ed. 2017. *English Usage Guides*. Oxford University Press.

———. 2019. *Describing Prescriptivism*. Routledge.

Varzi, Achille C. 2000. "Mereological Commitments." *Dialectica* 54:283–305.

———. 2011. "On Doing Ontology without Metaphysics." *Philosophical Perspectives* 25:407–23.

———. 2013. "Undetached Parts and Disconnected Wholes." In *Johanssonian Investigations*, edited by C. Svennerlind, J. Almäng, and R. D. Ingthorsson, 696–708. Ontos Verlag.

———. 2014. "Realism in the Desert." In *Metaphysics and Ontology without Myths*, edited by F. Bacchini, S. Caputo, and M. Dell'Utri, 16–31. Cambridge Scholars.

Väyrynen, Pekka. 2013. *The Lewd, the Rude and the Nasty*. Oxford University Press.

———. 2014. "Essential Contestability and Evaluation." *Australasian Journal of Philosophy* 92:471–88.

Vedantam, Shankar. 2006. "For Pluto, a Smaller World after All." *Washington Post*, August 25, 2006.

Vermeulen, Inga. 2018. "Verbal Disputes and the Varieties of Verbalness." *Erkenntnis* 83:331–48.

Vessonen, Elina. 2017. "Psychometrics versus Representational Theory of Measurement." *Philosophy of the Social Sciences* 47:330–50.

———. 2019. "Operationalism and Realism in Psychometrics." *Philosophy Compass* 14:e12624.

———. 2021a. "Conceptual Engineering and Operationalism in Psychology." *Synthese* 199:10615–37.

———. 2021b. "Respectful Operationalism." *Theory & Psychology* 31:84–105.

Viola, Tullio. 2019. "From Vague Symbols to Contested Concepts." *History and Theory* 58:233–51.

Wagenknecht, Susann, and Jessica Pflüger. 2018. "Making Cases." *Zeitschrift für Soziologie* 47:289–305.

Waismann, Friedrich. (1956) 1968. *How I See Philosophy*. Macmillan.

Wakefield, Jerome C. 1992. "The Concept of Mental Disorder." *American Psychologist* 47:373–88.

Walden, Kenneth. 2015. "The *Euthyphro* Dilemma." *Philosophy and Phenomenological Research* 90:612–39.

Waldron, Jeremy. 1995. "The Wisdom of the Multitude." *Political Theory* 23:563–84.

———. 2002. "Is the Rule of Law an Essentially Contested Concept (in Florida)?" *Law and Philosophy* 21:137–64.

Wall, Mike. 2011. "Pluto's Planet Title Defender." Space.com, August 24, 2011. https://www.space .com/12710-pluto-defender-alan-stern-dwarf-planet-interview.html.

Wallace, David Foster. 2009. *This Is Water*. Little, Brown.

Wallace, R. Jay. 2020. "Practical Reason." In *The Stanford Encyclopedia of Philosophy*, Spring 2020 ed., edited by E. N. Zalta. Metaphysics Research Lab, Center for the Study of Language and Information, Stanford University.

"Wallace Resolution Reinstated." 1992. *Perspectives* 15 (2): 12.

Wallace, Walter L. 1971. *The Logic of Science in Sociology*. Aldine-Atherton.

———. 1990. "Standardizing Basic Concepts in Sociology." *American Sociologist* 21:352–58.

———. 1991. "Standardizing Basic Sociological Concepts." *Perspectives* 14 (1): 1–2.

———. 1992. "Metatheory, Conceptual Standardization, and the Future of Sociology." In *Metatheorizing*, edited by G. Ritzer, 53–68. Sage.

———. 1995. "Why Sociology Doesn't Make Progress." *Sociological Forum* 10:313–18.

———. 1996. "Progress in Sociology." *Sociological Forum* 11:631–37.

Wallerstein, Immanuel. 2007. "Eurocentrism and Its Avatars." *Sociological Bulletin* 46:21–39.

Walmsley, Jan. 2001. "Normalisation, Emancipatory Research and Inclusive Research in Learning Disability." *Disability & Society* 16:187–205.

Walmsley, Jan, and Kelly Johnson. 2003. *Inclusive Research with People with Learning Disabilities.* Jessica Kingsley.

Waters, C. Kenneth. 2018. "Ask Not 'What *Is* an Individual?'" In *Individuation, Process, and Scientific Practices*, edited by O. Bueno, R.-L. Chen, and M. B. Fagan, 91–113. Oxford University Press.

Watts, Richard J. 2011. *Language Myths and the History of English.* Oxford University Press.

Weber, Max. 1904. "Die 'Objektivität' sozialwissenschaftlicher und sozialpolitischer Erkenntnis." *Archiv für Sozialwissenschaft und Sozialpolitik* 19:22–87.

———. (1919) 1946. "Science as a Vocation." In *From Max Weber*, edited and translated by H. H. Gerth and C. Wright Mills, 129–56. Oxford University Press.

———. 1922. *Gesammelte Aufsätze zur Wissenschaftslehre.* Verlag von J.C.B. Mohr (Paul Siebeck).

Weinberg, Justin. 2020. "A Resignation at Philosophical Studies and a Reply from the Editors." *Daily Nous*, June 12, 2020. https://dailynous.com/2020/06/12/resignation-philosophical -studies-reply-editors/.

Weintraub, David A. 2006. *Is Pluto a Planet?* Princeton University Press.

———. 2015. "NASA Missions May Re-elevate Pluto and Ceres from Dwarf Planets to Full-On Planet Status." *Conversation*, February 25, 2015. https://theconversation.com/nasa-missions -may-re-elevate-pluto-and-ceres-from-dwarf-planets-to-full-on-planet-status-36081.

Weisberg, Michael. 2003. "When Less Is More." PhD dissertation, Stanford University.

———. 2006. "Forty Years of 'The Strategy.'" *Biology & Philosophy* 21:623–45.

Weiskopf, Daniel Aaron. 2009. "The Plurality of Concepts." *Synthese* 169:145–73.

Weitz, Morris. 1972. "Open Concepts." *Revue Internationale de Philosophie* 26:86–110.

Wells, Ronald A. 1973. *Dictionaries and the Authoritarian Tradition.* Mouton.

Weng, Jeffrey. 2018. "What Is Mandarin?" *Journal of Asian Studies* 77:611–33.

———. 2020. "Uneasy Companions." *Theory and Society* 49:75–100.

Werbach, Kevin. 1994. "Looking It Up." *Harvard Law Review* 107:1437–54.

Werenfels, Samuel. (1702) 1711. *A Discourse of Logomachys, or Controversys about Words, So Common among Learned Men.* J. Darby.

Werner, Michael, and Bénédicte Zimmermann. 2006. "Beyond Comparison." *History and Theory* 45:30–50.

Westerhoff, Jan. 2007. "The Madhyamaka Concept of *Svabhāva*." *Asian Philosophy* 17:17–45.

Whitaker, C.W.A. 1996. *Aristotle's "De Interpretatione."* Oxford University Press.

White, James. 1979. "The Plant as a Metapopulation." *Annual Review of Ecology and Systematics* 10:109–45.

Whiting, Jennifer E. 1986. "Form and Individuation in Aristotle." *History of Philosophy Quarterly* 3:359–77.

Whooley, Owen. 2010. "Diagnostic Ambivalence." *Sociology of Health & Illness* 32:452–69.

———. 2019. *On the Heels of Ignorance*. University of Chicago Press.

Wijsen, Lisa D., Denny Borsboom, and Anna Alexandrova. 2022. "Values in Psychometrics." *Perspectives on Psychological Science* 17:788–804.

Wilholt, Torsten. 2009. "Bias and Values in Scientific Research." *Studies in History and Philosophy of Science* 40:92–101.

Wilkins, John S. 2003. "How to Be a Chaste Species Pluralist-Realist." *Biology & Philosophy* 18:621–38.

———. 2009a. *Defining Species*. Peter Lang.

———. 2009b. *Species*. University of California Press.

Wilkins, John S., and Malte C. Ebach. 2014. *The Nature of Classification*. Palgrave Macmillan.

Williams, Bernard. 1985. *Ethics and the Limits of Philosophy*. Harvard University Press.

———. 2005. *In the Beginning Was the Deed*. Princeton University Press.

Williams, David M., and Malte C. Ebach. 2018. "A Cladist Is a Systematist Who Seeks a Natural Classification." *Biology & Philosophy* 33:10.

Williams, Iwan P., Edward L. G. Bowell, Edward Tedesco, Guy J. Consolmagno, Giovanni B. Valsecchi, Bo Å Gustafson, Ingrid Mann, et al. 2007. "Working Group on Definition of Planet." In *Reports on Astronomy 2002–2005: Proceedings IAU Symposium No. XXVIA, 2006*, edited by O. Engvold, 189. International Astronomical Union.

Williams, Iwan P., and Jocelyn Bell Burnell. 2006. "What It Takes to Make a Planet." *Astronomy & Geophysics* 47:5.16–17.

Williams, James. 2018. *Stand out of Our Light*. Cambridge University Press.

Williams, Raymond. (1958) 1960. *Culture and Society, 1780–1950*. Doubleday.

———. 1976. *Keywords*. Oxford University Press.

Williamson, Timothy. 1994. *Vagueness*. Routledge.

Wilson, Jack. 1999. *Biological Individuality*. Cambridge University Press.

Wilson, Robert A., Matthew J. Barker, and Ingo Brigandt. 2007. "When Traditional Essentialism Fails." *Philosophical Topics* 35:189–215.

Wirth, Louis, ed. 1940. *Eleven Twenty-Six*. University of Chicago Press.

Witteveen, Joeri. 2016. "Suppressing Synonymy with a Homonym." *Journal of the History of Biology* 49:135–89.

Wittgenstein, Ludwig. (1953) 2009. *Philosophical Investigations*. 4th ed. Translated by G.E.M. Anscombe, P.M.S. Hacker, and Joachim Schulte. Wiley-Blackwell.

———. 1978. *Remarks on the Foundations of Mathematics*. Translated by G.E.M. Anscombe. Rev. ed. MIT Press.

Wolfsdorf, David. 2003a. "Socrates' Pursuit of Definitions." *Phronesis* 48:271–312.

———. 2003b. "Understanding the 'What-Is-F?' Question." *Apeiron* 36:175–88.

———. 2004. "The Socratic Fallacy and the Epistemological Priority of Definitional Knowledge." *Apeiron* 37:35–67.

Wong, Wan-chi. 2006. "Understanding Dialectical Thinking from a Cultural-Historical Perspective." *Philosophical Psychology* 19:239–60.

Wray, K. Brad. 2015. "Pessimistic Inductions." *International Studies in the Philosophy of Science* 29:61–73.

Wright, Erik Olin. 2010. *Envisioning Real Utopias*. Verso.

Wylie, Alison. 2012. "Feminist Philosophy of Science." *Proceedings and Addresses of the American Philosophical Association* 86:47–76.

Young, Iris Marion. 2000. *Inclusion and Democracy*. Oxford University Press.

Young, James O. 2018. "The Coherence Theory of Truth." In *The Stanford Encyclopedia of Philosophy*, Fall 2018 ed., edited by E. N. Zalta. Metaphysics Research Lab, Center for the Study of Language and Information, Stanford University.

Yuhas, Alan. 2015. "Who You Calling a Dwarf?" *Guardian*, July 15, 2015.

Zerubavel, Eviatar. 1991. *The Fine Line*. Free Press.

———. 1996. "Lumping and Splitting." *Sociological Forum* 11:421–33.

———. 2020. *Generally Speaking*. Oxford University Press.

Zetterberg, Hans L. (1954) 1965. *On Theory and Verification in Sociology*. 3rd ed. Bedminster.

Zimmer, Benjamin. 2006a. "Pluto Is a Dwarf Planet, but Not a Planet." Language Log, August 24, 2006. http://itre.cis.upenn.edu/~myl/languagelog/archives/003495.html.

———. 2006b. "New Planetary Definition a 'Linguistic Catastrophe'!" Language Log, August 25, 2006. http://itre.cis.upenn.edu/myl/languagelog/archives/003504.html.

———. 2007. "Pluto Got Plutoed, but It Still Won WOTY." Language Log, January 5, 2007. http://itre.cis.upenn.edu/~myl/languagelog/archives/004010.html.

Zuboff, Shoshana. 2019. *The Age of Surveillance Capitalism*. PublicAffairs.

INDEX

Page numbers in *italics* indicate figures and tables.

A NOTE ON THE TYPE

This book has been composed in Arno, an Old-style serif typeface in the classic Venetian tradition, designed by Robert Slimbach at Adobe.

GPSR Authorized Representative: Easy Access System Europe - Mustamäe tee 50, 10621 Tallinn, Estonia, gpsr.requests@easproject.com